Fifth Workshop on Scholarly Document Processing (SDP 2025)

Vienna, Austria
31 July 2025

ISBN: 979-8-3313-2416-2

Printed from e-media with permission by:

Curran Associates, Inc.
57 Morehouse Lane
Red Hook, NY 12571

Some format issues inherent in the e-media version may also appear in this print version.

Association for Computational Linguistics
209 N. Eighth Street
Stroudsburg, Pennsylvania 18360

Phone: 1-570-476-8006
Fax: 1-570-476-0860

acl@aclweb.org

Additional copies of this publication are available from:

Curran Associates, Inc.
57 Morehouse Lane
Red Hook, NY 12571 USA
Phone: 845-758-0400
Fax: 845-758-2633
Email: curran@proceedings.com
Web: www.proceedings.com

SDP 2025

Fifth Workshop on Scholarly Document Processing

Proceedings of the Workshop

July 31, 2025

Message from the SDP 2025 Organizing Committee

Welcome to the Fifth Workshop on Scholarly Document Processing (SDP) at ACL 2025. As the body of scholarly literature grows, automated methods in NLP, text mining, information retrieval, document understanding etc. are needed to address issues of information overload, disinformation, reproducibility, and more. Though progress has been made, there are significant unique challenges to processing scholarly text that require dedicated attention. The goal of the Scholarly Document Processing series of workshops is to provide a venue for addressing these challenges, as well as a platform for tasks and resources supporting the processing of scientific documents. Our long-term objective is to establish scholarly and scientific texts as an essential domain for NLP research, to supplement current efforts on web text and news articles. This workshop builds on the success of prior workshops: the SDP workshop held at ACL in 2024, COLING in 2022, NAACL in 2021 and EMNLP in 2020, and the SciNLP workshop held at AKBC 2020 and AKBC 2021. As in previous years, we have sought to bring together researchers and practitioners from various backgrounds focusing on different aspects of scholarly document processing. We believe that the interdisciplinary nature of the ACL venues greatly assists in encouraging submissions from a diverse set of fields.

Organizing Committee

Program Chairs

Tirthankar Ghosal, Oak Ridge National Laboratory, USA
Philipp Mayr, GESIS - Leibniz Institute for the Social Sciences, Germany
Amanpreet Singh, Allen Institute for AI, USA
Aakanksha Naik, Allen Institute for AI, USA
Georg Rehm, Deutsches Forschungszentrum für Künstliche Intelligenz GmbH (DFKI) and Humboldt-Universität zu Berlin, Germany
Dayne Freitag, SRI International, USA
Dan Li, Elsevier, Netherlands
Sonja Schimmler, Technische Universität Berlin and Fraunhofer FOKUS, Germany
Anita De Waard, Elsevier, Netherlands

Program Committee

Reviewers

Raia Abu Ahmad, Anurag Acharya, Daniel Acuna, Akiko Aizawa, Hamed Alhoori, Tamjid Azad, Ibrahim Al Azher

Fabio Barth, Ekaterina Borisova, Ioana Buhnila

Yupeng Cao, Soham Chitnis

Anita De Waard, Jay DeYoung, James Dunham, Nicolau Duran-Silva

Dayne Freitag

German Gritsai

Allan Hanbury, Tosho Hirasawa, Sameera Horawalavithana

Daisuke Ikeda

Yavuz Selim Kartal, Roman Kern, Petr Knoth, Buse Sibel Korkmaz

Dan Li, Xinyuan Lu

Biswadip Mandal, Yoshitomo Matsubara, Philipp Mayr, Shufan Ming, Miftahul Jannat Mokarrama

Wolfgang Otto

Antonio Pieri

Tohida Rehman, Allen G Roush

Sebastian Schellhammer, Pierre Senellart, Amanpreet Singh, Neil R. Smalheiser, Wojtek Sylwestrzak

Sotaro Takeshita, Hiroki Teranishi

Sharmila Upadhyaya, Aida Usmanova

Boris Veytsman

Taro Watanabe

Shiyuan Zhang, Wuhe Zou

Table of Contents

Program

Thursday, July 31, 2025

17:00 - 09:00	*For the final SDP2025 Program Schedule, see the workshop website:https://sdproc.org/2025/program.html.*

Overview of the Fifth Workshop on Scholarly Document Processing

Tirthankar Ghosal[a] **Philipp Mayr**[b]
Anita de Waard[c] **Aakanksha Naik**[d] **Amanpreet Singh**[d]
Dayne Freitag[e] **Georg Rehm**[f,g] **Sonja Schimmler**[h,i] **Dan Li**[c]

Abstract

The workshop on Scholarly Document Processing (SDP) started in 2020 to accelerate research, inform policy, and educate the public on natural language processing for scientific text. The fifth iteration of the workshop, SDP 2025 was held at the 63rd Annual Meeting of the Association for Computational Linguistics (ACL 2025) in Vienna as a hybrid event. The workshop saw a great increase in interest, with 26 submissions, of which 11 were accepted for the research track. The program consisted of a research track, invited talks and four shared tasks: (1) SciHal25: Hallucination Detection for Scientific Content, (2) SciVQA: Scientific Visual Question Answering, (3) ClimateCheck: Scientific Fact-checking of Social Media Posts on Climate Change, and (4) Software Mention Detection in Scholarly Publications (SOMD 25). In addition to the four shared task overview papers, 18 shared task reports were accepted. The program was geared towards NLP, information extraction, information retrieval, and data mining for scholarly documents, with an emphasis on identifying and providing solutions to open challenges.

1 Workshop description

Scholarly literature serves as the primary vehicle for scientists and academics to record and disseminate their findings, playing a vital role in driving knowledge forward and enhancing human well-being.

As the volume of scholarly literature continues to grow, automated methods in NLP, information retrieval, text mining, and document understanding are increasingly essential to address challenges such as information overload, disinformation, and reproducibility (Hołyst et al., 2024). While notable progress has been made, scholarly texts present unique characteristics that demand dedicated research efforts. This workshop aims to serve as a venue for tackling these challenges and to foster the development of tasks and resources specific to scientific document processing. Our long-term goal is to establish scholarly and scientific texts as a core domain within NLP research, complementing ongoing work on web and news content.

The first Scholarly Document Processing (SDP) workshop was co-located online with the EMNLP 2020 conference (Chandrasekaran et al., 2020), and provided a dedicated venue for those working on SDP to submit and discuss their research. Following this success and the demonstrated need for venues to foster discussions around scholarly NLP, SDP 2021 co-located with NAACL (Beltagy et al., 2021), SDP 2022 with COLING (Cohan et al., 2022), SDP 2024 (Ghosal et al., 2024) with ACL again aimed to connect researchers and practitioners from different communities working with scientific literature and data and created a premier meeting point to facilitate discussions on open problems in SDP.

SDP 2025 invited submissions from all communities that explore both the applications and challenges of processing scholarly and scientific documents. Relevant topics included, but were not limited to, large language models (LLMs) for science, representation learning, information

[a]Oak Ridge National Laboratory, USA
[b]GESIS – Leibniz Institute for the Social Sciences, Germany
[c]Elsevier, Netherlands
[d]Allen Institute for AI, USA
[e]SRI International, USA
[f]Deutsches Forschungszentrum für Künstliche Intelligenz GmbH (DFKI), Germany
[g]Humboldt-Universität zu Berlin, Germany
[h]Fraunhofer FOKUS, Germany
[i]Technische Universität Berlin, Germany

Proceedings of the Fifth Workshop on Scholarly Document Processing (SDP 2025), pages 1–6

extraction, document understanding, summarization, and question-answering. We also welcomed work on discourse modeling, argumentation mining, network analysis, bibliometrics and scientometrics, as well as research integrity and reproducibility – including new challenges introduced by generative AI. Additional areas of interest included peer review technologies, metadata and indexing, dataset availability, research infrastructure, and digital libraries. We further encouraged contributions on improving inclusion and representation in scholarly work, designing LLM-based interfaces for interacting with scientific documents, and examining the broader societal impact of scholarly communication.

2 Program

The SDP 2025 workshop consisted of keynote talks, a research track and a shared task track. SDP 2025 received 26 submissions for the research track, of which 11 were accepted (42% acceptance rate). Since the workshop will be hybrid, there will be both in-person and virtual presentations at the conference venue and online. Topics of the presentations run the gamut, and include: Scientific Misconduct Detection, Scholarly Impact Prediction, Novelty Assessment in Scientific Literature, Information Extraction from Scientific PDFs, Dataset Reference Extraction, Citation and Document Attribution, Literature Discovery via Natural Language Queries, Mathematical Term Disambiguation, LaTeX Code Generation Evaluation, Clinical Trial Translation Prediction, Climate Misinformation Mapping, Abstract Screening in Systematic Reviews. As expected, we see a sharp increase in papers that employ large language models for downstream SDP tasks. The full program with links to papers, videos and posters is available at https://sdproc.org/2025/program.html.

3 Shared Task Track

SDP 2025 hosted four shared tasks. All four shared tasks had their own organizing committees consisting of several members of the SDP 2025 organizers and/or other collaborators. Detailed overview papers of the shared tasks are referred to and followed in the proceedings.

3.1 Hallucination Detection for Scientific Content (SciHal25)

Organizers: Dan Li, Bogdan Palfi, Colin Kehang Zhang

Generative AI-powered academic research assistants are transforming how research is conducted. These systems enable users to pose research-related questions in natural language and receive structured, concise summaries supported by relevant references. However, hallucinations – unsupported claims introduced by large language models – pose a significant challenge to fully trusting these automatically generated scientific answers.

The SciHal25 task (Li et al., 2025) invites participants to detect hallucinated claims in answers to research-oriented questions. This task is formulated as a multi-label classification problem, each instance consists of a question, an answer, an extracted claim, and supporting reference abstracts. Participants are asked to label claims under two subtasks: (1) coarse-grained detection with labels Entailment, Contradiction, or Unverifiable; and (2) fine-grained detection with a more detailed taxonomy including 8 types. The dataset consists of claim-level annotations designed to evaluate the factual consistency between claims in generated answers and their cited references within scientific retrieval-augmented generation (RAG) systems. The data are primarily derived from Scopus AI, an in-house research assistant tool powered by a RAG system indexing millions of scientific abstracts. The dataset is divided into 3,592 training, 500 validation, and 500 test instances. Subtask 1 saw 83 submissions across 9 teams while subtask 2 saw 38 submissions across 6 teams, resulting in a total of 5 published technical reports. System reports from top three participating teams as well as an overview paper summarizing future directions are included in the workshop proceedings.

3.2 SciVQA: Scientific Visual Question Answering

Organizers: Ekaterina Borisova and Georg Rehm

Data visualisations such as figures (i. e., charts and diagrams) are ubiquitous in scholarly publications. Researchers use *scientific figures* to present and compare results with prior works as well as to enhance the understanding of their findings (Clark and Divvala, 2016). Hence, extracting and interpreting information from figures is beneficial for a wide array of tasks in scholarly document processing, including visual question answering (VQA). However, reasoning over scientific figures is challenging as they are inherently multimodal, diverse in types, and contain domain-specific concepts (Meng et al., 2024; Zhou et al., 2023; Huang et al., 2024).

The SciVQA shared task (Borisova et al., 2025) aims to shed light on the capabilities of current multimodal large language models to recognise and link visual elements (i. e., colour, shape, size, height, direction, position) of scientific figures with textual content (e. g., captions, legends, axis labels) for the VQA task. Participants were invited to develop VQA systems based on the novel SciVQA dataset containing 3,000 images of scientific figures from the ACL Anthology[1] and arXiv[2], and a total of 21,000 QA pairs.[3] The key focus of the SciVQA challenge is on closed-ended QA pairs, both *visual*, i. e., addressing visual attributes of a figure, and *non-visual*, i. e., not targeting visual elements of a figure. SciVQA was hosted on the Codabench platform (Xu et al., 2022), and the submitted systems were evaluated using precision, recall, and F1 scores of ROUGE-1, ROUGE-L (Lin, 2004), and BERTScore (Zhang* et al., 2020).[4] The competition attracted 20 registered participants, with seven submissions to the leaderboard and five papers reporting the solutions.

3.3 ClimateCheck: Scientific Fact-checking of Social Media Posts on Climate Change

Organizers: Raia Abu Ahmad, Aida Usmanova, and Georg Rehm

The rapid spread of climate-related discourse on social media has created new opportunities for public engagement, but it has also amplified the spread of mis- and disinformation (Fownes et al., 2018; Al-Rawi et al., 2021). As online platforms increasingly shape public understanding of scientific issues, it becomes essential to develop tools that can link everyday claims to trustworthy sources. While NLP has made significant strides in tasks such as misinformation detection (Aldwairi and Alwahedi, 2018; Aïmeur et al., 2023), scientific entity extraction (Hafid et al., 2022; Hughes and Song, 2024), and scientific document understanding (Dagdelen et al., 2024), the challenge of grounding social media claims about climate change in scientific literature remains largely underexplored.

To bridge this gap, we organised ClimateCheck (Abu Ahmad et al., 2025b), a shared task aimed at automating the verification of climate-related claims from social media using scholarly publications as evidence. Hosted on Codabench (Xu et al., 2022) during April/May 2025, the task included two subtasks: (1) Retrieving relevant scientific abstracts for a given claim, and (2) Classifying the claim's veracity based on the retrieved evidence. The competition drew 27 registered users and 13 active teams, 10 of which submitted to the leaderboazed. Participants worked with a curated dataset of 435 climate-related claims written in lay language and a corpus of 394,269 scientific abstracts (Abu Ahmad et al., 2025a). In Subtask I, abstracts retrieval, systems were evaluated using Recall@K ($K = 2, 5, 10$) and Binary Preference to account for incomplete annotations. In Subtask II, claim verification, classification performance was measured using the weighted F1-score and Recall@10 from the previous subtask to encourage both accuracy and evidence coverage. The ClimateCheck dataset and evaluation suite are publicly available, providing a resource for further research on bridging scientific knowledge and public discourse.[5,6]

3.4 Software Mention Detection in Scholarly Publications (SOMD 25)

Organizers: Sharmila Upadhyaya, Wolfgang Otto, Frank Krüger, Stefan Dietze

Scientific research is increasingly data-centric, and software plays a vital role across disciplines by enabling the collection, analysis, and interpretation of research data. As such, software has emerged as a critical scholarly artifact whose identification is essential for ensuring the transparency, reproducibility, and collaborative nature of scientific inquiry. However, the heterogeneous and informal nature of software mentioned in scholarly publications presents ongoing challenges for accurate detection and disambiguation. To ad-

[1]https://aclanthology.org

[2]https://arxiv.org

[3]https://huggingface.co/datasets/katebor/SciVQA

[4]https://www.codabench.org/competitions/5904/

[5]https://huggingface.co/datasets/rabuahmad/climatecheck

[6]https://huggingface.co/datasets/rabuahmad/climatecheck_publications_corpus

dress this, we organized the second iteration of the Software Mention Detection (SOMD2025[7]) shared task as part of the Scholarly Document Processing (SDP) workshop at ACL 2025. The objective of SOMD2025 is to foster community-driven development of joint frameworks for Named Entity Recognition (NER) and Relation Extraction (RE) targeting software mentions and their associated attributes. This edition builds on the previous SOMD2024 task but emphasizes a joint evaluation setting, better reflecting real-world information extraction pipelines. The shared task consists of two phases: Phase I focuses on model development using a gold-standard dataset. At the same time, Phase II introduces an out-of-distribution (OOD) test set to evaluate generalizability. Despite 18 registered participants, only six teams completed two phases and submitted system descriptions. Participants applied diverse strategies, including joint and pipeline architectures, leveraging pre-trained language models and data augmentation using LLM-generated samples. The evaluation was based on a macro-averaged F1 score for NER and RE components, reported as the SOMD score. The top-performing systems achieved a SOMD score of 0.89 in Phase I and 0.63 in Phase II, underscoring the difficulty of generalization in OOD scenarios. These results show clear improvements over the baselines and show that while current methods perform well in in-distribution data, generalization remains a significant challenge.

4 Workshop Review and Outlook

SDP is evolving along with other fields of AI. The increasing maturity of generative LLMs provides new opportunities and poses new challenges. The way in which tasks traditionally associated with literature mining are addressed has changed dramatically over the life of the workshop series. Generative AI has not obviated tasks such as retrieval, extraction, and summarization, but has enabled researchers to explore interesting variants of these tasks and to shift focus from understanding to prediction. The same burgeoning of research, attributable to generative AI's democratizing effect, has created new problems for the conduct of science, raising interest in automated support for peer review and the enforcement of scholarly integrity.

As we consider future iterations of the workshop, we are discussing ways to respond to these trends. With SDP 2025 we have begun to present a more varied set of shared tasks, each highlighting challenges unique to the automated processing of the scholarly literature. As we proceed with planning and advertising, a key objective will be to elicit high-quality submissions from researchers interested in the use and meta-linguistic aspects of scholarly communication.

5 Conclusion

The Workshop on Scholarly Document Processing is part of a virtual cycle. Advances in SDP have given rise to powerful new tools, such as Google's Co-Scientist or Elsevier's ScienceDirect AI, that derive value from the communications of scholars and return value to scholars through sophisticated new forms of research facilitation. To the extent that these tools succeed, both the pace of scholarly discovery and the volume of scholarly communication will increase.

But SDP research is not just an amplifier. We believe and hope that the research fostered at our workshop will open new lines of inquiry across a range of disciplines and relieve scientists of tedious or rote aspects of their labor. We hope that our work will ultimately increase the number and diversity of people that can make meaningful scholarly contributions.

6 Program Committee

1. Aida Usmanova, Leuphana Universität Lüneburg
2. Akiko Aizawa, National Institute of Informatics
3. Allan Hanbury, Complexity Science Hub & Technische Universität Wien
4. Allen G Roush, Oracle
5. Anita De Waard, Utrecht University
6. Antonio Pieri, Elsevier
7. Biswadip Mandal, University of Texas at Dallas
8. Boris Veytsman, Chan Zuckerberg Initiative & George Mason University
9. Buse Sibel Korkmaz, Imperial College London
10. Dan Li, Elsevier
11. Daniel Acuna, University of Colorado at Boulder

[7]https://www.codabench.org/competitions/5840/

12. Dayne Freitag, SRI International
13. Ekaterina Borisova, Technische Universität Berlin & Deutsches Forschungszentrum für Künstliche Intelligenz GmbH (DFKI)
14. Fabio Barth, Deutsches Forschungszentrum für Künstliche Intelligenz GmbH (DFKI)
15. Hamed Alhoori, Northern Illinois University
16. Hiroki Teranishi, Nara Institute of Science and Technology & RIKEN
17. Ibrahim Al Azher, Northern Illinois University
18. Ioana Buhnila, University of Lorraine
19. James Dunham, Georgetown University
20. Jay DeYoung, Allen Institute for Artificial Intelligence
21. Miftahul Jannat Mokarrama, Northern Illinois University
22. Neil R. Smalheiser, University of Illinois at Chicago
23. Nicolau Duran-Silva, Universitat Pompeu Fabra
24. Petr Knoth, Open University
25. Philipp Mayr, GESIS – Leibniz Institute for the Social Sciences
26. Pierre Senellart, Ecole Normale Supérieure
27. Raia Abu Ahmad, Deutsches Forschungszentrum für Künstliche Intelligenz GmbH (DFKI)
28. Roman Kern, Know Center GmbH & Technische Universität Graz
29. Sameera Horawalavithana, Pacific Northwest National Laboratory
30. Sebastian Schellhammer, GESIS – Leibniz Institute for the Social Sciences
31. Sharmila Upadhyaya, GESIS – Leibniz Institute for the Social Sciences
32. Shiyuan Zhang, University of Illinois at Urbana-Champaign
33. Soham Chitnis, New York University
34. Sotaro Takeshita, University of Mannheim
35. Tamjid Azad, Northern Illinois University
36. Taro Watanabe, Nara Institute of Science and Technology
37. Tohida Rehman, Jadavpur University
38. Tosho Hirasawa, Tokyo Metropolitan University
39. Wojtek Sylwestrzak, University of Warsaw
40. Wolfgang Otto, GESIS – Leibniz Institute for the Social Sciences
41. Xinyuan Lu, National University of Singapore
42. Yoshitomo Matsubara, Yahoo!
43. Yupeng Cao, Stevens Institute of Technology
44. Wuhe Zou, Netease Group

Acknowledgements

The organizers wish to thank all those who contributed to this workshop series: The researchers who submitted papers, the keynote speakers, the many reviewers who generously offered their time and expertise, and the participants of the workshop.
Philipp Mayr received funding from Deutsche Forschungsgemeinschaft under grant: MA 3964/8-2; the OUTCITE project (Backes et al., 2024) and the European Union under the Horizon Europe grant OMINO - Overcoming Multilevel INformation Overload (Hołyst et al., 2024) under grant number 101086321.
Georg Rehm was supported through the project NFDI for Data Science and Artificial Intelligence (NFDI4DS) as part of the non-profit association National Research Data Infrastructure (NFDI e. V.). The NFDI is funded by the Federal Republic of Germany and its states.

References

Raia Abu Ahmad, Aida Usmanova, and Georg Rehm. 2025a. The ClimateCheck dataset: Mapping social media claims about climate change to corresponding scholarly articles. In *Proceedings of the 5th Workshop on Scholarly Document Processing (SDP)*, Vienna, Austria.

Raia Abu Ahmad, Aida Usmanova, and Georg Rehm. 2025b. The ClimateCheck shared task: Scientific fact-checking of social media claims about climate change. In *Proceedings of the 5th Workshop on Scholarly Document Processing (SDP)*, Vienna, Austria.

Esma Aïmeur, Sabrine Amri, and Gilles Brassard. 2023. Fake news, disinformation and misinformation in social media: a review. *Social Network Analysis and Mining*, 13(1):30.

Ahmed Al-Rawi, Derrick O'Keefe, Oumar Kane, and Aimé-Jules Bizimana. 2021. Twitter's fake news discourses around climate change and global warming. *Frontiers in Communication*, 6:729818.

Monther Aldwairi and Ali Alwahedi. 2018. Detecting fake news in social media networks. *Procedia Computer Science*, 141:215–222.

Tobias Backes, Anastasiia Iurshina, Muhammad Ahsan Shahid, and Philipp Mayr. 2024. Comparing Free Reference Extraction Pipelines. *International Journal on Digital Libraries*.

Iz Beltagy, Arman Cohan, Guy Feigenblat, Dayne Freitag, Tirthankar Ghosal, Keith Hall, Drahomira Herrmannova, Petr Knoth, Kyle Lo, Philipp Mayr, Robert Patton, Michal Shmueli-Scheuer, Anita de Waard, Kuansan Wang, and Lucy Lu Wang. 2021. Overview of the second workshop on scholarly document processing. In *Proceedings of the Second Workshop on Scholarly Document Processing*, pages 159–165, Online. Association for Computational Linguistics.

Ekaterina Borisova, Nikolas Rauscher, and Georg Rehm. 2025. SciVQA 2025: Overview of the first scientific visual question answering shared task. In *Proceedings of the 5th Workshop on Scholarly Document Processing (SDP)*, Vienna, Austria. Association for Computational Linguistics.

Muthu Kumar Chandrasekaran, Guy Feigenblat, Dayne Freitag, Tirthankar Ghosal, Eduard Hovy, Philipp Mayr, Michal Shmueli-Scheuer, and Anita de Waard. 2020. Overview of the First Workshop on Scholarly Document Processing (SDP). In *Proceedings of the First Workshop on Scholarly Document Processing*, pages 1–6, Online. Association for Computational Linguistics.

Christopher Clark and Santosh Divvala. 2016. Pdffigures 2.0: Mining figures from research papers. In *2016 IEEE/ACM Joint Conference on Digital Libraries (JCDL)*, pages 143–152.

Arman Cohan, Guy Feigenblat, Dayne Freitag, Tirthankar Ghosal, Drahomira Herrmannova, Petr Knoth, Kyle Lo, Philipp Mayr, Michal Shmueli-Scheuer, Anita de Waard, and Lucy Lu Wang. 2022. Overview of the third workshop on scholarly document processing. In *Proceedings of the Third Workshop on Scholarly Document Processing*, pages 1–6, Gyeongju, Republic of Korea. Association for Computational Linguistics.

John Dagdelen, Alexander Dunn, Sanghoon Lee, Nicholas Walker, Andrew S Rosen, Gerbrand Ceder, Kristin A Persson, and Anubhav Jain. 2024. Structured information extraction from scientific text with large language models. *Nature Communications*, 15(1):1418.

Jennifer R Fownes, Chao Yu, and Drew B Margolin. 2018. Twitter and climate change. *Sociology Compass*, 12(6):e12587.

Tirthankar Ghosal, Amanpreet Singh, Anita De Waard, Philipp Mayr, Aakanksha Naik, Orion Weller, Yoonjoo Lee, Zejiang Shen, and Yanxia Qin. 2024. Overview of the fourth workshop on scholarly document processing. In *Proceedings of the Fourth Workshop on Scholarly Document Processing (SDP 2024)*, pages 1–6.

Salim Hafid, Sebastian Schellhammer, Sandra Bringay, Konstantin Todorov, and Stefan Dietze. 2022. Scitweets-a dataset and annotation framework for detecting scientific online discourse. In *Proceedings of the 31st ACM International Conference on Information & Knowledge Management*, pages 3988–3992.

Janusz A. Hołyst, Philipp Mayr, Michael Thelwall, Ingo Frommholz, Shlomo Havlin, Alon Sela, Yoed N. Kenett, Denis Helic, Aljoša Rehar, Sebastijan R. Maček, Przemysław Kazienko, Tomasz Kajdanowicz, Przemysław Biecek, Boleslaw K. Szymanski, and Julian Sienkiewicz. 2024. Protect our environment from information overload. *Nature Human Behaviour*, 8:402–403.

Kung-Hsiang Huang, Hou Pong Chan, Yi R. Fung, Haoyi Qiu, Mingyang Zhou, Shafiq Joty, Shih-Fu Chang, and Heng Ji. 2024. From pixels to insights: A survey on automatic chart understanding in the era of large foundation models.

Anthony James Hughes and Xingyi Song. 2024. Identifying and aligning medical claims made on social media with medical evidence. In *Proceedings of the 2024 Joint International Conference on Computational Linguistics, Language Resources and Evaluation (LREC-COLING 2024)*, pages 8580–8593.

Dan Li, Bogdan Palfi, Colin Kehang Zhang, Jaiganesh Subramanian, Adrian Raudaschl, Yoshiko Kakita, Anita Dewaard, Zubair Afzal, and Georgios Tsatsaronis. 2025. Overview of the scihal25 shared task on hallucination detection for scientific content. In *The 5th Workshop on Scholarly Document Processing @ ACL 2025*.

Chin-Yew Lin. 2004. ROUGE: A package for automatic evaluation of summaries. In *Text Summarization Branches Out*, pages 74–81, Barcelona, Spain. Association for Computational Linguistics.

Fanqing Meng, Wenqi Shao, Quanfeng Lu, Peng Gao, Kaipeng Zhang, Yu Qiao, and Ping Luo. 2024. ChartAssistant: A universal chart multimodal language model via chart-to-table pre-training and multitask instruction tuning. In *Findings of the Association for Computational Linguistics: ACL 2024*, pages 7775–7803, Bangkok, Thailand. Association for Computational Linguistics.

Zhen Xu, Sergio Escalera, Adrien Pavão, Magali Richard, Wei-Wei Tu, Quanming Yao, Huan Zhao, and Isabelle Guyon. 2022. Codabench: Flexible, easy-to-use, and reproducible meta-benchmark platform. *Patterns*, 3(7):100543.

Tianyi Zhang*, Varsha Kishore*, Felix Wu*, Kilian Q. Weinberger, and Yoav Artzi. 2020. BERTScore: Evaluating text generation with BERT. In *International Conference on Learning Representations*.

Mingyang Zhou, Yi Fung, Long Chen, Christopher Thomas, Heng Ji, and Shih-Fu Chang. 2023. Enhanced chart understanding via visual language pretraining on plot table pairs. In *Findings of the Association for Computational Linguistics: ACL 2023*, pages 1314–1326, Toronto, Canada. Association for Computational Linguistics.

TeXpert: A Multi-Level Benchmark for Evaluating LaTeX Code Generation by LLMs

Sahil Kale[1*] **Vijaykant Nadadur**[1]
[1]Knowledgeverse AI
{sahil, vrn}@k-v.ai

Abstract

LaTeX's precision and flexibility in typesetting have made it the gold standard for the preparation of scientific documentation. Large Language Models (LLMs) present a promising opportunity for researchers to produce publication-ready material using LaTeX with natural language instructions, yet current benchmarks completely lack evaluation of this ability. By introducing TeXpert, our benchmark dataset with natural language prompts for generating LaTeX code focused on components of scientific documents across multiple difficulty levels, we conduct an in-depth analysis of LLM performance in this regard and identify frequent error types. Our evaluation across open and closed-source LLMs highlights multiple key findings: LLMs excelling on standard benchmarks perform poorly in LaTeX generation with a significant accuracy drop-off as the complexity of tasks increases; open-source models like DeepSeek v3 and DeepSeek Coder strongly rival closed-source counterparts in LaTeX tasks; and formatting and package errors are unexpectedly prevalent, suggesting a lack of diverse LaTeX examples in the training datasets of most LLMs. Our dataset, code, and model evaluations are available on GitHub. [1]

1 Introduction

LaTeX is a highly versatile and widely adopted document preparation system built over the TeX typesetting program (LaTeX). With research-specific advantages including robust handling of mathematical equations, simple formatting commands, and straightforward management of references, it is a popular choice to produce publication-ready scientific material (Bos and McCurley, 2023).

The recent emergence of LLMs across various applications (García-Ferrero et al., 2024; Sherifi et al., 2024; Zhao et al., 2024) coupled with improved instruction-following ability (Yin et al., 2023; He et al., 2024) prompts an essential research question: "*Can LLMs generate publication-ready LaTeX code for components of scientific documents from natural language instructions?*". Through this research, we aim to evaluate the capability of LLMs in generating syntactically and logically accurate LaTeX code (which we refer to as accurate LaTeX code generation or simply LaTeX generation) and analyse the main types of errors they encounter.

While certain aspects of LaTeX code generation with LLMs, especially for mathematical content (Zou et al., 2024; Zhang et al., 2024), have been significantly studied, a comprehensive study of LLMs' LaTeX generation ability for various components commonly used in scientific documents (such as tables, figures, bibliography, etc.) remains unexplored. We believe a comprehensive benchmark for evaluating LLMs on LaTeX generation offers two key benefits: analysing common errors LLMs make in generating LaTeX code can provide format and error-based hints for flagging AI-generated research material (Chamezopoulos et al., 2024), and delineating the complexity of LaTeX tasks that LLMs can reliably perform can greatly reduce researchers' effort on formatting and typesetting.

In this work, we evaluate a diverse range of closed-source and open-source LLMs on their LaTeX generation capabilities. The main contributions of this paper can be stated as follows:

1. We introduce TeXpert, a benchmark designed to evaluate LLMs in generating accurate LaTeX code from natural language instructions, focused on commands in scientific documents
2. We evaluate popular open and closed-source LLMs on TeXpert by computing the success rate across three difficulty classes
3. We provide comprehensive insights pertaining to LLM limitations in LaTeX generation and identify frequent error types

*Corresponding author. Email: sahil@k-v.ai

[1]https://github.com/knowledge-verse-ai/TeXpert

Proceedings of the Fifth Workshop on Scholarly Document Processing (SDP 2025), pages 7–16
July 31, 2025

2 Related Work

Existing works on the evaluation of LLMs treat LaTeX-based tasks only as a peripheral component or limit their scope to specific output formats. The ability of LLMs to generate mathematical LaTeX equations from various sources has been explored in datasets like MATH (Hendrycks et al., 2021), MathBridge (Jung et al., 2024) and STEM-POM (Zou et al., 2024). Similarly, the STRUC-BENCH dataset (Tang et al., 2024) contains natural language inputs to test LLMs' LaTeX generation ability specific only to tabular content. The im2latex-100k dataset (Deng et al., 2017) also focuses on the narrow aspect of testing the ability of LLMs to convert images of mathematical formulae into LaTeX code, while Image2struct (Roberts et al., 2024) includes testing vision-language models in extracting structured LaTeX information from images.

A straightforward idea to evaluate the natural language to LaTeX ability of LLMs would be to generate free-to-use LaTeX templates [2] representing various document styles and formats using textual queries. However, these templates are often too large to be directly generated by large language models (LLMs) and are constrained only to a standard set of basic commands, limiting their applicability in this research. Several instruction-following benchmarks for LLMs evaluate their ability to follow natural language commands (Qin et al., 2024; Chen et al., 2024); however, there is a notable absence of datasets specifically designed to assess models in LaTeX code generation for scientific material.

Identifying and acting upon this need, we present TeXpert, an organised dataset designed to evaluate LLMs' capability to generate syntactically and logically correct LaTeX code from textual descriptions, focused on scientific document components.

3 Dataset Construction

To assess LLMs' capability to convert unstructured textual descriptions to LaTeX code, we build a benchmark dataset by following the process described in Figure 1. The process involves two major steps:

Collecting atomic LaTeX commands: We begin by systematically analyzing a range of data sources and scientific document templates to collect atomic LaTeX commands (details of sources and methodology are provided in Appendix A.1). These atomic commands, representing the minimal functional units commonly used in scientific writing and typically consisting of a backslash followed by a keyword and optional arguments, were extracted to form the basis of our dataset. The commands were then classified into 5 categories based on their purpose, as shown in Table 1. By adding an extra base step of collecting atomic commands commonly found in scientific formats, we regulate the scope of our final dataset containing LaTeX code generation tasks.

Generating TeXpert using atomic LaTeX commands: We curate a structured benchmark dataset containing natural language instructions for generating LaTeX code for various elements of scientific content using a combination of manual effort and LLM-based command generation. We build our dataset incrementally (while restricting the domain to atomic commands collected in the previous step to ensure specificity to scientific document components) using three different classes, namely Simple, Average and Hard, by increasing the complexity of tasks, the number of distinct atomic commands

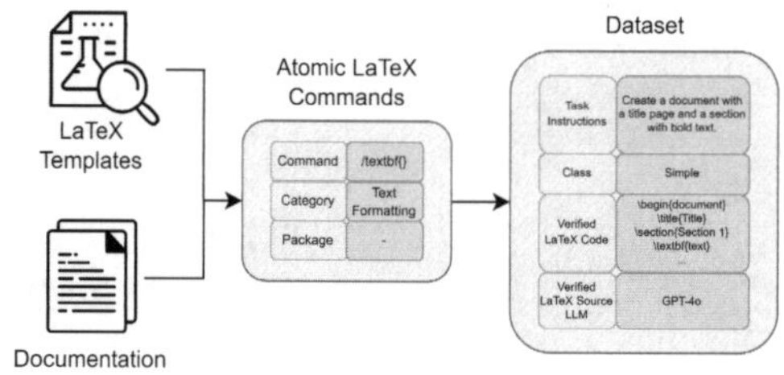

Figure 1: Process used to construct TeXpert, along with the dataset schema

Category	Atomic commands	Example
Text Formatting	86	\textbf
Equations and Symbols	83	\arcsin
Document Structure	75	\subsubsection{ }
Citation and References	39	\bibliographystyle {style}
Tables and Figures	36	\cellcolor{color}
Total	319	

Table 1: Details of the atomic LaTeX commands used to build TeXpert

[2] https://www.overleaf.com/latex/templates

and components of scientific documents needed, adding package requirements, and so on.

In order to classify the final task complexity as Simple, Average or Hard, we use specific constraints based on the number of commands, packages and components, precise description of which, along with a few examples, is found in Table 6 in Appendix A.2. With a focus on a small but high-quality dataset, we manually verify every row across all three classes in our dataset to ensure clear LaTeX generation requirements and consistency with the difficulty constraints. Our final dataset, named TeXpert, thus contains instructions and a classification label based on difficulty. After experimentation, we also add columns with a LaTeX code satisfying all requirements (if generated by any LLM) for future fine-tuning, along with the LLM that generated this correct code, resulting in the final schema in Figure 1. Statistics of our dataset are shown in Table 2.

4 Experimental Setup

We utilise a systematic evaluation framework to assess LLMs' ability to generate syntactically correct LaTeX code from natural language prompts using the TeXpert dataset. We experiment with a wide range of open-source LLMs including Mistral Large 24.11 (AI, 2024b), Codestral (AI, 2024a), DeepSeek V3 (DeepSeek-AI, 2024), and DeepSeek Coder 33b (Guo et al., 2024) as well as multiple high-performance closed-source models including GPT-4o (OpenAI, 2024b), GPT-4o-mini (OpenAI, 2024a), Gemini 1.5 Flash (Team, 2024), Claude 3.5 Sonnet (Anthropic, 2024) and Grok 2-1212 (xAI, 2024).

For each sample across the three difficulty levels in TeXpert, we provide the LLM with a prompt containing task instructions for LaTeX code generation (provided in Figure 5 in Appendix B). During generation, model parameters were set to predetermined values to ensure deterministic outputs, as detailed in Table 11 in Appendix B. Detailed model configurations are provided in Section B.3 in Appendix B. Rule-based extraction techniques are used to extract the LaTeX code from the response.

We then evaluate each LLM's response with GPT-4o as a judge, using a predefined evaluation prompt (refer to Figure 4 in Appendix B) to compute success rates and classify error types (described in Table 7 in Appendix B). The evaluation prompt was iteratively refined through manual spot checks of evaluation outputs, focusing on clarity, correctness, and alignment with evaluation criteria. This process continued until the prompt consistently yielded reliable and interpretable results, as per our judgment. For the hard set, we also provide manually generated and verified LaTeX code as a reference during evaluation, to help identify all requirements of the task. To mitigate potential evaluation bias from using the same model family as the judge, we use DeepSeek v3 as an evaluator for GPT-4o and GPT-4o-mini.

5 Result Discussion

The accuracy of LaTeX generation for scientific documents across difficulty classes is presented in Table 3 and visualised in Figure 2. The overall distribution of error types across all difficulty levels is presented in Table 4 and Figure 3, while individual error distributions for Simple, Average, and Hard difficulty classes are also provided in Tables 8, 9 and 10 in Appendix B.2, respectively. From Table 3, we can infer that GPT-4o outshines all other LLMs in LaTeX code generation, closely followed by DeepSeek v3. DeepSeek Coder 33b provides the best performance on the most complex tasks.

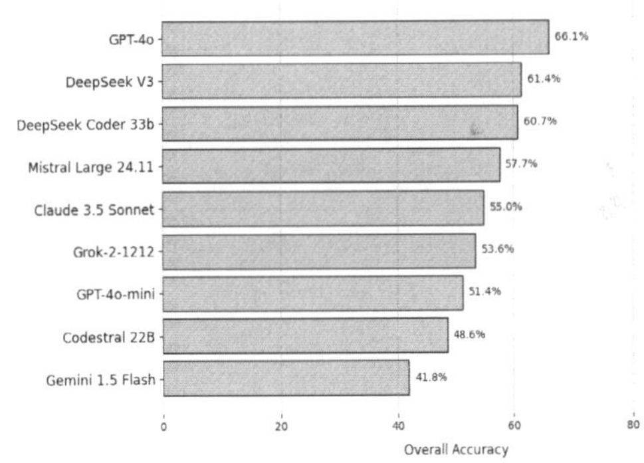

Figure 2: Overall accuracy for LaTeX generation tasks by various LLMs

LaTeX generation tasks expose fundamental LLM shortcomings: Even models that perform highly on other benchmarks like GPT-4o and Mistral Large fail to achieve over 80% and 60% accuracy in simple and average sets, respectively. This reveals a critical capability gap in using LLMs for formatting scientific documents in LaTeX, most likely due to the scarcity of LaTeX examples in training datasets.

Hard LaTeX tasks reveal a universal limitation

Difficulty Class	No. of samples	Average length of textual instructions	Average no. of atomic LaTeX commands	Average no. of extra LaTeX packages
Simple	250	115.8 ± 24 characters	10.9 ± 7.2	0.5 ± 0.8
Average	150	299.1 ± 85.7 characters	51.2 ± 29.2	3.6 ± 2.4
Hard	40	558.4 ± 216.7 characters	85.9 ± 31.0	6.6 ± 2.0

Table 2: Statistics of the TeXpert dataset, organised by difficulty class

Model	Accuracy %			
	Simple	Average	Hard	Overall
Closed-Source Models				
GPT-4o-mini	62.4	45.3	5	51.4
GPT-4o	**78.8**	58.7	15	**66.1**
Claude-3.5 Sonnet	62.8	56.7	0	55.0
Gemini 1.5 Flash	53.6	33.3	0	41.8
Grok 2 1212	62.4	52.0	5	53.6
Open-Source Models				
Mistral Large 24.11	64.4	**59.33**	10	57.7
Codestral 22B	60.8	41.3	0	48.6
DeepSeek V3	71.2	58.7	10	61.4
DeepSeek Coder 33b	69.2	58.0	**17.5**	60.7

Table 3: Main accuracy results (in %). Values in bold indicate the best accuracy for each difficulty class

Model	Error Types in %				
	CE	SE	LE	PE	FE
Closed-Source Models					
GPT-4o-mini	0.0	1.3	53.7	23.2	21.7
GPT-4o	0.0	2.1	59.1	15.2	23.6
Claude-3.5 Sonnet	0.0	5.3	44.3	29.9	20.6
Gemini 1.5 Flash	3.4	2.0	52.3	21.6	20.8
Grok-2 1212	1.2	5.3	46.5	25.5	21.4
Open-Source Models					
Mistral Large 24.11	0.0	2.5	53.0	20.8	23.7
Codestral 22B	0.6	2.8	52.5	18.8	25.3
DeepSeek V3	1.2	3.8	54.3	18.7	22.0
DeepSeek Coder 33b	0.4	2.6	54.0	20.5	22.5

Table 4: Overall error distribution for LaTeX generation tasks by various LLMs. CE = Capability Error, SE = Syntax Error, LE = Logical Error, PE = Package Error, FE = Formatting Error

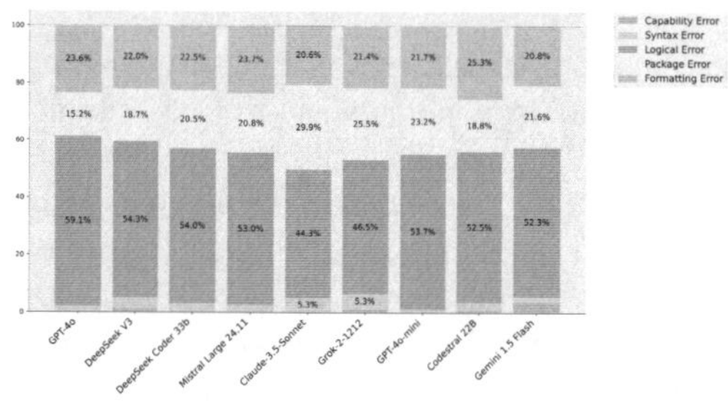

Figure 3: Error distribution for LaTeX generation tasks by various LLMs

across models: Accuracy across the Simple and Average sets remains consistent across models, however, models show a dramatic performance cliff on hard tasks, with Claude and Gemini completely failing. This consistent degradation pattern clearly shows a threshold on the number and complexity of instructions for LaTeX generation using LLMs, which can be presumed to lie between instruction statistics for the Average and Hard sets in Table 2.

Open-source models strongly rival closed-source ones in LaTeX generation: Open-source models like DeepSeek V3 and DeepSeek Coder 33b perform well on par with frontier closed-source models like GPT-4o and Claude-3.5-Sonnet in overall accuracy with minimal capability errors as well. Notably, DeepSeek Coder 33b greatly outperforms Claude 3.5 Sonnet and Grok 2 in the Hard set. This demonstrates the potential of open-source models to provide powerful yet cost-effective alternatives.

6 Error Analysis

In this section, we provide a brief analysis of the most common error types and probable sources during LaTeX generation by LLMs. From our perspective, most powerful LLMs still struggle to provide error-free code due to basic oversights like missing packages and unfaithful instruction following. It is encouraging to see minimal capability errors and syntax errors. We leave an in-depth analysis of the root cause of errors to the future scope.

Logical errors dominate: Logical errors consistently account for the majority of issues across LLMs, highlighting struggles to fully satisfy task requirements. In all the cases we analysed, the most pronounced errors across all model variants were focused on missed instructions and wrong structural placement, especially in GPT-4o-mini and all open-source models. Similarly, error clustering in multiple equation and table generation tasks indicates that LLMs like DeepSeek v3 and Mistral Large struggle with maintaining long-range consistency. We believe these errors likely arise from weak structural understanding inherent in LLMs, limited exposure to LaTeX context, and misalignment between pretraining tasks and formal document generation.

Frequent formatting lapses: Notably, formatting errors occur far more frequently than we anticipated in all the LLMs we experimented with. Analysis of the evaluations reveals that these errors primarily involve incorrect environment selection and malformed tables or captions accompanying large tables or figures. Such issues indicate limited structural understanding and inadequate grounding in LaTeX syntax, even in larger models like DeepSeek v3 and GPT-4o, showing that scale alone is not the solution. We speculate that these errors stem from a scarcity of training data and examples specifically addressing table formatting and related constructs.

Package errors are concerning: Package errors are prominently caused by improper or incomplete inclusion and configuration of essential LaTeX packages, especially bibliography-related ones, most prominent in Claude 3.5 Sonnet. GPT-4o has the lowest share of missing packages, showing encouraging signs that more inclusive training data might mitigate this issue, although Codestral's minimal package error rate also suggests potential for alternative approaches to reduce them further. Additionally, the use of non-standard or incompatible packages, especially in DeepSeek and Mistral models, is concerning and may point to LLMs hallucinating or making up packages to fill reasoning gaps. Overall, package issues suggest a fundamental gap in dependency management and environment consistency within LaTeX code generated by LLMs.

7 Conclusion

We curate TeXpert, a comprehensive benchmark designed to challenge LLMs to evaluate their LaTeX code generation capability from natural language prompts. Our dataset consists of a total of 440 high-quality samples, organised by difficulty. Our findings reveal that LaTeX generation is still an underperforming skill in LLMs and that there is a need to include LaTeX package details and complex layouts in the training data for LLMs to improve their capability in this task. By making the code and dataset for TeXpert publicly available, we hope to support and encourage further research within the community.

Limitations

Our research marks a significant step forward in providing a benchmark for evaluating the LaTeX generation capabilities of LLMs. However, we acknowledge the limitations of our work as follows:

- **Limited dataset size:** The Hard set's restricted size of 40 samples is a possible challenge in the generalisability of our findings. To address this, we encourage future work to increase the number and complexity of hard examples to broaden the benchmark's effectiveness.
- **Fine-tuning models and improved prompts:** Using our dataset to fine-tune models and reduce logical and package errors in LaTeX-based tasks is another straightforward extension to our work, along with checking advanced prompting structures for performance improvements.
- **Additional LaTeX sources and applications:** While our work focuses on generating LaTeX code for only scientific documents, incorporating sources and tasks for other document types, such as resumes and books, would broaden the research scope.

References

Asma Ben Abacha, Wen wai Yim, Yujuan Fu, Zhaoyi Sun, Meliha Yetisgen, Fei Xia, and Thomas Lin. 2025. Medec: A benchmark for medical error detection and correction in clinical notes. *Preprint*, arXiv:2412.19260.

Mistral AI. 2024a. Codestral. Accessed: 2025-01-05.

Mistral AI. 2024b. Mistral large. Accessed: 2025-01-05.

Anthropic. 2024. Model card claude 3 addendum. Accessed: 2025-01-05.

Joppe W. Bos and Kevin S. McCurley. 2023. Latex, metadata, and publishing workflows. *Preprint*, arXiv:2301.08277.

Savvas Chamezopoulos, Drahomira Herrmannova, Anita De Waard, Drahomira Herrmannova, Domenic Rosati, and Yury Kashnitsky. 2024. Overview of the DagPap24 shared task on detecting automatically generated scientific paper. In *Proceedings of the Fourth Workshop on Scholarly Document Processing (SDP 2024)*, pages 7–11, Bangkok, Thailand. Association for Computational Linguistics.

Xinyi Chen, Baohao Liao, Jirui Qi, Panagiotis Eustratiadis, Christof Monz, Arianna Bisazza, and Maarten de Rijke. 2024. The SIFo benchmark: Investigating the sequential instruction following ability of large language models. In *Findings of the Association for Computational Linguistics: EMNLP 2024*, pages 1691–1706, Miami, Florida, USA. Association for Computational Linguistics.

DeepSeek-AI. 2024. Deepseek-v3 technical report. *Preprint*, arXiv:2412.19437.

Yuntian Deng, Anssi Kanervisto, Jeffrey Ling, and Alexander M. Rush. 2017. Image-to-markup generation with coarse-to-fine attention. *Preprint*, arXiv:1609.04938.

Iker García-Ferrero, Rodrigo Agerri, Aitziber Atutxa Salazar, Elena Cabrio, Iker de la Iglesia, Alberto Lavelli, Bernardo Magnini, Benjamin Molinet, Johana Ramirez-Romero, German Rigau, Jose Maria Villa-Gonzalez, Serena Villata, and Andrea Zaninello. 2024. MedMT5: An open-source multilingual text-to-text LLM for the medical domain. In *Proceedings of the 2024 Joint International Conference on Computational Linguistics, Language Resources and Evaluation (LREC-COLING 2024)*, pages 11165–11177, Torino, Italia. ELRA and ICCL.

Daya Guo, Qihao Zhu, Dejian Yang, Zhenda Xie, Kai Dong, Wentao Zhang, Guanting Chen, Xiao Bi, Y. Wu, Y. K. Li, Fuli Luo, Yingfei Xiong, and Wenfeng Liang. 2024. Deepseek-coder: When the large language model meets programming – the rise of code intelligence. *Preprint*, arXiv:2401.14196.

Qianyu He, Jie Zeng, Qianxi He, Jiaqing Liang, and Yanghua Xiao. 2024. From complex to simple: Enhancing multi-constraint complex instruction following ability of large language models. In *Findings of the Association for Computational Linguistics: EMNLP 2024*, pages 10864–10882, Miami, Florida, USA. Association for Computational Linguistics.

Dan Hendrycks, Collin Burns, Saurav Kadavath, Akul Arora, Steven Basart, Eric Tang, Dawn Song, and Jacob Steinhardt. 2021. Measuring mathematical problem solving with the math dataset. *Preprint*, arXiv:2103.03874.

Kyudan Jung, Sieun Hyeon, Jeong Youn Kwon, Nam-Joon Kim, Hyun Gon Ryu, Hyuk-Jae Lee, and Jaeyoung Do. 2024. Mathbridge: A large corpus dataset for translating spoken mathematical expressions into $latex$ formulas for improved readability. *Preprint*, arXiv:2408.07081.

LaTeX. An introduction to LaTeX. `https://www.latex-project.org/about/`. Accessed: 2025-01-04.

OpenAI. 2024a. Gpt-4o mini: Advancing cost-efficient intelligence. Accessed: 2025-01-05.

OpenAI. 2024b. Gpt-4o system card. Accessed: 2025-01-05.

Yiwei Qin, Kaiqiang Song, Yebowen Hu, Wenlin Yao, Sangwoo Cho, Xiaoyang Wang, Xuansheng Wu, Fei Liu, Pengfei Liu, and Dong Yu. 2024. InFoBench: Evaluating instruction following ability in large language models. In *Findings of the Association for Computational Linguistics: ACL 2024*, pages 13025–13048, Bangkok, Thailand. Association for Computational Linguistics.

Josselin Somerville Roberts, Tony Lee, Chi Heem Wong, Michihiro Yasunaga, Yifan Mai, and Percy Liang. 2024. Image2struct: Benchmarking structure extraction for vision-language models. *Preprint*, arXiv:2410.22456.

Betim Sherifi, Khaled Slhoub, and Fitzroy Nembhard. 2024. The potential of llms in automating software testing: From generation to reporting. *Preprint*, arXiv:2501.00217.

Xiangru Tang, Yiming Zong, Jason Phang, Yilun Zhao, Wangchunshu Zhou, Arman Cohan, and Mark Gerstein. 2024. Struc-bench: Are large language models really good at generating complex structured data? *Preprint*, arXiv:2309.08963.

Gemini Team. 2024. Gemini 1.5: Unlocking multimodal understanding across millions of tokens of context. *Preprint*, arXiv:2403.05530.

xAI. 2024. Grok 2. Accessed: 2025-01-05.

Wenpeng Yin, Qinyuan Ye, Pengfei Liu, Xiang Ren, and Hinrich Schütze. 2023. LLM-driven instruction following: Progresses and concerns. In *Proceedings of the 2023 Conference on Empirical Methods in Natural Language Processing: Tutorial Abstracts*, pages 19–25, Singapore. Association for Computational Linguistics.

Renrui Zhang, Dongzhi Jiang, Yichi Zhang, Haokun Lin, Ziyu Guo, Pengshuo Qiu, Aojun Zhou, Pan Lu, Kai-Wei Chang, Peng Gao, and Hongsheng Li. 2024. Mathverse: Does your multi-modal llm truly see the diagrams in visual math problems? *Preprint*, arXiv:2403.14624.

Yiyun Zhao, Prateek Singh, Hanoz Bhathena, Bernardo Ramos, Aviral Joshi, Swaroop Gadiyaram, and Saket Sharma. 2024. Optimizing LLM based retrieval augmented generation pipelines in the financial domain. In *Proceedings of the 2024 Conference of the North*

American Chapter of the Association for Computational Linguistics: Human Language Technologies (Volume 6: Industry Track), pages 279–294, Mexico City, Mexico. Association for Computational Linguistics.

Jiaru Zou, Qing Wang, Pratyush Thakur, and Nickvash Kani. 2024. Stem-pom: Evaluating language models math-symbol reasoning in document parsing. *Preprint*, arXiv:2411.00387.

A Curation of TeXpert - Additional Details

A.1 Data Collection and Sources

To build the core of our TeXpert dataset, we manually extracted atomic commands from the Overleaf documentation listed in row 1 of Table 5 and from 25 documents each in LaTeX template repositories given in rows 2 and 3 of Table 5. This approach ensured a diverse range of document formats and LaTeX commands commonly used in scientific materials. For each document, a Python script using regular expressions was used to extract atomic LaTeX commands. These commands were then manually verified and grouped into five categories based on their function, as shown in Table 1. This process was intended to focus the dataset on commonly used LaTeX elements in scientific writing.

A.2 Difficulty constraints

Table 6 shows the constraints followed while classifying samples into difficulty classes (Simple/Average/Hard) during the generation of tasks in the TeXpert dataset. A randomly chosen example from each set is also provided for reference.

B Experimentation - Additional Details

B.1 Prompts

The prompts used during experimentation to evaluate responses using GPT-4o/DeepSeek v3 as a judge and to generate LaTeX code using natural language instructions and are given in Figures 4 and 4 respectively.

B.2 Error descriptions and distribution

Details of error types along with examples are given in Table 7. Additionally, the individual error distributions for Simple, Average, and Hard difficulty classes for each LLM are given in Tables 8, 9 and 10 respectively.

B.3 Model parameters

We report the generation parameters for all models used in our experiments to ensure transparency and reproducibility. All models were accessed through provider APIs, and the common parameter settings used across all models (except Anthropic models) are listed in Table 11. The model sizes of all closed-source models are approximate and taken from Abacha et al. (2025).

OpenAI Models: We run our experiments on two flagship models, GPT-4o (~200B parameters) and GPT-4o-mini (~8B parameters). We use the OpenAI Python SDK to access the models via API, specifying `seed=1234` and `n=1` along with the parameter values listed in Table 11, to ensure maximum determinism in responses. All other parameters are kept to default values.

DeepSeek Models: We use two recently released models, DeepSeek v3 (~671B parameters) and DeepSeek Coder (~33B parameters). DeepSeek models were accessed using the OpenAI Python SDK by specifying the DeepSeek URL endpoint and authentication details. Here too, we set `seed=1234` and `n=1` along with the parameter values listed in Table 11 during experimentation, keeping the rest to default values.

Mistral Models: We experiment with two powerful models, Mistral-Large-Instruct-2411 (~123B parameters) and Codestral-22B-v0.1 (~22B parameters). Both models were accessed using the official API in Mistral Python SDK, with an extra parameter `random_seed=1234` along with values in Table 11, with the rest as default.

Google AI Models: The Gemini 1.5 flash model was accessed using the official Google Generative AI Python SDK. Within the Generation Config, we set parameters values to those mentioned in Table 11, along with `candidate_count=1` and the rest as default.

xAI Models: We use a recently released Grok-2-1212 model by xAI, accessed using the OpenAI Python SDK by specifying the xAI endpoint. Here too, we set `seed=1234` and `n=1` along with the parameter values listed in Table 11 during experimentation, keeping the rest to default values.

Anthropic Models: The Claude 3.5 Sonnet model (~175B parameters) was accessed via the official Anthropic Python SDK. Due to limited configurable parameters, only `temperature=0.0`, `top_p=1`, and `max_tokens=8096` were explicitly set, with all other settings left at their defaults.

Data Source	URL
Overleaf Documentation	`https://www.overleaf.com/learn`
Overleaf Academic Journal Templates	`https://www.overleaf.com/latex/templates/tagged/academic-journal`
LaTeX Templates (Creodocs)	`https://www.latextemplates.com/cat/academic-journals`

Table 5: Primary sources used for collecting atomic LaTeX commands

Difficulty Class	Length of textual instructions	No. of atomic LaTeX Commands	No. of extra LaTeX packages	No. of specific formatting instructions (for tables, figures, etc.)	Example
Simple	<200 characters	10–20	<2	<2	Create a document with centered text in one block and justified text in another block.
Average	200–500 characters	12–80	2–5	2–5	Create a document with two sections. The first section should contain an aligned set of equations. The second section should contain a centered table, and the table should reference a figure placed in the first section.
Hard	500+ characters	80+	5+	5+	Your task is to produce a scientific research paper for arXiv that has a title page with author names, abstract and keywords, table of contents, and several sections. Add a 3x3 table that has lists in the second column, and figures with bold captions in last column. On every page except the first, add a footer with a signature image. Add an appendix that includes a table with header row entirely merged. Finally, add a custom bibliography.

Table 6: Description of constraints used during classification of tasks in TeXpert with a few examples

Error Type	Description	Examples
Capability Error	The LLM fails or denies to provide a valid response or says the task is out of its capability.	• LLM responds with: "Sorry, I cannot..." • LLM does not include any code in response
Syntax Error	The code generated by the LLM does not follow valid LaTeX syntax.	• Missing closing braces • Unescaped special characters
Logical Error	Mismatches between user instructions and the code logic, i.e., requirements given in natural language are not satisfied by the LaTeX code.	• Table headers omitted when explicitly requested • Missing components in code
Package Error	Required LaTeX packages are missing or commands do not match the document type.	• Using `\includegraphics` without importing the `graphicx` package
Formatting & Referencing Error	Layout issues like inconsistent alignment, font size, or spacing; improper formatting for cross-references, citations, or labels.	• Misaligned tables with inconsistent widths • Using `\ref{sec:1}` without defining `\label{sec:1}`

Table 7: Description and examples of error types used during evaluation of generated LaTeX code by LLMs

Prompt for evaluating LaTeX code

You are a judge tasked with evaluating the given LATEX CODE against the TASK INSTRUCTIONS.

Analyse the LaTeX code thoroughly to determine if it

satisfies the instructions completely and without errors.

Check every line and command with utmost care for the following types of errors:

1. Capability Error: The LLM fails or denies to provide a valid response or says the task is out of its capability.

Examples:

- LLM responds with: "Sorry, I cannot..."
- LLM does not include any code in response at all.

2. Syntax Error: The code does not follow valid LaTeX syntax.

Examples:

- Missing closing braces.
- Unescaped special characters.

3. Logical Error: The code does not fulfill all requirements as given in the task instructions.

Examples:

- Table headers omitted when explicitly requested.
- Missing components or incorrect logic in the code.

4. Package Error: Necessary LaTeX packages for the code are missing, or commands used are incompatible with the document type.

Examples:

- Using \includegraphics without importing the graphicx package.
- Using \chapter in a document class that does not support chapters.

5. Formatting Errors: Errors in layout, alignment, spacing, or referencing. But, make sure to ignore errors where the LaTeX code is missing the 'references.bib' file, it is not needed anywhere!

Examples:

- Misaligned tables with inconsistent column widths.
- Using custom references like \ref{sec:1} without defining \label{sec:1}.

YOUR TASK:

Evaluate the LATEX CODE for errors of the above types. If no errors are present, return 'error' as 'No' in below format. Provide your evaluation only and only in the following Python dictionary format:

```{ "error": "Yes" or "No",

"error_types": list of error types if error is 'Yes', else empty list,

"description": "description of error(s) encountered if error is 'Yes', else empty string" }

```

Figure 4: System prompt used to evaluate LaTeX code generated by LLMs using GPT-4o/DeepSeek v3 as-a-judge

Prompt for LaTeX code generation

You are a helpful LaTeX code assistant.

Your main job is to produce syntactically correct and logically accurate LaTeX code based on instructions given as TASK INSTRUCTIONS.

Make sure to follow each and every small instruction given in the task instructions.

The LaTeX code need not always be for an entire document if not specified, you can give code only according to the parts required.

Your output should be enclosed within ```latex and ``` only.
Do not give any output other than the LaTeX code, please!

Figure 5: System prompt used to generate LaTeX code using LLMs for given textual instructions

Model	Error Types in % - Simple Set				
	CE	SE	LE	PE	FE
Closed-Source Models					
GPT-4o mini	0	0	57	37.4	5.6
GPT-4o	0	6.3	66.67	17.5	9.5
Claude-3.5 Sonnet	0	13.6	36.8	41.6	8
Gemini 1.5 Flash	5.7	2.9	55	27.9	8.6
Grok-2 1212	3.6	9.9	43.2	41.4	1.8
Open-Source Models					
Mistral Large 24.11	0	7.6	55.5	28.6	8.4
Codestral 22B	1.7	5	60.3	22.3	10.7
DeepSeek V3	3.5	5.9	52.9	30.6	7.1
DeepSeek Coder 33b	0	2.2	54.4	36.7	6.7

Table 8: Error distribution for LaTeX generation tasks from the Simple set by various LLMs. CE = Capability Error, SE = Syntax Error, LE = Logical Error, PE = Package Error, FE = Formatting Error

Model	Error Types in % - Average Set				
	CE	SE	LE	PE	FE
Closed-Source Models					
GPT-4o mini	0	1.6	55.9	11.8	30.7
GPT-4o	0	0	58.3	15.7	26
Claude-3.5 Sonnet	0	1	48.5	24.8	25.7
Gemini 1.5 Flash	4.6	0.7	53.6	16.3	24.8
Grok-2 1212	0	3.6	54.5	17.4	24.5
Open-Source Models					
Mistral Large 24.11	0	0	54.1	17.3	28.6
Codestral 22B	0	1.3	53.9	16.2	28.6
DeepSeek V3	0	2.2	60	11.1	26.7
DeepSeek Coder 33b	1.1	4.2	56.8	7.4	30.5

Table 9: Error distribution for LaTeX generation tasks from the Average set by various LLMs. CE = Capability Error, SE = Syntax Error, LE = Logical Error, PE = Package Error, FE = Formatting Error

Model	Error Types in % - Hard Set				
	CE	SE	LE	PE	FE
Closed-Source Models					
GPT-4o mini	0	2.4	48.2	20.5	28.9
GPT-4o	0	0	52.3	12.3	35.4
Claude-3.5 Sonnet	0	1.2	47.6	23.2	28
Gemini 1.5 Flash	0	2.4	48.2	20.5	28.9
Grok-2 1212	0	2.5	41.8	17.7	38
Open-Source Models					
Mistral Large 24.11	0	0	49.3	16.4	34.2
Codestral 22B	0	2.2	43.3	17.8	36.7
DeepSeek V3	0	3.2	50	14.5	32.3
DeepSeek Coder 33b	0	1.4	50.7	17.4	30.4

Table 10: Error distribution for LaTeX generation tasks from the Hard set by various LLMs. CE = Capability Error, SE = Syntax Error, LE = Logical Error, PE = Package Error, FE = Formatting Error

Generation Parameters	
`temperature`	`0.0`
`top_p`	`1.0`
`max_tokens`	`8096`
`frequency_penalty`	`0.0`
`presence_penalty`	`0.0`

Table 11: Generation parameters used across all models

MathD2: Towards Disambiguation of Mathematical Terms

Shufan Jiang*[1,2], Mary Ann Tan*[1,2], and Harald Sack[1,2]

[1]FIZ Karlsruhe – Leibniz Institute for Information Infrastructure, Eggenstein-Leopoldshafen, Germany
[2]Karlsruhe Institute of Technology, Karlsruhe, Germany
{shufan.jiang, ann.tan, harald.sack}fiz-karlsruhe.de

Abstract

In mathematical literature, terms can have multiple meanings based on context. Manual term disambiguation across scholarly articles demands massive efforts from mathematicians. This paper addresses the challenge of automatically determining whether two or more definitions of a mathematical term are semantically different. Specifically, the difficulties of understanding how contextualized textual representation can help solve the problem are investigated. A new dataset MathD2 for mathematical term disambiguation is constructed with ProofWiki's disambiguation pages. Then three approaches based on contextualized textual representation are studied: (1) supervised classification based on the embeddings of concatenated definitions and titles; (2) zero-shot prediction based on semantic textual similarity (STS) between definition and title and (3) zero-shot LLM prompting. The first two approaches achieve accuracy greater than 0.9 on the ground truth dataset, demonstrating the effectiveness of our methods for automatic disambiguation of mathematical definitions. Our dataset and source code are available here: https://github.com/sufianj/MathTermDisambiguation.

1 Introduction

Mathematical scholarly articles contain highly structured statements, such as definitions, axioms, theorems, and proofs. Despite adhering to strict conventions and consistent usage of terminologies, these articles cannot be easily searched or explored through traditional keyword searches.

Mathematical definitions are rich sources of information. The terms defined therein known as *definienda* (singular: *definiendum*) can be automatically extracted. Extracted terms can be used to populate a knowledge base (KB), thereby facilitating knowledge discovery. In addition, these terms are utilized to index relevant mathematical statements and articles for efficient lookup.

To this end, several initiatives have emerged: Argot (Berlioz, 2021) is a collection of term-definition pairs automatically extracted from mathematical papers, allowing users to retrieve all definitions of a given term, while MathMex (Durgin et al., 2024) is a recent search engine for mathematical definitions based on the semantic similarity between a user's query and the definition. Both projects show promising usage of different word embeddings.

Existing research in this area focuses on automatically extracting mathematical definitions from scholarly articles (Berlioz, 2023; Nakagawa et al., 2004; Sun and Zhuge, 2023; Vanetik et al., 2020) and disambiguating definienda (Berlioz, 2021; Jiang and Senellart, 2023). Definienda disambiguation involves identifying and connecting terms to their corresponding mathematical definitions in a reference KB. It is particularly challenging when identical terms for the same concept are defined in various ways (e.g., "path") or when polysemous terms (e.g., "block") refer to distinct concepts in various subtopics (see Table 1). Argot cannot disambiguate polysemous terms, while MathMex cannot guarantee that the retrieved definitions accurately define the queried term.

For this study, ProofWiki[1] serves as the reference list. It is a crowd-sourced online collection of categorized mathematical proofs, including 500 disambiguation pages [2]. Similar to Wikipedia, these disambiguation pages list identical terms, each linking to a dedicated article. The heading of each article is composed of a unique title, appended by the category where the term can be found (e.g. algebra or

*These authors contributed equally to this work.

[1]https://ProofWiki.org/wiki/Main_Page
[2]ProofWiki Disambiguation Pages, https://proofwiki.org/wiki/Category:Definition_Disambiguation_Pages

Proceedings of the Fifth Workshop on Scholarly Document Processing (SDP 2025), pages 17–30
July 31, 2025

Definiendum	Definition in Source Article
block	A *block* in H is a maximal set of tightly-connected hyperedges. (Ergemlidze et al., 2019)
block	A *block* of indices is a set of numbers S where every term $SG_{a,b}(s)$ depends on the same value via division, for all $s \in S$. (Kupin, 2011)
path	If the vertices $v_0, v_1, \ldots, v_k$ of a walk W are distinct then W is called a *Path*. A path with n vertices will be denoted by P_n. P_n has length $n-1$. (Kalayathankal et al., 2015)
path	Let $G = (V, E)$ be a graph. A *path* in a graph is a sequence of vertices such that from each of its vertices there is an edge to the next vertex in the sequence. This is denoted by $P = (u = v_0, v_1 \ldots, v_k = v)$, where $(v_i, v_{i+1}) \in E$ for $0 \leq i \leq k-1$. (Perera and Mizoguchi, 2012)

Table 1: Definitions extracted from different scholarly articles (Jiang and Senellart, 2023). The definition of "path" has different formulations. The notion of "block" has different meanings.

geometry).

This work addresses the following research questions:

RQ1. How well can contextualized word embeddings help the disambiguation of mathematical terms?

RQ2. Which architectures and pre-training strategies are best suited for this task?

RQ3. How well do models trained in the preceding learning paradigm of pre-train + fine-tune compare with state-of-the-art (SOTA) *Instruction-Tuned* Large Language Models (LLMs)?

The main contributions of this work are:

- `MathD2` - a new dataset for **Math**ematical **D**efiniendum **D**isambiguation.
- Exploration of **three different approaches** demonstrating how the disambiguation task can benefit from contextualized semantic representations.
- **Experiment-supported evidence** highlighting the efficiency of sentence embeddings for the addressed disambiguation task.

2 Related Work

The challenges posed by this task are:

(a) the lack of labeled datasets for equivalent mathematical definitions – there is only one example for each definiendum and definition;

(b) the limited number of disambiguation pages;

(c) the unstructured nature of definitions that combine mathematical notations, formulas, and general discourse.

To address (a), entity linking and sentence similarity approaches for mathematical terms are reviewed. To tackle (b) and (c), transformer models (Vaswani et al., 2023) are employed for their capabilities to produce rich, contextualized representations.

Contextualized representations produced by BERT (Bidirectional Encoder Representations from Transformers) (Devlin et al., 2019) encode the meaning of a word according to its context. This means that polysemous words have several, more accurate representations depending on their location in the sentence. BERT is pre-trained on two key tasks: Masked Language Modeling (MLM), where random tokens in a sentence are masked and predicted based on context, and Next Sentence Prediction (NSP), which trains BERT to determine whether a sentence follows another in a discourse. Pre-training with MLM is widely applied for domain adaptation, especially when there is a dearth of data for fine-tuning (Mishra et al., 2021; Jiang et al., 2022). In addition, fine-tuning BERT for specific downstream tasks and domains is straightforward. For instance, by combining BERT's output with a classification layer, it has been adapted for mathematical notation prediction (Jo et al., 2021), definiendum extraction (Jiang and Senellart, 2023) and mathematical statement extraction (Mishra et al., 2024). The Natural Language Inferernce (NLI) datasets (Bowman et al., 2015; Williams et al., 2018) used by BERT's NSP pre-training are related to the task at hand. A piece of supporting evidence is AcroBERT (Chen et al., 2023), an entity linker that reuses BERT for NSP's pre-trained weights and is fine-tuned to link acronyms to their long forms. AcroBERT outperforms BERT and other domain-adapted BERT-based models.

However, the nature of the BERT's pre-training tasks makes it unsuitable for measuring semantic similarity. Sentence BERT (SBERT) [3] (Reimers and Gurevych, 2019) modifies the architecture of BERT to produce meaningful sentence embeddings that can be compared using cosine similarity. Out-of-the-box SBERT achieves superior performance across varied classification tasks involving mathematical texts (Steinfeldt and Mihaljević, 2024). In one such task, the proponents measure the similarity of SBERT embeddings between an input text and the combination of titles and abstracts of mathematical publications in arXiv [4] and zbMATH [5] to predict the classification code of the respective repositories. In the same vein, this study aims to evaluate the effectiveness of semantic textual similarity in linking definitions to titles. Since BERT for NSP and SBERT require different domain adaptation strategies (Reimers and Gurevych, 2019; Steinfeldt and Mihaljević, 2024), this work first identifies the architecture that performs better for the task.

Since the release of powerful LLMs, these models have been applied to various Information Extraction (IE) tasks, including entity linking. Particularly for long-tail entities, LLMAEL (Xin et al., 2024) instructed LLMs to augment the context by expanding entity mentions. The augmented context then serves as additional input to the entity disambiguation component of an IE pipeline (Xin et al., 2024). Meanwhile, (Vollmers et al., 2025) attempted to use LLMs in several IE pipeline components: first by prompting the LLM to identify entity mentions (NER), followed by context expansion using prompts reminiscent of LLMAEL's. Additional experiments conducted in this paper aim to find out the comparability of the proposed textual similarity models and LLMs in identifying another example of long-tail entities embodied by mathematical terms.

[3]https://huggingface.co/sentence-transformers/all-mpnet-base-v2

[4]https://arxiv.org/

[5]https://zbmath.org/

3 Methodology

Mathermatical term disambiguation is formalized as an entity linking task, where the entities refer to the unique article titles in ProofWiki. That is, given (1) a definition and an ambiguous definiendum and (2) a dictionary that maps the ambiguous definiendum to entities, the goal is to find the title that best matches the definition. The proposed method is described in two steps. First, the ground truth dataset is constructed. Second, three applicable approaches are considered.

3.1 Construction of the `MathD2` Dataset

A dump of the whole ProofWiki was extracted on the 5th of February, 2025, using WikiTeam (WikiTeam). This dump is then parsed with the disambiguation pages serving as a jump-off point for constructing the dictionary and the corpus used for training the proposed models.

The dictionary is composed of a list of terms and their corresponding candidate titles. Each term has a disambiguation page. This page contains links to associated articles, where each article is assigned a unique title.

The list of candidate titles for the dictionary is extracted from the hierarchical list of articles on each disambiguation page. It is important to note that not all articles appearing on a term's disambiguation page are automatically added as candidates for that term.

In addition, the hierarchy of topics is also taken into account when building the dictionary. More specific topics, or those belonging to the lower levels in the hierarchy, take precedence over higher level topics, when the former are also included in the latter's definition. The disambiguation page of "Equivalence" [6] illustrates this example: "Logical Equivalence" is not included in the candidate list of the term "Equivalence", since it is included already in the definitions of both "Semantic Equivalence" and "Provable Equivalence."

Aside from the hierarchy, the surface forms of the topics listed on the disambiguation page are also taken into account. Topics that do not include the term in question are not added as candidates (See "Set Theory" from the disambiguation page of the term, "Loop" [7].

[6]https://proofwiki.org/wiki/Definition:Equivalence

[7]https://proofwiki.org/wiki/Definition:Loop

Finally, terms mapped to less than two titles are removed. Table 2 shows (definition, title) pairs extracted from the disambiguation page of "Bilinear Form [8]."

The training corpus is extracted from the articles of the candidate titles. Only the *Definition* sections are utilized. They undergo post-processing which involves parsing of redirects and converting LaTeX content into plain text.

The `MathD2` dataset contains 365 ambiguous terms, mapping to 1984 *definition-title* pairs. For the finetuning in Section 3.2, the dataset is split for 5-fold cross validation as follows:

- 20% ambiguous terms and the corresponding *definition-title* pairs make a test set $test_{term}$. These terms are not seen in the training set, thereby testing model's ability to generalize on unseen ambiguous terms.
- of the 80% remaining ambiguous terms, the split between the training set and the second test set ($test_{title}$) is dependent on the number of (definition, title) pairs for each term. If a term has less than 8 (definition, title) pairs, all the pairs are are assigned to the training set. When the term has more than 8 definitions, the first 8 of those (definition, title) pairs are assigned to the training set, while the rest are assigned to $test_{title}$. Terms having not more than 8 definitions are automatically assigned to the training set. The purpose of $test_{title}$ is to evaluate the model's generalizability on new candidate titles to seen ambiguous terms.

The key difference between the two tests is that $test_{term}$ only contains unseen terms and the corresponding unseen candidate titles, while $test_{title}$ includes only seen terms and candidate titles not seen in the training set. Since there are more candidate titles per term on average in textittest$_{\text{title}}$, these terms are more ambiguous, making the test more difficult than $test_{term}$. This is reflected in the results shown on Table 4. In addition, inference on $test_{title}$ takes more time due to additional pairwise comparisons.

In the fine-tuning of Section 3.2, for each ambiguous term, two definitions and their titles are randomly selected to make positive pairs, and the titles of two other random definitions to make negative pairs. Table 3 shows the MathD2 dataset statistics. All approaches are evaluated on the 5 folds of 2 test sets.

3.2 Classification Based on One Concatenated Embedding

Following the finetuning setup of AcroBERT (Chen et al., 2023), BERT for NSP is adapted to build a supervised sentence pair classifier to link definitions to their page titles in ProofWiki. Every pair of (definition, candidate title with the matching ambiguous term in ProofWiki) is concatenated as an input sequence. The sequence begins with a [CLS] token, followed by a candidate title, a [SEP] token, and then the definition, ending with [SEP]. The input sequence passes through BERT's transformer layers. These layers produce contextual embeddings for each token in the sequence. Then, the embedding of [CLS] is fed into a softmax classification layer, which outputs a score to judge how coherent the concatenated sequence is. The pair with the highest score is selected as the final predicted output. First the out-of-box BERT for NSP serves as the baseline to see how well the pre-retained natural language inference model can describe the entailment between the titles and definitions. Then the pretrained BERT for NSP is finetuned with the training set using a triplet loss function

$$\mathcal{L} = \max\left\{0, \lambda - d_{\text{neg}} + d_{\text{pos}}\right\}$$

which aims to assign higher scores to the titles that match the input definition while reducing the scores of irrelevant candidates. $\lambda = 0.2$ is the margin value, and d_{pos} and d_{neg} are the distances for positive pairs (good matches of definition and title) and negative pairs (definition and irrelevant candidate title), respectively. This approach is implemented with PyTorch (Paszke et al., 2019) and transfomers (Wolf et al., 2020). The batch size is chosen among [8, 16, 32]. The learning rate is chosen among [1e-5, 2e-6] for Adam optimizer. The learning rate exponentially decays at a rate of 0.95 every 1000 steps. The model is trained with the training dataset for 200 epochs. After each epoch, a checkpoint (copy of the current model weights) is saved. Each checkpoint is then evaluated with the test dataset so that test data do not impact the model weights. The best evaluation scores are recorded in Appendix B.

[8] https://proofwiki.org/wiki/Definition:Bilinear_Form

Definition	Title
Let R be a ring. Let R_R denote the R-module R. Let M_R be an R-module. A bilinear form on M_R is a bilinear mapping $B : M_R \times M_R \to R_R$.	Definition: Bilinear Form (Linear Algebra)
A bilinear form is a linear form of order 2.	Definition: Bilinear Form (Polynomial Theory)

Table 2: Data extracted from a ProofWiki disambiguation page.

Fold	1	2	3	4	5
Train					
Term	292	292	292	292	292
Pairs	1153	1181	1181	1160	1169
Test$_{\text{term}}$					
Term	73	73	73	73	73
Pairs	412	362	342	445	423
Test$_{\text{title}}$					
Term	48	49	49	42	48
Pairs	419	441	461	379	392

Table 3: Cross-validation splits statistics. Terms in Test$_{\text{title}}$ sets are also in Train sets.

3.3 Zero-shot Prediction Based on Semantic Textual Similarity

A shortcoming of the previous solution is that the NSP inference has to be run for every (definition, title) pair mapped to an ambiguous term. Motivated to make a computationally more efficient solution, the sentence embeddings of the definitions and titles are explored. In this setup, the sentence embedding of the titles and the definitions only need to be calculated once. For the definition and each candidate title with the matching ambiguous term, the title with the highest cosine similarity to the embedding of the definition is selected as the final predicted output. To explore the potential benefits of different pretraining corpus and related tasks, the following models are studied:

- Out-of-box SBERT (`SBERT-all-mpnet-base-v2`) (Reimers and Gurevych, 2019).
- Mean pooled out-of-box BERT, to compare with the pretraining of SBERT.
- Mean pooled CC-BERT (Mishra et al., 2021), a from-scratch model pretrained with MLM on mathematical papers. This experiment studies the impact of domain-specific MLM pretraining and domain-specific tokenization, comparing to mean pooled out-of-box BERT.
- The best-performing sentence transformers for Semantic Textual Similarity(STS) tasks for short mathematical text as reported in (Steinfeldt and Mihaljević, 2024), including `Bert-MLM_arXiv-MP-class_zbMath` (Steinfeldt and Mihaljević, 2024) (noted as Adapted SBERT in Table 4), `SBERT-all-MiniLM-L6-v2` (Wang et al., 2020), and `SBERT-all-MiniLM-L12-v2` (Wang et al., 2020).

Following SBERT's default setting (Reimers and Gurevych, 2019), the mean pooling strategy is used to calculate the sentence embeddings with out-of-box BERT and CC-BERT.

3.4 LLM Prompting

Recently, Large Language Models (LLMs) have been incorporated to improve entity disambiguation tasks (Xin et al., 2024). Experiments conducted with LLMs are framed as a Zero-Shot Open Generative Question and Answer, where the LLM is instructed to identify the correct article title given a mathematical term and its ProofWiki definition as context.

In order to get the best results from the LLM, the prompt is constructed following best practices:

1. **Task Description.** "`Your task is to find the correct article title given a mathematical term and definition as context.`"
2. **Hallucination Prevention.** "`Reply with "I don't know" when uncertain.`"
3. **Expectation Setting.** "`Only select one answer from the provided list. Do not provide justifications.`"
4. **Multiple Choice.** "`Identify the correct title from this list:[...]`"

The LLMs used for testing are open-source and are

categorized as *Instruction-tuned* models (Zhang et al., 2024). These LLMs undergo a supervised fine-tuning step with a dataset consisting of human instructions paired with their desired generated outputs. The list of titles provided in the prompt are extracted from the dictionary mentioned in Section 3.1. Answers are only considered correct when the article title in the ground truth exists in full in the LLM's answer as in Example 1.

```
<s> [INST] Your task is to
find ...
Identify the correct
definition title from this
list: ...
[/INST] Indexing Set /
Term"</s>
```

Example 1: An Example of a Precise Response from `Mistral-7B-Instruct-v0.2`.

As can be seen in Example 2, there are instances when the LLM insists on providing lengthy justifications to its answer. Even when the text in the ground truth exists in the justification, this kind of answer will still be considered as incorrect.

```
<s> [INST] Your task is to
find ...
...following mathematical
definition as context:
Let G be a group...
[/INST] I don't know. The
term "complex" in the given
context refers to a subset
of a group...
```

Example 2: An Example of a response from `Mistral-7B-Instruct-v0.2` not following instructions.

The different LLMs used for the experiments are prompted with identical instructions. Inference call arguments, such as `max_tokens` or `temperature`, are adapted from the Hugging Face model card specifications pages.

4 Results and Discussion

4.1 Overall Performance

The evaluation measure used for comparison is *Accuracy* or micro F1-score (Equation 1) (Shen et al., 2015). Macro F1-score is not considered due to the characteristic of the test set, where there is only a single sample for each definition-title pair.

$$F1_{micro} = Acc = \frac{\text{\# correctly identified title}}{\text{\# of titles}} \tag{1}$$

Table 4 shows the experimental results of all three methods. Overall, the best-performing models are finetuned BERT for NSP, and generic SBERT-like models for STS. The differences between these models are not statistically significant (see Appendix B.1). Notably, the out-of-the-box SBERT demonstrated excellent performance with much less inference time.

Regarding the NSP approach, finetuned BERT on the MathD2 dataset significantly outperforms out-of-box BERT, validating AcroBERT's set-up, the informativeness of MathD2 data for finetuning, and the helpfulness of BERT's pretrained weights.

Regarding the STS approach, the performance of SBERT models is aligned with the results of (Reimers and Gurevych, 2019) and (Steinfeldt and Mihaljević, 2024). The experiments with the mean pooled out-of-box BERT and CC-BERT show that MLM domain-adaptation over mathematical papers slightly improves this task but is far less efficient than adapted SBERT, which has been pre-trained with fewer data but on a better task.

Given that both BERT for NSP and SBERT are pretrained on NLI tasks (Devlin et al., 2019; Reimers and Gurevych, 2019), it may be deduced that: i) Compared to using the [CLS] representation of concatenated sequences, using separated sentence embeddings captures more information for our task. ii) SBERT's pretraining on (title, abstract) pairs from S2ORC dataset (Lo et al., 2020) helps to better understand the entailment between titles and body texts. However, Bert-MLM_arXiv-MP-class_zbMath, the domain-adapted SBERT model [9] that the authors of (Steinfeldt and Mihaljević, 2024) fine-tuned with multiple tasks using titles and abstracts of mathematical papers does not yield better results. This might be due to the model being solely trained on titles and abstracts, diminishing the model's representational capacity for both formulas and general text.

In comparison, the results of the zero-shot experiments with LLMs are worse than those of the other

[9] https://huggingface.co/math-similarity/Bert-MLM_arXiv-MP-class_arXiv

Model	Approach	Test_{term}	Test_{title}
BERT (Devlin et al., 2019)	NSP	84.6	84.0
BERT(finetuned)	NSP	**92.3**	**91.6**
BERT(mean pooled)	STS	39.9	27.2
CC-BERT (Mishra et al., 2021)	STS	44.0	32.7
SBERT-all-mpnet-base-v2 (Reimers and Gurevych, 2019)	STS	**92.8**	**91.9**
SBERT-all-MiniLM-L6-v2	STS	91.6	**91.4**
SBERT-all-MiniLM-L12-v2	STS	**92.6**	**91.4**
Adapted SBERT (Steinfeldt and Mihaljević, 2024)	STS	59.8	48.4
Mistral-7B-Instruct-v0.2 (Jiang et al., 2023)	LLM-Instruct	45.9	50.4
Mistral-7B-Instruct-v0.3	LLM-Instruct	60.0	52.1
Meta-Llama-3-8B-Instruct	LLM-Instruct	75.0	71.9

Table 4: Averaged accuracy scores of five tests. Values are reported as $\rho \cdot 100$. Best scores are in bold. Detailed results and pairwise t-statistics can be found in Appendix B.

approaches. When running the experiments on older GPUs, some samples caused out-of-memory runtime errors due to the lengthy ProofWiki definition sections. For example, the definition section of *Matrix Product* [10] have matrices within it which could have caused the error. One solution is to limit the maximum token size during inference to 255. However, this curtails contexts that may help the model disambiguate highly ambiguous terms.

Error Type	Mistral v2	Mistral v3	Llama v3.1
NP	20.6	0.0	2.2
NFI	169.8	126.0	73.4
LB	3.2	1.0	0.4
WP	21.0	33.4	23.2

Table 5: Average Number of Errors per Type Produced by LLMs on 5 $\texttt{test}_{\texttt{term}}$ sets. NP = No Prediction, NFI = Not Following Instructions , LB = Learning Bias, WP = Wrong Prediction. Detailed error distribution is given in Appendix B.1.

4.2 Errors Generated by LLMs

In order to understand the types of errors encountered by LLMs, all responses from the $\texttt{test}_{\texttt{term}}$ split that are considered incorrect are manually scrutinized. These amounted to almost a quarter of $\texttt{test}_{\texttt{term}}$.

Appendix A provides examples of each category of errors. Erroneous LLM responses are of the following types:

1. **No Prediction (NP)**. This is when the LLM responds with *"I don't know."*

2. **Not Following Instructions (NFI).** These are scenarios when the LLM chose answers not included in the list of choices or when the answer is in the justification.

3. **Learning Bias (LB).** This is when the LLM 's answer is closest to the ground truth (e.g. "Degrees of Arc" instead of "Degree of Arc."). NFIs and LBs are often hard distinguish. As a rule of thumb, an error is considered an NFI, when the LLMs try to change the categorical structure of the titles into prose (e.g. "Right Distributive Operation" instead of "Distributive Operation/Right", as provided in the list of choices).

4. **Wrong Prediction (WP).** These errors are easy to distinguish. In most cases, the incorrect answers are included in the list of candidates.

Existing literature points to the tendencies of LLMs to hallucinate (Huang et al., 2025). Among the aforementioned error types, NFIs and LBs errors exhibit this behavior. Instead of admitting uncertainty or the lack of knowledge, these errors show that the model regresses to making up answers. Our experimental results also show that when the number of candidates increases, Mistral models are more likely to produce NFI errors (see Figure B.1 and Figure B.2 in Appendix B.1), and the correct rate decreases correspondingly.

Table 5 shows that older models, such as `Mistral-7B-Instruct-v0.2`, are likely not to know the answer with the highest number NPs and

[10] https://proofwiki.org/wiki/Definition:Matrix_Product

not follow explicit instructions (NFIs). Compared to its predecessor, `Mistral-7B-Instruct-v0.3` did not abstain from making predictions (0% NPs) but produced more wrong predictions. Not surprisingly, it is more likely to follow instructions than its predecessor. While the best performing model is `Meta-Llama-3-8B-Instruct` with considerable fewer errors across the board.

4.3 Limitations

An interesting finding is that all three approaches make some common mistakes, indicating the limits of using only semantic representations. The most common error is when the definition statement includes nested definitions. Another typical error is that the predicted result is in the correct category but not the definiendum, mainly when the definition contains morphemes in the predicted title or when the definition does not contain some morphemes in the expected title. For example, the definition of "Consequence Function" starts with "Let **G** be a game..." [11] , and the predicted title is "Definition:Consequence(Game Theory)' [12] . Thus, enhancing sentence embedding's comprehension of semantic and syntactic knowledge of mathematical definitions is still worth investigating. Other common mistakes reveal the noises in the dataset due to errors in Proofwiki [13], or automatic scrapping and LaTeXconversion of irregular ProofWiki pages.

Practical Considerations: One reason for comparing traditional transformer-based model paradigm of Pre-train+Fine-Tune and Large Language Models is the consideration of computing resource constraints. SOTA LLMs, such as `Meta-Llama-3-8B-Instruct`, require Cuda libraries with version 12.0 (Nvidia, 2024).

Experiments involving BERT/SBERT-based models are conducted on NVIDIA Tesla V100S-PCIE 32GB having compute capability of 5.0 with 14.5 TFLOPS [14]. On the other hand, experiments with LLMs used NVIDIA A100 80GB PCIe with with 19 TFLOPS, belonging to a line of Graphics Processing Units (GPUs) with compute capability of 7.0.

Compute capability dictates how much computing resources are required to run experiments. Newer LLMs require higher versions of Cuda. Cuda libraries require a specific version of NVIDIA drivers, and consequently, the array of GPUs capable of running the driver version.

5 Conclusion and Future Works

This work introduces `MathD2`, a new dataset for mathematical term disambiguation extracted from ProofWiki. Two entity-linking approaches have been implemented and shown to yield advantages in the usage of contextualized embeddings to differentiate mathematical definitions. The experimental results proved the efficiency and effectiveness of using out-of-the-box SBERT.

Additional experiments with SOTA LLMs also show that the proposed models performed better and have fewer computing resource constraints. Moreover, error analysis shows the inherent tendency of LLMs to hallucinate.

Further work is planned on applying the proposed approaches to scholarly papers. Regarding the closed scores of the best models, evaluation with more data and significance tests are planned. In addition, the current approach is to be extended to include document-level representation and citation information to differentiate definitions in scholarly papers. This work also indicates the need for further study on building sentence transformers that benefit from domain-specific MLM and task-related pre-training.

6 Acknowledgements

We would like to express our gratitude to Frank Pöhlmann who dedicated his time and editing experience to provide valuable feedback and constructive criticism on this paper.

References

Luis Berlioz. 2021. ArGoT: A Glossary of Terms extracted from the arXiv. *Electronic Proceedings in Theoretical Computer Science*, 342:14–21.

Luis Berlioz. 2023. *Hierarchical Representations from Large Mathematical Corpora*. Ph.D. thesis, University of Pittsburgh.

[11] https://proofwiki.org/wiki/Definition:Consequence_Function

[12] https://proofwiki.org/wiki/Definition:Consequence_(Game_Theory)

[13] For example, the definiendum in https://proofwiki.org/wiki/Definition:Ideal_of_Algebra/Right_Ideal should be *right ideal*, but is wrongly written as *left ideal*.

[14] TeraFLOPS specifies the number of floating point operations per second that the hardware can accomplish.

Samuel R. Bowman, Gabor Angeli, Christopher Potts, and Christopher D. Manning. 2015. A large annotated corpus for learning natural language inference. In *Proceedings of the 2015 Conference on Empirical Methods in Natural Language Processing*, pages 632–642, Lisbon, Portugal. Association for Computational Linguistics.

Lihu Chen, Gael Varoquaux, and Fabian M. Suchanek. 2023. GLADIS: A general and large acronym disambiguation benchmark. In *Proceedings of the 17th Conference of the European Chapter of the Association for Computational Linguistics*, pages 2073–2088, Dubrovnik, Croatia.

Jacob Devlin, Ming-Wei Chang, Kenton Lee, and Kristina Toutanova. 2019. Bert: Pre-training of deep bidirectional transformers for language understanding. In *Proceedings of the 2019 Conference of the North American Chapter of the Association for Computational Linguistics: Human Language Technologies, Volume 1 (Long and Short Papers)*, pages 4171–4186.

Shea Durgin, James Gore, and Behrooz Mansouri. 2024. Mathmex: Search engine for math definitions. In *European Conference on Information Retrieval*, pages 194–199. Springer.

Beka Ergemlidze, Ervin Győri, and Abhishek Methuku. 2019. 3-uniform hypergraphs without a cycle of length five. *arXiv preprint arXiv:1902.06257*.

Lei Huang, Weijiang Yu, Weitao Ma, Weihong Zhong, Zhangyin Feng, Haotian Wang, Qianglong Chen, Weihua Peng, Xiaocheng Feng, Bing Qin, and Ting Liu. 2025. A survey on hallucination in large language models: Principles, taxonomy, challenges, and open questions. *ACM Transactions on Information Systems*, 43(2):1–55.

Albert Q. Jiang, Alexandre Sablayrolles, Arthur Mensch, Chris Bamford, Devendra Singh Chaplot, Diego de las Casas, Florian Bressand, Gianna Lengyel, Guillaume Lample, Lucile Saulnier, Lélio Renard Lavaud, Marie-Anne Lachaux, Pierre Stock, Teven Le Scao, Thibaut Lavril, Thomas Wang, Timothée Lacroix, and William El Sayed. 2023. Mistral 7b. *Preprint*, arXiv:2310.06825.

Shufan Jiang, Rafael Angarita, Stéphane Cormier, Julien Orensanz, and Francis Rousseaux. 2022. Choubert: Pre-training french language model for crowdsensing with tweets in phytosanitary context. In *International Conference on Research Challenges in Information Science*, pages 653–661. Springer.

Shufan Jiang and Pierre Senellart. 2023. Extracting definienda in mathematical scholarly articles with transformers. *IJCNLP-AACL 2023*, page 31.

Hwiyeol Jo, Dongyeop Kang, Andrew Head, and Marti A Hearst. 2021. Modeling mathematical notation semantics in academic papers. In *Findings of the Association for Computational Linguistics: EMNLP 2021*, pages 3102–3115.

Sunny Joseph Kalayathankal et al. 2015. Operations on covering numbers of certain graph classes. *arXiv preprint arXiv:1506.03251*.

Elizabeth Kupin. 2011. Subtraction division games. *arXiv preprint arXiv:1201.0171*.

Kyle Lo, Lucy Lu Wang, Mark Neumann, Rodney Kinney, and Daniel Weld. 2020. S2ORC: The semantic scholar open research corpus. In *Proceedings of the 58th Annual Meeting of the Association for Computational Linguistics*, pages 4969–4983, Online. Association for Computational Linguistics.

Shrey Mishra, Yacine Brihmouche, Theo Delemazure, Antoine Gauquier, and Pierre Senellart. 2024. First steps in building a knowledge base of mathematical results. In *Proceedings of the Fourth Workshop on Scholarly Document Processing (SDP 2024)*, pages 165–174.

Shrey Mishra, Lucas Pluvinage, and Pierre Senellart. 2021. Towards extraction of theorems and proofs in scholarly articles. In *DocEng '21: ACM Symposium on Document Engineering 2021, Limerick, Ireland, August 24-27, 2021*, pages 25:1–25:4. ACM.

Koji Nakagawa, Akihiro Nomura, and Masakazu Suzuki. 2004. Extraction of Logical Structure from Articles in Mathematics. In Andrea Asperti, Grzegorz Bancerek, and Andrzej Trybulec, editors, *Mathematical Knowledge Management*, volume 3119, pages 276–289. Springer Berlin Heidelberg, Berlin, Heidelberg. Series Title: Lecture Notes in Computer Science.

Nvidia. 2024. Cuda12 support for v100 gpu.

Adam Paszke, Sam Gross, Francisco Massa, Adam Lerer, James Bradbury, Gregory Chanan, Trevor Killeen, Zeming Lin, Natalia Gimelshein, Luca Antiga, et al. 2019. Pytorch: An imperative style, high-performance deep learning library. *Advances in neural information processing systems*, 32.

KKKR Perera and Yoshihiro Mizoguchi. 2012. Bipartition of graphs based on the normalized cut and spectral methods. *arXiv preprint arXiv:1210.7253*.

Nils Reimers and Iryna Gurevych. 2019. Sentence-BERT: Sentence embeddings using Siamese BERT-networks. In *Proceedings of the 2019 Conference on Empirical Methods in Natural Language Processing and the 9th International Joint Conference on Natural Language Processing (EMNLP-IJCNLP)*, pages 3982–3992, Hong Kong, China. Association for Computational Linguistics.

Wei Shen, Jianyong Wang, and Jiawei Han. 2015. Entity linking with a knowledge base: Issues, techniques, and solutions. *IEEE Transactions on Knowledge and Data Engineering*, 27(2):443–460.

Christian Steinfeldt and Helena Mihaljević. 2024. Evaluation and domain adaptation of similarity models for short mathematical texts. In *International Conference on Intelligent Computer Mathematics*, pages 241–260. Springer.

Yutian Sun and Hai Zhuge. 2023. Discovering patterns

of definitions and methods from scientific documents. *arXiv preprint arXiv:2307.01216*.

Natalia Vanetik, Marina Litvak, Sergey Shevchuk, and Lior Reznik. 2020. Automated discovery of mathematical definitions in text. In *Proceedings of the Twelfth Language Resources and Evaluation Conference*, pages 2086–2094.

Ashish Vaswani, Noam Shazeer, Niki Parmar, Jakob Uszkoreit, Llion Jones, Aidan N. Gomez, Lukasz Kaiser, and Illia Polosukhin. 2023. Attention is all you need. *Preprint*, arXiv:1706.03762.

Daniel Vollmers, Hamada Zahera, Diego Moussallem, and Axel-Cyrille Ngonga Ngomo. 2025. Contextual augmentation for entity linking using large language models. In *Proceedings of the 31st International Conference on Computational Linguistics*, pages 8535–8545, Abu Dhabi, UAE. Association for Computational Linguistics.

Wenhui Wang, Furu Wei, Li Dong, Hangbo Bao, Nan Yang, and Ming Zhou. 2020. Minilm: Deep self-attention distillation for task-agnostic compression of pre-trained transformers. *Advances in Neural Information Processing Systems*, 33:5776–5788.

WikiTeam. Wikiteam. Original-date: 2014-06-25T10:18:03Z.

Adina Williams, Nikita Nangia, and Samuel Bowman. 2018. A broad-coverage challenge corpus for sentence understanding through inference. In *Proceedings of the 2018 Conference of the North American Chapter of the Association for Computational Linguistics: Human Language Technologies, Volume 1 (Long Papers)*, pages 1112–1122, New Orleans, Louisiana. Association for Computational Linguistics.

Thomas Wolf, Lysandre Debut, Victor Sanh, Julien Chaumond, Clement Delangue, Anthony Moi, Pierric Cistac, Tim Rault, Rémi Louf, Morgan Funtowicz, Joe Davison, Sam Shleifer, Patrick von Platen, Clara Ma, Yacine Jernite, Julien Plu, Canwen Xu, Teven Le Scao, Sylvain Gugger, Mariama Drame, Quentin Lhoest, and Alexander M. Rush. 2020. Transformers: State-of-the-art natural language processing. In *Proceedings of the 2020 Conference on Empirical Methods in Natural Language Processing: System Demonstrations*, pages 38–45, Online. Association for Computational Linguistics.

Amy Xin, Yunjia Qi, Zijun Yao, Fangwei Zhu, Kaisheng Zeng, Xu Bin, Lei Hou, and Juanzi Li. 2024. Llmael: Large language models are good context augmenters for entity linking. *Preprint*, arXiv:2407.04020.

Shengyu Zhang, Linfeng Dong, Xiaoya Li, Sen Zhang, Xiaofei Sun, Shuhe Wang, Jiwei Li, Runyi Hu, Tianwei Zhang, Fei Wu, and Guoyin Wang. 2024. Instruction tuning for large language models: A survey. *Preprint*, arXiv:2308.10792.

Appendices

A Error Analysis of LLMs' Response

Below are examples of actual LLM answers according to the type of error specified in Section 4.

1. No Prediction (NP).

   $\texttt{Test}_{\texttt{term-idx}}$: `269`
   Ground Truth: `Composition of Ratio`
   Answer: `I don't know`

2. Not Following Instructions (NFI).

   $\texttt{Test}_{\texttt{term-idx}}$: `51`
   Context: `Identify the correct definition title from this list: ['Image (Relation Theory)/Mapping/Mapping', 'Image (Relation Theory)/Relation/Relation', 'Direct Image Mapping/Mapping', 'Direct Image Mapping/Relation', 'Direct Image of Sheaf']`
   Ground Truth: `Direct Image of Sheaf`
   Answer: `Direct Image Mapping/Sheaf`

3. Learning Bias (LB).

   $\texttt{Test}_{\texttt{term-idx}}$: `338`
   Ground Truth: `Cut-Vertex`
   Answer: `Vertex Cut`

4. Wrong Prediction (WP).

   $\texttt{Test}_{\texttt{term-idx}}$: `2`
   Context: `Complex analysis is a branch of mathematics that studies complex functions.`
   Ground Truth: `Analysis/Complex`
   Answer: `Complex Function`

B Detailed Results

Table 6 and Table 7 show the 5-fold cross-validation accuracy scores.

B.1 Comparing Performance of Models

Table 8 and Table 9 compare models with close scores in Table 6 and Table 7. Paired Student's t-test is used to determine if one model is significantly better than another. Given $n = 5$ folds, let d_i represent the difference in accuracy between Model A and Model B for the i-th fold:

$$d_i = \text{Accuracy}_A^{(i)} - \text{Accuracy}_B^{(i)}, \quad i = 1, 2, \ldots, 5$$

Mean difference

$$\bar{d} = \frac{1}{n}\sum_{i=1}^{n} d_i$$

Sample standard deviation

$$s_d = \sqrt{\frac{1}{n}\sum_{i=1}^{n}(d_i - \bar{d})^2}$$

Standard Error

$$\text{SE} = \frac{s_d}{\sqrt{n}}$$

t-statistic

$$t = \frac{\bar{d}}{\text{SE}} = \frac{\bar{d}}{s_d/\sqrt{n}}$$

Degrees of Freedom $\text{DF} = n - 1 = 4$

Two-Tailed p-value

$$p\text{-value} = 2 \cdot P(T \geq |t|) \quad \text{where } T \sim t_{\text{DF}=4}$$

We consider the difference between the performance of two ML models to be statistically significant if p-value is smaller than 0.05.

Model	Approach	**Test$_{term}$ 1**	**Test$_{term}$ 2**	**Test$_{term}$ 3**	**Test$_{term}$ 4**	**Test$_{term}$ 5**
BERT	NSP	0.799	0.873	0.868	0.845	0.844
BERT (finetuned)	NSP	0.903	**0.972**	**0.927**	0.910	0.903
BERT (mean pooled)	STS	0.381	0.434	0.453	0.369	0.359
CC-BERT (mean pooled)	STS	0.427	0.448	0.462	0.434	0.430
SBERT-all-mpnet-base-v2	STS	**0.923**	0.936	0.918	0.928	**0.934**
SBERT-all-MiniLM-L6-v2	STS	0.871	0.923	**0.927**	0.935	0.922
SBERT-all-MiniLM-L12-v2	STS	0.893	0.939	0.921	**0.942**	**0.934**
Adapted SBERT	STS	0.568	0.655	0.611	0.580	0.577
Mistral-7B-Instruct-v0.2	LLM	0.483	0.506	0.421	0.456	0.430
Mistral-7B-Instruct-v0.3	LLM	0.619	0.635	0.667	0.526	0.556
Meta-Llama-3-8B-Instruct	LLM	0.731	0.815	0.719	0.780	0.707

Table 6: Accuracy scores on new terms. The best scores are in bold.

Model	Approach	**Test$_{title}$ 1**	**Test$_{title}$ 2**	**Test$_{title}$ 3**	**Test$_{title}$ 4**	**Test$_{title}$ 5**
BERT	NSP	0.847	0.823	0.833	0.850	0.847
BERT (finetuned)	NSP	0.926	**0.927**	0.911	0.900	**0.918**
BERT (mean pooled)	STS	0.258	0.274	0.260	0.290	0.278
CC-BERT (mean pooled)	STS	0.329	0.336	0.315	0.319	0.337
SBERT-all-mpnet-base-v2	STS	0.896	0.923	**0.928**	**0.934**	0.916
SBERT-all-MiniLM-L6-v2	STS	0.924	0.909	0.911	0.910	0.916
SBERT-all-MiniLM-L12-v2	STS	**0.928**	0.902	0.915	0.913	0.911
Adapted SBERT	STS	0.494	0.485	0.479	0.472	0.487
Mistral-7B-Instruct-v0.2	LLM	0.492	0.499	0.495	0.533	0.503
Mistral-7B-Instruct-v0.3	LLM	0.506	0.522	0.505	0.549	0.523
Meta-Llama-3-8B-Instruct	LLM	0.747	0.703	0.709	0.683	0.753

Table 7: Accuracy scores on new titles. The best scores are in bold.

Model 1	Model 2	t-statistic t	p-value p	Significant
SBERT-all-mpnet-base-v2	BERT (finetuned)	0.405	0.706	no
BERT (finetuned)	SBERT-all-MiniLM-L12-v2	-0.222	0.835	no
SBERT-all-MiniLM-L12-v2	SBERT-all-MiniLM-L6-v2	2.160	0.097	no
BERT (finetuned)	BERT	7.637	0.002	yes
BERT (mean pooled)	CC-BERT (mean pooled)	-3.197	0.033	yes
Mistral-7B-Instruct-v0.3	Mistral-7B-Instruct-v0.2	-4.928	0.008	yes

Table 8: Comparing models on new terms. Statistical significance: $p < 0.05$

Model 1	Model 2	t-statistic t	p-value p	Significant
SBERT-all-mpnet-base-v2	BERT (finetuned)	0.272	0.819	no
BERT (finetuned)	SBERT-all-MiniLM-L12-v2	0.377	0.753	no
SBERT-all-MiniLM-L12-v2	SBERT-all-MiniLM-L6-v2	-0.013	0.992	no
BERT (finetuned)	BERT	8.921	0.001	yes
BERT (mean pooled)	CC-BERT (mean pooled)	-7.759	0.002	yes
Mistral-7B-Instruct-v0.3	Mistral-7B-Instruct-v0.2	-7.948	0.002	yes

Table 9: Comparing models on new titles. Statistical significance: $p < 0.05$

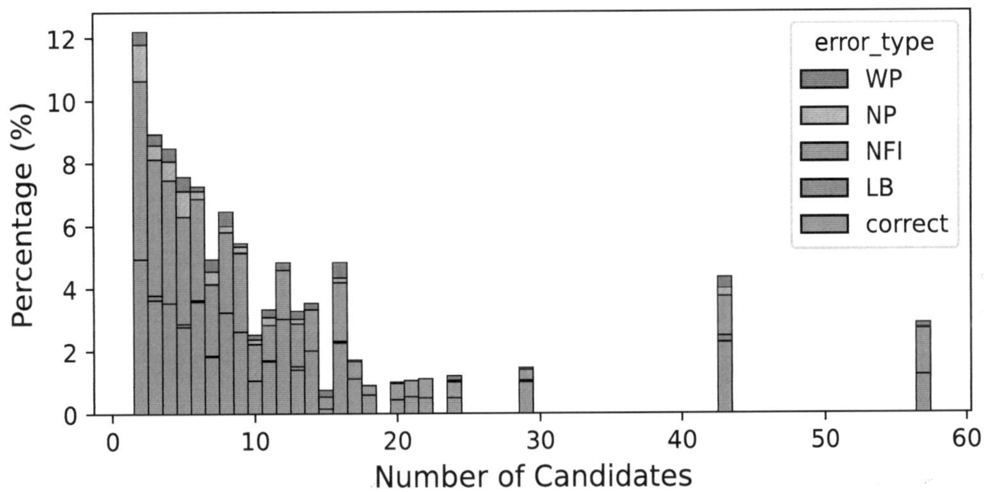

Figure B.1: Error Type Distribution by Candidate Number - mistralv2. NP = No Prediction, NFI = Not Following Instructions , LB = Learning Bias, WP = Wrong Prediction. The proportion of grey in a bar grows when the number of candidates increases, suggesting that NFI is more likely to happen when given more options.

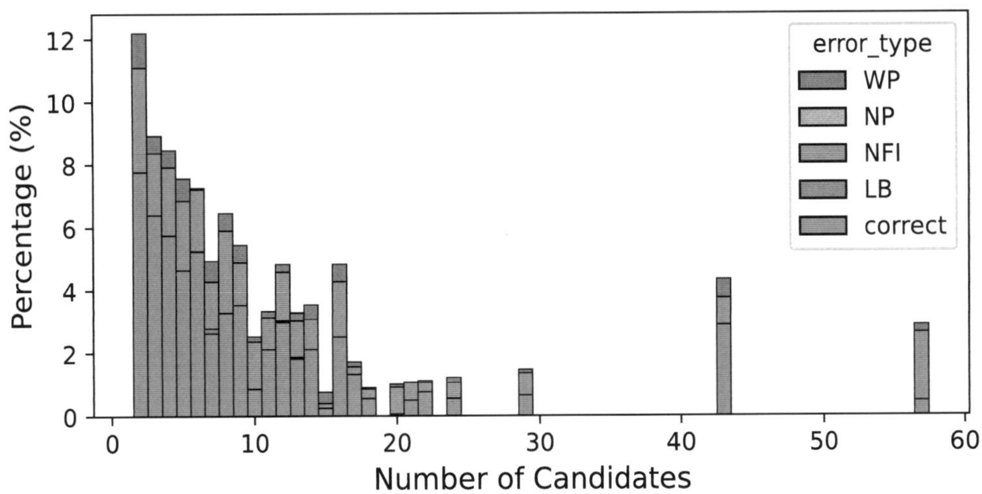

Figure B.2: Error Type Distribution by Candidate Number - mistralv3. NP = No Prediction, NFI = Not Following Instructions , LB = Learning Bias, WP = Wrong Prediction. The proportion of grey in a bar grows when the number of candiadtes increases, suggesting that NFI is more likely to happen when given more options.

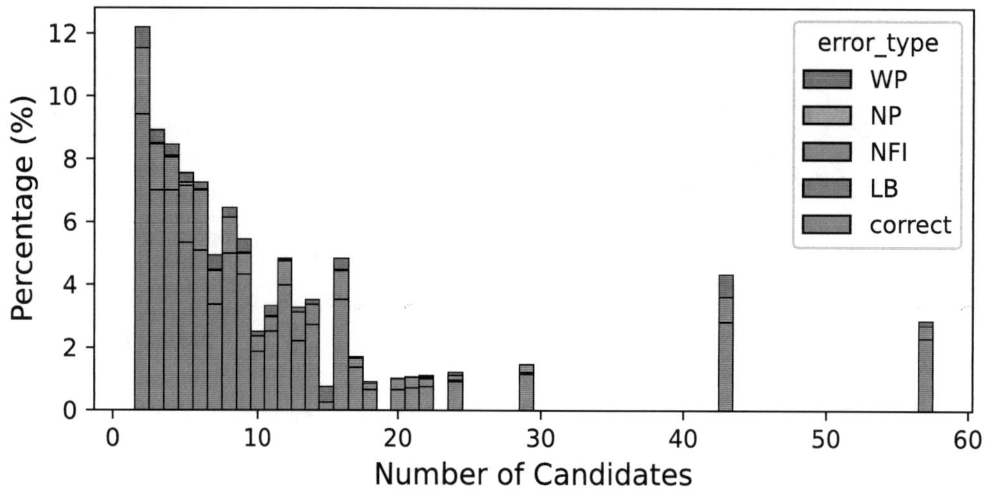

Figure B.3: Error Type Distribution by Candidate Number - llama3. NP = No Prediction, NFI = Not Following Instructions , LB = Learning Bias, WP = Wrong Prediction.

GraphTranslate: Predicting Clinical Trial Translation using Graph Neural Networks on Biomedical Literature

Emily Muller and **Justin Boylan-Toomey** and **Jack Ekinsmyth**
Arne Robben and **María De La Paz Cardona** and **Antonia Langfelder**
Wellcome Trust
London UK

Abstract

The translation of basic science into clinical interventions represents a critical yet prolonged pathway in biomedical research, with significant implications for human health. While previous translation prediction approaches have focused on citation-based and metadata metrics or semantic analysis, the complex network structure of scientific knowledge remains under-explored. In this work, we present a novel graph neural network approach that leverages both semantic and structural information to predict which research publications will lead to clinical trials. Our model analyses a comprehensive dataset of 19 million publication nodes, using transformer-based title and abstract sentence embeddings within their citation network context. We demonstrate that our graph-based architecture, which employs attention mechanisms over local citation neighbourhoods, outperforms traditional convolutional approaches by effectively capturing knowledge flow patterns (F1 improvement of 4.5 and 3.5 percentage points for direct and indirect translation). Our metadata is carefully selected to eliminate potential biases from researcher-specific information, while maintaining predictive power through network structural features. Notably, our model achieves state-of-the-art performance using only content-based features, showing that language inherently captures many of the predictive features of translation. Through rigorous validation on a held-out time window (2021), we demonstrate generalisation across different biomedical domains and provide insights into early indicators of translational research potential. Our system offers immediate practical value for research funders, enabling evidence-based assessment of translational potential during grant review processes. The code for GraphTranslate is available at `https://github.com/wellcometrust/graph-translate`.

1 Introduction

The path from scientific discovery to clinical application remains a critical challenge in biomedical research. Although laboratory research and preclinical studies can lead to advances in scientific understanding, translating these findings into real-world clinical interventions that directly benefit patients is a complex process involving multiple stages, including experimental validation, regulatory approval, and clinical trials, each of which introduces uncertainty and challenges (Contopoulos-Ioannidis et al., 2008). Moreover, despite substantial global investment in medical research and development, only a tiny fraction of basic research findings successfully translate into clinical treatments (Contopoulos-Ioannidis et al., 2003). This inefficiency in the translation pipeline, combined with the decades-long timeframe typically required for bench-to-bedside translation (Morris et al., 2011), creates an urgent need for tools that can identify promising translational research early in its lifecycle.

Previous approaches to predicting translational success have primarily relied on citation patterns and metadata features, or focused solely on semantic analysis of research content (Nelson et al., 2022; Padilla-Cabello et al., 2022). While these methods have shown promise, they often overlook the complex network of scientific knowledge through which research findings propagate towards clinical applications. Citation networks represent more than just academic impact—they capture the flow of knowledge from fundamental discoveries towards clinical implementation. However, effectively modelling these knowledge transmission pathways requires both understanding the semantic content of research and its structural position within the broader scientific landscape.

We address this challenge by introducing a graph neural network architecture that integrates

Proceedings of the Fifth Workshop on Scholarly Document Processing (SDP 2025), pages 31–41
July 31, 2025 ©2025 Association for Computational Linguistics

both semantic and structural information from research publications. By analysing a comprehensive dataset of 19 million publications using transformer-based embeddings within their citation network context, our model captures subtle patterns in how knowledge flows from basic science towards clinical applications. Crucially, we demonstrate that content-based features inherently encode many signals predictive of translational potential, allowing us to achieve state-of-the-art performance while minimising reliance on potentially biased metadata features. As a result, this approach offers practical value in identifying promising translational research early, helping researchers, funders, and institutions prioritise high-impact projects.

2 Related Work

Recent academic enquiry has focused on predicting the relationship between a paper and its translational outcomes via citation analysis. Hutchins et al. discovered a complex relationship between a paper's content, its citing articles, and citation rates, affecting its likelihood of being cited in clinical articles (Hutchins et al., 2019b). The study used human-annotated Medical Subject Headings (MeSH) and 22 features in a random forest model to predict translational success. The model achieved good accuracy with just two years of data, and the authors showed diminishing improvement when more years of data were added. This is crucial because early identification facilitates translation prediction within the timeframe of a grant.

The predictive power of MeSH tags is attributed to its identification of the clinical stage a paper lies (Hutchins et al., 2019b). The use of MeSH terms, however, is limiting, as it requires extensive human labelling. As an alternative, modern natural language processing methods can also identify the translational stage of a paper (Li et al., 2023). Full-MLP-CNN model predicted patent citations (AUROC = 0.915) and guidelines and policy documents (AUROC = 0.918) without MeSH terms (Nelson et al., 2022). This model used sentence embeddings of the title and abstract alongside extensive metadata from the Microsoft Academic Graph (MAG). This included Microsoft's ranking features based on eigencentrality. These features assess the scientific network surrounding entities such as papers, journals, or authors, with the rank of the paper emerging as the most influential metadata feature.

The Full-MLP-CNN study did not address how the age of the paper affects the accuracy of the prediction. This is important as, when time limited, more complex network measures can perform poorly compared to citation counts (Mariani et al., 2016). However, Microsoft explicitly sought to mitigate this age bias in their entity centrality metrics via reinforcement learning (Wang et al., 2019). In fact, a time-balanced network centrality measure has been shown to be more effective than simple citation counts in identifying Nobel Prize winning papers even in the first few years (Mariani et al., 2016). This indicates that even a time-limited citation network structure contains valuable information for translation prediction. The DELPHI model is a clear example of this (Weis and Jacobson, 2021). It combined article and journal metadata alongside a time-limited citation network to predict 5-year post-publication time-balanced network centrality using only 2 years of data, while identifying seminal biotechnology papers.

Nelson et al. found that removing citation metadata features had a moderate reduction in predictive performance. This is supported by Li et al., who expanded on the NIH study using a total of 91 citation and MeSH based features to predict the clinical citation count of papers (Li et al., 2022). The authors found the expanded citation network from paper references were more influential than those of the predicted paper or its early citations (Xin Li, Xuli Tang and Qukai Cheng, 2022). Beinat et al. meanwhile, showed within the fields of dementia and cancer, translation could be predicted without any citation network data (Beinat et al., 2024). They used an array of article metadata features alongside title and abstract embeddings in a CatBoost model to predict patent (AUROC = 0.84) and clinical trial citations (AUROC = 0.81) for dementia research.

Removing citation features is attractive, as it allows for translation prediction without any time delay. However, models from Nelson et al., and Beinat et al. use an array of researcher features in their models, raising concerns about increased model bias. While author popularity may relate to past translational success, it is difficult to separate this from potential structural biases when predicting future success. We argue that assessing a paper's translational potential should not consider personal researchers attributes such as h-index, institution or country.

Evidence suggests that both paper content and a

time-limited scientific network structure around papers can be used to effectively predict biomedical translation. However, no study to date has successfully integrated both elements. Our graph neural network approach combines paper embeddings alongside a time-limited scientific network structure to achieve this. The final model successfully predicts translational impact without depending on extensive feature engineering (MeSH), a now discontinued service (MAG), and minimises bias by excluding sensitive author features.

3 Methodology

3.1 Data

3.1.1 Wellcome Academic Graph

Our dataset was extracted from our custom-built graph database deployed on AWS Neptune, the Wellcome Academic Gaph (WAG). WAG is a network model of the academic landscape, with nodes representing academic entities and edges representing interactions between these entities. It is modeled on the retired Microsoft Academic Graph (Sinha et al., 2015) and tailored to meet our organisation's analysis requirements, including but not limited to enhanced coverage of grant funding data. WAG currently contains over 346 million academic entities (covering scientific publications dating back to the year 1665), connected by 2.9 billion edges. The underlying source data are based on Dimensions (Digital Science) (Herzog et al., 2020), a commercially available scientific research database commonly used by research funders, which we augmented with internal data. The latest version of WAG includes an enrichment layer to add pre-computed metrics and relationships to the graph. Figure 1a shows part of the graph schema relevant for GraphTranslate. Dimensions covers a wide range of articles from open- and closed-access journals (Singh et al., 2021), as well as clinical trial records from 15 registries (as of 2023) (Resources, 2018). Instead of citations from clinical trial publications, we use citations provided as part of these clinical trial records as the target label to predict translation.

3.1.2 Preprocessing

The data were filtered to include only publications related to medical science, as defined by the ANZSRC Field of Research (FoR) codes from 2020 (of Statistics, 2020), which are provided as part of the source data of the publication. The following

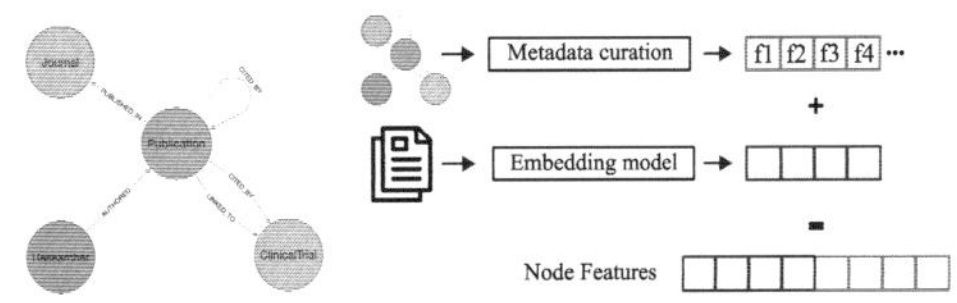

(a) Graph schema (b) Publication node features

Figure 1: Academic graph database schema and the construction of publication node embeddings.

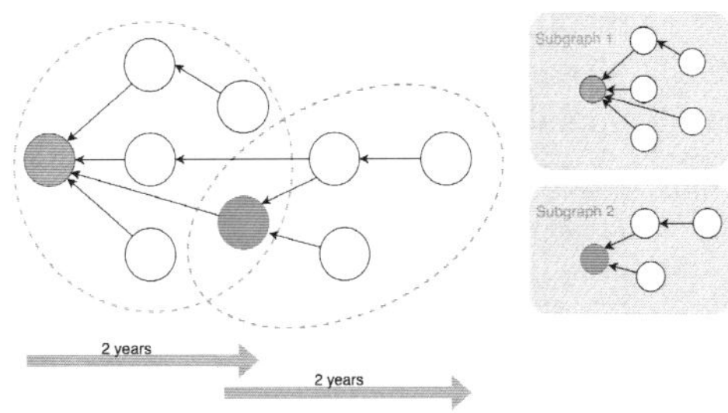

Figure 2: Citation data loading.

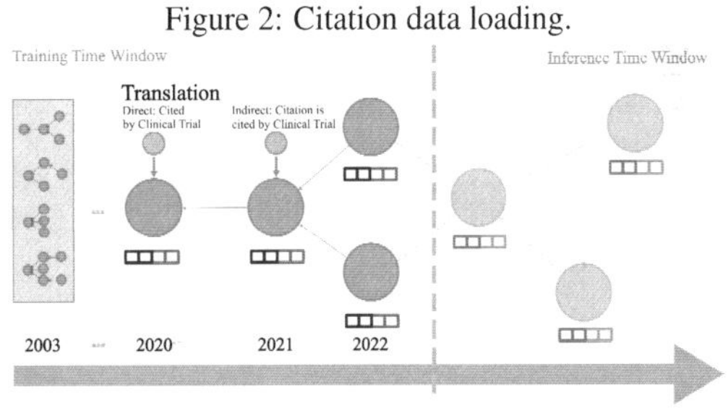

Figure 3: Temporal diagram of translation prediction.

Division-level FoR codes were selected based on our own exploratory analysis of publications historically cited by clinical trials: Biomedical and Clinical Sciences (32), Health Sciences (42), and Psychology (52). In addition, we limited our dataset to research articles by filtering on article-type tags. This was done to ensure that any performance metrics of the resulting models are both realistic (by excluding articles which will conceivably never be cited by a clinical trial) and indicative of translational potential of original research (by excluding review articles, among others). The publications' local citation network was extracted within a 2-year time window used for graph modeling, a time period previously identified as sufficient for predicting citation by a clinical article (Hutchins et al., 2019b). As shown in Figure 2, this was done by loading each year's publication nodes together with citations covering their respective 2-year time window as distinct sub-graphs.

3.1.3 Text Embeddings

Given our focus on semantic information as a key node feature for prediction, we included only those articles which had English language titles and abstracts available. Non-English texts were filtered out using the Google Compact shallow language detector network (Google). Semantic node features were created by converting titles and abstracts to text embeddings using SciBERT, a language model pre-trained on a multi-domain corpus of scientific publications, released in 2019 (Beltagy et al., 2019). Titles and abstracts were concatenated and tokenized. To produce fixed-length embeddings, longer texts were truncated while shorter texts were padded to the maximum sequence length of 512 tokens. 768-dimensional representations of titles and abstracts were produced by applying mean-pooling to the token-level embeddings generated by the model.

3.1.4 Graph Loader

We preprocessed the citation network by filtering out publications that received no citations (approximately 51% of the dataset) and those lacking required metadata fields. The final dataset was split into training (80%), validation (10%), and test (10%) sets for each year.

For training efficiency and to address class imbalance (1.7% positive cases), we downsampled the majority class in the training set to achieve a 1:1 ratio. The validation and test sets maintain their original class distributions to reflect real-world conditions. We implemented a custom PyTorch Geometric DataLoader with a batch size of 256 to handle the large-scale graph structure, using neighbor sampling with a maximum of 500 nodes in the first layer and 1000 nodes in the second to manage memory constraints.

3.2 GNN Model

3.2.1 Model architecture

We implemented a binary node classifier using a graph neural network (GNN) approach. GNNs are typically built on the assumption that the input graph is undirected. However, we hypothesised that our citation network's inherent directionality carries predictive value indicative of translation. Specifically, we hypothesized that data from publications cited by the article in question (i.e., past publications) are less informative than the citations an article receives after its publication. To leverage this directional information in our model, we used a Directed Graph Neural Network (Dir-GNN) architecture as first described by Rossi et al. (Rossi et al., 2023). We considered 2-hop citation neighborhoods when updating our node features for translational prediction, implemented using two graph convolutional layers for message passing. We compared the following graph convolutional layers, which are available as part of Pytorch Geometric: a simple graph convolutional operator (GCNConv) (Kipf and Welling, 2017), a GraphSAGE operator (SAGEConv) (Hamilton et al., 2018), and a graph attentional operator (GATConv) (Veličković et al., 2018). We applied the ReLU activation function and dropout after each convolutional layer. Our best performing model was trained using two GATConv layers with 32 hidden dimensions. Furthermore, we implemented jumping knowledge layer aggregation as part of our GNN architecture, which was based on concatenation of the model's hidden representations (Xu et al., 2018). Finally, a linear output layer was used to generate logits for binary classification.

3.2.2 Model training

Our GNN model was implemented in PyTorch Geometric. We used the Adam optimiser with a learning rate of 1e-3. Models were trained for 50 epochs with early stopping based on validation loss with a patience of 5 epochs. The hidden dimension was set to 32 with 2 graph attention layers. Dropout of 0.2 was applied after each layer. Model training was performed on a cloud compute instance with a Nvidia A10G GPU. Hyperparameters were determined through systematic grid search optimisation.

4 Experiments

To evaluate the efficacy of our graph-based approach for predicting research translation into clinical trials, we conducted four sets of experiments designed to test key hypotheses about model performance, feature importance, early detection capabilities and comparison to previous literature.

4.1 Graph Neural Networks vs. Linear Baseline

Our first experiment compares the predictive performance of our graph-based approach against a traditional linear baseline. Both models were trained on identical datasets comprising academic publications and their associated clinical trial citations. The baseline architecture consists of three linear layers (64 units each) with dropout regularisation (p=0.1). Our proposed graph model implemented two Graph Attention layers (GATConv) with 32-dimensional hidden representations and dropout (p=0.2). For comprehensive evaluation, we considered both direct (publications cited by clinical trial) and indirect (publications' citation is cited by clinical trial) connections between publications and clinical trials in our network structure.

4.2 Publication Node Metadata

We evaluated model performance with different types of metadata features: citation count, Field of Research classifications (FoR), Research Activity Classifications (RAC) (, UKCRC), journal impact metrics, and historical clinical trial participation by any authors. FOR classifications provide broad labeling of fields such as Biological Sciences (top-level class) and Ecology (second-level class). RAC classifications are specific to health-related research with 48 distinct codes organised into eight overarching groups. We obtained historic journal metrics data from Scimago API for each publication (Scimago, 2024). Historic clinical trial participation of an author required that any author be previously associated with a publication directly linked to a clinical trial (not cited). To manage high-dimensional feature spaces (>32 dimensions), we applied Principal Component Analysis (PCA) and retain the top 32 principal components. These reduced metadata embeddings are concatenated with the document text embeddings before being passed through the network.

4.3 Early Detection Performance

To assess the model's capability for early identification of translational research potential, we evaluated direct translation prediction on recent publications in the inference time window (2021). This experiment particularly focuses on the model's ability to identify longer pathways of translational research early on.

4.4 Evaluation

We evaluated the performance of our direct model on NIH's publicly available dataset: iCite (Hutchins et al., 2019a). We removed the feature which links authors to previous clinical trials and retrained our model for inference on this dataset using the same hyperparameters and early stopping. After removing publications without any citations or embeddings, there are a total of 5 million publications between 2003 and 2020. There is a 50% translational rate in this dataset.

Table 1: Validation dataset performance comparison between Linear Model and Graph Neural Network.

Model	AUROC	Recall	Precision	F1	AP
Dir. Linear Model	0.786	0.653	0.088	0.155	0.092
Dir. GNN	0.831	0.647	0.120	0.203	0.132
Indir. Linear Model	0.783	0.390	0.675	0.494	0.532
Indir. GNN	0.818	0.647	0.618	0.632	0.596

5 Results

5.1 Citations

Our dataset comprises 19 million publications and 127 million citation edges from 2003 to 2020 within the training window. Among these publications, 1.7% were identified as directly translational and 14.3% identified as indirectly translational. Analysis reveals average translation times of 6 ± 4 years for a clinical trial citation. The inference window (2021) contains 1.4 million publications, with 0.6% identified as translational. Publications are labeled as translational if they have been cited by a clinical trial as of April 2024. Evaluation of predictions using post-April 2024 clinical trial citations are reported for the test performance.

5.2 Baseline Model Performance Comparison

Our graph neural network (GNN) architectures demonstrate superior performance compared to baseline linear models across both direct and indirect translation prediction tasks. Both GNN models, which incorporate only embedding-based node attributes, effectively capture not only the semantic context of the target publication but also the structural information from its citation neighborhoods. This dual representation leads to improved overall performance metrics, with the direct translation GNN achieving an F1 score improvement of 4.5 percentage points (0.155 vs 0.203) and average precision increase of 4 percentage points. Similarly, the indirect translation GNN demonstrates an F1 score improvement of 12.8 percentage points (0.494 vs 0.632) and average precision of 4% over its linear counterpart.

5.3 Impact of Node Metadata Features

Analysis of different node metadata features reveals varying contributions to model performance. Re-

Table 2: Validation dataset performance comparison for metadata features.

Metadata	AUROC	Recall	Precision	F1	AP
Embeddings	0.831	0.647	0.120	0.203	0.132
+Cite	0.846	0.751	0.105	0.184	0.132
+Cite+Journal	0.722	0.337	0.136	0.194	0.072
+Cite+FOR	0.845	0.794	0.095	0.170	0.135
+Cite+RAC	0.831	0.685	0.130	0.218	0.151
+Cite+FOR+RAC	0.834	0.772	0.110	0.192	0.144
+Cite+Prev.Trial	**0.855**	**0.802**	**0.101**	**0.179**	**0.138**
+Cite+Prev.Trial+FOR	0.855	0.797	0.100	0.178	0.137
+Cite+Prev.Trial+RAC	0.849	0.666	0.145	0.239	0.161

Table 3: Test dataset performance for direct and indirect metadata models.

Model	AUROC	Recall	Precision	F1	AP
Direct GNN	0.852	0.788	0.107	0.188	0.148
Indirect GNN	0.815	0.551	0.662	0.601	0.551

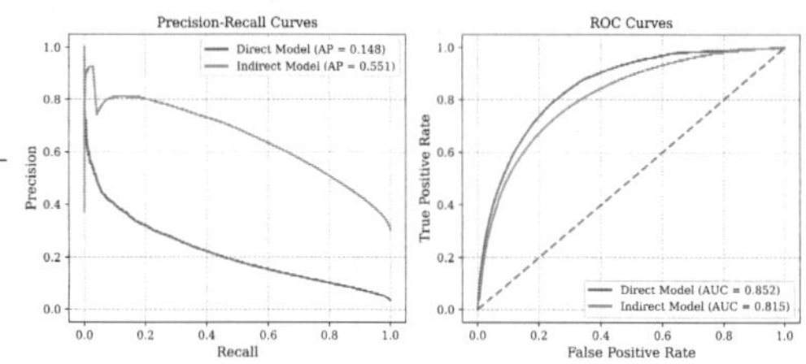

Figure 4: Precision-Recall and ROC curves for direct and indirect test performance.

search Activity Classification (RAC) codes provide the strongest performance boost, increasing the average precision (AP) to 0.151. These codes, which specifically categorise health and clinical research domains, offer an additional health-oriented perspective for assessing translational potential. However, their impact is limited by sparse coverage, with only 13% of publications having RAC annotations.

Fields of Research (FOR) codes, despite their broader coverage across the citation network (>80%), do not significantly improve either F1 or AP scores. Author-based features derived from previous clinical trial associations demonstrate the second-highest performance improvement (AP increase of 0.138), representing the marginal increased gain in scenarios where RAC codes are unavailable. Contrary to guideline/policy and patent prediction (Nelson et al., 2022), the inclusion of journal-based metrics (e.g., impact factor, citation counts) degraded model performance, suggesting that traditional bibliometric measures may not be reliable indicators of translational potential.

5.4 Test Performance

The final direct and indirect models trained on the embeddings, citation count and researcher linked clinical trials were used to measure test performance metrics as shown in Table 3, and precision-recall and ROC curves, as shown in Figure 4. The indirect model is able to substantially improve the precision on the test dataset. This is owing to a more balanced dataset with 14.3% of publications being indirectly cited by a trial.

A closer inspection of the performance metrics across the years show that the accuracy metrics are non-stationary over time, with more recent years suffering a degradation (see Appendix Figure 6). This is most likely due to the recency of these publications and the limited time elapsed to complete clinical trial citations compared to previous years. The assumption, therefore, is that a proportion of the false positives are incorrectly labeled as such. In order to validate this, we collected new Clinical Trials (as at January 2025). Analysis of Clinical Trials data post April 2024 reveals 5,421 new trials linked to 48,021 historic publications. Of these newly translated publications, 1,373 intersect with our test set. When accounting for these recent trials, 0.5% of all test publications were initially mislabeled as false positives. The updated precision scores per year are shown in Appendix Figure 7, with more recent years having a greater proportion of incorrectly labeled false positives. This indicates our model's ability to identify publications with future translational potential.

Appendix Figure 8 demonstrates varying performance for different fields of research. For health sub-domains: neuroscience, reproductive medicine, health and clinical sciences have the highest precision scores (above the global average). These fields represent scientific domains which may often include animal or human participants, positioning them closer to translational outcomes. On the other hand, the health fields with lower precision include biological sciences, medical biotechnology, engineering and microbiology. While a proportion of this can be attributed to longer translation pathways, certain fields continue to demonstrate increased performance pre-2010 (see Appendix Figure 9 - clinical sciences increases by 4 percentage points compared to biological sciences which increased by 1 percentage point). This indicates that the model is better at identifying translation in certain biomedical domains using the publication text and network neighbourhood.

Table 4: Inference performance for direct model.

Model	AUROC	Recall	Precision	F1	AP
Direct GNN	0.728	0.327	0.135	0.191	0.080

5.5 Early Detection Performance

Recall that on average it takes approximately 6 years to obtain a citation from a clinical trial (based on the Wellcome Academic Graph data). Since the inference time window includes publications from 2021, publications have accrued only 3.25 of post-publication citations, resulting in incomplete ground labels, as indicated by a low citation rate in the inference time window (0.6% versus 1.7%). This results in a degradation of the model recall as shown in Table 4. We would expect these results to be recovered once a more complete time window has elapsed.

The translation model predicts the field of immunology to have the greatest number of translational publications in 2021. This is followed by epidemiology and medical microbiology. These are predicted to translate at a rate of close to 4%. However, the precision score is likely to reduce that rate by a factor of 10 for true translation proportion. These fields reflect the translational contribution towards understanding Covid-19 during the pandemic (in the test dataset immunology had a translation rate of 2%).

We updated Clinical Trial citations by importing data after April 2024 up until January 2025. This led to incorrect false positives for the inference time window to have a 1.4% error rate. The correctly predicted publications have a very high median citation count (median > 100), indicative of high impact translational research (see Appendix Figure 11). In contrast the set of false negatives have a much lower citation count (median $\approx$ 10). The Research Activity Codes (RAC) associated with higher proportion of false negatives (see Appendix Figure 12) include individual care needs, organisation and delivery of services and primary prevention interventions to modify behaviours or promote wellbeing. These fields represent research close to translational science, and as shown by (Li et al., 2024), can have a low number of overall non-clinical citations. Lower citation count is not only a feature used for prediction, but also reduces the aggregated network neighbourhood effects for the GNN model prediction.

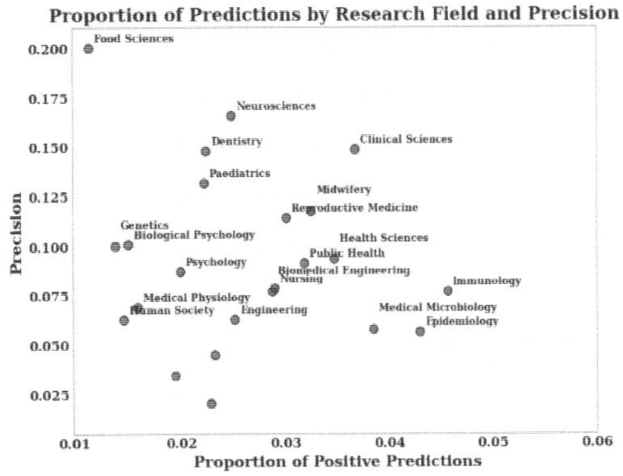

Figure 5: Proportion of positive predictions per field of research versus precision.

Table 5: Inference performance for NIH iCite dataset.

Source	AUROC	Accuracy	F1
Direct GNN	0.85	0.78	0.64
NIH RF (Hutchins et al., 2019b)	0.80	0.84	0.56

5.6 iCite Evaluation

Table 5 shows the performance of our model on the sampled iCite dataset. For completeness, we also show the reported results from the original model which incorporated MeSH categories of the original publication and its' first-order citations. The original publication reports a translation rate of 30% compared to our 50% (Hutchins et al., 2019b). This is most likely due to the time frame: the authors use publications from 1994 - 2014. Our model outperforms the NIH model on the iCite dataset using only embedding and citation count as features. This demonstrates the ability of title and abstract embeddings to encode information on a meaningful scale for understanding clinical trial translation. Since our model does not need any research codes such as MeSH, it can be applied to a broader set of research publications outside of the PubMeD archive.

5.7 Discussion

Our work presents the first application of graph neural networks to model research translation by incorporating local citation network structures. Following (Hutchins et al., 2019b), we use a two-year post-publication citation window, optimising for early detection while maintaining predictive power. However, our approach differs significantly in dataset scope - while their study focused exclusively on PubMed-indexed publications, we analyse a broader spectrum of biological and health sciences research, resulting in a more realistic but challenging 1.7% translation rate. This wider scope leads to lower F1 scores (0.19 versus 0.56), reflecting the inherent difficulty of prediction in a more imbalanced, real-world setting. We find that our model outperforms the model from NIH when predicting on the NIH-iCite dataset leading to increased AUC and F1 scores (0.64 versus 0.56 and 0.85 versus 0.80).

Our results demonstrate that graph neural networks, particularly through attention mechanisms, more effectively capture translation patterns compared to linear combinations of node, MeSH and citation features. The inclusion of Research Activity Classification (RAC) codes provides the highest performance boost, potentially serving a similar role to the MeSH-based features in Hutchins et al. (Hutchins et al., 2019b). However, the marginal improvement from RAC codes suggests our node embeddings already encode much of this information. Additionally, MeSH terms only cover a subset of publications (associated with PubMeD), therefore an embedding based approach to quantifying research content allows for greater generalisability. Notably, contrary to Nelson et al. (Nelson et al., 2022), we found no performance improvement from journal metrics, though this may reflect our focus on clinical trials rather than guidelines and policy citations.

In an early prediction time window, our model maintains precision capabilities while experiencing expected recall reduction due to the time lag between publication and clinical trial citation. Correct predictions correlate with early citation impact, while false positives concentrate in fields with typically longer translation pathways, such as biological mechanisms and oncology research. This pattern suggests our model effectively captures domain-specific translation dynamics.

In future work, a time-normalised PageRank measurement could improve model performance without relying directly on citations. Unlike (Nelson et al., 2022), we deliberately excluded potentially biased features such as researcher demographic or impact scores to avoid potential bias from academics with a longer career history or from certain well funded-geographies. Model performance might be further improved by incorporating local citation networks (references) to provide additional insights into knowledge flow patterns, an approach that has shown promise in predicting clinical citation patterns (Li et al., 2022).

Limitations

Our study has several important limitations that should be considered when interpreting results and applying the model:

Temporal Constraints

The model requires at least 2 years of citation data post-publication to make reliable predictions. This creates an inherent delay in assessment capabilities, limiting its use for real-time funding decisions. Since research grants themselves require time to produce outputs, funders would need to wait a minimum of 2 years from grant award date to assess translation potential. Consequently, this approach is more suitable for retrospective analysis of research portfolios where manual labeling would be impractical or unfeasible.

Limited Translation Outcomes

Our current implementation defines translation narrowly through citation in clinical trials. This definition excludes other important translation pathways such as patents, policy documents, clinical guidelines, commercial products, and public health interventions. In addition, it does not differentiate between phases of Clinical Trials. A more comprehensive model would incorporate these diverse translation outcomes to better reflect the multifaceted nature of research impact beyond the clinical trial pathway.

Interpretability Challenges

The complex interactions captured by graph neural networks limit straightforward interpretation of why specific research is predicted to translate. This "black box" aspect may limit acceptance by funding bodies or policymakers who require transparent decision-making rationale.

Ethics Statement

As authors submitting research to the ACL conference, we affirm our commitment to ethical standards through honest reporting, accurate data, and rigorous scientific methods. Our work provides transparent details for reproducibility, acknowledging ethical considerations, particularly regarding privacy, fairness, and potential misuse. We've respected copyrights and intellectual property, obtaining necessary permissions and crediting sources.

Our research promotes diversity, inclusion, and equity, deliberately avoiding biases related to gender, race, ethnicity, or any other characteristic. Compliance with ethical guidelines, including those by ACL and our institutions, remains paramount. By submitting this paper, we assert adherence to these standards and pledge to address any ethical concerns arising during the review.

References

Matilda Beinat, Julian Beinat, Mohammed Shoaib, and Jorge Gomez Magenti. 2024. Machine learning to promote translational research: predicting patent and clinical trial inclusion in dementia research. *Brain Communications*, 6(4):fcae230.

Iz Beltagy, Kyle Lo, and Arman Cohan. 2019. Scibert: A pretrained language model for scientific text. In *Conference on Empirical Methods in Natural Language Processing*.

D. G. Contopoulos-Ioannidis, G. A. Alexiou, T. C. Gouvias, and J. P. Ioannidis. 2008. Life cycle of translational research for medical interventions. *Science*, 321(5894):1298–1299.

Despina G Contopoulos-Ioannidis, Evangelia Ntzani, and JP Ioannidis. 2003. Translation of highly promising basic science research into clinical applications. *The American journal of medicine*, 114(6):477–484.

Google. Compact language detector v3 (cld3).

William L. Hamilton, Rex Ying, and Jure Leskovec. 2018. Inductive representation learning on large graphs.

Christian Herzog, Daniel Hook, and Stacy Konkiel. 2020. Dimensions: Bringing down barriers between scientometricians and data. *Quantitative Science Studies*, 1(1):387–395.

B Ian Hutchins, Kirk L Baker, Matthew T Davis, Mario A Diwersy, Ehsanul Haque, Robert M Harriman, Travis A Hoppe, Stephen A Leicht, Payam Meyer, and George M Santangelo. 2019a. The nih open citation collection: A public access, broad coverage resource. *PLoS biology*, 17(10):e3000385.

B Ian Hutchins, Matthew T Davis, Rebecca A Meseroll, and George M Santangelo. 2019b. Predicting translational progress in biomedical research. *PLoS biology*, 17(10):e3000416.

Thomas N. Kipf and Max Welling. 2017. Semi-supervised classification with graph convolutional networks.

Xin Li, Xuli Tang, and Qikai Cheng. 2022. Predicting the clinical citation count of biomedical papers using multilayer perceptron neural network. *Journal of Informetrics*, 16(4):101333.

Xin Li, Xuli Tang, and Wei Lu. 2023. Tracking biomedical articles along the translational continuum: a measure based on biomedical knowledge representation. *Scientometrics*, 128(2):1295–1319.

Xin Li, Xuli Tang, and Wei Lu. 2024. How biomedical papers accumulated their clinical citations: a large-scale retrospective analysis based on pubmed. *Scientometrics*, 129(6):3315–3339.

Manuel Sebastian Mariani, Matúš Medo, and Yi-Cheng Zhang. 2016. Identification of milestone papers through time-balanced network centrality. *Journal of Informetrics*, 10(4):1207–1223.

Zoë Slote Morris, Steven Wooding, and Jonathan Grant. 2011. The answer is 17 years, what is the question: understanding time lags in translational research. *Journal of the royal society of medicine*, 104(12):510–520.

Amy PK Nelson, Robert J Gray, James K Ruffle, Henry C Watkins, Daniel Herron, Nick Sorros, Danil Mikhailov, M Jorge Cardoso, Sebastien Ourselin, Nick McNally, et al. 2022. Deep forecasting of translational impact in medical research. *Patterns*, 3(5).

Australian Bureau of Statistics. 2020. Australian and new zealand standard research classification (anzsrc).

Javier Padilla-Cabello, Antonio Santisteban-Espejo, Ruben Heradio, Manuel J Cobo, Miguel A Martin-Piedra, and Jose A Moral-Munoz. 2022. Methods for identifying biomedical translation: A systematic review. *American Journal of Translational Research*, 14(4):2697.

Dimensions Resources. 2018. A Guide to the Dimensions Data Approach.

Emanuele Rossi, Bertrand Charpentier, Francesco Di Giovanni, Fabrizio Frasca, Stephan Günnemann, and Michael Bronstein. 2023. Edge directionality improves learning on heterophilic graphs.

Scimago. 2024. Journal and country rank.

Vivek Kumar Singh, Prashasti Singh, Mousumi Karmakar, Jacqueline Leta, and Philipp Mayr. 2021. The journal coverage of web of science, scopus and dimensions: A comparative analysis. *Scientometrics*, 126(6):5113–5142.

Arnab Sinha, Zhihong Shen, Yang Song, Hao Ma, Darrin Eide, Bo-June Hsu, and Kuansan Wang. 2015. An overview of microsoft academic service (mas) and applications. In *Proceedings of the 24th international conference on world wide web*, pages 243–246.

UK Clinical Research Collaboration (UKCRC). 2024. Research activity code health research classification system (rac hrcs).

Petar Veličković, Guillem Cucurull, Arantxa Casanova, Adriana Romero, Pietro Liò, and Yoshua Bengio. 2018. Graph attention networks.

Kuansan Wang, Iris Shen, Charles Huang, Chieh-Han Wu, Darrin Eide, Yuxiao Dong, Junjie Qian, Anshul Kanakia, Alvin Chen, and Rick Rogahn. 2019. A review of microsoft academic services for science of science studies. *Frontiers in Big Data*, 2:45.

James W Weis and Joseph M Jacobson. 2021. Learning on knowledge graph dynamics provides an early warning of impactful research. *Nature Biotechnology*, 39(10):1300–1307.

Keyulu Xu, Chengtao Li, Yonglong Tian, Tomohiro Sonobe, Ken ichi Kawarabayashi, and Stefanie Jegelka. 2018. Representation learning on graphs with jumping knowledge networks.

A Appendix

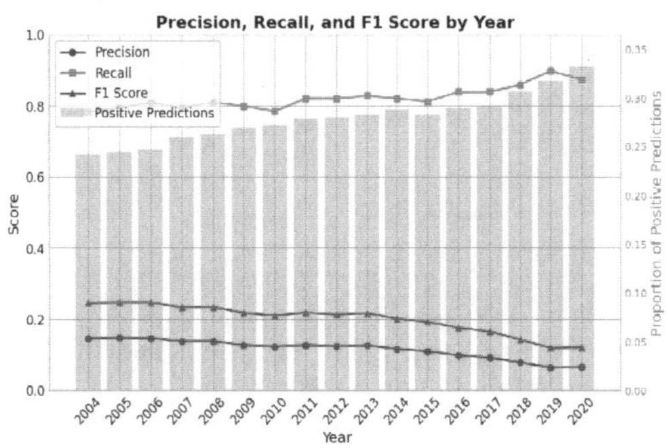

Figure 6: Test set performance metrics for direct clinical trial translation prediction.

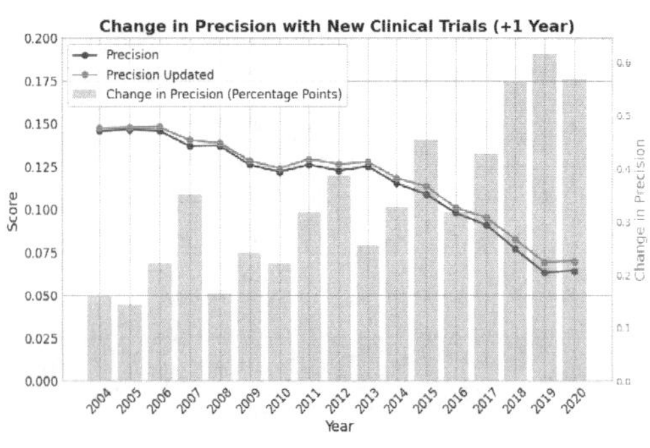

Figure 7: Test set precision metrics including updated metrics for newly translated publications.

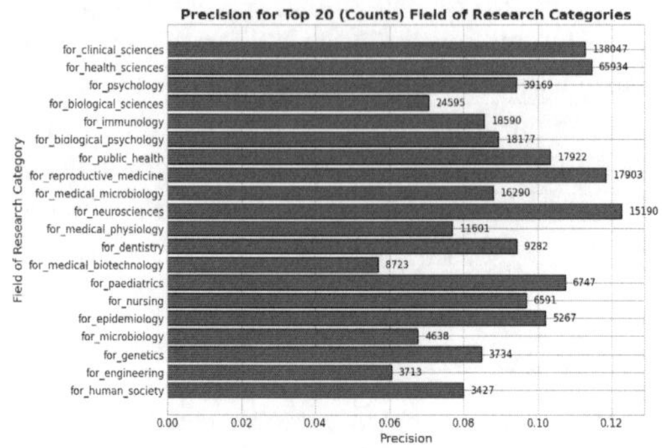

Figure 8: Test set precision metrics for most commonly appearing fields of research (total test set counts shown in brackets).

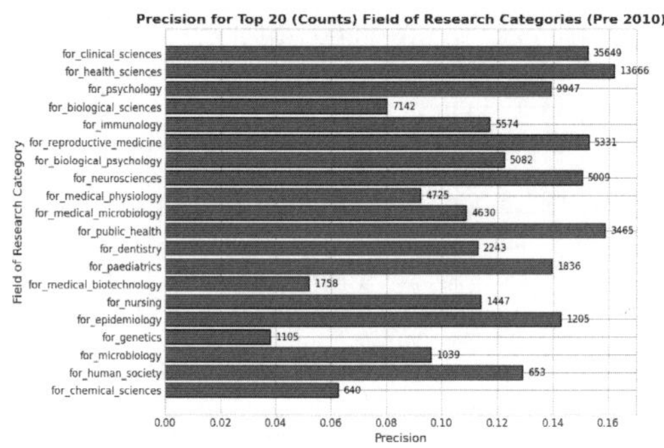

Figure 9: Test set precision metrics for most commonly appearing fields of research (pre-2010 only).

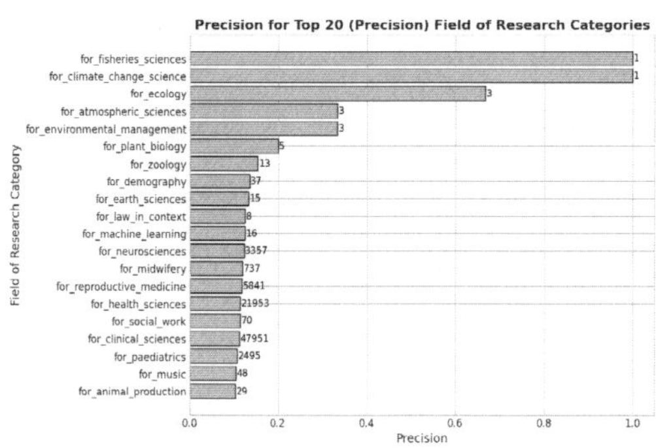

Figure 10: Test set precision metrics highest performing fields (total positive number of publicatoins shown in brackets).

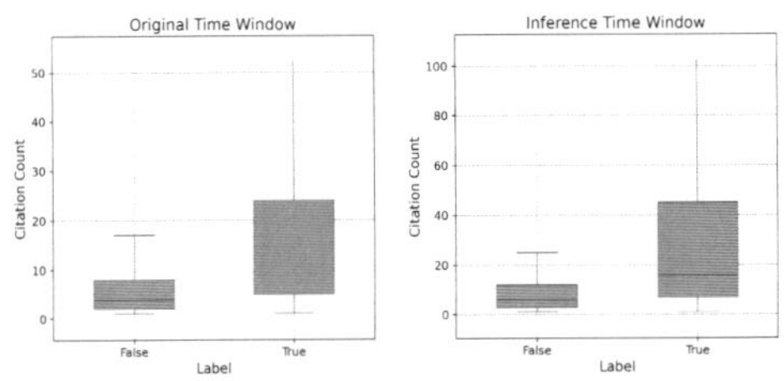

Figure 11: Distribution of citation count in training (left) and inference time window.

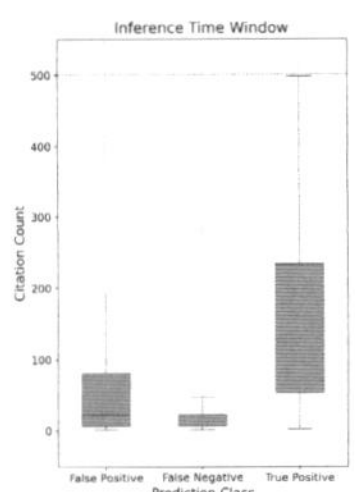

Figure 12: Citation count distribution in each inference prediction class.

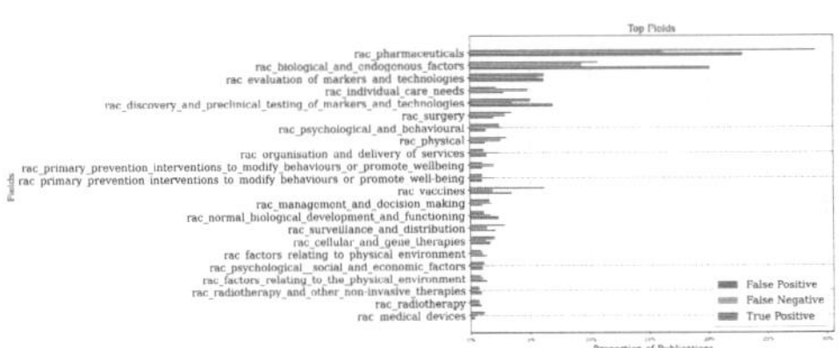

Figure 13: Proportion of RAC research fields in each inference prediction class.

The ClimateCheck Dataset: Mapping Social Media Claims About Climate Change to Corresponding Scholarly Articles

Raia Abu Ahmad[1,2], **Aida Usmanova**[3], **Georg Rehm**[1,4]

[1]Deutsches Forschungszentrum für Künstliche Intelligenz GmbH (DFKI), Berlin, Germany
[2]Technische Universität Berlin, Germany [3]Leuphana Universität Lüneburg, Germany
[4]Humboldt-Universität zu Berlin, Germany
Corresponding author: raia.abu_ahmad@dfki.de

Abstract

The rapid spread of misinformation on and through social media poses a significant challenge to public understanding of climate change and evidence-based policymaking. While natural language processing techniques have been used to analyse online discourse on climate change, no existing resources link social media claims to scientific literature. Thus, we introduce ClimateCheck, a human-annotated dataset that connects 435 unique, climate-related English claims in lay language to scientific abstracts. Each claim is connected to at least one and at most seventeen abstracts, resulting in 3,048 annotated claim-abstract pairs. The dataset aims to facilitate fact-checking and claim verification by leveraging scholarly document processing to improve access to scientific evidence in online discussions about climate change.

1 Introduction

Social media serves as a powerful tool to discuss critical issues such as climate change. However, it also accelerates the spread of misinformation (Fownes et al., 2018; Al-Rawi et al., 2021), making it increasingly difficult to ensure an informed public and create evidence-based policies.

Natural language processing techniques have proven valuable in analysing online discourse on pressing topics (Stede and Patz, 2021). A particularly promising application is linking social media discussions to peer-reviewed scholarly articles, fostering an evidence-based public dialogue (Sarrouti et al., 2021). However, previous efforts have primarily focused on the biomedical domain (Saakyan et al., 2021; Mohr et al., 2022) and, to the best of our knowledge, no resources have been developed to facilitate this connection for climate change discourse among the public.

To address this, we introduce **ClimateCheck**, a human-annotated dataset that links atomic English claims in lay language to scientific abstracts related to climate change. Our work aims to support fact-checking efforts and promote scientifically grounded discussions on climate change.

This paper describes the detailed process of developing the ClimateCheck dataset, which consists of four main stages, illustrated in Figure 1: (1) Collection of claims, (2) Collection of publications, (3) Linking claims to abstracts, and (4) Manual annotation of claim-abstract pairs.

We collected claims from several existing sources and decomposed them into an atomic, scientifically check-worthy form. Claims were either directly extracted from social media or synthetically generated using text style transfer techniques. We then sourced abstracts from scholarly articles in climate change and environmental sciences using existing research registries. To efficiently link claims and abstracts, we employed a pooling strategy popularised by TREC (Voorhees, 2005; Harman, 2011), as seen in similar datasets (Wadden et al., 2022). The relevant abstracts for each claim were first retrieved via a sparse retrieval method, followed by a neural cross-encoder for re-ranking. Then, state-of-the-art models identified abstracts containing supporting or refuting evidence. This resulted in claim-abstract pairs manually annotated by five graduate students in climate sciences. We adopt an existing annotation scheme (Thorne et al., 2018a), where each pair is annotated as *supports*, *refutes*, or *not enough information (NEI)*.

This process resulted in 1,325 unique English claims, of which we employ 435 for running the ClimateCheck shared task (Abu Ahmad et al., 2025). We split the data into training and testing sets with 259 and 176 unique claims, respectively. Each claim in the training data is linked to at least one and at most five abstracts based on our own linking approach, while for the testing data, we annotate additional claim-abstract pairs based on the submissions of participants, result-

Proceedings of the Fifth Workshop on Scholarly Document Processing (SDP 2025), pages 42–56
July 31, 2025

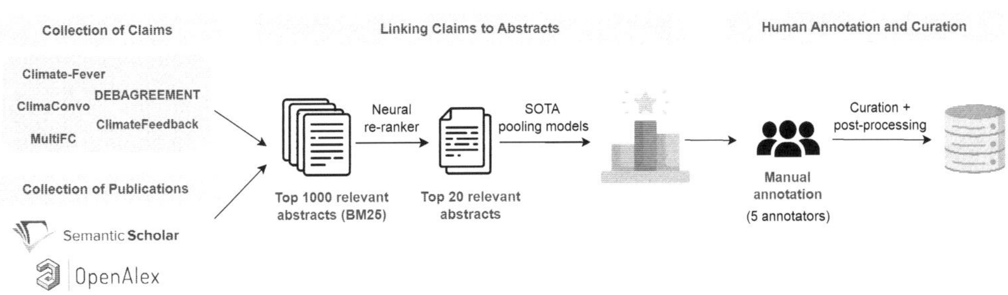

Figure 1: Process of developing the ClimateCheck dataset consisting of four main steps: (1) Collection of claims, (2) Collection of publications, (3) Linking claims to abstracts, and (4) Manual annotation of claim-abstract pairs.

ing in a maximum number of seventeen connected abstracts per claim. The overall process results in **3,048** claim-abstract pairs manually annotated with a total inter-annotator agreement (IAA) score of 0.69 using Cohen's κ.

The rest of the paper is structured as follows. Section 2 reviews existing datasets for scientific fact-checking in general, mentioning those specific to the climate sciences domain. Sections 3, 4, 5, and 6 respectively explain the processes of collecting claims, collecting publications, linking them, and annotating claim-abstract pairs. Importantly, each process is followed by either manual or automatic evaluation to ensure that no errors propagate to the next step.[1] Lastly, Section 7 presents the performance of pooling models on the annotated data and Section 8 concludes our paper.

2 Related Work

Several datasets have been developed for fact-checking across various domains. Fact Extraction and VERification (FEVER, Thorne et al., 2018b) is a benchmark that established a baseline for evidence-based claim verification using Wikipedia as a corpus. Likewise, Wikipedia Citation Entailment (WiCE, Kamoi et al., 2023) is a dataset of fine-grained natural claims mapped to Wikipedia articles that also provides entailment judgements for each subclaim. Although FEVER and WiCE cover a broad range of general knowledge claims, their evidence pool lacks the depth of scientific expertise required to verify domain-specific claims. Similarly, X-Fact (Gupta and Srikumar, 2021) is a multilingual benchmark designed for fact-checking general claims across 25 languages, but does not focus on scholarly publications as evidence sources.

Several fact-checking datasets use scientific literature as an evidence source. For example, SciFact (Wadden et al., 2020) is a benchmark for scientific claim verification in which claims are fact-checked against peer-reviewed biomedical abstracts, with claims annotated as supported or refuted based on evidence sentences. SciFact-Open (Wadden et al., 2022) extends this to an open-domain setting, requiring the retrieval of relevant abstracts before verification. However, a key distinction from our approach is that SciFact and SciFact-Open derive claims from scientific documents rather than public discourse. Closer comparisons to our work are HealthVer (Sarrouti et al., 2021), COVID-Fact (Saakyan et al., 2021), and CoVERT (Mohr et al., 2022), which link social media claims to scientific publications. However, all three are limited to the biomedical domain.

When it comes to climate-related fact-checking efforts, Climate-FEVER (Diggelmann et al., 2020) is, to our knowledge, the only publicly available dataset designed to assess the veracity of claims about climate change. It follows a FEVER-like approach, where claims sourced from English news articles are linked to evidential sentences from Wikipedia. While Climate-FEVER is a valuable resource, it does not align directly with our goal of connecting public discourse in lay language to scientific publications. Other climate-focused fact-checking efforts (Leippold et al., 2024; Augenstein et al., 2019) rely on claims extracted from dedicated fact-checking websites such as Science Feedback[2] and Skeptical Science.[3]

[1] https://github.com/ryabhmd/climatecheck

[2] https://science.feedback.org

[3] https://skepticalscience.com

3 Collection of Claims

To collect claims about climate change, we used five existing sources: (1) Climate-Fever (Diggelmann et al., 2020), (2) DEBAGREEMENT (Pougué-Biyong et al., 2021), (3) ClimaConvo (Shiwakoti et al., 2024), (4) ClimateFeedback,[4] and (5) MultiFC (Augenstein et al., 2019). Some of these directly extract text from social media, while others utilise claims from other sources, such as news outlets. In order to match the claims with the purpose of this dataset, text that was extracted directly from social media platforms underwent a process of claim detection (Section 3.1) and atomic claim generation (Section 3.2), while text extracted from other sources was converted to social media text style using text style transfer techniques (Section 3.3).

3.1 Scientific Claim Detection

Some of the reused datasets were not developed explicitly for fact-checking, thus, raw text did not necessarily contain claims. These include ClimaConvo, a dataset of tweets on climate change originally annotated for relevance, stance, hate speech, and humour (Shiwakoti et al., 2024), as well as DEBAGREEMENT (Pougué-Biyong et al., 2021), a dataset gathered from Reddit, which includes submissions and posts from January 2015 to May 2021 on r/climatechange.[5]

To filter these datasets, we first used an environmental claim detection model fine-tuned on ClimateBERT (Stammbach et al., 2023) to obtain an initial list of potential claims. Then, we manually reviewed the text classified as claims, as well as the text classified as non-claims with a probability of less than 80%. This was done to ensure that we get the maximum number of claims possible from the datasets, without missing any false negatives produced by the claim detection model.

Since the two aforementioned datasets are general public discussions, we noticed that some claims did not refer to scientific topics, rather discussing current political news about climate change. To detect those, we utilised the gemini-1.5-flash model (Gemini Team et al., 2023) in a zero-shot setting, with the self-ask (Press et al., 2023) and rephrase-and-respond (Deng et al., 2023) prompting methods (see Appendix A). This model was selected due to its open availability, fast response time, and competitive performance relative to other models. The model was asked to return a confidence percentage along with its prediction, of which we manually reviewed claims with at least 90% confidence. If any doubt was encountered in terms of the scientific check-worthiness of a claim, it was kept in the dataset, aiming for the climate sciences annotators to decide during the annotation phase of the project.

3.2 Atomic Claim Generation

Fact-checking tasks usually decompose texts to *atomic claims*, which are defined as statements that convey a single, clear, indivisible, and context-independent proposition or piece of information that can be evaluated as true or false (Zhang et al., 2024). More specifically, a *scientific atomic claim* is defined as a statement expressing a finding about one aspect of a scientific entity or process, which can be verified from a single source (Wadden et al., 2020).

Since tweets and posts on Reddit can sometimes contain several atomic claims, we processed them using the gemini-1.5-flash model to extract single atomic claims (see Appendix A). The results were manually reviewed and refined by two near-native English speakers. The instructions given to the refinement process consisted of: (1) Check that the claim indeed exists in the original text; (2) Check that the original text contains the same claim with minimal edits, preserving the original linguistic style; and (3) Check that the claim is atomic using the aforementioned definition. If not, the claim was rephrased to an atomic form when possible. The allowed alterations were replacing pronouns with nouns, adding a subject or an object to elucidate the context, and/or splitting a conjunctional sentence into several atomic claims. Table 7 in Appendix B shows an example of a tweet with several scientific atomic claims, followed by the model output and manual alterations.

3.3 Text Style Transfer

A key objective of this work is to bridge public discourse and scientific knowledge. To that end, we aimed to collect claims that not only reflect discourse on climate change, but also follow the linguistic style in which public conversations usually occur: informal and using colloquial language such as slang, abbreviations, and unconventional grammar (Benamara et al., 2018; Pavlick and Tetreault, 2016). Prior work has shown that such

[4]https://science.feedback.org/climate-feedback

[5]https://www.reddit.com/r/climatechange/

Original Claim	Synthetic Claim
Both the extent and thickness of Arctic sea ice has declined rapidly over the last several decades.	The Arctic sea ice is in trouble! It's been shrinking rapidly in both size and thickness. We gotta do something to turn this around! #SeaIce #ClimateChange

Table 1: Sample of an original claim from a news source and its synthetic tweet-like output.

specialised language requires appropriate datasets and models (Antypas et al., 2023; Barbieri et al., 2022), and recently, Cao et al. (2025) demonstrated that retrieval models underperform when queries are written informally, proving the importance of linguistic registers in datasets used to train and/or fine-tune models.

To be able to reuse datasets that were not developed from social media sources, we rephrased claims to resemble language typically used on social media, inspired by recent research on using large language models (LLMs) for text style transfer (Mukherjee et al., 2024). We used the gemini-1.5-flash model and various prompting techniques, such as role prompting (Schulhoff et al., 2024), rephrase-and-respond, self-ask, and external attention prompting (EAP, Chang et al., 2024) to generate three tweet-style rephrasings per claim (see Appendix A). We then evaluated each rephrased claim based on: (1) BERTScore for similarity to original claim, (2) GPT-2-based perplexity for fluency, and (3) Style classification confidence for text style. These specific evaluation metrics were chosen based on a recent survey on text style transfer (Mukherjee et al., 2024). To develop a style classifier, we fine-tuned BERT-base (Devlin et al., 2019) on a dataset of social media vs. non-social media text. To avoid a classification based on topic rather than style, the texts in both categories dealt with the climate domain. Non-social media sentences were gathered from scientific abstracts, Wikipedia articles, and IPCC reports,[6] and social media texts were taken from the ClimaConvo and DEBAGREEMENT datasets.[7]

To choose a tweet-style representative for each claim, we selected the highest scoring rephrasing as the final output. Tables 1 and 2 present a sample of a rephrased claim and the evaluation averages for all claims, respectively. The results suggest that the rephrased claims are fluent, semantically similar to the original claims, and stylistically similar to social media rather than formal text.

Metric	Score
Perplexity	34.54
BERTScore	72.93
Class. prob. of "social-media" class	99.87

Table 2: Average evaluation scores of the chosen synthetic tweets.

The processes described above resulted in **1,325** English claims. Table 3 summarises the claims by source and original style, and Figure 2 presents four claim samples from various sources.

To illustrate topic diversity in the final set of claims, we ran BERTopic (Grootendorst, 2022) and grouped the results into 16 clusters based on keywords and representative documents. These clusters were then reviewed and named manually, the results of which are shown in Figure 3. To connect the clusters with existing work, we looked for representative (sub-)topics in climate change. However, existing topic lists and taxonomies are usually developed based on official documents and reports rather than public discourse (Sica et al., 2023), or focus on misinformation in discourse rather than presenting neutral topics (Coan et al., 2021). That being said, we manually mapped our resulting clusters to the topics of the World Data Center for Climate (WDCC),[8] as well as the taxonomy presented by Sica et al. (2023). The results are shown in Appendix B.

4 Collection of Publications

To build the corpus of scholarly publications, we first queried S2ORC (Lo et al., 2020) via its bulk search API using "climate change" as the search term and filtered the results to the Environmental Sciences field, yielding 210,237 publications. To better simulate a real-life fact-checking environment with millions of available studies, we expanded the corpus using OpenAlex (Priem et al., 2022), filtering for open-access English publications on climate change, which yielded 826,531

[6]https://www.ipcc.ch/data/

[7]The classification model is available at https://huggingface.co/rabuahmad/cc-tweets-classifier

[8]https://www.wdc-climate.de/ui/topics

Dataset	Source	Original Style	No. of Claims
Climate-Fever	News Articles	Formal	741
DEBAGREEMENT	Reddit	Informal	274
ClimaConvo	Twitter	Informal	164
ClimateFeedback	Media	Formal	97
MultiFC	Diverse	Formal	49
Total			**1325**

Table 3: Overview of datasets reused to collect climate change-related claims.

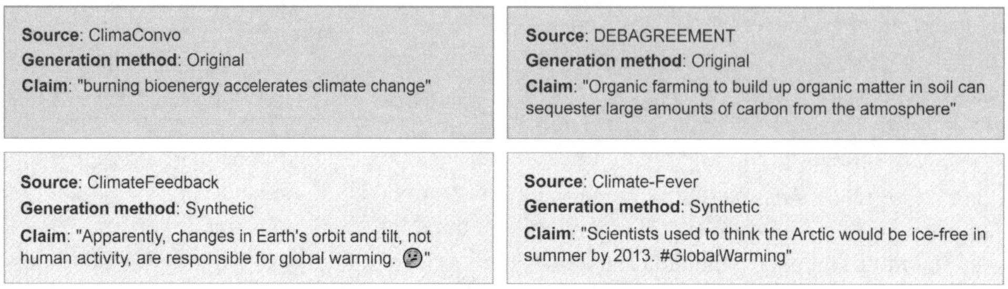

Figure 2: Samples of claims in the dataset.

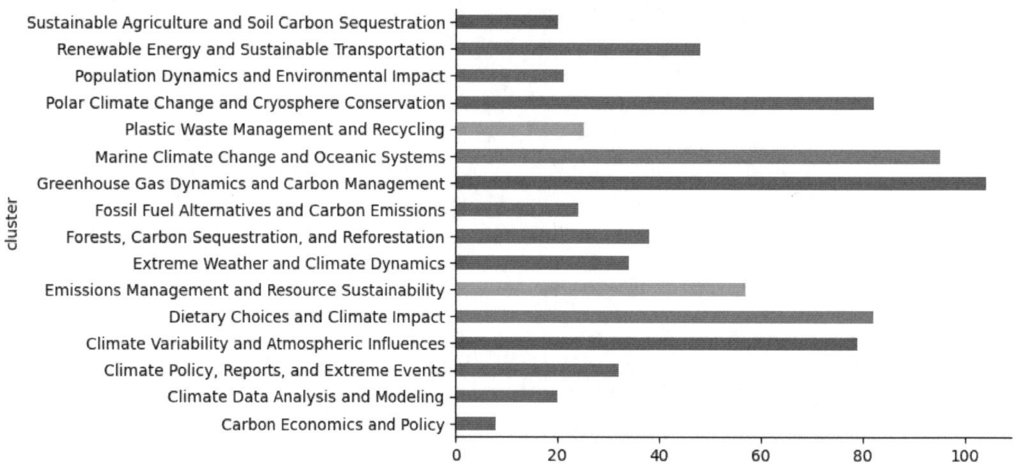

Figure 3: Distribution of represented topics in the collected claims; produced automatically using BERTopic.

articles. After merging and deduplicating by DOI, we further filtered out non-English[9] publications and those missing abstracts or full-text URLs, resulting in a corpus of 835,659 publications. Upon inspection, we noticed that some publications in the corpus were noisy, consisting of think-pieces and various non-peer-reviewed documents. Thus, we filtered out publications with less than 10 citations as a quality measure, chosen based on similar prior research (Wadden et al., 2022). The final corpus consists of **394,269** publications.[10]

5 Linking Claims to Publications

Following retrieval strategies popularised by the TREC competitions (Voorhees, 2005; Harman, 2011; Wadden et al., 2022), we linked each claim to relevant abstracts of scholarly articles using a sparse retrieval method, followed by a neural reranker. We then employed a pooling approach, using six state-of-the-art models to classify each

[9]Using https://github.com/fedelopez77/langdetect

[10]The publications corpus is available at https://huggingface.co/datasets/rabuahmad/climatecheck_publications_corpus

claim-abstract pair as "Supports", "Refutes", or "NEI". If an abstract was classified as evidentiary (i. e., either supports or refutes) by at least three models, the claim-abstract pair was added to the annotation pool.

For the sparse retrieval step, we used BM25 (Robertson et al., 2009), a method that relies on TF-IDF keyword matching, to get the top 1000 abstracts per claim. Then, we used a BERT-based neural cross-encoder[11] trained on the MS MARCO passage ranking task[12] to re-rank the retrieved abstracts per claim. For the pooling step, we chose six models based on the following criteria: (1) Open source, (2) Available on Hugging Face for ease of implementation, (3) Parameter size falls between 120M and 15B due to a limit in compute resources, (4) State-of-the-art performance on language understanding, natural language inference (NLI), and/or claim verification tasks. We checked the last criterion using the SuperGLUE,[13] OpenLLM,[14] and MTEB[15] leaderboards.

Consequently, three sequence classification models and three causal LLMs were chosen: 1. RoBERTa-large, fine-tuned on the MNLI dataset,[16] 2. DeBERTa-xxlarge, fine-tuned on the MNLI dataset,[17] 3. XLM-RoBERTa, fine-tuned on the XNLI dataset,[18] 4. Yi-1.5-Chat with a 16K context window (Young et al., 2024), 5. Qwen 1.5-14B-Chat (Bai et al., 2023), and 6. Llama3.1 8B-Instruct.[19] Due to compute and time limitations, the top 20 abstracts from the re-ranking phase were considered. Causal models were prompted using zero-shot role prompting and chain-of-thought (Wei et al., 2022) techniques (see prompt in Appendix A). We used HuggingFace's pipeline object[20] with the default text generation hyperparameters, disabling sampling, thus effectively selecting the most likely next token at each step. For sequence classification models, we used the default forward pass without any adjustments.

To prepare the annotation corpus, a maximum of five abstracts per claim were considered, preferring higher-ranking evidentiary abstracts. Interestingly, the output of the linking phase resulted in a total of **1,167** unique claims connected to a minimum of 1 and a maximum of 5 abstracts. Hence, 158 claims were naturally filtered out due to not resulting in any connected abstracts in the pooling process. These were indeed non-scientifically check-worthy claims that were mistakenly left in the data during the claim collection process (see examples in Appendix B).

6 Annotation Process

To annotate the corpus of claim-abstract pairs, we hired five part-time graduate students (master's). All students have strong expertise in climate sciences, as evidenced by their academic records, and are enrolled in English-language programmes dealing with different aspects of climate sciences. Their English proficiency was proven by providing official results from certified English language tests. We used the INCEpTION (Klie et al., 2018) annotation tool, which offers an automatic calculation of IAA and allows multiple users and roles (Borisova et al., 2024).

The annotation process followed these steps: (1) Read the claim carefully. (2) Read the abstract carefully. (3) Label the pair as one of the following: **"Supports"**: If the abstract supports the claim. **"Refutes"**: If the abstract refutes the claim. **"NEI"**: If the abstract does not provide sufficient information. Annotators were explicitly asked to decide only based on the given abstract, not on their prior knowledge.

To account for mistakes in the data preparation process in terms of creating atomic claims, the annotators were asked to report cases that were manually reviewed. If a claim was shortened to an atomic form, both annotators were updated and asked to annotate with the new version of the claim. Additionally, if an annotator encountered a claim that is not check-worthy against scientific articles, it was disregarded.[21]

Due to time and resource restrictions, the first version of the dataset contains a total of 435

[11]https://huggingface.co/cross-encoder/ms-marco-MiniLM-L-12-v2

[12]https://github.com/microsoft/MSMARCO-Passage-Ranking

[13]https://gluebenchmark.com/leaderboard

[14]https://huggingface.co/spaces/open-llm-leaderboard/open_llm_leaderboard#/

[15]https://huggingface.co/spaces/mteb/leaderboard

[16]https://huggingface.co/FacebookAI/roberta-large-mnli

[17]https://huggingface.co/microsoft/deberta-v2-xxlarge-mnli

[18]https://huggingface.co/joeddav/xlm-roberta-large-xnli

[19]https://huggingface.co/meta-llama/Llama-3.1-8B-Instruct

[20]https://huggingface.co/docs/transformers/en/main_classes/pipelines

[21]Full guidelines given to annotators are available at: https://github.com/ryabhmd/climatecheck/blob/master/ClimateCheck%20Annotation%20Guidelines.pdf

unique claims resulting in 1,815 annotated claim-abstract pairs. We split those into training and testing sets, where the former includes 259 unique claims and 1,144 claim-abstract pairs, while the latter 176 unique claims with 671 claim-abstract pairs. Each document was annotated by two students and curated by a third in case of disagreement. For administrative reasons, we had two annotation groups for the training data, and three for the testing data, each group consisting of two annotators given the same documents.

The dataset was used for the ClimateCheck shared task (Abu Ahmad et al., 2025), where we annotated a subset of claim-abstract pairs from the submissions of participants on a weekly basis, using claims from the test set. This resulted in 1,233 additional manually annotated claim-abstract pairs, with a total of **3,047** documents overall. Figure 4 shows the number of claims as a function of the number of connected abstracts, and Table 4 displays the distribution of labels in each split.[22]

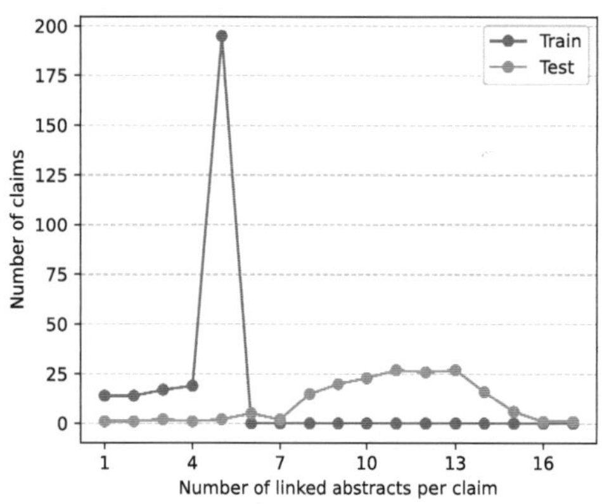

Figure 4: Distribution of the number of abstracts connected to unique claims in the train and test splits.

	Train	Test	Total
Supports	446	749	1195
Refutes	241	266	507
NEI	457	889	1346
Total	1144	1904	3048

Table 4: Label distribution in the train and test splits of the dataset.

The quality of annotations is evaluated based on IAA using Cohen's κ for pairwise comparisons (Cohen, 1960). While this metric was introduced to account for chance agreement, interpretive and widely-used guidelines, such as those by Landis and Koch (1977), suggest that values between 0.61 and 0.80 indicate substantial agreement. Our annotation process achieved an overall Cohen's κ score of 0.69, suggesting a high level of consistency among annotators. Throughout the project, special attention was paid to the agreement score, with the curator flagging claims with low IAA across all associated abstract pairs as potentially vague. Those were then reviewed and rephrased when necessary. The final IAA results are shown in Table 5, indicating individual group agreements in each data split. Importantly, the overall scores are weighted averages, taking the number of annotated documents into account.

Group	IAA	# of Documents
Training Data		
Group 1	0.74	607
Group 2	0.71	537
Overall	0.73	1144
Testing Data		
Group A	0.68	570
Group B	0.62	576
Group C	0.68	758
Overall	0.66	1904
Total	**0.69**	**3048**

Table 5: IAA results for annotated claim-abstract pairs measured using Cohen's κ.

7 Performance of Pooling Models

After finalising the annotations for both the train and test sets, we evaluated the pooling models on the task of claim verification using all annotated documents. The results are shown in Table 6, reported using weighted scores of precision (P), recall (R) and F1, as well as accuracy (Acc.). The sequence classification models were not fine-tuned on the dataset, and the causal models were prompted in a zero-shot setting (see Appendix A).

We note that the sequence classification models achieve similar levels of performance, ranging between an F1 score of 0.31 - 0.33 and an accuracy score of 0.43, with an overwhelming bias toward predicting the NEI class. The results of these models indicate frequent misclassifications of true evidentiary classes, indicating a limitation in models fine-tuned on general NLI datasets, such as MNLI

[22]The ClimateCheck dataset is publicly available at https://huggingface.co/datasets/rabuahmad/climatecheck

and XNLI, when it comes to their applicability to more domain-specific data. We hypothesise that the climate jargon in claims, technical terminology in abstracts, and the overall complex causal structures in claim-abstract pairs is not well represented in standard benchmarks, further supporting the need for domain- and register-specific datasets like ClimateCheck.

In contrast, instruction-tuned LLMs show a significantly better performance, with Yi-1.5-9B-Chat-16K achieving the best F1 and accuracy scores, both 0.61. This suggests that such models have more generalised reasoning abilities and contextual understanding, likely due to their exposure to such data during training. Interestingly, Yi outperformed Qwen by a large margin, despite having fewer parameters, showing that more parameters does not necessarily mean better performance.

Among causal LMs, Yi achieves a relatively balanced precision and recall scores, suggesting that it captures claim-abstract relations with minimal trade-off. However, other models show a clear precision-recall gap, with a pronounced emphasis on weighted precision at the expense of recall. This indicates that while models are highly reliable to make an accurate classification, they miss a significant portion of true instances, generating more false negatives.

Model	P	R	F1	Acc.
roberta-large-mnli	0.40	0.43	0.32	0.43
deberta-v2-xxlarge-mnli	0.39	0.42	0.33	0.43
xlm-roberta-large-xnli	0.40	0.43	0.31	0.43
Yi-1.5-9B-Chat-16K	0.65	**0.61**	**0.61**	**0.61**
Qwen1.5-14B-Chat	0.65	0.53	0.47	0.53
Llama-3.1-8B-Instruct	**0.66**	0.50	0.52	0.50

Table 6: Performance of the six pooling models on the ClimateCheck annotated data using a zero-shot setting.

8 Conclusion

This paper introduces our work of constructing **ClimateCheck**, a human-annotated dataset designed to bridge the gap between social media claims about climate change and corresponding scientific literature. Our dataset consists of 435 unique English claims in lay language, each linked to up to seventeen relevant scientific abstracts, resulting in **3,048** claim-abstract pairs. Claims were fetched from existing resources and refined into atomic, scientifically check-worthy statements, while abstracts were retrieved from open-access climate science publications. We employed BM25 and a neural cross-encoder to rank abstracts per claim, followed by a pooling approach using state-of-the-art models to select the most relevant evidentiary abstracts for annotation. To ensure high-quality annotations, we conducted a structured human annotation process with five graduate students in climate sciences. With this work, our aim is to advance climate-related fact-checking research, fostering a more scientifically grounded public discourse on climate change. Further work can utilise our dataset for tasks such as detecting scientifically check-worthy statements on social media, retrieving relevant publications, and verifying climate-related claims.

Limitations

Although we believe the dataset to be a valuable resource for scientific fact-checking models, it still has several limitations. First, claims are limited to the English language, which hinders improvements in cross-lingual applications that bridge global public discussions with scientific documents. In addition, when linking claims to publications, we only considered abstracts, not the full texts of publications, which might contain more relevant information on a query. During the same step, we filtered abstracts from publications with less than 10 citations as a quality measure, removing informative publications with a smaller citation count. This creates a limitation that could be mitigated in future work by filtering based on other criteria, such as the venue of publication. Additionally, due to time constraints and annotator capacity limitations, we only annotated about a third of the unique claims we originally extracted. However, we plan to release a second version of the dataset with more unique claims in the training data. That being said, we acknowledge that the annotation process is limited in that it is done on a paragraph-level, thus specific sentences that are most informative cannot be connected directly to the claim.

Ethical Statement

The ClimateCheck dataset does not contain sensitive or personal information and is collected from open-source resources. ClimaConvo tweets were preprocessed and thus cannot be traced back to their original form and remain anonymous. Annotators were compensated through a typical payment scheme and have been informed about the further use of the annotations.

Acknowledgements

This work was supported by the consortium NFDI for Data Science and Artificial Intelligence (NFDI4DS)[23] as part of the non-profit association National Research Data Infrastructure (NFDI e. V.). The consortium is funded by the Federal Republic of Germany and its states through the German Research Foundation (DFG) project NFDI4DS (no. 460234259). We thank the annotators: Emmanuella Asante, Farzaneh Hafezi, Senuri Jayawardena, Shuyue Qu, and Gokul Udayakumar for their work.

References

Raia Abu Ahmad, Aida Usmanova, and Georg Rehm. 2025. The ClimateCheck shared task: Scientific fact-checking of social media claims about climate change. In *Proceedings of the 5th Workshop on Scholarly Document Processing (SDP)*, Vienna, Austria.

Ahmed Al-Rawi, Derrick O'Keefe, Oumar Kane, and Aimé-Jules Bizimana. 2021. Twitter's fake news discourses around climate change and global warming. *Frontiers in Communication*, 6:729818.

Dimosthenis Antypas, Asahi Ushio, Francesco Barbieri, Leonardo Neves, Kiamehr Rezaee, Luis Espinosa-Anke, Jiaxin Pei, and Jose Camacho-Collados. 2023. SuperTweetEval: A challenging, unified and heterogeneous benchmark for social media NLP research. In *Findings of the Association for Computational Linguistics: EMNLP 2023*, pages 12590–12607, Singapore. Association for Computational Linguistics.

Isabelle Augenstein, Christina Lioma, Dongsheng Wang, Lucas Chaves Lima, Casper Hansen, Christian Hansen, and Jakob Grue Simonsen. 2019. Multifc: A real-world multi-domain dataset for evidence-based fact checking of claims. In *Proceedings of the 2019 Conference on Empirical Methods in Natural Language Processing and the 9th International Joint Conference on Natural Language Processing (EMNLP-IJCNLP)*, pages 4685–4697.

Jinze Bai, Shuai Bai, Yunfei Chu, Zeyu Cui, Kai Dang, Xiaodong Deng, Yang Fan, Wenbin Ge, Yu Han, Fei Huang, Binyuan Hui, Luo Ji, Mei Li, Junyang Lin, Runji Lin, Dayiheng Liu, Gao Liu, Chengqiang Lu, Keming Lu, Jianxin Ma, Rui Men, Xingzhang Ren, Xuancheng Ren, Chuanqi Tan, Sinan Tan, Jianhong Tu, Peng Wang, Shijie Wang, Wei Wang, Shengguang Wu, Benfeng Xu, Jin Xu, An Yang, Hao Yang, Jian Yang, Shusheng Yang, Yang Yao, Bowen Yu, Hongyi Yuan, Zheng Yuan, Jianwei Zhang, Xingxuan Zhang, Yichang Zhang, Zhenru Zhang, Chang Zhou, Jingren Zhou, Xiaohuan Zhou, and Tianhang Zhu. 2023. Qwen technical report. *arXiv preprint arXiv:2309.16609*.

Francesco Barbieri, Luis Espinosa Anke, and Jose Camacho-Collados. 2022. XLM-T: Multilingual language models in Twitter for sentiment analysis and beyond. In *Proceedings of the Thirteenth Language Resources and Evaluation Conference*, pages 258–266, Marseille, France. European Language Resources Association.

Farah Benamara, Diana Inkpen, and Maite Taboada. 2018. Introduction to the special issue on language in social media: Exploiting discourse and other contextual information. *Computational Linguistics*, 44(4):663–681.

Ekaterina Borisova, Raia Abu Ahmad, Leyla Garcia-Castro, Ricardo Usbeck, and Georg Rehm. 2024. Surveying the FAIRness of annotation tools: Difficult to find, difficult to reuse. In *Proceedings of The 18th Linguistic Annotation Workshop (LAW-XVIII)*, pages 29–45, St. Julians, Malta. Association for Computational Linguistics.

Tianyu Cao, Neel Bhandari, Akhila Yerukola, Akari Asai, and Maarten Sap. 2025. Out of style: Rag's fragility to linguistic variation. *arXiv preprint arXiv:2504.08231*.

Yuan Chang, Ziyue Li, and Xiaoqiu Le. 2024. Guiding large language models via external attention prompting for scientific extreme summarization. In *Proceedings of the Fourth Workshop on Scholarly Document Processing (SDP 2024)*, pages 226–242.

Travis G Coan, Constantine Boussalis, John Cook, and Mirjam O Nanko. 2021. Computer-assisted classification of contrarian claims about climate change. *Scientific reports*, 11(1):22320.

Jacob Cohen. 1960. A coefficient of agreement for nominal scales. *Educational and psychological measurement*, 20(1):37–46.

Yihe Deng, Weitong Zhang, Zixiang Chen, and Quanquan Gu. 2023. Rephrase and respond: Let large language models ask better questions for themselves. *arXiv preprint arXiv:2311.04205*.

Jacob Devlin, Ming-Wei Chang, Kenton Lee, and Kristina Toutanova. 2019. Bert: Pre-training of deep bidirectional transformers for language understanding. In *Proceedings of the 2019 Conference of the North American Chapter of the Association for Computational Linguistics: Human Language Technologies, Volume 1 (Long and Short Papers)*, pages 4171–4186.

[23]https://www.nfdi4datascience.de

Thomas Diggelmann, Jordan Boyd-Graber, Jannis Bulian, Massimiliano Ciaramita, and Markus Leippold. 2020. Climate-fever: A dataset for verification of real-world climate claims. *arXiv preprint arXiv:2012.00614*.

Jennifer R Fownes, Chao Yu, and Drew B Margolin. 2018. Twitter and climate change. *Sociology Compass*, 12(6):e12587.

Google Gemini Team, Rohan Anil, Sebastian Borgeaud, Jean-Baptiste Alayrac, Jiahui Yu, Radu Soricut, Johan Schalkwyk, Andrew M Dai, Anja Hauth, Katie Millican, et al. 2023. Gemini: a family of highly capable multimodal models. *arXiv preprint arXiv:2312.11805*.

Maarten Grootendorst. 2022. Bertopic: Neural topic modeling with a class-based tf-idf procedure. *arXiv preprint arXiv:2203.05794*.

Ashim Gupta and Vivek Srikumar. 2021. X-fact: A new benchmark dataset for multilingual fact checking. In *Proceedings of the 59th Annual Meeting of the Association for Computational Linguistics and the 11th International Joint Conference on Natural Language Processing (Volume 2: Short Papers)*, pages 675–682.

Donna Harman. 2011. *Information retrieval evaluation*. Morgan & Claypool Publishers.

Ryo Kamoi, Tanya Goyal, Juan Diego Rodriguez, and Greg Durrett. 2023. Wice: Real-world entailment for claims in wikipedia. In *Proceedings of the 2023 Conference on Empirical Methods in Natural Language Processing, EMNLP 2023, Singapore, December 6-10, 2023*, pages 7561–7583. Association for Computational Linguistics.

Jan-Christoph Klie, Michael Bugert, Beto Boullosa, Richard Eckart De Castilho, and Iryna Gurevych. 2018. The inception platform: Machine-assisted and knowledge-oriented interactive annotation. In *Proceedings of the 27th international conference on computational linguistics: System demonstrations*, pages 5–9.

J Richard Landis and Gary G Koch. 1977. The measurement of observer agreement for categorical data. *biometrics*, pages 159–174.

Markus Leippold, Saeid Ashraf Vaghefi, Dominik Stammbach, Veruska Muccione, Julia Bingler, Jingwei Ni, Chiara Colesanti-Senni, Tobias Wekhof, Tobias Schimanski, Glen Gostlow, et al. 2024. Automated fact-checking of climate change claims with large language models. *arXiv preprint arXiv:2401.12566*.

Kyle Lo, Lucy Lu Wang, Mark Neumann, Rodney Kinney, and Daniel S Weld. 2020. S2orc: The semantic scholar open research corpus. In *Proceedings of the 58th Annual Meeting of the Association for Computational Linguistics*, pages 4969–4983.

Isabelle Mohr, Amelie Wührl, and Roman Klinger. 2022. Covert: A corpus of fact-checked biomedical covid-19 tweets. In *Proceedings of the Thirteenth Language Resources and Evaluation Conference*, pages 244–257.

Sourabrata Mukherjee, Mateusz Lango, Zdenek Kasner, and Ondrej Dušek. 2024. A survey of text style transfer: Applications and ethical implications. *arXiv preprint arXiv:2407.16737*.

Ellie Pavlick and Joel Tetreault. 2016. An empirical analysis of formality in online communication. *Transactions of the Association for Computational Linguistics*, 4:61–74.

John Pougué-Biyong, Valentina Semenova, Alexandre Matton, Rachel Han, Aerin Kim, Renaud Lambiotte, and Doyne Farmer. 2021. Debagreement: A comment-reply dataset for (dis) agreement detection in online debates. In *Thirty-fifth Conference on Neural Information Processing Systems Datasets and Benchmarks Track (Round 2)*.

Ofir Press, Muru Zhang, Sewon Min, Ludwig Schmidt, Noah A Smith, and Mike Lewis. 2023. Measuring and narrowing the compositionality gap in language models. In *Findings of the Association for Computational Linguistics: EMNLP 2023*, pages 5687–5711.

Jason Priem, Heather Piwowar, and Richard Orr. 2022. Openalex: A fully-open index of scholarly works, authors, venues, institutions, and concepts. *arXiv preprint arXiv:2205.01833*.

Stephen Robertson, Hugo Zaragoza, et al. 2009. The probabilistic relevance framework: Bm25 and beyond. *Foundations and Trends® in Information Retrieval*, 3(4):333–389.

Arkadiy Saakyan, Tuhin Chakrabarty, and Smaranda Muresan. 2021. Covid-fact: Fact extraction and verification of real-world claims on covid-19 pandemic. In *Proceedings of the 59th Annual Meeting of the Association for Computational Linguistics and the 11th International Joint Conference on Natural Language Processing (Volume 1: Long Papers)*, pages 2116–2129.

Mourad Sarrouti, Asma Ben Abacha, Yassine M'rabet, and Dina Demner-Fushman. 2021. Evidence-based fact-checking of health-related claims. In *Findings of the Association for Computational Linguistics: EMNLP 2021*, pages 3499–3512.

Sander Schulhoff, Michael Ilie, Nishant Balepur, Konstantine Kahadze, Amanda Liu, Chenglei Si, Yinheng Li, Aayush Gupta, HyoJung Han, Sevien Schulhoff, et al. 2024. The prompt report: A systematic survey of prompting techniques. *arXiv preprint arXiv:2406.06608*.

Shuvam Shiwakoti, Surendrabikram Thapa, Kritesh Rauniyar, Akshyat Shah, Aashish Bhandari, and Usman Naseem. 2024. Analyzing the dynamics of climate change discourse on twitter: A new annotated corpus and multi-aspect classification. In *Proceedings of the 2024 Joint International Conference on Computational Linguistics, Language Resources and Evaluation (LREC-COLING 2024)*, pages 984–994.

Francesco Sica, Francesco Tajani, Mª Paz Sáez-Pérez, and José Marín-Nicolás. 2023. Taxonomy and indicators for esg investments. *Sustainability*, 15(22):15979.

Dominik Stammbach, Nicolas Webersinke, Julia Bingler, Mathias Kraus, and Markus Leippold. 2023. Environmental claim detection. In *Proceedings of the 61st Annual Meeting of the Association for Computational Linguistics (Volume 2: Short Papers)*, pages 1051–1066.

Manfred Stede and Ronny Patz. 2021. The climate change debate and natural language processing. In *Proceedings of the 1st Workshop on NLP for Positive Impact*, pages 8–18.

James Thorne, Andreas Vlachos, Christos Christodoulopoulos, and Arpit Mittal. 2018a. Fever: a large-scale dataset for fact extraction and verification. In *Proceedings of the 2018 Conference of the North American Chapter of the Association for Computational Linguistics: Human Language Technologies, Volume 1 (Long Papers)*, pages 809–819.

James Thorne, Andreas Vlachos, Oana Cocarascu, Christos Christodoulopoulos, and Arpit Mittal. 2018b. The fact extraction and verification (fever) shared task. *EMNLP 2018*, 80(29,775):1.

EM Voorhees. 2005. Trec: Experiment and evaluation in information retrieval.

David Wadden, Shanchuan Lin, Kyle Lo, Lucy Lu Wang, Madeleine van Zuylen, Arman Cohan, and Hannaneh Hajishirzi. 2020. Fact or fiction: Verifying scientific claims. In *Proceedings of the 2020 Conference on Empirical Methods in Natural Language Processing (EMNLP)*, pages 7534–7550.

David Wadden, Kyle Lo, Bailey Kuehl, Arman Cohan, Iz Beltagy, Lucy Lu Wang, and Hannaneh Hajishirzi. 2022. Scifact-open: Towards open-domain scientific claim verification. *arXiv preprint arXiv:2210.13777*.

Jason Wei, Xuezhi Wang, Dale Schuurmans, Maarten Bosma, Fei Xia, Ed Chi, Quoc V Le, Denny Zhou, et al. 2022. Chain-of-thought prompting elicits reasoning in large language models. *Advances in neural information processing systems*, 35:24824–24837.

Alex Young, Bei Chen, Chao Li, Chengen Huang, Ge Zhang, Guanwei Zhang, Guoyin Wang, Heng Li, Jiangcheng Zhu, Jianqun Chen, et al. 2024. Yi: Open foundation models by 01. ai. *arXiv preprint arXiv:2403.04652*.

Zhihao Zhang, Yixing Fan, Ruqing Zhang, and Jiafeng Guo. 2024. A claim decomposition benchmark for long-form answer verification. In *China Conference on Information Retrieval*, pages 41–53. Springer.

A Prompts

Scientific Check-worthiness Prompt

Task: Check-worthiness detection.
Definition: Given a claim, identify if it can be fact-checked **against scientific publications in environmental sciences** to determine their accuracy or truthfulness.
Constraints:
1. Keep in mind that the answer of whether the fact is check-worthy is referring to fact-checking against ***scholarly publications in environmental sciences only and not any other field of science***.
2. For every claim, provide the degree of confidence in the answer you provide. The number should be between 0 and 1 with a higher number indicating higher confidence.
3. Give the output in a json format 'result': 'check-worthy', 'confidence': 0.8
4. Before giving your answer, rewrite the prompt, expand the task at hand, and only then respond.
5. If you have follow-up questions, generate them and then answer them before giving the final output.
Claim: [claim]
Output:

Atomic Claim Generation Prompt

Task: Given an input text, give a list of atomic claims in it. Atomic claims are verifiable statements **expressing a finding about one and only one aspect of a scientific entity or process**, which can be verified from a single source.
Constraints:
1. The output should only split different sentences in the input text so that each sentence contains one claim.
2. ** It is extremely important in this task that the style of the text, including the used words and characters, should not be changed, and the text itself should not be rephrased. Claims should be copy-pasted. **
3. ** Each claim should be self-contained without needing more context. A claim should have a subject, a predicate and an object. If a sentence in the input text needs more context to be understood completely, it should not be included in the list of answers. **
4. Before giving your answer, rewrite the prompt, expand the task at hand, and only then respond.
5. If you have follow-up questions, generate them and then answer them before giving the final output.
6. Give your answers in a list in JSON format.
Examples: [examples]
Input text: [text]
Output:

Text Style Transfer Prompt

Task: Given a claim extracted from a news article, produce a rephrasing as if you are a layperson tweeting about it.
Constraints:
1. Take into account stylistic features of social media text such as use of slang and informal language.
2. Do not overdo your text generations. Keep them plausible enough to believe a human wrote them.
3. Introduce variance in rhetoric and syntactic structures of your tweets. **Not every tweet needs to contain a question.**
4. **Generate tweets in a neutral tone. Do not add irony or satire.**
5.**Keep the scientific claim that is present in the original claim**
6. Give three output options in a JSON format that includes a list of the tweets.
7. Before giving your answer, rewrite the prompt, expand the task at hand, and only then respond.
8. If you have follow-up questions, generate them and then answer them before giving the final output.
Examples of tweets about a similar topic: [examples]
Claim: [claim]
Output:

Pooling Models Prompt

You are an expert claim verification assistant with vast knowledge of climate change, climate science, environmental science, physics, and energy science.
Your task is to check if the Claim is correct according to the Evidence. Generate 'Supports' if the Claim is correct according to the Evidence, or 'Refutes' if the claim is incorrect or cannot be verified. Or 'Not enough information' if you there is not enough information in the evidence to make an informed decision.
Evidence: [abstract]
Claim: [claim]
Provide the final answer in a Python list format.
Let's think step-by-step:

B Additional Samples and Figures

B.1 Atomic Claim Generation

Original Text	Plastics are not only a primary marine pollutant but also a significant driver of the climate crisis. Emissions from plastic production will reach a billion tons per year by 2030, and plastic in the environment releases methane and ethylene in a feedback loop. #FridaysforFuture
Gemini-1.5 Output	['Plastics are not only a primary marine pollutant but also a significant driver of the climate crisis.', 'Emissions from plastic production will reach a billion tons per year by 2030.', 'plastic in the environment releases methane and ethylene in a feedback loop.']
Manual Refinement	['Plastics are a primary marine pollutant.', 'Plastics are a significant driver of the climate crisis.', 'Emissions from plastic production will reach a billion tons per year by 2030.', 'plastic in the environment releases methane in a feedback loop.', plastic in the environment releases ethylene in a feedback loop']

Table 7: Example of processing social media text into atomic claims.

B.2 Filtered Claims

The following list contains ten example claims that were filtered out during the linking process. These claims did not result in any linked abstracts that met our criteria of having at least three evidentiary predictions from the pooling models.

1. So, Benny Peiser has backtracked on his criticism. Interesting... Wonder what made him change his mind?
2. people are trying to dispose of plastics in Uganda by burning
3. Florida needs to step up its game when it comes to business regulations. Ranking 45th out of 50 states is not a good look.
4. The 2016 Future Energy Jobs Act is Illinois' most significant climate legislation.
5. Obama warned the U.S. Coast Guard that global warming is the biggest threat to the military and the world. We gotta take climate change seriously! #ClimateAction #ClimateCrisis
6. Google will run entirely on green energy 24/7 without requiring carbon offsets at all by 2030.
7. Luxury *non-*gas cars need to be celebrated.
8. Carbicrete's process is carbon-negative.
9. They also said the company failed to keep adequate servicing records
10. United Kingdom has a special responsibility to provide moral and political leadership on the climate crisis.

B.3 Topic Distribution of Claims

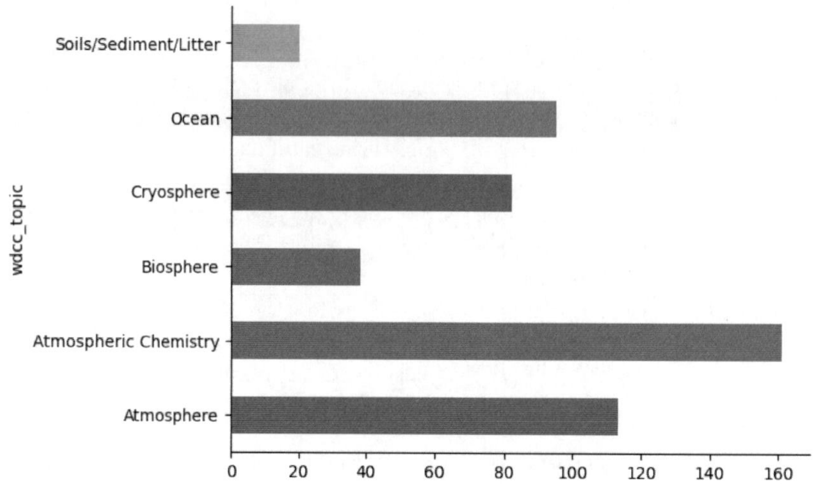

Figure 5: Distribution of represented WDCC topics in the collected claims, made by mapping BERTopic clusters to topics manually.

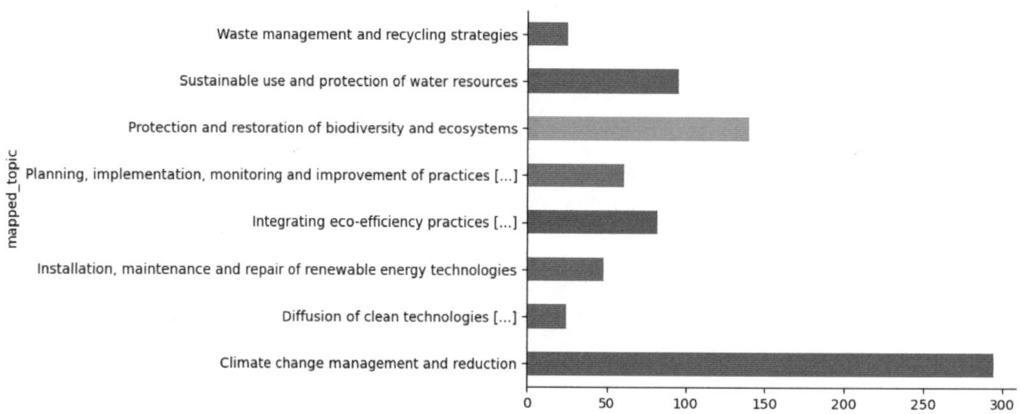

Figure 6: Distribution of claim topics according to the environmental section of the taxonomy presented by Sica et al. (2023).

Analyzing the Evolution of Scientific Misconduct Based on the Language Of Retracted Papers

Christof Bless[1,2] *, **Andreas Waldis**[1,4], **Angelina Parfenova**[1,3],
Maria Andueza Rodriguez[1,5], **Andreas Marfurt**[1]
[1]Lucerne University of Applied Sciences and Arts,
[2]Leibniz University Hannover,
[3]Technical University of Munich,
[4]Technical University of Darmstadt,
[5]University of Fribourg

Abstract

Amid rising numbers of organizations producing counterfeit scholarly articles, it is important to quantify the prevalence of scientific misconduct. We assess the feasibility of automated text-based methods to determine the rate of scientific misconduct by analyzing linguistic differences between retracted and non-retracted papers. We find that retracted works show distinct phrase patterns and higher word repetition. Motivated by this, we evaluate two misconduct detection methods, a mixture distribution approach and a Transformer-based one. The best models achieve high accuracy (>0.9 F1) on detection of paper mill articles and automatically generated content, making them viable tools for flagging papers for closer review. We apply the classifiers to more than 300,000 paper abstracts, to quantify misconduct over time and find that our estimation methods accurately reproduce trends observed in the real data.

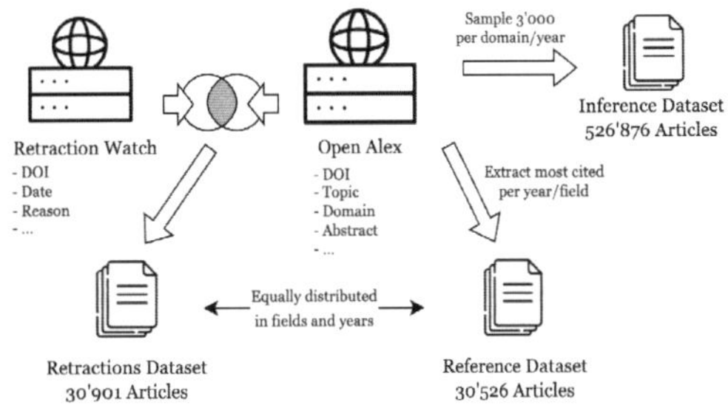

Figure 1: We create a dataset of retracted papers by merging resources from `retractionwatch.org` and `openalex.org`. We add to that a reference dataset of non-retracted articles to train various classifiers for identifying papers with scientific misconduct. Finally, we estimate the development of misconduct over time by running a classifier on a large inference dataset of papers from diverse domains.

1 Introduction

The integrity of scientific research is increasingly threatened by the rise of so-called *paper mills*, for-profit organizations that produce and sell fraudulent academic manuscripts to researchers, academics, or students who are under pressure to publish in peer-reviewed journals (Candal-Pedreira et al., 2022; Abalkina, 2023). Often disguised as editing or translation services, paper mills sell manuscripts, author slots on peer-reviewed papers, and citations for existing papers (COPE, 2025; Christopher, 2021). Papers produced by paper mills can have negative consequences for society as they circulate false claims, erode trust in science, or lead to unjustified academic promotions (Byrne et al., 2022; Fanelli et al., 2021).

Since 2010, at least 5402 retracted papers have been connected to paper mills according to the Retraction Watch database (The Center for Scientific Integrity, 2018). This would be around 2 in every 10,000 papers indexed by Scopus in the same time frame. However, this number reflects only cases where the paper mill activity was uncovered. The real number of fabricated papers is likely considerably higher due to their convincing nature (Oransky et al., 2021; Brainard and You, 2018).

In this paper, we evaluate the feasibility of estimating the true rate of scientific misconduct by analyzing linguistic differences between retracted and non-retracted papers and specifically papers retracted for reasons of scientific misconduct. Based on preliminary data review, the central hypothesis is that paper mill articles share a distinctive writing style characterized by words and phrases stemming from the methods used to produce these articles. We conjecture that the automated tools and/or human ghostwriters share a common style or produce unusual expressions (Cabanac et al., 2021).

To investigate this hypothesis, we construct a text corpus of retracted and non-retracted articles (Figure 1 and Section 2) and assess linguistic characteristics of retracted papers (Section 3). Next,

* Corresponding author: christof.bless@hslu.ch

Proceedings of the Fifth Workshop on Scholarly Document Processing (SDP 2025), pages 57–71
July 31, 2025

we evaluate the performance of two text-based misconduct detection methods – a mixture distribution model and a Transformer-based text classifier – and apply them to an inference corpus stretching a 42-year time-frame (Sections 4 & 5).

We find that (1) retracted articles have distinctive language patterns and lower lexical diversity than non-retracted articles, (2) paper mill content is detected with an F1 score of 0.93, (3) there is high correlation ($\rho = 0.79$) between the models' estimates and the observed rate of misconduct retractions, and (4) predicted rates of misconduct are hard to interpret but accurately capture trends. More details on the results can be found in Section 6 and a relation to previous work in Section 7.

The **main contributions** of our work are (1) a balanced dataset of retracted and non-retracted articles, containing abstracts and full-text sections, (2) a quantification model based on a mixture distribution to directly estimate the rate of papers containing misconduct from a collection of articles and (3) three Transformer-based classifiers each classifying one of the labels *paper mill*, *randomly generated content* and *falsification*.

We make our code, data, and trained models available on GitHub[1].

2 A Dataset of Retractions

Figure 1 gives an overview of the provenance and size of the datasets used in this study. We utilize a dataset of retracted papers originating from the blog `retractionwatch.com` merged with information from the scientific publication repository `openalex.org` (see Subsection 2.1). Then, we crawl open-access PDF articles from the web to add full-text data to this dataset (see Subsection 2.2). For comparative analysis, we create a reference corpus of non-retracted articles with the same temporal and topical distribution (see Subsection 2.3).

2.1 Retraction Watch Text Corpus

Scientific publishers usually issue paper retractions through their platforms in the form of retraction notices. Typically, retraction notices don't contain extensive information about the backgrounds of a retraction and often go unnoticed by the community (Marcus and Oransky, 2014). To combat this, journalists Ivan Oransky and Adam Marcus started their blog `retractionwatch.com`, where they publish retractions alongside the background stories they manage to investigate. This also led to the creation of the Retraction Watch database consisting of 55,520 entries of retracted articles with associated reasons and nature of retraction.

Reason labels. In the data, there are 106 distinct reason labels, and each record can be assigned multiple reasons (3.6 on average). We identify the biggest reasons linked to scientific misconduct that are potentially recognizable from the paper's text as *Paper Mill*, *Falsification/Fabrication of Data*, and *Randomly Generated Data*. Filtering the retractions by these three reasons results in sub-datasets containing 3,605, 3,090, and 1,016 articles, respectively. Whenever we speak of misconduct hereafter, it will refer to papers tagged with one of these three reasons.

OpenAlex data. The Retraction Watch dataset does not include any content-related data. We use the platform `openalex.org` (Priem et al., 2022) to gather the text of abstracts as well as information about authors, publishers, affiliations, and topics of the papers. OpenAlex is a repository of more than 240 million scholarly documents, which mainly consists of data from the Microsoft Academic Graph (Sinha et al., 2015) and Crossref[2], but also combines information from other metadata sources. Merging the Retraction Watch data with OpenAlex reduces the number of articles in the corpus to 30,901, of which 19,472 have a plain text abstract available. In some cases of retractions, instead of the abstract, we find a retraction notice. Considering that we want to find latent signals of retracted articles, we filter out these cases by excluding abstracts containing the substring "retract".

Domains and fields. OpenAlex employs a three-tiered hierarchy for the research area of a paper, with the *domain* at the top, following a *field* and *subfield* categories. These categorizations allow us to conduct our analyses within and across fields.

2.2 Full-Text Extraction

OpenAlex does not publish any full-text content of articles. Instead, we can often retrieve PDF links of open-access papers through the API. We collect these PDF documents where possible. The PDF documents are converted to raw text by a PDF to

[1] `https://github.com/Christof93/language-of-scientific-misconduct.git`

[2] `https://www.crossref.org/`

Section	Number of Articles
Abstract	19,472
Introduction	6,783
Related Work	1,589
Methods	1,301
Result & Discussion	5,177
Conclusion	5,300

Table 1: Count of retracted articles grouped by successfully extracted sections.

markdown converter[3]. To extract content-related text snippets from the full-text, we employ a simple regular expression matching algorithm that detects sections according to a number of section title variants. We determine the section titles by looking at the frequency distribution of all section titles and choosing titles that fulfill two requirements: (1) the section they preface is likely content-related and (2) they occur very frequently. We group the resulting list of section titles into these five categories: introduction, related work, method, results/discussion, and conclusion (see in Table 5 in Appendix A) for the mapping of titles to categories. This approach ensures that we keep the article contents instead of appendices, tables, references, or even meta information such as the retraction notice prepended to many retracted articles. It also allows filtering and analyzing the content by section type. About 50% of the PDF links allow automated retrieval, and we manually download an additional 1,306 documents to bolster the record. Table 1 shows the total articles and sections obtained.

2.3 Reference Corpus

For our analysis, we construct a parallel reference corpus of non-retracted articles sampled from OpenAlex. Since a random sample of research articles might potentially include a small number of soon-to-be-retracted papers we try to reduce noise by extracting only the top cited articles from OpenAlex, assuming that they are less likely to be fraudulent. For each year and field in the retraction corpus, we collect exactly the same number of articles for the reference corpus. We gather the same information for this dataset and download freely accessible PDF documents where possible.

[3]https://pypi.org/project/pymupdf4llm/

3 Language Characteristics of Retracted Papers

To analyze linguistic differences between retracted and non-retracted papers, we compare log-odds of word and n-gram occurrences (Subsection 3.1) and investigate the significance of differences in word repetitions (Subsection 3.2).

3.1 Characteristic Expressions

We conduct a log-odds analysis, identifying words that are significantly overrepresented in one corpus versus the other. We apply a chi-square independence test to assess whether frequency differences between corpora were statistically significant, only considering tokens and n-grams meeting the significance threshold of $p < 0.05$. According to the analysis, retracted papers overuse certain adverbs and verbs across all domains in the dataset. Illustrative examples can be found when restricting the dataset by domains and fields.

Computer science. For example, in the field of computer science (a subfield of the physical sciences domain) phrases such as *becoming more and more*, *relatively*, and *developed rapidly* had significantly higher log-odds ratios compared to non-retracted papers. Verbs like *analyzes*, *brought*, and *realized* are also disproportionately more common in computer science retractions.

Physical sciences. In the overall physical sciences domain we find a significantly higher frequency of adverbs such as *erefore* (likely an error in PDF conversion of therefore), *gradually*, *comprehensively*, *vigorously*, and *organically* in retracted works. These adverbs are rather vague and unspecific, which might be a reason why they occur less in evidence-based non-retracted papers.

Social science. In the Social Sciences domain, similar patterns emerged. Adverbs like *accurately, vigorously,* and *scientifically* were more frequent in retracted papers, suggesting that authors needlessly overemphasize results. Non-retracted papers in all domains displayed a higher frequency of cautious and precise language. Terms like *i.e.*, *thereof, ideally* and *likely* were more common.

3.2 Lexical Diversity

Examining some of the retracted articles, we notice that they often feature repeated use of the same words, sometimes even within the same sentence. To test this assumption, we calculate the

	Sentence Level			Document Level		
POS Tag	Ret TTR	Ref TTR	CLES	Ret TTR	Ref TTR	CLES
VERB	0.982	0.987	0.492	0.794	0.873	0.348
ADJ	0.960	0.974	0.480	0.683	0.771	0.368
NOUN	0.924	0.946	0.456	0.571	0.679	0.326
ADV	0.988	0.992	0.497	0.805	0.890	0.377

Table 2: Mean type-token ratio (TTR) for retracted (Ret) and reference (Ref) texts and Common Language Effect Size (CLES) values between them, at sentence and document level.

type-token ratio (TTR) as a measure of lexical diversity (Baayen, 2001) for selected parts of speech (adjective, adverb, noun, and verb) at both the document and sentence levels (see Table 2).

We consider a Mann-Whitney *U* test (Mann and Whitney, 1947) to establish the significance of differences in TTR between retracted and non-retracted sentences and documents. The Kolmogorov-Smirnov test (Massey, 1951) confirms that TTR distributions in both corpora are not normal, justifying the use of Mann-Whitney. According to the test, differences between retracted and non-retracted type-token ratios are significant for all selected POS tags ($p < 0.001$).

TTR difference effect size. The Common Language Effect Size (CLES) scores (see Table 2) indicate that differences in lexical diversity within sentences are very small between retracted and reference papers (close to 0.5, which would indicate no difference). Per document, the differences are more pronounced. Lower CLES values at the document level, particularly for nouns (0.3258) and adjectives (0.3681), suggest that retracted papers exhibit lower lexical diversity, meaning they rely more on repetitive phrasing or expressions.

4 Identifying Scientific Misconduct

The language analysis results in Section 2 suggest that retracted papers can be identified through statistical methods based on the differing linguistic structure. Building on this, we focus on specifically identifying retractions involving scientific misconduct next. We present two methods to achieve this, a quantification framework based on a mixture distribution (Subsection 4.1) and a classifier fine-tuned on a pre-trained Transformer model (Subsection 4.2).

4.1 Distributional Quantification Framework

Inspired by recent successes in measuring usage of LLM-generated language, we adapt the *distributional LLM quantification* framework from Liang et al. (2024b) to measure the fraction of research articles that contain language typical of scientific misconduct. The Distributional Quantification Framework (DQF) determines the most likely mixture ratio of two probability distributions pre-calculated on the training data. Let $\mathcal{P}$ denote the distribution of the reference text and $\mathcal{Q}$ that of the type of text we want to quantify. $\mathcal{P}(x)$ and $\mathcal{Q}(x)$ will denote the likelihood of text x under $\mathcal{P}$ or $\mathcal{Q}$ respectively. A collection of texts is described by a mixture of these two distributions:

$$\mathcal{D}_\alpha(X) = (1-\alpha)\mathcal{P}(X) + \alpha\mathcal{Q}(X) \quad (1)$$

where α is the mixture parameter determining the fraction of examples belonging to the text type.

$\mathcal{P}$ and $\mathcal{Q}$ are estimated from training data – in our case a corpus of non-retracted articles $X_\mathcal{P}$ and a collection of retracted scientific articles $X_\mathcal{Q}$ (Section 2).

To estimate $\mathcal{P}$ as $\hat{\mathcal{P}}$, the method relies on occurrence probabilities of the tokens t from both text corpora. The estimated probability $\hat{p}(t)$ of a token in the reference corpus is defined as:

$$\hat{p}(t) = \frac{\sum_{x \in X_\mathcal{P}} \mathbb{1}\{t \in x\}}{|X_\mathcal{P}|} \quad (2)$$

i.e., the number of texts containing the token divided by the total number of texts in the specific corpus. Analogously for $X_\mathcal{Q}$, $\hat{\mathcal{Q}}$, and $\hat{q}(t)$. The probability of a text x under $\hat{\mathcal{P}}$ is subsequently given by:

$$\hat{\mathcal{P}}(x) = \prod_{t \in x} \hat{p}(t) \times \prod_{t \notin x} (1 - \hat{p}(t)) \quad (3)$$

and $\hat{\mathcal{Q}}(x)$ can be derived similarly using $\hat{q}(t)$.

Finally, to infer the coefficient α for an unseen collection of texts $\{x_i\}_{i=1}^n$,the DQF uses maximum likelihood estimation under the estimated mixture distribution $\hat{\mathcal{D}} = (1-\alpha)\hat{\mathcal{P}}(X_\mathcal{P}) + \alpha\hat{\mathcal{Q}}(X_\mathcal{Q})$:

$$\hat{\alpha} = \underset{\alpha \in [0,1]}{\text{argmax}} \sum_{i=1}^{n} log((1-\alpha)\hat{\mathcal{P}}(x_i) + \alpha\hat{\mathcal{Q}}(x_i)) \quad (4)$$

This step will be used to infer an α estimator representing the fraction of texts in a collection exhibiting the style of $\mathcal{Q}$.

4.2 Transformer-based Classifier

As a comparison to the DQF, we also train Transformer-based classifiers. We adopt the commonly used fine-tuning paradigm and train a randomly initialized classification head on top of a pre-trained Transformer encoder model.[4] Specifically, we use four Transformer encoders pre-trained on general text (BERT (Devlin et al., 2019), RoBERTa (Liu et al., 2019), DeBERTa-v3 (He et al., 2021), ModernBert (Warner et al., 2024)) and three encoders adapted to the scientific domain (SciBERT (Beltagy et al., 2019), SciDeBERTa (Kim et al., 2023), and ClinicalBERT (Wang et al., 2023)). We fine-tune these classifiers with a batch size of 16 and a learning rate of $2 \cdot 10^{-5}$, and select the best model across five epochs based on evaluation set performances. To ensure the reliability of our results, we repeat this process for five different randomly generated seeds and report the average performance.

5 Experiments

We evaluate the DQF and Transformer approaches at the level of the document collection and the individual documents. First, we infer the ratio of papers retracted for misconduct from a collection of articles using the DQF (Section 5.1). Second, we compare both approaches by classifying misconduct on the document level (Section 5.2). Finally, we use both the best-performing Transformer from Section 5.2 and the DQF to quantify misconduct through inference on a collection of randomly sampled research articles to explore temporal trends (Section 5.3).

5.1 Quantification of Misconduct

With the DQF, we can infer the ratio of papers involved in misconduct directly from a collection of articles. To evaluate the performance of the DQF on this task, we test its predicted α on constructed mixtures of retracted and non-retracted text fragments and determine how close the estimate is to the true ratio. We follow these steps:

1. We split the data into 50% training and 50% test examples for both the retracted and reference corpus. We run an experiment for each combination of considered sections (e.g. abstract + introduction) and parts of speech.

2. From the test set, we construct 11 variants with different ratios of retracted and reference examples, going from 0% retracted examples to 100% in increments of 10%.

3. We evaluate if the model predicts the appropriate α ratio by considering the difference between prediction and true ratio. For subsequent experiments, we choose the configuration with the closest α estimate to the true ratio.

4. We repeat steps 1 and 2 using the best model from step 3 on subsets of the data filtered by all combinations of domain, field, and retraction reason.

In the following, we report the results of this evaluation approach for the DQF method.

Relying on verbs and adverbs leads to the best estimate. The results of the configuration search from step 3 for the DQF estimator can be found in Table 3. Generally, including the sections *abstract*, *introduction*, and *conclusion* and the POS-tags *verb* and *adverb* leads to the best results. Only relying on adverbs leads to the closest estimates in social sciences, but the bootstrapping variance is high due to data scarcity. the DQF can estimate the ratio α on the document or the sentence level. Running it on the sentence level increases performance across all domains.

Domain	Sections	POS Tags	Mean Error
Health Sciences	A, I	VERB, ADV	0.075 ± 0.011
Life Sciences	A, I	VERB, ADV	0.081 ± 0.010
Social Sciences	A, I, C	ADV	0.063 ± 0.036
Physical Sciences	I, C	VERB, ADV	0.064 ± 0.013

Table 3: Best-performing mixture model per domain with corresponding setting of document sections and POS Tags. A, I, and C stand for abstract, introduction, and conclusion, respectively. ADV means adverbs.

Quantifying paper mill content works better than falsified data. DQF results for specific misconduct retraction reasons can be found in Figure 2. In the case of paper mill quantification, we observe that the method overestimates the true ratio by maximally 15% if the test data entirely consists of non-retracted sentences and underestimates it by around 11% for completely retracted data. The top subplot in Figure 2 shows that the method does not perform well for the retraction reason of falsification. A possible explanation would be that falsification

[4] See Appendix B.1 for more details.

Model	PM	RGC	F&F
BERT	0.905	0.920	0.770
RoBERTa	0.905	0.904	0.779
DeBERTa-v3	0.916	0.911	0.770
ModernBert	0.914	0.903	0.779
ClinicalBERT	0.895	0.886	0.709
SciBERT	0.911	0.914	**0.797**
SciDeBERTa	**0.926**	**0.934**	**0.797**
DQF	0.854	0.798	0.727

Table 4: Different models' F1 on detecting misconduct types: Paper Mill (PM), Randomly Generated Content (RGC), and Falsification and Fabrication of Data (F&F).

happens on the level of experimental results or data and is not directly visible in the article text. This finding is also confirmed by the Transformer-based classifier (see Figure 4b) and inference results (see Figure 8 in Appendix B.3). We also evaluate the performance for the categories *randomly generated content* and *peer review fraud*, which both have similar results (see Figure 5 in Appendix B.2).

5.2 Document-Level Detection

For the misconduct classifier, we look at individual articles. For all misconduct reason subsets of the retraction corpus, we sample an equal-sized subset from the reference corpus matching the distributions of years and scientific fields. Then, we further split the data into training, development, and test sets according to a 60:15:25 split, keeping the label distribution balanced for all sets. We separately fine-tune different Transformer classifiers to perform binary classification for each reason of misconduct. The results are shown in Table 4.

SciDeBERTa is the strongest model on average. Detecting falsification is again the hardest task, as discussed in the previous experiment. Generally, models pre-trained on scientific text perform better than their base models, as we can see when we compare SciBERT to BERT and SciDeBERTa to DeBERTa.

DQF performs worse at classification. To assess the performance of the DQF in a document classification setting and compare it to the Transformer-based classifiers, we replicate the experiment for this approach. We first learn estimators for the distributions $\mathcal{P}$ and $\mathcal{Q}$ on the training set. Then, we infer the estimated α parameter for each document in the development set and measure precision and recall for different classification thresholds. The corresponding precision-recall curve for the paper mill detector on the development set can be found in Figure 6 in Appendix B.2. We take the α threshold producing the best F1 score on the development set to create the final classifier evaluated on the test set. Table 4 shows that the DQF approach performs considerably worse on the test set than the Transformer-based classifiers.

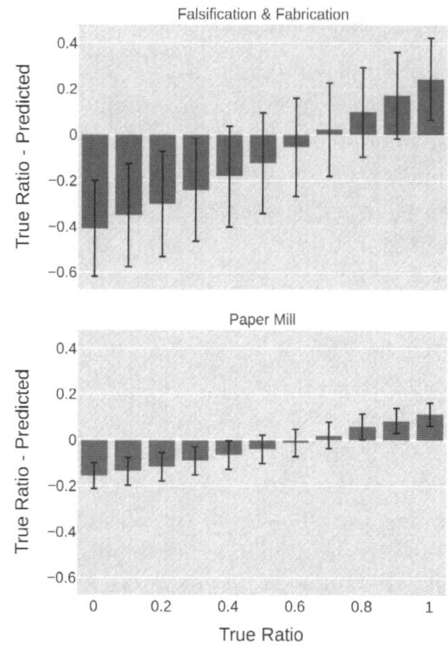

Figure 2: Differences between true ratio and DQF α on a test set of retracted and non-retracted sentences, constructed with ratios $\{0, 0.1, ..., 0.9, 1\}$. Retractions are due to *Falsification* (top) and *Paper Mill* (bottom). Error bars indicate the confidence interval.

5.3 Misconduct over Time

Next, we turn to estimating scientific misconduct over time by running our best-performing Transformer classifier and the DQF on a much larger inference dataset. We sample 12,000 papers per year from 1980 to 2024 from the OpenAlex API. The sample is divided equally among the four domains defined by OpenAlex: *Health Sciences*, *Life Sciences*, *Physical Sciences*, and *Social Sciences*. Any reportedly retracted articles are excluded from the sampling process. In total, we find 526,876 articles, 390,474 of which have an abstract available. We apply the best DQF model from Section 5.1 for each misconduct reason and each of the four domains to the inference dataset's paper abstracts.

The results for the paper mill model can be found in Figure 3, and for falsification and randomly generated content in Figures 7 and 8 in Appendix B.3.

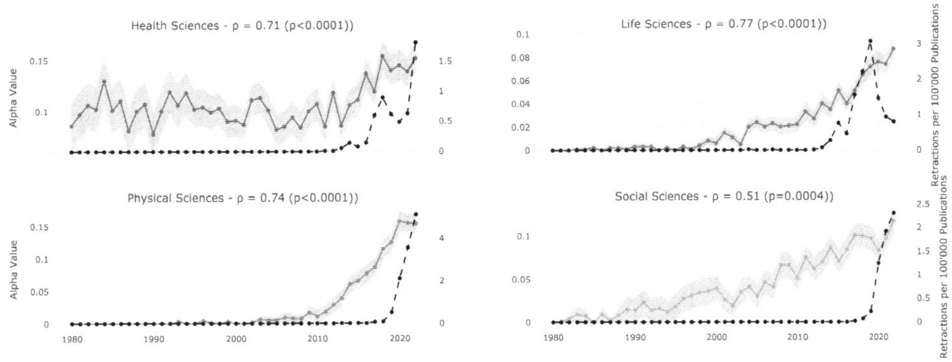

Figure 3: DQF α value signifying the fraction of articles attributed to the *paper mill* category with confidence interval in the shaded area (left y-axis) compared to confirmed paper mill retractions as a fraction of total published articles (right y-axis) per domain. ρ denotes Pearson correlation between the two curves with associated p-value.

To get an impression of the reliability of these results, we overlay the number of confirmed retractions per 100,000 publications listed by the Retraction Watch dataset on the right y-axis. While the α estimate is several orders of magnitude larger than the confirmed retraction ratio, we can observe that the correlation is significant, especially for the domains of Life and Physical Sciences.

Further, we run inference with a Transformer-based classifier on the same dataset. The results in Figure 4 are produced by SciDeBERTa, the best-performing classifier on paper mill and randomly generated content detection. The Figure shows the averaged results across all domains, for the reasons of paper mill and falsification.

Correlation between confirmed and predicted ratios is high. We see a high correlation to the reported retraction for the best-performing paper mill classifier (Figure 4a) and a slightly negative correlation for the falsification classifier (Figure 4b). As mentioned above, we expect that the retractions that fall into the falsification category do not have a strong signal since the falsification might often be limited to study data as opposed to textual content – especially in the health sciences domain where this type of misconduct is most prevalent. The results for the randomly generated content category are omitted from Figure 4, but reported in Table 6 in Appendix B.4. Similar to paper mill, the classification of randomly generated content is significantly correlated with the reported results at $\rho = 0.75$.

SciDeBERTa classifier estimates are higher than those of other methods. Compared to the DQF results, the SciDeBERTa classifier produces a higher rate of misconduct papers at up to 20% predicted positive rate. This is double the rate predicted by ModernBERT and the DQF. We list the inferred rates of the paper mill papers from the Transformer-based classifier grouped by domains in Figure 9 in Appendix B.4. The estimate seems more stable in the health sciences compared to the DQF results in Figure 3.

6 Discussion

In this section, we revisit the most important results and discuss implications of the findings.

The DQF estimates seem as accurate as the classifier-based ones except in health sciences. We observe that the DQF approach seems to function well in the domains of life sciences and physical sciences and a little less in social sciences. For health sciences, it returns seemingly overestimated and highly varying results. This might be explained by the widespread use of formulaic language in the health sciences domain.

The α is not a precise estimate for the true ratio of misconduct. Our methods estimate that 10–15% of papers are involved in misconduct. The evaluation in Figure 2 shows that the method tends to overestimate the α for a low ground-truth ratio. This indicates that the actual ratio is likely smaller. This method may not be precise enough to reliably detect small effects. Rather than providing an exact fraction of misconduct cases, the α value should be interpreted as the proportion of papers that exhibit writing style similarities with paper-milled papers

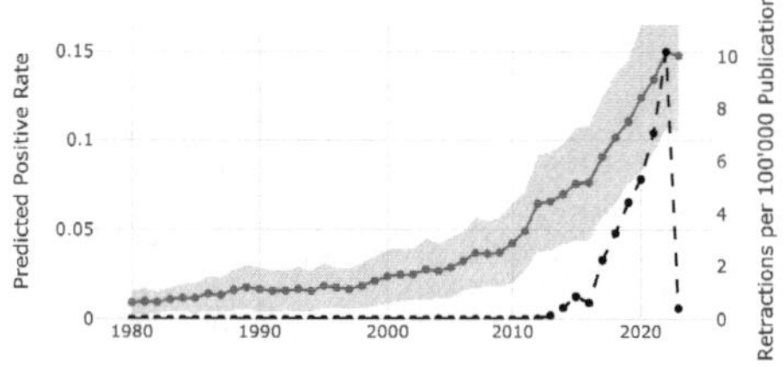

(a) $\rho = 0.79$ $(p < 0.0001)$

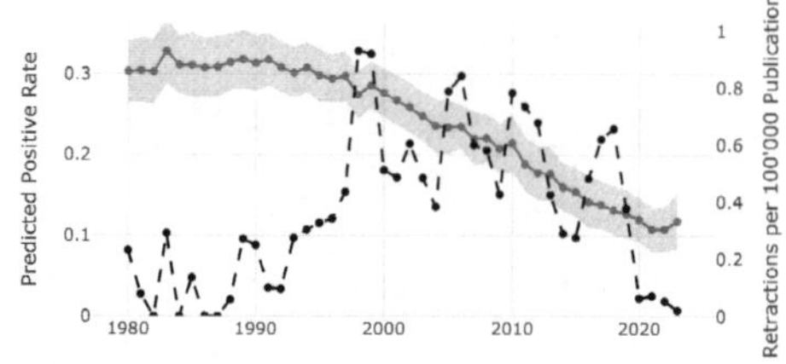

(b) $\rho = -0.17$ $(p = 0.266)$

Figure 4: SciDeBERTa-based positive prediction rate for detection of *paper mill* (a) and *falsification/fabrication* (b) on the left y-axis compared to confirmed retractions per 100,000 publications on the right y-axis. Pearson correlation ρ between the two curves is given with the associated p-value.

or have a slightly higher-than-average probability of resulting from misconduct. In many cases, the estimated ratio correlates strongly with the reported number of misconduct-related retractions, as the inference study shows.

Trend analysis is a promising application of these models. The practical use case of this becomes clear if we examine the median delay between the date of publication and the date of retraction in our data, which is 475 days, with the 80th percentile at 3.6 years. The DQF method delivers a computationally efficient way to estimate how the incidence of certain types of misconduct changes in real time in a large collection of scientific articles. This could be used, for example, to measure the effectiveness of anti-fraud policies at large publishers.

7 Related Work

Many studies examine the phenomenon of retractions and misconduct (Wray and Andersen, 2018; Candal-Pedreira et al., 2022; Feng et al., 2020; Nath et al., 2006; Parker et al., 2024) but they primarily focus on metadata such as citation information rather than textual content. (Sharma et al., 2024) use the Retraction Watch dataset to analyze author collaboration networks. (Hu and Xu, 2020) and (Vuong, 2019) study linguistic characteristics of retraction notices but not the article content. We do not find any datasets that combine information about retractions with the content of the associated articles. Especially looking at the full text and not only abstracts.

Detection of scientific misconduct. The extensive use of LLM chatbots has led to numerous works focusing on identifying AI-generated content in scientific articles and peer reviews. (Liang et al., 2024b,a) and (Yu et al., 2024) investigate detecting modified sentences by OpenAI's GPT-3 and GPT-4o models. Earlier work from (Gehrmann et al., 2019) trains a model to distinguish human-written sentences from GPT-2 generated ones. (Cabanac and Labbé, 2021) present a detection method that identifies "tortured phrases" which they attribute to using scientific text generators such as SciGen. However, their work is limited to articles from a single journal.

Aside from detecting AI-generated text, some authors explore more general methods to automatically detect fraud and misconduct in science. (Usman and Balke, 2024, 2023) use citation information from retraction cascades to identify potentially retractable articles. (Horton et al., 2020) use Benford's law to identify falsified data specifically. Similar to our work, (Razis et al., 2023) use a Transformer-based model for paper mill content detection. Our work presents a new dataset for this task, which stems from a wider range of science domains and is slightly larger. Further, we extend their analysis by more pre-trained models and an analysis of large-scale inference on a longitudinal dataset.

8 Conclusion

In this work, we find distinct linguistic patterns in articles retracted for misconduct, such as overuse of certain expressions and frequent repetition of adjectives, nouns, and adverbs. Based on these findings, we train a distributional quantification framework and a Transformer-based classifier to track growth trends of scientific misconduct. Our classifier achieves an F1 score of 0.93 in detecting paper mill articles and automatically generated content, making it a viable option for flagging fraudulent papers for human review. Further, we show that a computationally simpler approach based on a mixture distribution model can estimate trends of misconduct in life and physical sciences. However, in health sciences, the Transformer-based classifier performs better. For future work, we will investigate how metadata such as citation networks and affiliation can be incorporated into detecting misconduct and lead to increased performance in cases where the text-based approach does not yield sufficient results.

Limitations

This study has several limitations. First, the underlying Retraction Watch dataset is compiled by volunteer journalists, making its coverage inconsistent. For instance, retractions were reported more frequently during the platforms early years, disproportionately affecting recently published papers, and little is known about the annotation process of reason labels. Additionally, many older retracted papers may no longer be accessible online, as their records have likely been lost.

Furthermore, as was shown in the study, α values do not necessarily reflect the true proportion of paper-milled articles. The estimates can not be taken at face value but serve as a tool to investigate trend evolution.

Finally, availability of text (abstracts and full-text) has limited the size of our text corpus. For the misconduct reason of *falsification*, the dataset is particularly small potentially impacting the accuracy of the resulting classifier. Also, while it might have a positive impact on performance we intentionally exclude non-content-related metadata about publications from the training process to isolate the influence of language. Future work will extend on this.

Ethics Statement

Our work recognizes the ethical implications of predicting misconduct based on individual articles, as false positives could lead to serious reputational harm and may be perceived as slander by the affected authors and/or institutions. Therefore, we emphasize that our method should not be used for definitive individual accusations but rather for statements about collections of articles and trend estimation.

Furthermore, we are aware that releasing an instance-based classification method carries the risk of reverse engineering, allowing malicious actors to manipulate accordingly their writing, in order to evade detection while still perpetrating scientific misconduct. However, we believe that the benefits of transparency outweigh this risk, as security through obscurity is rarely an effective strategy in the long term.

Finally, we acknowledge that our classifier may introduce bias against non-native English speakers, as variations in vocabulary and lexical diversity could influence predictions. Furthermore, low-price text rewriting and translation services may unintentionally produce text that resembles the linguistic patterns associated with misconduct, potentially leading to unfair penalties for individuals. Addressing these biases is a critical area for future work.

Acknowledgements

Special thanks are extended to our colleagues Luca Mazzola and Alexander Denzler at HSLU for their feedback. Furthermore, we thank Oliver Karras and Sören Auer from the Leibniz Information Centre for Science and Technology University Library (TIB) in Hannover for their feedback and support.

References

Anna Abalkina. 2023. Publication and collaboration anomalies in academic papers originating from a paper mill: Evidence from a russia-based paper mill. *Learned Publishing*, 36(4):689702.

R. Harald Baayen. 2001. *Word Frequency Distributions*. Springer Netherlands.

Iz Beltagy, Kyle Lo, and Arman Cohan. 2019. SciBERT: A pretrained language model for scientific text. In *Proceedings of the 2019 Conference on Empirical Methods in Natural Language Processing and the 9th International Joint Conference on Natural Language Processing (EMNLP-IJCNLP)*, pages 3615–3620, Hong Kong, China. Association for Computational Linguistics.

Jeffrey Brainard and Jia You. 2018. What a massive database of retracted papers reveals about science publishing's death penalty'. *Science*. Accessed: 2024-12-23.

Jennifer A Byrne, Yasunori Park, Reese A K Richardson, Pranujan Pathmendra, Mengyi Sun, and Thomas Stoeger. 2022. Protection of the human gene research literature from contract cheating organizations known as research paper mills. *Nucleic Acids Research*, 50(21):1205812070.

Guillaume Cabanac and Cyril Labbé. 2021. Prevalence of nonsensical algorithmically generated papers in the scientific literature. *Journal of the Association for Information Science and Technology*, 72(12):14611476.

Guillaume Cabanac, Cyril Labbé, and Alexander Magazinov. 2021. Tortured phrases: A dubious writing style emerging in science. evidence of critical issues affecting established journals.

Cristina Candal-Pedreira, Joseph S Ross, Alberto Ruano-Ravina, David S Egilman, Esteve Fernández, and Mónica Pérez-Ríos. 2022. Retracted papers originating from paper mills: cross sectional study. *BMJ*, page e071517.

Jana Christopher. 2021. The raw truth about paper mills. *FEBS Letters*, 595(13):17511757.

COPE. 2025. Systematic manipulation of the publishing process: Paper mills. Accessed: 2025-01-14.

Jacob Devlin, Ming-Wei Chang, Kenton Lee, and Kristina Toutanova. 2019. BERT: Pre-training of deep bidirectional transformers for language understanding. In *Proceedings of the 2019 Conference of the North American Chapter of the Association for Computational Linguistics: Human Language Technologies, Volume 1 (Long and Short Papers)*, pages 4171–4186, Minneapolis, Minnesota. Association for Computational Linguistics.

Daniele Fanelli, Julie Wong, and David Moher. 2021. What difference might retractions make? an estimate of the potential epistemic cost of retractions on meta-analyses. *Accountability in Research*, 29(7):442459.

Lingzi Feng, Junpeng Yuan, and Liying Yang. 2020. An observation framework for retracted publications in multiple dimensions. *Scientometrics*, 125(2):14451457.

Sebastian Gehrmann, Hendrik Strobelt, and Alexander Rush. 2019. GLTR: Statistical detection and visualization of generated text. In *Proceedings of the 57th Annual Meeting of the Association for Computational Linguistics: System Demonstrations*. Association for Computational Linguistics.

Pengcheng He, Jianfeng Gao, and Weizhu Chen. 2021. DeBERTaV3: Improving DeBERTa using electra-style pre-training with gradient-disentangled embedding sharing. *CoRR*, abs/2111.09543.

Joanne Horton, Dhanya Krishna Kumar, and Anthony Wood. 2020. Detecting academic fraud using benford law: The case of professor james hunton. *Research Policy*, 49(8):104084.

Guangwei Hu and Shaoxiong (Brian) Xu. 2020. Agency and responsibility: A linguistic analysis of culpable acts in retraction notices. *Lingua*, 247:102954.

Eunhui Kim, Yuna Jeong, and Myung-Seok Choi. 2023. MediBioDeBERTa: Biomedical language model with continuous learning and intermediate fine-tuning. *IEEE Access*, 11:141036–141044.

Weixin Liang, Zachary Izzo, Yaohui Zhang, Haley Lepp, Hancheng Cao, Xuandong Zhao, Lingjiao Chen, Haotian Ye, Sheng Liu, Zhi Huang, Daniel A. McFarland, and James Y. Zou. 2024a. Monitoring AI-modified content at scale: A case study on the impact of ChatGPT on AI conference peer reviews.

Weixin Liang, Yaohui Zhang, Zhengxuan Wu, Haley Lepp, Wenlong Ji, Xuandong Zhao, Hancheng Cao, Sheng Liu, Siyu He, Zhi Huang, Diyi Yang, Christopher Potts, Christopher D Manning, and James Y. Zou. 2024b. Mapping the increasing use of LLMs in scientific papers. In *First Conference on Language Modeling*.

Yinhan Liu, Myle Ott, Naman Goyal, Jingfei Du, Mandar Joshi, Danqi Chen, Omer Levy, Mike Lewis, Luke Zettlemoyer, and Veselin Stoyanov. 2019. RoBERTa: A robustly optimized BERT pretraining approach. *CoRR*, abs/1907.11692.

H. B. Mann and D. R. Whitney. 1947. On a test of whether one of two random variables is stochastically larger than the other. *The Annals of Mathematical Statistics*, 18(1):5060.

Adam Marcus and Ivan Oransky. 2014. What studies of retractions tell us. *Journal of Microbiology & Biology Education*, 15(2):151154.

Frank J. Massey. 1951. The kolmogorov-smirnov test for goodness of fit. *Journal of the American Statistical Association*, 46(253):6878.

Sara B Nath, Steven C Marcus, and Benjamin G Druss. 2006. Retractions in the research literature: misconduct or mistakes? *Medical Journal of Australia*, 185(3):152154.

Ivan Oransky, Stephen E Fremes, Paul Kurlansky, and Mario Gaudino. 2021. Retractions in medicine: the tip of the iceberg. *European Heart Journal*, 42(41):42054206.

Lisa Parker, Stephanie Boughton, Lisa Bero, and Jennifer A. Byrne. 2024. Paper mill challenges: past, present, and future. *Journal of Clinical Epidemiology*, 176:111549.

Jason Priem, Heather Piwowar, and Richard Orr. 2022. OpenAlex: A fully-open index of scholarly works, authors, venues, institutions, and concepts.

Gerasimos Razis, Konstantinos Anagnostopoulos, Omiros Metaxas, Stefanos-Dimitrios Stefanidis, Hong Zhou, and Ioannis Anagnostopoulos. 2023. Papermill detection in scientific content. In *2023 18th International Workshop on Semantic and Social Media Adaptation &; Personalization (SMAP)18th International Workshop on Semantic and Social Media Adaptation &; Personalization (SMAP 2023)*, page 16. IEEE.

Kiran Sharma, Aanchal Sharma, Jazlyn Jose, Vansh Saini, Raghavraj Sobti, and Ziya Uddin. 2024. Exploring structural dynamics in retracted and non-retracted author's collaboration networks: A quantitative analysis.

Arnab Sinha, Zhihong Shen, Yang Song, Hao Ma, Darrin Eide, Bo-June (Paul) Hsu, and Kuansan Wang. 2015. An overview of microsoft academic service (MAS) and applications. In *Proceedings of the 24th International Conference on World Wide Web*, WWW 15, page 243246. ACM.

The Center for Scientific Integrity. 2018. The retraction watch database. ISSN: 2692-4579. [Cited: 2024-08-22].

Muhammad Usman and Wolf-Tilo Balke. 2023. *On Retraction Cascade? Citation Intention Analysis as a Quality Control Mechanism in Digital Libraries*, page 117131. Springer Nature Switzerland.

Muhammad Usman and Wolf-Tilo Balke. 2024. *Tracing the Retraction Cascade: Identifying Non-retracted but Potentially Retractable Articles*, page 109126. Springer Nature Switzerland.

QuanHoang Vuong. 2019. The limitations of retraction notices and the heroic acts of authors who correct the scholarly record: An analysis of retractions of papers published from 1975 to 2019. *Learned Publishing*, 33(2):119130.

Guangyu Wang, Xiaohong Liu, Zhen Ying, Guoxing Yang, Zhiwei Chen, Zhiwen Liu, Min Zhang, Hongmei Yan, Yuxing Lu, Yuanxu Gao, et al. 2023. Optimized glycemic control of type 2 diabetes with reinforcement learning: a proof-of-concept trial. *Nature Medicine*, 29(10):2633–2642.

Benjamin Warner, Antoine Chaffin, Benjamin Clavié, Orion Weller, Oskar Hallström, Said Taghadouini, Alexis Gallagher, Raja Biswas, Faisal Ladhak, Tom Aarsen, Nathan Cooper, Griffin Adams, Jeremy Howard, and Iacopo Poli. 2024. Smarter, better, faster, longer: A modern bidirectional encoder for fast, memory efficient, and long context finetuning and inference. *CoRR*, abs/2412.13663.

K. Brad Wray and Line Edslev Andersen. 2018. Retractions in science. *Scientometrics*, 117(3):20092019.

Sungduk Yu, Man Luo, Avinash Madasu, Vasudev Lal, and Phillip Howard. 2024. Is your paper being reviewed by an LLM? investigating AI text detectability in peer review. In *Neurips Safe Generative AI Workshop 2024*.

A Dataset Creation

This section contains the table with mappings from section category to section title variants that were used to extract full-text of article sections (Table 5).

B Additional Details of the Experiments

In this section, we find all the details needed for reproducing the experiments (Subsection B.1), validation set performance from the DQF evaluation (Subsection B.2), and additional results from the inference study from the DQF (Section B.3 and Transformer-based classifier (Section B.4).

B.1 Used Language Models

All experiments are conducted on a single Nvidia RTX A6000 GPU equipped with 48GB of memory. The models utilized are sourced from the Hugging Face model hub:

- `bert-base-uncased`
- `roberta-base`
- `microsoft/deberta-v3-base`
- `answerdotai/ModernBERT-base`
- `allenai/scibert_scivocab_uncased`
- `KISTI-AI/Scideberta-full`
- `medicalai/ClinicalBERT`

B.2 Additional DQF Evaluation Results

This section contains the DQF evaluation results for peer review fraud and randomly generated content (Figure 5) and the precision-recall curve from finding the DQF detector threshold on the development set (Figure 6).

B.3 Additional DQF Inference Results

In this section, results of the DQF approach on the inference dataset can be found. Figure 7 shows inference of the randomly generated content, and Figure 8 shows that of the falsification estimation model on the large inference corpus.

B.4 Additional Transformer-based Classifier Inference Results

This section contains the remaining inference results of the Transformer-based classifier. Table 6 subsumes the mean positive prediction rate and Pearson correlation for all models and reasons on the inference data. More detailed results per domain and over the years can be found in Figure 9 for paper mill detection by the SciDeBERTa model and for falsification detection by the SciBERT model (best performing on this task) in Figure 10.

Section	Section Title Variants
Introduction	[Objectives, Objective, Background, Introduction]
Related Work	[Related Work, Related Works, State of the Art, Literature Review]
Methods	[Methods, Method, Patients and Methods, Methods and Materials, Methodology]
Result & Discussion	[Discussion, Discussions, Statistical Analysis, Results and Analysis, Results and Discussion, Result and Discussion, Result Analysis, Result, Results, Analysis of Results, Experimental Results, Analysis of Experimental Results, Result Analysis and Discussion, Results and Discussions, Experimental Results and Analysis]
Conclusion	[Conclusion, Conclusions, Authors Conclusions]

Table 5: Mapping of Section Title Variants to Standardized Sections.

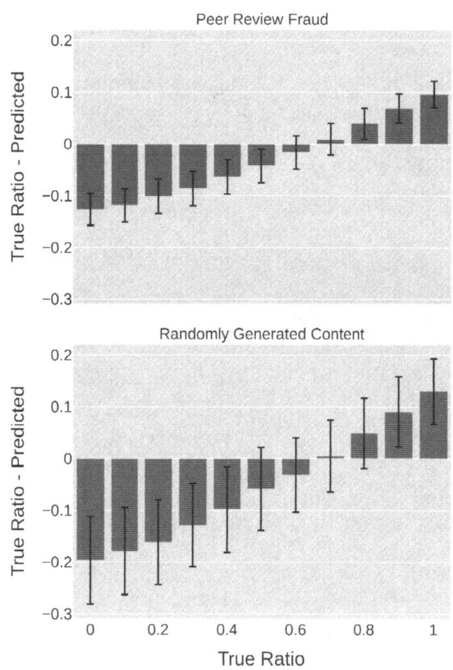

Figure 5: Differences between true ratio and DQF α on a testset partitioned into retracted and non-retracted sentences according to ratios $\{0, 0.1, ..., 0.9, 1\}$. Retractions for reasons of peer review fraud (top) and randomly generated content (bottom).

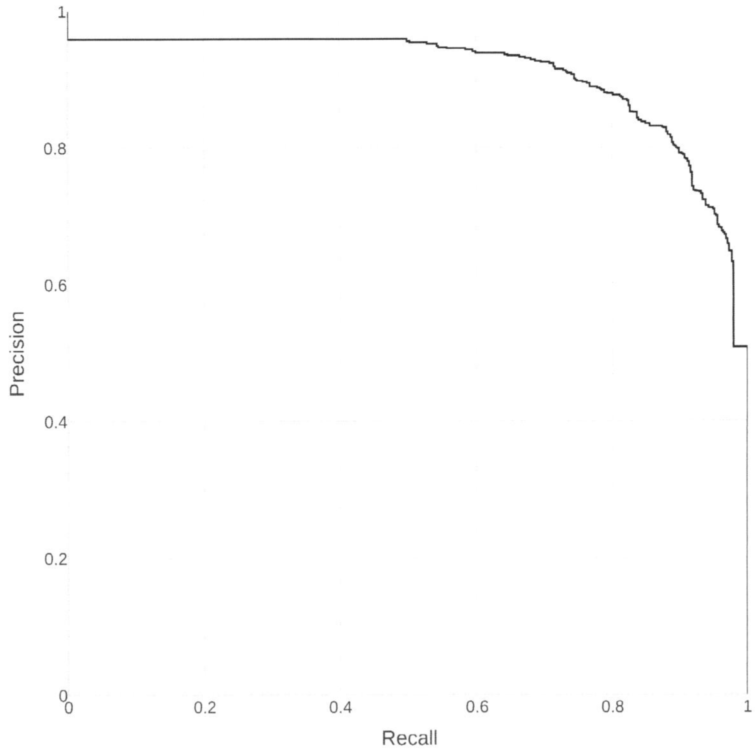

Figure 6: Evaluation of the DQF α used as a detector on the same training and development set as the Transformer-based classifier. The curve shows precision and recall for different thresholds of α values to determine whether a paper should be labeled Paper Mill or not.

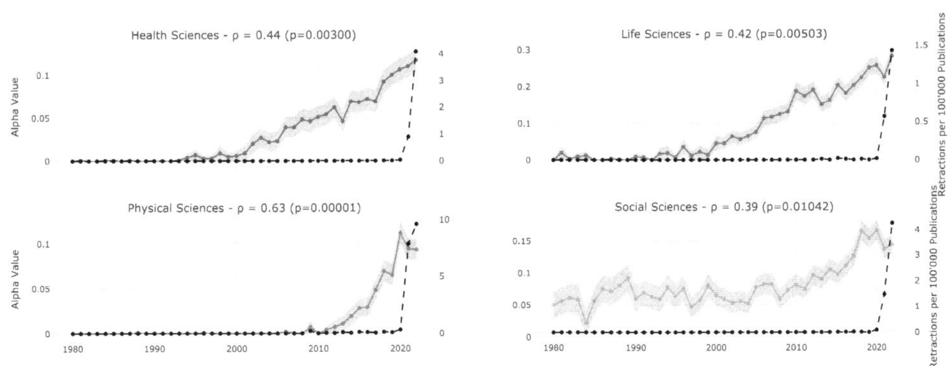

Figure 7: DQF α value signifying the fraction of articles identified as randomly generated content with confidence interval in the shaded area (left y-axis) compared to confirmed randomly generated content retractions (right y-axis) per science domain. ρ denotes Pearson correlation between the two curves with associated p-value.

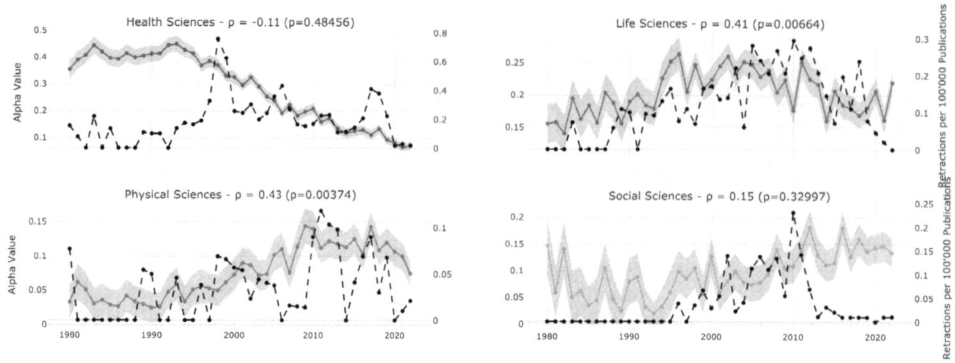

Figure 8: DQF α value signifying the fraction of articles identified as falsification with confidence interval in the shaded area (left y-axis) compared to confirmed falsification retractions (right y-axis) per science domain. ρ denotes Pearson correlation between the two curves with associated p-value.

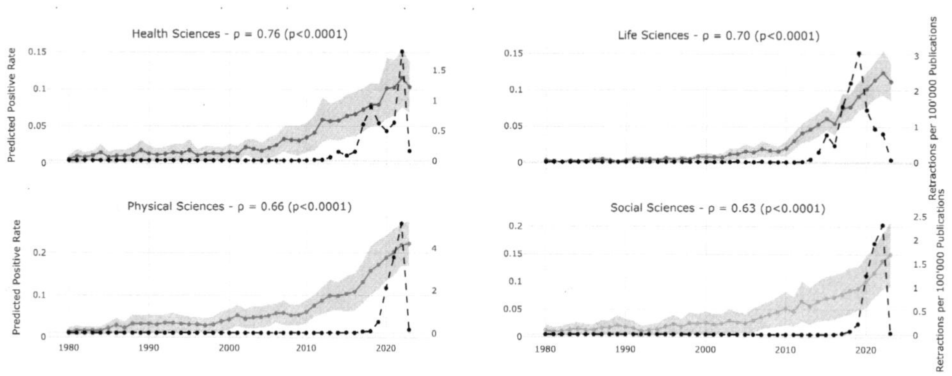

Figure 9: Predicted positive rate of the SciDeBERTa-based classifier on the paper mill detection task (left y-axis) compared to confirmed paper mill retractions (right y-axis) per domain. Pearson correlation ρ between the two curves is displayed with associated p-value.

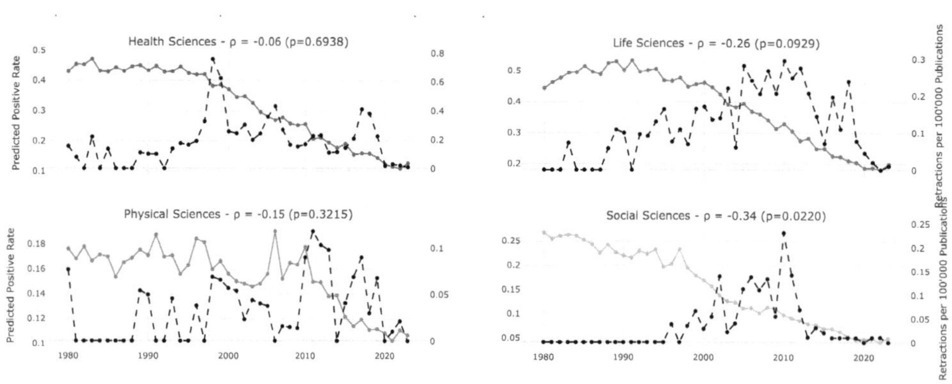

Figure 10: Predicted positive rate of the SciBERT-based classifier on the falsification detection task (left y-axis) compared to confirmed paper mill retractions (right y-axis) per domain. Pearson correlation ρ between the two curves is displayed with associated p-value.

Model	Reason	Mean PPR	Correlation
SciDeBERTa	Paper Mill	0.05	$\rho = 0.78$ (p=0.00000)
SciDeBERTa	Falsification	0.25	$\rho = -0.31$ (p=0.04236)
SciDeBERTa	Generated Content	0.03	$\rho = 0.63$ (p=0.00000)
BERT	Paper Mill	0.07	$\rho = 0.75$ (p=0.00000)
BERT	Falsification	0.26	$\rho = -0.23$ (p=0.12545)
BERT	Generated Content	0.05	$\rho = 0.56$ (p=0.00007)
SciBERT	Paper Mill	0.05	$\rho = 0.78$ (p=0.00000)
SciBERT	Falsification	0.25	$\rho = -0.23$ (p=0.12722)
SciBERT	Generated Content	0.03	$\rho = 0.61$ (p=0.00001)
ClinicalBERT	Paper Mill	0.07	$\rho = 0.76$ (p=0.00000)
ClinicalBERT	Falsification	0.17	$\rho = -0.28$ (p=0.06148)
ClinicalBERT	Generated Content	0.08	$\rho = 0.55$ (p=0.00010)
ModernBert	Paper Mill	0.03	$\rho = 0.79$ (p=0.00000)
ModernBert	Falsification	0.31	$\rho = -0.17$ (p=0.26445)
ModernBert	Generated Content	0.03	$\rho = 0.64$ (p=0.00000)
DeBERTa-v3	Paper Mill	0.05	$\rho = 0.80$ (p=0.00000)
DeBERTa-v3	Falsification	0.39	$\rho = -0.24$ (p=0.11783)
DeBERTa-v3	Generated Content	0.04	$\rho = 0.62$ (p=0.00001)
RoBERTa	Paper Mill	0.03	$\rho = 0.79$ (p=0.00000)
RoBERTa	Falsification	0.26	$\rho = -0.25$ (p=0.10302)
RoBERTa	Generated Content	0.06	$\rho = 0.57$ (p=0.00006)

Table 6: Mean positive prediction rates (PPR) and correlation coefficients for different models and reasons.

Collage: Decomposable Rapid Prototyping for Co-Designed Information Extraction on Scientific PDFs

Sireesh Gururaja[1*] **Yueheng Zhang**[2*]
Guannan Tang[2] **Tianhao Zhang**[2] **Kevin Murphy**[2] **Yu-Tsen Yi**[2] **Junwon Seo**[2]
Anthony Rollett[2] **Emma Strubell**[1,2]
[1]Language Technologies Institute, School of Computer Science
[2]Department of Materials Science and Engineering
Carnegie Mellon University
sgururaj@cs.cmu.edu, yuehengz@andrew.cmu.edu

Abstract

Recent years in NLP have seen the continued development of domain-specific information extraction tools for scientific documents, alongside the release of increasingly multimodal pretrained language models. While applying and evaluating these new, general-purpose language model systems in specialized domains has never been easier, it remains difficult to compare them with models developed specifically for those domains, which tend to accept a narrower range of input formats, and are difficult to evaluate in the context of the original documents. Meanwhile, the general-purpose systems are often black-box and give little insight into preprocessing (like conversion to plain text or markdown) that can have significant downstream impact on their results.

In this work, we present Collage, a tool intended to facilitate the co-design of information extraction systems on scientific PDFs between NLP developers and scientists by facilitating the rapid prototyping, visualization, and comparison of different information extraction models on the content of scientific PDFs. For scientists, Collage provides side-by-side visualization and comparison of multiple models of different input modalities in the context of the PDF content they are applied to; for developers, Collage allows the rapid deployment of new models by abstracting away PDF preprocessing and visualization into easily extensible software interfaces. We also enable both developers and scientists to inspect, debug, and better understand modeling pipelines by providing granular views of intermediate states of processing. We demonstrate our system in the context of information extraction to assist with literature review in materials science.

1 Introduction

In recent years, systems based on large language models (LLMs) have broadened the public visibility of developments in NLP. With the advent of tools that have publicly accessible, user-friendly interfaces, experts in specialized domains outside NLP are empowered to use and evaluate these models inside their domains, for example to automatically mine insights from scientific literature. Further, an increasing number of these tools are multimodal, handling not only text, but frequently images, or even PDFs directly. However, despite the accessibility of these tools, the processing pipelines they employ remain as end-to-end black boxes and provide little interpretability or debuggability in case of failure. Further, these systems usually rely only on large, deployed models, potentially leaving other user priorities, such as interpretability, efficiency, or domain specialization, unaddressed.

Domain specific research in domains like clinical (Naumann et al., 2023), legal (Preoțiuc-Pietro et al., 2023), and scientific (Knoth et al., 2020; Co-

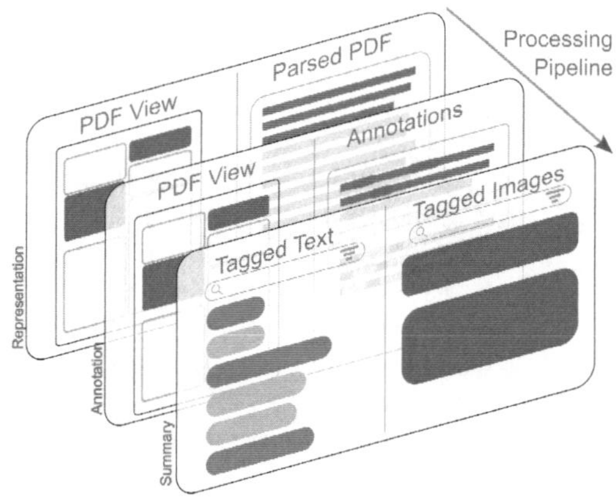

Figure 1: Collage allows users to inspect multiple models in different modalities by presenting a stage-by-stage, decomposed view of the PDF modeling pipeline. Here, we see a PDF composed of text and tables, with entities from different models shown in red and yellow. The summary view shows extracted content, while annotations and inspection views allow the user to step back in the modeling pipeline

[*] Equal contribution.

Proceedings of the Fifth Workshop on Scholarly Document Processing (SDP 2025), pages 72–82

han et al., 2022) NLP have long histories. Models in these areas remain less accessible; in order to run and evaluate these models on your own data, custom code is often needed. Further, because many of these models are text-only, evaluating their results in the context of their eventual use — for example, directly on a PDF — poses a challenge.

This paper presents Collage, a tool that facilitates the rapid prototyping, visualization, and comparison, of multiple models across modalities on the contents of scientific PDF documents. Collage was designed to address the interface between developers of NLP-based tools for scientific documents and the scientists who are the intended users of those tools. To address scientists' needs, we ground our design in a series of interviews with domain experts in multiple fields, with a particular focus on materials science. Further, in cases where model results may not meet scientists' or developers' expectations, we visualize the intermediate representation at each step, giving the user a granular view of the modeling pipeline, allowing shared debugging processes between developers and users. Collage is domain-agnostic, and can visualize any model that conforms to one of its three interfaces - for token classification models, text generation models, and image/text multimodal models. We provide implementations of these interfaces that allow the use of any HuggingFace token classifier, multiple LLMs, and several additional models without requiring users to write any code. All of the interfaces are easily implemented, and we provide instructions and reference implementations in our repository [1].

2 Motivation

Collage is based on collected themes from interviews with 15 professionals across materials science, law, and policy, in which the authors ask about their practices for working with large collections of documents. For a reasonable scope, we focus on the 9 materials scientists in our sample, whose responses concern their process of literature review. We focus on three themes that emerged consistently from these interviews to inform our design of Collage:

Varied focuses. One of the most prominent themes to emerge in our interviews is the variety of focuses that scientists, even in very closely related subfields, can have when reading a paper and evaluating it for relevance to their purpose. While many participants focused on paper metadata, such as the reputation of the publication venue or citation count, others focused on cues from within the content of the paper. For the design of Collage, we focus on accelerating co-design of models that address specific information extraction needs on paper content, by reducing the burden of deploying new models on PDF content, and providing a shared, user-friendly view of the results upon which scientists and developers can base subsequent efforts.

Information in tables. As pointed out above, many of our participants relied heavily on information provided in tables, rather than solely in the document text. As such, an important concern in the design of Collage would be to allow multimodality in the models that it interfaces with and visualizes.

Older documents. Our participants noted that they regularly work with documents across a wide time range. Several participants noted that the work that they relied on most frequently were technical reports from the 1950s to the 1970s. These reports are now digitized, but are otherwise highly variable in their accessibility to modern processing tools:

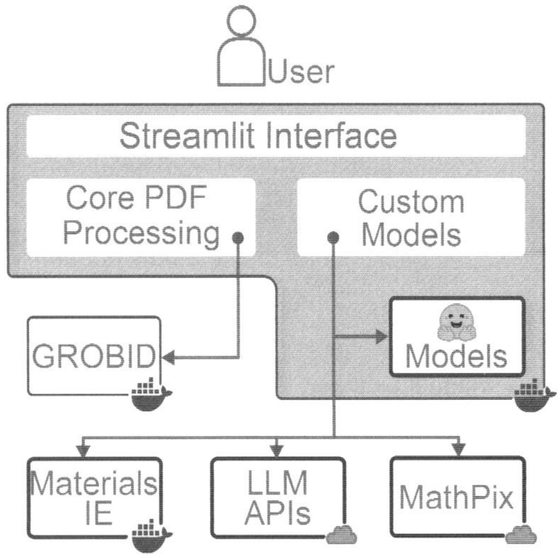

Figure 2: System architecture with currently implemented models. All custom models implement our interfaces, outline color indicates which: Token Classification, Text Generation, or Image Processing. [Docker icon] indicates components running in the same Docker container, and [cloud icon] indicates models running in the cloud. "Materials IE" refers to materials-specific models, like ChemDataExtractor.

[1] github.com/gsireesh/ht-max

The OCR used when digitizing them can be inaccurate, they often contain noise in the scanned images, and layouts are less standardized. This can lead to confusion on whether issues with performance are the fault of models themselves, or preprocesing choices that cause that degraded performance. We therefore aim to provide an interface that allows users to inspect intermediate stages of processing, to better understand where a model may have failed, and what subsequent development should target next: whether better performing models, or better preprocessing.

3 Design and Implementation

We conceptualize our system in three parts: PDF representation, which parses and makes the content of PDFs easily available to downstream usage; modeling, i.e. applying multiple models to that PDF representation, backed by common software interfaces, which facilitate the rapid extension of the set of available models; and a frontend graphical interface that allows users to visualize and compare the results of those models on uploaded PDFs. We discuss the design choices and implementation details of each stage in the following subsections, and show an architectural overview in Figure 2.

3.1 PDF Representation

To produce a PDF representation amenable to our later processing, we build a pipeline on top of the PaperMage library (Lo et al., 2023), which provides a convenient set of abstractions for handling multimodal PDF content. PaperMage allows the definition of `Recipes`, i.e. combinations of processing steps that can be reused. We base our pipeline off of its `CoreRecipe` pipeline, which identifies visual and textual elements of a paper, such as tables and paragraphs.

We then introduce several new components to the `CoreRecipe`, to make the paper representation more suitable to our use case. First, we introduce a parser based on Grobid (GRO, 2008–2023), which provides a semantic grouping of paragraphs into structural units, allowing us to segment processing and results by paper section. Second, to address issues with text segmentation in scientific documents, we replace PaperMage's default segmenter (based on PySBD) with a SciBERT (Beltagy et al., 2019)-based SciSpaCy (Neumann et al., 2019) pipeline.

At the end of this stage of processing, we have the PaperMage representation of a document, in the form of `Entity` objects, organized in `Layers`. `Entity` objects can be e.g. individual paragraphs by section or index, images of tables, and individual sentences.

```
class LiteLlmCompletionPredictor(TextGenerationPredictorABC):
  def __init__(
    self,
    model_name: str,
    api_key: str,
    prompt_generator_function: Callable[[str], List[LLMMessage
        ]],
    entity_to_process="reading_order_sections",
  ):
    super().__init__(entity_to_process)
    self.model_name = model_name
    self.api_key = api_key
    self.generate_prompt = prompt_generator_function

  def generate_from_entity_text(self, entity: Entity) -> str:
    messages = [asdict(m) for m in self.generate_prompt(entity.
        text)]
    llm_response = completion(
      model=self.model_name, api_key=self.api_key, messages=
          messages, max_tokens=2500
    )
    response_text = llm_response.choices[0].message.content
    return response_text
```

Figure 3: Partial implementation of the `TextGenerationPredictor` to allow LLM predictions given an `Entity` extracted from the PDF. `LLMMessage` is a data class wrapper around the system and user messages for LLMs in the OpenAI format. Not shown are the property declarations; full listing can be found in our code repository.

3.2 Modeling and Software Interfaces

To facilitate the easy implementation of new information extraction tools, we define common interfaces that simplify the process of adding additional processing to a document's content. These interfaces standardize three kinds of annotation on PDF content, allowing users convenient access to the PDF's content as images or strings (though they can access the PaperMage representation) and automatically handling visualization in several supported formats. This requires users to implement only a few simple functions in the modalities their models already use. All models currently in Collage are implementations of these interfaces. We describe the interfaces, the requirements for implementation, and current implementations below. All interfaces are defined in the `papermage_components/interfaces` package of our repository. In order to add a new custom processor, users must define a class that extends one of the interfaces specified below, and then register their predictor in the `local_model_config.py` module.

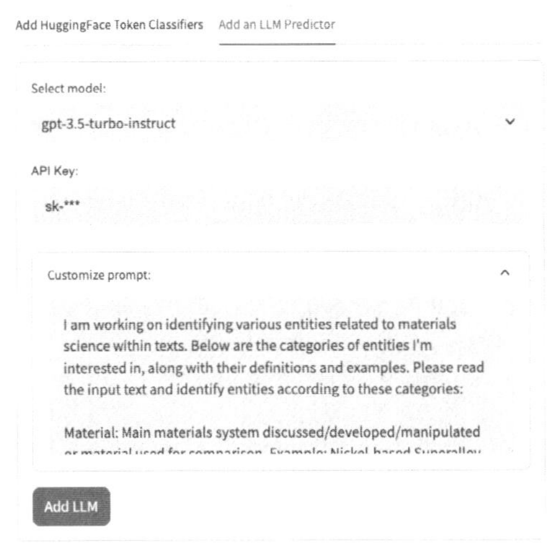

Figure 4: LLM Selector, as it appears in the File Upload view. Users specify an LLM to query, enter their API key, customize the prompt for an LLM, and repeat for any number of LLMs and prompts.

Token Classification Interface: This interface is intended for any model that produces annotations of spans in text, i.e. most "classical" NER or event extraction models. Users are required to extend the `TokenClassificationPredictorABC` class and override the `tag_entities_in_batch` method, which takes a list of strings to tag, and produces a list of lists of tagged entities per-sentence. Tagged entities are expected to have the start and end character offsets, and the interface's code automatically handles mapping indices from the sentence level to the document level, and visualizing annotated text using the displaCy visualizer [2].

To demonstrate this interface, we provide two implementations: one with a common materials information extraction system, ChemDataExtractor2 (Swain and Cole, 2016; Mavracic et al., 2021), which we wrap in a simple REST API and Dockerize to streamline environment and setup, as well as a predictor that can apply any HuggingFace model that conforms to the `TokenClassification` task on the HuggingFace Hub[3].

Text Generation Interface: Given the prominence of large language model-based approaches, this interface is designed to allow for text-to-text prediction. Users are required to extend the `TextGenerationPredictorABC` class, and to implement the `generate_from_entity_text()` method, which takes and returns a string. This basic setup allows users to e.g. prompt an LLM and display the raw response. A popular prompting method, however, is to request structured data e.g. in the form of JSON. To accommodate this, and to allow for aggregating LLM predictions into a table, users can also implement the `postprocess_text_to_dict()` method. The default implementation of this method attempts to deserialize the entirety of the LLM response into a dictionary, but users can implement custom logic.

Our implementation of this interface uses LiteLLM[4], a package that allows accessing multiple commercial LLM services behind the same API. We allow users to specify the endpoint/model, their own API key, and a prompt, and display predictions from that model. We show a partial implementation of this predictor in Figure 3, and a sample of its results in Figure 5.

Image Prediction Interface: Given the focus on tables and charts that many of our interview participants discussed, and the fact that table parsing is an active research area, we additionally provide an interface for models that parse images, the `ImagePredictorABC` in order to handle multimodal processing, including tables. This interface allows users two options of method to override: In cases where only image inputs are needed (e.g. if a table extractor performs its own OCR), the `process_image()` method; in cases where the method is inherently multimodal, implementors can instead override the `process_entity()` method, which allows them full access to PaperMage's multimodal `Entity` representation. This interface requires implementors to return at least one of three types of data: a raw string representation, which we view as useful for e.g. image captioning tasks; a tabular dictionary representation, for the case of table parsing; or a list of bounding boxes, in the case of models that segment images. Implementations of this interface are free to return more than one type of output; all of them will be visualized in the frontend.

We demonstrate implementations of both types. For raw image outputs, we implement a predictor that calls the MathPix API[5], a commercial service for PDF understanding. For the multimodal approach, we implement a predictor that builds on

[2]`https://demos.explosion.ai/displacy-ent`
[3]Model list available here.

[4]`https://docs.litellm.ai/`
[5]`https://mathpix.com/`

the Microsoft Table Transformer model (Smock et al., 2023). This model predicts bounding boxes around table cells, which we then cross-reference with extracted PDF text in the PaperMage representation to provide parsed table output. An example of parsed table output from this predictor can be seen in figure 5.

3.3 Visualization Frontend

We present the results of the PDF processing in an interactive tool built using Streamlit[6] that allows the user – whether scientist or developer – to upload a PDF, define a processing pipeline, and inspect the results of that processing pipeline at each stage. More concretely, after the paper is uploaded and processed, we present the results of the pipeline in three views, in decreasing order of abstraction from the paper. The intention of this is to first show the user the potential output of their chosen pipeline for a given paper, then allow them to inspect each step of the pipeline that led to that final output. Each view is described in more detail below, and has a screenshot in Appendix A.

File Upload and Processing. The first view we present to a user allows them to upload a file, and to define the processing pipeline applied to that file. Basic PDF processing is always performed, and users can then toggle which custom models will be run. Users can additionally specify any number of HuggingFace token classification models or LLMs with the provided widget, which allows users to search the HuggingFace Hub, select LLMs, and customize the prompts for them. We show a view of the LLM model selector in Figure 4.

File Overview. This view presents the high-level extracted information from the paper, as candidates for what could be shown to the user as part of their search process. In particular, we show a two-column view, with tables of tagged entities from both token-level predictors and LLMs on the left, and the processed content of images on the right. Users can filter based on sections, to e.g. find materials mentioned in the methods section of a paper. If the user finds the content extracted with the pipeline useful, the model and processing pipeline could be further developed into a more integrated prototype. If not, the user can proceed to the succeeding views, to see where models may have failed.

[6]`https://streamlit.io`

Annotations. This view allows the user to compare the results of models in the context of the PDF. We present another two-column view, in which the PDF is visualized on the left, and allows the user to select a paragraph or table at a time, and visualize the results of each model on it. In the case of text annotation, we visualize the entities identified by token prediction models as well as predictions from LLMs. In the case of images, all of the available output types from the image processing interface are visualized. We show a composite screenshot of this interface in Figure 5.

Representation Inspection. This view presents visualization of the PDF representation available to any downstream processing that the user might select. In the sidebar, users can choose to visualize any PaperMage `Layer`, i.e. set of `Entity` objects, tagged by the basic processing steps. Then, in a view similar to the raw annotations view, they can see all of those entities highlighted on the PDF in the left-side column. Once the user selects an object, they see the raw content extracted from that object in the right-side column, in the form of its image representation and the text extracted from it, along with the option to view how the text is segmented into sentences. This view allows users to inspect how the PDF processing choices may have affected the text they send to models, which often have significant effects on their downstream performance (Camacho-Collados and Pilehvar, 2018).

4 Addressing Needs from Interviews

Our system is specifically designed to respond to the concerns raised in our interviews. First, to accommodate the varied processes of materials scientists, we design interfaces that allow for easy implementation of new models into our framework; our existing implementations of those interfaces also allow for the application of multiple LLMs and HuggingFace models directly in the context of the PDFs under review. This allows users to search for and evaluate models that suit their existing workflows. For tables, we both provide an interface and implementations that allow the comparison of proprietary and open-source table parsing systems. Extending this work to new table models and evaluating them is simplified by our software and visualization interfaces. Our inspection view is designed to address concerns about older PDFs: in being able to inspect the results of processing, users and engineers of this system can identify fail-

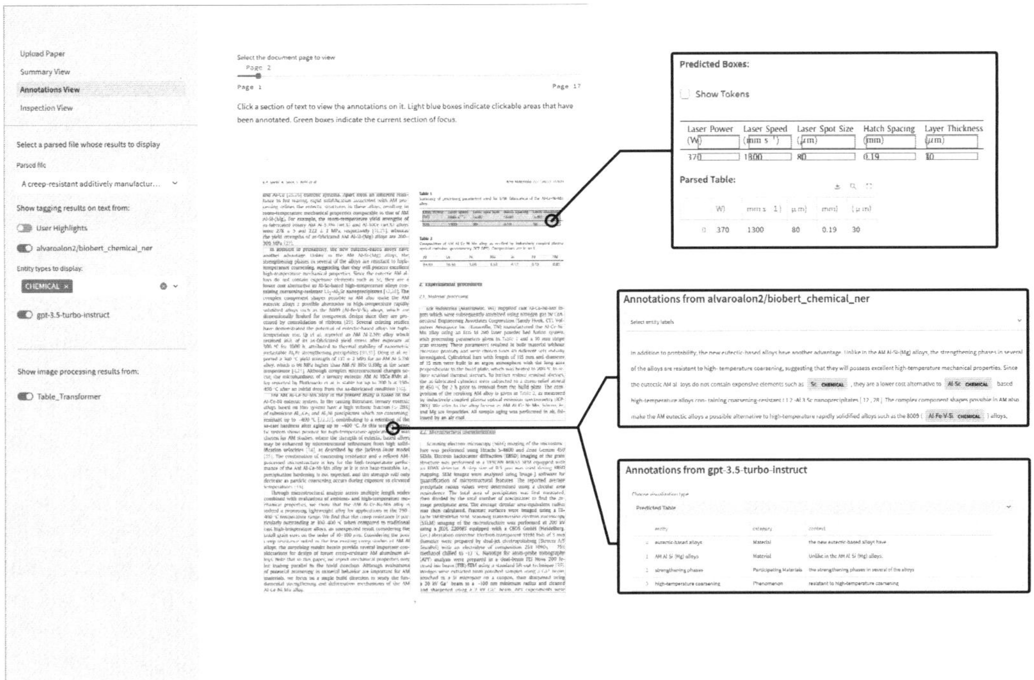

Figure 5: The annotations view. On the left, a screenshot showing the sidebar, allowing file and model selection, and the left pane, a visualization of the PDF with clickable regions highlighted. On the right, screenshots showing visualizations from the Table Transformer model with bounding boxes and parsed table (top), a HuggingFace transformer model with token-level tags (middle), and GPT-3.5 Turbo, with JSON output parsed into a table (bottom).

ure modes in both the upstream and downstream processing.

5 Co-design with Collage

In this section, we walk through an example of how Collage might facilitate the development of an information extraction pipeline for a materials scientist. In this scenario, Bob, a materials scientist, wishes to extract the synthesis parameters of a class of materials called zeolites from a dataset of PDFs from the 1980s to the 2010s. Papers discussing Zeolite synthesis often report parameters both in the text of the paper as well as in tables, so multimodal extraction is crucial. He has worked with Alice, an NLP developer, before but they have not yet collaborated on this project.

Evaluating off-the-shelf models. Bob begins in Collage by trying to see if there is an existing model that already works for his case. Using the HuggingFace model selector in the upload paper view, he searches for tagging models, but only finds models trained on general scientific or biomedical text, not materials. He is, however, able to write a prompt for an LLM model to extract this information, and he adds predictors that call out to two popular commercial models to extract the information that he's interested in. He uploads a recent paper that he's been reading, and waits for Collage to process it.

Finding modeling opportunities. Once Collage has processed the paper, Bob heads to the **summary view**, and compares the results from the two commercial models. He's able to view the parameters that they extracted, filtered by section, to develop an understanding of what heuristics might get him the information he wants: parameters identified in the related works section, for example, are frequently irrelevant to his search. In the summary view, he's also able to see the tables that Collage has identified and parsed with the Table-Transformer and MathPix models, along with their labels and captions, and the tagged bounding boxes for the table cells.

To make sure those annotations are reasonable, he heads to the **annotations view**, where he can visualize the extracted information side-by-side with the original PDF content, and compare the annotations from his two LLMs. He's also able to check whether the table detection model has predicted sensible bounding boxes that both don't exclude content like table footnotes, but also don't include irrelevant, non-table content. He notes that while the table parsing from both models is reasonable, the paper he's reading reports values in ratios that may not be comparable across papers. To have a single pipeline that produces normalized results, he'd like to use a multimodal LLM, but in Collage currently, LLMs can only be applied to text. He decides to get in touch with Alice, to see if she can develop an LLM-based table information extraction model.

Prototype model development. Alice begins work on a table information extraction tool, but there are a lot of possible options to evaluate: should she use a multimodal model and process the table in image format? Should she linearize the table into text, and have a text-only LLM work with it? In Collage, both options involve little more than implementing the LLM call, so it's easy to do both and then compare. For the multimodal case, Alice extends the **image predictor interface**, which allows her to receive as input the cropped image of any element on the page and pass that to an LLM; for the text-only case, Alice can easily access the underlying document representation use the already identified and parsed tables (which are in a DataFrame-compatible format) and convert them into markdown for her linearization. She is able to return a dictionary in the same schema for both predictors, which will automatically be visualized in the frontend as a Pandas dataframe. She commits her code, registers the predictors, and asks Bob to take a look in the Collage interface.

In-context evaluation. Bob then re-processes his paper through Collage, making sure to check the boxes for Alice's new table parsing predictors. In the summary view, he's able to compare the predicted, normalized tables to the original PDF, to verify that the models are performing the normalization correctly. He then picks the better performing model, and asks Alice to create a pipeline that can process his entire dataset. Alice is able to take the predictor, add it to the PaperMage recipe that underlies Collage, and run it over Bob's set of PDF documents, adding a step to export the parsed tables that Bob saw in the Collage interface.

Diagnosing errors. Bob looks through the parsed tables from processing all of the PDFs, and notes that for the older PDFs, the parsed content doesn't look right. He'd like to diagnose the problem. Because the processing that Alice and Bob run on these documents is the same as that underlying Collage, the results can be visualized in the tool, even if they were not directly processed through it. Bob loads the representation of the parsed older document, and is able to view the results from the model that didn't look right. While the bounding boxes for the table look correct in the annotations view, he's also able to see in the **inspection view** that the text detected within the table has not been correctly OCR'd. He can now contact Alice to see if there's a fix for that problem, but in the meantime, he can examine the visualizations for his PDFs to understand how the publication year might affect whether the deployed suite of models can correctly extract and normalize information, and what the cutoff year might be for the results to be trustworthy.

In this case, Collage enables Bob to self-serve cutting-edge NLP for his own use case, requiring that he involve Alice only when Collage's functionality needs extension. When that happens, Bob and Alice can both see results in the same interface, and can discuss errors and how to prioritize new work. When Alice develops new predictors to address Bob's needs, she is required to do no PDF processing or visualization, which are built into the tool, and Bob can evaluate and compare the results of these new predictors in the same interface he's been using the whole time. For debugging, both Bob and Alice have access to the same representation and visualization as a shared source of truth, and collaborate to involve both NLP and subject matter expertise in how to fix the problem. Collage can accelerate the process of collaboration between NLP developers and scientists, allowing for co-design and rapid prototyping with a shared representation.

6 Related Work

Collage situates itself at the intersection of tools that offer reading assistance for scientific PDFs and tools that partially automate the process of literature review by means of information extraction. Tools for scientific PDFs often focuses on interfaces that augment the existing PDF with new information, such as citation contexts (Rachatasumrit et al., 2022; Nicholson et al., 2021), or highlights that aid skimming (Fok et al., 2023). However, most of these works are designed around and purpose-built for specific models. By contrast, Collage draws from projects like PaperMage (Lo et al., 2023), by attempting to be model-agnostic, while at the same time providing a visual interface to prototype and evaluate those models.

Scientific information extraction and literature review automation also have long histories. Collage's focus on materials science was driven by the field's existing investment into data-driven design (Himanen et al., 2019; Olivetti et al., 2020), which focuses on using information extraction tools to build up knowledge graphs to inform future materials research. This adds to the existing body of work in chemical and material information extraction, including works like ChemDataExtractor (Swain and Cole, 2016; Mavracic et al., 2021) and MatSciBERT (Gupta et al., 2022). Works like Dagdelen et al. (2024) showcase the growing interest in LLM-based extraction; as LLMs increasingly become multimodal, this capability is likely to be used for tasks like scientific document understanding. While all of these tools are intended to be applied to documents from the materials science domain, they do not share an interface: most tools expect plain text, some, like ChemDataExtractor allow HTML and XML documents, and some work with images. Collage aims to be a platform on which multiple competing approaches can be evaluated, regardless of the input and output formats they require.

7 Conclusion

In this work, we present Collage, a system designed to facilitate co-design and rapid prototyping of mixed modality information extraction on PDF content between scientists and NLP developers. We focus on a case study in the materials science domain, that allows materials scientists to evaluate models for their ability to assist in literature review. We intend for this work to be a platform on which to evaluate further modeling work in this area.

Ethics and Broader Impacts

Our interview protocol was evaluated and approved by the Carnegie Mellon University Institutional Review Board as STUDY2023_00000431.

In developing a tool to facilitate the automated processing of scientific PDFs, we feel that it is important to acknowledge that that automation may propagate the biases of the underlying models. Particularly in the case of English that does not reflect the training corpora that models were built on top of, models can perform poorly, leading to fewer results from those papers, and the potential to inadvertently exclude them. However, we hope that in providing a tool to inspect model outputs before such automation tools are deployed, that we can encourage critical evaluation and uses of these tools.

Acknowledgements

Research was sponsored by the Army Research Laboratory and was accomplished under Cooperative Agreement Number W911NF-22-2-0121. The views and conclusions contained in this document are those of the authors and should not be interpreted as representing the official policies, either expressed or implied, of the Army Research Laboratory or the U.S. Government. The U.S. Government is authorized to reproduce and distribute reprints for Government purposes notwithstanding any copyright notation herein.

References

2008–2023. Grobid. https://github.com/kermitt2/grobid.

Iz Beltagy, Kyle Lo, and Arman Cohan. 2019. Scibert: A pretrained language model for scientific text. *arXiv preprint arXiv:1903.10676*.

Jose Camacho-Collados and Mohammad Taher Pilehvar. 2018. On the role of text preprocessing in neural network architectures: An evaluation study on text categorization and sentiment analysis. In *Proceedings of the 2018 EMNLP Workshop BlackboxNLP: Analyzing and Interpreting Neural Networks for NLP*, pages 40–46, Brussels, Belgium. Association for Computational Linguistics.

Arman Cohan, Guy Feigenblat, Dayne Freitag, Tirthankar Ghosal, Drahomira Herrmannova, Petr Knoth, Kyle Lo, Philipp Mayr, Michal Shmueli-Scheuer, Anita de Waard, and Lucy Lu Wang, editors. 2022. *Proceedings of the Third Workshop on Scholarly Document Processing*. Association for Computational Linguistics, Gyeongju, Republic of Korea.

John Dagdelen, Alexander Dunn, Sanghoon Lee, Nicholas Walker, Andrew S. Rosen, Gerbrand Ceder, Kristin A. Persson, and Anubhav Jain. 2024. Structured information extraction from scientific text with large language models. *Nature Communications*, 15(1):1418. Publisher: Nature Publishing Group.

Raymond Fok, Hita Kambhamettu, Luca Soldaini, Jonathan Bragg, Kyle Lo, Andrew Head, Marti A. Hearst, and Daniel S. Weld. 2023. Scim: Intelligent Skimming Support for Scientific Papers. In *Proceedings of the 28th International Conference on Intelligent User Interfaces*, pages 476–490. ArXiv:2205.04561 [cs].

Tanishq Gupta, Mohd Zaki, NM Anoop Krishnan, and Mausam. 2022. Matscibert: A materials domain language model for text mining and information extraction. *npj Computational Materials*, 8(1):102.

Lauri Himanen, Amber Geurts, Adam Stuart Foster, and Patrick Rinke. 2019. Data-driven materials science: status, challenges, and perspectives. *Advanced Science*, 6(21):1900808.

Petr Knoth, Christopher Stahl, Bikash Gyawali, David Pride, Suchetha N. Kunnath, and Drahomira Herrmannova, editors. 2020. *Proceedings of the 8th International Workshop on Mining Scientific Publications*. Association for Computational Linguistics, Wuhan, China.

Kyle Lo, Zejiang Shen, Benjamin Newman, Joseph Z Chang, Russell Authur, Erin Bransom, Stefan Candra, Yoganand Chandrasekhar, Regan Huff, Bailey Kuehl, et al. 2023. Papermage: A unified toolkit for processing, representing, and manipulating visually-rich scientific documents. In *Proceedings of the 2023 Conference on Empirical Methods in Natural Language Processing: System Demonstrations*, pages 495–507.

Juraj Mavracic, Callum J Court, Taketomo Isazawa, Stephen R Elliott, and Jacqueline M Cole. 2021. Chemdataextractor 2.0: Autopopulated ontologies for materials science. *Journal of Chemical Information and Modeling*, 61(9):4280–4289.

Tristan Naumann, Asma Ben Abacha, Steven Bethard, Kirk Roberts, and Anna Rumshisky, editors. 2023. *Proceedings of the 5th Clinical Natural Language Processing Workshop*. Association for Computational Linguistics, Toronto, Canada.

Mark Neumann, Daniel King, Iz Beltagy, and Waleed Ammar. 2019. ScispaCy: Fast and robust models for biomedical natural language processing. In *Proceedings of the 18th BioNLP Workshop and Shared Task*, pages 319–327, Florence, Italy. Association for Computational Linguistics.

Josh M. Nicholson, Milo Mordaunt, Patrice Lopez, Ashish Uppala, Domenic Rosati, Neves P. Rodrigues, Peter Grabitz, and Sean C. Rife. 2021. scite: A smart citation index that displays the context of citations and classifies their intent using deep learning. *Quantitative Science Studies*, 2(3):882–898.

Elsa A Olivetti, Jacqueline M Cole, Edward Kim, Olga Kononova, Gerbrand Ceder, Thomas Yong-Jin Han, and Anna M Hiszpanski. 2020. Data-driven materials research enabled by natural language processing and information extraction. *Applied Physics Reviews*, 7(4).

Daniel Preoțiuc-Pietro, Catalina Goanta, Ilias Chalkidis, Leslie Barrett, Gerasimos (Jerry) Spanakis, and Nikolaos Aletras, editors. 2023. *Proceedings of the Natural Legal Language Processing Workshop 2023*. Association for Computational Linguistics, Singapore.

Napol Rachatasumrit, Jonathan Bragg, Amy X. Zhang, and Daniel S Weld. 2022. CiteRead: Integrating Localized Citation Contexts into Scientific Paper Reading. In *27th International Conference on Intelligent User Interfaces*, IUI '22, pages 707–719, New York, NY, USA. Association for Computing Machinery.

Brandon Smock, Rohith Pesala, and Robin Abraham. 2023. Aligning benchmark datasets for table structure recognition. In *International Conference on Document Analysis and Recognition*, pages 371–386. Springer.

Matthew C. Swain and Jacqueline M. Cole. 2016. ChemDataExtractor: A Toolkit for Automated Extraction of Chemical Information from the Scientific Literature. *Journal of Chemical Information and Modeling*, 56(10):1894–1904. Publisher: American Chemical Society.

A Appendix: Screenshots of Interface Views

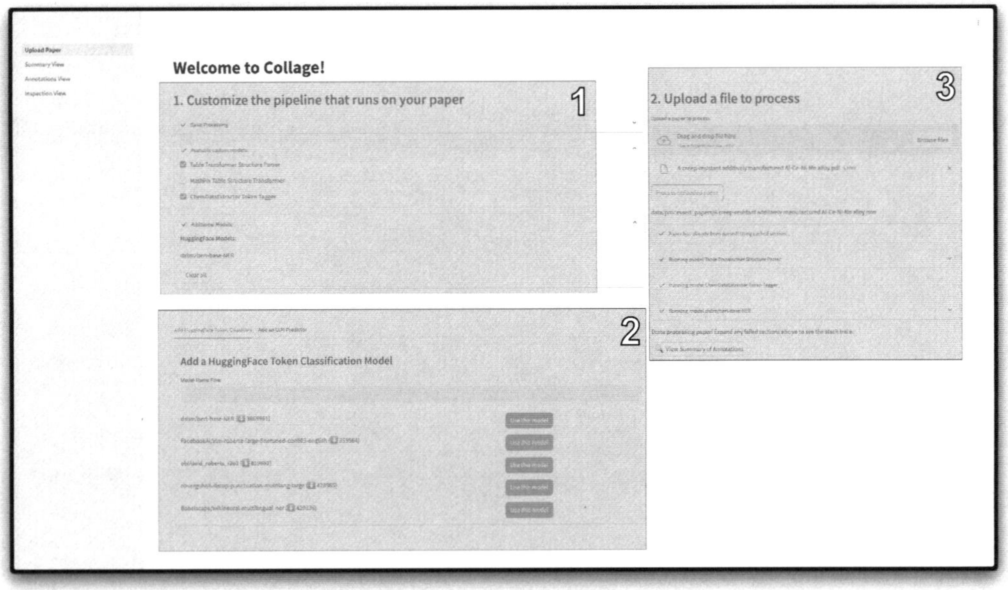

Figure 6: The Upload Paper view, showing (1) The currently selected models, (2) widget for selecting HuggingFace and LLM Classifiers, (3) File upload and progress visualization.

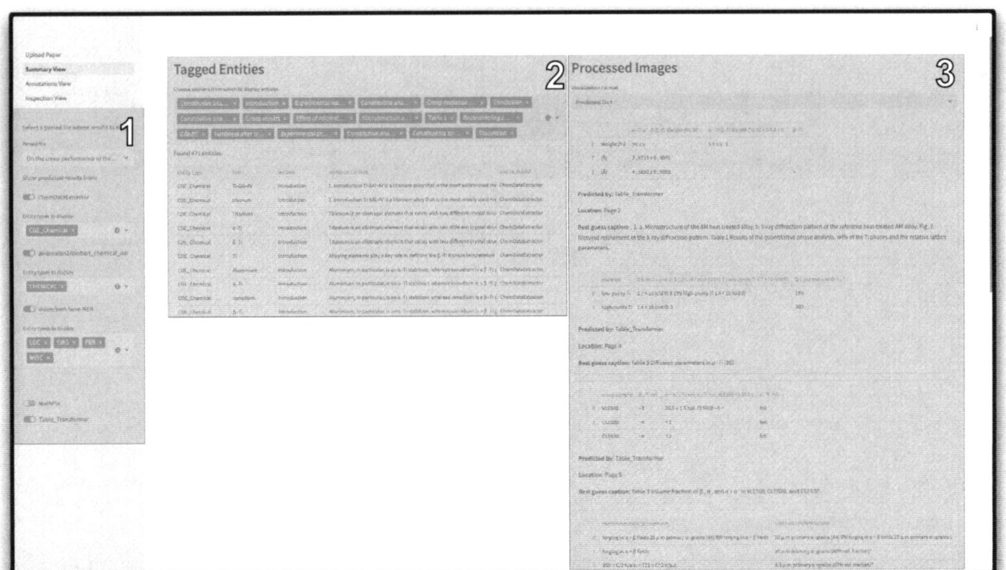

Figure 7: The Summary view, showing (1) the sidebar allowing model and entity type selection, (2) visualized tagged entities from the selected tagging models, (3) visualized image processing results.

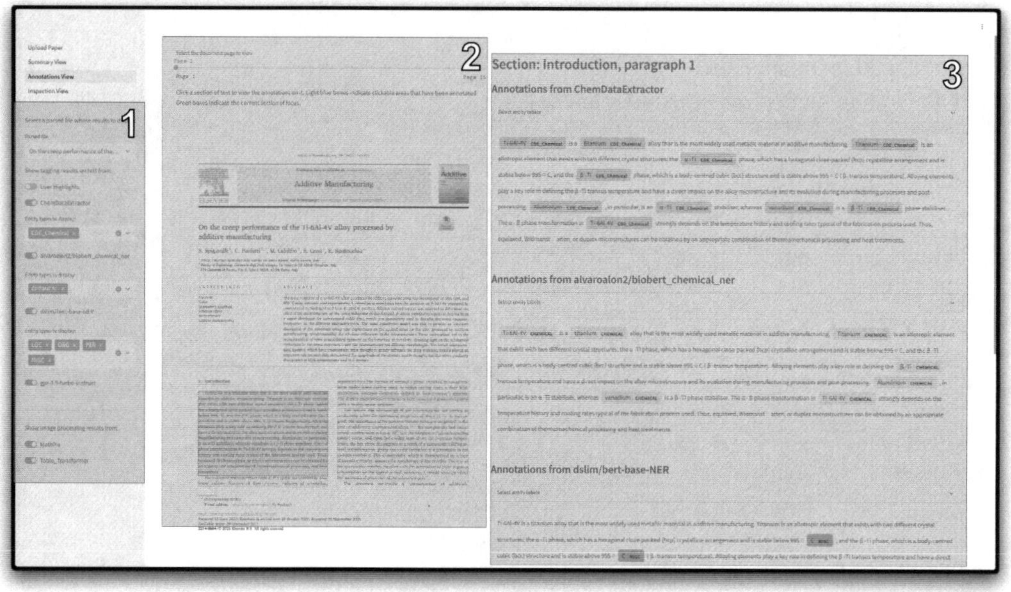

Figure 8: The Annotations view, showing (1) the sidebar allowing model and entity type selection, (2) the visualized PDF, showing clickable regions (3) visualized annotations on the clicked region.

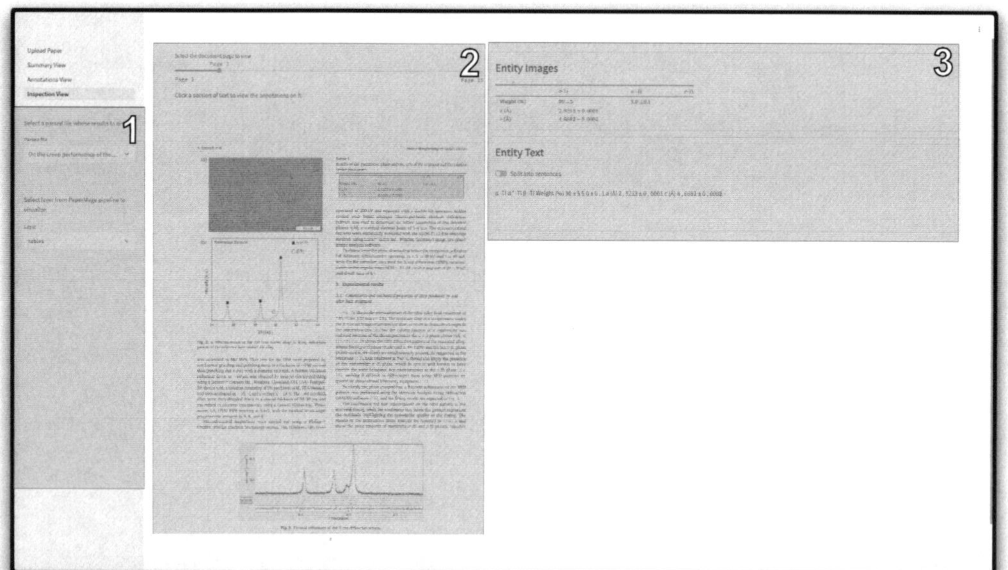

Figure 9: The Inspection view, showing (1) the sidebar allowing PaperMage layer selection, (2) the visualized PDF, showing clickable regions (3) the image and the text of the selected `Entity`

Literature discovery with natural language queries

Anna Kiepura[†], **Jessica Lam**[†], **Nianlong Gu**[‡]
Richard H.R. Hahnloser[†]
[†]Institute of Neuroinformatics, University of Zurich and ETH Zurich, Switzerland
{akiepura, lamjessica, rich}@ini.ethz.ch
[‡]Linguistic Research Infrastructure, University of Zurich, Switzerland
nianlong.gu@uzh.ch

Abstract

Literature discovery is a critical component of scientific research. Modern discovery systems leveraging Large Language Models (LLMs) are increasingly adopted for their ability to process natural language queries (NLQs). To assess the robustness of such systems, we compile two NLQ datasets and submit them to nine widely used discovery platforms. Our findings reveal that LLM-based search engines struggle with precisely formulated queries, often producing numerous false positives. However, precision improves when LLMs are used not for direct retrieval but to convert NLQs into structured keyword-based queries. As a result, hybrid systems that integrate both LLM-driven and keyword-based approaches outperform purely keyword-based or purely LLM-based discovery methods.

1 Introduction

Scientific research heavily relies on the ability to discover and assimilate relevant literature (Patel and Patel, 2019). Traditional literature search methods, whether through publisher-specific databases (e.g., *Nature*[1]) or generic academic search engines (e.g., *Google Scholar*[2]), primarily use keyword-based queries processed via inverted indexes and ranking algorithms such as BM25 (Robertson et al., 2009). While these conventional approaches are effective, they often struggle with nuanced, concept-driven queries.

Recent advancements in artificial intelligence, particularly the rise of Large Language Models (LLMs) and LLM-powered chatbots (e.g. *Consensus*[3]), have enabled a more intuitive and context-aware search experience. However, despite their convenience, LLM-driven retrieval systems lack formal guarantees of accuracy (Liu et al., 2023). This limitation can lead to erroneous search results, including false positives (retrieving irrelevant papers) and false negatives (overlooking relevant papers), potentially impacting the reliability of literature discovery. To systematically assess these challenges, we conduct an evaluation of various literature search engines using natural language queries (NLQs).

We find that existing platforms are not equipped to handle NLQs, with most papers retrieved being incorrect, but that using LLMs to parse NLQs into structured queries interpretable by these platforms highly boosts retrieval performance. Our contributions are:

1. We introduce two manually curated datasets[4] designed for systematic evaluation of literature discovery platforms on NLQs.
2. We benchmark the performance of nine popular literature discovery platforms on our datasets.
3. We investigate the ability of LLMs to transform NLQs into structured formats and analyze their impact on retrieval effectiveness.

2 Related work

Literature discovery, or the task of finding relevant papers (either to cite in a given sentence (Jeong et al., 2019; Kieu et al., 2020; Gu et al., 2022; Nogueira et al., 2020)) or to answer an input question (Menick et al., 2022; Gao et al., 2023; Dehghan et al., 2024)), has been a long-standing research focus in the realm of scientific document processing. Sun et al. (2024) and Ajith et al. (2024) showed that well-instructed LLMs outperform the more typical, nearest-neighbour based methods in re-ranking papers on relevance to the input query, in part due to the LLM ability to generalise across synonyms and imprecise queries.

However, because generation-based search en-

[1]nature.com/search/advanced
[2]scholar.google.com
[3]consensus.app
[4]https://github.com/annamkiepura/lit_discovery

Proceedings of the Fifth Workshop on Scholarly Document Processing (SDP 2025), pages 83–95
July 31, 2025 ©2025 Association for Computational Linguistics

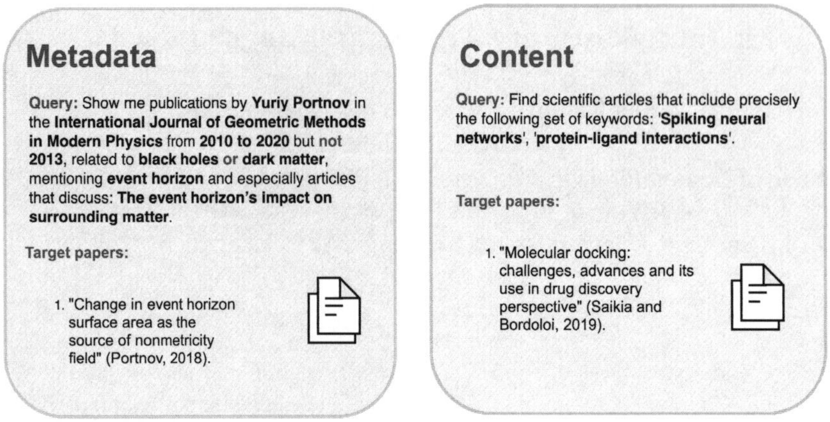

Figure 1: Example queries from the **Metadata** and **Content** datasets with the corresponding target papers (Portnov, 2018; Saikia and Bordoloi, 2019).

gines are prone to hallucination (Liu et al., 2023), grounding LLM-powered literature discovery platforms by referencing a paper database remains key. Retrieving information from most databases involves submitting structured queries that are interpretable by said databases. To reduce the need for learning about the structure accepted by each database, much research has gone into automatically translating NLQs into structured queries (Zhong et al., 2018). A typical approach was to manually craft a mapping table between mentioned keywords and database properties (Montgomery et al., 2020), but these tables are often too rigid to effectively handle query ambiguity and complexity. In contrast, recent works have successfully used LLMs for this mapping problem (Lei et al., 2024), and in this work, we explore whether this effectiveness extends to the specific context of precise NLQs for literature discovery.

3 Methods

A key principle of effective retrieval systems is to provide users with fine-grained control over retrieval behaviour (Schleith et al., 2022; Kandula et al., 2024). In literature discovery, this control would include enabling researchers to specify authors, venue, publication year, and topics of interest. Alternatively, researchers might seek papers on multidisciplinary topics defined by one or several keywords that are rarely used together. Such complex queries are well-suited to classical search engines but may pose challenges for LLMs, which we seek to explore.

3.1 Datasets

We manually created two NLQ datasets for scientific literature discovery. A NLQ can specify conditions on paper metadata (e.g., publication year) and content (e.g. specific keywords to appear in the paper). We also allow for combining conditions with the boolean operators AND (e.g., papers are about vaccines and COVID-19) and OR (e.g., papers are authored by John Moore or Steven Johnes).

The first **Metadata** dataset contains requirements on paper metadata and content and was constructed as follows:

1. We first selected a research domain (e.g., biomedical science), then came up with relevant keywords (e.g., vaccines) and publisher (e.g., Nature).
2. Next, we continuously added conditions on the paper metadata until the publisher's search engine could find only very few papers relevant to the topic while meeting all conditions.
3. We consolidated the keywords and the conditions into a NLQ, and linked each NLQ to the papers found on the corresponding publisher's website in Step 2 (target papers).

The second **Content** dataset focuses on restricted paper content and was designed by tying the query with the paper content rather than its metadata. Specifically, this dataset contains NLQs that combine keywords that rarely co-occur within single papers:

1. First, we identified suitable keyword combi-

Statistic	Meta.	Cont.
Queries	30	30
Conditions per query	3 - 9	2 - 4
Tokens per query	18 - 66	16 - 22
Target papers per query	1 - 5	N/A
TTR	0.45	0.32
RTTR	13.85	8.98

Table 1: Basic statistics of the **Metadata** dataset. TTR - Type-Token Ratio, RTTR - Root Type-Token Ratio (Torruella and Capsada, 2013).

nations (e.g. "connectomics", "entropy maximization", "diffusion tensor imaging").

2. Then, we translated each combination into an NLQ: "Find scientific articles that include precisely the following set of keywords:...'. We also experimented with increasing the verbosity of queries by further characterizing the keyword combinations, see Appendix D.

3. For this dataset, there are no predefined target papers. Every paper retrieved by the engines is classified as correctly retrieved if it contains all target keywords.

In total, we constructed 30 NLQs for **Metadata** and 30 NLQs for **Content**. Figure 1 shows example NLQs and Table 1 lists basic statistics.

3.2 Literature discovery systems

We compared search engines powered by **lexical** similarity, **semantic** similarity, or **chatbots**. A more detailed description of each platform is available in Appendix E.

Lexicality *Google Scholar*[5] is a free search engine that indexes scholarly works and relies primarily on lexical matching. It retrieves results based on exact keywords and phrases, making search accuracy dependent on precise wording.

Semantics *Semantic Scholar* (Kinney et al., 2023) is one of the largest open-sourced platforms for scientific literature discovery. It uses a two-stage search engine: the first stage efficiently finds many relevant papers and the second stage more carefully reranks these papers by semantic relevance. The open-sourced search engine of *SciLit* (Gu and Hahnloser, 2023) is similar, but additionally supports sophisticated metadata filtering options. The closed-sourced *Elicit*[6] is an LLM-powered platform for biomedical literature using semantic similarity[7].

Chatbots *Consensus*[8] and *Perplexity*[9] are both popular closed-sourced chatbots for getting answers from real-world information sources. We also included *Floatz*[10] and *Zeta-Alpha*[11], two closed-sourced platforms combining LLMs, semantic search and indexing. Additionally, we compared against *ChatGPT-4o*[12], a general-purpose closed-sourced chatbot.

3.3 NLQ Parsing

Additionally, we investigated how parsing the original NLQ into a structured query aligning with the specific engine's specifications affects retrieval performance. This part of the analysis was possible only for platforms which specify their structured query format.

For *SciLit*[13] and *Semantic Scholar*[14], we followed the provided documentation on their discovery engines to convert NLQs into structured queries. Next, we benchmarked the retrieval performance using the structured queries. The conversion was performed with a GPT-4o-mini model under a few-shot setting (Appendix A).

Note that our dataset's queries were not fully compatible with the *Semantic Scholar* API: (1) strict keyword filtering (exact word matches), (2) logical OR functionality for metadata fields (e.g., limiting to papers from *Nature* OR *Science*), and (3) exclusion queries (e.g., ignoring specific authors) are not supported. To optimize our use of *Semantic Scholar*, we curated a small dataset comprising 15 queries that align with the platform's API constraints (Appendix B). For the **Metadata** dataset, content and author requirements were merged into the "query" field, while venue and year constraints were assigned to their respective fields. OR conditions were interpreted as AND conditions, and exclusions were disregarded. For the **Content** dataset, keyword-based constraints were entered into the "query" field.

Google Scholar lacks an official API constructing structured searches. Based on empirical anal-

[5] scholar.google.com

[6] elicit.org

[7] support.elicit.com/en/articles/552705

[8] consensus.app

[9] perplexity.ai

[10] floatz.ai/

[11] zeta-alpha.com/

[12] openai.com/index/hello-gpt-4o/

[13] github.com/nianlonggu/SciLit

[14] api.semanticscholar.org/api-docs

ysis of query structure and results, we proposed a parsing scheme, detailed in Appendix C. However, without an official documentation, optimal query formatting cannot be guaranteed.

3.4 Performance analysis

For both **Metadata** and **Content** queries, we evaluated retrieval performance by comparing each platform's output against the target papers. Papers present in the target list were classified as "correct papers", whereas the non-targets were classified as "incorrect papers". Additionally, any non-existent papers returned by the platforms were categorized as "hallucinated papers". For each platform, we computed average Precision, Recall, and F-1 across the $N = 30$ queries:

$$\text{Precision} = \frac{1}{N}\sum_{q=1}^{N}\frac{\text{Correctly Retrieved}_q}{\text{Total Retrieved}_q}$$

$$\text{Recall} = \frac{1}{N}\sum_{q=1}^{N}\frac{\text{Correctly Retrieved}_q}{\text{Total Targets}_q}$$

$$\text{F1} = \frac{1}{N}\sum_{q=1}^{N}2 \times \frac{\text{Precision}_q \times \text{Recall}_q}{\text{Precision}_q + \text{Recall}_q}$$

4 Results and discussion

Overall, the examined platforms rarely hallucinated papers. For **Metadata** queries, only Perplexity suggested one hallucinated paper, while all other platforms suggested none. No hallucinations were observed for **Content** queries.

Systems Struggled with Precise Queries Table 2 highlights the challenges most search engines face with precise NLQs. For **Metadata**, precision remains low, except for *SciLit* + LLM parsing, *Google Scholar* + LLM parsing, *ChatGPT-4o*, and *Perplexity*. The highest Recall scores were achieved by *Google Scholar* + LLM parsing, *SciLit* + LLM parsing, *Perplexity*, and *ChatGPT-4o*. In terms of F1 score, *Google Scholar* + LLM parsing, *SciLit* + LLM parsing, *ChatGPT-4o*, and *Perplexity* outperformed other platforms, with *Google Scholar* + LLM parsing delivering the best overall performance. For the **Content** dataset, precision is notably high for *Google Scholar* + LLM parsing, *Google Scholar*, and *Zeta-Alpha*, but remains low for other platforms. Only *Google Scholar* + LLM parsing demonstrated consistently high Recall and F1 scores, making it the top performer on this dataset. *SciLit* and *Semantic Scholar* perform poorly on **Content**, even with LLM parsing.

	Metadata			**Content**		
	P	R	F1	P	R	F1
Elicit	0.08	0.41	0.12	0.03	0.10	0.04
Zeta-Alpha	0.23	0.19	0.20	0.60	0.31	0.39
Consensus	0.08	0.33	0.11	0.01	0.05	0.02
Floatz	0.10	0.10	0.10	0.22	0.09	0.11
Perplexity	0.55	0.57	0.52	0.10	0.09	0.08
ChatGPT-4o	0.61	0.53	0.55	0.19	0.11	0.13
SciLit	0.01	0.01	0.01	0.00	0.03	0.01
+ LLM parsing	0.78	0.76	0.76	0.42	0.17	0.23
Semantic Scholar	0.00	0.00	0.00	0.00	0.00	0.00
+ LLM parsing	0.28	0.48	0.32	0.04	0.05	0.03
Google Scholar	0.03	0.02	0.02	0.64	0.37	0.44
+ LLM parsing	**0.80**	**0.80**	**0.79**	**0.96**	**0.98**	**0.96**

Table 2: Performance of search engines based on **Metadata** and **Content** datasets in terms of **P**recision, **R**ecall, and **F1**. Metrics exclude hallucinated papers. "+ LLM parsing" indicates NLQ converted into a structured query.

The performance metrics are computed by pooling together the target papers obtained across all platforms, but these two platforms use only S2AG (Wade, 2022), which is likely much smaller than the *Google Scholar* paper database. Thus, there were likely many papers that could have never been retrieved in the first place from these two platforms.

LLM Parsing Enhances Discovery Performance For the three platforms that support using structured queries (namely, *SciLit*, *Semantic Scholar*, *Google Scholar*), we found improved retrieval performance on both datasets when we parsed NLQs with an LLM into a structured format. A smaller performance boost was observed for *Semantic Scholar*, likely due to poor compatibility of our dataset's NLQs with its API. The poor performance achieved without LLM parsing is likely due to these three platforms being designed for queries that are keyword- or semantically dense, not for queries that are phrased as instructions.

5 Conclusion

Our findings highlight key strengths and limitations of LLM-based literature discovery systems. While these systems struggle with precise NLQs, LLM parsing significantly enhances retrieval performance, particularly when integrated with structured search engines. This suggests that hybrid approaches combining LLM-based and structured retrieval methods are more promising for literature discovery and could bridge the gap between the flexibility of human-like queries and the structured nature of conventional search engines, effectively mitigating the challenges posed by ambiguous or instruction-based NLQs. Additionally, LLM-based systems prove valuable in scenarios where structured queries are not feasible or when queries do not conform to strict database formats. Future work should explore refining hybrid methodologies to further optimize retrieval accuracy and relevance.

Limitations

Due to resource constraints, only the free software versions were evaluated. Additionally, we designed only 60 queries because of the extensive work of manually constructing them and of examining the retrieved papers. Also, our precise queries may not be representative of the imprecise queries researchers might submit in practice. In future work, it may therefore be worthwhile to design queries that creatively combine requests for precise content in the midst of imprecise interests, which would call for human evaluation due to the lack of a gold standard.

References

Anirudh Ajith, Mengzhou Xia, Alexis Chevalier, Tanya Goyal, Danqi Chen, and Tianyu Gao. 2024. LitSearch: A retrieval benchmark for scientific literature search. In *Proceedings of the 2024 Conference on Empirical Methods in Natural Language Processing*, pages 15068–15083, Miami, Florida, USA. Association for Computational Linguistics.

Iz Beltagy, Kyle Lo, and Arman Cohan. 2019. SciBERT: A pretrained language model for scientific text. In *Proceedings of the 2019 Conference on Empirical Methods in Natural Language Processing and the 9th International Joint Conference on Natural Language Processing (EMNLP-IJCNLP)*, pages 3615–3620, Hong Kong, China. Association for Computational Linguistics.

Mohammad Dehghan, Mohammad Ali Alomrani, Sunyam Bagga, David Alfonso-Hermelo, Khalil Bibi, Abbas Ghaddar, Yingxue Zhang, Xiaoguang Li, Jianye Hao, Qun Liu, Jimmy Lin, Boxing Chen, Prasanna Parthasarathi, Mahdi Biparva, and Mehdi Rezagholizadeh. 2024. Ewek-qa: Enhanced web and efficient knowledge graph retrieval for citation-based question answering systems. *Preprint*, arXiv:2406.10393.

Tianyu Gao, Howard Yen, Jiatong Yu, and Danqi Chen. 2023. Enabling large language models to generate text with citations. *Preprint*, arXiv:2305.14627.

Nianlong Gu, Yingqiang Gao, and Richard H. R. Hahnloser. 2022. Local citation recommendation with hierarchical-attention text encoder and scibert-based reranking. *Preprint*, arXiv:2112.01206.

Nianlong Gu and Richard H.R. Hahnloser. 2023. SciLit: A platform for joint scientific literature discovery, summarization and citation generation. In *Proceedings of the 61st Annual Meeting of the Association for Computational Linguistics (Volume 3: System Demonstrations)*, pages 235–246, Toronto, Canada. Association for Computational Linguistics.

Chanwoo Jeong, Sion Jang, Hyuna Shin, Eunjeong Park, and Sungchul Choi. 2019. A context-aware citation recommendation model with bert and graph convolutional networks. *Preprint*, arXiv:1903.06464.

Hemanth Kandula, Damianos Karakos, Haoling Qiu, Benjamin Rozonoyer, Ian Soboroff, Lee Tarlin, and Bonan Min. 2024. Querybuilder: Human-in-the-loop query development for information retrieval. *Preprint*, arXiv:2409.04667.

Binh Thanh Kieu, Inigo Jauregi Unanue, Son Bao Pham, Hieu Xuan Phan, and Massimo Piccardi. 2020. Learning neural textual representations for citation recommendation. *Preprint*, arXiv:2007.04070.

Rodney Kinney, Chloe Anastasiades, Russell Authur, Iz Beltagy, Jonathan Bragg, Alexandra Buraczynski, Isabel Cachola, Stefan Candra, Yoganand Chandrasekhar, Arman Cohan, Miles Crawford, Doug Downey, Jason Dunkelberger, Oren Etzioni, Rob Evans, Sergey Feldman, Joseph Gorney, David Graham, Fangzhou Hu, Regan Huff, Daniel King, Sebastian Kohlmeier, Bailey Kuehl, Michael Langan, Daniel Lin, Haokun Liu, Kyle Lo, Jaron Lochner, Kelsey MacMillan, Tyler Murray, Chris Newell, Smita Rao, Shaurya Rohatgi, Paul Sayre, Zejiang Shen, Amanpreet Singh, Luca Soldaini, Shivashankar Subramanian, Amber Tanaka, Alex D. Wade, Linda Wagner, Lucy Lu Wang, Chris Wilhelm, Caroline Wu, Jiangjiang Yang, Angele Zamarron, Madeleine Van Zuylen, and Daniel S. Weld. 2023. The semantic scholar open data platform. *Preprint*, arXiv:2301.10140.

Janice Y. Kung. 2023. Elicit. *The Journal of the Canadian Health Libraries Association*, 44(1):15–8. © Kung. No competing interests declared.

Fangyu Lei, Jixuan Chen, Yuxiao Ye, Ruisheng Cao, Dongchan Shin, Hongjin Su, Zhaoqing Suo, Hongcheng Gao, Wenjing Hu, Pengcheng Yin, Victor Zhong, Caiming Xiong, Ruoxi Sun, Qian Liu, Sida Wang, and Tao Yu. 2024. Spider 2.0: Evaluating language models on real-world enterprise text-to-sql workflows. *Preprint*, arXiv:2411.07763.

Nelson F. Liu, Tianyi Zhang, and Percy Liang. 2023. Evaluating verifiability in generative search engines. *Preprint*, arXiv:2304.09848.

Kyle Lo, Lucy Lu Wang, Mark Neumann, Rodney Kinney, and Daniel Weld. 2020. S2ORC: The semantic scholar open research corpus. In *Proceedings of the 58th Annual Meeting of the Association for Computational Linguistics*, pages 4969–4983, Online. Association for Computational Linguistics.

Smriti Mallapaty. 2024. Can google scholar survive the ai revolution? *Nature*, 635:797–798.

Jacob Menick, Maja Trebacz, Vladimir Mikulik, John Aslanides, Francis Song, Martin Chadwick, Mia Glaese, Susannah Young, Lucy Campbell-Gillingham, Geoffrey Irving, and Nat McAleese. 2022. Teaching language models to support answers with verified quotes. *Preprint*, arXiv:2203.11147.

Mahdi Naser Moghadasi and Yu Zhuang. 2020. Sent2vec: A new sentence embedding representation with sentimental semantic. In *2020 IEEE International Conference on Big Data (Big Data)*, pages 4672–4680.

Chantal Montgomery, Haruna Isah, and Farhana Zulkernine. 2020. Towards a natural language query processing system. *Preprint*, arXiv:2009.12414.

Rodrigo Nogueira, Zhiying Jiang, Kyunghyun Cho, and Jimmy Lin. 2020. Navigation-based candidate expansion and pretrained language models for citation recommendation. *Preprint*, arXiv:2001.08687.

Mimansha Patel and Nitin Patel. 2019. Exploring research methodology: Review article. *International Journal of Research and Review*, 6(3):48–55. Review Article.

Yuriy A. Portnov. 2018. Change in event horizon surface area as the source of nonmetricity field. *International Journal of Geometric Methods in Modern Physics*, 15(06):1850104.

Stephen Robertson, Hugo Zaragoza, et al. 2009. The probabilistic relevance framework: Bm25 and beyond. *Foundations and Trends® in Information Retrieval*, 3(4):333–389.

Surovi Saikia and Manobjyoti Bordoloi. 2019. Molecular docking: Challenges, advances and its use in drug discovery perspective. *Current Drug Targets*, 20(5):501–521.

Johannes Schleith, Hella-Franziska Hoffmann, Milda Norkute, and Brian Cechmanek. 2022. Human-in-the-loop information extraction increases efficiency and trust. In *Mensch und Computer 2022 – Workshopband*, Darmstadt, Germany. Gesellschaft für Informatik e.V.

Weiwei Sun, Lingyong Yan, Xinyu Ma, Shuaiqiang Wang, Pengjie Ren, Zhumin Chen, Dawei Yin, and Zhaochun Ren. 2024. Is chatgpt good at search? investigating large language models as re-ranking agents. *Preprint*, arXiv:2304.09542.

Joan Torruella and Ramon Capsada. 2013. Lexical statistics and tipological structures: A measure of lexical richness. In *5th International Conference on Corpus Linguistics (CILC2013)*, volume 95, pages 447–454. Elsevier Ltd.

Alex D. Wade. 2022. The semantic scholar academic graph (s2ag). In *Companion Proceedings of the Web Conference 2022*, WWW '22, page 739, New York, NY, USA. Association for Computing Machinery.

Victor Zhong, Caiming Xiong, and Richard Socher. 2018. Seq2SQL: Generating structured queries from natural language using reinforcement learning.

A LLM parsing into structured queries (SciLit)

To parse the NLQs from the **Metadata** dataset into the structured format required by the SciLit API, we used GPT-4o with the prompt in Figure 2.

Example input query: "Show me publications by Yuriy Portnov in the International Journal of Geometric Methods in Modern Physics from 2010 to 2020 but not 2013, related to black holes or dark matter, and especially articles that discuss: The event horizon's impact on surrounding matter. "

Output structured query: {"Semantic Query": "The event horizon's impact on surrounding matter.", "Keywords": ["Author.FullName: Yuriy Portnov", "Venue: International Journal of Geometric Methods in Modern Physics", "2010..2020", "!2013", "black holes|dark matter"]}.

The prompt for **Content** queries is in Figure 3.

Example input query: "Find scientific articles that include precisely the following set of keywords: 'Piezoelectric materials', 'cellular mechanotransduction', 'ultrasound stimulation'. "

Example output (structured query): ['Piezoelectric materials', 'cellular mechanotransduction', 'ultrasound stimulation']

B Semantic Scholar Custom Dataset and LLM parsing into structured queries (Semantic Scholar)

As the queries in **Metadata** and **Content** are not fully suitable for the *Semantic Scholar* API, we composed a smaller dataset of 15 queries that are fully suitable with their API, **Semantic Scholar Custom**. Queries in **Semantic Scholar Custom** are much simpler than in **Metadata** and **Content**. Specifically, they do not include strict keyword filtering (returning papers containing an exact word match), OR functions (e.g., papers published in Nature OR Science), or exclusions (e.g., papers not authored by Steven Jones, or papers published between 2010 and 2020 but excluding 2018).

Example query from Semantic Scholar Custom dataset: "Find papers on deep reinforce-

I will give you a query text, your task is to extract two sources of information from the text: 1) Semantic Query and 2) Keywords. This query text is a natural language about how I want to query the scientific literature database. You should parse the query text and extract the information in the following steps:

Step 1: Identify the semantic query. You need to inspect the query text and check if there is any text (e.g., some sentences or paragraphs) that the user intends to use as the semantic query to find semantically similar papers. If there is no semantic query specified in the query text, then set the semantic query as an empty string "".

Step 2: Extract keywords. You need to parse the query text and extract keywords mentioned in the query text that are supposed to be used as filters when doing search. The keywords include four and ONLY 4 types:

1. AuthorFullNames: After extracting all authors' full names, prefix each extracted author name with a special string "Author.FullName:".
2. Venue: Extract venue or journal mentioned in the query text, and prefix each extracted venue with a special string "Venue:".
3. PublicationDate: Extract keywords of years or a range of years. If the publication date keywords are a range of years, express the year keywords in the form "Start-Year..End-Year". For individual years, extract the year itself.
4. GeneralKeywords: Extract the keywords that are mentioned in the query text but do not belong to other keyword types. Extract the keywords as they are (maximum three words). Do not copy the semantic query directly as a general keyword, and correct any spelling mistakes in the extracted keywords.

Step 3: Check the NOT logic operation for each extracted keyword. Prefix excluded keywords with "!" where appropriate.

Step 4: Check the OR logic operation between multiple post-processed keywords in Step 3. If there is an OR logic specified between keywords, use the "|" character to join them.

Step 5: Convert the extracted semantic query and the post-processed and extracted keywords into a machine-readable JSON format:

```
==== Start of the JSON ====
{
"Semantic Query": Put the extracted semantic query here,
"Keywords": Put the post-processed and extracted keywords as a list [k1, ..., kn]
}
==== End of the JSON ====
```

Have a look at a few examples below:

Example 1:
Query: Find the papers of Jimmy White and Tom Anderson from 2010 to 2020 but not in 2015, published in Nature or Science, on the topic of neuron morphology or machine lerning but not animal behavior, especially related to the statement like: axonal and dendritic arbors as key functional components of neural processing and fundamental determinants of neural circuits.
Keywords: { "Semantic Query": "Axonal and dendritic arbors as key functional components of neural processing and fundamental determinants of neural circuits.", "Keywords": ["Author.FullName:Jimmy White", "Author.FullName:Tom Anderson", "Venue:Nature|Venue:Science", "2010..2020", "!2015", "neuron morphology|machine learning", "!animal behavior"] }

Example 2:
Query: Show me papers of John Wick or Robert Smith, about zebra finch but not zebra fish, published on nature communications or PLOS Biology from 2010 to 2024 but not the year 2018. Especially show me the papers related to the content: Juvenile birds learn from adults.
Keywords: { "Semantic Query": "Juvenile birds learn from adults.", "Keywords": ["Author.FullName:John Wick|Author.FullName:Robert Smith", "Venue:Nature Communications|Venue:PLOS Biology", "2010..2024", "!2018", "zebra finch", "!zebra fish"] }

Example 3:
Query: I want to search for papers related to machine learning and zebra finch, authored by Anja Zai and, from 2020 to 2020.
Keywords: { "Semantic Query": "", "Keywords": ["Author.FullName:Anja Zai", "2020..2022", "machine learning","zebra finch"] }
In Example 3, the query contained no text that can be attributed to semantic query, therefore I set the semantic query as an empty string.

Following the instruction above, please parse the following query text step by step:

Figure 2: Prompt for GPT-4o to parse **Metadata** queries into a structure suitable for SciLit.

I will give you a query text, and your task is to extract a list of keywords that should appear in the retrieved papers according to the query. Have a look at the few examples below:

Example 1:
Query: "Find scientific articles that that include precisely the following set of keywords: 'mechanotransduction', 'photosynthesis', 'Calvin Cycle'. "
Keywords: ['mechanotransduction', 'photosynthesis', 'Calvin Cycle']

Example 2:
Query: "Find scientific articles that that include precisely the following set of keywords: 'red blood cells', 'glucometer', 'diabetes'. "
Keywords: ['red blood cells', 'glucometer', 'diabetes']

Following the instruction above, please parse the following query text step by step:

Figure 3: Prompt for GPT-4o to parse **Content** queries into a structure suitable for SciLit.

ment learning authored by David Silver published in NeurIPS since 2021."

We then benchmarked the performance of Semantic Scholar on **Semantic Scholar Custom** queries without LLM parsing and with LLM parsing in two different versions. Version v1, the structured query had 'query', 'venue', 'year', and 'author' parameters, while version v2 had only 'query', 'venue', and 'year' parameters, while the information corresponding to the author was included in the 'query' parameter.

For version **v1**, we used the prompt in Figure 4.

Example input query: "Find papers on deep reinforcement learning authored by David Silver published in NeurIPS after 2021."

Example output (structured query): {'query': 'deep reinforcement learning', 'venue': 'NeurIPS', 'year': '2021-', 'author': 'David Silver'}

For version **v2**, we used the prompt in Figure 5.

Example input query: "Find papers on deep reinforcement learning authored by David Silver published in NeurIPS since 2021."

Example output (structured query): 'query': 'deep reinforcement learning David Silver', 'venue': 'NeurIPS', 'year': '2021-'

As shown in Table 3, LLM parsing v2 yielded the best performance. Hence, we used this version of parsing for the **Metadata** and **Content** datasets.

	P	R	F1
Semantic Scholar	0.00	0.00	0.00
+ LLM parsing_v1	0.01	0.02	0.01
+ LLM parsing_v2	**0.07**	**0.09**	**0.07**

Table 3: Comparison of Semantic Scholar performance based on benchmark queries from the Semantic Scholar custom dataset. Metrics include **P**recision, **R**ecall, and **F1**.

C LLM parsing into structured queries (Google Scholar)

We parsed the NLQs from **Metadata** into the structure that we speculate is consistent with Google Scholar using GPT-4o with the prompt in Figure 6.

Example input query: "I need papers written by Daniel Sheridan and Probir Chakravarty published after 1999 about pituitary stem cells and their roles in regulation of reproductive functions. "

Example output (structured query): (author:"Daniel Sheridan" AND author:"Probir Chakravarty") "pituitary stem cells" "regulation of reproductive functions" year(2000:)

Then, we transformed each structured query into a URL for Google Scholar by extracting relevant filter parameters and encoding them properly. For the above example, the resulting URL is as follows:

```
https://scholar.google.com/scholar?hl=en&
as_sdt=0%2C5&as_q=%28author%3A%22Daniel%
20Sheridan%22%20AND%20author%3A%22Probir%
20Chakravarty%22%29%20%20%22pituitary%20stem%
20cells%22%20%22regulation%20of%20reproductive%
20functions%22&as_epq=&as_oq=&as_occt=any&as_
sauthors=&as_publication=&as_ylo=2000
```

For **Content**, we followed Appendix A.

D Content Dataset - Expanded Query

For each keyword combination in the **Content** dataset, an expanded query was constructed as follows: "Give me the papers in {domain} on the topic of {topic} that contain precisely the following keywords: {keywords}". Domain and Topic were manually specified for each query given the key-

I will give you a text that describes how I want to query the scientific literature database. You task is to parse and extract (1) the semantic query, and (2) the filter parameters from the text. Follow these steps:

Step 1: Extract filter parameters that should be used as filters on the papers to be returned. If a filter parameter is described as a term to be avoided, do not extract it. For each of the three filter parameters types below, extract the corresponding information and process it as follows:
1. venue: Identify all publication venues, conferences, or journal names mentioned, then concatenate them with commas but no spaces.
2. year: Identify the first requirement on publication year mentioned. If exactly one year is described, then extract just the year. If a range of years is described, then express the range by in the form "start-end". If only the start year is described, then write it as "start-", and if only the end year is described, then write it as "-end".
3. author: Identify all author names mentioned and concatenate them with commas but no spaces.

Step 2: Identify the semantic query. This refers to any part of the text describes what the papers of interest should be about, and it may be words, phrases, sentences, or paragraphs. It should include all meaningful phrases that were not extracted above. If no semantic query is described in the text, then set the semantic query as an empty string "".

Step 3: Put the semantic query and the processed filter parameters together into a machine-readable JSON object:
==== Start of the JSON ====
{
"query": Put the extracted semantic query here,
"venue": Put the extracted venue requirement here,
"year": Put the extracted year requirement here,
"author": Put the extracted author requirement here
}
==== End of the JSON ====

Here are a few examples:

Example 1:
Query: Find the papers of Jimmy White and Tom Anderson published in Nature or Science in 2010, on the topic of neuron morphology or machine learning but not animal behavior, especially related to the statement like: axonal and dendritic arbors as key functional components of neural processing and fundamental determinants of neural circuits.
Output: {
"query": "Axonal and dendritic arbors as key functional components of neural processing and fundamental determinants of neural circuits neuron morphology machine learning",
"year": "2010",
"venue": "Nature,Science",
"author": "Jimmy White,Tom Anderson
}

Example 2:
Query: Show me papers of John Wick and Robert Smith, about zebra finch but not zebra fish, published in nature communications or PLOS Biology before 2020. Especially show me the papers related to the content: Juvenile birds learn from adults.
Output: {
"query": "Juvenile birds learn from adults zebra finch",
"venue": "Nature Communications,PLOS Biology"
"year": "-2019",
"author": "John Wick,Robert Smith"
}

Example 3:
Query: I want to search for papers related to machine learning and biomedical applications, authored by Yoshua Bengio since 2023.
Output: {
"query": "machine learning and biomedical applications",
"venue": "",
"year": "2023-",
"author": "Yoshua Bengio"
}
Following the instructions above, please parse the following query description text:

Figure 4: Prompt for GPT-4o to parse **Custom** queries into a structure suitable for Semantic Scholar, version 1.

I will give you a text that describes how I want to query the scientific literature database. You task is to parse and extract (1) the semantic query, and (2) the keywords from the text. Follow these steps:

Step 1: Extract keywords that should be used as filters on the papers to be returned. If a keyword is described as a term to be avoided, do not extract it. For each of the three keyword types below, extract the corresponding information and process it as follows:
1. venue: Identify all publication venues, conferences, or journal names mentioned, then concatenate them with commas but no spaces.
2. year: Identify the first requirement on publication year mentioned. If exactly one year is described, then extract just the year. If a range of years is described, then express the range by in the form "start-end". If only the start year is described, then write it as "start-", and if only the end year is described, then write it as "-end".

Step 2: Identify the semantic query. This refers to any part of the text describes what the papers of interest should be about, and it may be words, phrases, sentences, or paragraphs. It should include all meaningful phrases that were not extracted above. If no semantic query is described in the text, then set the semantic query as an empty string "".

Step 3: Put the semantic query and the processed keywords together into a machine-readable JSON object:
==== Start of the JSON ====
{
"query": Put the extracted semantic query here.
"venue": Put the extracted venue requirement here.
"year": Put the extracted year requirement here.
}
==== End of the JSON ====

Here are a few examples:

Example 1:
Query: Find the papers of Jimmy White and Tom Anderson published in Nature or Science in 2010, on the topic of neuron morphology or machine learning but not animal behavior, especially related to the statement like: axonal and dendritic arbors as key functional components of neural processing and fundamental determinants of neural circuits.
Output: {
"query": "Axonal and dendritic arbors as key functional components of neural processing and fundamental determinants of neural circuits Jimmy White Tom Anderson neuron morphology machine learning",
"year": "2010",
"venue": "Nature,Science",
}

Example 2:
Query: Show me papers of John Wick or Robert Smith, about zebra finch but not zebra fish, published in nature communications or PLOS Biology before 2020. Especially show me the papers related to the content: Juvenile birds learn from adults.
Output: {
"query": "Juvenile birds learn from adults John Wick Robert Smith zebra finch",
"venue": "Nature Communications,PLOS Biology"
"year": "-2019",
}

Example 3:
Query: I want to search for papers related to machine learning and biomedical applications, authored by Yoshua Bengio since 2023.
Output: {
"query": "machine learning and biomedical applications Yoshua Bengio",
"venue": "",
"year": "2023-"
}

Following the instructions above, please parse the following query description text step by step:

Figure 5: Prompt for GPT-4o to parse **Custom** queries into a structure suitable for Semantic Scholar, version 2.

Help me translate natural language queries into structured format required by Google Scholar. Follow these steps:

Step 1: First, extract author information from the query (if there is any). Use author's name, and prepend it with 'author:'. For example: 'author:Jones'.
If the query specifies two authors with AND operation, specify that as follows: (author:"Gao" AND author:"Gu").
If the query specifies two authors with OR operation, specify that as follows: (author:"Gupta" OR author:"Srivastava").

Step 2: Then, extract venue information from the query (if there is any).
Prepend it with 'source:'. For example: 'source:Nature'. If the query specifies two venues with OR operation, specify that as follows: (source:"Science" OR source:"Nature").

Step 3: Then, extract year information from the query (if there is any).
If the query specifies a years range, specify that as follows: year(2020:2022). If the query specifies a given year, specify that as follows: year(2015).
If the query specifies upper (inclusive) bound for year, specify that as follows: year(:2000).
If the query specifies lower (inclusive) bound for year, specify that as follows: year(2015:).

Step 4: Then, extract keywords from the query (if there are any). Put them inside double quotation mark, for example "quantum mechanics".
If there is an OR operation, specify this as follows: ("deep learning" OR "reinforcement learning").
If there is AND operation, specify it as follows: "diabetes" "glucometer".

Step 5: In addition, you can include NOT operation using a dash in the following way: -"dataset" (when we want to exclude papers containing the keywords "dataset").
You can also use the NOT operation for year: -year:2009 (excludes papers published in 2009).
You can use the NOT operation for author: (author:"Johns" -author:"Smiths") (when you want to retrieve papers written by Johns but excluding the ones co-authored by Smiths).
You can use the NOT operation for venue: -source:"arXiv" (when you want to exclude papers published in arXiv).

Step 6: Finally, concatenate all conditions into one structured queries using a single space to separate different parameters.

Have a look at the few examples below:

Example 1:
Query: Find papers authored by Saleska and Mackelprang between 2013 and 2020, particularly the ones mentioning permafrost and Arctic environments.
Target output: (author:"Saleska" AND author:"Mackelprang") year(2013:2020) "permafrost" "Arctic environments"

Example 2:
Query: Find papers published in Science or Nature about deep learning or reinforcement learning.
Target output: (source:"Science" OR source:"Nature") ("deep learning" OR "reinforcement learning")

Example 3:
Query: Give me papers written by Yuriy Portnov, published in International Journal of Geometric Methods in Modern Physics, about black holes or dark matter.
Target output: author:"Yuriy Portnov" source:"International Journal of Geometric Methods in Modern Physics" ("black holes" OR "dark matter")

Following the instructions above, please parse the following query description text step by step:

Figure 6: Prompt for GPT-4o to parse **Metadata** queries into a structure suitable for Google Scholar.

word combination. Example: "Give me research papers in Biotechnology on the topic of Enzyme Engineering that contain precisely the following keywords: 'Metalloenzyme catalysis', 'directed evolution', 'biofuel production'. "

The retrieval results obtained with the expanded query are summarized in Table 4.

Method	P	R	F1
Google Scholar	**0.56**	**0.30**	**0.37**
Elicit	0.05	0.10	0.06
Zeta-Alpha	0.52	0.28	0.34
Consensus	0.02	0.08	0.03
Perplexity	0.12	0.11	0.10
Floatz	0.04	0.02	0.03
GPT-4o	0.17	0.15	0.14
Semantic Scholar	0.00	0.00	0.00
SciLit	0.00	0.00	0.00

Table 4: Performance of search engines based on **Content** dataset with expanded queries in terms of **P**recision, **R**ecall, and **F1**. Metrics exclude hallucinated papers.

E Search Engines

The majority of the platforms included in our analysis are not open-source and do not fully disclose the details of their underlying databases or search algorithms. As a result, our descriptions are based on publicly available information and general observations about their functionality rather than a complete technical breakdown of their inner workings.

- **Google Scholar** is a widely used academic search engine that indexes scholarly literature from a vast array of sources, including publisher websites, institutional repositories, preprint servers, and open-access archives. While its exact database composition is proprietary, it continuously crawls and aggregates research papers, theses, books, and conference proceedings. For search, it primarily performs a keyword-based search, supporting Boolean operators, phrase searches, and field-specific queries. Beyond simple keywords matching, Google Scholar incorporates citation-based ranking to prioritize influential papers. Additionally, it employs semantic search techniques to understand the query intent and retrieve conceptually relevant papers (Mallapaty, 2024).

- **Semantic Scholar** primarily uses the Semantic Scholar Open Research Corpus (S2ORC) (Lo et al., 2020) as its database. Unlike traditional keyword-based search engines, it leverages Machine Learning to enhance search relevance and understanding. When a user submits a query, Semantic Scholar applies keyword-based search, citation analysis, and semantic search techniques to retrieve the most relevant papers. It ranks the results based on factors like citation count, influence score, and content similarity, rather than just exact keyword matches.

- **Consensus** leverages the same database as Semantic Scholar, updating it on a monthly basis. For paper searching, it integrates LLMs with a specialized Vector Search system. When a user enters a textual query into the chatbot interface, the input undergoes preprocessing (e.g., stopword removal). Subsequently, a hybrid approach combining keyword search and Vector Search is applied to the abstracts and titles of all papers in the database to determine a relevance score for each document. This score is then refined using additional metadata, such as citation count, study design, and publication date, to re-rank the results and generate a final list of the top 10 most relevant papers.

- **Perplexity** uses LLMs like GPT-4o[15] and Claude 3[16] to interpret the context and nuances of user queries. After a user enters a query, the query is first passed through an LLM. Then, a real-time web search is conducted, retrieving information from sources such as as articles, websites, and academic journals. The extracted insights are then synthesised into a response. Following, citations to sources are added to the output text, enabling users to verify information.

- **SciLit** is the only fully open-source platform in our analysis. It utilizes multiple scientific text corpora (S2ORC (Lo et al., 2020), PMCOA[17], arXiv[18], bioArxiv[19], and medRxiv[20]), structuring each corpus as a separate SQLite database. It indexes research papers using

[15] https://openai.com/index/hello-gpt-4o/

[16] https://claude.ai/

[17] https://healthdata.gov/dataset/PubMed-Central-Open-Access-Subset-PMC-OA-/3vwy-a2x4/about_data

[18] https://info.arxiv.org/help/bulk_data.html

[19] https://www.biorxiv.org/tdm

[20] https://www.medrxiv.org/

both an inverted index for keyword-based retrieval and an embedding index for semantic search. SciLit first applies Boolean filtering to refine results based on keywords, and then ranks the filtered papers by computing cosine similarity between their Sent2Vec (Moghadasi and Zhuang, 2020) embeddings and the user query. Finally, SciBERT (Beltagy et al., 2019) is used for re-ranking, ensuring that the most relevant papers appear at the top.

- **Elicit** utilizes the Semantic Scholar database, updating the collection weekly with newly added research papers. Unlike traditional search engines, it does not rely on keyword-based queries or controlled vocabulary. Instead, users are encouraged to input full research questions, such as "How does iron supplementation affect anemia?". Upon receiving a query, Elicit retrieves the eight most relevant papers and extracts key insights or variables based on user preferences (Kung, 2023).

- **Floatz** integrates with a wide range of open-source databases and publisher sources, including Elsevier[21], Clarivate[22], PubMed[23], and preprint repositories. If a specific paper is not available in its databases, it leverages integrations like OpenAlex[24] to retrieve the necessary information. While details about its search functionality are limited, Floatz combines LLMs, semantic search, indexing, and knowledge-building algorithms to process user queries effectively.

- **Zeta-Alpha** operates on its own indexed database, incorporating sources such as arXiv, conference proceedings, blogs, and GitHub repositories. Additionally, users can upload their own documents and references, which are then indexed using the platform's neural search technology. For search, Zeta-Alpha employs a hybrid approach that combines traditional keyword-based search - supporting Boolean operators, phrase searches, and field-specific queries - with neural vector search and fine-tuned LLMs, such as Zeta-Alpha-E5-Mistral[25].

- **GPT-4o** Unlike other platforms in our analysis, GPT-4o is a general-purpose AI model designed for a wide range of tasks, not specifically for retrieving scientific literature. It does not index or query academic databases like Google Scholar or Semantic Scholar but instead generates responses based on pre-trained knowledge.

F Implementation details

We used the free versions of all listed platforms, entering each query manually into their search interfaces and recording the retrieved papers. For chatbot-based search systems, paper titles were manually extracted from the responses. If a chatbot found no exact matches but suggested alternatives, we labeled it as "no paper retrieved." No platform-specific filters were applied to ensure evaluation was based solely on NLQs.

For search engines like *Consensus* and *Elicit*, which returned many papers, we analyzed only papers appearing before pressing the "Load More" or "More Results" buttons, which is 10 papers at most. Documents other than research papers, such as books, reviews, and theses, were excluded.

[21] https://www.elsevier.com/
[22] https://mjl.clarivate.com/home
[23] https://pubmed.ncbi.nlm.nih.gov/
[24] https://openalex.org/
[25] https://huggingface.co/zeta-alpha-ai/Zeta-Alpha-E5-Mistral

Literature-Grounded Novelty Assessment of Scientific Ideas

Simra Shahid[1] **Marissa Radensky**[2] **Raymond Fok**[2]
Pao Siangliulue[3] **Daniel S. Weld**[3] **Tom Hope**[3]
[1]Microsoft [2]University of Washington [3]Allen Institute for AI
simrashahid@microsoft.com {radensky, rayfok}@cs.washington.edu
{paos, danw, tomh}@allenai.org

Abstract

Automated scientific idea generation systems have made remarkable progress, yet the automatic evaluation of idea novelty remains a critical and underexplored challenge. Manual evaluation of novelty through literature review is labor-intensive, prone to error due to subjectivity, and impractical at scale. To address these issues, we propose the **Idea Novelty Checker**, an LLM-based retrieval-augmented generation (RAG) framework that leverages a two-stage retrieve-then-rerank approach. The Idea Novelty Checker first collects a broad set of relevant papers using keyword and snippet-based retrieval, then refines this collection through embedding-based filtering followed by facet-based LLM re-ranking. It incorporates expert-labeled examples to guide the system in comparing papers for novelty evaluation and in generating literature-grounded reasoning. Our extensive experiments demonstrate that our novelty checker achieves approximately 13% higher agreement than existing approaches. Ablation studies further showcases the importance of the facet-based re-ranker in identifying the most relevant literature for novelty evaluation.

1 Introduction

Novelty evaluation is foundational for determining whether ideas in scientific research, product development, or creative ideation introduce meaningful innovation relative to prior work. Yet, as the volume of published literature grows exponentially, manual verification of originality becomes impractical. This is further complicated by the inherent subjectivity of novelty judgments, which is why experts can more easily decide on similarity of two ideas (Picard et al., 2023) and often struggle to articulate why one idea is more novel than another. Further the evaluation becomes subjective as it also depends on personal knowledge and intuition gained from scientific literature (Ahmed et al., 2018; Picard et al., 2023).

Automated systems attempt to address this challenge by defining novelty as differences observed while comparing new ideas against prior work with similarity measures, but they exhibit critical limitations. Prior work has evolved from using n-gram frequency and lexical metrics (TF-IDF, LDA) (Wang et al., 2019; Sarica et al., 2019) to semantic embeddings (G'omez-P'erez et al., 2022; Su et al., 2024) that capture similarity but don't capture paraphrased variations of ideas and papers. Moreover, while recent approaches have adopted LLM-augmented pipelines to generate numerical scores (1-10) (Bougie and Watanabe, 2024; Wang et al., 2024) or provide binary classifications (novel versus not novel) (Lu et al., 2024; Li et al., 2024; Si et al., 2024; Su et al., 2024), they do not ground the rationales in existing works and frequently fail to capture subtle variations in phrasing, resulting in the misclassification of well-documented ideas as novel (Beel et al., 2025; Gupta and Pruthi, 2025). This shortcoming makes it difficult for researchers to distinguish novel ideas from incremental contributions or subtle cases of plagiarism (Gupta and Pruthi, 2025).

Moreover, all these approaches hinge on the successful retrieval of relevant literature for a given idea, a task that remains inherently challenging (Mysore et al., 2022; Mysore et al.; Stevenson and Merlo, 2022; Eger et al., 2019; Xu et al., 2014; Freestone and Karmaker, 2024). Prior works (Si et al., 2024; Lu et al., 2024) extract keywords from the idea to search for papers, so important work can easily be missed if the relevant paper does not have the exact keyword. This undermines the reliability of the novelty evaluation process.

We address these gaps with Idea Novelty Checker, a retrieval-augmented LLM pipeline that assesses an idea's novelty by comparing it to a set of the most relevant papers. First, Idea Novelty Checkercollects a broad set of relevant papers using keyword and snippet-based retrieval, as well as

Proceedings of the Fifth Workshop on Scholarly Document Processing (SDP 2025), pages 96–113
July 31, 2025 ©2025 Association for Computational Linguistics

by retrieving papers similar to any seed papers provided. Next, an embedding-based similarity search filters this large collection, and a facet-based LLM re-ranker (Sun et al., 2023b) further narrows the set by comparing idea facets (purpose, mechanism, evaluation, and application) with those in the retrieved papers. Finally, expert-annotated in-context examples of *novel* and *not novel* ideas guide the system in generating literature-grounded rationales, mitigating subjectivity in novelty judgments.

In our experiments, we compared Idea Novelty Checkerwith baselines such as zero-shot prompting, prompt optimization approaches (DSPY and TextGRAD), and expert-based OpenReview examples. Our results show that expert-annotated in-context examples significantly improve classification performance. Comparisons with systems like AI Scientist and AI Researcher further demonstrate that our Idea Novelty Checkerachieves higher agreement with expert judgments, and our ablation studies shows that the combined retrieval and two-stage re-ranking are critical for identifying the most relevant papers.

Our contributions are as follows:

- We introduce Idea Novelty Checker, a retrieval-augmented LLM pipeline that automatically evaluates the novelty of scientific ideas. We plan to release our code and expert-collected data[1] to support work in automatic scientific discovery and provide literature-grounded novelty evaluations.
- We conducted a formative study in which experts evaluated ideas for novelty. The study revealed two key challenges to consider for novelty evaluation: clarifying what constitutes novelty given its subjectivity, and identifying relevant literature to assess it. This directly shaped the design of Idea Novelty Checker.
- Our method integrates keyword-based and snippet-based retrieval, followed by a two-stage re-ranker with embedding similarity and facet-based LLM re-ranking to identify key literature related to the given idea.
- We present extensive evaluations, ablation studies, and qualitative analyses that demonstrate the effectiveness of our novelty checker over existing approaches. Additionally, we discuss prompt sensitivity in LLMs for novelty evaluation further highlighting the importance of clear novelty definitions.

[1]anonymous.4open.science/r/idea_novelty_checker

2 Related Work

Automated approaches to novelty assessment in scientific literature have evolved considerably. Early methods relied on lexical similarity metrics, such as TF-IDF, LSA, and LDA (Wang et al., 2019; Sarica et al., 2019), but these techniques struggled to capture paraphrased concepts. Semantic embedding methods (G'omez-P'erez et al., 2022) improved on this by identifying deeper relationships, yet they are confined to surface-level comparisons (Mysore et al., 2022; Mysore et al.).

Retrieval-augmented LLM systems have emerged as a promising alternative, evaluating novelty either on a numerical scale (e.g., 1–10) (Bougie and Watanabe, 2024; Wang et al., 2024) or with binary classification (Li et al., 2024; Lu et al., 2024). AI Researcher (Si et al., 2024) uses a Swiss-system tournament ranking to compare ideas pairwise for *similarity* and *novelty* against individual papers. If any comparison has sufficient similarity, the idea is not novel. Another notable work is AI Scientist (Lu et al., 2024) that employs an iterative process in which an LLM generates queries from a research idea to retrieve relevant papers via the Semantic Scholar API (Kinney et al., 2023). The LLM then compares the idea against these papers until a clear decision is reached or a preset iteration limit is met. However, this approach has several limitations. First, it depends on keyword-based retrieval methods to get the most relevant papers to an idea, which may fail if the relevant papers do not contain the exact keywords. Second, comparing an idea against a large number of retrieved papers (sometimes over 100) can introduce known issues that LLMs often overlook instructions within a prompt (Loya et al., 2023; Sclar et al., 2024; Joshi et al., 2024). Finally, the decision of novelty evaluation relies on string matching for phrases like "decision made: novel" or "decision made: not novel." If such a decision is not reached, the idea is automatically considered novel. Independent evaluations (Beel et al., 2025) have further highlighted challenges in AI Scientist's novelty assessments, noting that the system can misclassify well-established concepts (micro-batching for stochastic gradient descent) as novel.

Our work builds on these insights by combining retrieval-then-rerank methods (Zhou et al., 2022; Naik et al., 2021) and uses expert-annotated examples to ensure that our novelty evaluations are grounded in the relevant literature.

3 Formative Study on Challenges in Evaluating Novelty

Evaluating idea novelty in scientific literature is inherently challenging because the criteria for novelty are subjective and can be defined in multiple ways. We conducted a formative study, referred to as the expert-annotated study throughout the paper, where the first and second authors reviewed the novelty of ideas based on the most relevant papers.

To assess idea novelty relative to existing literature, our study engaged experts who evaluated 51 ideas, comprising of 46 generated by the Scideator system (Radensky et al., 2024) and 5 adapted from accepted and rejected papers from OpenReview (ICLR 22, NeurIPS 23).[2] Each idea was classified into one of three categories: novel, moderately novel, or not novel. For every idea, we identified the most relevant papers through a two-step process: candidate papers were initially gathered using keyword-based queries and subsequently re-ranked using an LLM-based reranker (Sun et al., 2023b) according to their overall relevance to the idea.

The experts achieved a moderate agreement (Cohen's Kappa = 0.64). A key challenge identified was that experts sometimes relied on their broader domain knowledge rather than restricting their judgments to the most relevant papers, as the top papers alone were often not sufficient. Additionally, using three categories led to disagreements, as the distinction between novel and moderate novelty is itself subjective.

Building on these observations, we conducted a second study to minimize the influence of external knowledge. In this study, experts were instructed to base their judgments solely on the provided papers, and the categories were simplified to just two: novel and not novel.

Inspired by prior work (Portenoy et al., 2022; Kang et al., 2022; Chan et al., 2018; Suh et al., 2024; Srinivasan and Chan, 2024; Choi et al., 2024; Kang et al., 2024; Radensky et al., 2024) that categorizes research ideas into core facets such as purpose (the problem being addressed by the paper) and mechanism (the proposed solution to the problem), we define novelty as follows: An idea is considered novel if it differs from all retrieved papers in at least one core facet for the topic at hand—namely, purpose (i.e., a distinct objective), mechanism (i.e., a distinct technical approach), or evaluation (i.e., a distinct validation method). An idea is also considered novel if it uniquely combines these facets or applies them to a new application domain.

Using this controlled framework, we reannotated a set of ideas and evaluated 51 ideas, comprising of 34 new ones generated by Radensky et al. (2024) and 17 from the previous study where external knowledge had influenced novelty judgments. By narrowing the focus to the relevant papers alone, we observed fewer disagreements and achieved a higher agreement rate (Cohen's Kappa = 0.68). Of the 8 instances of disagreement, in 4 cases one expert overlooked details from the paper, in 2 cases the experts differed in their perception of subtle contributions to novelty, and in the remaining 2 cases no specific comments were provided.

This formative study highlights that a robust novelty checker depends critically on high-quality retrieval and a well-defined notion of novelty. These findings directly inform our methodology described in the following section.

4 Methodology: Idea Novelty Checker

Based on our formative study findings, our novelty checker is designed with two key components that address the two critical challenges: C1 ensuring high-quality retrieval of papers relevant to the idea for novelty assessment and C2 establishing clear criteria for judging novelty. The challenge C1 arises from the vast space of overlapping papers—there are hundreds of millions of potential matches. To address this, our system first filters the scientific literature to collect the most relevant papers for a given idea (see Section 4.1 and Step 1 and 2 in Figure 1). The input idea is then compared to each paper in this collection by prompting an LLM (see Section 4.2).

In tackling challenge C2, which arises from the inherent subjectivity and multiple definitions of novelty, the novelty checker leverages expert-labeled examples of *novel* and *not novel* ideas from the formative study. It generates reasoning grounded not only in comparisons against the most relevant papers but also in the standardized definition of novelty introduced earlier, which helps counteract subjectivity (see Step 3 in Figure 1). Below, we detail these two components.

[2] Fewer examples were taken from OpenReview since the primary focus was on evaluating ideas from Scideator.

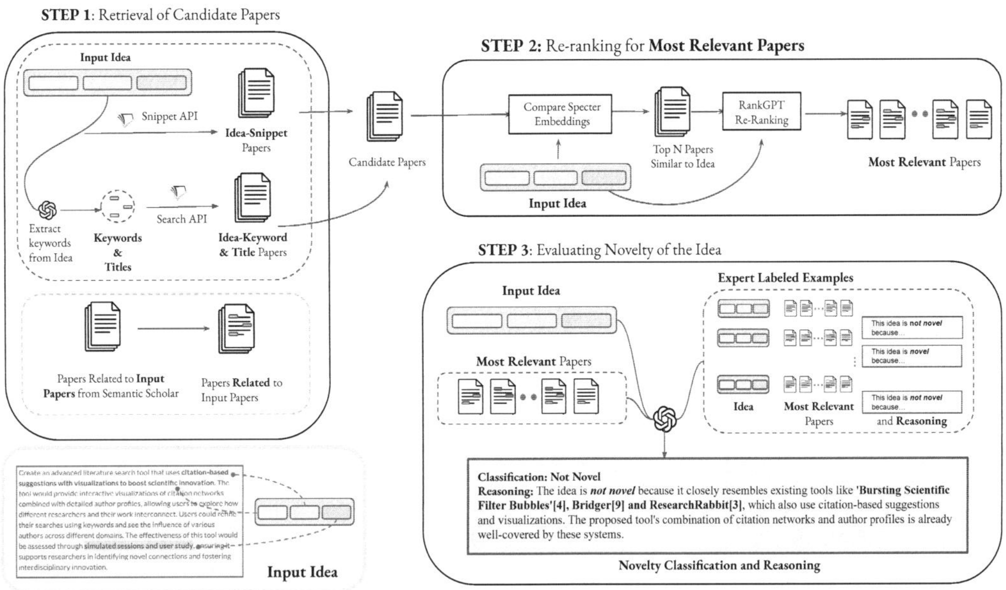

Figure 1: Our Idea Novelty Checker follows a retrieve-then-rerank approach for novelty evaluation. First, it gathers a broad set of papers relevant to an idea using query expansion (extracting keywords and titles from the idea) and snippet search (using the entire idea as input). Optionally, if seed papers are provided, we retrieve papers similar to these seed papers. Next, a two-stage re-ranking process is applied, where an embedding-based ranking strategy filters the large collection to top-N papers, followed by a facet-based LLM re-ranker to identify the top-k most relevant papers. Finally, these top-k papers are used to assess the idea's novelty, guided by in-context examples that evaluate novelty with grounded reasoning.

4.1 Most Relevant Papers to Idea

Following established information retrieval practices (Gao et al., 2024; Nouriinanloo and Lamothe, 2024; Abdallah et al., 2025; Meng et al., 2024; Sun et al., 2023a; Baldelli et al., 2024), our pipeline uses a two-phase approach for identifying the most relevant papers to a given idea. First, we gather a broad set of candidate papers related to the idea. Then, we re-rank these candidates in two steps: first using embedding-based similarity, and then applying LLM-based re-ranking to facet-based similarity.

STEP 1: Retrieval of Candidate Papers

To accurately assess the novelty of an idea, it is crucial to compare it against a comprehensive collection of papers that cover the various facets of the idea. For a given idea and its corresponding papers (if any) used to generate the idea, we find more related papers to these input seed papers using the Semantic Scholar API [3]. However, simple retrieval methods often overlook important aspects of an idea (Mysore et al., 2022; Wang et al., 2023). To improve the paper collection's coverage we follow (Lu et al., 2024; Si et al., 2024) and employ a query-based retrieval method, where search queries are generated corresponding to different keywords related to the idea, and queried through the Semantic Scholar Search API (Kinney et al., 2023). Corresponding to each search query, papers are added to the collection of relevant papers. We prompt the LLM (LLM_{query}) to generate these search queries based on the keywords and potential titles related to the idea.

Next, we also employ Semantic Scholar's snippet search[4], which is trained to identify similar snippets (approximately 500 words of text) in other papers. We leverage the context size of this retrieval mechanism by incorporating the entire idea into the snippet search. Finally, we combine the seed papers and their related works with the papers retrieved from the two Semantic Scholar based query-retrieval method. This combined set form the candidate papers for the ideation process.

[3]api.semanticscholar.org/api-docs/recommendations

[4]api.semanticscholar.org/api-docs/#tag/Snippet-Text

STEP 2: Re-ranking for Most Relevant Papers To identify the papers most likely to overlap with the candidate idea, we implement a two-stage re-ranking process that combines embedding-based filtering with an LLM-based re-ranking approach. To identify the papers most likely to overlap with the candidate idea, we implement a two-stage re-ranking process that combines embedding-based filtering with an LLM-based re-ranking approach.

First, we employ **embedding-based filtering** to compute the semantic similarity between the idea and each paper in our collection of papers from STEP 1. We select the top N papers with the highest cosine similarity between their embeddings and the idea embedding. While this embedding-based ranking efficiently narrows down the collection of papers, it is limited in its capacity to capture deeper and more contextual relationships between different facets of the idea and the papers, in comparison to powerful state-of-art LLMs (Reimers and Gurevych, 2019).

To address these limitations we employ a popularly used **LLM-based re-ranker**, RankGPT (Sun et al., 2023b), which refines the initial ranking of candidate papers by examining how relevant each paper is to the idea. We change relevance criteria to match it with each key facet of the idea. RankGPT goes beyond simple surface similarities by comparing the papers against the idea's application domain, purpose, mechanism, and evaluation. It follows a clear set of priorities: first, it favors papers that match all key facets of the idea; then, it prefers those that align with the application domain and purpose; next, it considers papers that share similarities in purpose, mechanism, or evaluation; and finally, it ranks lower those that only partially match or address related facets. This approach ensures that the final ranking accurately reflects the relevance and depth of each paper in connection with the idea. We refer to the LLM used for RankGPT as ($LLM_{rankgpt}$).

This collection of k-most relevant papers is used by the novelty checker in the next step to evaluate the idea's novelty.

4.2 Idea Novelty Evaluation

To assess an idea's novelty, we prompt an LLM ($LLM_{novelty}$) with both the idea and its top-k relevant papers. The LLM outputs a binary classification (novel or not novel) accompanied by reasoning based on the top-k retrieved literature. To guide the LLM's judgment, we include $n_{examples}$ in-context examples drawn from our formative study, where $n_{examples}$ is treated as a hyperparameter. These examples reflect the experts' criteria for novelty: an idea is considered novel if it differs from all retrieved papers in at least one core facet—namely, purpose (i.e., objective of idea), mechanism (i.e., technical approach), evaluation (i.e., validation method), a unique combination of these facets, or if it applies the same facets to a new application domain.

5 Implementation & Baselines

Dataset: From our formative study, we collected 67 consensus-labeled examples (39 labeled as novel and 28 as non-novel). We split into training and test sets (35 for training and 32 for testing) with a balanced distribution of novel and non-novel ideas. Please refer to Table 4 in the Appendix for sample examples.

Baselines: We evaluated multiple baselines to benchmark our novelty assessment approach. First, we employed a zero-shot prompt as a straightforward baseline, and further refined this manually written prompt using Anthropic's prompt generator[5]. We also applied popular prompt optimization techniques such as DSPy (Khattab et al., 2023) and TextGRAD (Yuksekgonul et al., 2024), which optimize the prompt instructions using a train/validation split created from formative study examples.

As an alternative to using in-context examples from the formative study, we extracted reviews from ICLR and NeurIPS submissions via the OpenReview API (OpenReview). These reviews comprise aspects such as *strengths, presentation, limitations, soundness, weaknesses, questions, confidence, contribution, summary,* and *rating*. The input title and abstract were adapted to match the ideas in the training data using a style-change prompt[6]. After rigorous filtering, we identified approximately 8,156 submissions discussing idea novelty and manually selected reviews that specifically evaluated the core idea rather than the entire paper. From these, we randomly sampled 20 idea-review pairs to serve as an additional baseline with different in-context examples.

In addition to these baselines, we also compare our novelty checker '*prompt*' with that of AI Sci-

[5]https://docs.anthropic.com/en/docs/build-with-claude/prompt-engineering/prompt-generator

[6]All prompts are provided in the anonymised codebase.

entist (Lu et al., 2024) (different from its paper reviewer) and AI Researcher (Si et al., 2024) on the same test set of ideas and fixed top 10 papers. We compare **only the prompts to assess novelty** of these two approaches with ours, rather than the entire system, because the test set containing the novelty judgments by experts were based on a fixed set of the 10 most relevant papers for each idea. Since different retrieval methods could introduce new papers and potentially change novelty classification, we standardize the most relevant papers to ensure a fair comparison of the prompts alone. Additionally, since both setups require a different style of input idea, we adapted the ideas to match the requirements of each system.

Implementation Settings: For our novelty evaluation system, we use SPECTER-2 (Cohan et al., 2020) as the default embedding model. Initially, we retrieve the top N =100 papers using these embeddings, from which the top k =10 most relevant papers are selected for comparison with the input idea. The default language model for the idea keyword extraction (LLM_{query}), re-ranking process ($LLM_{rankgpt}$), and novelty evaluation ($LLM_{novelty}$) is gpt-4o[7]. Expert-labeled data from the formative study is incorporated as in-context examples in the novelty checker. We experimented with various numbers of in-context examples (comprising idea-paper pairs along with their novelty class and reviews) and found that the best performance was achieved using 15 idea examples (random seed 100). For the OpenReview examples, the best setup involved 5 idea-review pairs. For DSPy we used 2 bootstrapped examples, and trained both DSPy and TextGRAD for 12 prompt iterations.

6 Experiments

In this section, we first compare different baselines on the dataset for novelty evaluations (Section 6.1). Next we present our findings from ablation studies that shows the imporance of each component in our approach (Section 6.2). ablations studies We supplement these findings with qualitative examples of expert-labeled ideas and compare our setup with recent novelty checkers (Section 6.3). We conclude with insights from prompt optimization experiments that highlights the sensitivity of LLMs to prompt variations for novelty evaluation tasks (Section 6.4).

[7]We used the model "gpt-4o" during August and September 2024.

6.1 Comparing Novelty Checker Prompts

Our experiments show that incorporating expert-annotated data as in-context examples significantly enhances novelty classification accuracy compared to zero-shot prompts, DSPY, TextGRAD, and setups using OpenReview examples (Table 1).Since OpenReview reviews do not reference the associated papers, we evaluated our expert-labeled examples both with and without including relevant papers to ensure a fair comparison. Notably, even when we excluded the relevant papers from the expert-labeled examples, our approach still outperformed the OpenReview baseline.

Additionally, we compared two configurations for DSPY, one with reasoning and one without. Our expert-labeled prompt consistently achieved higher performance than the prompt optimizations produced by these methods, and we posit that the number of examples for train/validation were not sufficient for prompt optimisers with gpt-4o. The TextGRAD prompt optimiser did not improve upon its initial system prompt. It provided valuable insights into the LLM's prompt sensitivity, which we further discuss in Section 6.4.

Our approach achieved over **10 times more agreement with expert-labeled examples** compared to AI Scientist, and **approximately 13% higher agreement** than AI Researcher, further validating the effectiveness of our novelty checker. It is important to note that AI Scientist defaults to "not novel" when it fails to reach a conclusion in novelty evaluation (18 out of 32 times), which may have impacted its agreement rates. We also present some qualitative examples in Figures 2, 3 and 4 of the Appendix, showcasing how these approaches evaluate the novelty of an idea.

6.2 Ablation Studies

Setup: To assess the contribution of each component in our novelty checker, we conducted ablation studies using 58 ideas (comprising 13 'not novel' instances from our test set and 45 NLP papers from the literature). For this experiment, we focus on the 'not novel' cases, since the ideas labeled novel in expert-labeled test data can vary with different retrieved paper sets. In our ablations, we considered the following variations: (i) **Complete System:** Uses both keyword and snippet retrieval (each returning the top-k documents based on Semantic Scholar's ranking), embedding filtering, and facet-based RankGPT re-ranking; (ii) **RankGPT Rele-**

Models	Accuracy	Precision	Recall	F1	Cohen Kappa
Zero Shot Setting					
Zero Shot	0.68	0.76	0.64	0.65	-
+ improved prompt using Anthropic prompt generator	0.68	0.70	0.64	0.64	-
Prompt Optimizers					
DSPy					
- with idea, most relevant papers, class	0.68	0.83	0.62	0.58	-
- with idea, most relevant papers, class, reasoning	0.66	0.82	0.58	0.52	
TextGRAD					
- with idea, most relevant papers, class	0.78	0.76	0.76	0.76	-
In-context Setting					
Open-Review Examples					
- with idea & review (i.e., reasoning)	0.59	0.55	0.51	0.43	-
Expert Labeled Examples					
- with idea, reasoning	0.75	0.76	0.77	0.75	-
- with idea, most relevant papers, class	0.78	0.77	0.76	0.77	-
- with idea, most relevant papers, class, reasoning	0.81	0.84	0.78	0.79	0.59
Other Novelty Checkers					
AI Scientist (Lu et al., 2024)	0.47	0.55	0.53	0.44	0.05
AI Researcher (Si et al., 2024)					
- GPT-4o	0.78	0.81	0.74	0.75	0.52
- CLAUDE-3-5-SONNET	0.56	0.63	0.61	0.56	0.19

Table 1: Experimental Results using gpt-4o on expert-annotated dataset.

vance: Used the same retrieval methods (keyword and snippet) plus embedding filtering, but replaced the facet-based RankGPT re-ranker with one based on general relevance (Sun et al., 2023b). This variation differs from the complete system only in the LLM re-ranking component, allowing us to assess the importance of facet-based re-ranking; (iii) **Embedding Filtering:** Omits the LLM re-ranker entirely, relying only on the embedding-based filtering. This setup allows us to assess the importance of the LLM re-ranking step; and (iv) **Snippet Retrieval** and **Keyword Retrieval**: Each of these setups returned the top-k documents from their respective retrieval method (without embedding filtering or any LLM re-ranking), leveraging the inherent ranking/scoring provided by Semantic Scholar. This setup allows to assess the importance of both re-ranking steps. This structured setup enabled us to isolate the contribution of each component (retrieval method vs. re-ranking strategy) and evaluate whether they collectively brought key papers for novelty assessment into the top 10. We use o3-mini for evaluating novelty (Step 3) and gpt-4o for re-ranking (Step 2).

Classification Analysis: Table 2 shows that the complete system, which employs facet-based re-ranking in RankGPT, significantly outperforms its ablated variants in accuracy. The results demonstrate that methods relying only on keyword or snippet-based retrieval have much lower accuracy, and even alternate re-ranking strategies with a single embedding-based reranker or both embedding and general relevance RankGPT are insufficient to consistently bring key papers into the most relevant paper set. These findings show that combining facet-based reranking with embedding is critical for identifying the most relevant papers.

Table 2: Accuracy of predicting "not novel".

Method	Accuracy
Complete System	89.66%
- Relevance RankGPT	13.79%
- Embedding Filtering	10.34%
- Snippet Retrieval	8.62%
- Keyword Retrieval	5.17%

Analysis of the Most Relevant Papers: Table 3 compares the top-10 most relevant papers retrieved under each ablation setting with those from the complete system. Approximately 30% of the papers differ when using either embedding-based or general relevance RankGPT. Additionally, notable rank shifts are observed between the facet-based and relevance-based LLM rerankers. In contrast, without the reranking steps, both snippet and keyword retrieval exhibit minimal overlap with the final system's top results, highlighting the importance of the reranker stage.

6.3 Qualitative Analysis

Table 4 in the Appendix shows examples from our training set, including an idea, its most relevant papers, and the corresponding expert reasoning.

Table 3: Comparing rank and overlap in retrieved papers with each variant to the complete system. *Overlap* indicates how many papers overlap on average with the complete system top-10 papers. *Rank Shift* measures the average absolute difference in rank positions (only among overlapping papers).

Method	Overlap (↑)	Rank Shift (↓)
Relevance RankGPT	7.97	0.67
Embedding Filtering	7.93	0.84
Snippet Retrieval	2.88	1.85
Keyword Retrieval	1.17	1.39

While assessing novelty, we add both the titles and abstracts of the most relevant papers for each idea.

Figures 2, 3, and 4 in the Appendix qualitatively compare novelty evaluations by AI Scientist, AI Researcher, and Idea Novelty Checker (ours) on two research ideas. Idea Novelty Checker provides concise justifications for its novelty decisions by referencing key similarities and differences with existing works. For example, in Example 1, it correctly identifies the idea as 'novel' by highlighting these aspects. In contrast, AI Researcher evaluates each paper individually, classfying an idea as 'not novel' if any paper is considered citable; but in our examples, none of the papers were flagged as citable despite sharing similar purposes, leading to a 'novel' classification. Due to space constraints, we show insights only from the first paper for each example. Figure 4 indicates that while AI Scientist's judgments generally align with the ground truth and offer actionable suggestions, it sometimes misinterprets the idea—as in Figure 3, where its focus shifts from the idea to the accompanying code.

6.4 Prompt Sensitivity

In our experiments with TextGrad, we investigated how specific prompt instructions influence an LLM's ability to classify the novelty of an idea. Figures in Appendices 5, 6, and 7 present the accuracy of various prompts optimized with TextGrad on our dataset (train=25, validation = 10, test = 32).

Prompts with both non-zero and zero validation accuracy included various instructions for evaluating the novelty of ideas, such as assessing the uniqueness of methods and their comparison to existing research. Through this prompt optimization process, we observed interesting ways in which LLMs may evaluate novelty, like considering historical context, frequency of similar studies, comparative analysis with existing works, examining arguments for both novel and non-novel perspectives. However, prompts without these specific instructions also influenced accuracy, suggesting the complexity of novelty evaluation with LLMs.

Notably, some prompts with similar instructions showed different performance on validation data. For example, both prompt 3 (accuracy = 0) and prompt 9 (accuracy = 0.6) include instructions to evaluate if the idea introduces unique methodologies, and how it compares to existing work. However, the difference in their performance suggests that subtle variations in wording and instruction framing can significantly impact the classification performance. It remains unclear why certain prompts perform better despite having similar instructions.

Our analysis highlights the LLM's sensitivity to prompt design when assessing novelty of an idea. Even minor variations in wording and structure can lead to substantial performance changes, emphasizing the need for careful prompt engineering and well-chosen in-context examples to guide the LLM for idea novelty evaluation.

7 Conclusion

In this work, we propose Idea Novelty Checker, a retrieval-augmented pipeline for evaluating the novelty of scientific ideas and generating literature-grounded rationales. Our formative study highlighted two main challenges in evaluating novelty: (1) retrieving the most relevant papers from a vast corpus, and (2) establishing a fixed notion of novelty due to its inherent subjectivity. To address the latter, we incorporate expert-annotated examples in our novelty checker where we consider an idea to be novel within a given topic domain if it (1) differs from all retrieved papers in at least one core facet—namely, purpose (a new objective), mechanism (a distinct technical approach), or evaluation (a distinct validation method); (2) uniquely combines these facets; or (3) applies them to a new application domain.

Our experiments on an expert-annotated dataset demonstrate that Idea Novelty Checker outperforms two well-known recent baselines, and our ablation studies confirm the importance of each component in our system. Furthermore, qualitative comparisons and analyses of prompt sensitivity provide additional insights into novelty evaluation.

8 Limitations & Future Work

While Idea Novelty Checker is superior in many aspects, it also has some limitations. For instance, due to context size constraints (with fifteen in-context examples for both *novel* and *not novel* categories), our analysis is restricted to the top 10 retrieved papers, which may disproportionately influence the overall novelty assessment. Additionally, our definition of novelty relies on expert annotations, and the same annotators who provided the in-context examples also classified the test ideas. This could potentially give our approach an advantage in understanding our view of novelty. Moreover, many of the ideas used for testing were generated by the same system (Radensky et al., 2024) that produced the in-context examples, although some ideas were sourced from OpenReview.

In future work, we aim to address these limitations by expanding the literature scope using tools such as DeepResearch and ScholarQA and further refining our novelty evaluation to view novelty as a continuum rather than binary classification.

References

Abdelrahman Abdallah, Bhawna Piryani, Jamshid Mozafari, Mohammed Ali, and Adam Jatowt. 2025. Rankify: A comprehensive python toolkit for retrieval, re-ranking, and retrieval-augmented generation.

Faez Ahmed, Sharath Kumar Ramachandran, Mark D. Fuge, Samuel T. Hunter, and Scarlett R. Miller. 2018. Interpreting idea maps: Pairwise comparisons reveal what makes ideas novel. *Journal of Mechanical Design*.

Davide Baldelli, Junfeng Jiang, Akiko Aizawa, and Paolo Torroni. 2024. Twolar: A two-step llm-augmented distillation method for passage reranking. *ArXiv*, abs/2403.17759.

Joeran Beel, Min-Yen Kan, and Moritz Baumgart. 2025. Evaluating sakana's ai scientist for autonomous research: Wishful thinking or an emerging reality towards 'artificial research intelligence' (ari)?

Nicolas Bougie and Narimasa Watanabe. 2024. Generative adversarial reviews: When llms become the critic. *ArXiv*, abs/2412.10415.

Joel Chan, Joseph Chee Chang, Tom Hope, Dafna Shahaf, and Aniket Kittur. 2018. Solvent: A mixed initiative system for finding analogies between research papers. *Proceedings of the ACM on Human-Computer Interaction*, 2(CSCW):1–21.

DaEun Choi, Sumin Hong, Jeongeon Park, John Joon Young Chung, and Juho Kim. 2024. Creative-connect: Supporting reference recombination for graphic design ideation with generative ai. In *Proceedings of the CHI Conference on Human Factors in Computing Systems*, pages 1–25.

Arman Cohan, Sergey Feldman, Iz Beltagy, Doug Downey, and Daniel S. Weld. 2020. Specter: Document-level representation learning using citation-informed transformers. *ArXiv*, abs/2004.07180.

DeepResearch. Deepresearch. `https://openai.com/index/introducing-deep-research/`.

Steffen Eger, Andreas Rücklé, and Iryna Gurevych. 2019. Pitfalls in the evaluation of sentence embeddings. *ArXiv*, abs/1906.01575.

Matthew Freestone and Shubhra (Santu) Karmaker. 2024. Revisiting word embeddings in the llm era.

Jingtong Gao, Bo Chen, Xiangyu Zhao, Weiwen Liu, Xiangyang Li, Yichao Wang, Zijian Zhang, Wanyu Wang, Yuyang Ye, Shanru Lin, Huifeng Guo, and Ruiming Tang. 2024. Llm-enhanced reranking in recommender systems. *ArXiv*, abs/2406.12433.

Jos'e Manuel G'omez-P'erez, Andr'es Garc'ia-Silva, Rosemarie Leone, Mirko Albani, Moritz Fontaine, Charles Poncet, Leopold Summerer, Alessandro Donati, Ilaria Roma, and Stefano Scaglioni. 2022. Artificial intelligence and natural language processing and understanding in space: A methodological framework and four esa case studies. *ArXiv*, abs/2210.03640.

Tarun Gupta and Danish Pruthi. 2025. All that glitters is not novel: Plagiarism in ai generated research.

Ishika Joshi, Simra Shahid, Shreeya Venneti, Manushree Vasu, Yantao Zheng, Yunyao Li, Balaji Krishnamurthy, and Gromit Yeuk-Yin Chan. 2024. Coprompter: User-centric evaluation of llm instruction alignment for improved prompt engineering. *ArXiv*, abs/2411.06099.

Hyeonsu B Kang, David Chuan-En Lin, Nikolas Martelaro, Aniket Kittur, Yan-Ying Chen, and Matthew K Hong. 2024. Biospark: An end-to-end generative system for biological-analogical inspirations and ideation. In *Extended Abstracts of the CHI Conference on Human Factors in Computing Systems*, pages 1–13.

Hyeonsu B Kang, Xin Qian, Tom Hope, Dafna Shahaf, Joel Chan, and Aniket Kittur. 2022. Augmenting scientific creativity with an analogical search engine. *ACM Transactions on Computer-Human Interaction*, 29(6):1–36.

Omar Khattab, Arnav Singhvi, Paridhi Maheshwari, Zhiyuan Zhang, Keshav Santhanam, Sri Vardhamanan, Saiful Haq, Ashutosh Sharma, Thomas T.

Joshi, Hanna Moazam, Heather Miller, Matei Zaharia, and Christopher Potts. 2023. Dspy: Compiling declarative language model calls into self-improving pipelines. *arXiv preprint arXiv:2310.03714*.

Rodney Michael Kinney, Chloe Anastasiades, Russell Authur, Iz Beltagy, Jonathan Bragg, Alexandra Buraczynski, Isabel Cachola, Stefan Candra, Yoganand Chandrasekhar, Arman Cohan, Miles Crawford, Doug Downey, Jason Dunkelberger, Oren Etzioni, Rob Evans, Sergey Feldman, Joseph Gorney, David W. Graham, F.Q. Hu, Regan Huff, Daniel King, Sebastian Kohlmeier, Bailey Kuehl, Michael Langan, Daniel Lin, Haokun Liu, Kyle Lo, Jaron Lochner, Kelsey MacMillan, Tyler C. Murray, Christopher Newell, Smita R Rao, Shaurya Rohatgi, Paul Sayre, Zejiang Shen, Amanpreet Singh, Luca Soldaini, Shivashankar Subramanian, A. Tanaka, Alex D Wade, Linda M. Wagner, Lucy Lu Wang, Christopher Wilhelm, Caroline Wu, Jiangjiang Yang, Angele Zamarron, Madeleine van Zuylen, and Daniel S. Weld. 2023. The semantic scholar open data platform. *ArXiv*, abs/2301.10140.

Long Li, Weiwen Xu, Jiayan Guo, Ruochen Zhao, Xinxuan Li, Yuqian Yuan, Boqiang Zhang, Yuming Jiang, Yifei Xin, Ronghao Dang, Deli Zhao, Yu Rong, Tian Feng, and Li Bing. 2024. Chain of ideas: Revolutionizing research via novel idea development with llm agents. *ArXiv*, abs/2410.13185.

Manikanta Loya, Divya Sinha, and Richard Futrell. 2023. Exploring the sensitivity of LLMs' decision-making capabilities: Insights from prompt variations and hyperparameters. In *Findings of the Association for Computational Linguistics: EMNLP 2023*, pages 3711–3716, Singapore. Association for Computational Linguistics.

Chris Lu, Cong Lu, Robert Tjarko Lange, Jakob N. Foerster, Jeff Clune, and David Ha. 2024. The ai scientist: Towards fully automated open-ended scientific discovery. *ArXiv*, abs/2408.06292.

Chuan Meng, Negar Arabzadeh, Arian Askari, Mohammad Aliannejadi, and Maarten de Rijke. 2024. Ranked list truncation for large language model-based re-ranking. *ArXiv*, abs/2404.18185.

Sheshera Mysore, Arman Cohan, and Tom Hope. 2022. Multi-vector models with textual guidance for fine-grained scientific document similarity. In *Proceedings of the 2022 Conference of the North American Chapter of the Association for Computational Linguistics: Human Language Technologies*, pages 4453–4470.

Sheshera Mysore, Tim O'Gorman, Andrew McCallum, and Hamed Zamani. Csfcube–a test collection of computer science research articles for faceted query by example.

Aakanksha Naik, Sravanthi Parasa, Sergey Feldman, Lucy Lu Wang, and Tom Hope. 2021. Literature-augmented clinical outcome prediction. *ArXiv*, abs/2111.08374.

Baharan Nouriinanloo and Maxime Lamothe. 2024. Re-ranking step by step: Investigating pre-filtering for re-ranking with large language models. *ArXiv*, abs/2406.18740.

OpenReview. Openreview. `https://openreview.net/`.

Cyril Picard, Kristen M. Edwards, Anna C. Doris, Brandon Man, Giorgio Giannone, Md Ferdous Alam, and Faez Ahmed. 2023. From concept to manufacturing: Evaluating vision-language models for engineering design. *ArXiv*, abs/2311.12668.

Jason Portenoy, Marissa Radensky, Jevin D West, Eric Horvitz, Daniel S Weld, and Tom Hope. 2022. Bursting scientific filter bubbles: Boosting innovation via novel author discovery. In *Proceedings of the 2022 CHI Conference on Human Factors in Computing Systems*, pages 1–13.

Marissa Radensky, Simra Shahid, Raymond Fok, Pao Siangliulue, Tom Hope, and Daniel S. Weld. 2024. Scideator: Human-llm scientific idea generation grounded in research-paper facet recombination. *ArXiv*, abs/2409.14634.

Nils Reimers and Iryna Gurevych. 2019. Sentence-bert: Sentence embeddings using siamese bert-networks. In *Conference on Empirical Methods in Natural Language Processing*.

Serhad Sarica, Jianxi Luo, and Kristin L. Wood. 2019. Technology knowledge graph based on patent data. *Expert Syst. Appl.*, 142.

ScholarQA. Scholarqa. `https://scholarqa.allen.ai/chat/`.

Melanie Sclar, Yejin Choi, Yulia Tsvetkov, and Alane Suhr. 2024. Quantifying language models' sensitivity to spurious features in prompt design or: How i learned to start worrying about prompt formatting. In *The Twelfth International Conference on Learning Representations*.

Chenglei Si, Diyi Yang, and Tatsunori Hashimoto. 2024. Can llms generate novel research ideas? a large-scale human study with 100+ nlp researchers. *ArXiv*, abs/2409.04109.

Arvind Srinivasan and Joel Chan. 2024. Improving selection of analogical inspirations through chunking and recombination. In *Proceedings of the 16th Conference on Creativity & Cognition*, pages 374–397.

Suzanne Stevenson and Paola Merlo. 2022. Beyond the benchmarks: Toward human-like lexical representations. *Frontiers in Artificial Intelligence*, 5.

Haoyang Su, Renqi Chen, Shixiang Tang, Zhenfei Yin, Xinzhe Zheng, Jinzhe Li, Biqing Qi, Qi Wu, Hui Li, Wanli Ouyang, Philip Torr, Bowen Zhou, and Nanqing Dong. 2024. Many heads are better than one: Improved scientific idea generation by a llm-based multi-agent system.

Sangho Suh, Meng Chen, Bryan Min, Toby Jia-Jun Li, and Haijun Xia. 2024. Luminate: Structured generation and exploration of design space with large language models for human-ai co-creation. In *Proceedings of the CHI Conference on Human Factors in Computing Systems*, pages 1–26.

Weiwei Sun, Lingyong Yan, Xinyu Ma, Pengjie Ren, Dawei Yin, and Zhaochun Ren. 2023a. Is chatgpt good at search? investigating large language models as re-ranking agent. *ArXiv*, abs/2304.09542.

Weiwei Sun, Lingyong Yan, Xinyu Ma, Shuaiqiang Wang, Pengjie Ren, Zhumin Chen, Dawei Yin, and Zhaochun Ren. 2023b. Is chatgpt good at search? investigating large language models as re-ranking agents. In *Proceedings of the 2023 Conference on Empirical Methods in Natural Language Processing*, pages 14918–14937.

Jianyou Wang, Kaicheng Wang, Xiaoyue Wang, Prudhviraj Naidu, Leon Bergen, and Ramamohan Paturi. 2023. Doris-mae: scientific document retrieval using multi-level aspect-based queries. In *Proceedings of the 37th International Conference on Neural Information Processing Systems*, pages 38404–38419.

Kai Wang, Boxiang Dong, and Junjie Ma. 2019. Towards computational assessment of idea novelty. In *Hawaii International Conference on System Sciences*.

Wenxiao Wang, Lihui Gu, Liye Zhang, Yunxiang Luo, Yi Dai, Chen Shen, Liang Xie, Binbin Lin, Xiaofei He, and Jieping Ye. 2024. Scipip: An llm-based scientific paper idea proposer. *ArXiv*, abs/2410.23166.

Chang Xu, Yalong Bai, Jiang Bian, Bin Gao, G. Wang, X. Liu, and Tie-Yan Liu. 2014. Rc-net: A general framework for incorporating knowledge into word representations. *Proceedings of the 23rd ACM International Conference on Conference on Information and Knowledge Management*.

Mert Yuksekgonul, Federico Bianchi, Joseph Boen, Sheng Liu, Zhi Huang, Carlos Guestrin, and James Zou. 2024. Textgrad: Automatic" differentiation" via text. *arXiv preprint arXiv:2406.07496*.

Yucheng Zhou, Tao Shen, Xiubo Geng, Chongyang Tao, Can Xu, Guodong Long, Binxing Jiao, and Daxin Jiang. 2022. Towards robust ranker for text retrieval. *ArXiv*, abs/2206.08063.

Table 4: **Expert-labeled examples from annotation study**

Example 1

Idea: Develop a **natural language processing classifier designed to improve scientific paper revisions** by automatically identifying and categorizing reviewer comments that are most likely to lead to substantial and actionable revisions. The system would be trained on a **manually-labeled dataset analysis** of scientific review comments and the corresponding paper edits, leveraging features such as linguistic cues, sentiment, and comment specificity to predict the likelihood of a comment being acted upon. This classifier could then be used to prioritize reviewer feedback, helping authors focus on the most impactful suggestions first.

Most Relevant Papers:

1. ARIES: A Corpus of Scientific Paper Edits Made in Response to Peer Reviews
2. Can large language models provide useful feedback on research papers?
3. A Dataset of Peer Reviews (PeerRead): Collection, Insights and NLP Applications
4. arXivEdits: Understanding the Human Revision Process in Scientific Writing
5. Characterizing Text Revisions to Better Support Collaborative
6. Can We Automate Scientific Reviewing?
7. DeepReviewer: Collaborative Grammar & Innovation Neural Network for Paper Review
8. Aspect-based Sentiment Analysis of Scientific Reviews
9. Aspect-based sentiment analysis of online peer reviews and prediction of paper acceptance
10. ReviVal: Towards Automatically Evaluating the Informativeness of Peer Reviews

Reasoning: The idea is **novel** because it uniquely focuses on prioritizing reviewer comments for actionable revisions, which is not explicitly addressed in ARIES[1] or other works like ReviVal[10].

Example 2

Idea: Develop a **systematic review-based framework** designed **to align LLM evaluation with human preferences**, ensuring that evaluation criteria are continuously refined based on comprehensive reviews of user feedback and emerging model behaviors. This framework will utilize **content analysis of user interactions and feedback** to identify patterns and areas of improvement. The effectiveness of this framework will be assessed through a **qualitative study** involving iterative cycles of user feedback and criteria refinement.

Most Relevant Papers:

1. EvalLM: Interactive Evaluation of Large Language Model Prompts on User-Defined Criteria
2. Humanely: Human evaluation of LLM yield, using a novel web-based evaluation tool
3. Evaluation of Code Generation for Simulating Participant Behavior in Experience Sampling Method by Iterative In-Context Learning of a Large Language Model
4. Human-Centered Evaluation and Auditing of Language Models
5. Aligning Model Evaluations with Human Preferences: Mitigating Token Count Bias in Language Model Assessments
6. Who Validates the Validators? Aligning LLM-Assisted Evaluation of LLM Outputs with Human Preferences
7. Human-Centered Design Recommendations for LLM-as-a-judge
8. CheckEval: Robust Evaluation Framework using Large Language Model via Checklist
9. Discovering Language Model Behaviors with Model-Written Evaluations
10. Prometheus 2: An Open Source Language Model Specialized in Evaluating Other Language Models

Reasoning: The idea is **not novel** because it closely resembles existing frameworks like EvalLM[1] and HumanELY[2], which already align LLM evaluations with human preferences using user-defined criteria and human feedback.

Figure 2: Two example ideas used as the basis for comparison in subsequent figures, evaluated by Idea Novelty Checker (Ours), AI Scientist, and AI Researcher.

Example 1

IDEA: Develop a system that uses a *faceted author representation* of digital learning resource (DLR) creators based on their educational materials and inferred teaching personas. This system would aim *to support ubiquitous learning* by helping learners discover novel educators and materials that offer innovative perspectives. *Usability testing of learning resources* would be conducted to ensure the system enhances the learning experience by balancing relevance and novelty, thus boosting the accessibility and discoverability of diverse educational content.

MOST RELEVANT PAPERS:

(1) Bursting Scientific Filter Bubbles: Boosting Innovation via Novel Author Discovery
(2) Bridger: Toward Bursting Scientific Filter Bubbles and Boosting Innovation via Novel Author Discovery
(3) Novel Algorithmic Recommendation Engine for Diverse Content Discovery
(4) ComLittee: Literature Discovery with Personal Elected Author Committees
(5) Explanations in Open User Models for Personalized Information Exploration
(6) AMiner: Mining Deep Knowledge from Big Scholar Data
(7) Similar researcher search in academic environments
(8) VeTo-web: A Recommendation Tool for the Expansion of Sets of Scholars
(9) From Who You Know to What You Read: Augmenting Scientific Recommendations with Implicit Social Networks
(10) DiscipLink: Unfolding Interdisciplinary Information Seeking Process via Human-AI Co-Exploration

EXPERT-LABELED CLASS: Novel

Example 2

IDEA: Develop a **Co-Creative Interaction Framework** for LLM-assisted evaluations to **align llm evaluation with human preferences**. This framework will map out detailed interaction models between human evaluators and LLMs, including turn-taking, communication protocols, and iterative feedback loops. The framework will be evaluated through **qualitative study** involving user testing and thematic analysis of evaluator experiences, capturing how well the framework supports alignment with human preferences and identifying areas for iterative improvement.

MOST RELEVANT PAPERS:

(1) EvalLM: Interactive Evaluation of Large Language Model Prompts on User-Defined Criteria
(2) Human-Centered Design Recommendations for LLM-as-a-judge
(3) CheckEval: Robust Evaluation Framework using Large Language Model via Checklist
(4) Human-Centered Evaluation and Auditing of Language Models
(5) Prometheus 2: An Open Source Language Model Specialized in Evaluating Other Language Models
(6) Who Validates the Validators? Aligning LLM-Assisted Evaluation of LLM Outputs with Human Preferences
(7) Evaluation of Code Generation for Simulating Participant Behavior in Experience Sampling Method by Iterative In-Context Learning of a Large Language Model
(8) Discovering Language Model Behaviors with Model-Written Evaluations
(9) LLM Comparator: Visual Analytics for Side-by-Side Evaluation of Large Language Models
(10) Do LLMs Meet the Needs of Software Tutorial Writers? Opportunities and Design Implications

EXPERT-LABELED CLASS: Novel

Figure 3: Reviews corresponding to idea 1 in Figure 2.

Method	Review
SCIDEATOR (Ours)	The idea is **novel** because it introduces the concept of faceted author representation specifically for digital learning resource (DLR) creators, focusing on their educational materials and inferred teaching personas to support ubiquitous learning. This approach is distinct from related works like Bridger[1][2], which focus on scientific author discovery, and ComLittee[4], which supports authorcentric exploration in research. The proposed system aims to enhance the discoverability of diverse educational content, balancing relevance and novelty, which is not explicitly addressed in the related papers.
AI Scientist	THOUGHT: The proposed research presents an innovative approach to language models. The rough goal is to train a model to predict the next character in a sequence in order to be able to capture the semantic meaning of the entire sequence, which can be used in language models. This approach is not uncommon, though, as there are many areas where we must generate predictions of the next likely character, which can be used in order to understand the entire meaning of the text. This model aims to improve upon traditional models by locally training the model on the use of characters rather than words. Of particular note is the fact that the model uses a scaled gradient descent method which changes how the weights are updated, a method that is very new and, thus, is a key point of innovation. While that is extremely novel, a model that works on the character level is not. The primary new technique here is the use of a momentum of the gradient, which is used to improve learning. The model uses a technique similar to many current models. It is possible that it could be used with different parameters, though, to learn more or to learn in a more effective way than other models. This approach has been suggested many times over the years, but it is promising to pursue. It is, however, a novel approach to the existing technology. However, we must consider the existing literature and how it might overlap with this proposition. I will now proceed to search for related publications that may be relevant in order to establish a definitive argument regarding the novelty of the proposed model. RESPONSE: "‘json\n\n "Query": "Character-level language models"\n\n"‘\n I believe this should identify any previous work or existing lines of research that are most similar to the proposed model. This will confirm whether this is actually a novel concept. My primary concern is understanding if this is a novel or an existing work, as this is a model that could potentially be used for many purposes. There is a good chance that it might have already been proposed. I hope that this search will bring more clarity to the argument. **If decision is not made, default is: not novel.**
AI Researcher	Proposed Research Problem and Approach: Project Proposal: The research problem is the limited accessibility and discoverability of innovative educational content due to the lack of effective representation and utilization of diverse teaching personas and educational materials of DLR creators. The approach involves developing a faceted author representation based on creators' educational materials and inferred teaching personas to enhance the discovery of novel educational content. Paper Abstract: The research problem is the isolation of scientific research and information overload, which limit awareness and hinder innovation. The approach involves constructing a faceted representation of authors from their papers and inferred personas to balance relevance and novelty in discovering new scholars and their work. Summary and Differences: - Project Proposal Summary: Enhancing the discovery of digital learning resources by developing a faceted author representation based on educational materials and teaching personas. - Paper Abstract Summary: Facilitating the discovery of new scholars and their work by constructing a faceted author representation from scientific papers and inferred personas to balance relevance and novelty. - Differences: - The project proposal focuses on digital learning resources and educational content, aiming to improve the learning experience. - The paper abstract focuses on scientific research and scholars, aiming to boost innovation and bridge diverse scientific communities. No .... *The comparison with other papers has been truncated due to space limitations. All papers in the most relevant set are marked as "Binary Judgment: No", which implies it* ***should not be cited as similar work to the idea.*** **Classification: novel**

Figure 4: Reviews corresponding to idea 2 in Figure 2.

Method	Review
SCIDEATOR (Ours)	The idea is **novel** because it introduces a CoCreative Interaction Framework specifically designed to align LLM evaluation with human preferences through detailed interaction models, including turntaking, communication protocols, and iterative feedback loops. This approach is distinct from related works like EvalLM[1], which focuses on iterative refinement of prompts, and EvaluLLM[2], which leverages LLMs as customizable judges but does not map out detailed interaction models. Additionally, CheckEval[3] and Prometheus 2[5] focus on evaluation frameworks and opensource evaluators, respectively, without the cocreative interaction aspect. The proposed framework's emphasis on qualitative studies and thematic analysis to capture evaluator experiences further differentiates it from existing methods.

AI Scientist	THOUGHT:\n The proposed idea involves designing a framework for co-creative interaction between human evaluators and Large Language Models (LLMs), focusing on aspects like turn-taking and communication protocols. It also emphasizes qualitative study and thematic analysis. This is a very specific angle that combines human-computer interaction and AI evaluation. While several existing papers discuss LLM evaluation frameworks, human-centered design, and human involvement in evaluation (e.g., EvalLM, EvaluLLM, and other papers from the results), the specific focus on co-creative interaction frameworks with detailed interaction models and iterative feedback loops may not have been explored thoroughly.\n\n Additionally, the idea looks at aligning evaluations with human preferences which is a nuanced approach. Therefore, a more targeted query to ascertain if any existing literature discusses similar co-creative frameworks or detailed interaction models involving human evaluators and LLMs is necessary. The current results do not seem to cover this specific angle in depth. **Decision made: novel** RESPONSE:\n"'json\n\n "Query": "Co-creative interaction framework LLM evaluation"\n\n"'
AI Researcher	Proposed Research Problem and Approach: - Project Proposal: - Problem: Current LLM evaluation methods often fail to align with human preferences. - Approach: Develop a Co-Creative Interaction Framework (CCIF) that includes detailed interaction models between human evaluators and LLMs, facilitating turn-taking, communication protocols, and iterative feedback loops to better align LLM evaluations with human preferences. - Paper Abstract: - Problem: Developers must iteratively revise prompts by evaluating outputs to diagnose weaknesses, which is effort-intensive and context-specific. - Approach: Present EvalLM, an interactive system for iteratively refining prompts by evaluating multiple outputs on user-defined criteria, using an LLM-based evaluator to provide feedback and improve prompts. - Differences: - The project proposal focuses on aligning LLM evaluations with human preferences through a co-creative interaction framework involving detailed interaction models. - The paper abstract focuses on refining LLM prompts through an interactive system that evaluates outputs based on user-defined criteria. No .... *The comparison with other papers has been truncated due to space limitations. All papers in the most relevant set are marked as "Binary Judgment: No", which implies it* ***should not be cited as similar work to the idea.*** **Classification: novel**

Figure 5: **Performance trends of test accuracy across prompts during prompt optimization with TextGRAD.**

Highlighted text shows unique instructions used to evaluate the novelty of ideas. The final test accuracy was 0.78125, showing that none of the optimized prompts (1 to 12) improved over the original.

Prompt Number	Validation Accuracy	Prompt Text
Starting Prompt	0.8	You are a classifier. Given a research idea and related papers, classify the idea as 'novel' or 'not novel' Respond in two lines: Review: <This is the review you will generate after comparing idea with related papers.> Classification:<novel or not novel label according to your review/rationale>
1	0	You are a classifier. Given a research idea and related papers, classify the idea as 'novel' or 'not novel'. A novel idea introduces a unique, groundbreaking concept or approach not previously covered in the literature. A not novel idea reiterates or slightly modifies existing research. Consider the historical context and frequency of similar studies when making your classification. Focus on identifying unique, groundbreaking elements that differentiate the idea from existing research. Do not rely solely on keywords or the mention of a controlled setting to determine novelty. If the classification is ambiguous, indicate uncertainty and suggest a human review. Respond with only the classification label: 'novel' or 'not novel'.
2	0.7	You are a classifier. Classify the research idea as 'novel' or 'not novel' based on the related papers. Provide a brief review and directly state the classification. Review: <This is the review you will generate after comparing the idea with related papers.> Classification: <novel or not novel label according to your review/rationale> Example: Review: The idea is unique as it combines adaptive interfaces with AI explanations, which is not covered in the provided papers. Classification: novel.
3	0	You are a classifier. Given a research idea and related papers, classify the idea as 'novel' or 'not novel.' Respond in two lines: Review: Provide a detailed review comparing the idea with related papers. Include specific examples and details from the referenced papers to justify your classification. Highlight both similarities and differences between the proposed idea and existing methodologies. Ensure your review is concise and precise, focusing on the main arguments. Classification: Based on the review, classify the idea as 'novel' or 'not novel' according to the following criteria: - Uniqueness of the approach - Originality of the application - Novelty of the results Provide specific references or evidence from the papers mentioned to support your classification. Use assertive language to clearly convey your classification.

Figure 6: contd. TextGrad Prompt Optimisation.

Prompt Number	Validation Accuracy	Prompt Text
4	0.7	You are a classifier. Classify the research idea as 'novel' or 'not novel' based on the related papers. Respond concisely: Review: <brief review> Classification: <novel or not novel>
5	0	You are a classifier. Given a research idea and related papers, classify the idea as 'novel' or 'not novel.' Respond in two lines: 1. **Review**: Provide a detailed review comparing the idea with related papers. Include specific examples and details from the referenced papers to justify your classification. Highlight both similarities and differences between the proposed idea and existing methodologies. Ensure your review is concise and precise, focusing on the main arguments. 2. **Classification**: Based on the review, classify the idea as 'novel' or 'not novel' according to the following criteria: - Uniqueness of the approach - Originality of the application - Novelty of the results - Provide specific references or evidence from the papers mentioned to support your classification. - Use assertive language to clearly convey your classification.
7	0.3	You are a classifier. Given a research idea and related papers, classify the idea as 'novel' or 'not novel' based on the following criteria: 1. **Definition of Novelty** : - A 'novel' idea introduces a unique, groundbreaking concept, methodology, or significant improvement over existing work. - A 'not novel' idea closely aligns with existing work without significant innovation. 2. **Contextual Instructions** : - If the idea involves common methodologies or well-known techniques, explicitly mention these aspects in your review. - Consider the historical context and frequency of similar studies when making your classification. 3. **Comparative Analysis** : - Compare the proposed idea with existing systems or technologies mentioned in the related papers. Highlight similarities to justify the classification. 4. **Evidence and Examples** : - Provide specific examples or evidence from the related papers that demonstrate the lack of novelty. 5. **Structured Format** : - Use a structured format with sections such as 'Introduction,' 'Evaluation Criteria,' 'Comparative Analysis,' and 'Conclusion' to present your review. Respond in two lines: Review: <This is the review you will generate after comparing the idea with related papers.> Classification: <novel or not novel label according to your review/rationale>
8	0	You are a classifier. Given a research idea and related papers, classify the idea as 'novel' or 'not novel'. Respond in two lines: 1. Review: Provide a detailed review that includes specific references to the related papers, highlighting similarities and differences. Include direct quotes or specific sections from the related papers that support your classification. 2. Classification: Use precise terminology to classify the idea as 'novel' or 'not novel' based on your review/rationale. Avoid vague terms and be specific in your justification.

Figure 7: contd. TextGrad Prompt Optimisation.

Prompt Number	Validation Accuracy	Prompt Text
9	0.6	You are a classifier. Given a research idea and related papers, classify the idea as 'novel' or 'not novel'. Definition of Novel: An idea is 'novel' if it introduces a new concept, methodology, or significant improvement that is not already well-documented in the provided papers. Criteria for Evaluation: 1. Uniqueness of the approach. 2. Combination of elements. 3. Presence of similar frameworks in the literature. Instructions: 1. Compare the proposed idea's methodology, scope, and application with those described in the related papers. 2. Highlight specific aspects of the idea and compare them with the related papers. 3. Provide a detailed review based on the comparison. 4. Conclude with a classification of 'novel' or 'not novel' based on this comparison. Respond in the following format: Review: <This is the review you will generate after comparing the idea with related papers.> Classification: <novel or not novel label according to your review/rationale>
10	0.6	You are a classifier. Given a research idea and related papers, classify the idea as 'novel' or 'not novel'. A novel idea introduces a unique, groundbreaking concept or approach not previously covered in the literature. A not novel idea reiterates or slightly modifies existing research. Consider the historical context and frequency of similar studies when making your classification. Respond in two lines: Review: <one-sentence review> Classification: <novel or not novel> Ensure your response is concise and uses simple language. Avoid unnecessary details.
11	0.6	You are a classifier. Given a research idea and related papers, classify the idea as 'novel' or 'not novel'. Respond with: 1. Review: Provide a concise review in no more than two sentences, comparing the idea with related papers. Ensure your review includes a clear rationale for why the idea is classified as 'novel' or 'not novel'. Avoid using uncertain terms like 'appears' or 'seems' . 2. Classification: Use the term 'novel' or 'not novel' consistently based on your review. Example: Review: The proposed idea of developing a human-centric explainable AI system is novel because it uniquely combines explainable AI techniques with iterative improvement through human feedback and predictive models. Classification: novel
12	0.5	You are a classifier. Given a research idea and related papers, classify the idea as 'novel' or 'not novel'. Respond in two lines: Review: <Provide a detailed review comparing the idea with related papers, including specific examples and reasons for your classification. Mention existing tools or research that cover similar capabilities.> Classification: <novel or not novel label according to your review/rationale. Use the term 'novel' consistently in both your review and classification. Ensure your response is detailed yet concise, avoiding unnecessary verbosity.>

Data Gatherer: LLM-Powered Dataset Reference Extraction from Scientific Literature

Pietro Marini[1], **Aécio Santos**[1], **Nicole Contaxis**[2], **and Juliana Freire**[1,3]
[1]Tandon School of Engineering
[2]Grossman School of Medicine
[3]Center for Data Science
New York University

Abstract

Despite growing emphasis on data sharing and the proliferation of open datasets, researchers face significant challenges in discovering relevant datasets for reuse and systematically identifying dataset references within scientific literature. We present Data Gatherer, an automated system that leverages large language models to identify and extract dataset references from scientific publications. To evaluate our approach, we developed and curated two high-quality benchmark datasets specifically designed for dataset identification tasks. Our experimental evaluation demonstrates that Data Gatherer achieves high precision and recall in automated dataset reference extraction, reducing the time and effort required for dataset discovery while improving the systematic identification of data sources in scholarly literature.

1 Introduction

The increasing availability of data has accelerated scientific progress. Genomic and proteomic data sharing, for example, has enabled scientists to develop approaches that rely on access to large amounts of data (JB et al., 2020). Policies and frameworks like the FAIR Principles (Wilkinson et al., 2016) and FORCE11's Joint Declaration of Data Citation Principles (Altman et al., 2015) and changing researchers practices have contributed to increasing the amount of data available. Yet, finding datasets for reuse and identifying datasets referenced in research papers remain a challenging and labor-intensive task (Castelo et al., 2021; Borgman and Groth, 2025; Tsueng et al., 2023; Griffiths et al., 2022).

In contrast to journal article and book citation practices that use standardized formats (e.g., citation styles, DOIs), dataset references are inconsistent, ambiguous, and dispersed throughout scholarly documents, making systematic discovery difficult. PubMed and PubMed Central, for example, make some dataset mentions available through LinkOut Resources which links to external resources. They also allow researchers to search for articles that contain associated data in their Data Availability Statement (DAS), a structured section of articles that describe datasets used, or inside similar sections. However, these indexes are not currently able to surface dataset mentions fully, especially those embedded in the article text.

Even when datasets are explicitly referenced, their mentions are often ambiguous. The same dataset may be cited under different names, abbreviations, or project titles across multiple papers. Some papers provide only partial accession codes or omit repository information, making it difficult to resolve the dataset's location. DAS's, for example, may erroneously state that all data from a study is included in the paper (Federer et al., 2018). Common issues like typos, incorrect identifiers, and broken links further hinder discovery.

To locate datasets included in papers, researchers, librarians and data curators then have to undertake the labor-intensive process of manually searching, cross-referencing, and verifying dataset mentions. Mentions may include metadata such as accession codes, repository names, URLs, or informal descriptions. They can be embedded in figure captions, tables, supplementary materials, citations, or structured article sections like a DAS rather than explicitly listed in the main text.

Recent advances in Large Language Models (LLMs) present unprecedented opportunities for automating the discovery and extraction of dataset mentions from scientific literature. LLMs demonstrate superior capability in recognizing complex patterns in natural language text, enabling them to identify dataset references across diverse formats and naming conventions while distinguishing them from superficially similar entities such as gene and experiment identifiers. This can lead to significant improvements in automated extraction.

Proceedings of the Fifth Workshop on Scholarly Document Processing (SDP 2025), pages 114–123
July 31, 2025 ©2025 Association for Computational Linguistics

Contributions. We introduce Data Gatherer[1], an open-source, LLM-powered system that automates the identification and extraction of structured dataset records from scientific publications. Our system addresses the labor-intensive manual processes currently employed by researchers and librarians for dataset discovery. The design and development of Data Gatherer was informed by a collaboration with biomedical researchers specializing in proteomics and genomics, ensuring the tool addresses real-world requirements. To evaluate the effectiveness of Data Gatherer, we develop two benchmark datasets: (1) a high-quality collection carefully curated and validated by an expert librarian to ensure accuracy and completeness, and (2) a larger-scale dataset constructed through the systematic integration of existing databases that maintain associations between research articles and their referenced datasets. These benchmarks enable a comprehensive evaluation across different scales and quality standards. We present the results of an experimental evaluation which show that Data Gatherer achieves recall of up to 99.4% and precision up to 91.1% across our benchmark datasets.

In summary, our main contributions are: (1) an LLM-powered pipeline for automated identification and extraction of dataset references from scholarly documents (Section 5); (2) development and curation of two benchmark datasets for evaluation of dataset extraction methods (Section 4); and (3) an experimental evaluation of our data extraction methods using different LLMs (Section 6).

2 Related Work

The related work on the extraction of dataset mention from scientific literature falls in two main categories, which we describe below.

Datasets for Information Extraction from Scientific Literature. Several datasets have been developed to facilitate research in scientific information extraction. Anzaroot and McCallum (2013) introduced a dataset for fine-grained citation field extraction, focusing on segmenting citation strings into components like title and authors. Cheung et al. (2024) presented PolyIE, a dataset for extracting entities and relations specific to polymer materials. Zhang et al. (2024) created SciER, a dataset for entity and relation extraction with a focus on datasets, methods, and tasks. While these datasets facilitate various aspects of scientific information extraction, such as citation parsing and domain-specific entity extraction, we focus on a different task: the extraction of dataset references from the scientific literature on proteomics and genomics.

The Data Citation Corpus, created by Make Data Count in collaboration with the Chan Zuckerberg Initiative, is a comprehensive list of data citations from articles and preprints meant to facilitate the creation and use of data metrics similar to bibliometrics used to measure the impact of other scholarly outputs (e.g., H-index, Impact Factor, and the RCR) (Make Data Count, 2025). The Data Citation Corpus is in part compiled using machine learning methods that leverage SciBERT-based Named Entity Recognition (Istrate, 2023). Make Data Count does not make these data citation location tools publicly available. In contrast, our tool is open source and freely accessible to researchers, and instead of focusing on the creation of data metrics, our goal is to enable users to identify all mentions of datasets within a collection of articles to facilitate data discovery and reuse.

Dataset Discovery and Citation Analysis. Early approaches to dataset mention extraction relied on statistical methods. Ghavimi et al. (2016) present a semi-automatic approach combining dictionary-based matching with similarity measures to identify dataset references and link them to existing dataset registries. Zeng and Acuna (2020) propose using a bidirectional LSTM with a CRF inference mechanism for dataset mention detection. Kumar et al. (2021) propose DataQuest, a BERT-based entity recognition model with POS-aware embeddings, utilizing a two-stage pipeline for dataset sentence classification and mention extraction. These methods face important limitations that constrain their practical applicability. First, they typically require domain-specific training data, limiting their transferability across research disciplines. Second, the relatively small model sizes and training corpora restrict their ability to capture the full diversity of dataset naming conventions and referencing patterns found in scientific literature. Third, these methods often struggle with implicit or contextual dataset references that require deeper semantic understanding beyond surface-level pattern matching. Our work addresses these limitations by leveraging the robust information extraction capabilities of large language models trained on extensive, diverse corpora. This approach enables more generalizable extraction across domains while reducing dependence on manually curated training data.

[1] `https://github.com/VIDA-NYU/data-gatherer`

3 Problem Definition

We aim to automatically discover and extract dataset references from scholarly publications, focusing on citations accessible in academic documents available on the Web.

Definition 1. Given a publication P (e.g., a URL or DOI that refers to a scholarly article), the goal is to build a function $\mathcal{F}$ that extracts a structured set of records $\{(d_i, r_i)\}$ from P, i.e., $\mathcal{F}(P) = \{(d_1, r_1), (d_2, r_2), ..., (d_n, r_n)\}$, where d_i is the dataset identifier, typically an accession code or another type of dataset reference, and r_i is the repository name or reference (e.g., a plain text string or a URL pointing to the repository). □

We consider a dataset reference valid if its identifier d_i exists in the repository r_i. To evaluate the ability of different approaches to identify and extract valid dataset references correctly, we built two benchmark datasets that are detailed in Section 4.

4 The `DataRef` Benchmarks

To evaluate `Data Gatherer`, we constructed two datasets using distinct methodologies: (1) `DataRef-EXP` was manually curated by an expert librarian who identified and reviewed publication web pages on PubMed Central, selecting articles to ensure a diverse representation of dataset citation formats; (2) `DataRef-REV` was built by combining metadata from two online resources: ProteomeCentral,[2] a portal that aggregates dataset information from repositories within the ProteomeXchange consortium (Deutsch et al., 2023), and the Gene Expression Omnibus (GEO) repository.[3] Below we detail the data curation approach for each of these datasets. The datasets are available for download at https://doi.org/10.5281/zenodo.15549086.

4.1 `DataRef-EXP` Dataset

The `DataRef-EXP` dataset was created through systematic manual selection and curation of scholarly journal articles to ensure a comprehensive representation of dataset citation formats and referencing patterns. The articles were exclusively sourced from PubMed Central (PMC)[4] for two important reasons. First, PMC provides open access to the full text of articles via an API, eliminating potential copyright restrictions and technical barriers to systematically download journal articles. Second, PMC's advanced filtering capabilities enable targeted identification of articles containing explicit data references, particularly through their Data Availability Statements (DAS). DAS explicitly document the datasets employed in research and provides access information or retrieval instructions. While DAS quality varies across publications—with many exhibiting incomplete metadata or outdated access links—their presence serves as a reliable indicator for articles likely to contain dataset references. This filtering mechanism streamlined the curation process by pre-selecting articles with higher probability of containing relevant dataset mentions.

A total of 21 journal articles were selected, containing 48 dataset references. Journal articles were chosen in order to maximize the variation in how included datasets were referenced, enabling a comprehensive evaluation of the Data Gatherer's ability to extract dataset mentions across various formats. For example, some journal articles were chosen in which all dataset mentions were included in the DAS while other journal articles included dataset mentions in figures, in tables, or within the text. Additionally, some articles were chosen due to errors in dataset mentions, like inaccurate accession numbers or incomplete dataset information (e.g., an accession number but no named repository).

4.2 `DataRef-REV` Dataset

The second benchmark dataset was constructed using a systematic reverse-engineering methodology that leverages structured metadata exports from established scientific data repositories: ProteomeCentral and Gene Expression Omnibus (GEO). ProteomeCentral is a valuable source for ground truth data, offering curated metadata for 23,348 publicly available datasets, including dataset identifiers and one or more valid related paper DOIs or PubMed identifiers. It aggregates datasets from various repositories and links them to citing publications, making it a great starting point for locating papers that contain dataset references. Similarly, GEO is a public functional genomics data repository managed by the National Center for Biotechnology Information (NCBI). GEO provides programmatic access through a REST API that allowed us to retrieve 165,078 dataset identifiers with valid references to publications that mention them.

A limitation of `DataRef-REV` is that it only contains references to datasets from repositories that are part of the ProteomeXchange consortium or

[2] `https://proteomecentral.proteomexchange.org/`
[3] `https://www.ncbi.nlm.nih.gov/geo/`
[4] `https://pmc.ncbi.nlm.nih.gov/`

the GEO – it is possible that there may be datasets mentioned in the paper that are not deposited in these repositories. However, an advantage is that it is automatically generated, allowing us to obtain a much larger number of dataset references compared to DataRef-EXP (manually curated).

Dataset Construction Details. Each dataset entry includes a unique identifier, typically an accession code, along with the corresponding repository name, such as PRIDE, MassIVE, iProX, jPOST, PeptideAtlas, or PanoramaPublic. Additionally, the metadata contains information about citing publications, including their DOI or PubMed Central ID (PMCID) when available, as well as the title and keywords associated with the dataset. To ensure high-quality metadata, entries lacking a DOI or publication link were discarded, guaranteeing that each dataset-reference pair has an associated paper reference. As a result, DataRef-REV contains 397,263 dataset references records from 244,847 papers to 188,426 datasets.

To supplement the structured metadata, we implemented an automated data-fetching pipeline to retrieve full-text HTML versions of citing publications. Using Selenium, we systematically accessed publisher web sites and extracted the HTML source of each article when it was available. By integrating full-text data with structured repository metadata, we ensure that our dataset reflects both formally registered dataset citations and real-world citation practices in scholarly writing.

5 The Data Gatherer Tool

Data Gatherer was designed to automatically extract dataset references from scientific publications by processing both HTML web pages and XML responses as discussed in Section 3. It employs LLMs to identify references and construct links that enable the retrieval of the dataset. We have explored two main strategies: Full-Document Read (FDR) and Retrieve-Then-Read (RTR).

5.1 Retrieve-Then-Read (RTR)

The RTR method is a two-step process designed to improve efficiency in dataset reference extraction by leveraging the structural elements of full-text documents for scientific articles. It first locates specific target sections of the papers where dataset mentions are likely to appear, such as the DAS and similar sections. Then, it collects the textual content from the target sections and feeds them to an LLM using a few-shot prompt to extract dataset references (we provide prompts in the Appendix 7). We use the RTR approach for two main reasons. First, by drastically reducing the input length, RTR lowers both inference time and computational cost. Second, if the retrieval step is effective, it preserves most of the relevant information needed for extraction, allowing the language model to focus on likely regions of interest. However, retrieval must be precise: naïve or hard-coded retrieval rules may miss the critical passages and lead to lower recall.

Since RTR relies on structured documents, it currently applies only to open-access articles from PubMed Central (PMC), but the method can be extended to other sources with similar structural cues.

Rule-Based Section Retrieval. We developed a rule-based retrieval method to identify the sections of the raw XML/HTML documents that are likely to contain references to the dataset. It uses a combination of CSS selectors and XPath expressions, which we defined after various trial-and-error experiments on publications comprising diverse forms of dataset citation records. The retrieval rules, which are configured in a JSON file, are organized in two levels: general rules apply to the raw input data regardless of the specific publisher, and the remaining rules are tailored for use only in specific domains.

LLM-Based Dataset Extraction. Following section retrieval, we apply LLM-based extraction and instruct the LLM to output dataset references in JSON format using a structured few-shot prompting approach. Multiple prompt variations were tested and refined to improve extraction precision.

5.2 Full-Document Read (FDR)

To avoid the costs associated with manually defining rules for locating target sections, we consider an alternative approach that utilizes an LLM-based extraction pipeline to process the entire document. Instead of processing only specific sections of the article, we use the entire document text. While this method is more adaptable to various publishers, it has some drawbacks. Specifically, it only works with LLMs that support relatively long context windows and requires them to handle a significantly larger input, which increases costs.

HTML Preprocessing & Filtering. Before passing documents to the LLM, we perform an HTML normalization step to remove non-informative elements, such as scripts, styles, images, iframes, buttons, and metadata tags. This preprocessing ensures that only relevant text-based content is considered, reducing noise and improving dataset extraction performance and costs.

Handling Long HTML Documents. We use only LLMs that support long-context windows, with gpt-4o-mini (128K tokens) being the model with the smallest context limit. In cases where documents exceed this limit, the content is truncated until it fits the model context size constraints.

6 Experimental Evaluation

We evaluated Data Gatherer's performance using DataRef-EXP and DataRef-REV (Section 4). Due to the size of the DataRef-REV dataset, we used a sample consisting of 1,883 dataset citation records from 1,242 PubMed Central articles. Performance was assessed by using precision and recall metrics calculated for each paper and then averaged over the set of papers to compute the average precision and average recall. Since identifiers are typically unique across repositories (e.g., DOIs), we compare only the identifiers to determine matches. To account for common identifier variations (e.g., DOI: 10.6019/PXD123456 vs. Accession Code: PXD123456), we consider both exact or partial matches (e.g., substring match) for dataset identifiers.

We report the results in Table 1, which includes a comparison of different LLMs and extraction methods for the two datasets. Both methods (FDR and RTR) attain high precision and recall. gpt-4o-mini attains higher precision than gemini-2.0-flash for both methods on the DataRef-EXP dataset, but not for DataRef-REV. Note that the *maximum* recall on DataRef-EXP is generally lower, which is expected since the dataset was designed to include a high variety of difficult cases. Moreover, the RTR method struggles to obtain high recall in DataRef-REV dataset, potentially due to the low coverage of the manually curated rules, which may lead to missing important parts of the input. Despite of the low recall, the RTR method seems to improve precision in some cases.

While not conclusive, these results suggest that reducing the input size can help improve the cost (due to smaller input size) and the precision of long-context models (at the cost of decreasing the recall in some cases). Thus, more accurate and general RTR methods could be beneficial to improve the overall results. We also note that the results reported on the DataRef-REV dataset are limited, specially precision, since it may be possible that the models identify correct datasets that are not included in the ground truth (see section 4).

Dataset	Model	Method	Precision	Recall
DataRef-EXP	gpt-4o-mini	FDR	0.843	0.821
		RTR	**0.911**	**0.905**
	gemini-2.0-flash	FDR	0.704	**0.817**
		RTR	**0.880**	0.802
DataRef-REV	gpt-4o-mini	FDR	**0.853**	**0.985**
		RTR	0.684	0.635
	gemini-2.0-flash	FDR	0.754	**0.994**
		RTR	**0.803**	0.563

Table 1: Comparison of different LLMs, and methods (FDR, RTR) on DataRef-EXP vs DataRef-REV.

7 Conclusion

Researchers, librarians, and data curators currently spend significant amounts of time locating dataset mentions in scholarly papers. They perform this work both to locate datasets for secondary analysis projects and also to ensure a paper's conclusions are well-supported by the data. To ease this time-intensive and difficult task, we designed Data Gatherer to automatically find and parse dataset mentions in articles. As new methodologies in the sciences increasingly rely on access to large amounts of open data this tool can have a notable impact on the way that researchers, data curators, and librarians find, review, and aggregate data to meet the promise of these new methods.

Limitations

Our work has several limitations. The retrieve-then-read (RTR) approach only supports the PubMed Central (PMC) structure, so it requires extra effort to extend it to other repositories. The full-document read (FDR) approach aims to resolve this limitation by processing the full document, however, this limits the number of LLMs that can be used and may increase processing costs. Regardless of the strategy, the system can miss dataset references or output incorrect references. It also relies on LLM capabilities, which can be limited in ambiguous contexts. Additionally, our evaluation datasets, DataRef-EXP and DataRef-REV, may not fully represent all dataset citation practices since their size is limited and mainly cover papers related to proteomics and genomics research fields.

Acknowledgements

This work was supported by NSF awards IIS-2106888 and OAC-2411221, the DARPA ASKEM program Agreement No. HR0011262087, and the ARPA-H BDF program. The views, opinions, and findings expressed are those of the authors and should not be interpreted as representing the official views or policies of the DARPA, ARPA-H, the U.S. Government, or NSF.

References

Micah Altman, Christine Borgman, Mercè Crosas, and Maryann Matone. 2015. An introduction to the joint principles for data citation. *Bulletin of the Association for Information Science and Technology*, 41(3):43–45.

Sam Anzaroot and Andrew McCallum. 2013. A new dataset for fine-grained citation field extraction. In *ICML Workshop on Peer Reviewing and Publishing Models (PEER)*.

Christine L. Borgman and Paul Groth. 2025. From Data Creator to Data Reuser: Distance Matters. *Harvard Data Science Review*, 7(2). Https://hdsr.mitpress.mit.edu/pub/2mvqwgmf.

Sonia Castelo, Rémi Rampin, Aécio Santos, Aline Bessa, Fernando Chirigati, and Juliana Freire. 2021. Auctus: A dataset search engine for data discovery and augmentation. *Proceedings of the VLDB Endowment*, 14(12):2791–2794.

Jerry Cheung, Yuchen Zhuang, Yinghao Li, Pranav Shetty, Wantian Zhao, Sanjeev Grampurohit, Rampi Ramprasad, and Chao Zhang. 2024. PolyIE: A dataset of information extraction from polymer material scientific literature. In *Proceedings of the 2024 Conference of the North American Chapter of the Association for Computational Linguistics: Human Language Technologies (Volume 1: Long Papers)*, pages 2370–2385.

Eric W Deutsch, Nuno Bandeira, Yasset Perez-Riverol, Vagisha Sharma, Jeremy J Carver, Luis Mendoza, Deepti J Kundu, Shengbo Wang, Chakradhar Bandla, Selvakumar Kamatchinathan, and 1 others. 2023. The proteomexchange consortium at 10 years: 2023 update. *Nucleic Acids Research*. PMID: 36370099, DOI: `https://doi.org/10.1093/nar/gkac1040`.

Lisa M. Federer, Christopher W. Belter, Douglas J. Joubert, Alicia Livinski, Ya-Ling Lu, Lissa N. Snyders, and Holly Thompson. 2018. Data sharing in PLOS ONE: An analysis of data availability statements. *PLOS ONE*, 13(5):e0194768.

Behnam Ghavimi, Philipp Mayr, Sahar Vahdati, and Christoph Lange. 2016. Identifying and improving dataset references in social sciences full texts. In *Positioning and Power in Academic Publishing: Players, Agents and Agendas*, pages 105–114. IOS Press.

Emily Griffiths, Rebecca M Joseph, George Tilston, Sarah Thew, Zoher Kapacee, William Dixon, and Niels Peek. 2022. Findability of UK health datasets available for research: a mixed methods study. *BMJ Health Care Inform*, 29(1):e100325.

Ana-Maria Istrate. 2023. Building the Open Global Data Citation Corpus – Chan Zuckerberg Initiative. Publisher: Zenodo Version Number: 1.0.

Byrd JB, Greene AC, Prasad DV, Jiang X, and Greene CS. 2020. Responsible, practical, genomic data sharing that accelerates research. *Nature Reviews Genetics*.

Sandeep Kumar, Tirthankar Ghosal, and Asif Ekbal. 2021. DataQuest: An approach to automatically extract dataset mentions from scientific papers. In *Towards Open and Trustworthy Digital Societies: 23rd International Conference on Asia-Pacific Digital Libraries, ICADL 2021, Virtual Event, December 1–3, 2021, Proceedings 23*, pages 43–53. Springer.

Make Data Count. 2025. Open data metrics require open infrastructure: Data Citation Corpus. `https://makedatacount.org/find-a-tool/`.

Ginger Tsueng, Marco A. Alvarado Cano, José Bento, Candice Czech, Mengjia Kang, Lars Pache, Luke V. Rasmussen, Tor C. Savidge, Justin Starren, Qinglong Wu, Jiwen Xin, Michael R. Yeaman, Xinghua Zhou, Andrew I. Su, Chunlei Wu, Liliana Brown, Reed S. Shabman, Laura D. Hughes, the NIAID Systems Biology Data Dissemination Working Group, and Serdar Turkarslan. 2023. Developing a standardized but extendable framework to increase the findability of infectious disease datasets. *Scientific Data*, 10(1):99.

Mark D. Wilkinson, Michel Dumontier, IJsbrand Jan Aalbersberg, Gabrielle Appleton, Myles Axton, Arie Baak, Niklas Blomberg, Jan-Willem Boiten, Luiz Bonino Da Silva Santos, Philip E. Bourne, Jildau Bouwman, Anthony J. Brookes, Tim Clark, Mercè Crosas, Ingrid Dillo, Olivier Dumon, Scott Edmunds, Chris T. Evelo, Richard Finkers, and 34 others. 2016. The FAIR Guiding Principles for scientific data management and stewardship. *Scientific Data*, 3(1):160018.

Tong Zeng and Daniel Acuna. 2020. Finding datasets in publications: the syracuse university approach. In *Rich Search and Discovery for Research Datasets*, pages 158–165. SAGE.

Qi Zhang, Zhijia Chen, Huitong Pan, Cornelia Caragea, Longin Jan Latecki, and Eduard Dragut. 2024. SciER: An entity and relation extraction dataset for datasets, methods, and tasks in scientific documents. In *Proceedings of the 2024 Conference on Empirical Methods in Natural Language Processing*, pages 13083–13100.

Appendix: LLM Prompts

The prompts used in our experiments for both the Retrieve-Then-Read (RTR) method are given in Figure 1 and Figure 2, while Figure 3 and Figure 4 show the prompts used in the FDR method.

Role: system
Content:
You are a specialized assistant that extracts dataset references from the content of scientific papers. You must output a JSON array of objects, where each object has the following keys: 'dataset_identifier', 'data_repository', and 'dataset_webpage'. Follow the structure of the provided examples exactly.

Role: user
Content:
Extract dataset references based on the examples below:

Example 1:
Content: "The study used dataset EGAS00001000925, which is available at the European Genome Archive."
Response:

```
[
  {
    "dataset_identifier": "EGAS00001000925",
    "data_repository": "European Genome Archive",
    "dataset_webpage": "https://ega-archive.org/studies/EGAS00001000925"
  }
]
```

Example 2:
Content: "Proteomics data was obtained from PRIDE, accession PXD029821."
Response:

```
[
  {
    "dataset_identifier": "PXD029821",
    "data_repository": "PRIDE",
    "dataset_webpage": "https://www.ebi.ac.uk/pride/archive/projects/PXD029821"
  }
]
```

Example 3:
Content: "The repository dbGaP hosts the dataset phs001366.v1.p1 at this location."
Response:

```
[
  {
    "dataset_identifier": "phs001366.v1.p1",
    "data_repository": "dbGaP",
    "dataset_webpage": "https://www.ncbi.nlm.nih.gov/projects/gap/cgi-bin/study.
    cgi?study_id=phs001366.v1.p1"
  }
]
```

Now process the following content:

Content: {content}

Figure 1: Prompt for Gemini to extract dataset references from small HTML elements, used for the RTR method.

Role: system
Content:
You are a specialized assistant that extracts dataset references from the content of scientific papers. You must output a JSON array of objects, where each object has the following keys: 'dataset_identifier', 'data_repository', and 'dataset_webpage'. Follow the structure of the provided examples exactly. We will not wrap the json codes in JSON markers.

Role: user
Content:
Extract dataset references based on the examples below:

Example 1:
Content: "The study used dataset EGAS00001000925, which is available at the European Genome Archive."
Response:

```
[
  {
    "dataset_identifier": "EGAS00001000925",
    "data_repository": "European Genome Archive",
    "dataset_webpage": "https://ega-archive.org/studies/EGAS00001000925"
  }
]
```

Example 2:
Content: "Proteomics data was obtained from PRIDE, accession PXD029821."
Response:

```
[
  {
    "dataset_identifier": "PXD029821",
    "data_repository": "PRIDE",
    "dataset_webpage": "https://www.ebi.ac.uk/pride/archive/projects/PXD029821"
  }
]
```

Example 3:
Content: "The repository dbGaP hosts the dataset phs001366.v1.p1 at this location."
Response:

```
[
  {
    "dataset_identifier": "phs001366.v1.p1",
    "data_repository": "dbGaP",
    "dataset_webpage": "https://www.ncbi.nlm.nih.gov/projects/gap/cgi-bin/study.
    cgi?study_id=phs001366.v1.p1"
  }
]
```

Now process the following content:

Content: {content}

Figure 2: Prompt for GPT to extract dataset references from small HTML elements, used for the RTR method.

Role: model
Content:
I am a large language model trained to be informative and comprehensive. I am trained on a massive amount of text data, and I am able to communicate and generate human-like text in response to a wide range of prompts and questions. For this task, I will act as a specialized assistant that can identify datasets mentioned in a publication and create a summary suitable for non-specialists.
The output should be a JSON array of objects, where each object has the following keys:
- "dataset_identifier": This is any alphanumeric string (maybe including punctuation marks) that uniquely identifies or provides access to a dataset.
- "repository_reference": This is the URL or reference to the data repository where the dataset can be found.
Here are some examples for reference:

```
[
  'dataset_identifier' => 'EGAS00001000925',
  'repository_reference' => 'https://ega-archive.org/datasets/EGAS00001000925',

  'dataset_identifier' => 'GSE69091',
  'repository_reference' => 'https://www.ncbi.nlm.nih.gov/geo/query/acc.cgi?acc=
    GSE69091',

  'dataset_identifier' => 'PRJNA306801',
  'repository_reference' => 'https://www.ncbi.nlm.nih.gov/bioproject/?term=
    PRJNA306801',

  'dataset_identifier' => 'phs003416.v1.p1',
  'repository_reference' => 'dbGaP',

  'dataset_identifier' => 'PXD049309',
  'repository_reference' => 'https://www.ebi.ac.uk/pride/archive/projects/
    PXD049309',

  'dataset_identifier' => 'IPX0004230000',
  'repository_reference' => 'http://www.iprox.org',

  'dataset_identifier' => 'MSV000092944',
  'repository_reference' => 'https://massive.ucsd.edu/',

  'dataset_identifier' => 'n/a',
  'repository_reference' => 'https://data.broadinstitute.org/ccle_legacy_data/
    mRNA_expression/'
]
```

Role: user
Content: Given the information that I am going to share:
1) the webpage in HTML format that you have to extract datasets information from.
2) a sample of already known data repositories.
Please return a JSON array of objects where each object has the following structure:
- 'dataset_identifier': The dataset identifier (a code). If not found, set it to "n/a".
- 'repository_reference': The URL or reference to the data repository. If not found, set it to "n/a".
Please follow these strict instructions:
- The output must be a valid JSON array of objects.
- Each object must contain the keys 'dataset_identifier' and 'repository_reference'.
- Any other output format will be considered invalid.
Below is the input data that you will use to generate the output:

1) html => {content}

2) repos => {repos}

Figure 3: Prompt for Gemini to extract dataset references from full documents normalized, used for the FDR method.

Role: system
Content:
I am a large language model trained to be informative and comprehensive. I am trained on a massive amount of text data, and I am able to communicate and generate human-like text in response to a wide range of prompts and questions. For this task, I will act as a specialized assistant that can identify datasets mentioned in a publication and create a summary suitable for non-specialists.
The output should be a JSON array of objects, where each object has the following keys:
- 'dataset_identifier': This is any alphanumeric string (maybe including punctuation marks) that uniquely identifies or provides access to a dataset.
- 'repository_reference': This is the URL or reference to the data repository where the dataset can be found.
Here are some examples for reference:

```
[
  'dataset_identifier' => 'EGAS00001000925',
  'repository_reference' => 'https=>//ega-archive.org/datasets/EGAS00001000925',

  'dataset_identifier' => 'GSE69091',
  'repository_reference' => 'Gene Expression Omnibus (GEO)',

  'dataset_identifier' => 'PRJNA306801',
  'repository_reference' => 'https=>//www.ncbi.nlm.nih.gov/bioproject/?term=
    PRJNA306801',

  'dataset_identifier' => 'phs003416.v1.p1',
  'repository_reference' => 'dbGaP',

  'dataset_identifier' => 'PXD049309',
  'repository_reference' => 'https=>//www.ebi.ac.uk/pride/archive/projects/
    PXD049309',

  'dataset_identifier' => 'IPX0004230000',
  'repository_reference' => 'http=>//www.iprox.org',

  'dataset_identifier' => 'MSV000092944',
  'repository_reference' => 'https=>//massive.ucsd.edu/',

  'dataset_identifier' => 'n/a',
  'repository_reference' => 'https://data.broadinstitute.org/ccle_legacy_data/
    mRNA_expression/'
]
```

Role: user
Content:
I have a webpage in HTML format ({content}) and a list of known data repositories ({repos}). Please return a JSON array of objects, where each object has the structure:
- 'dataset_id': The dataset identifier (a code). If not found, set it to 'n/a'.
- 'repository_reference': The URL or reference to the data repository. If not found, set it to 'n/a'.

Ensure the output is a plain JSON array, not nested inside another structure, and not an Unterminated string.

Input:
content => {content}
repos => {repos}

Figure 4: Prompt for GPT to extract dataset references from full documents normalized, used for the FDR method.

Predicting The Scholarly Impact of Research Papers Using Retrieval-Augmented LLMs

Tamjid Azad[†], **Ibrahim Al Azher**[†], **Sagnik Ray Choudhury**[‡], **Hamed Alhoori**[†]
[†]Northern Illinois University, [‡]University of North Texas
tamjidazad@gmail.com, iazher@niu.edu, sagnik.raychoudhury@unt.edu, alhoori@niu.edu

Abstract

Assessing a research paper's scholarly impact is an important phase in the scientific research process; however, metrics typically take some time after publication to accurately capture the impact. Our study examines how Large Language Models (LLMs) can predict scholarly impact accurately. We utilize Retrieval-Augmented Generation (RAG) to examine the degree to which the LLM performance improves compared to zero-shot prompting. Results show that LLama3-8b with RAG achieved the best overall performance, while Gemma-7b benefited the most from RAG, exhibiting the most significant reduction in Mean Absolute Error (MAE). Our findings suggest that retrieval-augmented LLMs offer a promising approach for early research evaluation. Our code and dataset for this project are publicly available [1] [2].

1 Introduction

Evaluating the impact of a research paper is important to the scientific process, as researchers, funding agencies, and policymakers must make informed decisions (Akella et al., 2021). Typically, impact has been measured using bibliometric indicators, such as citation counts, h-index, i-index, and journal impact factors (Gupta et al., 2023; Waltman, 2016), as well as field-normalized metrics such as Field Citation Ratio (FCR) and Relative Citation Ratio (RCR) (Hutchins et al., 2016; Purkayastha et al., 2019). While each of these metrics provides useful insights into a paper's impact (Gupta et al., 2023), they depend on citation data, which takes time to accumulate.

The delay in assessing the scholarly impact can cause a challenge when making decisions in certain situations. For example, organizations that allocate funding for investments may need to assess the potential of new publications to guide funding, or domains that are evolving quickly may need to identify influential work that is important for directing researchers' attention. While alternative metrics such as altmetrics attempt to capture the engagement of the public immediately through social media and news coverage (Thelwall et al., 2013; Shahzad et al., 2022; Shaikh et al., 2023), they also rely on data after publication and thus cannot provide a true preemptive evaluation.

In this study, we estimate the scholarly impact of research papers by analyzing their content using Large Language Models (LLMs). LLMs have opened new possibilities for evaluating impact (Zhang et al., 2023), allowing researchers to rigorously analyze the research paper is content for more insights (de Winter, 2024; Zhao et al., 2025; Thelwall, 2025). However, despite these models being trained on a vast corpus, their knowledge is fixed at the time of training, so they can't dynamically access external sources during inference (Wang et al., 2024a).

This limitation means that for predicting scholarly impact, LLMs cannot evaluate how a new paper compares to prior related studies or assess its contribution in the context of ongoing research. Since a paper's influence often depends on how original it is compared to prior work and how relevant it is to ongoing research, (James et al., 2023; De Silva et al., 2017), comparing it to other studies is essential for accurately assessing its potential impact.

To address this concern, we use a technique called Retrieval Augmented Generation (RAG), where the retriever collects external sources that are semantically similar to the query being evaluated. These sources are sent to the LLM as context to give a more informed response (Gao et al., 2023). In the context of scientific articles, recent work shows that RAG improves the generation of structured scientific content, such as future work

[1]Code
[2]Dataset

Proceedings of the Fifth Workshop on Scholarly Document Processing (SDP 2025), pages 124–131
July 31, 2025 ©2025 Association for Computational Linguistics

statements, by grounding predictions in relevant prior research (Azher et al., 2025). RAG could potentially be valuable in the case of impact prediction, where we use prior literature to help LLM reason better. In our study, we will be addressing the following research questions:

RQ1: Does RAG improve the overall performance of LLM compared to zero-shot for scholarly impact prediction?

RQ2: How well do predictions from LLMs generalize across different research disciplines?

RQ3: How often did RAG improve or degrade LLM performance among individual papers?

2 Dataset Collection

We collected research articles published between 2018 and 2022 across five disciplines: Computer Science, Mathematics, Engineering, Physical Sciences, and Psychology. For each discipline and year, we randomly sampled 2,000 articles, extracting their titles, abstracts, and FCR scores from Dimensions.ai[3]. This creates a diverse dataset, sufficient to test the generalizability of prediction models. The FCR adjusts a paper's citation count by comparing it to the average citations of papers in the same field and publication year (Hutchins et al., 2016). Since FCR is an unbounded metric with no upper limit, we used the empirical cumulative distribution function (ECDF) to normalize its values within a $0 - 1$ range for each discipline and publication year. This makes our data more consistent and suitable for the model to learn and analyze for prediction (Kwok et al., 2023).

We then preprocessed the title and abstract columns by converting text to lowercase, discarding special characters, and removing abstracts with fewer than 100 tokens. Based on the ECDF-normalized FCR values, each article was categorized into one of three impact levels: *low* ($0 - 0.33$), *medium* ($0.34 - 0.66$), or *high* ($0.67 - 1$) impact level. These categorical labels were used to examine the distribution of impact levels within the dataset. To mitigate class imbalance and reduce the risk of model overfitting or bias toward dominant citation patterns, we removed overrepresented classes.

We then evaluated the readability of each paper's abstract using the textstat[4] library. These readability metrics were used as additional input features to quantify the ease or difficulty of text comprehension. Since readability can influence citation patterns, including these metrics enables us to investigate its potential role in the LLM's ability to predict scholarly impact (Ante, 2022; Wang et al., 2022). We used the Flesch Reading Ease (FRE) score[5], where higher values indicate more readable text, and the Gunning Fog Index (GFI)[6], which estimates the years of education required to comprehend the text (DuBay, 2004).

After preprocessing, the dataset consisted of $6,000$ research articles, each containing its title, abstract, abstract readability scores, and normalized FCR scores. In the experiment, we divided the dataset into a knowledge base containing $5,400$ papers (90% used for retrieval) and a test set of 600 papers (10% used to evaluate the model's predictions).

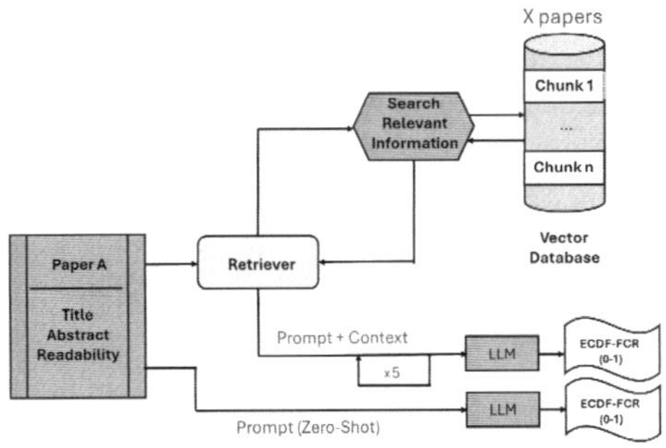

Figure 1: Overview of the RAG and Zero-shot workflow to predict the normalized FCR score.

3 Methodology

Figure 1 illustrates our workflow, which uses RAG to assist the LLM in making its prediction. The experiment used three LLMs (LLama3-8b, Mistral-7b, and Gemma-7b) and a retrieval-augmented setup that combined dense retrieval for contextual grounding and self-consistency to improve prediction reliability. Besides RAG, we used zero-shot as a baseline to assess how much the retriever actually benefited the LLM performance.

3.1 Large Language Models

Zero-Shot Prompting: We use zero-shot as a baseline, where we instruct the LLM to predict the nor-

[3]https://www.dimensions.ai/

[4]https://pypi.org/project/textstat/

[5]https://readable.com/readability/flesch-reading-ease-flesch-kincaid-grade-level/

[6]https://readable.com/readability/gunning-fog-index/

malized FCR score (ECDF-FCR) using just the title and abstract of the paper. Previous research has demonstrated the efficacy of zero-shot approaches for tasks such as predicting citation intent, displaying LLM's ability to perform well without additional fine-tuning (Koloveas et al., 2025; Alvarez et al., 2024). As such, zero-shot prompting serves as a benchmark for evaluating our RAG approach (Kumagai et al., 2024).

Self-Consistency: Our implementation of the RAG approach will also utilize self-consistency to further improve the reliability of the predictions. will involve prompting the LLM five times per paper and using the median score as the normalized FCR output. Self-consistency is particularly important in prediction tasks, as it improves the robustness of the model by reducing variance in the response and ensuring that the most consistent response is selected (Nguyen et al., 2024).

3.2 Retrieval-Augmented Generation

Dense Retrieval: Since RAG can be implemented in several ways, we settled on using the dense retrieval approach, which extracts the most comparable documents from a corpus given a query. This is accomplished by representing each document as an embedding and using a search method to efficiently compare pairwise similarities. Unlike keyword retrieval methods, dense retrieval maps documents and queries to a shared embedding space, allowing more semantic matching (Shi et al., 2023).

Facebook AI Similarity Search: FAISS[7] (Facebook AI Similarity Search) is an open-source library designed to find similar items in large datasets, especially when using high-dimensional vectors (Ghadekar et al., 2023; Douze et al., 2024). It supports various search methods, such as L2 distance, cosine similarity, or approximate nearest neighbors (ANN) for vector databases, making it scalable to extensive document collections.

4 Experimental Setup

We evaluated the LLM performance in both the zero-shot (Figure 2, Appendix) and RAG (Figure 3, Appendix) using two types of input sets: **(1)** text only (Title, Abstract) and **(2)** text with readability (Title, Abstract, Flesch Reading Ease, Gunning Fog Index).

We downloaded each model from Ollama[8] to run locally with the default configurations. We implemented a dense retrieval approach using FAISS to identify the most relevant research papers from the knowledge base. The FAISS index was created using the IndexFlatIP method, which is well-suited for cosine similarity search when used with normalized embeddings. Since we used SciBERT to generate the embeddings, we normalized each vector before indexing to ensure that the inner product search approximated the cosine similarity.

To efficiently compute embeddings, we processed research papers in batches of $1,000$, using parallel execution with four workers to speed up the computation. The resulting embeddings were stored directly in FAISS, enabling a flat, brute-force retrieval strategy. During the retrieval phase, the title and abstract of each input paper were encoded using SciBERT and used to query the FAISS index. The retriever will then find five papers that are the most semantically similar to the query containing the test paper and pass them to the LLM, where it will then use those five papers as context when predicting the normalized FCR score.

To evaluate the performance of the LLMs, we measured accuracy and ranking quality using Mean Absolute Error (MAE) and Normalized Discounted Cumulative Gain (NDCG). MAE quantifies accuracy by calculating the average difference between predicted and actual impact scores, with lower values indicating higher accuracy. NDCG assesses how well the model ranks papers by impact, comparing its predicted rankings of FCR scores to their actual rankings, where a value closer to 1 means that it is more accurate at ranking high-impact papers.

5 Results and Discussion

RQ1: Performance of LLMs in Zero-Shot vs. Retrieval-Augmented Generation. The results for zero-shot and RAG predictions are presented in Table 1. In zero-shot, LLama3-8b consistently outperformed Mistral and Gemma-7b in all features, achieving the lowest MAE of 0.222 and the highest NDCG of 0.936 when readability was a part of the input. In contrast, the other models had weaker performance, with Mistral-7b averaging an MAE of 0.304 and an NDCG of 0.918 between the two sets of features, and Gemma-7b receiving 0.309 and 0.916. These findings are consistent with previous research that used LLama3-8b to predict normalized citation counts for newly published articles

[7]https://github.com/facebookresearch/faiss

[8]https://ollama.com/search

Model	Title + Abstract		+ FRE, GFI	
	MAE	NDCG	MAE	NDCG
LLama3-8b	**0.227**	**0.929**	**0.222**	**0.936**
Mistral-7b	0.317	0.923	0.291	0.917
Gemma-7b	0.314	0.910	0.304	0.923

(a) Zero-shot Performance

Model + RAG	Title + Abstract		+ FRE, GFI	
	MAE	NDCG	MAE	NDCG
LLama3-8b + RAG	**0.182**	0.947	**0.195**	**0.953**
Mistral-7b + RAG	0.246	**0.955**	0.260	0.941
Gemma-7b + RAG	0.237	0.940	0.217	0.941

(b) LLM w/ RAG Performance

Table 1: Side-by-side comparison of Zero-shot and RAG performance. Metrics include MAE and NDCG across two input sets: (1) Title + Abstract and (2) Title, Abstract, Flesch Reading Ease (FRE), Gunning Fog Index (GFI).

(Zhao et al., 2025).

After integrating RAG with LLM, the performance of each model for predicting research paper impact improved, although the degree of improvement varied. Gemma-7b had the most substantial gains, reducing its MAE to 0.237 (a 0.077 decrease from zero-shot) with text-only input and 0.217 (a decrease of 0.087) when readability was considered, indicating the model depends on the external context for making its prediction. Mistral-7b also benefited, especially in text-only, where its MAE dropped to 0.246 (a reduction of 0.071). In contrast, LLama3-8b experienced the smallest improvements from RAG, with MAE reductions of 0.045 and 0.027, but still had the lowest MAE out of all models.

RQ2: LLM Prediction Generalizable Across Domains. The influence of RAG on the accuracy of the prediction varied across different domains (Figure 4, Appendix), with some fields benefiting more than others. Computer Science and Engineering showed the most significant improvements across most models, with Gemma-7b showing a reduction in MAE of 0.105 in both fields, the most substantial gain among all domains. Mistral also showed strong improvements, decreasing its MAE by 0.055 in Computer Science and 0.059 in Engineering, while LLama3-8b showed the highest improvement in Engineering only.

RQ3: How Often RAG Improve or Degrade LLM performance. To assess whether the retriever improved or worsened the LLM performance, we compared the absolute prediction error of RAG and zero-shot for each paper across all LLMs. Overall, RAG achieved a performance superior to zero-shot in $57-59\%$ in all cases (Mistral-7B: $1,369$, LLaMA3-8B: $1,376$, Gemma-7B: $1,409$), while zero-shot outperformed RAG in $36-38\%$ of cases (Mistral-7B: 873, LLaMA3-8B: 908, Gemma-7B: 874). This further shows that the context provided by the retriever generally improved the prediction but was not universally effective. These results reveal that while RAG can help, it also introduces noise or conflicting information, a challenge also addressed in Astute RAG, which investigates how to detect and mitigate such retrieval failures in LLMs (Wang et al., 2024b).

6 Conclusion

The evaluation process provides insight into a paper's impact and contribution to the research community. Our study attempts to expedite that process by prompting an LLM with a paper's title, abstract, and abstract readability. To improve the LLM response, we also incorporate RAG, which retrieves relevant papers as context when LLM makes its prediction, offering a faster alternative for assessing impact. While RAG improved the prediction overall, its inconsistent performance in some instances highlights the need to refine the retrieval approach further.

Limitations and Future Works

Our study has some limitations that allow opportunities for further improvement. First, the retrieval mechanism returned irrelevant or low-quality documents, sometimes degrading the prediction. Secondly, the input features for the text are limited to only the title and abstract, which overlooks other sections that could help the LLM. Lastly, because FCR requires at least two years of citation data, the ground truth is unavailable for recently published papers, preventing us from evaluating the performance of newer work. Future work will improve retrieval quality by experimenting with more techniques such as hybrid retrieval or re-ranking methods to match relevant documents better. Furthermore, we will expand the input beyond just the title and abstract, such as the introduction, methodology, and limitations (Azher et al., 2024), so that the model has more content to work with.

References

Akhil Pandey Akella, Hamed Alhoori, Pavan Ravikanth Kondamudi, Cole Freeman, and Haiming Zhou. 2021. Early indicators of scientific impact: Predicting citations with altmetrics. *Journal of Informetrics*, 15(2):101128.

Carlos Alvarez, Maxwell Bennett, and Lucy Lu Wang. 2024. Zero-shot scientific claim verification using llms and citation text. In *Proceedings of the Fourth Workshop on Scholarly Document Processing (SDP 2024)*, pages 269–276.

Lennart Ante. 2022. The relationship between readability and scientific impact: Evidence from emerging technology discourses. *Journal of Informetrics*, 16(1):101252.

Ibrahim Al Azher, Miftahul Jannat Mokarrama, Zhishuai Guo, Sagnik Ray Choudhury, and Hamed Alhoori. 2025. Futuregen: Llm-rag approach to generate the future work of scientific article. *arXiv:2503.16561*.

Ibrahim Al Azher, Venkata Devesh Reddy Seethi, Akhil Pandey Akella, and Hamed Alhoori. 2024. Limtopic: Llm-based topic modeling and text summarization for analyzing scientific articles limitations. In *Proceedings of the 24th ACM/IEEE Joint Conference on Digital Libraries*, pages 1–12.

Pali UK De Silva, Candace K Vance, Pali UK De Silva, and Candace K Vance. 2017. Measuring the impact of scientific research. *Scientific scholarly communication: the changing landscape*, pages 101–115.

Joost de Winter. 2024. Can chatgpt be used to predict citation counts, readership, and social media interaction? an exploration among 2222 scientific abstracts. *Scientometrics*, 129(4):2469–2487.

Matthijs Douze, Alexandr Guzhva, Chengqi Deng, Jeff Johnson, Gergely Szilvasy, Pierre-Emmanuel Mazaré, Maria Lomeli, Lucas Hosseini, and Hervé Jégou. 2024. The faiss library. *arXiv:2401.08281*.

William H. DuBay. 2004. The principles of readability. Technical Report ED490073, ERIC Clearinghouse.

Yunfan Gao, Yun Xiong, Xinyu Gao, Kangxiang Jia, Jinliu Pan, Yuxi Bi, Yi Dai, Jiawei Sun, Haofen Wang, and Haofen Wang. 2023. Retrieval-augmented generation for large language models: A survey. *arXiv:2312.10997*, 2.

Premanand P Ghadekar, Sahil Mohite, Omkar More, Praiwal Patil, Shubham Mangrule, et al. 2023. Sentence meaning similarity detector using faiss. In *2023 7th International Conference On Computing, Communication, Control And Automation (ICCUBEA)*, pages 1–6. IEEE.

Shikha Gupta, Naveen Kumar, and Subhash Bhalla. 2023. Citation metrics and evaluation of journals and conferences. *Journal of Information Science*, page 01655515231151411.

B Ian Hutchins, Xin Yuan, James M Anderson, and George M Santangelo. 2016. Relative citation ratio (rcr): a new metric that uses citation rates to measure influence at the article level. *PLoS biology*, 14(9):e1002541.

Mathew James, Vikas Palakkat, and Gareth JF Jones. 2023. Identifying influential citations in scientific papers. In *2023 31st Irish Conference on Artificial Intelligence and Cognitive Science (AICS)*, pages 1–4. IEEE.

Paris Koloveas, Serafeim Chatzopoulos, Thanasis Vergoulis, and Christos Tryfonopoulos. 2025. Can llms predict citation intent? an experimental analysis of in-context learning and fine-tuning on open llms. *arXiv:2502.14561*.

Atsutoshi Kumagai, Tomoharu Iwata, and Yasuhiro Fujiwara. 2024. Zero-shot task adaptation with relevant feature information. In *Proceedings of the AAAI Conference on Artificial Intelligence*, volume 38, pages 13283–13291.

Wai Meng Kwok, George Streftaris, and Sarat Chandra Dass. 2023. A novel target value standardization method based on cumulative distribution functions for training artificial neural networks. In *2023 IEEE 13th Symposium on Computer Applications & Industrial Electronics (ISCAIE)*, pages 250–255. IEEE.

Alex Nguyen, Dheeraj Mekala, Chengyu Dong, and Jingbo Shang. 2024. When is the consistent prediction likely to be a correct prediction? *arXiv:2407.05778*.

Amrita Purkayastha, Eleonora Palmaro, Holly J Falk-Krzesinski, and Jeroen Baas. 2019. Comparison of two article-level, field-independent citation metrics: Field-weighted citation impact (fwci) and relative citation ratio (rcr). *Journal of informetrics*, 13(2):635–642.

Murtuza Shahzad, Hamed Alhoori, Reva Freedman, and Shaikh Abdul Rahman. 2022. Quantifying the online long-term interest in research. *Journal of Informetrics*, 16(2):101288.

Abdul Rahman Shaikh, Hamed Alhoori, and Maoyuan Sun. 2023. Youtube and science: models for research impact. *Scientometrics*, 128(2):933–955.

Weijia Shi, Sewon Min, Maria Lomeli, Chunting Zhou, Margaret Li, Gergely Szilvasy, Rich James, Xi Victoria Lin, Noah A Smith, Luke Zettlemoyer, et al. 2023. In-context pretraining: Language modeling beyond document boundaries. *arXiv:2310.10638*.

Mike Thelwall. 2025. In which fields do chatgpt 4o scores align better than citations with research quality? *arXiv preprint arXiv:2504.04464*.

Mike Thelwall, Stefanie Haustein, Vincent Larivière, and Cassidy R Sugimoto. 2013. Do altmetrics work? twitter and ten other social web services. *PloS one*, 8(5):e64841.

Ludo Waltman. 2016. A review of the literature on citation impact indicators. *Journal of informetrics*, 10(2):365–391.

Fali Wang, Zhiwei Zhang, Xianren Zhang, Zongyu Wu, Tzuhao Mo, Qiuhao Lu, Wanjing Wang, Rui Li, Junjie Xu, Xianfeng Tang, et al. 2024a. A comprehensive survey of small language models in the era of large language models: Techniques, enhancements, applications, collaboration with llms, and trustworthiness. *arXiv:2411.03350*.

Fei Wang, Xingchen Wan, Ruoxi Sun, Jiefeng Chen, and Sercan Ö. Arık. 2024b. Astute rag: Overcoming imperfect retrieval augmentation and knowledge conflicts for large language models. *Preprint*, arXiv:2410.07176.

Shan Wang, Xiaojun Liu, and Jie Zhou. 2022. Readability is decreasing in language and linguistics. *Scientometrics*, 127(8):4697–4729.

Yang Zhang, Yufei Wang, Kai Wang, Quan Z Sheng, Lina Yao, Adnan Mahmood, Wei Emma Zhang, and Rongying Zhao. 2023. When large language models meet citation: A survey. *arXiv:2309.09727*.

Penghai Zhao, Qinghua Xing, Kairan Dou, Jinyu Tian, Ying Tai, Jian Yang, Ming-Ming Cheng, and Xiang Li. 2025. From words to worth: Newborn article impact prediction with llm. In *Proceedings of the AAAI Conference on Artificial Intelligence*, volume 39, pages 1183–1191.

Appendix

```
prompt = " You are an expert in evaluating the scholarly impact of research papers.
Given a research paper, predict its normalized FCR score, between 0 and 1, where 0 is
the lowest impact and 1 is the highest impact.

**New Paper:**
Title: the far side of mars two distant marsquakes detected by insight
Abstract: abstract for over three earth years the marsquake service has been analyzing
the data sent back from the seismic experiment for interior structure the seismometer
placed on the surface of mars by nasa insight lander. Although by October 2021, the
mars seismic catalog included 951 events, until recently...
Return only a number. Do not add explanations or text. " '''
--------------------------------------------------------------------------------
Output: 0.304
```

Figure 2: Prompt for Zero-shot with text only feature set.

```
prompt = " You are an expert in evaluating the scholarly impact of research papers.
Given a research paper, predict its normalized FCR score, between 0 and 1, where 0 is
the lowest impact and 1 is the highest impact.

**Context Papers:**
"Title: how to determine the early warning threshold value of meteorological factors on
influenza through big data analysis and machine learning
Abstract: Infectious diseases are a major health challenge for the worldwide population.
Since their rapid spread can cause great distress to the real world, in addition to taking
appropriate measures to curb the spread of infectious diseases..."
Flesch Reading Ease: 26.85
Gunning Fog Index: 15.69
FCR Score: 0.201

"Title: carbon emission of construction materials and reduction strategy take prefabricated
construction in China as an example Abstract: The rapid development of urbanization has
made the building industry a major source of carbon emissions. As the goal of carbon
neutrality becomes clearer, the construction industry faces serious challenges in energy
conservation and emission..."
Flesch Reading Ease: 31.31
Gunning Fog Index: 14.01
FCR Score: 0.149
--------------------------------------------------------------------------------
**New Paper:**
"Title: leveraging user comments for the construction of recycled water infrastructure
evidence from an eyetracking experiment Abstract: Building sufficient recycled water in-
frastructure is an effective way to address water shortages and environmental degradation,
playing a strategic role in resource conservation, ecological protection, and sustainable
development. Although recycled water is environmentally..."
Flesch Reading Ease: 5.7
Gunning Fog Index: 23.56
Return only a number. Do not add explanations or text.
"
--------------------------------------------------------------------------------
Output: 0.433
```

Figure 3: Prompt using RAG with full feature set (text and readability).

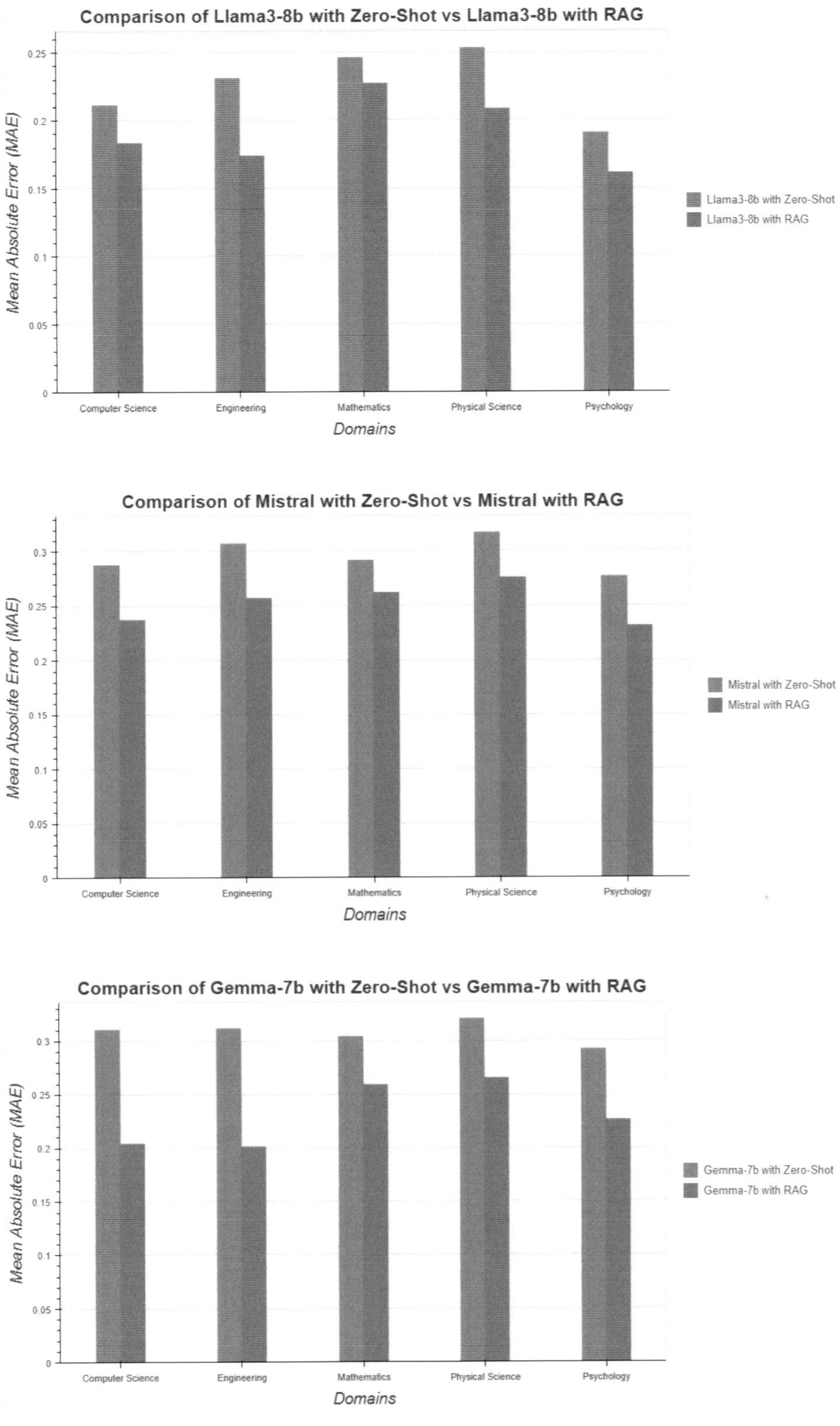

Figure 4: Comparison of MAE across domains for LLama3-8b, Mistral, and Gemma-7b using Zero-shot and RAG approach.

Document Attribution:
Examining Citation Relationships using Large Language Models

Vipula Rawte[1*], Ryan Rossi[2], Franck Dernoncourt[2], Nedim Lipka[2]

[1]Adobe Inc. [2]Adobe Research

vrawte@adobe.com

Abstract

As Large Language Models (LLMs) are increasingly applied to **document-based tasks** - such as document summarization, question answering, and information extraction - where user requirements focus on retrieving information from provided documents rather than relying on the model's parametric knowledge, ensuring the trustworthiness and interpretability of these systems has become a critical concern. A central approach to addressing this challenge is *attribution*, which involves tracing the generated outputs back to their source documents. However, since LLMs can produce inaccurate or imprecise responses, it is crucial to assess the reliability of these citations.

To tackle this, our work proposes two techniques. (1) A **zero-shot** approach that frames attribution as a straightforward textual entailment task. Our method using `flan-ul2` demonstrates an improvement of 0.27% and 2.4% over the best baseline of ID and OOD sets of AttributionBench Li et al. (2024), respectively. (2) We also explore the role of the **attention mechanism** in enhancing the attribution process. Using a smaller LLM, `flan-t5-small`, the F1 scores outperform the baseline across almost all layers except layer 4 and layers 8 through 11.

1 Introduction

Attribution in Large Language Models refers to tracing the origins of information embedded in the model's outputs. This involves identifying the specific datasets, documents, or text segments contributing to the generated response. Attribution is essential for verifying the information's provenance, ensuring the generated content's accuracy and reliability, and addressing concerns regarding plagiarism, accountability, and transparency in AI systems. Attribution methods typically involve mapping responses to the relevant data sources that influenced the model's generation.

In LLMs, attribution systematically links the model's outputs to their source materials, facilitating the identification of the exact documents, datasets, or references that informed the generated response. The primary goal is to uphold transparency, validate factual correctness, and give proper credit to sources. This process is critical for maintaining the credibility and accountability of generative AI systems.

Attribution methods are fundamental for enhancing the interpretability and dependability of LLMs. They support the model's output by providing citations or references, improving accuracy, and reducing the risk of misinformation. This ensures that each response is substantiated by relevant evidence, forming a basis for assessing the sufficiency and relevance of the underlying data.

Research on LLM attribution methodologies encompasses citation generation, claim verification, and hallucination detection techniques. These strategies are aimed at improving the quality and reliability of LLM-generated content. However, challenges remain in implementing adequate attribution, including the need for robust validation mechanisms, managing cases where sources influence the model's reasoning indirectly, handling structured data or non-textual sources (e.g., tables, figures, or images), and addressing the complexities of multi-lingual or cross-lingual data. Overcoming these challenges is essential for successfully integrating attribution methods within LLMs.

As AI and machine learning systems become increasingly prevalent, the demand for accountability, transparency, and reliability intensifies. Attribution techniques are pivotal in achieving these objectives, positioning them as a key area of research and development to advance AI technologies and ensure their responsible deployment.

The main **contributions** of this work are:

[*]Work done while the first author was an intern at Adobe Research

Proceedings of the Fifth Workshop on Scholarly Document Processing (SDP 2025), pages 132–136
July 31, 2025 ©2025 Association for Computational Linguistics

- A simple zero-shot prompting technique following the idea of textual entailment.
- An attention-based binary classification technique exploring whether attention could help achieve the attribution better.

2 Related Work

Attribution in LLMs has become a vital research area focused on tracing content origins and ensuring accuracy and accountability. Key studies have introduced various techniques and addressed challenges in this field.

Pasunuru et al. (2023) propose a minimal-supervision method for eliciting attributions, improving scalability, and reducing the need for extensive human input. An interactive visual tool for attribution is introduced Lee et al. (2024), aiming to enhance transparency by making attributions more accessible to non-technical users. Zhou et al. (2024) explore attribution in low-resource settings, emphasizing its potential to explain model behavior when data and resources are limited.

The Captum interpretability library is used in Miglani et al. (2023) for generative LLMs, offering insights into the factors influencing model predictions. Khalifa et al. (2024) argue that source-aware training enhances attribution by linking knowledge to specific sources, improving content reliability. The issue of false attribution, stressing the need for more accurate methodologies, is highlighted in Adewumi et al. (2024).

Bohnet et al. (2023) focus on attribution in question-answering systems, proposing methods for evaluating and modeling attributions in QA contexts. A survey of LLM attribution research, summarizing key techniques, challenges, and developments, is provided in Li et al. (2023). Lastly, Yue et al. (2023) explores the automated evaluation of attribution, aiming to streamline validation processes in practical applications.

3 Method and Experimental Setup

The attribution task defined in AttributionBench Li et al. (2024) is framed as a binary classification problem, where the objective is to determine whether a given claim is attributable to its associated references. The work in AttributionBench explores this problem using both zero-shot inference and fine-tuning of LLMs. Similarly, our formulation adopts the same approach to the problem. However, we restrict our methodology to zero-shot experiments due to computational limitations. Additionally, we also investigate if attention layers could help improve the attribution.

3.1 Zero-shot Textual Entailment

We frame this attribution task as a textual entailment problem to ensure simplicity and efficiency.

Textual entailment refers to the relationship between two text fragments, typically a premise and a hypothesis, where the goal is to determine whether the premise entails the hypothesis. Formally, given two sentences S_1 (premise) and S_2 (hypothesis), textual entailment can be defined as a binary relation $\text{Entail}(S_1, S_2)$, where:

$$\text{Entail}(S_1, S_2) = \begin{cases} 1, & \text{if } S_1 \text{ entails } S_2 \\ 0, & \text{otherwise} \end{cases}$$

Here, S_1 entails S_2 if the meaning of S_1 logically supports or guarantees the truth of S_2. The task is to model this relation using techniques, such as deep learning models, to predict this entailment relationship based on large corpora of annotated text pairs.

Why zero-shot Textual Entailment? The core challenge in zero-shot textual entailment is to build models that can generalize well to unseen tasks and relationships, relying purely on contextual understanding rather than task-specific fine-tuning. This is typically achieved through techniques like transfer learning, where models use their broad language understanding to handle specific inference tasks on the fly. For example, a model may be able to infer whether the statement "It is raining outside" entails "The ground is wet" without having been specifically trained on this exact inference.

QUESTION: how much of the world's diamonds does de beers own?

RESPONSE: De Beers owns 40% of the world's diamonds.

CLAIM: De Beers owns 40% of the world's diamonds.

REFERENCE: Title: Diamond Section: Industry, Gem-grade diamonds. The De Beers company, as the world's largest diamond mining company, holds a dominant position in the industry, and has done so since soon after its founding in 1888 by the British businessman Cecil Rhodes.

.....

.....

De Beers sold off the vast majority of its diamond stockpile in the late 1990s - early 2000s and the remainder largely represents working stock (diamonds that are being sorted before sale). This was well documented in the press but remains little known to the general public.

Setting	Model (Size)	ExpertQA (#=612)			Stanford-GenSearch (#=600)			AttributedQA (#=230)			LFQA (#=168)			ID-Avg.
		F1 ↑	FP ↓	FN ↓	F1 ↑	FP ↓	FN ↓	F1 ↑	FP ↓	FN ↓	F1 ↑	FP ↓	FN ↓	F1 ↑
Zero-shot Li et al. (2024)	FLAN-T5 (770M)	38.2	1.3	47.4	73.5	15	11.5	80.4	12.2	7.4	37.2	0	48.2	57.3
	FLAN-T5 (3B)	55.6	15.8	27.9	74	17.2	8.7	79.8	15.2	4.8	75.3	6.5	17.9	71.2
	AttrScore-FLAN-T5 (3B)	55.7	32.4	9.6	64.6	27.3	6.5	80.5	16.5	2.6	71.4	21.4	6.5	68.1
	FLAN-T5 (11B)	52	36.4	7.5	59.2	32.7	5	78.6	18.3	2.6	79.8	10.1	10.1	67.4
	T5-XXL-TRUE (11B)	54.5	17.8	27.3	68.5	16.2	15.3	**85.2**	7.8	7	80.4	1.2	17.9	72.2
	FLAN-UL2 (20B)	59.4	22.5	18	72.5	19.2	8	82.5	13	4.3	80.1	4.2	15.5	73.6
	AttrScore-Alpaca (7B)	47.4	11.1	37.7	68.6	21.2	9.8	79	14.8	6.1	68.7	10.1	20.8	65.9
	GPT-3.5 (w/o CoT)	55.3	30.4	12.1	62	30.5	3.8	74.7	20.9	3.5	72.6	22	4.2	66.2
	GPT-3.5 (w/ CoT)	**60.4**	23	16.2	66.1	25.5	7.2	78.9	14.3	6.5	73.4	19.6	6.5	69.7
	GPT-4 (w/o CoT)	56.5	32.8	8	59.8	33.2	3.5	81	15.7	3	71.6	23.2	4.2	67.2
	GPT-4 (w/ CoT)	59.2	26.3	13.9	71.7	19.5	8.5	82.2	10	7.8	80.2	14.9	4.8	73.3
Our Zero-shot	gpt4-o (05-13-2024)	52	13.1	33	64.7	**14**	21.2	71.5	10	18.3	81.14	23.8	15.47	64.1
	flan-ul2 (20B)	55	32.7	10	**75.2**	16	8.7	84.16	20.86	12.17	**85.38**	16.6	13.09	**73.8**

Table 1: We evaluate our zero-shot approach against the AttributionBench. Results highlighted in **bold** denote the highest performance. Our method performs better than existing approaches on the Stanford-GenSearch and LFQA sub-datasets. The average ID achieved using our method with `flan-ul2` is **73.8**, representing the highest value.

```
Answer the question with ONLY a 'YES'
or 'NO.' Does the REFERENCE entail the
CLAIM?
```

Figure 1: For our zero-shot experiments, we used this prompt template to query the LLM for determining whether the REFERENCE entails the CLAIM.

In our problem formulation, we task the LLM with a textual entailment problem by utilizing the prompt outlined in Fig. 1. This process involves evaluating the relationship between the given claim and its associated references, as defined in AttributionBench.

3.2 Attention-based attribution

Given the computational limitations, we designed experiments using a single LLM, specifically the `flan-t5-small` model, to analyze attention layers in addressing the attribution task.

Experimental Setup: We utilized the attention weights from each layer as input to a fully connected layer for binary attribution classification. We did this for all 12 layers.

4 Results and Analysis

In the initial phase of our evaluation of the attribution task, we conduct zero-shot experiments. The framework presented in AttributionBench is divided into two key components: in-distribution (ID) and out-of-distribution (OOD) sampling of the dataset. In their experimental setup, AttributionBench employs F1 score, False Positive (FP), and False Negative (FN) rates as evaluation metrics. Consistent with their methodology, we adopt the same metrics - **F1**, **FP**, and **FN** - for the evaluation in this study.

4.1 Evaluation Metrics

F1: The F1 score is a metric used to evaluate the performance of a classification model, specifically its balance between precision and recall.

FP: The False Positive Rate (FP) is a measure used to evaluate the performance of a classification model, specifically in binary classification tasks. It quantifies the proportion of negative instances that are incorrectly classified as positive.

FN: The False Negative (FN) is a metric used to evaluate the performance of classification models. It represents the proportion of actual positive instances incorrectly classified as negative.

4.2 Zero-shot

In this zero-shot setup, we formulate the attribution binary classification task as a simple *textual entailment* problem. To do so, we prompt the LLM using the template shown in Fig. 1. We compare our zero-shot method with the baseline zero-shot approach given in Li et al. (2024). With this simple question, we outperform the baselines in both ID and OOD sets.

We present our zero-shot experimental results in Table 1 for ID data distribution. We mainly used two LLMs: `gpt4-o` Achiam et al. (2023) and `flan-ul2` Raffel et al. (2020). We observe that `flan-ul2` performs better with F1 accuracy metrics in Stanford-GenSearch and the LFQA subdataset. The best ID-average (`flan-ul2`) = **73.8**.

Similar to the results observed for in-distribution (ID) data, the highest-performing model for out-of-distribution (OOD) tasks, as presented in Table 2, is `flan-ul2`, specifically for the AttrScore-GenSearch and HAGRID sub-datasets. When evaluating the OOD performance, our approach, leveraging the `flan-ul2` model, achieves the highest average score, reaching an impressive value of

Setting	Model (Size)	BEGIN (# = 436)			AttrScore-GenSearch (# 162)			HAGRID (# = 1013)			OOD-Avg.
		F1 ↑	FP ↓	FN ↓	F1 ↑	FP ↓	FN ↓	F1 ↑	FP ↓	FN ↓	F1 ↑
Zero-shot Li et al. (2024)	FLAN-T5 (770M)	79.6	9.2	11.2	80.8	6.2	13	75.9	13.1	10.9	78.8
	FLAN-T5 (3B)	80.2	13.3	6.4	82	6.2	11.7	79	16.9	3.8	80.4
	AttrScore-FLAN-T5 (3B)	78.9	17.7	3	76.3	16.7	6.8	68.6	26.9	2.6	74.6
	FLAN-T5 (11B)	72.3	25	1.1	78.1	16.7	4.9	64.5	30.6	2	71.6
	T5-XXL-TRUE (11B)	**86.4**	4.8	8.7	76.4	2.5	20.4	78.6	14.4	6.8	80.5
	Flan-UL2 (20B)	82.2	13.1	4.6	87.7	5.6	6.8	73.9	21.4	3.9	81.3
	AttrScore-Alpaca (7B)	75.9	20.4	3	82.1	6.8	11.1	73.9	19.9	5.6	77.3
	GPT-3.5 (w/o CoT)	79.4	15.8	4.4	76.7	18.5	4.3	70.1	25.2	2.8	75.4
	GPT-3.5 (w/ CoT)	77.6	14.9	7.3	82.1	11.1	6.8	74	19.7	5.1	77.9
	GPT-4 (w/o CoT)	77.5	19.7	2.1	84.3	14.2	1.2	72.1	23.9	2.8	78
	GPT-4 (w/ CoT)	77.5	18.3	3.7	83.3	8	8.6	75.9	18.5	5.2	78.9
Our Zero-shot	gpt4-o (05-13-2024)	79.69	42.66	5.5	**88.24**	17.28	7.4	76.54	42.37	14.41	81.48
	flan-ul2 (20B)	81.55	32.56	8.71	88.05	9.87	13.5	**80.71**	42.79	6.36	**83.43**

Table 2: We evaluate our zero-shot approach against the AttributionBench. Results highlighted in **bold** denote the highest performance. Our method performs better than existing approaches on the AttrScore-GenSearch and HAGRID sub-datasets. The out-of-distribution (OOD) average achieved with our approach utilizing the `flan-ul2` model is the highest, reaching a value of **83.43**.

83.43. This demonstrates the robustness and superior generalization capability of the `flan-ul2` model across both ID and OOD settings.

4.3 Using Attention layers

Preliminary results comparing zero-shot and varying attention layers on the LFQA attribution subset are presented in Table 3. We present layer-wise performance results for all three evaluation metrics. Although the results are mixed, the F1 scores generally outperform the baseline across nearly all layers, except for layers 4 and 8 to 11. Additionally, lower values of false positives (FP) and false negatives (FN) compared to the zero-shot baseline suggest improved performance.

	LFQA (#=168)		
	F1 ↑	FP ↓	FN ↓
Our Zero-shot	20	17.85	86.9
using attention			
layer 1	66.67	100	0
layer 2	66.93	98.8	0
layer 3	66.67	100	0
layer 4	0	0	100
layer 5	66.13	100	1.19
layer 6	66.13	100	1.19
layer 7	65.6	100	2.38
layer 8	10.31	9.52	94.04
layer 9	2.35	0	98.8
layer 10	0	0	100
layer 11	66.67	100	0
layer 12	66.93	98.8	0

Table 3: With balanced classes (84 each Class 0/1) using `flan-t5-small`, F1 scores exceed the baseline across most layers, except 4 and 8–11, indicating improved performance, further supported by reduced false positives and false negatives.

5 Conclusion and Future Work

In this paper, we conducted zero-shot experiments on AttributionBench to assess the performance of textual entailment-based approaches for attribution tasks. Our findings show that even without fine-tuning, a simple zero-shot textual entailment approach outperforms the existing baseline in both in-distribution and out-of-distribution settings. Notably, `flan-ul2` demonstrated strong performance across these scenarios, underscoring its robustness and suitability for such tasks. We also preliminary analyzed attention layer behavior using the smaller `flan-t5-small` model. The results suggest that attention mechanisms could provide valuable insights for improving attribution performance.

We plan to overcome computational limitations for future work by conducting fine-tuning experiments. We aim to use more advanced LLMs to perform a deeper analysis of attention layers. This could provide further actionable insights to refine performance and yield more robust findings.

6 Limitations

Limitation 1: Although fine-tuning could enhance the results beyond zero-shot, it comes with additional computational overhead. Therefore, we restricted our experiments to zero-shot settings in this paper and demonstrated how a straightforward zero-shot textual entailment approach can further improve performance.

Limitation 2: Regarding exploring attention mechanisms to enhance the performance of the attribution task, we were similarly restricted by computational limitations. Consequently, we could not utilize computationally demanding models for this analysis. Instead, the experiments were conducted using a lightweight model, `flan-t5-small`.

References

Josh Achiam, Steven Adler, Sandhini Agarwal, Lama Ahmad, Ilge Akkaya, Florencia Leoni Aleman, Diogo Almeida, Janko Altenschmidt, Sam Altman, Shyamal Anadkat, et al. 2023. Gpt-4 technical report. *arXiv preprint arXiv:2303.08774*.

Tosin Adewumi, Nudrat Habib, Lama Alkhaled, and Elisa Barney. 2024. On the limitations of large language models (llms): False attribution. *Preprint*, arXiv:2404.04631.

Bernd Bohnet, Vinh Q. Tran, Pat Verga, Roee Aharoni, Daniel Andor, Livio Baldini Soares, Massimiliano Ciaramita, Jacob Eisenstein, Kuzman Ganchev, Jonathan Herzig, Kai Hui, Tom Kwiatkowski, Ji Ma, Jianmo Ni, Lierni Sestorain Saralegui, Tal Schuster, William W. Cohen, Michael Collins, Dipanjan Das, Donald Metzler, Slav Petrov, and Kellie Webster. 2023. Attributed question answering: Evaluation and modeling for attributed large language models. *Preprint*, arXiv:2212.08037.

Muhammad Khalifa, David Wadden, Emma Strubell, Honglak Lee, Lu Wang, Iz Beltagy, and Hao Peng. 2024. Source-aware training enables knowledge attribution in language models. In *First Conference on Language Modeling*.

Seongmin Lee, Zijie J. Wang, Aishwarya Chakravarthy, Alec Helbling, ShengYun Peng, Mansi Phute, Duen Horng Chau, and Minsuk Kahng. 2024. Llm attributor: Interactive visual attribution for llm generation. *Preprint*, arXiv:2404.01361.

Dongfang Li, Zetian Sun, Xinshuo Hu, Zhenyu Liu, Ziyang Chen, Baotian Hu, Aiguo Wu, and Min Zhang. 2023. A survey of large language models attribution. *Preprint*, arXiv:2311.03731.

Yifei Li, Xiang Yue, Zeyi Liao, and Huan Sun. 2024. AttributionBench: How hard is automatic attribution evaluation? In *Findings of the Association for Computational Linguistics: ACL 2024*, pages 14919–14935, Bangkok, Thailand. Association for Computational Linguistics.

Vivek Miglani, Aobo Yang, Aram Markosyan, Diego Garcia-Olano, and Narine Kokhlikyan. 2023. Using captum to explain generative language models. In *Proceedings of the 3rd Workshop for Natural Language Processing Open Source Software (NLP-OSS 2023)*, pages 165–173, Singapore. Association for Computational Linguistics.

Ramakanth Pasunuru, Koustuv Sinha, Armen Aghajanyan, LILI YU, Tianlu Wang, Daniel M Bikel, Luke Zettlemoyer, Maryam Fazel-Zarandi, and Asli Celikyilmaz. 2023. Eliciting attributions from llms with minimal supervision.

Colin Raffel, Noam Shazeer, Adam Roberts, Katherine Lee, Sharan Narang, Michael Matena, Yanqi Zhou, Wei Li, and Peter J Liu. 2020. Exploring the limits of transfer learning with a unified text-to-text transformer. *Journal of machine learning research*, 21(140):1–67.

Xiang Yue, Boshi Wang, Ziru Chen, Kai Zhang, Yu Su, and Huan Sun. 2023. Automatic evaluation of attribution by large language models. In *Findings of the Association for Computational Linguistics: EMNLP 2023*, pages 4615–4635, Singapore. Association for Computational Linguistics.

Wei Zhou, Heike Adel, Hendrik Schuff, and Ngoc Thang Vu. 2024. Explaining pre-trained language models with attribution scores: An analysis in low-resource settings. In *Proceedings of the 2024 Joint International Conference on Computational Linguistics, Language Resources and Evaluation (LREC-COLING 2024)*, pages 6867–6875, Torino, Italia. ELRA and ICCL.

SOMD2025: A Challenging Shared Task for Software Related Information Extraction

Sharmila Upadhyaya[1] **Wolfgang Otto**[1] **Frank Krüger**[2] **Stefan Dietze**[1,3]
[1]GESIS — Leibniz Institute for the Social Sciences, Cologne, Germany
[2]Wismar University of Applied Sciences, Wismar, Germany
[3]Heinrich-Heine-University Düsseldorf, Germany
{sharmila.upadhyaya, wolfgang.otto, stefan.dietze}@gesis.org
frank.krueger@hs-wismar.de

Abstract

The use of software in acquiring, analyzing, and interpreting research data underscores its role as an essential artifact of scientific inquiry. Understanding and tracing the provenance of software in research helps in reproducible and collaborative research works. In this paper, we present an overview of our second iteration of the **So**ftware **M**ention **D**etection (SOMD) shared task as a part of the Scholarly Document Processing (SDP) workshop, that will be held in conjunction with ACL in 2025. The objective of this shared task is to encourage participants to reevaluate the methodologies employed in the tasks of joint named entity recognition (NER) and relation extraction (RE) for software mentions using the gold standard benchmark that has been provided. Our shared task has two phases of challenges. First, the participants focus on implementing a joint framework for NER and RE for the given dataset. Furthermore, the second phase encompasses an out-of-distribution dataset, which is utilized to assess the generalizability of the methodologies proposed in Phase I. The competition, which transpired from March to April of 2025, garnered the participation of 18 individuals and spanned a duration of two months. Four teams have finished the competition and submitted full system descriptions. Participants applied various approaches, including joint and pipeline models, and explored data augmentation with LLM-generated samples. The evaluation was based on a macro F1 score for both NER and RE, with the average reported as the SOMD score. The winning teams achieved a SOMD score of 0.89 in Phase I and 0.63 in Phase II, demonstrating the challenge of generalization.

1 Introduction

Scientific research is becoming progressively data-centric, and software plays an important role across disciplines by enabling the analysis, processing, and modeling of research data. As such, it has emerged as a key scholarly artifact, essential not only for conducting research but also for ensuring the reproducibility and advancement of scientific knowledge. To ensure transparency and reproducibility of scientific work, it is essential to identify the software used and trace its provenance, thus encouraging collaboration among scientists/researchers. Software mentions in scholarly publications are heterogeneous, informal, and in widespread use. Therefore, identifying and disambiguating software mentions, while attending to its metadata, is an essential yet challenging task. Various Knowledge Graph resources, such as OpenAire (Manghi et al., 2019) and SoftwareKG (Schindler et al., 2020), link open-access articles to the software used, supporting the need for robust methods to identify, extract, link, and disambiguate software mentions.

Various existing citation principles regarding software usage and mentions(Katz et al., 2021; Smith et al., 2016) promote knowledge sharing and innovation. However, these principles are not always strictly followed in all works, resulting in informal and incomplete information regarding the software mentioned or used (Schindler et al., 2024). Robust Information Extraction (IE) methods help to detect and disambiguate software mentions and related metadata. SOMESCI (Schindler et al., 2021) is a manually curated gold standard corpus about software mentioned in scientific articles, providing training samples for Named Entity Recognition (NER), Relation Extraction(RE), Entity Disambiguation(ED), and Entity Linking(EL). Based on this dataset, the SOMD2024 shared task was organized to advance research on automatic detection and analysis of software mentions in scholarly articles. The task challenged participants to develop methods for (i) Detecting Software Mentions, (ii) Identifying Associated Attributes, and (iii) Classifying the Relations between Software

Proceedings of the Fifth Workshop on Scholarly Document Processing (SDP 2025), pages 137–145
July 31, 2025 ©2025 Association for Computational Linguistics

and their Attributes.

In this paper, we present the Software Mention Detection shared task (SOMD2025)—the successor to SOMD2024 (Krüger et al., 2024). The goal is to advance the field through community-driven development and evaluation of new methods. SOMD2025 builds on the success of the previous edition. But while the first iteration focused on establishing NER, attribute detection and RE for software mentions in separate subtasks, SOMD2025 emphasizes a joint evaluation of these subtasks. Our task advances the development of a pipeline for IE components (NER; RE) for scientific knowledge. These pipelines serve as an initial step for functions such as metadata enrichment, semantic linking, and knowledge graph construction from scholarly articles, aligning with NFDI4DS's[1] and BERD@NFDI's[2] broader mission of supporting the research data lifecycle and providing infrastructures. We focus on the discovery and traceability of the software mentioned in research publications—a crucial step in the reproducibility of research.

In addition to learning and evaluating the joint NER and RE framework, we introduce an out-of-distribution (OOD) test set to assess the generalizability of the models—a significantly more challenging benchmark compared to the in-distribution data. We hosted the two subsequent phases of the competition in the CodaBench platform (Xu et al., 2022). Phase I aims at model development, where we provide gold-standard training and test splits to the participants. Phase II challenges participants to apply their models from Phase I on an out-of-distribution dataset comprised of scholarly documents that were not part of the training or test set used in Phase I. Although 18 participants registered, only three teams submitted for Phase I and five teams made submission for Phase II. Four of them submitted a system description for the workshop proceedings. To encourage future research, we have transformed Phase 2 into an Open Submission Phase that will allow further development of IE systems for our task.[3]

We provide the competition details in the rest of the paper. We include the task description and the evaluation metrics in section 3 and a description of the dataset for both phases in section 3.2. We summarize results in section 5, where we compare the methods of different participants.

[1]https://www.nfdi4datascience.de/

[2]https://www.berd-nfdi.de/

[3]https://www.codabench.org/competitions/5840/

2 Related Work

Software Mention Recognition. Early efforts in recognizing software mentions in scientific articles relied on manual analysis of small corpora (Howison and Bullard, 2016; Nangia and Katz, 2017) or targeted extraction of specific tools (Li et al., 2017, 2016). Automatic approaches such as rule-based systems and bootstrapping offered moderate performance (Pan et al., 2015; Duck et al., 2016). Deep learning models, particularly BiLSTM-CRF architectures (Schindler et al., 2020), improved accuracy but required more robust annotated datasets. Recently, transformer-based models like SciBERT trained on the SoMeSci corpus (Schindler et al., 2022, 2021) achieved state-of-the-art NER results. Importantly, SoMeSci also includes annotations for software attributes (e.g., version, license) (Schindler et al., 2021) and their links to software mentions, providing a foundation for relation extraction. Similarly, SoftwareKG (Schindler et al., 2020) offers a knowledge graph of software entities and metadata mined from scientific literature, further highlighting the need for integrated NER and RE.

SOMD Shared Task. The SOMD2024 shared task built upon these efforts by targeting software mention detection, attribute recognition, and relation classification using the SoMeSci corpus (Schindler et al., 2021). Participants explored diverse modeling approaches, including large language models and encoder/decoder architectures (Khan et al., 2024; Otto et al., 2024; Thi et al., 2024; Nguyen Xuan et al., 2024). Unlike the prior edition, which handled tasks independently, this year's task emphasizes joint learning and evaluation of NER and RE to encourage integrated solutions.

Joint NER and Relation Extraction. Joint learning of NER and RE has emerged as a robust alternative to traditional pipeline approaches, which often suffer from error propagation. Integrated models have demonstrated improved accuracy and efficiency by simultaneously extracting entities and their relations (Hennen et al., 2024; Huguet Cabot and Navigli, 2021; Wadden et al., 2019; Ye et al., 2022a). While these models have been widely adopted in general and biomedical domains, only a few efforts—such as SoMeSci and SoftwareKG—explicitly address relation-level modeling in the software domain. Their contributions underscore

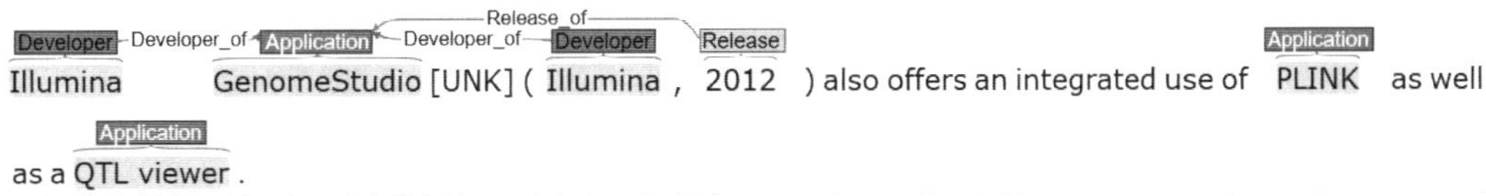

Figure 1: Illustration of NER and relation extraction annotations in the input data.

the growing importance of joint models in domain-specific information extraction. Prior studies consistently show joint frameworks outperform pipeline systems (Li and Ji, 2014), addressing limitations in earlier methods (Zeng et al., 2014; Zhang et al., 2017).

3 Task Description

We focus on the discovery and traceability of the software mentioned in research publications—a crucial step to ensure the reproducibility of research. For this purpose, we propose Information Extraction of software and related metadata, including Named Entity Recognition and Relation Extraction. We approach the concept of software as a form of research artifact, with software-related IE serving as a foundational element in the construction of Research Knowledge Graphs (RKGs) (Schindler et al., 2021; Karmakar et al., 2023). These RKGs, in turn, are built upon a foundation of scholarly articles, thereby facilitating the aggregation and organization of research findings. We encourage participants to build robust and generalizable NLP methods, i.e., models for software mentions, attribute detection, and relation extraction. An instance of a sentence with annotated software mentions, attributes, and relations is illustrated in Figure1.

SOMD2024 (Krüger et al., 2024) had hosted these problems as three independent subtasks. SOMD2025 combines these three subtasks into an end-to-end setup for training and evaluation. We endorse jointly learning the automatic extraction of software mentions, its attributes, and their relations from scholarly documents. Our task belongs to the well-known problem in information extraction, i.e., Joint Learning Paradigm for NER and RE (Li and Ji, 2014; Huguet Cabot and Navigli, 2021; Hennen et al., 2024). We have two phases of competition. We provide the labeled dataset for phase I, supporting model training. It contains three aligned files per instance: a tokenized text file, a NER label file, and a relation label file, each line corresponding to a sentence. The NER file uses IOB2 tagging with entity types such as Application, Abbreviation, and Version. The relation file encodes binary relations as <relation_type> <head_index> <tail_index>, with indices referencing the starting tokens (0-based). The test set in Phase I and II includes only the tokenized text, and participants are required to submit predicted NER and relation files. Full format details are available on the competition page[4].

3.1 Shared Task Schedule

Phase I: Model Development. Given the labeled gold dataset, participants develop an initial model for joint NER and RE for the gold standard dataset. Participants submit their outcomes on an unlabeled test/development set with the same distribution as a training set as they belong to the same original dataset.

Phase II: To test the generalizability of Phase I approaches, we deliver in Phase II an out-of-distribution test set for the same task. The goal of this phase is to adapt and refine models designed for Phase I to handle out-of-distribution data effectively.

Open Submission Phase: After the end of the competition, we initialize an open submission phase inviting researchers to submit their results on the benchmark dataset from Phase II. This phase is not part of the competition but an initiative encouraging ongoing collaboration and facilitating long-term engagement within the research community.

3.2 Dataset

We utilize the gold standard SoMeSci (Schindler et al., 2021) corpus for Phase I, which comprises 3756 manually annotated software mentions from 1367 PubMed Central articles. It supports Named Entity Recognition, Relation Extraction, Entity Disambiguation, and Entity Linking. Annotations include software version, developer, URL, citations,

[4]https://www.codabench.org/competitions/5840/

mention type (e.g., usage, creation), and software type (e.g., application, plugin). There are a total of 7237 labeled entities across 47,524 sentences. We resample the original corpus to create predefined training and testing splits for NER and RE. We manually add negative samples, i.e., sentences without entities and relations, to better simulate real-world data scenarios. We show the statistics of the overall dataset and individual entity label and relation label distributions in Table 3.

For Phase II, we sample PubMed Central Open Access scientific articles. We automatically annotate these articles using a state-of-the-art model (Schindler et al., 2022) based on SciBERT (Beltagy et al., 2019), trained on the SoMeSci gold-standard benchmark dataset (Schindler et al., 2021), to extract software mentions, their attributes, and the relations between them. We consider this a weakly labeled dataset. The overall statistics of detected named entities and relations are provided in the Table 4. To create a gold standard labeled test set, five annotators; three are master's students in relevant fields, and two PhD candidates reviewed and corrected the weakly labeled test set. We use the same annotation guidelines as the original SOMESCI corpus to ensure consistency. Table 4 compares dataset statistics before (weakly annotated) and after review.

3.3 Scoring Metric

We use the same evaluation metrics for all phases. We evaluate the NER and RE performance using the F1 score on exact matches. We opted for the macro F1 score as our dataset is imbalanced, as shown in Table 3 and 4. This decision ensures equal evaluation importance for all classes, regardless of the class frequency. As a final metric to evaluate the competing approaches, we use the mean of macro F1 for NER and macro F1 for RE. This 'F1 SOMD' called metric favors IE systems, which are able to perform well on both tasks, i.e., NER and RE.

3.4 Submissions

The shared task competition encompassed two phases from February 24 to April 3, 2025. Registration began on February 24, followed by the initial training and test data release on February 27. Phase I ran from February 27 to March 25, during which participants could submit up to 5 daily runs. Phase II started with a new dataset release on March 25 and closed on April 3, allowing five daily submissions. The open post-evaluation phase on Codabench allows 10 daily submissions per participant, enabling further experimentation and result refinement.

4 Participants and Approaches

A total of 18 teams registered for the SOMD2025 shared task. Three teams participated fully by submitting results in both Phase I and Phase II, as well as providing a system description. These teams were the TU Graz Data Team (TUGraz), a team from the Nepal-based company EKbana, and one participant from the Universidade de Aveiro (UAveiro). Additionally, there was one late participation, consisting of a master's student from the Georgia Institute of Technology and an independent researcher (psr123), who submitted only for Phase II and provided a system description.

These four teams are referred to as the final participants in this paper. One further participant submitted results in Phase II but did not provide a system description and is therefore not discussed further. All final participants used the open submission phase to further test and refine their approaches after the conclusion of Phase II. In this section, we introduce the four final approaches alongside two baseline models.

4.1 Approaches

All final participants employed finetuning approaches, with some leveraging additional training data, as detailed in Table 1. All teams utilized pretrained language models (PLMs). The largest model used for finetuning was DeBERTa v3, comprising up to 418 million parameters, including the embedding layer (He et al., 2021a,b). The largest model applied for generating embeddings without layer finetuning was the Multilingual E5 instruct model with 560 million parameters (Wang et al., 2024). One participant incorporated a graph neural network (GNN) based on the words of parsed input sentences, with edges defined by their dependency tree (UAveiro). Additionally, this team used DeepSeek v3 (Liu et al., 2024) to classify detected relation types. Regarding loss strategies, only one team (TUGraz) and our baseline approach adopted a joint loss for NER and RE. The remaining teams trained RE and NER modules separately and applied a pipeline approach for inference on the test data.

In terms of data augmentation and generated training data, two out of four approaches utilized addi-

Table 1: Overview of approaches used in SOMD2025. The loss strategy reflect the usage of joint learning for the NER and RE task in contrast to train separate models with separate losses.

Team	Model Architecture	PLM	Loss Strategy	Data Augmentation
TUGraz	Transformer	DeBERTa v3	joint	—
EKbana	Transformer + Adapter	ModernBERT	separate	SOMD2024 + LLM Generated
psr123	Transformer	DeBERTa v3	separate	Negative Samples + LLM Generated
UAveiro	GNN + Transformer	Multilingual E5	separate	—
Baseline	HGERE (Transf. + GNN)	SciBERT	joint	—

tional training data. One team (psr123) augmented the training data specifically with sentences from the same domain as the test set that contain no mentions, to expose the model to negative examples. Another team (EKbana) used the SOMD2024 dataset as additional training data. Furthermore, new training samples were generated using large language models (LLMs) by both EKbana and psr123.

4.2 Baseline Model

Recent work has shown that supervised NER and RE with small language models can achieve strong performance on scholarly information extraction tasks (Yan et al., 2023; Zhang et al., 2024). Among the current approaches, joint models that unify entity and relation prediction have gained attention for their ability to capture dependencies between tasks. In our experiments, we adopt HGERE (Yan et al., 2023) as a joint baseline model. HGERE extends the marker-based PL-Marker framework (Ye et al., 2022b) by introducing a hypergraph neural network that models interactions between subjects, objects, and relations. We selected HGERE due to its effective integration of task components and its demonstrated performance in similar domains.

5 Results

In this section, we present the results of the SOMD2025 shared task, including performance scores for both phases of the competition. For this section, we focus on the more challenging Phase II test set because it better illustrates the generalization capabilities of the used IE models. We compare the results of all final participating teams, highlight the top-performing systems, and contrast them with baseline models. Additionally, we include results from the non-competitive open submission phase as including unpublished Codabench results reported in the corresponding system descriptions of the teams. This provides further insight into model improvements beyond the official evaluation period. The main results can be found in Table 2, illustrating TUGraz as the winner of the challenging Phase II with a SOMD score of 0.63. The TU Graz team used a joint loss for NER and RE and was not dependent on data augmentation to achieve that score.

Note that two of four teams were not able to submit RE results in time, illustrating the hurdle to overcome to switch from well-established NER models to RE models. The leading competing approaches, TUGraz (0.69 SOMD score in the non-competitive version for Phase II) and our proposed baseline model HGERE (0.62 SOMD score for Phase II), both employ a joint loss for the NER and RE tasks without utilizing additional training data. The UAverio performance results report that an unconventional approach utilizing a dependency graph-based representation of language is not able to achieve the same results as transformer-based approaches. Transformer-based approaches are able to use attention to mitigate information between all tokens directly.

6 Discussion

6.1 The Role of LLMs

None of the participants used prompting of LLMs as a final competition approach. But some of the approaches used LLMs in other roles. TUGraz is the only team reporting performances for prompting approaches without any finetuning. They tested only NER in Phase I, achieving a macro F1 of 0.39 with Gemini 2 in a zero-shot approach. Additionally, they reported results of LLaMA 3 8B (Grattafiori et al., 2024) finetuning for Phase I, a SOMD score of 0.66. Compared to finetuning approaches based on smaller language models, these results led the team to the decision not to pursue this direction further.

Two other teams, EKbana and psr123, experimented with synthetic training data generated by LLMs. Team psr123 used existing entities from available training samples and asked models to

Table 2: macro F1 score Results for SOMD2025 Shared Task. SOMD score is the mean of NER and RE macro F1.

Submission	Team	Phase I (macro F1)			Phase II (macro F1)		
		SOMD	NER	RE	SOMD	NER	RE
official	TUGraz	88	90	**85**	**63**	**68**	**57**
	EKbana	***89***	***93***	84	55	64	46
	psr123	–	–	–	32	65	0
	UAverio	39	45	34	15	30	0
non-competitive	TUGraz	–	–	–	*69*	*77*	*62*
	Baseline	*89*	91	*87*	62	68	57
	EKbana	–	–	–	60	69	50
	psr123	–	–	–	56	65	47
	UAverio	–	–	–	22	44	0

produce new contexts mentioning the same entities. They experimented with synthetic data from three different models, with the best configuration (samples generated with Mistral 7B) resulting in a performance gain of 6% points for macro F1 NER. The observed performance gain can be primarily attributed to a significant increase in precision. Team EKbana attempted to tweak results in the out-of-distribution based Phase II by searching for new vocabulary in the Phase II test set sentences compared to Phase I data. They then used these new terms as input to produce new training examples, aiming to adapt their Phase I model to the new distribution of the test data. This approach led to a performance boost of 0.09 SOMD score after several experiments utilizing this data. Whether this approach is generalizable to other distribution shifts, such as domain shift, remains to be proven in future research.

The last usage example among participants was the role of a relation classifier in UAverio's approach. Their model outputs relation candidates in the form of entity mentions and they prompted a Deepseek v3 model to identify the correct relation direction and label. Nonetheless, the overall mediocre performance does not provide valuable interpretability regarding the promise of this approach.

6.2 The Impact of Additional Training Data

Team psr123 showed that adding negative sentences (i.e., sentences without any software mentions) significantly improved the performance of their RE model, from 0.15 to 0.47 macro F1 on the Phase II test set. However, team TUGraz demonstrated that a similar experiment using DeBERTa v3 (He et al., 2021a) with a separate loss for RE achieved a higher RE macro F1 of 0.56 without additional negative samples. This suggests that a deeper analysis of implementation details and hyperparameter settings is needed to accurately assess the impact of adding negative examples.

Team EKbana's use of SOMD2024 data as additional training data for Phase I deserves special attention. As described in Section 3.2, the SOMD2025 Phase I data is a resampled version of the SOMD2024 dataset. This results in data leakage when SOMD2024 data is used for training. EKbana's Phase I result in Table 2 should be interpreted with this in mind.

6.3 Loss Strategy

Team TUGraz highlighted the effectiveness of using a joint loss for NER and RE in their system description. Their experiments showed a performance improvement of 1 to 10 SOMD score points compared to training with separate losses. Our Baseline approach, which also relies on a joint loss, supports the conclusion that selecting an appropriate model architecture—and in particular, the loss function—is more critical than adding extra training data, whether synthetically generated or composed of additional negative sentences. A well-defined experimental setup and careful design choices enabled team TUGraz to achieve the best performance and win the shared task.

7 Conclusion

The SOMD2025 shared task addressed the challenge of extracting software mentions, attributes, and relations from scientific articles using a joint NER and RE framework. With two evaluation phases, including an out-of-distribution test set, the task emphasized both extraction accuracy and model generalizability. Participating teams employed diverse strategies, including pretrained language models, graph-based architectures, and data augmentation using LLMs. Results show that while current methods perform well on in-distribution data, generalization remains a significant challenge.

Table 3: Dataset Overview: Sentence Statistics, Entity and Relation Label Distributions(Phase I)

(a) Dataset Split Summary. **Pos.** denotes the number of sentences that have both entities and relations. Neg. denotes the number of sentences that have no relation label. Negatives are split into (i) sentences with entities but no relations, and (ii) sentences with neither entities nor relations.

Split	# Sents	Pos.	Neg. (Ent/None)
Train	1149	1021	16 / 112
Test	203	182	3 / 18

(b) Entity Label Distribution

Entity	Train	Test
Application	1232	217
Version	904	168
Developer	616	125
Citation	382	53
ProgrammingEnvironment	234	37
URL	216	32
PlugIn	211	34
OperatingSystem	146	22
Release	69	13
Abbreviation	58	4
Extension	43	7
License	43	7
SoftwareCoreference	14	1
AlternativeName	14	2

(c) Relation Label Distribution

Relation	Train	Test
Version_of	904	168
Developer_of	623	126
Citation_of	387	53
URL_of	218	32
PlugIn_of	141	25
Release_of	69	13
Abbreviation_of	58	4
Specification_of	53	14
Extension_of	44	7
License_of	40	7
AlternativeName_of	14	2

The top systems showed improvements over previous baselines, particularly in Phase I, and provided valuable insights into joint learning strategies and training data choices. The shared task supports sustained progress in software-related information extraction from scholarly texts by continuing with an open, ongoing submission phase.

8 Limitations

The current setup of the SOMD shared task is constrained by the lack of a representative distribution of negative samples across both the training and test sets. Furthermore, the scope of the research is limited to the biomedical domain, as determined by the selection of relevant open access publications. Additionally, the methodology of the shared task does not incorporate a disambiguation step, which is identified as a direction for future work.

9 Acknowledgment

This work has received funding through the DFG projects NFDI4DS (grant number 460234259) and BERD@NFDI (grant number 460037581). We thank both NFDI4DS and BERD@NFDI for their funding and support. Special thanks go to all institutions and individuals contributing to the association and its goals.

References

Iz Beltagy, Kyle Lo, and Arman Cohan. 2019. Scibert: A pretrained language model for scientific text. In *Proceedings of EMNLP*.

Geraint Duck, Goran Nenadic, Michele Filannino, Andy Brass, David L Robertson, and Robert Stevens. 2016. A survey of bioinformatics database and software usage through mining the literature. *PloS one*, 11(6):e0157989.

Aaron Grattafiori, Abhimanyu Dubey, Abhinav Jauhri, Abhinav Pandey, Abhishek Kadian, Ahmad Al-Dahle, Aiesha Letman, Akhil Mathur, Alan Schelten, Alex Vaughan, Amy Yang, Angela Fan, Anirudh Goyal, Anthony Hartshorn, Aobo Yang, Archi Mitra, Archie Sravankumar, Artem Korenev, Arthur Hinsvark, and 542 others. 2024. The llama 3 herd of models. *Preprint*, arXiv:2407.21783.

Pengcheng He, Jianfeng Gao, and Weizhu Chen. 2021a. Debertav3: Improving deberta using electra-style pre-training with gradient-disentangled embedding sharing. *Preprint*, arXiv:2111.09543.

Pengcheng He, Xiaodong Liu, Jianfeng Gao, and Weizhu Chen. 2021b. Deberta: Decoding-enhanced bert with disentangled attention. In *International Conference on Learning Representations*.

Table 4: Phase-2 Dataset Overview: Sentence Statistics, Entity and Relation Label Distributions. The reviewed set is a manually corrected subset of the weakly labeled data.

(a) Entity Label Distribution

Entity Type	Weak	Reviewed
Application	662	363
Version	135	96
Developer	47	20
Citation	216	187
ProgrammingEnvironment	70	24
URL	84	70
PlugIn	38	20
OperatingSystem	7	2
Release	10	10
Abbreviation	19	12
Extension	7	6
License	-	-
SoftwareCoreference	4	3
AlternativeName	18	17

(b) Relation Label Distribution

Relation Type	Weak	Reviewed
Version_of	134	96
Developer_of	41	20
Citation_of	173	187
URL_of	72	70
PlugIn_of	22	13
Release_of	8	10
Abbreviation_of	16	12
Specification_of	12	-
Extension_of	5	6
License_of	-	7
AlternativeName_of	14	17

Moritz Hennen, Florian Babl, and Michaela Geierhos. 2024. ITER: Iterative transformer-based entity recognition and relation extraction. In *Findings of the Association for Computational Linguistics: EMNLP 2024*, pages 11209–11223, Miami, Florida, USA. Association for Computational Linguistics.

James Howison and Julia Bullard. 2016. Software in the scientific literature: Problems with seeing, finding, and using software mentioned in the biology literature. *Journal of the Association for Information Science and Technology*, 67(9):2137–2155.

Pere-Lluís Huguet Cabot and Roberto Navigli. 2021. REBEL: Relation extraction by end-to-end language generation. In *Findings of the Association for Computational Linguistics: EMNLP 2021*, pages 2370–2381, Punta Cana, Dominican Republic. Association for Computational Linguistics.

Saurav Karmakar, Matthäus Zloch, Fidan Limani, Benjamin Zapilko, Sharmila Upadhyaya, Jennifer D'Souza, Leyla J. Castro, Georg Rehm, Marcel R. Ackermann, Harald Sack, Zeyd Boukhers, Sonja Schimmler, Danilo Dessí, Peter Mutschke, and Stefan Dietze. 2023. Research knowledge graphs in nfdi4ds. In *INFORMATIK 2023 - Designing Futures: Zukünfte gestalten*, pages 909–918. Gesellschaft für Informatik e.V., Bonn.

Daniel S Katz, Neil P Chue Hong, Tim Clark, August Muench, Shelley Stall, Daina Bouquin, Matthew Cannon, Scott Edmunds, Telli Faez, Patricia Feeney, and 1 others. 2021. Recognizing the value of software: a software citation guide. *F1000Research*, 9:1257.

AmeerAli Khan, Qusai Ramadan, Cong Yang, and Zeyd Boukhers. 2024. Falcon 7b for software mention detection in scholarly documents. In *International Workshop on Natural Scientific Language Processing and Research Knowledge Graphs*, pages 278–288. Springer Nature Switzerland Cham.

Frank Krüger, Saurav Karmakar, and Stefan Dietze. 2024. Somd@ nslp2024: Overview and insights from the software mention detection shared task. In *International Workshop on Natural Scientific Language Processing and Research Knowledge Graphs*, pages 247–256. Springer.

Frank Krüger, Saurav Karmakar, and Stefan Dietze. 2024. Somd@nslp2024: Overview and insights from the software mention detection shared task. In *Natural Scientific Language Processing and Research Knowledge Graphs: First International Workshop, NSLP 2024, Hersonissos, Crete, Greece, May 27, 2024, Proceedings*, page 247–256, Berlin, Heidelberg. Springer-Verlag.

Kai Li, Xia Lin, and Jane Greenberg. 2016. Software citation, reuse and metadata considerations: An exploratory study examining lammps. *Proceedings of the Association for Information Science and Technology*, 53(1):1–10.

Kai Li, Erjia Yan, and Yuanyuan Feng. 2017. How is r cited in research outputs? structure, impacts, and citation standard. *Journal of Informetrics*, 11(4):989–1002.

Qi Li and Heng Ji. 2014. Incremental joint extraction of entity mentions and relations. In *Proceedings of the 52nd Annual Meeting of the Association for Computational Linguistics (Volume 1: Long Papers)*, pages 402–412, Baltimore, Maryland. Association for Computational Linguistics.

Aixin Liu, Bei Feng, Bing Xue, Bingxuan Wang, Bochao Wu, Chengda Lu, Chenggang Zhao, Chengqi Deng, Chenyu Zhang, Chong Ruan, and 1 others. 2024. Deepseek-v3 technical report. *arXiv preprint arXiv:2412.19437*.

Paolo Manghi, Alessia Bardi, Claudio Atzori, Miriam Baglioni, Natalia Manola, Jochen Schirrwagen,

Pedro Principe, Michele Artini, Amelie Becker, Michele De Bonis, and 1 others. 2019. The openaire research graph data model. *Zenodo*.

Udit Nangia and Daniel S Katz. 2017. Understanding software in research: Initial results from examining nature and a call for collaboration. In *2017 IEEE 13th international conference on e-science (e-science)*, pages 486–487. IEEE.

Phi Nguyen Xuan, Quang Tran Minh, and Thin Dang Van. 2024. Abcd team at somd 2024: Software mention detection in scholarly publications with large language models. In *International Workshop on Natural Scientific Language Processing and Research Knowledge Graphs*, pages 267–277. Springer Nature Switzerland Cham.

Wolfgang Otto, Sharmila Upadhyaya, and Stefan Dietze. 2024. Enhancing software-related information extraction via single-choice question answering with large language models. In *International Workshop on Natural Scientific Language Processing and Research Knowledge Graphs*, pages 289–306. Springer.

Xuelian Pan, Erjia Yan, Qianqian Wang, and Weina Hua. 2015. Assessing the impact of software on science: A bootstrapped learning of software entities in full-text papers. *Journal of Informetrics*, 9(4):860–871.

David Schindler, Felix Bensmann, Stefan Dietze, and Frank Krüger. 2021. Somesci- a 5 star open data gold standard knowledge graph of software mentions in scientific articles. In *Proceedings of the 30th ACM International Conference on Information & Knowledge Management*, CIKM '21, page 4574–4583, New York, NY, USA. Association for Computing Machinery.

David Schindler, Felix Bensmann, Stefan Dietze, and Frank Krüger. 2022. The role of software in science: a knowledge graph-based analysis of software mentions in pubmed central. *PeerJ Computer Science*, 8:e835.

David Schindler, Tazin Hossain, Sascha Spors, and Frank Krüger. 2024. A multilevel analysis of data quality for formal software citation. *Quantitative Science Studies*, 5(3):637–667.

David Schindler, Benjamin Zapilko, and Frank Krüger. 2020. Investigating software usage in the social sciences: A knowledge graph approach. In *European Semantic Web Conference*, pages 271–286. Springer.

Arfon M Smith, Daniel S Katz, and Kyle E Niemeyer. 2016. Software citation principles. *PeerJ Computer Science*, 2:e86.

Thuy Nguyen Thi, Anh Nguyen Viet, and Thin Dang Van. 2024. Software mention recognition with a three-stage framework based on bertology models at somd 2024. *Natural Scientific Language Processing and Research Knowledge Graphs*, page 257.

David Wadden, Ulme Wennberg, Yi Luan, and Hannaneh Hajishirzi. 2019. Entity, relation, and event extraction with contextualized span representations. In *Proceedings of the 2019 Conference on Empirical Methods in Natural Language Processing and the 9th International Joint Conference on Natural Language Processing (EMNLP-IJCNLP)*, pages 5783–5788.

Liang Wang, Nan Yang, Xiaolong Huang, Linjun Yang, Rangan Majumder, and Furu Wei. 2024. Multilingual e5 text embeddings: A technical report. *arXiv preprint arXiv:2402.05672*.

Zhen Xu, Sergio Escalera, Adrien Pavão, Magali Richard, Wei-Wei Tu, Quanming Yao, Huan Zhao, and Isabelle Guyon. 2022. Codabench: Flexible, easy-to-use, and reproducible meta-benchmark platform. *Patterns*, 3(7).

Zhaohui Yan, Songlin Yang, Wei Liu, and Kewei Tu. 2023. Joint entity and relation extraction with span pruning and hypergraph neural networks. In *Proceedings of the 2023 Conference on Empirical Methods in Natural Language Processing*, pages 7512–7526, Singapore. Association for Computational Linguistics.

Deming Ye, Yankai Lin, Peng Li, and Maosong Sun. 2022a. Packed levitated marker for entity and relation extraction. In *Proceedings of the 60th Annual Meeting of the Association for Computational Linguistics (Volume 1: Long Papers)*, pages 4904–4917.

Deming Ye, Yankai Lin, Peng Li, and Maosong Sun. 2022b. Packed levitated marker for entity and relation extraction. In *Proceedings of the 60th Annual Meeting of the Association for Computational Linguistics (Volume 1: Long Papers)*, pages 4904–4917, Dublin, Ireland. Association for Computational Linguistics.

Daojian Zeng, Kang Liu, Siwei Lai, Guoliang Zhou, and Jun Zhao. 2014. Relation classification via convolutional deep neural network. In *Proceedings of the 25th International Conference on Computational Linguistics (COLING)*, pages 2335–2344.

Qi Zhang, Zhijia Chen, Huitong Pan, Cornelia Caragea, Longin Jan Latecki, and Eduard Dragut. 2024. SciER: An entity and relation extraction dataset for datasets, methods, and tasks in scientific documents. In *Proceedings of the 2024 Conference on Empirical Methods in Natural Language Processing*, pages 13083–13100, Miami, Florida, USA. Association for Computational Linguistics.

Yuhao Zhang, Victor Zhong, Danqi Chen, Gabor Angeli, and Christopher D. Manning. 2017. Position-aware attention and supervised data improve slot filling. In *Proceedings of the 2017 Conference on Empirical Methods in Natural Language Processing (EMNLP)*, pages 35–45.

From In-Distribution to Out-of-Distribution: Joint Loss for Improving Generalization in Software Mention and Relation Extraction

Stasa Mandic[1], **Georg Niess**[1], **Roman Kern**[1,2]
[1]Graz University of Technology, [2]Know Center
Correspondence: stasa.mandic@student.tugraz.at

Abstract

Identifying software entities and their semantic relations in scientific texts contributes to improved reproducibility and allows for the construction machine-readable knowledge graphs. However, models struggle with domain variability and sparse supervision. We address this by evaluating joint Named Entity Recognition (NER) and Relation Extraction (RE) models on the SOMD 2025 shared task, emphasizing generalization to out-of-distribution scholarly texts. We propose a unified training objective that jointly optimizes both tasks using a shared loss function and demonstrates that joint loss formulations can improve out-of-distribution robustness compared to disjoint training. Our results reveal significant performance gaps between in- and out-of-distribution settings, prompting critical reflections on modeling strategies for software knowledge extraction. Notably, our approach ranked 1st in Phase 2 (out-of-distribution) and 2nd in Phase 1 (in-distribution) in the SOMD 2025 shared task, showing strong generalization and robust performance across domains. All code is publicly available.[1]

1 Introduction

Software is crucial to scientific work, but identifying its mentions and relations in text is difficult due to ambiguity, limited supervision, and domain variation (Howison and Bullard, 2016; Pan et al., 2015). The Software Mention Detection (SOMD) shared task series addresses these challenges through benchmark datasets and evaluation frameworks. While the 2024 edition focused on pipeline approaches using full-text articles from the SoMeSci corpus (Dietze et al., 2024), the 2025 task shifts to joint modeling of NER and RE at the sentence level to reduce cascading errors (Li and Ji, 2014; Zeng et al., 2014; Cabot and Navigli, 2021).

In this work, we evaluate joint NER and RE models for software knowledge extraction under domain shift. We compare span-based (GLiNER (Kral et al., 2023)), encoder-based (BERT, SciBERT, and DeBERTa (Devlin et al., 2019; Beltagy et al., 2019; He et al., 2021)), and instruction-tuned architectures (Gemini and Llama (Team et al., 2023; Touvron et al., 2023)) on the SOMD 2025 benchmark. Our central research question is: **Does a joint loss objective improve generalization in multitask NER and RE models?** We find that joint loss boosts in-distribution performance and consistently mitigates degradation in out-of-distribution settings. This highlights its utility as a simple yet effective mechanism for improving robustness in extractive multitask learning.

2 Related Work

Extracting software mentions and their semantic relations from scientific texts is crucial for reproducibility and knowledge organization, yet software is often referenced informally, posing challenges for automatic identification and disambiguation (Schindler et al., 2021). Early approaches treated NER and RE as separate pipeline stages (Li and Ji, 2014; Zeng et al., 2014), but this modularity frequently led to cascading errors, particularly when entity boundaries were misidentified (Zhang et al., 2017). To mitigate these issues, recent work has shifted toward joint models that unify NER and RE within a single architecture. Span-based methods leverage contextualized representations to jointly encode entities and their relations (Wadden et al., 2019; Ye et al., 2022), while generation-based architectures such as REBEL (Cabot and Navigli, 2021) and iterative decoding frameworks (Hennen et al., 2024) aim to improve expressiveness and compositional generalization.

In addition, a growing body of work has focused on discourse-aware and document-level models,

[1]https://github.com/sm9ta/somd2025-joint-loss

Proceedings of the Fifth Workshop on Scholarly Document Processing (SDP 2025), pages 146–153
July 31, 2025 ©2025 Association for Computational Linguistics

which extend the context window beyond a single sentence. For example, Wadden et al. (2019) introduce a span-based architecture that propagates information across sentences using global context graphs, while Ye et al. (2022) use levitated markers to retain global coreference and discourse signals. Models like SciREX (Jain et al., 2020) further highlight the importance of integrating paragraph-level and document-level context to improve entity linking and relation reasoning in scientific documents. These approaches demonstrate that sentence-local models are often insufficient for resolving long-range dependencies, a limitation we also observe in our results. While much of the literature emphasizes architectural integration, fewer studies explore the role of joint loss optimization, i.e., coupling NER and RE learning via a shared objective (Sun et al., 2022; Zhang et al., 2022; Liu et al., 2023). We extend this line of research by comparing joint and disjoint loss formulations across model families and analyzing their impact on generalization, particularly under distribution shift.

In the SOMD 2024 shared task, participants explored alternatives to traditional pipeline systems. Thi et al. (2024) proposed a three-stage BERT-based pipeline, while Otto et al. (2024) used an instruction-tuned LLM for QA-style extraction. Others investigated few-shot adaptation with GPT-3.5/4 (Istrate et al., 2024) or token-level fine-tuning with Falcon-7B (Khan et al., 2024), highlighting the challenges of aligning LLMs with structured tasks. Building on these efforts, our work unifies evaluation across model types and emphasizes generalization under domain shift, responding to recent calls for more robust extraction frameworks (Krüger et al., 2024).

3 Task and Dataset

The SOMD 2025 task involves a two-phase sentence-level joint NER and RE on annotated scientific texts from the SoMeSci corpus (Schindler et al., 2021). The annotation schema includes 14 entity types and 11 relation types that can be found in Appendix A. In **Phase 1 (In-Distribution Validation Set)** models are trained and evaluated on 1,432 annotated sentences (train) and 256 test sentences, while in **Phase 2 (Out-of-Distribution Test Set)** 457 new test sentences from unseen domains are released without gold labels. Models are evaluated via leaderboard submissions, with an additional focus on generalization.

4 Method

4.1 Model Selection

In early experiments, we evaluated instruction-tuned decoder-based models (Gemini 2 and LLaMA 3 8B) in zero and few-shot configurations without fine-tuning. However, their performance was not satisfactory as they failed to follow SOMD's strict schema, hallucinated outputs, and lacked token-level precision, issues also noted in prior work (Otto et al., 2024; Istrate et al., 2024), which highlights the limitations of instruction-following LLMs in structured extraction. We therefore excluded them from joint training and focused on encoder-based models with proven suitability for NER and RE.

We selected DeBERTa-v3, SciBERT, and GLiNER based on their complementary strengths and empirical performance in previous NER and RE benchmarks. SciBERT is pretrained on 1.14M scientific papers from Semantic Scholar and is specifically optimized for the scientific domain (Beltagy et al., 2019), making it particularly suited to the SOMD corpus. DeBERTa-v3 incorporates disentangled attention and enhanced mask decoding, which improve generalization across domains, especially in out-of-distribution settings (He et al., 2021). GLiNER, a span-based model, provides strong performance on fine-grained entity recognition due to its ability to directly model entity spans without relying on token-level tagging (Kral et al., 2023). This is particularly useful in software-related texts where entity boundaries may be ambiguous.

Other prominent pretrained models such as RoBERTa or BioBERT were not included in our final evaluation due to domain misalignment (e.g., biomedical corpora in BioBERT (Lee et al., 2020)) or redundancy with DeBERTa in terms of architectural class. We also did not include models such as T5 (Raffel et al., 2020) or BART (Lewis et al., 2019), as their sequence-to-sequence format is less compatible with structured joint token- and span-level prediction. In the end, our goal was not exhaustive benchmarking, but rather a focused comparison across representative architectures: span-based (GLiNER), domain-specialized encoder (SciBERT), and general-purpose contextual encoder (DeBERTa) to assess how model inductive biases influence generalization under joint optimization.

4.2 Model Architecture

Given an input sentence $\mathbf{x} = \{x_1, x_2, \ldots, x_N\}$, the encoder produces hidden states $\mathbf{h} = \{h_1, h_2, \ldots, h_N\}$, which serve as the basis for downstream prediction tasks. On top of the encoder, we add two task-specific classification heads. The first is a token-level classifier for NER that predicts BIO-encoded entity labels for each token. The second head is a relation classifier that predicts the type of semantic relation between entity pairs, based on the concatenation of their respective token representations. For each candidate pair (i, j) of detected entities, their corresponding embeddings h_i and h_j are concatenated and passed to a feedforward classification layer. In the end, we evaluate multiple encoder backbones, including SciBERT, DeBERTa-v3-large, and GLiNER.
Figure 1 illustrates the architecture and information flow in our joint NER and RE model, including task-specific heads and shared optimization through a unified loss.

4.3 Joint Loss Objective

To encourage shared representations between NER and RE, we optimize a joint loss function. The NER loss is a masked token-level cross-entropy over K entity classes:

$$\mathcal{L}_{\text{NER}} = -\sum_{i=1}^{N} m_i \log \frac{\exp(z_{i,y_i})}{\sum_{k=1}^{K} \exp(z_{i,k})} \quad (1)$$

where m_i masks out incomplete tokens, z_i are the logits, and y_i are gold labels. The RE loss is computed over a set of candidate entity pairs $\mathcal{R}$, with L relation types (including a "no-relation" class):

$$\mathcal{L}_{\text{RE}} = -\sum_{(i,j)\in\mathcal{R}} \log \frac{\exp(z_{ij,r_{ij}})}{\sum_{l=1}^{L} \exp(z_{ij,l})} \quad (2)$$

The total loss is:

$$\mathcal{L} = \mathcal{L}_{\text{NER}} + \lambda \mathcal{L}_{\text{RE}} \quad (3)$$

where λ is a tunable weight (default $\lambda = 1$).

4.4 Training Setup

We fine-tune all models using AdamW with warm-up and early stopping. The training is done for 3 to 6 epochs depending on the model with batch size 8 and learning rate 3×10^{-5}. Dropout and gradient clipping are applied, and the best checkpoints are selected via dev set macro F1.

4.4.1 Joint Training Procedure

Algorithm 1 outlines our joint training procedure. For each batch, contextualized embeddings are computed, token-level predictions and loss for NER are obtained, and relation classification is performed on candidate entity pairs. The two losses are then combined into a single objective, and a joint backward pass is used to update all model parameters simultaneously. To evaluate the effect of shared optimization, we also implement a disjoint training variant where NER and RE tasks are optimized separately in isolated stages and gradients are not shared across tasks during training.

Algorithm 1 Joint Training for NER and Relation Extraction

Require: Training dataset $\mathcal{D} = \{(X, Y, \mathcal{R})\}$, where X denotes the input token sequence, Y the corresponding token labels, and $\mathcal{R}$ the relation annotations.

Initialize model parameters Θ (shared encoder, NER head, and RE head).
for each epoch **do**
  for each batch $(X, Y, \mathcal{R}) \in \mathcal{D}$ **do**
    $H \leftarrow \text{Encoder}(X)$ {Compute contextual representations}
    $Z^{\text{NER}} \leftarrow \text{NER\_Head}(H)$
    Compute masked NER loss using the cross-entropy loss CE$(\cdot)$:

$$\mathcal{L}_{\text{NER}} \leftarrow \sum_{i=1}^{N} m_i \, \text{CE}(Z_i^{\text{NER}}, y_i)$$

    Generate candidate entity pairs $\mathcal{C}$ from Y (using gold labels during training or predicted labels at inference).
    for each candidate pair $(i, j) \in \mathcal{C}$ **do**
      $r_{ij} \leftarrow \text{Concat}(H_i, H_j)$
      $Z_{ij}^{\text{RE}} \leftarrow \text{RE\_Head}(r_{ij})$
    end for
    Compute RE loss:

$$\mathcal{L}_{\text{RE}} \leftarrow \sum_{(i,j)\in\mathcal{C}} \text{CE}(Z_{ij}^{\text{RE}}, r_{ij}^{\text{gt}})$$

    Compute joint loss: $\mathcal{L} \leftarrow \mathcal{L}_{\text{NER}} + \mathcal{L}_{\text{RE}}$
    Perform backpropagation: update Θ using $\nabla\mathcal{L}$ (e.g., via AdamW with a linear scheduler).
  end for
end for

5 Results

We evaluate joint NER and RE models on the SOMD 2025 benchmark using span-based (GLiNER), encoder-based (SciBERT, DeBERTa-v3). All models are jointly fine-tuned using both a disjoint and unified loss objective and evaluated across in-distribution (Phase 1) and out-of-distribution (Phase 2) subsets while their performance is summarized in Table 1. We report total and macro-averaged F1, precision, and recall as per SOMD 2025 guidelines. NER is evaluated using token-level exact matches under the IOB2 scheme, while RE requires exact entity span and relation label matches. Phase 2 uses leaderboard submissions due to the current unavailability of gold annotations.

Phase 1: In-Distribution Performance We fine-tuned GLiNER, DeBERTa v3, and SciBERT on the official training split and evaluated them on the development set. GLiNER (base and large-v2.1) was fine-tuned with improved label alignment; SciBERT incorporated a feedforward classifier over span start tokens; and DeBERTa v3 (tasksource-nli) demonstrated stronger stability than its Microsoft variant. In the end, we report that GLiNER outperforms other models with a total F1 of 0.88, followed by DeBERTa-v3 (0.83) and SciBERT (0.79).

Phase 2: Out-of-Distribution Generalization In Phase 2, all models showed a noticeable drop in performance, highlighting the challenge of out-of-distribution generalization. DeBERTa v3 performed the best (Total F1: 0.69; NER: 0.79; RE: 0.62), likely due to its strong contextual modeling and robust sentence-level semantics. GLiNER followed with a Total F1 of 0.60, suggesting that it struggled more with semantic variability; and SciBERT remained competitive with Total F1 of 0.59, showing stable results across tasks despite its limited adaptability to unseen domains.

5.1 Effect of Joint Loss

Across all models, training with joint loss improved both in-distribution and out-of-distribution performance (Table 1). This indicates that joint loss might allow models to use interdependencies between entity recognition and relation extraction more effectively.

5.2 Error Analysis

All models experienced a notable performance decline from Phase 1 to Phase 2, underscoring the challenge of generalizing to out-of-distribution data. GLiNER, DeBERTa v3, and SciBERT dropped from total F1 scores of 0.88, 0.83, and 0.79 to 0.60, 0.69, and 0.59, respectively, corresponding to reductions of approximately 0.20–0.25. This drop was especially pronounced in relation extraction, where domain shifts introduced unfamiliar entity formats, longer and more nested mentions (e.g., *Stata Statistical Software: Release 13*), and cross-clause relations that proved difficult to capture. SciBERT was most affected, suggesting that domain-specific pretraining alone is insufficient to guarantee robustness across scientific subdomains.
A detailed entity- and relation-level analysis in Table 2 and 3 shows that GLiNER and DeBERTa v3 performed well on frequent and syntactically unambiguous entities such as URL, SoftwareCoreference, and OperatingSystem, where the high number of training examples and clear structure provided strong learning signals. They also handled common relation types like Citation_of and Developer_of with high accuracy. However, notable differences emerged in semantically complex and low-resource categories. DeBERTa v3 outperformed GLiNER on rare entities like Extension and its associated relation Extension_of, likely due to its stronger contextual representations and attention mechanisms. Conversely, GLiNER performed better on PlugIn and PlugIn_of, that might be indicating advantages of span-based architectures in handling regular syntactic patterns. Both models struggled with underrepresented or domain-specific relations such as License_of, AlternativeName_of, and Specification_of, where F1 scores dropped to zero, highlighting shared limitations in handling class imbalance and semantic drift.
In addition, an important constraint across all models seemed to be their reliance on sentence-level inputs, which prevented them from resolving longer-range dependencies or cross-sentence relationships. This restricted their ability to fully capture the context necessary for accurate entity and relation extraction in complex scholarly texts. Overall, these findings suggest that improving out-of-distribution generalization requires stronger pretraining objectives, more balanced annotation schemes, and model architectures capable of discourse-level reasoning.

Model	Phase 1 In-Distribution Validation Set							Phase 2 Out-of-Distribution Test Set						
	Total F1	Entity			Relation			Total F1	Entity			Relation		
		F1	P	R	F1	P	R		F1	P	R	F1	P	R
Disjoint Loss														
GLiNER	0.78	0.77	0.77	0.78	0.80	0.81	0.81	0.59	0.61	0.60	0.69	0.57	0.61	0.63
DeBERTa v3	0.80	0.78	0.77	0.80	0.81	0.81	0.84	0.59	0.63	0.60	0.70	0.56	0.59	0.60
SciBERT	0.75	0.79	0.79	0.79	0.72	0.68	0.77	0.53	0.56	0.59	0.59	0.50	0.59	0.52
Joint Loss														
GLiNER	0.88	0.90	0.87	0.94	0.85	0.88	0.85	0.60	0.66	0.65	0.73	0.53	0.58	0.56
DeBERTa v3	0.83	0.83	0.84	0.84	0.82	0.83	0.83	0.69	0.79	0.74	0.84	0.62	0.62	0.63
SciBERT	0.79	0.85	0.84	0.87	0.73	0.72	0.74	0.59	0.61	0.55	0.68	0.58	0.48	0.72

Table 1: Performance metrics for selected models in Phase 1 and Phase 2.

Entity Recognition (F1)		
Entity Type	**GLiNER**	**DeBERTa v3**
Application	0.765	0.732
Citation	0.837	0.903
Developer	0.667	0.667
PlugIn	0.435	0.346
Version	0.210	0.794
Extension	0.133	0.400
Release	0.667	0.727
URL	1.000	1.000
Abbreviation	0.529	0.750
ProgrammingEnvironment	0.957	0.936
OperatingSystem	1.000	1.000
SoftwareCoreference	1.000	1.000
AlternativeName	0.457	0.769

Table 2: Entity recognition F1 scores for GLiNER and DeBERTa v3.

Relation Extraction (F1)		
Relation Type	**GLiNER**	**DeBERTa v3**
Developer_of	0.650	0.652
Citation_of	0.682	0.683
Version_of	0.573	0.615
PlugIn_of	0.647	0.579
URL_of	0.787	0.595
Abbreviation_of	0.640	0.667
Release_of	0.522	0.705
Extension_of	0.250	0.545
AlternativeName_of	0.000	0.500
License_of	0.000	0.000
Specification_of	0.000	0.000

Table 3: Relation extraction F1 scores for GLiNER and DeBERTa v3.

6 Conclusion

We evaluate joint NER and RE models for extracting software mentions and relations in scientific texts, with a focus on out-of-distribution generalization. Our results show that a shared loss objective consistently boosts performance across architectures, indicating that multitask learning benefits not only from architectural integration but also from coupled optimization. This joint loss approach reduces error propagation and enhances robustness, making it a simple yet effective strategy for structured scientific information extraction.

Limitations

While our study offers valuable insights into joint NER and RE model generalization, it has limitations. First, restricting inputs to the sentence level may hinder models from capturing broader context or long-range dependencies, and future work should explore paragraph- or document-level modeling. Second, baseline Gemini and LLaMA were evaluated only in the first phase and due to low results were excluded from further training; adapting them to the domain may yield better results. Third, the limited size of the SOMD 2025 dataset may reduce the effectiveness of large models, especially for rare entities and relations.

References

Iz Beltagy, Kyle Lo, and Arman Cohan. 2019. SciBERT: A pretrained language model for scientific text. In *Proceedings of the 2019 Conference on Empirical Methods in Natural Language Processing and the 9th International Joint Conference on Natural Language Processing (EMNLP-IJCNLP)*, pages 3615–3620, Hong Kong, China. Association for Computational Linguistics.

Pierre Cabot and Roberto Navigli. 2021. REBEL: Relation extraction by end-to-end language generation. In *Proceedings of the 2021 Conference on Empirical Methods in Natural Language Processing*, pages 4110–4121, Online and Punta Cana, Dominican Republic. Association for Computational Linguistics.

Jacob Devlin, Ming-Wei Chang, Kenton Lee, and Kristina Toutanova. 2019. BERT: Pre-training of deep bidirectional transformers for language understanding. In *Proceedings of the 2019 Conference of the North American Chapter of the Association for Computational Linguistics: Human Language Technologies, Volume 1 (Long and Short Papers)*, pages 4171–4186, Minneapolis, Minnesota. Association for Computational Linguistics.

Stefan Dietze, Frank Krüger, and Saurav Karmarkar. 2024. SOMD: Software mention detection in scholarly publications. In *Proceedings of the International Workshop on Natural Scientific Language Processing and Research Knowledge Graphs (NSLP 2024)*, St. Julians, Malta. Springer.

Pengcheng He, Xiaodong Liu, Jianfeng Gao, and Weizhu Chen. 2021. DeBERTa: Decoding-enhanced BERT with disentangled attention. In *International Conference on Learning Representations (ICLR)*.

Moritz Hennen, Florian Babl, and Michaela Geierhos. 2024. ITER: Iterative transformer-based entity recognition and relation extraction. In *Findings of the Association for Computational Linguistics: EMNLP 2024*, pages 11209–11223, Miami, Florida, USA. Association for Computational Linguistics.

James Howison and Julia Bullard. 2016. Software in the scientific literature: Problems with seeing, finding, and using software mentioned in the biology literature. *Journal of the Association for Information Science and Technology*, 67(9):2137–2155.

Ana-Maria Istrate, Joshua Fisher, Xinyu Yang, Kara Moraw, Kai Li, Donghui Li, and Martin Klein. 2024. Scientific software citation intent classification using large language models. In *Proceedings of the International Workshop on Natural Scientific Language Processing and Research Knowledge Graphs (NSLP 2024)*, pages 80–99. Springer Nature Switzerland, Cham.

Sarthak Jain, Ankur Pal, Eric Lehman, and Byron C. Wallace. 2020. Scirex: A challenge dataset for document-level information extraction. In *Proceedings of the 58th Annual Meeting of the Association for Computational Linguistics*, pages 7506–7516, Online. Association for Computational Linguistics.

AmeerAli Khan, Qusai Ramadan, Cong Yang, and Zeyd Boukhers. 2024. Falcon 7b for software mention detection in scholarly documents. In *Proceedings of the International Workshop on Natural Scientific Language Processing and Research Knowledge Graphs (NSLP 2024)*, pages 278–288. Springer Nature Switzerland, Cham.

Tomas Kral, Milan Straka, and Jana Strakova. 2023. GLiNER: Generalist linker for named entity recognition. In *Findings of the Association for Computational Linguistics: ACL 2023*, pages 1710–1722, Toronto, Canada. Association for Computational Linguistics.

Frank Krüger, Saurav Karmakar, and Stefan Dietze. 2024. SOMD@NSLP2024: Overview and insights from the software mention detection shared task. In *Proceedings of the International Workshop on Natural Scientific Language Processing and Research Knowledge Graphs (NSLP 2024)*, pages 247–256. Springer.

Jinhyuk Lee, Wonjin Yoon, Sungdong Kim, Donghyeon Kim, Sunkyu Kim, Chan Ho So, and Jaewoo Kang. 2020. Biobert: a pre-trained biomedical language representation model for biomedical text mining. *Bioinformatics*, 36(4):1234–1240.

Mike Lewis, Yinhan Liu, Naman Goyal, Marjan Ghazvininejad, Abdelrahman Mohamed, Omer Levy, Ves Stoyanov, and Luke Zettlemoyer. 2019. BART: Denoising sequence-to-sequence pre-training for natural language generation, translation, and comprehension. *arXiv preprint*, arXiv:1910.13461.

Qi Li and Heng Ji. 2014. Incremental joint extraction of entity mentions and relations. In *Proceedings of the 52nd Annual Meeting of the Association for Computational Linguistics (Volume 1: Long Papers)*, pages 402–412, Baltimore, Maryland. Association for Computational Linguistics.

Yujie Liu, Linjun Yang, and Fei Huang. 2023. Joint extraction of entities and relations with shared parameters and task-specific decoders. *Knowledge-Based Systems*, 267:110192.

Wolfgang Otto, Sharmila Upadhyaya, and Stefan Dietze. 2024. Enhancing software-related information extraction via single-choice question answering with large language models. In *Proceedings of the International Workshop on Natural Scientific Language Processing and Research Knowledge Graphs (NSLP 2024)*, pages 289–306. Springer.

Xuelian Pan, Erjia Yan, Qianqian Wang, and Weina Hua. 2015. Assessing the impact of software on science: A bootstrapped learning of software entities in full-text papers. *Journal of Informetrics*, 9(4):860–871.

Colin Raffel, Noam Shazeer, Adam Roberts, Katherine Lee, Sharan Narang, Michael Matena, Yanqi Zhou, Wei Li, and Peter J. Liu. 2020. Exploring the limits of transfer learning with a unified text-to-text transformer. *Journal of Machine Learning Research*, 21(140):1–67.

David Schindler, Felix Bensmann, Stefan Dietze, and Frank Krüger. 2021. SoMeSci: A 5 star open data gold standard knowledge graph of software mentions in scientific articles. In *Proceedings of the 30th ACM International Conference on Information and Knowledge Management (CIKM)*, pages 4574–4583, New York, NY, USA. Association for Computing Machinery.

Kai Sun, Rui Zhang, and Xiang Ren. 2022. FS-NER: A few-shot joint entity and relation extraction framework. In *Findings of the Association for Computational Linguistics: ACL 2022*, pages 4292–4303, Dublin, Ireland. Association for Computational Linguistics.

Gemini Team, Rohan Anil, Sebastian Borgeaud, Jean-Baptiste Alayrac, Jiahui Yu, Radu Soricut, Johan Schalkwyk, Andrew M. Dai, Anja Hauth, Katie Millican, and 1 others. 2023. Gemini: A family of highly capable multimodal models. *arXiv preprint*, arXiv:2312.11805.

Thuy Nguyen Thi, Anh Nguyen Viet, Thin Dang Van, and Ngan Luu-Thuy Nguyen. 2024. Software mention recognition with a three-stage framework based on BERTology models at SOMD 2024. In *Proceedings of the International Workshop on Natural Scientific Language Processing and Research Knowledge Graphs (NSLP 2024)*, pages 257–266. Springer.

Hugo Touvron, Thibaut Lavril, Gautier Izacard, Xavier Martinet, Marie-Anne Lachaux, Timothée Lacroix, Baptiste Rozière, Naman Goyal, Eric Hambro, Faisal Azhar, and 1 others. 2023. LLaMA: Open and efficient foundation language models. *arXiv preprint*, arXiv:2302.13971.

David Wadden, Ulme Wennberg, Yi Luan, and Hannaneh Hajishirzi. 2019. Entity, relation, and event extraction with contextualized span representations. In *Proceedings of the 2019 Conference on Empirical Methods in Natural Language Processing and the 9th International Joint Conference on Natural Language Processing (EMNLP-IJCNLP)*, pages 5784–5789, Hong Kong, China. Association for Computational Linguistics.

Deming Ye, Yankai Lin, Peng Li, and Maosong Sun. 2022. Packed levitated marker for entity and relation extraction. In *Proceedings of the 60th Annual Meeting of the Association for Computational Linguistics (Volume 1: Long Papers)*, pages 4904–4917, Dublin, Ireland. Association for Computational Linguistics.

Daojian Zeng, Kang Liu, Siwei Lai, Guangyou Zhou, and Jun Zhao. 2014. Relation classification via convolutional deep neural network. In *Proceedings of COLING 2014, the 25th International Conference on Computational Linguistics: Technical Papers*, pages 2335–2344, Dublin, Ireland. Dublin City University and Association for Computational Linguistics.

Ningyu Zhang, Shumin Deng, Xiaozhi Zhang, Zhiyuan Tang, and 1 others. 2022. UniRE: A unified label space for entity relation extraction. In *Proceedings of the 2022 Conference on Empirical Methods in Natural Language Processing*, pages 217–228, Abu Dhabi, United Arab Emirates. Association for Computational Linguistics.

Yuhao Zhang, Victor Zhong, Danqi Chen, Gabor Angeli, and Christopher D. Manning. 2017. Position-aware attention and supervised data improve slot filling. In *Proceedings of the 2017 Conference on Empirical Methods in Natural Language Processing*, pages 35–45, Copenhagen, Denmark. Association for Computational Linguistics.

A Appendix

Model	Phase 1 In-Distribution Validation Set							Phase 2 Out-of-Distribution Test Set						
	Total F1	Entity			Relation			Total F1	Entity			Relation		
		F1	P	R	F1	P	R		F1	P	R	F1	P	R
BERT Uncased	0.67	0.75	0.73	0.79	0.60	0.59	0.61	–	–	–	–	–	–	–
Llama 3 8b Finetune	0.66	0.63	0.62	0.65	0.68	0.72	0.66	–	0.52	0.54	0.53	–	–	–
Gemini 2 Zero-Shot	–	0.39	0.37	0.44	–	–	–	–	–	–	–	–	–	–

Table 4: Performance metrics for the additional models we tested in Phase 1 and 2. Not all experiments were conducted for all models.

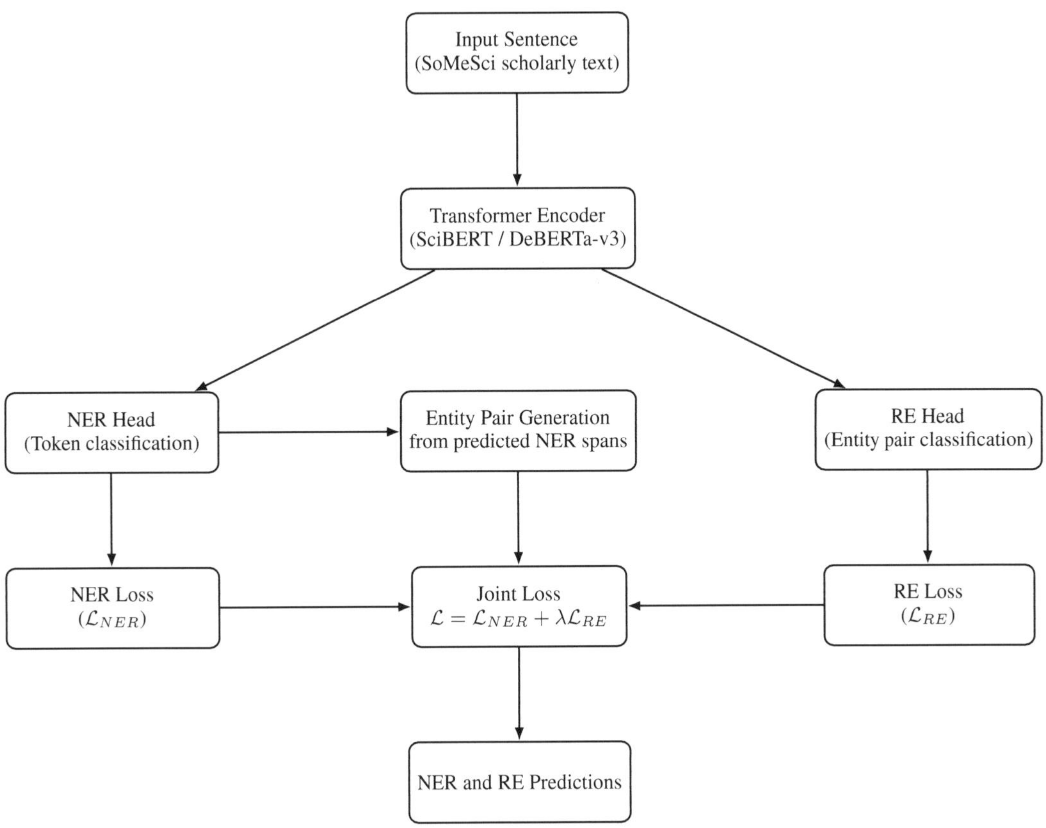

Figure 1: Architecture and data flow of our joint NER and RE model. The Transformer Encoder processes input tokens, which are used by two task-specific heads. NER predictions are used to generate entity pairs for RE. Each task contributes to the total loss, enabling joint optimization.

SOMD 2025: Fine-tuning ModernBERT for In- and Out-of-Distribution NER and Relation Extraction of Software Mentions in Scientific Texts

Projan Shakya*[1], Kristina Ghimire*[1], Kashish Bataju*[1], Ashwini Mandal*[1], Sadikshya Gyawali*[1], Manish Dahal*[1], Manish Awale*[1], Shital Adhikari [1,2], Sanjay Rijal[1,3], Vaghawan Ojha*[1]

[1]E.K. Solutions Pvt. Ltd., Nepal, [2]Steven Insititute of Technology, USA
[3]Institut de Física d'Altes Energies (IFAE), Spain
Correspondence: vaghawan.ojha@ekbana.net

Abstract

Software mentions are ubiquitous yet remains irregularly referenced among scientific texts. In this paper, we utilized the dataset and evaluation criteria defined by Software Mention Detection (SOMD 2025) competition to solve the problem of Named Entity Recognition (NER) and Relation Extraction (RE) in input sentences from scientific texts. During the competition, we achieved a leading F1 SOMD score of 0.89 in Phase I by first fine-tuning ModernBERT for NER, and then using the extracted entity pairs for RE. Additionally, we trained a model that jointly optimizes entity and relation losses, leading to an improvement in F1 SOMD score to 0.92. Retraining the same model on an augmented dataset, we achieved the second best F1 SOMD score of 0.55 in Phase II. In the Open Submission phase, we experimented with adaptive fine-tuning, achieving an F1 SOMD score of 0.6, with the best macro average for NER being 0.69. Our work shows the efficiency of fine-tuning a niche task like software mention detection despite having limited data and the promise of adaptive fine-tuning on Out of Distribution (OOD) dataset.

Keywords: *BERT, ModernBERT, Named Entity Recognition, Relation Extraction, SciDeBERTa, SOMD*

1 Introduction

Software is an integral part of scientific research and scholarly documents (Allen et al., 2018; Du et al., 2021). Despite its significance, software is often referenced informally rather than being formally cited in academic publications (Schindler et al., 2021). Automatically identifying these inconsistencies in mentioning software and their associated attributes can enhance the transparency, accessibility, and reproducibility of scientific research (Schindler et al., 2021). The Software Mention Detection 2025 (Sharmila et al.) challenge aimed to advance the development of robust models that can jointly detect software entities and classify their relations in scholarly documents. The goal of this competition was to automatically extract structured information about software used in scientific research, improving understanding and reproducibility. Named Entity Recognition (NER) and Relation Extraction (RE) are two of the most important classical problems in Natural Language Processing (NLP) (Nasar et al., 2021). Since relation depends on the inherent named entity, these two problems had been posed as a joint tasks in the challenge (Sharmila et al.). The SOMD 2025 shared task aimed to tackle this problem by offering two phases as below:

- Phase I: This task involved identifying 14 types of software-related entities in BIO format [1] and 11 types of relations between those entities.
- Phase II: This task aimed to extract the entities and relation with OOD [2] test set. A new evaluation dataset was provided, introducing a data distribution shift between Phase I and Phase II. The objective of this phase was to adapt the model trained on Phase I to an OOD test set.

In this paper, we experiment with various architectures and identify the most effective ones for the joint extraction of named entities and their relations. We focus on approaches that not only perform well in the given tasks but could also generalize to similar joint extraction problems in the future.

*All authors contributed equally

[1]BIO format - B for the beginning of the entity, I for the inside of the entity, and O for non-entity tokens.

[2]OOD - Out of Distribution

Proceedings of the Fifth Workshop on Scholarly Document Processing (SDP 2025), pages 154–163
July 31, 2025 ©2025 Association for Computational Linguistics

To this end, we fine-tuned encoder-only transformer models and evaluated their performance. In Phase I, our best-performing model was optimized by first performing NER through fine-tuning ModernBERT (Warner et al., 2024), followed by identifying relationships between the extracted entities. A different model trained after Phase I, referred to as the Modified Joint Model (see Section 4.1.4), later surpassed the performance of the previously best-performing model.

In Phase II, we augmented the training data using Large Language Model (LLM) generated examples and retrained the Modified Joint Model. During the Open Submission phase, we applied Adaptive fine-tuning (Ruder, 2021), which led to improvement in scores obtained during Phase II.

All relevant code and implementations have been made publicly available on GitHub[3] for reproducibility and further research.

2 Related Studies

NER and RE are key tasks in information extraction, with several models and datasets developed to improve their performance (Giorgi et al., 2019; Markus and Adrian, 2020; Nasar et al., 2021; Shang et al., 2022; Wang et al., 2022).

(Devlin et al., 2019) introduced BERT, an encoder-only transformer model, which became a standard for extracting contextual embeddings in NLP tasks. Building on BERT, DYGIE++ proposed a dynamic span graph approach for joint NER, RE, and event extraction, achieving F1 scores of 67.5% for NER and 48.4% for RE on the SciERC dataset. (Markus and Adrian, 2020) presented SpERT, an attention-based model for span-based joint entity and relation extraction, which achieved F1 scores of 70.33% for entity recognition and 50.84% for relation extraction on SciERC using SciBERT. (Huguet Cabot and Navigli, 2021) introduced REBEL, a sequence-to-sequence model based on BART, which achieved an F1 score of 92.02% for RE tasks on the NYT dataset by linearizing triplets into text sequences.

(Shang et al., 2022) proposed OneRel, a joint entity and relation extraction model, which treats the task as a triple classification problem and achieved an F1 score of 92.9% on the NYT dataset. (Hennen et al., 2024) introduced ITER, an encoder-based model utilizing FLAN-T5, which performed NER and RE in three parallelizable steps, achieving F1 scores of 91.7% for NER and 71.9% for RE on ACE05.

ModernBERT was introduced as a state-of-the-art encoder-only model, optimizing BERT with modern enhancements (Warner et al., 2024). Trained on 2 trillion tokens, it showed significant improvements across various domains, though its application in NER and RE remained unexplored. (Jeong and Kim, 2022) explored SciDeBERTa, a model specialized for scientific text, in SOMD to extract entities and relations with domain-aware contextual embeddings.

In SOMD 2024, A three-stage framework based on XLM-RoBERTa achieved a macro-averaged F1 score of 67.8%, ranking third in Sub-task I (NER), with steps for entity classification, extraction, and type classification (Thi et al., 2024).

In this paper, we experiment with ModernBERT and SciDeBERTa for generating contextual embedding in a joint model with an added fine-tuning layers for NER and RE, aiming to enhance the state of art performance specifically in software mention detection tasks.

3 Dataset Description

Phase-I

The given train dataset (Schindler et al., 2021) consisted of 1149 sentences with their corresponding entity and relation labels, while the test set (in-distribution) had 203 sentences. The class distributions of entities and relations in the SOMD 2025 train dataset are illustrated in Figure 1 and Figure 2 respectively.

Phase II

The test dataset for Phase II consisted of 220 OOD sentences without any entity or relation labels. To enhance model performance on the Phase II OOD test set, we augmented the Phase I train dataset by using Large Language Models (LLMs). The augmentation process is explained below:

Dataset Augmentation

We began by identifying Out-of-Vocabulary (OOV) entities from the Phase II OOD test set. These included version patterns (e.g., spaced formats like `v 2 . 2 . 1`), citation formats (e.g., `[ 5 ]`, `[ 4 , 7 ]`), application names, and other uncommon expressions. These entities introduced unfamiliar vocabulary, contributing to the distribution shift in OOD test set.

[3] `https://github.com/ekbanasolutions/somd-2025`

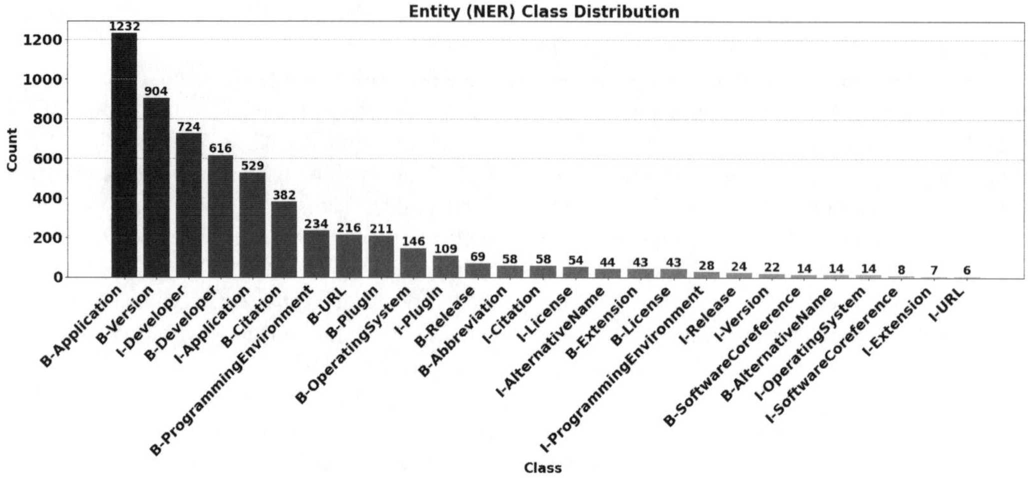

Figure 1: Class Distribution of Entities in the SOMD 2025 Training Dataset

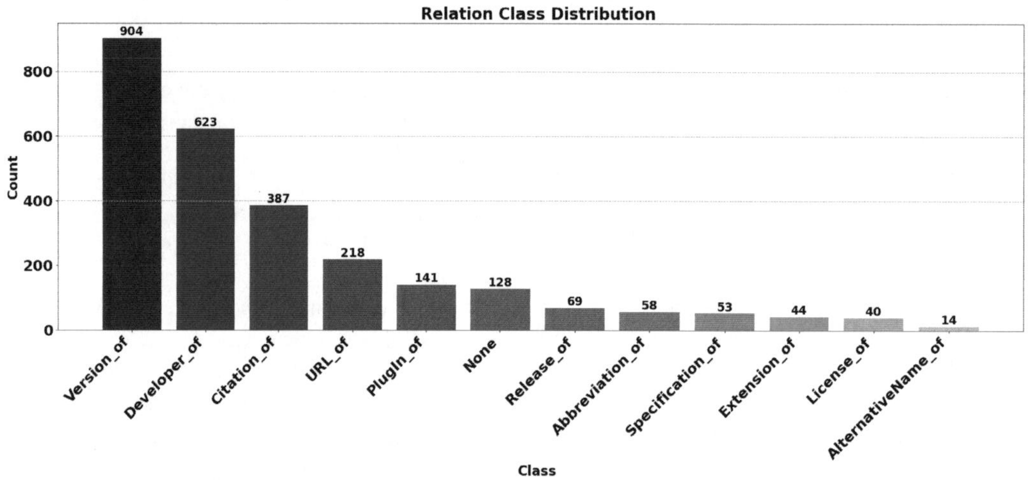

Figure 2: Class Distribution of Relations in the SOMD 2025 Training Dataset

Using the extracted keywords, we used GPT-4o, to generate natural language sentences. The sentence generation was guided by a carefully written prompt to ensure consistency and alignment with the task requirements. The prompt used to generate the sentences is shown in Appendix A.

The model was instructed to strictly maintain the mentioned formats. The generated sentences were then passed through our best-performing model after Phase I (Modified Joint Model, detailed in Section 4.1.4) to automatically assign entity and relation labels. These predictions were manually verified to correct missing or incorrect annotations and to filter out invalid samples. We refer to the curated dataset as LLM-Joint-Augmented dataset.

4 Methods

The methodologies employed in Phase I, Phase II and the Open Submission track are detailed in the following sections. For each phase, multiple methods are presented to reflect the step-by-step progression of our approach. These variations reflect iterative improvements made based on experimental results, showing the gradual development of our approach.

4.1 Phase I

In this phase, we evaluated two pre-trained language models: ModernBERT-base (Warner et al., 2024) and SciDeBERTa-cs (Jeong and Kim, 2022) to determine the most suitable base model for our downstream tasks. Based on experimental results (see Table 1), ModernBERT-base performed better and was chosen for the further fine-tuning.

4.1.1 NER Fine-tuning

We fine-tuned ModernBERT-base on the SOMD 2025 training dataset (Schindler et al., 2021), as detailed in Section 3, which was randomly split into 80% for training and 20% for development. The official SOMD 2025 test set was reserved for final evaluation. To adapt ModernBERT-base for Named Entity Recognition (NER), we appended task-specific layers to pre-trained ModernBERT-base. These layers were initialized using Xavier initialization to ensure stable convergence. We employed a hidden dropout rate of 0.4 during training, alongside an attention dropout rate of 0.3 to regularize the self-attention mechanism. The ReLU activation function was used in the additional layers and also a dropout layer with a rate of 0.3 was included for further regularization. This setup is referred to as the EntityModel architecture, illustrated in Figure 3.

4.1.2 RE Fine-tuning

After extracting the entities using the EntityModel, we performed Relation Extraction (RE) based on the identified entity pairs. The RelationModel is detailed in Figure 3. Hidden state was passed from the final layer of the EntityModel. To stabilize and accelerate the training process, we also applied Layer Normalization and Multi-Head Attention (MHA) was incorporated to capture the contextualized relationships between the entities. Finally, the [CLS] token, which summarizes the entire sentence, was concatenated with the final output of the contextualized entity pair. GELU was used as the activation function. To prevent overfitting, a dropout rate of 0.5 was used in the Feed Forward layers, while an attention dropout of 0.1 was applied to the attention heads. Additionally, weight decay of 0.1 was added to make the model more robust and prevent overfitting since our dataset consisted of limited amount of data. Linear learning rate scheduler was used with the initial learning rate being $5e-5$.

4.1.3 Few-Shot Prompting

We performed few-shot prompting for RE using GPT-4o, providing few carefully constructed examples. The model was instructed to follow a clear, step-by-step procedure to extract relations based solely on entities predicted by our fine-tuned NER

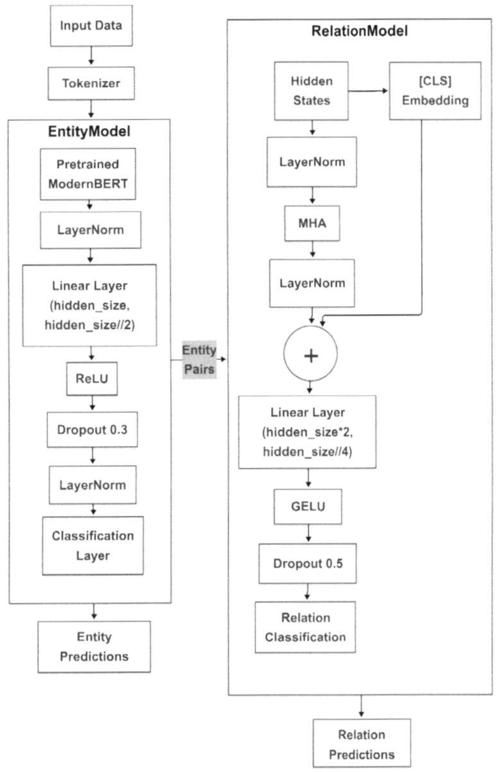

Figure 3: Model Architecture used in Phase I for NER and RE Fine-tuning

model detailed in Section 4.1.1. The model was explicitly instructed not to hallucinate any new relation classes.

4.1.4 Modified Joint Model (Post-Phase I)

After completing Phase I, we further experimented with a new architecture, which we refer to as the Modified Joint Model, designed to extract both entities and their relations.

For the entity extraction, we reused the same EntityModel, initializing it with the weights from our previously fine-tuned EntityModel in Section 4.1.1. To enable RE, we added additional layers on top of the EntityModel. Unlike the setup in Section 4.1.2, the RelationModel here followed a different architecture as shown in detail in Figure 4.

For relation extraction, we identified all non-"O" entity pairs predicted by EntityModel and concatenated their hidden states with the [CLS] token embedding to capture both local and global context. This combined representation was passed through two linear layers with ReLU activation and dropout of 0.4 for classification. Entity and relation losses were computed separately and summed to jointly

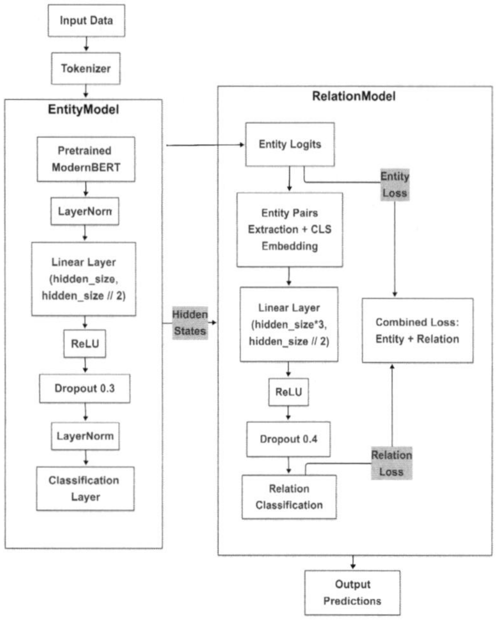

Figure 4: Model Architecture for Modified Joint Model

optimize both tasks in an end-to-end manner.

4.2 Phase II

In Phase II, we first used the trained Modified Joint Model detailed in Section 4.1.4, to infer on the provided OOD test data. In order to improve the score, we fine-tuned the ModernBERT-base model using a Masked Language Modeling (MLM) approach. The training process used the LLM-Joint-Augmented dataset as described in Section 3, by splitting it randomly into 80% training and 20% evaluation sets. Sentences were tokenized with a maximum length of 128 tokens and a masking probability of 15%. The model was trained for up to 60 epochs with early stopping (patience of 3) to prevent overfitting. The training configuration used a learning rate of $4e-4$ with weight decay of 0.01, batch sizes of 16, and FP16 precision for performance optimization. Then, for better generalization of OOD data provided in Phase II, we applied multiple approaches. The results from these approaches are presented in Table 2. Below we discuss some of the major approaches which improved the F1 scores.

4.2.1 Fine-tuning with Augmented Data

In this approach, we retrained our best-performing model (the Modified Joint Model, shown in Figure 4) using the MLM-pretrained ModernBERT-base on the LLM-Joint-Augmented dataset.

4.2.2 Separated Relation Classification

In this approach, we split relation classification into binary and multi-class tasks to reduce false positives. Two linear layers were added atop the Modified Joint Model: one used BinaryCrossEntropy to detect relation presence, and the other used CrossEntropy for relation type classification.

4.3 SOMD 2025 Open Submission

4.3.1 Adaptive fine-tuning

To perform better on the OOD evaluation set, we used Adaptive fine-tuning (Ruder, 2021) on the LLM-Joint-Augmented dataset, by adding three linear layers and a residual connection to ModernBERT-base in order to learn new features while preserving prior knowledge.

4.3.2 Fine-tuning ModernBERT

Given the limited improvements achieved with the previous approach, we fine-tuned ModernBERT-base from scratch (up to 20 layers) on the LLM-Joint-Augmented dataset. This resulted in a significant boost in NER score, increasing the F1 score by approximately 0.07, even without the use of adaptive layers. This yielded the highest NER F1 score among all participants and also led to improvements in the RE F1 score.

4.3.3 Post fine-tune Adaptation

Since fine-tuning ModernBERT up to layer 20 (Section 4.3.2) resulted in a significant improvement in NER performance, we incorporated the adaptive layer on top of the fine-tuned model. The adaptive layer followed the architecture described in Section 4.3.1. We experimented with various learning rates, batch sizes, and other hyperparameters to optimize performance. This overall approach is illustrated in Figure 5.

5 Results

After fine-tuning ModernBERT-base (Warner et al., 2024) on the SOMD 2025 dataset, we achieved an NER F1 score of 0.93. Another approach was fine-tuning SciDeBERTa-cs (Jeong and Kim, 2022), specifically at the 10th layer, which resulted an NER F1 score of 0.89. This comparative experiment made us more inclined towards ModernBERT-base for further experiments. Building on the fine-tuned ModernBERT-base model, we experimented with various architectures for RE, achieving an RE F1 score of 0.84, that resulted in an F1 SOMD score of 0.89 in Phase I. Notably, our second model

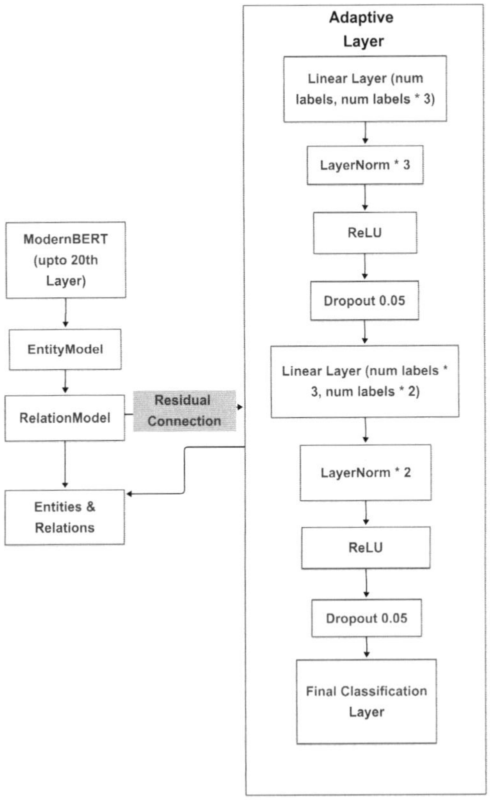

Figure 5: Model Architecture used in Section 4.3.3

(Modified Joint Model as shown in Figure 4), surpassed the previous approaches, achieving a higher overall F1 score of 0.92, as shown in Table 1. This result, however, was achieved after Phase I ended.

S.N.	Approach	NER	RE	F1 SOMD
1. NER fine-tuning (Section 4.1.1)				
	ModernBERT	0.93	-	-
	SciDeBERTa	0.89	-	-
2. RE fine-tuning (Section 4.1.2)				
	Baseline	0.93	0.80	0.87
	+ LayerNorm	0.93	0.80	0.87
	+ MultiHeadAttention	0.93	0.83	0.88
	+ GELU	0.93	**0.84**	**0.89**
3. Few-Shot Prompting (Section 4.1.3)				
	GPT-4o	-	0.38	-
4. Modified Joint Model (Section 4.1.4)				
	ModernBERT	**0.95**	**0.89**	**0.92**

Table 1: SOMD score for each approach of Phase I

In Phase II, we achieved SOMD score of 0.55 by fine-tuning the Modified Joint Model using the LLM-Joint-Augmented dataset, which was ranked the second-best in SOMD 2025. We obtained macro average F1 score of 0.64 for NER and 0.46 for RE. The precision, recall and F1 score for each entity and relation class in the test set of Phase I and Phase II are shown in Table 4 and Table 5.

After the phase was completed, we experimented with multiple approaches which resulted in improvement of the F1 score as mentioned in the Table 2. In open submission, we experimented with adaptive learning and further fine-tuning the model which resulted in an F1 SOMD score of 0.6 as explained in Section 4.3.3.

Approach	F1 SOMD
Phase II Submission	
Using Phase I Modified Joint Model (Section 4.1.4)	0.51
Fine-tuning with Augmented Data (Section 4.2.1)	**0.55**
Separated Relation Classification (Section 4.2.2)	0.54
Open Submission	
Adaptive Learning (Section 4.3.1)	0.57
Fine-tuning ModernBERT (Section 4.3.2)	0.58
Post fine-tune Adaptation (Section 4.3.3)	**0.60**

Table 2: SOMD F1 scores for different approaches in Phase II and Open Submission

All the macro F1 score for NER and RE are computed using exact match via seqeval library (Nakayama, 2018).

Limitations

The model demonstrated poor generalization to OOD dataset, as seen when transitioning from Phase I to Phase II of the SOMD 2025 dataset. A key challenge inherent to the task was heavy reliance of RE on accurate NER; thus, errors in NER propagated to RE, resulting in incorrect relation pairings. Another limitation was the class imbalance in the dataset, as illustrated in Figures 1 and 2. Furthermore, the entity hidden states along with the [CLS] token representation was passed through several layers for RE, which made the early errors have even bigger impact later. A notable limitation was also the unavailability of large corpus of sentences to fine-tune the model.

Discussion and Conclusion

Compared to the results reported in SOMD 2025[4], our model achieved the highest F1 score of 0.89 in Phase I, outperforming the *TU Graz Data Team*, which scored 0.88, and *gabrielrsilva*, who scored 0.39. Thus, our model attained the top performance among all participants in this phase. In Phase II, our model achieved an F1 score of 0.55, ranking second overall. The highest score in this phase was

[4]SOMD 2025 Results: `https://www.codabench.org/competitions/5840/#/results-tab`

Phase	F1 SOMD	NER (macro avg)			RE (macro avg)		
		F1	Precision	Recall	F1	Precision	Recall
Phase I	0.89	0.93	0.93	0.95	0.84	0.85	0.86
Post-Phase I (Modified Joint Model)	0.92	0.95	0.95	0.96	0.89	0.95	0.85
Phase II	0.55	0.64	0.67	0.65	0.46	0.69	0.39
Open Submission	0.60	0.69	0.74	0.69	0.51	0.71	0.42

Table 3: SOMD results for NER and RE in each phase

Entity	Phase I				Phase II			
	Precision	Recall	F1 score	Support	Precision	Recall	F1 score	Support
Abbreviation	1.0000	0.7500	0.8571	4	0.9000	0.7500	0.8182	12
AlternativeName	1.0000	1.0000	1.0000	2	1.0000	0.4118	0.5833	17
Application	0.9283	0.9539	0.9409	217	0.7120	0.7218	0.7168	363
Citation	1.0000	0.9811	0.9905	53	0.8744	0.9679	0.9188	187
Developer	0.9762	0.9840	0.9801	125	0.5882	0.5000	0.5405	20
Extension	0.8571	0.8571	0.8571	7	0.0000	0.0000	0.0000	6
License	1.0000	1.0000	1.0000	7	-	-	-	-
OperatingSystem	1.0000	1.0000	1.0000	22	1.0000	1.0000	1.0000	2
PlugIn	0.8750	0.8235	0.8485	34	0.3784	0.7000	0.4912	20
ProgrammingEnvironment	0.9474	0.9730	0.9600	37	0.9000	0.7500	0.8182	24
Release	0.9286	1.0000	0.9630	13	0.7000	0.7000	0.7000	10
SoftwareCoreference	0.5000	1.0000	0.6667	1	0.0000	0.0000	0.0000	3
URL	1.0000	1.0000	1.0000	32	1.0000	1.0000	1.0000	70
Version	0.9879	0.9702	0.9790	168	0.6911	0.8854	0.7763	96
Micro Avg	0.9586	0.9626	0.9606	722	0.7626	0.8012	0.7814	830
Macro Avg	0.9286	0.9495	0.9316	722	0.6726	0.6451	0.6433	830
Weighted Avg	0.9595	0.9626	0.9607	722	0.7663	0.8012	0.7778	830

Table 4: Precision, Recall, F1 score, and Support of Each Entity Class in Test Dataset of Phase I and Phase II

Relation	Phase I				Phase II			
	Precision	Recall	F1 score	Support	Precision	Recall	F1 score	Support
Developer_of	0.8722	0.9206	0.8958	126	0.8889	0.4000	0.5517	20
Citation_of	0.8276	0.9057	0.8649	53	0.6761	0.5134	0.5836	187
Version_of	0.8378	0.9226	0.8782	168	0.8600	0.4479	0.5890	96
PlugIn_of	0.9524	0.8000	0.8696	25	0.5882	0.7692	0.6667	13
URL_of	0.8286	0.9062	0.8657	32	0.4286	0.3000	0.3529	70
License_of	0.8571	0.8571	0.8571	7	0.0000	0.0000	0.0000	0
AlternativeName_of	1.0000	1.0000	1.0000	2	1.0000	0.1176	0.2105	17
Release_of	0.6667	0.9231	0.7742	13	1.0000	0.3000	0.4615	10
Abbreviation_of	1.0000	0.5000	0.6667	4	0.8000	0.6667	0.7273	12
Extension_of	0.7778	1.0000	0.8750	7	0.0000	0.0000	0.0000	6
Specification_of	0.6667	0.7143	0.6897	14	0.0000	0.0000	0.0000	0
Micro Avg	0.8392	0.9024	0.8697	451	0.6773	0.4432	0.5358	431
Macro Avg	0.8443	0.8591	0.8397	451	0.6935	0.3905	0.4604	431
Weighted Avg	0.8432	0.9024	0.8696	451	0.6984	0.4432	0.5267	431

Table 5: Precision, Recall, F1 score, and Support of Each Relation Class in Test Dataset of Phase I and Phase II

obtained by *TU Graz Data Team*, with scores of 0.63. In the Open Submission track, our model achieved an F1 SOMD score of 0.60, which, at the time of writing, ranked second overall, and attained the highest NER F1 score of 0.69 among all submissions.

Compared to SOMD 2024's results, our model achieved a higher F1 score in the NER task which was at the time divided into Subtask I and Subtask II. The top-performing team in Subtask I last year, *Team phinx*, had an F1 score of 0.74 (Xuan et al., 2024), while *Team ottowg* scored 0.838 (Otto et al., 2024) in Subtask II. Our model outperformed both of these benchmarks. However, in the RE task, our model showed a slight drop in performance. The top-performing team last year, *Team ottowg*, achieved an F1 score of 0.911. It is important to note that their approach (Otto et al., 2024) utilized a question-answering framework, which constrained the number of candidate entities and explicitly highlighted possible relations, thereby simplifying the task and potentially boosting performance.

Better results could have been achieved by pretraining a Masked Language Model (MLM) on a large corpus. This would have enabled the model to learn richer contextual representations of language, improving its ability to understand sentence structure and semantics. Consequently, leading to more accurate predictions for both entity recognition and relation extraction tasks. Pretraining provides a strong foundation, especially when fine-tuned on task-specific data, as it helps the model generalize better–particularly in low-resource settings or when dealing with unseen vocabulary and complex sentence structures (Zhou et al., 2022; Sonkar et al., 2022).

Since limited research has explored the use of ModernBERT for NER and RE, we initiated our study using it as the foundation. Our model was built on ModernBERT, and further enhanced through prior training on the NER task and adaptive fine-tuning. This combination enabled it to achieve strong performance on both in-domain and OOD datasets. While relation extraction under OOD conditions remains challenging, the results highlight the effectiveness of combining robust pretraining, task-specific fine-tuning, and a joint optimization strategy for software mention understanding.

6 Acknowledgments

We thank E.K. Solutions Pvt. Ltd. (EKbana Nepal) for kindly providing the time and resources needed to participate in this competition. We would also like to extend our gratitude to the SOMD 2025 competition organizers.

References

Alice Allen, Peter J. Teuben, and P. Wesley Ryan. 2018. Schroedinger's code: A preliminary study on research source code availability and link persistence in astrophysics. *The Astrophysical Journal Supplement Series*, 236(1):10.

Jacob Devlin, Ming-Wei Chang, Kenton Lee, and Kristina Toutanova. 2019. Bert: Pre-training of deep bidirectional transformers for language understanding. *Preprint*, arXiv:1810.04805.

Caifan Du, Johanna Cohoon, Patrice Lopez, and James Howison. 2021. Softcite dataset: A dataset of software mentions in biomedical and economic research publications. *Journal of the Association for Information Science and Technology*, 72(7):870–884.

John Giorgi, Xindi Wang, Nicola Sahar, Won Young Shin, Gary D. Bader, and Bo Wang. 2019. End-to-end named entity recognition and relation extraction using pre-trained language models. *Preprint*, arXiv:1912.13415.

Moritz Hennen, Florian Babl, and Michaela Geierhos. 2024. ITER: Iterative transformer-based entity recognition and relation extraction. In *Findings of the Association for Computational Linguistics: EMNLP 2024*, pages 11209–11223, Miami, Florida, USA. Association for Computational Linguistics.

Pere-Lluís Huguet Cabot and Roberto Navigli. 2021. REBEL: Relation extraction by end-to-end language generation. In *Findings of the Association for Computational Linguistics: EMNLP 2021*, pages 2370–2381, Punta Cana, Dominican Republic. Association for Computational Linguistics.

Yuna Jeong and Eunhui Kim. 2022. Scideberta: Learning deberta for science technology documents and fine-tuning information extraction tasks. *IEEE Access*, 10:60805–60813.

Eberts Markus and Ulges Adrian. 2020. *Span-Based Joint Entity and Relation Extraction with Transformer Pre-Training*. IOS Press.

Hiroki Nakayama. 2018. seqeval: A python framework for sequence labeling evaluation. Software available from https://github.com/chakki-works/seqeval.

Zara Nasar, Syed Waqar Jaffry, and Muhammad Kamran Malik. 2021. Named entity recognition and relation extraction: State-of-the-art. *ACM Comput. Surv.*, 54(1).

Wolfgang Otto, Sharmila Upadhyaya, and Stefan Dietze. 2024. Enhancing software-related information extraction via single-choice question answering with large language models. In *Proceedings of the Workshop on Natural Scientific Language Processing and Research Knowledge Graphs*, Cologne, Germany. GESIS - Leibniz Institute for the Social Sciences.

Sebastian Ruder. 2021. Recent Advances in Language Model Fine-tuning. `http://ruder.io/recent-advances-lm-fine-tuning`.

David Schindler, Felix Bensmann, Stefan Dietze, and Frank Krüger. 2021. Somesci- a 5 star open data gold standard knowledge graph of software mentions in scientific articles. In *Proceedings of the 30th ACM International Conference on Information & Knowledge Management*, CIKM '21, page 4574–4583, New York, NY, USA. Association for Computing Machinery.

Yu-Ming Shang, Heyan Huang, and Xian-Ling Mao. 2022. Onerel:joint entity and relation extraction with one module in one step. *Preprint*, arXiv:2203.05412.

Upadhyaya Sharmila, Otto Wolfgang, Krueger Frank, and Stefan Dietze. 5th workshop on scholarly document processing.

Shashank Sonkar, Zichao Wang, and Richard G. Baraniuk. 2022. Maner: Mask augmented named entity recognition for extreme low-resource languages. *Preprint*, arXiv:2212.09723.

Thuy Nguyen Thi, Anh Nguyen Viet, Thin Dang Van, and Ngan Nguyen Luu Thuy. 2024. Software mention recognition with a three-stage framework based on bertology models at somd 2024. *Preprint*, arXiv:2405.01575.

Xinyu Wang, Jiong Cai, Yong Jiang, Pengjun Xie, Kewei Tu, and Wei Lu. 2022. Named entity and relation extraction with multi-modal retrieval. *Preprint*, arXiv:2212.01612.

Benjamin Warner, Antoine Chaffin, Benjamin Clavié, Orion Weller, Oskar Hallström, Said Taghadouini, Alexis Gallagher, Raja Biswas, Faisal Ladhak, Tom Aarsen, Nathan Cooper, Griffin Adams, Jeremy Howard, and Iacopo Poli. 2024. Smarter, better, faster, longer: A modern bidirectional encoder for fast, memory efficient, and long context finetuning and inference. *Preprint*, arXiv:2412.13663.

Phi Nguyen Xuan, Quang Tran Minh, and Thin Dang Van. 2024. ABCD Team at SOMD 2024: Software Mention Detection in Scholarly Publications with Large Language Models. In *Proceedings of the Workshop on Natural Scientific Language Processing and Research Knowledge Graphs (NSLP-KG)*, Ho Chi Minh City, Vietnam. CEUR Workshop Proceedings.

Ran Zhou, Xin Li, Ruidan He, Lidong Bing, Erik Cambria, Luo Si, and Chunyan Miao. 2022. MELM: Data augmentation with masked entity language modeling for low-resource NER. In *Proceedings of the 60th Annual Meeting of the Association for Computational Linguistics (Volume 1: Long Papers)*, pages 2251–2262, Dublin, Ireland. Association for Computational Linguistics.

Appendix

A. Prompt to LLM for Data Augmentation

The following prompt was used, where {text} was dynamically replaced with the extracted OOV keywords:

> **System:** You are a helpful assistant that generates natural sentences. Return only the sentence without any additional text.
>
> **User:** Generate a natural sentence using these keywords: {text}. The sentence should include citations such as [1], [3 , 4], or formatted styles like (Battke et al . , 2010) or (Jellyfish , https://scicrunch.org/resolver/RRID: SCR_005491) [28]. The sentence should also follow version patterns like: v . 2 . 4 . 0, v 2 . 31 . 9, v 10, version 20170127, version 2 . 3 . 0, (v 0 . 36 . 5), etc. Some sentences should include the extensions like: SPSS / PASW , SAS / SPSS , R / RStudio, etc. Some sentences should include the applications like: R, Python, GraphPad Prism, etc. Some sentences should include the operating systems like: Windows, Linux, Mac OS, etc. Strictly maintain sentence extensions, versions, applications, operating systems, etc. as given examples.

Inductive Learning on Heterogeneous Graphs Enhanced by LLMs for Software Mention Detection

Gabriel Silva
IEETA, DETI, LASI, Univ. Aveiro, PT
grsilva@ua.pt

Mário Rodriges
IEETA, ESTGA, LASI, Univ. Aveiro, PT
mjfr@ua.pt

António Teixeira
IEETA, DETI, LASI, Univ. Aveiro, PT
ajst@ua.pt

Marlene Amorim
GOVCOPP, DEGEIT, Univ. Aveiro, PT
mamorim@ua.pt

Abstract

This paper explores the synergy between Knowledge Graphs (KGs), Graph Machine Learning (Graph ML), and Large Language Models (LLMs) for multilingual Named Entity Recognition (NER) and Relation Extraction (RE), specifically targeting software mentions within the SOMD 2025 challenge. We propose a methodology where documents are first transformed into heterogeneous KGs enriched with linguistic features (Universal Dependencies) and external knowledge (entity linking). An inductive GraphSAGE model, operating on PyTorch Geometric's 'HeteroData' structure with dynamically generated multilingual embeddings, performs node classification tasks. For NER, Graph ML identifies candidate entities and types, with an Large Language Model (LLM) (DeepSeek v3) acting as a validation layer. For RE, Graph ML predicts dependency path convergence points indicative of relations, while the LLM classifies the relation type and direction based on entity context. Our results demonstrate the potential of this hybrid approach, showing significant performance gains post-competition (NER Phase 2 Macro F1 improved to 43.6% from 29.5%, RE Phase 1 33.6% Macro F1), which are already described in this paper, and highlighting the benefits of integrating structured graph learning with LLM reasoning for information extraction.

1 Introduction

Advancing the capabilities of Natural Language Processing (NLP) often requires moving beyond the surface level of plain text to leverage richer, more structured information. While raw text provides the foundation, incorporating details like semantic relationships, external world knowledge, or task-specific metadata can significantly boost performance on complex understanding (Safuan and Ku-Mahamud, 2025). This necessity, however, introduces a significant challenge: developing frameworks capable of seamlessly handling diverse data formats and integrating multiple layers of annotations – ranging from word-level tags (like part-of-speech) to sentence-level labels (like sentiment) and document-level classifications (like topic).

KGs provide a notably flexible and powerful paradigm to address this complexity. By representing information as nodes (entities, concepts) and edges (relationships), KGs offer an inherently structured way to capture intricate connections within and beyond the text. This structure facilitates the coherent integration of various annotation types across different textual granularities, ensuring that, for instance, word-level syntactic information can coexist and relate to document-level semantic themes. Crucially, KGs excel at maintaining the explicit connections between linguistic units and associated knowledge, preserving context that might be lost in purely sequential models. Furthermore, the KG paradigm benefits from a mature and growing ecosystem of established standards, databases, and software tools for creation, querying, and reasoning.

Despite the clear advantages offered by KGs for representing rich, multi-level information, the recent trajectory of mainstream NLP research has largely centered on models that process raw text sequences directly. This past decade has been marked by significant breakthroughs: the fundamental contribution of distributional representations via Word Embeddings (Mikolov et al., 2013), the development of powerful sequential models like Bi-LSTMs (Lample et al., 2016), arguably the most impactful release with the Transformer architecture (Vaswani et al., 2017), followed by large pre-trained models such as BERT (Devlin et al., 2019) and BART (Lewis et al., 2020), and more recently, generative AI and LLMs such as ChatGPT (OpenAI, 2023). Although these methods have pushed the state-of-the-art by learning complex patterns from vast textual data, their primary focus on sequential text

Proceedings of the Fifth Workshop on Scholarly Document Processing (SDP 2025), pages 164–172
July 31, 2025

input means the potential synergies of explicitly integrating structured knowledge, as offered by KGs, remain relatively underexplored in many application areas.

The use of graphs has been previously demonstrated in adjacent fields, such as Open Information Extraction, particularly for the Chinese language, where graph-based approaches have yielded favorable results (Lyu et al., 2021). Initial research has also investigated the potential of integrating graphs and LLMs. The study by (Chen et al., 2024) examines the role of graphs as both enhancers and predictors. An example of the combined capabilities of graphs and LLMs is Microsoft GraphRAG (Edge et al., 2025), which aims to leverage their synergistic effects.

The research presented here is part of the 2025 Software Mention Detection (SOMD) competition. The primary contribution of this work is a multilingual NER and RE system that utilizes KGs, Graph ML, and LLMs.

2 Method

In this section, the methodology employed is described. We will outline the overall approach, describe the processing of the dataset and finally how to generate our predictions for both NER and RE.

2.1 Overall Process

The methodology presented involves converting input documents into a structured graph format. This intermediate representation is specifically designed to serve as input for various Graph ML algorithms. The overall system architecture that facilitates this process is illustrated in Figure 1.

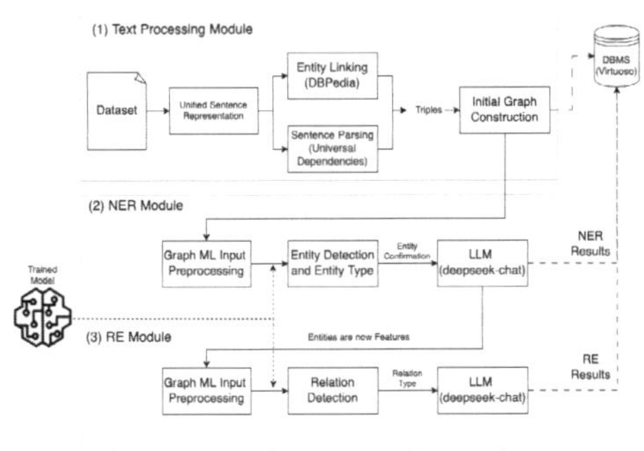

Figure 1: Overview of the current framework architecture

There are 3 crucial steps in this architecture. The first one is the Text Processing Module where we convert the dataset into our initial graph representation, we enrich our data by using making use Entity Linking and Universal Depedencies. The second step is the NER Module. In this module, the Graph ML algorithm performs two tasks: identifying entities and determining the type of each entity. The LLM serves as a confirmation layer when the Graph ML algorithm is uncertain about which type of entity to assign to a given word. The last step is the RE module, in this module our Knowledge Graph (KG) already has knowledge about the predicted entities and identifies where a relationship is present, then the LLM will decide which type of relationship exists between these two words based on their entity types.

2.2 Dataset Processing

In this work the only dataset used was the one provided by the competition. This dataset consists of 1,150 sentences for algorithm development, followed by two distinct testing phases. The first testing phase contains 203 sentences, while the second phase includes an additional 220 sentences. The first phase test set more closely resembles the training data, whereas the second phase serves as an out-of-domain evaluation.

As previously described, the text processing module is responsible for processing the dataset. Initially, texts are converted into a unified representation, ensuring consistent spacing around punctuation across all sentences and proper formatting of URLs, among other standardizations. This process may add or remove tokens from sentences, therefore, an additional attribute is maintained for each word to represent its mapping in the original sentence, enabling reconstruction at a later stage.

The second step of this text processing module involves performing Entity Linking. We query DBpedia for concepts identified in the sentences and establish links in our KG to the corresponding DBpedia nodes, this query is shown in Listing 1. We query DBPedia Software sub-set for concepts that contain the given word in English. Each DBPedia concept that is found is then added as a Class on our Graph with the connections found in the "class" query variable. Ideally, this step would engage with the entire DBpedia instance rather than this limited subset. However, at the time of preparing this work, access to a DBpedia dump was unavailable due to maintenance. In this step, we also parse the sentence using a Universal Dependencies (de Marneffe et al., 2014) parser to extract the syntactic dependencies and morphological features of each word.

Listing 1: DBPedia SPARQL Query. "word" is replaced with the term to query.

```
SELECT DISTINCT ?s ?label ?class WHERE {
    ?s rdf:type dbo:Software .
    ?s rdfs:label ?label .
    FILTER (lang(?label) = 'en') .
    ?label bif:contains "word" .
    ?s rdf:type ?class .
}
```

Each word has attributes including feats, their dependency graph, lemma, edges, and other characteristics defined in Universal Dependencies. Additionally, each word can be linked to the original sentence to which it belongs. We form each triple and upload this data into a triplestore (Virtuoso). For a more in-depth look at the process of building the graph from text can be read at (Silva et al., 2023, 2024). An example of the connections in the graph can be seen in Figure 2. We start at a sentence and navigate the graph through its dependency tree (Sentence -> ROOT word -> dependents). An example of what a "word" node looks like can be seen in Figure 3. This word did not have any connections to DBpedia, as such, the edges are not present.

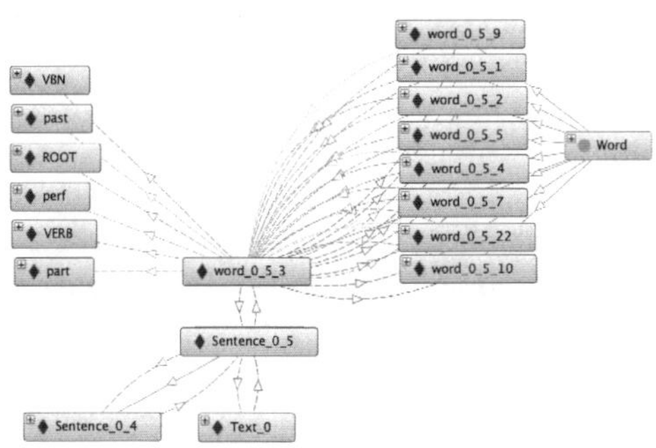

Figure 2: Example of the connections in a graph starting from a sentence.

2.2.1 Named Entity Recognition

For NER we add the entity tags without the BIO part to each word in our graph as an attribute. Words that do not represent an entity are simply tagged with "Nothing".

2.2.2 Relation Extraction

To represent relations between entities while treating the problem as a node classification task, we did not label the relations as edges in our graph. Instead, we made use of the dependency graph. For

Figure 3: Example of a word node for the word "ProctorU"

each pair of entities that form a relation, we traverse their dependency graph until we reach the word at which they converge. At this convergence point, we create an attribute and designate it as a relationship. To backtrack we simply look for the beginning of identities that converge in that word.

In Figure 4 we have an example of how we do this. The sentence from the test set "Standardized regression coefficients (SCR) were calculated using the sensitivity package of the R - project [50] ." has a relationship (sensitivity, PlugIn_of, R). In this example we can see that they both converge on the word "package" by following their dependency graphs:

sensitivity - package

R - project - of - package

This allows for a relation to be marked at the "package" word.

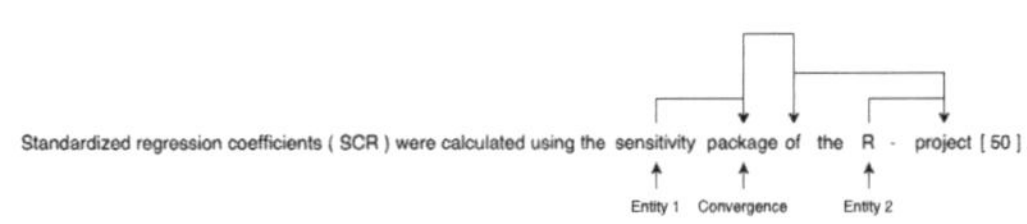

Figure 4: Using the Dependency Graph to get the convergence between two entities.

2.3 Prediction Process

In this subsection, we will elaborate on the process used to derive NER and RE results from the initial text.

2.3.1 Named Entity Recognition

Following the construction of the initial graph the format has to be adapted from triples to the Pytorch Geometric (PyG) (Fey and Lenssen, 2019) format. As part of this preparation pipeline, embeddings are generated for each word node. These embeddings are created using the "intfloat/multilingual-e5-large-instruct" model(Wang et al., 2024) from HuggingFace[1]. We chose this model due to its multilingual capabilities, performance and size according to the MTEB benchmark[2] (Muennighoff et al., 2023). These are intentionally not stored in the graph due to their large vector size. Instead, they are computed dynamically when required by the Machine Learning pipeline, just prior to converting the augmented graph into the PyG format.

Given the heterogeneous nature of the graph, which contains nodes and edges with diverse types and attributes, representing the complete edge information within a single tensor is not feasible. As a result, we utilize the HeteroData object[3] to structure the graph data for model training. Additionally, we adopted an inductive learning approach (Lachaud et al., 2023), selected for its improved applicability and generalizability to real-world scenarios where graph structures may evolve or be unseen during training. We use a GraphSAGE (Hamilton et al., 2018) based architecture. Our model for both tasks consists of 8 layers where each layer is a GraphSAGE layer, followed by normalization, ReLU and applying dropout with a learning rate of 0.01 and dropout of 0.3.

We train two distinct models: one that predicts whether a word corresponds to an entity, and another that predicts the type of the previously identified entities. If the output of the entity type prediction falls below a specified threshold, we validate the result using a LLM, specifically, we utilize DeepSeek v3 (deepseek-chat) (DeepSeek-AI et al., 2025) with queries adapted from the Microsoft RAG (Edge et al., 2025) GitHub repository. The NER query can be seen on Table 1 We utilize the five entity types with the highest likelihood identified by the Graph ML algorithm as grounding for our query.

Both predictions are then incorporated into our graph and transmitted to the RE Module. If two or more connected words are identified as entities we can add the respective BIO tags in conjunction with the entity tag, the one that comes first in the sentence will be tagged with the B and the following linked ones with I.

2.3.2 Relation Extraction

The RE process is similar to the NER process with the model architecture being the same. As discussed in Section 2.2.2 we identify the convergence point of each pair of words that form a relationship so in this step we want to predict which words are a convergence point. Once this convergence point is established, we just have to go through the identities that were identified in the previous step for a given the sentence.

The LLM in this prediction module is used to determine both the direction and type of the relationship. We ground the LLM by giving it the Entity type of each identified word and ask it to classify the relation type. The model used is the same as previously mention, DeepSeek V3. In instances where no convergence word is identified, we provide the LLM with the entities and ask it to identify if there are any relations present in the sentence. Table 2 shows the query used.

3 Results

This section presents the results of our training on the validation set and the performance on the test set for both phases of the competition. Every run was documented using the Weights & Biases platform (Biewald, 2020).

3.1 Named Entity Recognition

As previously outlined in the methods section, NER was categorized into two models: a binary model and an entity classification model.

3.1.1 Binary Model

The Binary Model performed well when identifying entities and non-entities. The model achieved an F1-Score of 93.6% with a recall and precision of 93.8% and 93.3% respectively on the validation set. Additionally, we plotted the ROC and Precision-Recall curves, as presented in Figures 56. The accuracy is not reported as it is not a relevant metric for this problem due to the imbalance in the dataset (number of words classified as entity vs non-entity).

[1]https://huggingface.co/intfloat/multilingual-e5-large-instruct

[2]https://huggingface.co/spaces/mteb/leaderboard

[3]https://pytorch-geometric.readthedocs.io/en/latest/generated/torch_geometric.data.HeteroData.html

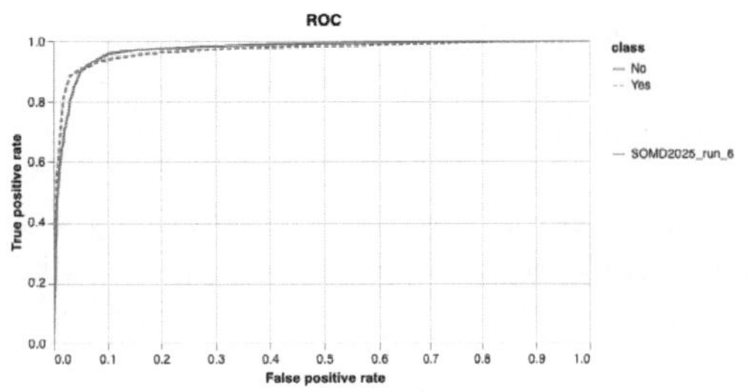

Figure 5: ROC Curve for the Entity Binary classification model.

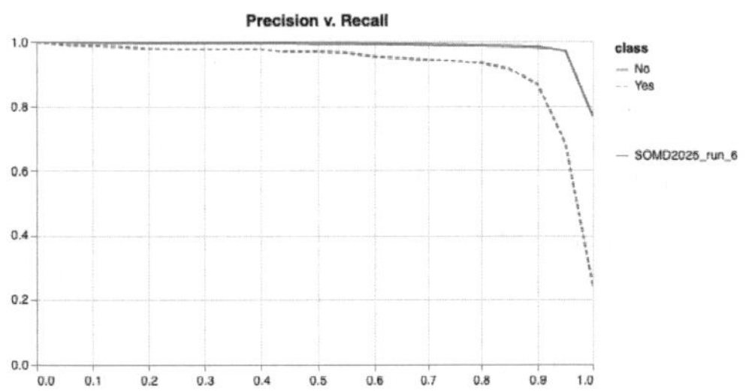

Figure 6: Precision-Recall curve for the Entity Binary classification model.

The F1-Score and corresponding curves indicate that the model demonstrated strong performance in accurately identifying whether a word is an entity.

3.1.2 Entity Type Model

Using the output from the previous model, the subsequent step was to add this prediction as an attribute for each word to identify the type of entity. Consequently, we trained a model with this additional attribute, which indicates whether a word is an entity, and aims to predict the type of entity present in the word. The training results yielded F1, Precision, and Recall scores of 70.5%, 70.7%, and 71.6%, respectively, on the validation set. A normalized confusion matrix is presented in Figure 7.

The model exhibited the greatest difficulty in identifying entities classified as "AlternativeName" and "SoftwareCoreference.". Additionally, it frequently confused "PlugIn" with "Application," with a misclassification rate exceeding fifty percent. This observation is further supported by the ROC curve presented in Figure 8.

During Phase 1, we evaluated the performance of the Graph ML model by submitting results without validation from the LLM. This approach resulted in a decrease in performance, thereby supporting our hypothesis that utilizing the LLM as a confirmation tool in cases of model uncertainty represents a viable strategy.

The results for Phase 1 of this model was a Macro-average F1 score of 44.6%, with Precision at 52.7% and Recall at 40.2%. In Phase 2, the results showed a decline, with an F1 score of 29.5%, Precision at 35.8%, and Recall at 27.3. Following the conclusion of Phase 2, we have successfully improved these metrics, resulting in current values of 43.6% for F1, 43.7% for Precision, and 45.2% for Recall, which are now comparable to the results of Phase 1.

3.2 Relation Extraction

The last part of the competition was the RE which we could only do after having identified the entities. As was previously described for RE we identify the word where two entities converge and tag it as a "relation", as such, the goal of this model is to find those convergence words. When these convergence words are found we can go through the identities and find which ones converge to that predicted word.

This model achieved an F1 score of 87.4%, precision of 88.1% and recall of 86.8%. Similarly to the binary model we can see the ROC and Precision vs Recall curves in Figure 9 and Figure 10.

Unfortunately we only managed to obtain relation results for the first phase of the competition with the scores being: 33.5% F1-Score, 38.4% Precision and 32.1% Recall. However, with the model for entities having significant improvements after the competition is ended, our hypothesis is that these better results will also show themselves in the RE portion of the work.

4 Conclusion

Although the results in the competition were not optimal compared to those of other participants, we have made significant improvements to the model during the ongoing open phase which are here presented, enhancing its competitiveness on the test set. In the NER task, the Phase 2 results yielded a Macro F1 score of 29.5% and a Micro F1 score of 37.4%. In this Open Submission phase, the scores have improved to 43.6% and 58%, respectively, increasing their competitiveness. Unfortunately, for RE, we were unable to obtain results for Phase 2 in a timely manner. Thus, the Phase 1 results were as follows: 33.6% F1-Score, 38.4% Precision and 32.1% Recall. With the improvements to the en-

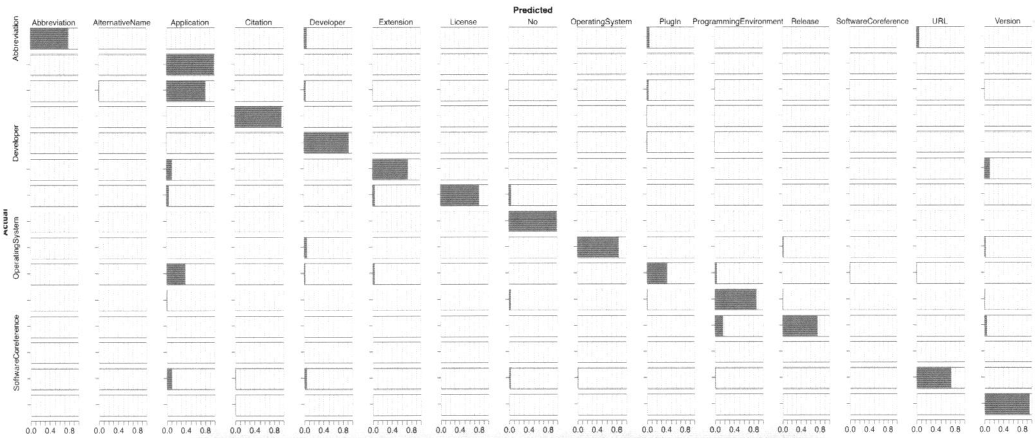

Figure 7: Normalized confusion matrix for the entity prediction model.

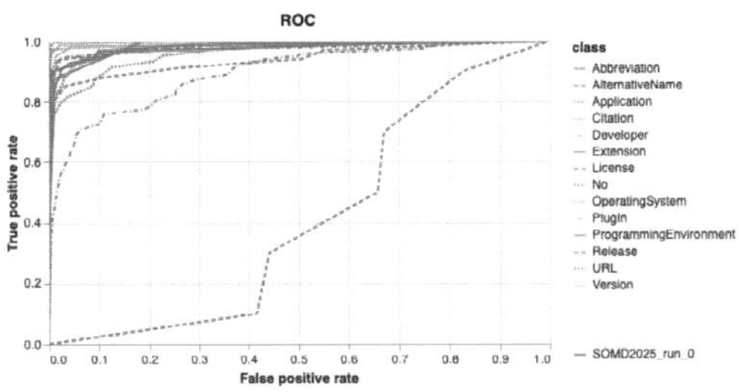

Figure 8: ROC Curves for the entity prediction model.

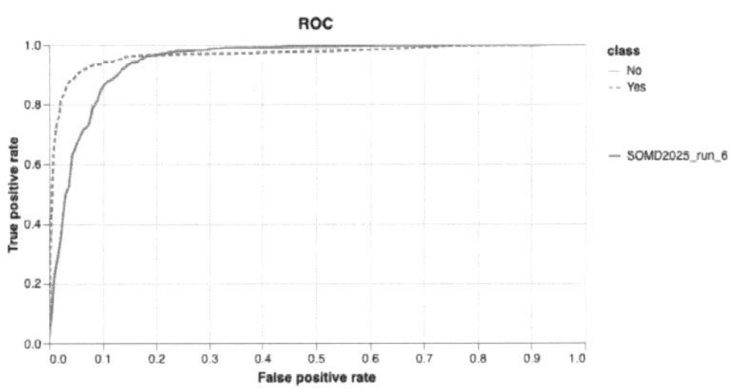

Figure 9: ROC Curves for the relation model.

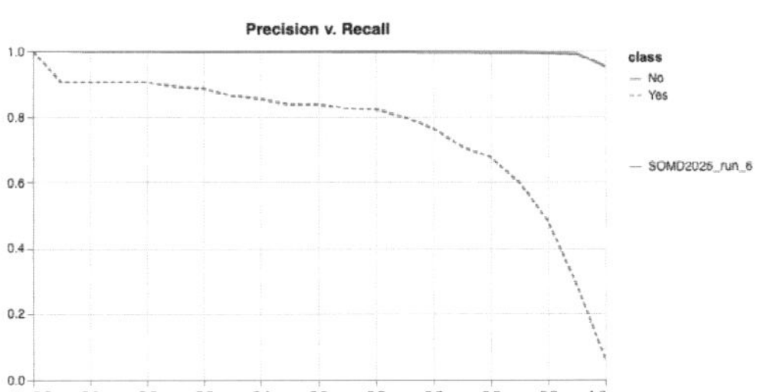

Figure 10: Precision-Recall curves for the relation model.

tity model, these numbers are expected to be even better.

Our model possesses several advantages, including being lightweight, easily adaptable to other problems (as no specific code or preprocessing was conducted for this dataset), and supporting multiple languages (as long as a parser is available).

Despite the promising methodology and its positive aspects, considerable work remains to enhance these results. The work here developed is available at: `https://github.com/gabrielrsilva11/SOMD2025`.

Future Work

- Incorporate additional external knowledge into our graph to enhance its ability to generalize knowledge. Furthermore, integrate DBpedia (Auer et al., 2007) into our KG.

- Testing various Graph ML models, including transformers (Hu et al., 2020), has the potential to significantly influence the results.

- Obtain additional data or a pre-trained model. The dataset utilized for training the graph machine learning algorithms was exclusively provided by the competition and comprises a total of 1,150 sentences.

5 Acknowledgements

This work was funded by FCT - Fundação para a Ciência e a Tecnologia (FCT) I.P., through national funds, within the scope of the UIDB/00127/2020 project (IEETA/UA, http://www.ieeta.pt/) and the scholarship UI/BD/153571/2022.

References

Sören Auer, Christian Bizer, Georgi Kobilarov, Jens Lehmann, Richard Cyganiak, and Zachary Ives. 2007.

Dbpedia: a nucleus for a web of open data. In *Proceedings of the 6th International The Semantic Web and 2nd Asian Conference on Asian Semantic Web Conference*, ISWC'07/ASWC'07, page 722–735. Springer-Verlag.

Lukas Biewald. 2020. Experiment tracking with weights and biases. Software available from wandb.com.

Zhikai Chen, Haitao Mao, Hang Li, Wei Jin, Hongzhi Wen, Xiaochi Wei, Shuaiqiang Wang, Dawei Yin, Wenqi Fan, Hui Liu, and Jiliang Tang. 2024. Exploring the potential of large language models (llms)in learning on graphs. *SIGKDD Explor. Newsl.*

Marie-Catherine de Marneffe, Timothy Dozat, Natalia Silveira, Katri Haverinen, Filip Ginter, Joakim Nivre, and Christopher D. Manning. 2014. Universal Stanford dependencies: A cross-linguistic typology. In *Proceedings of the Ninth International Conference on Language Resources and Evaluation (LREC'14)*, pages 4585–4592, Reykjavik, Iceland. European Language Resources Association (ELRA).

DeepSeek-AI, Aixin Liu, Bei Feng, Bing Xue, Bingxuan Wang, Bochao Wu, Chengda Lu, Chenggang Zhao, Chengqi Deng, and Chenyu Zhang et al. 2025. Deepseek-v3 technical report. *Preprint*, arXiv:2412.19437.

Jacob Devlin, Ming-Wei Chang, Kenton Lee, and Kristina Toutanova. 2019. Bert: Pre-training of deep bidirectional transformers for language understanding. In *North American Chapter of the Association for Computational Linguistics*.

Darren Edge, Ha Trinh, Newman Cheng, Joshua Bradley, Alex Chao, Apurva Mody, Steven Truitt, Dasha Metropolitansky, Robert Osazuwa Ness, and Jonathan Larson. 2025. From local to global: A graph rag approach to query-focused summarization. *Preprint*, arXiv:2404.16130.

Matthias Fey and Jan E. Lenssen. 2019. Fast graph representation learning with PyTorch Geometric. In *ICLR Workshop on Representation Learning on Graphs and Manifolds*.

William L. Hamilton, Rex Ying, and Jure Leskovec. 2018. Inductive representation learning on large graphs. *Preprint*, arXiv:1706.02216.

Ziniu Hu, Yuxiao Dong, Kuansan Wang, and Yizhou Sun. 2020. Heterogeneous graph transformer. In *Proceedings of The Web Conference 2020*, WWW '20, page 2704–2710, New York, NY, USA. Association for Computing Machinery.

Guillaume Lachaud, Patricia Conde-Cespedes, and Maria Trocan. 2023. Comparison between inductive and transductive learning in a real citation network using graph neural networks. In *Proceedings of the 2022 IEEE/ACM International Conference on Advances in Social Networks Analysis and Mining*, ASONAM '22, page 534–540. IEEE Press.

Guillaume Lample, Miguel Ballesteros, Sandeep Subramanian, Kazuya Kawakami, and Chris Dyer. 2016. Neural architectures for named entity recognition. *arXiv preprint arXiv:1603.01360*.

Mike Lewis, Yinhan Liu, Naman Goyal, Marjan Ghazvininejad, Abdelrahman Mohamed, Omer Levy, Veselin Stoyanov, and Luke Zettlemoyer. 2020. BART: Denoising sequence-to-sequence pre-training for natural language generation, translation, and comprehension. In *Proceedings of the 58th Annual Meeting of the Association for Computational Linguistics*.

Zhiheng Lyu, Kaijie Shi, Xin Li, Lei Hou, Juanzi Li, and Binheng Song. 2021. Multi-grained dependency graph neural network for chinese open information extraction. In *Advances in Knowledge Discovery and Data Mining*.

Tomas Mikolov, Kai Chen, Gregory S. Corrado, and Jeffrey Dean. 2013. Efficient estimation of word representations in vector space. In *International Conference on Learning Representations*.

Niklas Muennighoff, Nouamane Tazi, Loïc Magne, and Nils Reimers. 2023. Mteb: Massive text embedding benchmark. *Preprint*, arXiv:2210.07316.

R OpenAI. 2023. Gpt-4 technical report. *ArXiv*, 2303.

Safuan and Ku Ruhana Ku-Mahamud. 2025. Handling semantic relationships for classification of sparse text: A review. *Engineering Proceedings*, 84(1).

Gabriel Silva, Mário Rodrigues, António Teixeira, and Marlene Amorim. 2023. A Framework for Fostering Easier Access to Enriched Textual Information. In *12th Symposium on Languages, Applications and Technologies (SLATE 2023)*, volume 113 of *Open Access Series in Informatics (OASIcs)*, pages 2:1–2:14, Dagstuhl, Germany. Schloss Dagstuhl – Leibniz-Zentrum für Informatik.

Gabriel Silva, Mário Rodrigues, António Teixeira, and Marlene Amorim. 2024. First assessment of graph machine learning approaches to Portuguese named entity recognition. In *Proc. Int. Conference on Computational Processing of Portuguese*, pages 563–567. ACL.

Ashish Vaswani, Noam Shazeer, Niki Parmar, Jakob Uszkoreit, Llion Jones, Aidan N Gomez, Ł ukasz Kaiser, and Illia Polosukhin. 2017. Attention is all you need. In *Advances in Neural Information Processing Systems*, volume 30. Curran Associates, Inc.

Liang Wang, Nan Yang, Xiaolong Huang, Linjun Yang, Rangan Majumder, and Furu Wei. 2024. Multilingual e5 text embeddings: A technical report. *Preprint*, arXiv:2402.05672.

A Prompts Used

Table 1: Prompt Structure for entity identification

Section	Prompt Details
Target Activity	You are an intelligent assistant that helps a human analyst to identify the entity type of words in a Sentence.
Goal	Given a word or words identify their given entities based on a given list.
Steps	1. You are given a word or words. If there is more than one word identify if they belong to the same entity or are separate entities. - Each word is separated by a space, even if it is punctuation count it as a word. - You must ONLY classify the given words. DO NOT CLASSIFY ANY OTHER WORDS IN THE SENTENCE. 2. For the word or words given identify which entity they belong to from the list of given words. - Make sure to take into account the previous words into your classification. 3. Return output as a single list of all the word entity pairs in steps 1 and 2. Use **{record_delimiter}** as the list delimiter. DO NOT ADD ANY EXPLANATION. 4. Format each pair as <word> {delimiter} <entity_type>

Examples	`Example 1:`
	Words: IMB SPSS Inc .
	Entity types: No, Application, Developer, URL, Version, PlugIn, Citation, Extension, ProgrammingEnvironment, OperatingSystem, Release, Abbreviation, License, SoftwareCoreference, AlternativeName
	Sentence: The Pearson correlation coefficient between the two analyses was calculated using IBM Statistical Package for Social Sciences software (SPSS , ver. 21 ; IMB SPSS Inc . , Chicago , IL , USA) and differences were considered as statistically significant if the p - Value was < 0.05 .
	Output:
	IMB {delimiter} Developer
	{record_delimiter}
	SPSS {delimiter} Developer
	{record_delimiter}
	Inc {delimiter} Developer
	{record_delimiter}
	. {delimiter} Developer
	`Example 2:`
	Words: GNU
	Entity types: No, Application, Developer, URL, Version, PlugIn, Citation, Extension, ProgrammingEnvironment, OperatingSystem, Release, Abbreviation, License, SoftwareCoreference, AlternativeName
	Sentence: FamSeq is a free software package under GNU license (GPL v 3) , which can be downloaded from our website : http://bioinformatics.mdanderson.org/main/FamSeq , or from SourceForge : http://sourceforge.net/projects/famseq/ .
	Output:
	GNU {delimiter} No

Table 2: Prompt Structure for relation identification between entities

Section	Prompt Details
Target Activity	You are an intelligent assistant that helps a human analyst to identify relations between entities in a sentence.
Goal	Given a pair of words identify if a relationship exists between them and the type of relationship based on a list of options.
Steps	1. You are given a list of words by / in the form of word / word / ...) a sentence and a token count list which contains the ids of each token. Start by identifying if there is a relationship between the words. 2. In case there is a relationship, from the list of options given in Relationship Possibilities, choose the type of relationship that best suits these two words. You must ONLY choose a relationship from the relationship list. - Make sure to take into account the full sentence to identify the type of relationship. - A relationship CAN NOT have itself as the head token and the tail token. Ex: URL_of \t6\t6 3. In case a relationship is found the output should be in the format of: relationship \ttoken_id\ttoken_id - make sure the token_id count starts at 0 and has a maximum equal to the number of spaces in the sentence. 4. However if no relationship is found between the entities the output should be "None". DO NOT ADD ANY EXPLANATION.

Examples	`Example 1:`
	Words: Remote / Software / http://softwaresecure.com / ProctorU / http://proctoru.com
	Relationship Possibilities: Abbreviation_of, AlternativeName_of, Citation_of, Developer_of, Extension_of, License_of, PlugIn_of, Release_of, Specification_of, URL_of, Version_of
	Sentence: Depending on the course , instructor , and exam type , DE MCS students have taken exams at a regional location monitored by a paid proctor or have taken exams using commercial online proctoring services such as Remote Proctor Now from Software Secure (http://softwaresecure.com) or ProctorU (http://proctoru.com) .
	Tokens: 0 1 2 3 4 5 6 7 8 9 10 11 12 13 14 15 16 17 18 19 20 21 22 23 24 25 26 27 28 29 30 31 32 33 34 35 36 37 38 39 40 41 42 43 44 45 46 47 48 49 50 51
	Output: Developer_of \t41\t37;URL_of \t44\t37;URL_of \t49\t47
	`Example 2:`
	Words: Mutation / 3.10 / SoftGenetics
	Relationship Possibilities: Abbreviation_of, AlternativeName_of, Citation_of, Developer_of, Extension_of, License_of, PlugIn_of, Release_of, Specification_of, URL_of, Version_of
	Sentence: Sequence data were imported as AB 1 files into Mutation Surveyor v 3.10 (SoftGenetics , State College , PA) .
	Tokens: 0 1 2 3 4 5 6 7 8 9 10 11 12 13 14 15 16 17 18 19 20 21
	Output: Developer_of \t14\t9;Version_of\t12\t9

Extracting Software Mentions and Relations using Transformers and LLM-Generated Synthetic Data at SOMD 2025

Pranshu Rastogi
Independent Researcher
rastogipranshu29@gmail.com

Rajneesh Tiwari
MS student, CS, Georgia Institute of Technology
rtiwari37@gatech.edu

Abstract

Software is an essential building block of scientific activity, but it often does not receive official citation in scholarly literature. In order to enhance research accessibility and interpretability, we built a system that identifies software mentions and their properties (e.g., version numbers, URLs) as named entities, and classify relationships between them. We fine-tuned Deberta based models for the Named Entity Recognition (NER) task and handled Relation Extraction (RE) as a classification problem over entity pairs. Due to the small dataset size, we employed Large Language Models to create synthetic training data for augmentation. Our system achieved strong performance, with a **65%** F1 score on NER (ranking **2nd** in test phase) and a **47%** F1 score on RE and combined **56% F1 score**, showing significant performance of our approach in this area. Github:- pranshurastogi29/Named-entity-Relation-Extraction-SOMD-2025-ACL

1 Introduction

SOMD 2025[1] shared task focuses on software mention detection. Software which is firmly integrated into the fabric of contemporary scientific inquiry—not just as an experimental and analytic tool but also as a subject of theoretical discussion. In spite of its ubiquity, software regularly fails to receive systematic and formal citation in scholarly papers. Closing this gap calls for automated systems with the ability to detect and comprehend software mentions and their corresponding context in scholarly texts. In this paper, we introduce a system to address this task based on **Named Entity Recognition (NER)** and **Relation Extraction (RE)** methods. Our solution is built upon a heavily annotated dataset of **1,150** sentences (Schindler et al., 2021) of research articles, covering a wide variety of software-related entities and relationships. These are not limited to simple identifiers such as software names, but also encompass more involved constructions including versions, developers, licenses, and usage scenarios. The hierarchical annotation structure and BIO tagging scheme of the dataset allow for fine-grained entity recognition, and the relation annotations record informative relations—version relations and plugin relations—among entities.

For Named Entity Recognition (NER), we fine-tuned Deberta(He et al., 2021) (Base and Large) models on a provided dataset to detect different software-related entities. To enhance generalization, we created high-quality synthetic training data through instruction-guided Large Language Models (such Gemma-2-9b-it (Gemma Team et al., 2024), Mistral-7b-instruct-v0.1 (Jiang et al., 2023), Qwen2.5-7b-instruct(Yang et al., 2024)(Team, 2024).), from template-based on real examples. In Relation Extraction (RE), we cast the problem as a classification task over pairs of entities labeled by the NER model and fine-tunned Deberta (He et al., 2021) and ModernBERT (Warner et al., 2024) based encoders to predict the relationship type between software components. This end-to-end system obtained **65%** score on NER and **47%** for RE and **combined 56% F1 score**, testifying to the subtlety involved in identifying software references and their relationships within scientific texts.

2 Background

Software plays a fundamental role in research across many scientific disciplines, facilitating experimentation, simulation, analysis, and reproducibility. Despite its centrality, software is usually only informally discussed in academic literature and mostly absent of reference citations or proper metadata, which presents issues for subsequent indexing, reuse and reproducibility (Schindler et al., 2021). In order to address these issues, it is now common practice to automate the identification of

[1] https://sdproc.org/2025/somd25.html

Proceedings of the Fifth Workshop on Scholarly Document Processing (SDP 2025), pages 173–181
July 31, 2025

software mentions in academic writings and the various attributes of that mention. This commonly involves two natural language processing tasks: Named Entity Recognition (NER) and Relation Extraction (RE).

Commonly NER and RE have been looked at independently using pipeline-based approaches which lead to iterative errors, e.g. misidentified entities will lead to misidentified relationships (Zeng et al., 2014); (Zhang et al., 2017). In response to these limitations researchers have begun to shift away from independent modeling tasks to modeling both tasks, in a joint fashion, simultaneously and in turn improving performance and efficiency.

2.1 Related Work

One of the earliest joint extraction approaches was introduced by (Li and Ji, 2014), who proposed an incremental model that simultaneously identifies entities and their relations using shared contextual features. This joint modeling approach demonstrated clear advantages over pipeline systems in terms of accuracy and coherence.

Subsequent studies have leveraged transformer-based architectures to further improve the joint learning of NER and RE. (Wadden et al., 2019) presented a contextual span-based model that utilizes BERT-based embeddings to extract entities and relations jointly within a unified framework. Generative methods have also gained traction in this space. (Huguet Cabot and Navigli, 2021) proposed REBEL, a sequence-to-sequence model that reformulates relation extraction as a text generation task, simplifying the overall architecture and reducing dependency on complex feature engineering. Building upon these developments, (Hennen et al., 2024) introduced ITER, a transformer-based iterative refinement model for joint NER and RE that incrementally improves predictions through multiple passes, leading to state-of-the-art performance.

In the domain of software mention detection, the SoMeSci knowledge graph developed by (Schindler et al., 2021) represents a significant contribution. It provides a high-quality annotated dataset of software mentions from scientific articles, enabling the development and evaluation of machine learning models tailored to this specific use case.

2.2 Dataset or Task Description

The dataset is dominated by a high class imbalance on both relation and entity labels. Of the 2,680 relations in the dataset, only three types—Version of (33.7%), Developer of (23.2%), and Citation of (14.4%) total more than 70% of all instances. When you add URL of and PlugIn of, the top five relation types total almost 85% of the data. By comparison, less common relations such as Extension of and AlternativeName of occur much less often, indicating a long-tail distribution. Fig 2

At the entity level, about 82% of the 32,000 tokens have a non-entity tag ("O"). Among the real entity types, the most frequent ones are Application of (1,761 tokens) and Developer of (1,340 tokens), then come Version of (926 tokens) and Citation of (440 tokens).Table 1

2.3 Input and Output Format

The input consists of scholarly text (e.g., academic paper sentences), and the system outputs both entity-level annotations and inter-entity relations.

Example Input (text.txt): `{ "Input Text" : In this paper , we introduce the latest version of our computational analysis software , Comprehensive Analytical Software Tool ( CAST ) , now upgraded to version 5.2 . }`

NER Tags Output (train.entities.labels.txt): `{ "NER Label and Prediction Format" : O O O O O O O O O O O O O O O B-Application I-Application I-Application I-Application O B-Abbreviation O O O O O O B-Version O }`

This shows how entities are labeled using the BIO tagging scheme. For instance, "Comprehensive Analytical Software Tool" is an `Application`, "CAST" is an `Abbreviation`, and "5.2" is a `Version`.

Relation Output (train.relations.labels.txt): `{ "RE Label and Prediction Format": abbreviation of 20 15 ; version of 27 15 }`

This indicates that the entity at token index 20 ("CAST") is an abbreviation of the one starting at index 15 ("Comprehensive Analytical Software Tool"), and the entity at index 27 ("5.2") is its version.

2.4 Evaluation Criteria

Submissions are evaluated on two tasks: Named Entity Recognition (NER) and Relation Extraction (RE), using macro-averaged F1-scores. It averages the F1-score of each class without considering the class imbalance. This means that each class is treated equally, regardless of how many instances it has in the dataset. For final ranking, submissions

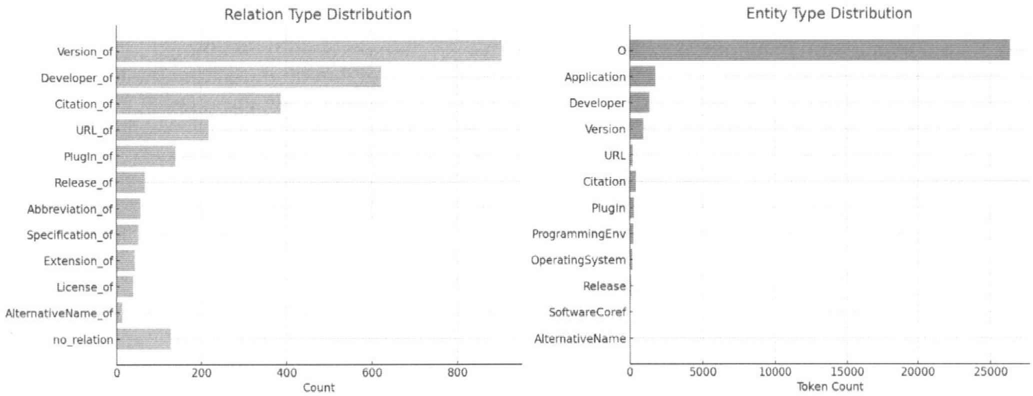

Figure 1: Label distribution in the dataset. Left: Relation Type Distribution. Right: Entity Type Distribution.

Entity Label	Count
O	26344
B-Application	1232
I-Application	529
B-Developer	616
I-Developer	724
B-URL	216
I-URL	6
B-Version	904
I-Version	22
B-PlugIn	211
I-PlugIn	109
B-Citation	382
I-Citation	58
B-Extension	43
I-Extension	7
B-ProgrammingEnvironment	234
I-ProgrammingEnvironment	28
B-OperatingSystem	146
I-OperatingSystem	14
B-Release	69
I-Release	24
B-Abbreviation	58
B-License	43
I-License	54
B-SoftwareCoreference	14
I-SoftwareCoreference	8
B-AlternativeName	14
I-AlternativeName	44

Table 1: Distribution of BIO entity labels in the annotated dataset

are scored using as the **average of the NER and RE Macro averaged F1-scores.**

3 System Overview

3.1 Named Entity Recognition

To address the NER problem, we designed a scalable and resilient pipeline based on Deberta-v3-large (He et al., 2021), an encoder-only transformer with high performance that can be easily well adapted towards challenging NER part of our problem. The model was selected precisely because it can support the difficulties of our dataset — software entities that tend to be fine-grained, vague, and sparsely located throughout the text. more than 80% of the dataset tokens are non-entities, which makes detection even harder. Deberta's disentangled attention and powerful contextual representations enable the model to detect subtle attention patterns between token in such cases. We add a token classification head on top of Deberta for the NER task.

3.1.1 Training Configuration and Implementation Strategy

For Named Entity Recognition (NER) we provided a comprehensive training procedure using a large-scale pre-trained transformer and prepared for and selected optimization and regularization methods. In this section we describe the complete training configuration such as model architecture, hyperparameters, data, and compute.

Model Architecture: We utilize the Deberta-v3-large (He et al., 2021), which offers strong contextual encoding through disentangled attention and enhanced mask decoding. A token classification head is placed atop the encoder to support the NER task, where each token is labeled based on the BIO tagging scheme for named entity spans. The same backbone is later extended for joint NER and RE learning in downstream settings.

Hyperparameter Settings: The model is fine-tuned using the following configuration:

- **Maximum sequence length:** 512 tokens
- **Learning rate:** 2.5e-5

Named Entity Recognition	Precision	Recall	F1-Score	Support
Abbreviation	0.6667	0.5000	0.5714	12
AlternativeName	0.5833	0.8235	0.6829	17
Application	0.6560	0.6198	0.6374	363
Citation	0.7245	0.7594	0.7415	187
Developer	0.3261	0.7500	0.4545	20
Extension	0.5000	0.1667	0.2500	6
OperatingSystem	0.5000	0.5000	0.5000	2
PlugIn	0.2449	0.6000	0.3478	20
ProgrammingEnvironment	0.8261	0.7917	0.8085	24
Release	1.0000	1.0000	1.0000	10
SoftwareCoreference	1.0000	1.0000	1.0000	3
URL	0.7746	0.7857	0.7801	70
Version	0.6250	0.7292	0.6731	96
Micro Avg	0.6438	0.6904	0.6663	830
Macro Avg	0.6482	0.6943	**0.6498**	830
Weighted Avg	0.6675	0.6904	0.6731	830
Relation Extraction				
Developer_of	0.2344	0.7500	0.3571	20
Citation_of	0.5321	0.7968	0.6381	187
Version_of	0.3901	0.7396	0.5108	96
PlugIn_of	0.1013	0.6154	0.1739	13
URL_of	0.4701	0.7857	0.5882	70
License_of	0.0000	0.0000	0.0000	0
AlternativeName_of	0.6522	0.8824	0.7500	17
Release_of	0.5263	1.0000	0.6897	10
Abbreviation_of	0.5000	0.5000	0.5000	12
Extension_of	0.0000	0.0000	0.0000	6
Specification_of	0.0000	0.0000	0.0000	0
Micro Avg	0.4240	0.7633	0.5452	431
Macro Avg	0.3785	0.6744	**0.4675**	431
Weighted Avg	0.4599	0.7633	0.5675	431

Table 2: Test Phase - Performance metrics for Named Entity Recognition (top) and Relation Extraction (bottom).

- **Learning rate scheduler:** Linear with warmup
- **Warmup ratio:** 10%
- **Weight decay:** 0.01
- **Batch size:** 8 (with gradient accumulation of 16 steps to simulate a batch size of 128)
- **Epochs:** 30
- **Evaluation strategy:** Epoch-based with best-model checkpointing
- **Mixed precision (AMP):** Enabled to accelerate training

These hyperparameters were chosen based on empirical tuning, as well as experience with prior work on transformer-based NER models. Our use of both warmup scheduling and weight decay regularization avoids overfitting, while gradient accumulation enables stable training under memory limitations.

Negative Sampling: Due to the highly imbalanced class distribution (over 80 % were non-entity tokens) we implement negative sampling during training with a downsampling ratio of 0.3. Thus, this approach allows the model to avoid the over-representation of non-entity classes and enhanced the sensitivity of the model in regard to minority classes (i.e. software-related entities).

3.1.2 Synthetic Data Generation for NER Using LLMs

To augment the training data for the Named Entity Recognition (NER) task, we use LLMs to generate synthetic text that maintains annotated entities while introducing significant variation. The general strategy is to pair two samples from the training set and combine their content into a single passage with all named entities from the original texts intact. This is achieved by combining the related entity labels into one consolidated mapping and token definition to maintain explicitly within a carefully designed prompt.The prompt instructs the LLM to paraphrase and merge the two texts both syntactically and semantically, promoting variability in sentence structure and wording without compromising entity coherence. By maintaining same tokens within the generated text, the method guarantees perfect label recovery, enabling us to label the generated text by mapping each token back to its respective entity type, or as non-entity where there is no match. We generate with samples using LLMs (such Gemma-2-9b-it (Gemma Team et al., 2024), Mistral-7b-instruct-v0.1 (Jiang et al., 2023), Qwen2.5-7b-instruct(Yang et al., 2024)(Team, 2024)). For examples check **Appendix A**

This process not only contributes linguistic diversity to the data set, but also creates more varied context by combining information from multiple samples. The pre-structured prompts form the centerpiece of this operation, which guide the LLM to maintaining both entity accuracy and task cohesiveness. Hence, the resulting data enriches the quality and generalizability of the NER model

3.2 Relation Extraction

For the Relation Extraction we used a contextaware strategy by concatenating the entire input text along with the recognized entities and associated entity types. This allowed the transformer based architectures such as Deberta (He et al., 2021) and ModernBERT (Warner et al., 2024) to utilize both sentence-level and entity-specific upon training.In our early experiments, we finetuned models on a multiclass classification configuration including 12 different relationship types. Trained using this configuration, models with both Deberta (He et al., 2021) and Modern BERT (Warner et al., 2024) with a macro-averaged F1 value of about 15% over the relation-level test set.

3.2.1 Model Architecture and Implementation Strategy

We adapted a transformer-based model with Deberta-v3-large (He et al., 2021) as the backbone encoder. The model has all hidden states from all layers and is instantiated with all dropout components (both hidden and attention) set to 0.1. The model includes a mean pooling layer which aggregates the token embeddings weighted by the attention mask with a linear head that projects to output classes. Given this setup, we were able to train the model efficiently using dual T4 GPU that are publicly available on Kaggle

Hyperparameter Settings: The following configuration summarizes the key hyperparameters used throughout our experiments:

- **Maximum sequence length:** 384 tokens
- **Batch size:** 64 (no accumulation needed)
- **Learning rate:** 4e-5 (encoder), 6e-5 (decoder)
- **Learning rate scheduler:** Linear decay
- **Warmup steps:** None
- **Epochs:** 6
- **Optimizer:** AdamW (β_1=0.9, β_2=0.999, ϵ=1e$-$6)
- **Weight decay:** 0.01
- **Gradient clipping:** 5000 (max norm)
- **Evaluation frequency:** Every 20 steps

Team	F1 NER	Precision	Recall
TU Graz Data Team	0.68	0.66	0.75
psr123 (Our Team)	0.65	0.65	0.69
Ekbana	0.64	0.67	0.65

Table 3: Comparison of system-level NER (Macro Average) metrics across different teams in Test Phase

3.2.2 Data Augmentation for RE

To address the relation extraction (RE) task, we design a strategy that pairs each sentence with two entity and their corresponding types, formatted as 'entity_type [SEP] entity_text'. For every document, we extract annotated entity pairs and label them with their respective relation types, such as `Developer_of` or `URL_of`. To augment the dataset and introduce harder negative samples, we generate additional entity pairs that do not appear in the original annotations and label them as `no_relation`. For example, if the annotated data contains a pair like `B-Developer [SEP] Software` and `B-Application [SEP] Remote` labeled as `Developer_of`, we add unannotated pairs like `B-Developer [SEP] Software` and `B-Application [SEP] ProctorU` with the `no_relation` Figure2 label. This augmentation process results in a more balanced and challenging training set, enabling the model to better differentiate true relations from coincidental entity co-occurrences. Each training sample ultimately takes the form of the sentence followed by the two entity spans, separated by `[SEP]` tokens: `[document text] [SEP] entity_1 [SEP] entity_2`. This design allows the transformer-based model to leverage full sentence context alongside focused entity information, thereby improving its ability to capture complex relationships in software-related text.

Reproducibility: Our entire pipeline which of NER and RE are implemented using the open

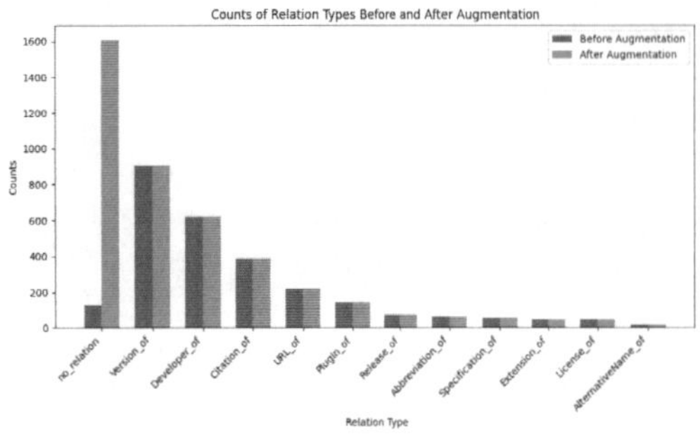

Figure 2: Label distribution after augmentation

source libraries. The design of pipeline is highly modularized, reproducible and easy-to-implement system. Complete configurations details are available in the code release.

Hardware Configuration: To maximize cost-efficiency and experimentation flexibility, our training and experiments used Kaggle's free GPU available environments. In particular, we used the newly released **T4 x2 dual-GPU** environment, which greatly improved the efficiency of training and allowed us to conduct more extensive ablation studies.

4 Performance Analysis

Experimentation Phase. In the experimentation stage, we investigated several modeling methods for the Named Entity Recognition (NER) task, mainly utilizing the Deberta-V3-Large (He et al., 2021) model with a token classification method. We started with a vanilla Deberta-V3-Large model and used a 4-fold cross-validation configuration. In this setup, we observed that the model trained on **Fold 1** achieved an **F1 score (macro average) of 60%** Table 4 on the test set. The other fold-trained models yielded similar validation performance, but none exceeded an F1 score of 60% on the test set.

To enhance generalization, we supplemented our training data with **synthetically generated datasets** produced using different large language models (LLMs), namely Gemma-2-9B-it (Gemma Team et al., 2024), Mistral-7B-Instruct-v0.1 (Jiang et al., 2023), and Qwen2.5-7B-Instruct(Yang et al., 2024)(Team, 2024). Among these, only the synthetic data generated by Mistral-7B-Instruct-v0.1 (Jiang et al., 2023) led to a significant improvement of **5%** in the F1 score. The datasets generated by Qwen2.5-7B-Instruct and Gemma-2-9B-it (Gemma Team et al., 2024) offered a modest **2% gain** Table 4 in a full-training scenario but did not surpass the performance of the Mistral-7B-Instruct-v0.1 (Jiang et al., 2023) based augmentation.

Our best-performing system was the final model: a Deberta-V3-Large (He et al., 2021) trained on the complete original training dataset, **augmented with synthetic data** from Mistral-7B-Instruct-v0.1 (Jiang et al., 2023). This configuration achieved a **macro-averaged F1 score of 65%** Table 4 on the official test set.

We also experimented with XLM-RoBERTa(Conneau et al., 2019) using the same setup, training it on the full dataset along with the additional synthetic data. However, it achieved only a **macro-averaged F1 score of 28% Table 4** on the NER task. This comparatively lower performance further reinforced our choice of and confidence in the Deberta-V3-Large (He et al., 2021) model for this task.

4.1 Performance of NER Test Phase

- **Best Performers:** The model did extremely well in "Release" and "SoftwareCoreference" with 100% Table 2 spot perfect F1-scores. What this indicates is that the model was consistently dependable in identifying these entities.The "ProgrammingEnvironment" entity also demonstrated good performance, which had an F1-score of 80.85% Table 2, and thus ensured that the model was capable of identifying this type as well.

- **Lower Performing Categories:** Other categories were tougher for the model. "Extension" had the worst F1-score of 25%Table 2. Entities "Developer" and "PlugIn" also had lower scores.

- **Overall Performance:** The macro average F1-score over all the NER classes was 65% Table 2, which shows consistent overall performance. Although the model performed well in most entity types, there is still some improvement to be made, particularly in dealing with rare or contextually ambiguous entities.

On the **Relation Extraction** A closer examination showed that more common relation classes were overfitted to and relations between unrelated tokens. To counter this, we employed a data augmentation method with negative examples, i.e., entity pairs having no relation among them, and

Task	Model / Setup	Precision	Recall	F1
NER	Deberta-V3-Large	0.5734	0.6612	0.5993
	Deberta-V3-Large (Full Fit + Mistral-7B)	0.6482	0.6943	**0.6498**
	Deberta-V3-Large (Full Fit + Gemma2-9B)	0.5875	0.6808	0.6199
	Deberta-V3-Large (Full Fit + Qwen2.5)	0.6657	0.6531	0.6215
	XLM-RoBERTa (Full Fit + Gemma2-9B)	0.2775	0.3104	0.2871
RE	Deberta-V3-Large	0.1025	0.4117	0.1543
	Modern BERT-Large	0.0878	0.4228	0.1379
	Deberta-V3-Large (Augmented Data)	0.3785	0.6744	**0.4675**
	Modern BERT-Large (Augmented Data)	0.3473	0.6702	0.4384

Table 4: Performance of different models and training setups on NER and RE tasks (Macro Averaged Scores)

thereby balancing the dataset and robust training. This improvement produced an increase in performance of substantial size, raising our test F1 measure to **47%, a gain of 32%**. Although we could not enter our RE results during the initial test period due to some constraints, we extend a sincere thanks to the workshop organizers for providing an open submission phase, which enabled us to enter our RE model. Our final submission uses a full-fit model trained on the entire relation extraction dataset along with our data augmentation, which gave us our best result of **47%** Table 2 macro-averaged F1.

4.2 Performance of RE Test Phase

- **Best Performers:** "AlternativeName_of" achieved a strong F1-score of 0.7500, demonstrating the model's ability to effectively identify this relation type."Citation_of" and "URL_of" also showed good performance, with F1-scores of 0.6381 and 0.5882, respectively.
- **Overall Performance:** The macro average F1-score for RE is 0.4675, indicating a relatively low overall performance in relation extraction.This result points to challenges in dealing with unbalanced or complex relation types, with a significant opportunity for improvement in handling these cases effectively.

5 Acknowledgments

We would like to thank the organisers of the Software Mention Detection (SOMD) shared task and the Scholarly Document Processing (SDP) workshop for running this competition. We also thank the anonymous reviewers for their insightful and constructive comments, which helped raise the standard of this manuscript considerably.

6 Conclusion

Our approach exhibits decent performance in addressing the task of RE and NER within the software space. In the case of NER, our model has a macro F1-score of **65%** Table 4, and entity categories such as Release and SoftwareCoreference have perfect recall and precision. Still some categories, particularly those that had sparse or confusing examples—such as PlugIn and Extension—were still hard to predict to the model. RE results were not good enough, as macro F1-scores of about 15% because of potential overfitting in over dominant relation classes and incorrect classification of no-relation entity pairs. This was solved by data augmentation process of adding hard negative samples, which boosted RE performance with the macro F1 improved to **47%**, reflecting on the strength of balancing the data and enhancing generalisation. We also investigated synthetic data augmentation with LLMs. Of these, only Mistral-7B demonstrated a definite performance boost (**5%** F1), Our best-performing model Deberta-V3-Large trained on the entire dataset with augmented data produced optimal overall performance, our system produces **combined macro F1** of **56%** Table 4. Overall, our findings highlight the potential of combining pretrained models with synthetic data to tackle complex information retrieval problems in scholarly text. Our hope is that this work will help to further develop better software mention detection systems.

References

Alexis Conneau, Kartikay Khandelwal, Naman Goyal, Vishrav Chaudhary, Guillaume Wenzek, Francisco Guzmán, Edouard Grave, Myle Ott, Luke Zettlemoyer, and Veselin Stoyanov. 2019. Unsupervised cross-lingual representation learning at scale. *CoRR*, abs/1911.02116.

Thomas Mesnard Gemma Team, Cassidy Hardin, Robert Dadashi, Surya Bhupatiraju, Laurent Sifre, Morgane Rivière, Mihir Sanjay Kale, Juliette Love, Pouya Tafti, Léonard Hussenot, and et al. 2024. Gemma.

Pengcheng He, Jianfeng Gao, and Weizhu Chen. 2021. Debertav3: Improving deberta using electra-style pre-training with gradient-disentangled embedding sharing.

Moritz Hennen, Florian Babl, and Michaela Geierhos. 2024. ITER: Iterative transformer-based entity recognition and relation extraction. In *Findings of the Association for Computational Linguistics: EMNLP 2024*, pages 11209–11223, Miami, Florida, USA. Association for Computational Linguistics.

Pere-Lluís Huguet Cabot and Roberto Navigli. 2021. REBEL: Relation extraction by end-to-end language generation. In *Findings of the Association for Computational Linguistics: EMNLP 2021*, pages 2370–2381, Punta Cana, Dominican Republic. Association for Computational Linguistics.

Albert Q. Jiang, Alexandre Sablayrolles, Arthur Mensch, Chris Bamford, Devendra Singh Chaplot, Diego de las Casas, Florian Bressand, Gianna Lengyel, Guillaume Lample, Lucile Saulnier, Lélio Renard Lavaud, Marie-Anne Lachaux, Pierre Stock, Teven Le Scao, Thibaut Lavril, Thomas Wang, Timothée Lacroix, and William El Sayed. 2023. Mistral 7b.

Qi Li and Heng Ji. 2014. Incremental joint extraction of entity mentions and relations. In *Proceedings of the 52nd Annual Meeting of the Association for Computational Linguistics (Volume 1: Long Papers)*, pages 402–412, Baltimore, Maryland. Association for Computational Linguistics.

David Schindler, Felix Bensmann, Stefan Dietze, and Frank Krüger. 2021. Somesci- a 5 star open data gold standard knowledge graph of software mentions in scientific articles. In *Proceedings of the 30th ACM International Conference on Information & Knowledge Management*, CIKM '21, page 4574–4583, New York, NY, USA. Association for Computing Machinery.

Qwen Team. 2024. Qwen2.5: A party of foundation models.

David Wadden, Ulme Wennberg, Yi Luan, and Hannaneh Hajishirzi. 2019. Entity, relation, and event extraction with contextualized span representations. In *Proceedings of the 2019 Conference on Empirical Methods in Natural Language Processing and the 9th International Joint Conference on Natural Language Processing (EMNLP-IJCNLP)*, pages 5784–5789, Hong Kong, China. Association for Computational Linguistics.

Benjamin Warner, Antoine Chaffin, Benjamin Clavié, Orion Weller, Oskar Hallström, Said Taghadouini, Alexis Gallagher, Raja Biswas, Faisal Ladhak, Tom Aarsen, Nathan Cooper, Griffin Adams, Jeremy Howard, and Iacopo Poli. 2024. Smarter, better, faster, longer: A modern bidirectional encoder for fast, memory efficient, and long context finetuning and inference.

An Yang, Baosong Yang, Binyuan Hui, Bo Zheng, Bowen Yu, Chang Zhou, Chengpeng Li, Chengyuan Li, Dayiheng Liu, Fei Huang, Guanting Dong, Haoran Wei, Huan Lin, Jialong Tang, Jialin Wang, Jian Yang, Jianhong Tu, Jianwei Zhang, Jianxin Ma, Jin Xu, Jingren Zhou, Jinze Bai, Jinzheng He, Junyang Lin, Kai Dang, Keming Lu, Keqin Chen, Kexin Yang, Mei Li, Mingfeng Xue, Na Ni, Pei Zhang, Peng Wang, Ru Peng, Rui Men, Ruize Gao, Runji Lin, Shijie Wang, Shuai Bai, Sinan Tan, Tianhang Zhu, Tianhao Li, Tianyu Liu, Wenbin Ge, Xiaodong Deng, Xiaohuan Zhou, Xingzhang Ren, Xinyu Zhang, Xipin Wei, Xuancheng Ren, Yang Fan, Yang Yao, Yichang Zhang, Yu Wan, Yunfei Chu, Yuqiong Liu, Zeyu Cui, Zhenru Zhang, and Zhihao Fan. 2024. Qwen2 technical report. *arXiv preprint arXiv:2407.10671*.

Daojian Zeng, Kang Liu, Siwei Lai, Guangyou Zhou, and Jun Zhao. 2014. Relation classification via convolutional deep neural network. In *Proceedings of COLING 2014, the 25th International Conference on Computational Linguistics: Technical Papers*, pages 2335–2344, Dublin, Ireland. Dublin City University and Association for Computational Linguistics.

Yuhao Zhang, Victor Zhong, Danqi Chen, Gabor Angeli, and Christopher D. Manning. 2017. Position-aware attention and supervised data improve slot filling. In *Proceedings of the 2017 Conference on Empirical Methods in Natural Language Processing*, pages 35–45, Copenhagen, Denmark. Association for Computational Linguistics.

Appendices

A Synthetic Data Generation for NER

Example of Synthetically Generated Data

Task: Merge and rephrase the following two texts at both syntactic and semantic levels while preserving specific tokens.

Text 1: *Significance was accepted at P $\leq$ 0.05, statistical power was 90%, and the analyses were performed in Statistical Package for Social Sciences version 20.0 (SPSS, Chicago, Illinois, USA).*

Text 2: *Microsoft Excel 2007 was used to compile the data and STATA Version 12.0 was used for statistical analyses [28].*

Required Tokens (to be preserved as-is): {`Microsoft`, `Excel`, `2007`, `12.0`, `[28]`, `Statistical`, `Package`, `for`, `Social`, `Sciences`, `20.0`, `SPSS`}

Generated Output Text:
In order to analyze the data, statistical significance was accepted at P $\leq$ 0.05 and the statistical power was determined to be 90%. The analyses were performed using **Statistical Package** for **Social Sciences** version **20.0**, commonly referred to as **SPSS**. Data compilation was carried out using **Microsoft Excel 2007**, while further statistical analysis was conducted using STATA version **12.0** ([28]).

Example 1: Synthetic NER sample

Example of Synthetically Generated Data

Task: Merge and rephrase the following two texts at both syntactic and semantic levels while preserving specific tokens.

Text 1: *In contrast to the original tool, ggsashimi internally generates an R script which uses the ggplot 2 library [5] for the graphical rendering.*

Text 2: *The pre-processed data files were imported into Agilent Mass Profiler Professional software (version 12.1) for further statistical analysis.*

Required Tokens (to be preserved as-is): {`ggsashimi`, `R`, `ggplot`, `2`, `[5]`, `Agilent`, `Mass`, `Profiler`, `Professional`, `version`, `12.1`}

Generated Output Text:
While **ggsashimi** internally generates an **R** script using the **ggplot 2** library [5] for graphical rendering, in contrast to the original tool, the pre-processed data files were imported into **Agilent Mass Profiler Professional** software (version **12.1**) for further statistical analysis.

Example 2: Synthetic NER sample

SciVQA 2025: Overview of the First Scientific Visual Question Answering Shared Task

Ekaterina Borisova[1,2], **Nikolas Rauscher**[1,2], **Georg Rehm**[1,3]

[1]Deutsches Forschungszentrum für Künstliche Intelligenz GmbH (DFKI)
[2]Technische Universität Berlin [3]Humboldt-Universität zu Berlin
Corresponding author: ekaterina.borisova@dfki.de

Abstract

This paper provides an overview of the First Scientific Visual Question Answering (SciVQA) shared task conducted as part of the Fifth Scholarly Document Processing workshop (SDP 2025). SciVQA aims to explore the capabilities of current multimodal large language models (MLLMs) in reasoning over figures from scholarly publications for question answering (QA). The main focus of the challenge is on closed-ended visual and non-visual QA pairs. We developed the novel SciVQA benchmark comprising 3,000 images of figures and a total of 21,000 QA pairs. The shared task received seven submissions, with the best performing system achieving an average F1 score of approx. 0.86 across ROUGE-1, ROUGE-L, and BertScore metrics. Participating teams explored various fine-tuning and prompting strategies, as well as augmenting the SciVQA dataset with out-of-domain data and incorporating relevant context from source publications. The findings indicate that while MLLMs demonstrate strong performance on SciVQA, they face challenges in visual reasoning and still fall behind human judgments.

1 Introduction

Graphical representations such as figures (e. g., charts and diagrams), combined with natural language, serve as essential tools for identifying patterns, analysing trends, and extracting insights from data. In academic research, this dual-modality is particularly prominent, with scientific publications conveying large amounts of valuable information through both unstructured text and (semi-)structured figures.

Automatically decoding and processing data from figures available in scholarly papers (i. e., *scientific figures*) can be beneficial for downstream tasks such as visual question answering (VQA). However, VQA over figures is challenging due to their diverse types (e. g., line charts, box plots, pie charts), multimodal nature (combining visuals, numerical data, text), and complex relationships between various components (e. g., axes and labels) (Meng et al., 2024; Zhou et al., 2023). For scientific figures, the task is further complicated by the presence of domain-specific terminology and principles (Huang et al., 2024). Hence, efficient VQA requires accurate information extraction, strong reasoning skills, and expertise in the target research field (Liu et al., 2023b; Li et al., 2024b; Meng et al., 2024).

Although VQA has been extensively studied (Wu et al., 2017), its application to scientific figures is still an emerging area of research (Ahmed et al., 2023). Existing real-world datasets are limited, containing figures sourced exclusively from arXiv [1] (Wang et al., 2024b; Roberts et al., 2024), ignoring other scientific contexts, such as peer-reviewed conference and journal publications. Furthermore, while several works examine the robustness of current multimodal large language models (MLLMs) for figure VQA (Islam et al., 2024; Mukhopadhyay et al., 2024; Wu et al., 2024), none specifically focus on extensive evaluation of models' abilities to accurately recognise, process, and link visual attributes (e. g., colour, shape, size) of scientific figures with textual content (e. g., captions, legends, axis labels).

To bridge the mentioned gaps and promote further research, we organised the *First Scientific Visual Question Answering* (SciVQA) shared task as part of the Fifth Scholarly Document Processing workshop (SDP 2025)[2] at ACL 2025. This challenge aims to shed light on the capabilities and limitations of current MLLMs in handling both

[1]https://arxiv.org
[2]https://sdproc.org/2025/

Proceedings of the Fifth Workshop on Scholarly Document Processing (SDP 2025), pages 182–210
July 31, 2025

questions addressing visual elements of scientific figures and those without visual information. Participants were invited to build VQA systems using a novel dataset of 3,000 images of scientific figures from two distinct sources, ACL Anthology[3] and arXiv, associated with a total of 21,000 visual and non-visual QA pairs. The competition attracted 20 registered teams, seven of which submitted their results. This paper presents an overview of the SciVQA shared task, including the dataset, baseline, and submitted systems description, summary of the results, comparison of automatic solutions to human performance, and an analysis of common challenges and errors faced by MLLMs.

2 Related work

Existing datasets. Previous efforts such as FigureQA (Kahou et al., 2018), DVQA (Kafle et al., 2018), LEAF-QA (Chaudhry et al., 2019), and PlotQA (Methani et al., 2020), rely on synthetic data with limited types of figures and template-based QA pairs. For instance, FigureQA focuses on bar, line, and pie charts plotted using the Bokeh library and associated with QA pairs generated from the fifteen predefined templates. DVQA is even more restricted in terms of figure variability, containing only bar plots generated with the Matplotlib library. While such datasets utilise the low-cost approach for data generation and annotation, they fail to reflect complexity and diversity of real-world figures and questions. Current benchmarks, including ChartQA (Masry et al., 2022), OpenCQA (Kantharaj et al., 2022), CharXiv (Wang et al., 2024b), SciFiBench (Roberts et al., 2024), and ChartQAPro (Masry et al., 2025a), comprise authentic images of figures with either human-written or manually validated synthetic QA pairs. However, only the latter three feature unbounded types of figures. Additionally, existing datasets vary in terms of the QA taxonomies they adopt. Among the commonly distinguished question categories are structural (understanding a figure's structure), retrieval (extracting information from a figure's components), and reasoning (operating on multiple figures' components), with binary (yes/no), multiple-choice, fixed or open vocabulary answers (Kafle et al., 2018; Chaudhry et al., 2019; Methani et al., 2020; Masry et al., 2022, 2025a). Recent works, CharXiv and ChartQAPro, also introduce the novel distinction between answerable and unanswerable questions. Although diverse benchmarks are available, those containing real-world scientific figures and questions remain scarce and are primarily limited to a single source – pre-prints from arXiv.

Modeling approaches. Earlier studies (Liu et al., 2023a; Kim et al., 2020; Masry et al., 2022; Methani et al., 2020; Liu et al., 2023b; Zhou et al., 2023) approach QA over figures with a two-stage process, i. e., the image of a figure is transformed into an underlying (semi-)structured table which then serves as part of a textual input to a language model. One of the main drawbacks of this method is the loss of visual information such as colour (e. g., purple box), shape (e. g., triangular marker), position (e. g., top right figure), height (e. g., between the highest and the lowest bars), direction (e. g., pointing toward the box), and size (e. g., largest segment) (Liu et al., 2023a; Kim et al., 2024; Wei et al., 2024), which prevents systems from answering questions that rely on these features (e. g., *"What is the minimum value of the* ***green line****?"*). With recent advances in vision and multimodality research, the focus has shifted towards an end-to-end VQA approach, i. e., leveraging images of figures directly using MLLMs, thus preserving visual aspects (Wang et al., 2024b; Masry et al., 2025b; Han et al., 2023; Zeng et al., 2024; Wei et al., 2024). While some works propose and utilise figure-oriented MLLMs, including ChartGemma (Masry et al., 2025b), ChartLlama (Han et al., 2023), UniChart (Masry et al., 2023), ChartAssistant (Meng et al., 2024), TinyChart (Zhang et al., 2024), and MultiModal Chart Assistant (Liu et al., 2024), others (Mukhopadhyay et al., 2024; Wu et al., 2024) also explore the capabilities of general-purpose MLLMs such as GPT-4o (OpenAI et al., 2024) and Gemini (Team et al., 2024) via prompt engineering. Despite the promising results of the current open- and closed-source MLLMs in VQA over figures (Islam et al., 2024; Mukhopadhyay et al., 2024; Wu et al., 2024), their effectiveness in accurately recognising and interpreting visual attributes (e. g., colour, shape, height) remains underexplored.

Compared to the existing works, the SciVQA shared task is intended to advance VQA over scientific figures, specifically focusing on exploring the capabilities of MLLMs to reason over questions addressing visual aspects of objects such as shape, size, position, height, direction or colour.

[3] https://aclanthology.org

3 Shared task overview

In the SciVQA challenge, the task is to develop multimodal QA systems using images of scientific figures, their captions, associated natural language QA pairs, and optionally additional metadata (e. g., figure type). The shared task was hosted on the Codabench platform (Xu et al., 2022) from April 1, 2025, to May 16, 2025.[4] In what follows, QA pair types schema (§3.1), dataset (§3.2), and metrics used for evaluation (§3.3) are described in detail.

3.1 Question answering pair types schema

As mentioned in §2, prior studies mainly rely on fixed templates for QA pairs generation. However, this approach restricts the diversity and naturalness of the resulting QA pairs. Due to these limitations, we defined a custom schema containing seven QA pair types. As shown in Figure 1, the QA pairs fall into two root classes: *closed-ended* and *unanswerable*. A closed-ended QA means that it is possible to answer a question based solely on a given data source, i. e., a figure image and/or optionally its caption. Thus, no additional resources such as the main text of a publication, other documents, figures or tables are required. In contrast, an unanswerable question implies that it is not possible to infer an answer solely from a given data (e. g., full paper text is required, values are not visible or missing).

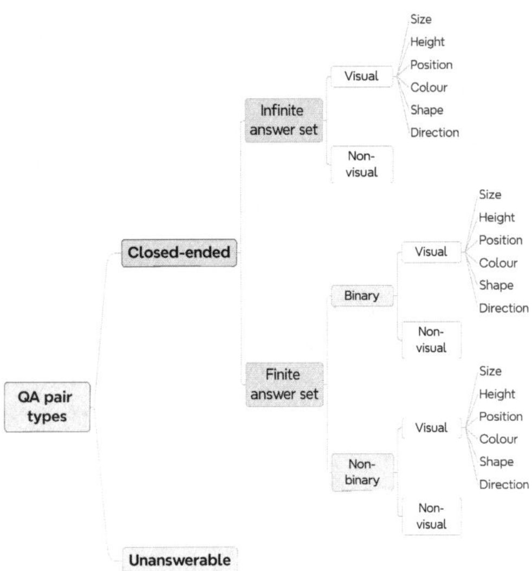

Figure 1: Question answering pair types schema.

At the second level of our schema, the categorisation is based on the fact that for a given question Q, there exists a set S of all possible answers $S = \{a_1, a_2, \ldots, a_N\}$, which can be either *infinite* or *finite*. Questions with an infinite S of answers simply do not have any predefined answer options, e. g., *"What is the approximate value of the loss at the 10th epoch for the green line?"*. On the contrary, questions with a finite S of answers are associated with a limited range of answer options. Such QA pairs fall into two subcategories: 1. *binary* – require a yes/no or true/false answer, e. g., *"Is the percentage of positive tweets equal to 15?"*; 2. *non-binary* – require to choose from a set of M predefined answer options where one or more are correct, e. g, *"What is the maximum value of the green bar at the threshold equal to 10?" – A: 5, B: 10, C: 300, D: None of the above*. Each of the discussed QA pair types can be *visual* and *non-visual*. Visual questions address or incorporate information on one or more of the six visual attributes of a figure, i. e., shape, size, position, height, direction or colour, e. g., *"In the **bottom left** figure, what is the value of the **blue line** at iteration 100?"*. Non-visual questions do not involve any of the mentioned six visual aspects of a figure, e. g, *"What is the minimum value of X?"*, *"What is the difference between the percentage of votes obtained for humour and non-humour tweets?"*. Table 3 (Appendix A) summarises QA pair types and their definitions, while Figure 4 (Appendix A) provides an example of an annotated figure.

3.2 SciVQA dataset

Data collection. The SciVQA dataset comprises 3,000 images[5] of real-world figures extracted from English scientific publications in Computational Linguistics (CL). The figure instances are collected from the two existing datasets, ACL-Fig (Karishma et al., 2023) and SciGraphQA (Li and Tajbakhsh, 2023). ACL-Fig is a corpus of 1,671 figure images extracted from ACL Anthology papers and automatically annotated for the type classification task. SciGraphQA is a dataset of 295,000 figure images from scholarly publications available on arXiv, annotated for multi-turn VQA. First, we extract all figures from the ACL-Fig dataset, excluding images of tables and those not depicting any trends or consisting solely of text, i. e., instances classified as algorithms, natural images, NLP rules/grammar, screenshots, maps, and word clouds. Then to obtain the remaining data, we take a random sample of

[4] `https://www.codabench.org/competitions/5904/`

[5] We restrict the dataset size due to constraints in both the annotation timeframe and the number of annotators available.

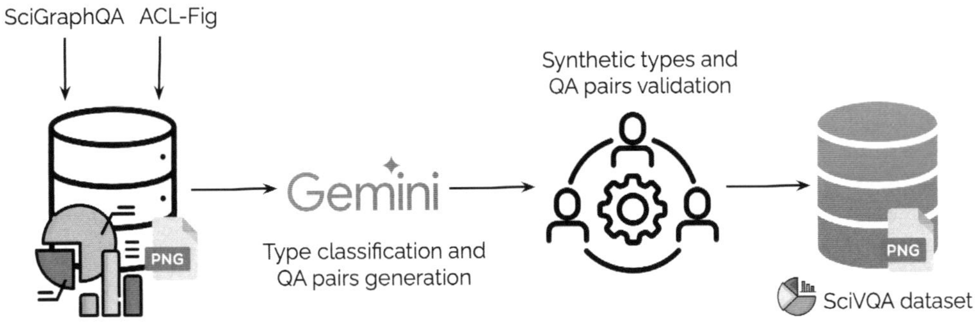

Figure 2: SciVQA dataset annotation pipeline.

figures from SciGraphQA that originated from papers tagged as Computation and Language (cs.CL). We also perform deduplication to ensure that only figures from papers not already included in the ACL-Fig subset are considered. Finally, we manually assess the quality of all collected images and substitute those which are unreadable due to low resolution or issues such as fully cropped y and x labels. We use PDFFigures 2.0 (Clark and Divvala, 2016) and MinerU (Wang et al., 2024a) to extract the respective figure images from the PDF files of scholarly papers. As a result, the SciVQA corpus contains 908 images from ACL-Fig and 2,092 images from SciGraphQA, fetched from scholarly papers published between 1994 and 2024.

Annotation. Inspired by recent studies (Li and Tajbakhsh, 2023; Li et al., 2024a) which leverage generative models like GPT-4 for generating QA pairs, we annotate the SciVQA dataset semi-automatically to reduce the manual effort and cost. The annotation process involves two main phases (see Figure 2): 1. synthetic QA pairs generation and figure type classification 2. followed by manual validation of the results.

In the initial stage, we perform automatic annotation based on figure images and captions using the free API tier of Gemini-1.5-Flash (Team et al., 2024).[6] First, we classify figures into types according to structural and stylistic characteristics, as this information can serve as useful metadata during VQA systems training. All figures are classified as either *compound*, i. e., contain multiple sub-figures which can be separated and constitute individual figure objects or *non-compound*, i. e., contain a single figure which cannot be decomposed into multiple standalone sub-figures. Additionally, we instruct Gemini to indicate the number of (sub-)figures in a given image. Following the ACL-Fig schema, we further categorise the figures in the SciGraphQA subset into one of the following eleven types: *line chart*, *bar chart*, *box plot*, *confusion matrix*, *pie chart*, *scatter plot*, *pareto chart*, *venn diagram*, *architecture diagram*, *neural networks*, and *tree*. Note that we exclude the *graph* class, as it is too generic and the model might overuse it. However, we retain it during the human validation phase since figures from ACL-Fig already include this label. Finally, we annotate each figure image from SciVQA with seven synthetic QA pairs according to the schema discussed in §3.1. For the unanswerable questions, we instruct the model to output the predefined statement *"It is not possible to answer this question based only on the provided data."*, and to generate four answer options for non-binary questions.[7] As a result, a total of 21,000 QA pairs are obtained. Prompt examples are provided in Figures 5-7 in Appendix B.

In the next phase, we manually validate synthetic QA pairs and figure type labels. We hire five master students with a strong theoretical background in CL and a high level of proficiency in English. We also involve three additional student assistants from our lab with the relevant expertise. As an annotation tool, we use Label Studio[8] since it allows both image and text input. Depending on their contracts, each annotator is assigned 133-520 images, i. e., 931-3,640 QA pairs. To mitigate potential bias from an annotator working primarily on a single figure type (e. g., line graph), we ensure that each student receives a diverse set of figures. In the annotation setup, students are pro-

[6]The use of Gemini-1.5-Flash was prohibited during the competition to eliminate any bias.

[7]The data preparation code is available in our GitHub repository: `https://github.com/esborisova/SciVQA`

[8]`https://labelstud.io`

vided with a figure image, its caption, type labels, and seven QA pairs with information on their types (see Figure 11 in Appendix C). For the figure classification, we also introduce an *other* category to account for instances outside the ACL-Fig schema. Annotators could specify a subclass if they know the specific type. Additionally, there is an option to request access to the source PDF file. However, since the task requires questions to be answerable without additional context, the annotators are instructed to consult the corresponding PDF file only in edge cases (e. g., unclear or unfamiliar terminology). The students are asked to either confirm or edit the synthetic annotations based on the evaluation criteria defined in the guidelines.[9] Note that no inter-annotator agreement is computed, as each data instance is validated by one student. The annotation project lasted for two months, including one week of training during which the annotators familiarised themselves with the guidelines, Label Studio, and completed a trial annotation of 20 images. As a result, 14,013 out of 21,000 (i. e., about 67%) QA pairs generated by Gemini are modified during this phase.

Each data point in the final annotated SciVQA dataset includes the PNG file of a figure and metadata such as QA pair, QA pair type, caption text, instance ID, image filename, figure ID, figure type labels, number of (sub-)figures, source paper ID and URL, venue, field (for arXiv data), and source dataset. The resulting corpus is split into train (70%), validation (10%), and test (20%) sets (see Table 4 in Appendix D) and is publicly available on Hugging Face.[10] The complete list of 32 figure type categories (extended from an initial eleven during manual validation), including statistics on their distribution in SciVQA are provided in Appendix E.

3.3 Evaluation metrics

Since the SciVQA dataset includes both non-binary questions, where the order of correctly predicted options can vary (e. g., A,B,C vs. C,B,A), and those requiring free-form answers, evaluation based on the exact match becomes insufficient. Therefore, we opted to use precision, recall and F1 scores of ROUGE-1, ROUGE-L (Lin, 2004), and BertScore (Zhang* et al., 2020) to capture both lexical and semantic similarity between gold references and predictions. The final ranking of the systems was determined based on the average F1 score across the three metrics. Specifically, for each system, we compute F1 scores of ROUGE-1, ROUGE-L, and BERTScore (across all questions), sum the results, and divide by the total number of metrics (i. e., three).

4 System descriptions

For the SciVQA challenge, we provide both a baseline model and human judgments to evaluate the task's difficulty and establish an upper-bound benchmark. In this section, we first outline our methodology for evaluating human performance on SciVQA. Then we describe our baseline model and the systems from five teams that submitted results to the leaderboard and corresponding reports.

Human judgments. To evaluate human performance on SciVQA, we distribute the test set across five annotators such that each receives 120 images and 840 associated QA pairs. Each student is assigned instances annotated by a different student to ensure they have not seen the questions before and have no prior knowledge of the gold answers. The task is to provide an answer given a figure image, its caption, type, and a question. Students are instructed to produce concise answers, use a template response for unanswerable questions (see §3.2), and indicate *"I don't know"* if they do not understand the question or believe no correct option is present in a multiple-choice scenario (non-binary questions). We use Label Studio configured similarly to the SciVQA human validation project (see Figure 12 in Appendix C).

Baseline. As a baseline, we use the closed-source GPT-4.1-mini model, since GPT-4 variants have demonstrated strong performance on VQA over figures (Mukhopadhyay et al., 2024; Wu et al., 2024; Wang et al., 2024b).[11] The model is run via API in a few-shot setting to enable in-context learning (Brown et al., 2020). We adopt role prompting (Schulhoff et al., 2025) to guide the model toward domain-specific reasoning, and dynamically select examples from the training set that are similar to the given test sample, as this strategy can enhance performance (Liu et al., 2022; Min et al., 2022). We

[9] https://github.com/esborisova/SciVQA/blob/main/data/SciVQA%20annotation%20guidelines.pdf

[10] https://huggingface.co/datasets/katebor/SciVQA

[11] The code for our baseline is available here: https://github.com/esborisova/SciVQA/tree/main/src/baseline

select five examples[12] matching the QA pair type and figure type of the query. If there are not enough samples with the same figure type, we randomly choose examples that share the same question type but differ in figure type. Note that for unanswerable instances, we exclude QA pair type metadata and provide two unanswerable examples along with three randomly selected samples from other question types, as including type information or using only unanswerable examples would reveal the gold answer. We define both the system prompt and the user prompt for the model. The former comprises the task instruction, examples of QA pairs, and metadata such as QA pair type (for answerable questions), figure caption, and its type (see Figure 8 in Appendix B). The user prompt includes the target question, its type (for answerable questions), an image of the target figure and its caption (see Figure 9 in Appendix B). We dynamically adjust answer format instructions based on the question type and post-process predictions to ensure they match the required structure.

ExpertNeurons. The team proposes Retrieval Augmented VQA with a Vision Language Model (RAVQA-VLM) framework (Bhat et al., 2025) which: 1. encodes images of figures and their associated metadata (caption, figure ID, type) into dense embeddings, 2. retrieves relevant context from the source scholarly papers using a dense passage retriever (Karpukhin et al., 2020), 3. and combines visual features, retrieved text, and the question as an input to an MLLM. ExpertNeurons adopts InternVL3-14B (Zhu et al., 2025) as a base model and conducts experiments using four settings. In the first, they use the vanilla version of InternVL3-14B, while in the second they fine-tune it on the SciVQA dataset using Low-Rank Adaptation (LoRa, Hu et al., 2022). The third setting additionally incorporates the RAVQA-VLM pipeline and enhances image sharpness using the Lanczos resampling technique (Turkowski, 1990; Duchon, 1979). The final approach augments the SciVQA training set with 2,500 ChartQA samples for fine-tuning InternVL3-14B.

THAii_LAB. This solution, QwenChart (Ventura et al., 2025), involves instruction fine-tuning of Qwen2.5-VL (Bai et al., 2025) models (7 and 72 billion parameters) on the SciVQA data using LoRa. THAii_LAB employs a dynamic prompting strategy with Chain-of-Thought (CoT, Wei et al., 2022) to convert each instance of SciVQA into conversation-based queries. The prompt includes task instructions, a figure image, its caption, a corresponding question, figure and question type details. Additionally, they evaluate the generalisation ability of QwenChart by testing it on out-of-domain data, namely the ChartQA benchmark.

Coling_UniA. The participants develop a system that leverages two MLLMs, InternVL3-78B and Pixtral-Large-Instruct-2411,[13] selecting the final answer based on model confidence level (Jaumann et al., 2025). The choice of model and prompting strategy is conditioned on the figure and QA pair types. For few-shot, they explore two main methods to retrieve candidate examples from the SciVQA training set: 1. using question similarity based on Sentence-BERT embeddings (Reimers and Gurevych, 2019), and 2. leveraging question and image similarity using embeddings from either CLIP (Radford et al., 2021) or BLIP-2 (Li et al., 2023). To improve MLLM configuration selection, Coling_UniA also merges rare figure types under a common category. For the experiments, they utilise the image of a figure, associated question, figure caption, and figure type labels.

florian. This team conducts a series of experiments with GPT-4o-mini and two variants of Qwen2.5-VL (7 billion and 32 billion parameters) (Schleid et al., 2025). They evaluate the performance of the models in zero- vs. one-shot setting and compare fine-tuning Qwen2.5-VL using the original SciVQA training split vs. its augmented version with additional instances from SpiQA (Pramanick et al., 2024) and ArXivQA (Li et al., 2024a). For all experiments, florian uses images of figures and their captions as an input.

Infyn. The team focuses on prompt engineering exploring the capabilities of InternVL3-8B, Qwen2.5-VL-7B-it, Bespoke-MiniChart-7B,[14] and Phi-4-multimodal (5.6 billion parameters) (Microsoft et al., 2025) models (Movva and Marupaka, 2025). Infyn designs a set of task-specific instructions for the zero-shot setting that incorporate the figure image, caption, figure type, and

[12]Due to API cost constraints, we limit the number of examples. However, including more samples could potentially lead to better results.

[13]`https://huggingface.co/mistralai/Pixtral-Large-Instruct-2411`

[14]`https://huggingface.co/bespokelabs/Bespoke-MiniChart-7B`

System	Rank	ROUGE-1			ROUGE-L			BertScore			Avg. F1
		F1	Precision	Recall	F1	Precision	Recall	F1	Precision	Recall	
Human	–	**0.8291**	**0.8347**	**0.8337**	**0.8285**	**0.8342**	**0.8330**	**0.9826**	**0.9822**	**0.9832**	**0.8801**
Baseline	–	0.7062	0.7139	0.7093	0.7055	0.7131	0.7086	0.9756	0.9762	0.9753	0.7957
ExpertNeurons	1	**0.8049**	**0.8086**	**0.8109**	**0.8043**	**0.8080**	**0.8103**	**0.9849**	**0.9850**	**0.9849**	**0.8647**
THAii_LAB	2	0.7899	0.7960	0.7949	0.7892	0.7953	0.7942	0.9839	0.9841	0.9840	0.8543
Coling_UniA	3	0.7862	0.7970	0.7860	0.7856	0.7964	0.7854	0.9817	0.9826	0.9812	0.8512
florian	4	0.7631	0.7658	0.7698	0.7621	0.7648	0.7689	0.9831	0.9830	0.9835	0.8361
Infyn	5	0.7350	0.7438	0.7437	0.7345	0.7434	0.7432	0.9787	0.9784	0.9795	0.8161
Soham Chitnis	6	0.7057	0.7190	0.7048	0.7052	0.7186	0.7043	0.9801	0.9820	0.9786	0.7970
psr123	7	0.6068	0.6089	0.6170	0.6056	0.6078	0.6156	0.9587	0.9590	0.9588	0.7237

Table 1: Evaluation results of the systems submitted to the SciVQA shared task, including human performance and baseline model. The highest scores are highlighted with grey shading and bold font. "Avg." denotes average F1 score across ROUGE-1, ROUGE-L, and BertScore.

QA pair type, which are then combined into a single baseline prompt. They further extend this prompt by including CoT and self-reflection reasoning (Wang et al., 2025). They evaluate individual models as well as an ensemble approach, in which either Qwen2.5-VL-7B-it, Bespoke-MiniChart-7B, or Phi-4-multimodal is selected depending on the given figure type.

5 Results

Human vs. automated systems. The final results for the SciVQA challenge are presented in Table 1. The human judgments outperform automatic systems, with a maximum gap of 23%. Overall, the accuracy across individual annotators is similar: the largest difference is up to 6% in recall values and up to 3% in average F1 score across ROUGE-1, ROUGE-L, and BertScore (see Table 5 in Appendix F). This could be partially attributed to the students' prior familiarity with the task and QA pair types. The questions could also be relatively simple for humans due to their closed-ended nature and the annotators' expertise in CL. Among all the predictions, 27 questions are answered with "I don't know", commonly due to unclear, ambiguous or incorrectly phrased questions. For instance, some questions fail to specify which subplot should be considered when an attribute is present in multiple subplots or they refer to a wrong attribute (e. g., colour, axis, value) in the graph.

Across all automatic solutions, five out of seven teams exceed our baseline. The highest scores are achieved by ExpertNeurons, using the fine-tuned InternVL3-14B model coupled with RAVQA-VLM and data augmentation. Their system surpasses our baseline by up to about 11%, while trailing behind human performance by approximately 2-3%. These findings suggest that including relevant context, along with cross-domain data, can enhance an MLLM's reasoning and generalisation abilities. QwenChart (with 7 billion parameters), proposed by THAii_LAB, ranks next. However, the team reports that their system does not generalise well to out-of-domain data, resulting in a performance drop on ChartQA. They also observe that model robustness varies depending on the question and figure type. In particular, QwenChart performs worst on infinite visual QA pairs and on figures categorised as other or containing multiple subplots with mixed types. Our baseline follows a similar trend, with visual questions, especially without predefined answer options, being more challenging for GPT-4.1-mini than non-visual ones (see Table 6 in Appendix G). THAii_LAB is closely followed by Coling_UniA, whose approach combines two MLLMs and confidence-based answer selection. The difference in scores is less than 1%. These results are interesting given that the two systems rely on different base MLLMs, prompting strategies, and learning approaches. Such a small gap highlights that while fine-tuning is effective, competitive performance can be achieved through carefully designed prompts. Similar to THAii_LAB, Coling_UniA notes that their model performs worse on infinite visual QA pair types.

Ranking fourth, florian falls behind the top three teams by about 2–5%. Their final system is based on Qwen2.5-VL (with 32 billion parameters) fine-tuned on the original SciVQA data. In line with prior observations, florian highlights that infinite visual QA pairs pose a challenge for the model. However, unlike ExpertNeurons, they find that augmenting SciVQA leads to reduced performance, although additional instances are sourced from schol-

Error type	Description
Visual attribute reasoning	Fails to correctly recognise visual attributes (e. g., colour, shape), comparing magnitudes or positions of those properties (e. g., "higher than", "below").
Text recognition and extraction	Fails to correctly extract labels, values, phrases, etc. This includes both cases with completely incorrect extraction and those failing to reproduce text labels, names, short phrases, exactly as they appear in the figure image or caption.
Numerical value formatting	Fails to output the correct precision (too few or too many decimal places), inconsistent/incorrect in handling of units (adding or omitting units) or representing ranges/approximate values.
Incomplete/partially correct list of items	Fails to output a complete list of expected items where all are correctly identified, e. g., for non-binary questions.
Arithmetic reasoning	Fails to correctly compute the value. This includes errors in addition, subtraction, multiplication, division, percentages, ratios or any arithmetic operation necessary for the correct response.
Other	Issues not covered by any of the five categories listed above.

Table 2: The list of error types and their definitions.

arly papers, matching the target domain. Such disparity may stem from imbalances in QA types as well as differences in format of QA pairs between SpiQA, ArXivQA and SciVQA. In this regard, figures and questions from ChartQA (used by ExpertNeurons) may be better aligned with the SciVQA dataset, especially since both include visual questions category. Infyn secures the fifth place, achieving an average F1 score of approximately 0.82 by using a model ensemble approach combined with custom prompts. Finally, Soham Chitnis and psr123 close the ranking falling behind other teams by up to about 11% and 20%, respectively. Notably, Soham Chitnis achieves scores comparable to our baseline, with a maximum difference of less than 1%. In contrast, the solution by psr123 does not surpass the SciVQA baseline, falling short by approximately 7% in average F1 score.

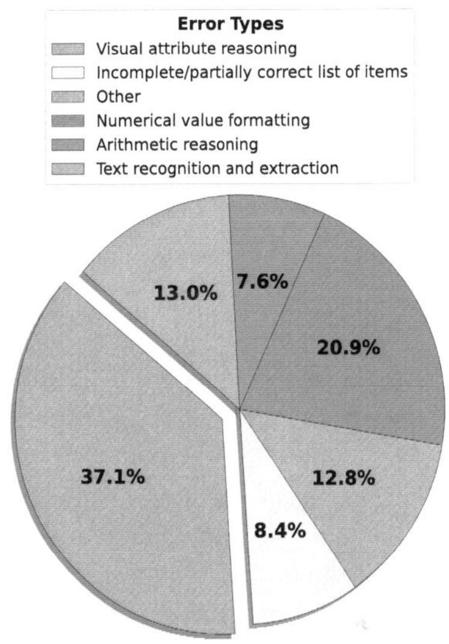

Figure 3: Distribution of error types in the predictions of the SciVQA baseline model.

Error analysis To gain insights into the common issues affecting performance, we conduct an error analysis based on the predictions from the SciVQA baseline. We identify 1,564 incorrectly answered questions based on an exact match between gold and predictions. Among those, 202 correspond to the unanswerable QA pair type, where the model simply produced an answer. To analyse the rest 1,362 cases, we generate an initial summary of errors with Gemini-2.5-Pro (see prompt in Figure 10 in Appendix B). Then we manually group those errors into the six categories listed in Table 2 and assign Google spreadsheets with 270-273 incorrectly predicted instances to five students for annotation. Additionally, we also include a "No errors" category to account for cases where the prediction is correct (e. g., gold is incorrect or incomplete).

Figure 3 shows the resulting distribution of error types, excluding the "No errors" cases. The examples of instances per error type are provided in Appendix H. The most common failures (37.1%) are associated with visual attribute reasoning. This finding, together with observations from the shared task participants, suggests that current MLLMs still struggle with interpreting visual information. Previous studies (Mukhopadhyay et al., 2024) also report challenges in MLLMs' visual reasoning such as errors associated with colour encoding, especially when it comes to similar shades. The second largest group of errors (20.9%) is related to numerical value formatting. The most frequent mismatches involve the absence of approximations or ranges and slight numerical discrepancies. This indicates that GPT-4.1-mini may not have fully learned the expected answer formatting from the given examples. Text recognition and extraction along with the other errors account for 13% and 12.8%, respectively. The former often includes failures in reproducing the required formatting of text (e. g., see Figure 19). For the "Other" category, we observe that annotators specify cases where either the gold answer is incorrect or both the gold answer and the prediction are valid. Similarly, several such cases appear under the "No errors" label. In total, 111 out of 4200 gold instances are flagged as being incorrect. Given the large scale of the dataset and the error-prone nature of manual annotation (Klie et al., 2024), one round of human validation of synthetic QA pairs may have been insufficient, resulting in some noise. Although the percentage of annotation errors is rather small (approximately 2.6%), they likely affected the final evaluation scores. Notably, the "Incomplete/partially correct list of items" category constitutes only 8% of all errors, followed by arithmetic reasoning failures (7.6%).

6 Conclusion

In this paper, we presented an overview of the first SciVQA shared task. The challenge attracted seven submissions, five of which outperformed our baseline. The results reveal that, while automated systems can achieve strong performance on the newly proposed SciVQA benchmark, they remain behind human judgments. Furthermore, the findings indicate that fine-tuning on cross-domain data, combined with relevant contextual information from source papers, leads to the best results. However, domain adaptation and data augmentation is not always required, and carefully designed prompting strategies can achieve very close results (about 2% gap). Additionally, we observe that current MLLMs struggle most with visual reasoning, as their accuracy drops on QA pairs addressing visual attributes of figures.

Limitations

Although this study sheds light on the abilities of current MLLMs to reason over scientific figures, it is not without limitations. First, the evaluation relies on automated metrics, ROUGE and BertScore, which may fall short when handling free-form answers. BertScore is also less suitable for non-binary questions, since answer options are short, leading to high similarity scores being assigned to distinct choices (e. g., A vs. B). Additional manual review could be beneficial for the analysis of prediction quality. Second, SciVQA provides a single gold reference, whereas multiple valid answers may exist. Extending the dataset to include several references could improve the fairness of the evaluation process. Third, the SciVQA test set contains a few annotation errors which can influence scoring. As a next step, we plan another manual revision to correct these errors and improve data quality. Finally, this study focuses solely on closed-ended QA in English, and we leave the extension of SciVQA to open-ended multilingual QA for future work.

Acknowledgments

The work received funding through the German Research Foundation (DFG) project NFDI for Data Science and Artificial Intelligence, NFDI4DS [15] (no. 460234259). We would like to thank Valentina Tretti, Radovan Milovic, Ardalan Khazraei, David Raul Carranza Navarrete, Shane John Paul Newton, Melina Plakidis, Emma Carballal, and Maria Francis for annotating the SciVQA data, error types, and conducting human evaluation. We also thank Raia Abu Ahmad for the fruitful discussions related to the dataset construction and competition set up.

Ethics statement

SciVQA does not contain any sensitive or personal data. The images of the figures used to construct the SciVQA benchmark are sourced from the publicly available datasets. We comply with their respective licenses and usage terms. The annotators were compensated according to a standard payment scheme and were informed about the intended use of their annotations.

References

Saleem Ahmed, Bhavin Jawade, Shubham Pandey, Srirangaraj Setlur, and Venu Govindaraju. 2023. Realcqa: Scientific chart question answering as a testbed for first-order logic. In *Document Analysis and Recognition - ICDAR 2023*, pages 66–83, Cham. Springer Nature Switzerland.

Shuai Bai, Keqin Chen, Xuejing Liu, Jialin Wang, Wenbin Ge, Sibo Song, Kai Dang, Peng Wang, Shijie Wang, Jun Tang, Humen Zhong, Yuanzhi Zhu, Mingkun Yang, Zhaohai Li, Jianqiang Wan, Pengfei Wang, Wei Ding, Zheren Fu, Yiheng Xu, and 8 others. 2025. Qwen2.5-vl technical report. *Preprint*, arXiv:2502.13923.

[15] 19https://www.nfdi4datascience.de

Nagaraj Bhat, Joydeb Mondal, and Srijon Sarkar. 2025. ExpertNeurons at SciVQA-2025: Retrieval augmented VQA with vision language model (RAVQA-VLM). In *Proceedings of the 5th Workshop on Scholarly Document Processing (SDP)*, Vienna, Austria. Association for Computational Linguistics.

Tom Brown, Benjamin Mann, Nick Ryder, Melanie Subbiah, Jared D Kaplan, Prafulla Dhariwal, Arvind Neelakantan, Pranav Shyam, Girish Sastry, Amanda Askell, Sandhini Agarwal, Ariel Herbert-Voss, Gretchen Krueger, Tom Henighan, Rewon Child, Aditya Ramesh, Daniel Ziegler, Jeffrey Wu, Clemens Winter, and 12 others. 2020. Language models are few-shot learners. In *Advances in Neural Information Processing Systems*, volume 33, pages 1877–1901. Curran Associates, Inc.

Ritwick Chaudhry, Sumit Shekhar, Utkarsh Gupta, Pranav Maneriker, Prann Bansal, and Ajay Joshi. 2019. LEAF-QA: Locate, encode & attend for figure question answering. *Preprint*, arXiv:1907.12861.

Christopher Clark and Santosh Divvala. 2016. Pdffigures 2.0: Mining figures from research papers. In *2016 IEEE/ACM Joint Conference on Digital Libraries (JCDL)*, pages 143–152.

Claude Duchon. 1979. Lanczos filtering in one and two dimensions. *Journal of Applied Meteorology - J APPL METEOROL*, 18:1016–1022.

Yucheng Han, Chi Zhang, Xin Chen, Xu Yang, Zhibin Wang, Gang Yu, Bin Fu, and Hanwang Zhang. 2023. ChartLlama: A multimodal LLM for chart understanding and generation. *Preprint*, arXiv:2311.16483.

Edward J Hu, Yelong Shen, Phillip Wallis, Zeyuan Allen-Zhu, Yuanzhi Li, Shean Wang, Lu Wang, and Weizhu Chen. 2022. LoRA: Low-rank adaptation of large language models. In *International Conference on Learning Representations*.

Kung-Hsiang Huang, Hou Pong Chan, Yi R. Fung, Haoyi Qiu, Mingyang Zhou, Shafiq Joty, Shih-Fu Chang, and Heng Ji. 2024. From pixels to insights: A survey on automatic chart understanding in the era of large foundation models. *Preprint*, arXiv:2403.12027.

Mohammed Saidul Islam, Raian Rahman, Ahmed Masry, Md Tahmid Rahman Laskar, Mir Tafseer Nayeem, and Enamul Hoque. 2024. Are large vision language models up to the challenge of chart comprehension and reasoning. In *Findings of the Association for Computational Linguistics: EMNLP 2024*, pages 3334–3368, Miami, Florida, USA. Association for Computational Linguistics.

Christian Jaumann, Annemarie Friedrich, and Rainer Lienhart. 2025. Coling-UniA at SciVQA 2025: Few-shot example retrieval and confidence-informed ensembling for multimodal large language models. In *Proceedings of the 5th Workshop on Scholarly Document Processing (SDP)*, Vienna, Austria. Association for Computational Linguistics.

Kushal Kafle, Brian Price, Scott Cohen, and Christopher Kanan. 2018. DVQA: Understanding data visualizations via question answering. In *2018 IEEE/CVF Conference on Computer Vision and Pattern Recognition*, pages 5648–5656.

Samira Ebrahimi Kahou, Vincent Michalski, Adam Atkinson, Akos Kadar, Adam Trischler, and Yoshua Bengio. 2018. FigureQA: An annotated figure dataset for visual reasoning. *Preprint*, arXiv:1710.07300.

Shankar Kantharaj, Xuan Long Do, Rixie Tiffany Leong, Jia Qing Tan, Enamul Hoque, and Shafiq Joty. 2022. OpenCQA: Open-ended question answering with charts. In *Proceedings of the 2022 Conference on Empirical Methods in Natural Language Processing*, pages 11817–11837, Abu Dhabi, United Arab Emirates. Association for Computational Linguistics.

Zeba Karishma, Shaurya Rohatgi, Kavya Shrinivas Puranik, Jian Wu, and C. Lee Giles. 2023. ACL-Fig: A dataset for scientific figure classification. *Preprint*, arXiv:2301.12293.

Vladimir Karpukhin, Barlas Oguz, Sewon Min, Patrick Lewis, Ledell Wu, Sergey Edunov, Danqi Chen, and Wen-tau Yih. 2020. Dense passage retrieval for open-domain question answering. In *Proceedings of the 2020 Conference on Empirical Methods in Natural Language Processing (EMNLP)*, pages 6769–6781, Online. Association for Computational Linguistics.

Dae Hyun Kim, Enamul Hoque, and Maneesh Agrawala. 2020. Answering questions about charts and generating visual explanations. In *Proceedings of the 2020 CHI Conference on Human Factors in Computing Systems*, CHI '20, page 1–13, New York, NY, USA. Association for Computing Machinery.

Wonjoong Kim, Sangwu Park, Yeonjun In, Seokwon Han, and Chanyoung Park. 2024. SIMPLOT: Enhancing chart question answering by distilling essentials. *Preprint*, arXiv:2405.00021.

Jan-Christoph Klie, Richard Eckart de Castilho, and Iryna Gurevych. 2024. Analyzing dataset annotation quality management in the wild. *Computational Linguistics*, 50(3):817–866.

Junnan Li, Dongxu Li, Silvio Savarese, and Steven Hoi. 2023. BLIP-2: bootstrapping language-image pre-training with frozen image encoders and large language models. In *Proceedings of the 40th International Conference on Machine Learning*, ICML'23. JMLR.org.

Lei Li, Yuqi Wang, Runxin Xu, Peiyi Wang, Xiachong Feng, Lingpeng Kong, and Qi Liu. 2024a. Multimodal ArXiv: A dataset for improving scientific comprehension of large vision-language models. In *Proceedings of the 62nd Annual Meeting of the Association for Computational Linguistics (Volume 1: Long Papers)*, pages 14369–14387, Bangkok, Thailand. Association for Computational Linguistics.

Shengzhi Li and Nima Tajbakhsh. 2023. SciGraphQA: A large-scale synthetic multi-turn question-answering dataset for scientific graphs. *Preprint*, arXiv:2308.03349.

Zhuowan Li, Bhavan Jasani, Peng Tang, and Shabnam Ghadar. 2024b. Synthesize step-by-step: Tools, templates and LLMs as data generators for reasoning-based chart VQA. In *2024 IEEE/CVF Conference on Computer Vision and Pattern Recognition (CVPR)*, pages 13613–13623, Los Alamitos, CA, USA. IEEE Computer Society.

Chin-Yew Lin. 2004. ROUGE: A package for automatic evaluation of summaries. In *Text Summarization Branches Out*, pages 74–81, Barcelona, Spain. Association for Computational Linguistics.

Fangyu Liu, Julian Eisenschlos, Francesco Piccinno, Syrine Krichene, Chenxi Pang, Kenton Lee, Mandar Joshi, Wenhu Chen, Nigel Collier, and Yasemin Altun. 2023a. DePlot: One-shot visual language reasoning by plot-to-table translation. In *Findings of the Association for Computational Linguistics: ACL 2023*, pages 10381–10399, Toronto, Canada. Association for Computational Linguistics.

Fangyu Liu, Francesco Piccinno, Syrine Krichene, Chenxi Pang, Kenton Lee, Mandar Joshi, Yasemin Altun, Nigel Collier, and Julian Eisenschlos. 2023b. MatCha: Enhancing visual language pretraining with math reasoning and chart derendering. In *Proceedings of the 61st Annual Meeting of the Association for Computational Linguistics (Volume 1: Long Papers)*, pages 12756–12770, Toronto, Canada. Association for Computational Linguistics.

Fuxiao Liu, Xiaoyang Wang, Wenlin Yao, Jianshu Chen, Kaiqiang Song, Sangwoo Cho, Yaser Yacoob, and Dong Yu. 2024. MMC: Advancing multimodal chart understanding with large-scale instruction tuning. In *Proceedings of the 2024 Conference of the North American Chapter of the Association for Computational Linguistics: Human Language Technologies (Volume 1: Long Papers)*, pages 1287–1310, Mexico City, Mexico. Association for Computational Linguistics.

Jiachang Liu, Dinghan Shen, Yizhe Zhang, Bill Dolan, Lawrence Carin, and Weizhu Chen. 2022. What makes good in-context examples for GPT-3? In *Proceedings of Deep Learning Inside Out (DeeLIO 2022): The 3rd Workshop on Knowledge Extraction and Integration for Deep Learning Architectures*, pages 100–114, Dublin, Ireland and Online. Association for Computational Linguistics.

Ahmed Masry, Xuan Long Do, Jia Qing Tan, Shafiq Joty, and Enamul Hoque. 2022. ChartQA: A benchmark for question answering about charts with visual and logical reasoning. In *Findings of the Association for Computational Linguistics: ACL 2022*, pages 2263–2279, Dublin, Ireland. Association for Computational Linguistics.

Ahmed Masry, Mohammed Saidul Islam, Mahir Ahmed, Aayush Bajaj, Firoz Kabir, Aaryaman Kartha, Md Tahmid Rahman Laskar, Mizanur Rahman, Shadikur Rahman, Mehrad Shahmohammadi, Megh Thakkar, Md Rizwan Parvez, Enamul Hoque, and Shafiq Joty. 2025a. ChartQAPro: A more diverse and challenging benchmark for chart question answering. *Preprint*, arXiv:2504.05506.

Ahmed Masry, Parsa Kavehzadeh, Xuan Long Do, Enamul Hoque, and Shafiq Joty. 2023. UniChart: A universal vision-language pretrained model for chart comprehension and reasoning. In *Proceedings of the 2023 Conference on Empirical Methods in Natural Language Processing*, pages 14662–14684, Singapore. Association for Computational Linguistics.

Ahmed Masry, Megh Thakkar, Aayush Bajaj, Aaryaman Kartha, Enamul Hoque, and Shafiq Joty. 2025b. ChartGemma: Visual instruction-tuning for chart reasoning in the wild. In *Proceedings of the 31st International Conference on Computational Linguistics: Industry Track*, pages 625–643, Abu Dhabi, UAE. Association for Computational Linguistics.

Fanqing Meng, Wenqi Shao, Quanfeng Lu, Peng Gao, Kaipeng Zhang, Yu Qiao, and Ping Luo. 2024. ChartAssistant: A universal chart multimodal language model via chart-to-table pre-training and multitask instruction tuning. In *Findings of the Association for Computational Linguistics: ACL 2024*, pages 7775–7803, Bangkok, Thailand. Association for Computational Linguistics.

Nitesh Methani, Pritha Ganguly, Mitesh M. Khapra, and Pratyush Kumar. 2020. PlotQA: Reasoning over scientific plots. *Preprint*, arXiv:1909.00997.

Microsoft, :, Abdelrahman Abouelenin, Atabak Ashfaq, Adam Atkinson, Hany Awadalla, Nguyen Bach, Jianmin Bao, Alon Benhaim, Martin Cai, Vishrav Chaudhary, Congcong Chen, Dong Chen, Dongdong Chen, Junkun Chen, Weizhu Chen, Yen-Chun Chen, Yi ling Chen, Qi Dai, and 57 others. 2025. Phi-4-mini technical report: Compact yet powerful multimodal language models via mixture-of-loras. *Preprint*, arXiv:2503.01743.

Sewon Min, Xinxi Lyu, Ari Holtzman, Mikel Artetxe, Mike Lewis, Hannaneh Hajishirzi, and Luke Zettlemoyer. 2022. Rethinking the role of demonstrations: What makes in-context learning work? In *Proceedings of the 2022 Conference on Empirical Methods in Natural Language Processing*, pages 11048–11064, Abu Dhabi, United Arab Emirates. Association for Computational Linguistics.

Prahitha Movva and Naga Harshita Marupaka. 2025. Enhancing scientific visual question answering through multimodal reasoning and ensemble modeling. In *Proceedings of the 5th Workshop on Scholarly Document Processing (SDP)*, Vienna, Austria. Association for Computational Linguistics.

Srija Mukhopadhyay, Adnan Qidwai, Aparna Garimella, Pritika Ramu, Vivek Gupta, and Dan Roth. 2024.

Unraveling the truth: Do VLMs really understand charts? a deep dive into consistency and robustness. In *Findings of the Association for Computational Linguistics: EMNLP 2024*, pages 16696–16717, Miami, Florida, USA. Association for Computational Linguistics.

OpenAI, Josh Achiam, Steven Adler, Sandhini Agarwal, Lama Ahmad, Ilge Akkaya, Florencia Leoni Aleman, Diogo Almeida, Janko Altenschmidt, Sam Altman, Shyamal Anadkat, Red Avila, Igor Babuschkin, Suchir Balaji, Valerie Balcom, Paul Baltescu, Haiming Bao, Mohammad Bavarian, Jeff Belgum, and 262 others. 2024. GPT-4 technical report. *Preprint*, arXiv:2303.08774.

Shraman Pramanick, Rama Chellappa, and Subhashini Venugopalan. 2024. SPIQA: A dataset for multimodal question answering on scientific papers. In *Advances in Neural Information Processing Systems*, volume 37, pages 118807–118833. Curran Associates, Inc.

Alec Radford, Jong Wook Kim, Chris Hallacy, Aditya Ramesh, Gabriel Goh, Sandhini Agarwal, Girish Sastry, Amanda Askell, Pamela Mishkin, Jack Clark, Gretchen Krueger, and Ilya Sutskever. 2021. Learning transferable visual models from natural language supervision. In *International Conference on Machine Learning*.

Nils Reimers and Iryna Gurevych. 2019. Sentence-BERT: Sentence embeddings using Siamese BERT-networks. In *Proceedings of the 2019 Conference on Empirical Methods in Natural Language Processing and the 9th International Joint Conference on Natural Language Processing (EMNLP-IJCNLP)*, pages 3982–3992, Hong Kong, China. Association for Computational Linguistics.

Jonathan Roberts, Kai Han, Neil Houlsby, and Samuel Albanie. 2024. SciFIBench: Benchmarking large multimodal models for scientific figure interpretation. In *Advances in Neural Information Processing Systems*, volume 37, pages 18695–18728. Curran Associates, Inc.

Florian Schleid, Jan Strich, and Chris Biemann. 2025. Visual question answering on scientific charts using fine-tuned vision-language models. In *Proceedings of the 5th Workshop on Scholarly Document Processing (SDP)*, Vienna, Austria. Association for Computational Linguistics.

Sander Schulhoff, Michael Ilie, Nishant Balepur, Konstantine Kahadze, Amanda Liu, Chenglei Si, Yinheng Li, Aayush Gupta, HyoJung Han, Sevien Schulhoff, Pranav Sandeep Dulepet, Saurav Vidyadhara, Dayeon Ki, Sweta Agrawal, Chau Pham, Gerson Kroiz, Feileen Li, Hudson Tao, Ashay Srivastava, and 12 others. 2025. The prompt report: A systematic survey of prompt engineering techniques. *Preprint*, arXiv:2406.06608.

Gemini Team, Rohan Anil, and Sebastian Borgeaud et. al. 2024. Gemini: A family of highly capable multimodal models. *Preprint*, arXiv:2312.11805.

Ken Turkowski. 1990. *Filters for common resampling tasks*, page 147–165. Academic Press Professional, Inc., USA.

Viviana Ventura, Lukas Kleybolte, and Alessandra Zarcone. 2025. Instruction-tuned QwenChart for chart question answering. In *Proceedings of the 5th Workshop on Scholarly Document Processing (SDP)*, Vienna, Austria. Association for Computational Linguistics.

Bin Wang, Chao Xu, Xiaomeng Zhao, Linke Ouyang, Fan Wu, Zhiyuan Zhao, Rui Xu, Kaiwen Liu, Yuan Qu, Fukai Shang, Bo Zhang, Liqun Wei, Zhihao Sui, Wei Li, Botian Shi, Yu Qiao, Dahua Lin, and Conghui He. 2024a. MinerU: An open-source solution for precise document content extraction. *Preprint*, arXiv:2409.18839.

Haozhe Wang, Chao Qu, Zuming Huang, Wei Chu, Fangzhen Lin, and Wenhu Chen. 2025. Vl-rethinker: Incentivizing self-reflection of vision-language models with reinforcement learning. *Preprint*, arXiv:2504.08837.

Zirui Wang, Mengzhou Xia, Luxi He, Howard Chen, Yitao Liu, Richard Zhu, Kaiqu Liang, Xindi Wu, Haotian Liu, Sadhika Malladi, Alexis Chevalier, Sanjeev Arora, and Danqi Chen. 2024b. Charxiv: Charting gaps in realistic chart understanding in multimodal LLMs. In *Advances in Neural Information Processing Systems*, volume 37, pages 113569–113697. Curran Associates, Inc.

Jason Wei, Xuezhi Wang, Dale Schuurmans, Maarten Bosma, Brian Ichter, Fei Xia, Ed H. Chi, Quoc V. Le, and Denny Zhou. 2022. Chain-of-thought prompting elicits reasoning in large language models. In *Proceedings of the 36th International Conference on Neural Information Processing Systems*, NIPS '22, Red Hook, NY, USA. Curran Associates Inc.

Jingxuan Wei, Nan Xu, Guiyong Chang, Yin Luo, BiHui Yu, and Ruifeng Guo. 2024. mChartQA: A universal benchmark for multimodal chart question answer based on vision-language alignment and reasoning. *Preprint*, arXiv:2404.01548.

Qi Wu, Damien Teney, Peng Wang, Chunhua Shen, Anthony Dick, and Anton van den Hengel. 2017. Visual question answering: A survey of methods and datasets. *Computer Vision and Image Understanding*, 163:21–40. Language in Vision.

Yifan Wu, Lutao Yan, Leixian Shen, Yunhai Wang, Nan Tang, and Yuyu Luo. 2024. ChartInsights: Evaluating multimodal large language models for low-level chart question answering. In *Findings of the Association for Computational Linguistics: EMNLP 2024*, pages 12174–12200, Miami, Florida, USA. Association for Computational Linguistics.

Zhen Xu, Sergio Escalera, Adrien Pavão, Magali Richard, Wei-Wei Tu, Quanming Yao, Huan Zhao, and Isabelle Guyon. 2022. Codabench: Flexible, easy-to-use, and reproducible meta-benchmark platform. *Patterns*, 3(7):100543.

Xingchen Zeng, Haichuan Lin, Yilin Ye, and Wei Zeng. 2024. Advancing multimodal large language models in chart question answering with visualization-referenced instruction tuning. *Preprint*, arXiv:2407.20174.

Liang Zhang, Anwen Hu, Haiyang Xu, Ming Yan, Yichen Xu, Qin Jin, Ji Zhang, and Fei Huang. 2024. TinyChart: Efficient chart understanding with program-of-thoughts learning and visual token merging. In *Proceedings of the 2024 Conference on Empirical Methods in Natural Language Processing*, pages 1882–1898, Miami, Florida, USA. Association for Computational Linguistics.

Tianyi Zhang*, Varsha Kishore*, Felix Wu*, Kilian Q. Weinberger, and Yoav Artzi. 2020. BERTScore: Evaluating text generation with BERT. In *International Conference on Learning Representations*.

Mingyang Zhou, Yi Fung, Long Chen, Christopher Thomas, Heng Ji, and Shih-Fu Chang. 2023. Enhanced chart understanding via visual language pre-training on plot table pairs. In *Findings of the Association for Computational Linguistics: ACL 2023*, pages 1314–1326, Toronto, Canada. Association for Computational Linguistics.

Jinguo Zhu, Weiyun Wang, Zhe Chen, Zhaoyang Liu, Shenglong Ye, Lixin Gu, Hao Tian, Yuchen Duan, Weijie Su, Jie Shao, Zhangwei Gao, Erfei Cui, Xuehui Wang, Yue Cao, Yangzhou Liu, Xingguang Wei, Hongjie Zhang, Haomin Wang, Weiye Xu, and 32 others. 2025. InternVL3: Exploring advanced training and test-time recipes for open-source multimodal models. *Preprint*, arXiv:2504.10479.

A Question answering pair types

Question answering pair type	Definition
Closed-ended	It is possible to answer a question based only on a given data source, i. e., a figure image and/or its caption. No additional resources such as the main text of a publication, other documents, figures or tables are required.
Unanswerable	It is not possible to infer an answer based solely on a given data source.
Infinite answer set	There are no predefined answer options.
Finite answer set	There is a limited range of answer options.
Binary	Requires a yes/no or true/false answer.
Non-binary	Requires to choose from a set of (four) predefined answer options where one or more are correct.
Visual	Addresses or incorporates information on one or more of the six visual attributes of a figure, i. e., shape, size, position, height, direction or colour.
Non-visual	Does not involve any of the six pre-defined visual aspects of a figure.

Table 3: The list of question answering pair types and their definitions.

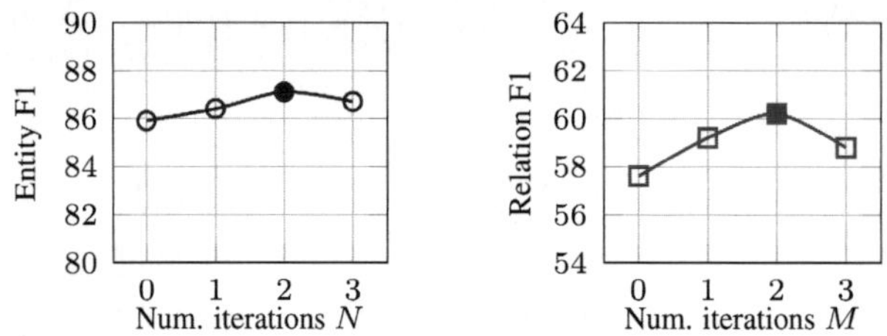

(a) Entity F1 with different number of CorefProp iterations N.

(b) Relation F1 with different number of RelProp iterations M.

Figure Caption: Figure 3: F1 score of each layer on ACE development set for different number of iterations. N = 0 or M = 0 indicates no propagation is made for the layer.

Question Type: Closed-ended infinite answer set visual
Question: What is the F1 score of the red line at M = 2?
Answer: 60

Question Type: Closed-ended infinite answer set non-visual
Question: What is the F1 score for the entity layer when there are no iterations?
Answer: 86

Question Type: Closed-ended finite answer set binary visual
Question: Is the highest F1 score for Entity in the left plot achieved at N=2?
Answer: Yes

Question Type: Closed-ended finite answer set binary non-visual
Question: Does the number of iterations impact the F1 score for both Entity and Relation?
Answer: Yes

Question Type: Closed-ended finite answer set non-binary visual
Question: Which graph shows the F1 score for RelProp iterations?
Answer options: A: The graph on the left B: The graph on the right C: Both graphs D: Neither graph
Answer: B

Question Type: Closed-ended finite answer set non-binary non-visual
Question: Which kind of F1 is above 75% for all iterations?
Answer options: A: Entity B: Relation C: Both D: Neither
Answer: A

Question Type: Unanswerable
Question: What is the F1 score of the entity layer after 2 iterations of propagation with N = 1 and M = 2?
Answer: It is not possible to answer this question based only on the provided data.

Figure 4: Example of a figure and seven question answering pair types associated with it. The sample is taken from the SciVQA training set.

B Prompts

Task: Generate a closed-ended visual question and an answer to it based on a given image of a scientific figure and caption.

Caption: Figure 4: Accuracy breakdown w.r.t. constituent height in unbiased trees derived from the syntactic task distances in our model (top) and the language modeling distances (bottom). A constituent is considered as correct if its boundaries correspond to a true constituent. The constituents heights are those in the predicted tree. Since constituents that represent the whole sentence always have correct boundaries, they are excluded from the calculation.

Constraints:
1. The question must be answerable solely based on the content of the image and provided caption.
2. The answer should be concise, requiring no external knowledge.
3. The question must incorporate information on visual attributes present in a scientific figure such as shape, size, position, color, direction, and height.
4. The answer must be short.

Output Format: JSON, with a single object containing the generated question and answer.

Examples: [{"question": "What is the maximum value of the green dashed line?","answer": "360"}] [{"question": "What is the value of the orange bar at the threshold y?","answer": "70"}]

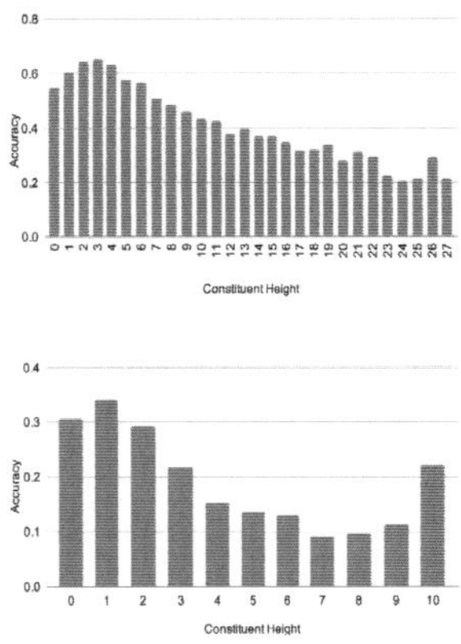


```json
[{"question": "What is the approximate accuracy of the blue bar at constituent height 2 in the bottom graph?", "answer": "0.3"}]
```

Figure 5: Example of a prompt for generating a closed-ended visual question with infinite answer set using Gemini-1.5-Flash.

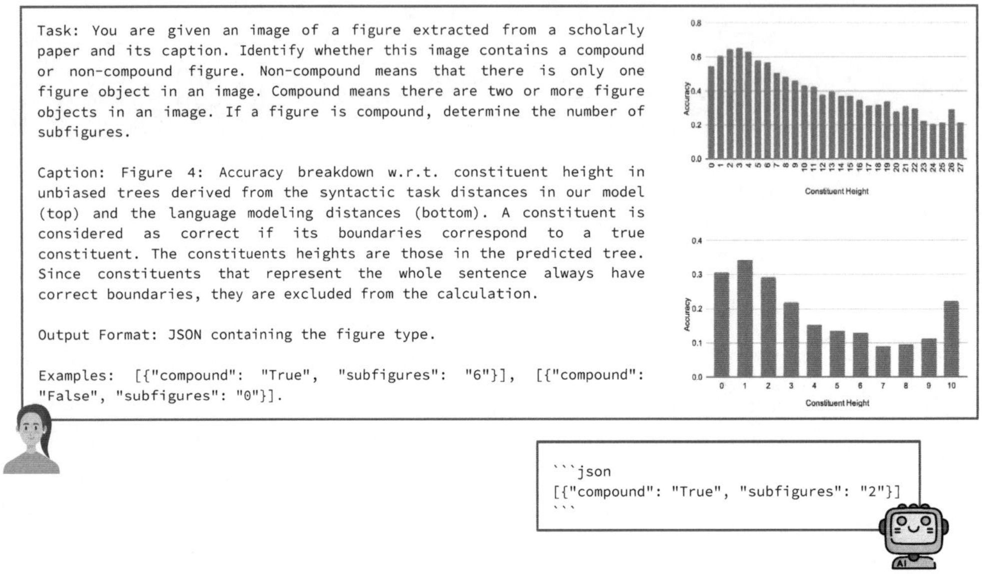

Figure 6: Example of a prompt for classifying figures into compound and non-compound using Gemini-1.5-Flash.

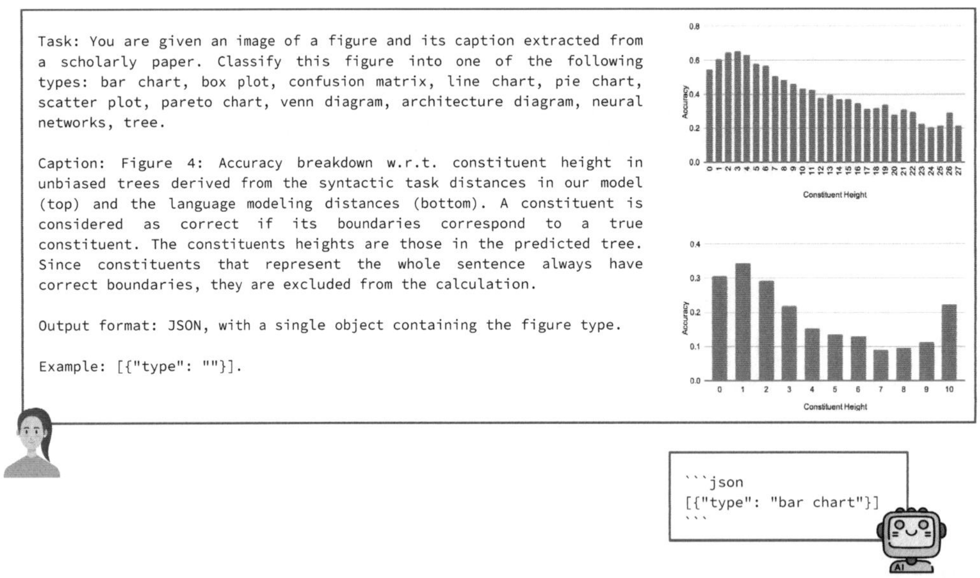

Figure 7: Example of a prompt for classifying figures into types using Gemini-1.5-Flash.

```
You are an expert scientific figure analyst specializing in academic publications.
Your task is to answer questions about scientific figures and their captions accurately and concisely.
Answer the given question based *solely* on the information visible in the figure and its provided caption.

The user message will include a 'Question Type'. Adhere strictly to the following rules for formatting your response
based on the question type:

- For 'closed-ended finite answer set binary visual' or 'closed-ended finite answer set binary non-visual':
- Respond ONLY with 'Yes' or 'No'.
- Do NOT add any other text, explanations, or punctuation.
- Your entire response must be exactly one word: either 'Yes' or 'No'.

- For 'closed-ended finite answer set non-binary visual' or 'closed-ended finite answer set non-binary non-visual':
- Identify the correct option(s) from the provided 'Answer Options'.
- Respond ONLY with the letter(s) of the correct option(s) as listed.
- For a single correct option, provide only its letter (e.g., 'B').
- For multiple correct options, list ALL correct letters separated by commas with NO SPACES (e.g., 'A,C,D').
- Ensure ALL correct options are listed and NO incorrect ones.
- Do NOT add any other text, explanations, or surrounding punctuation.

- For 'closed-ended infinite answer set visual' or 'closed-ended infinite answer set non-visual':
- Provide a brief, direct answer.
- This answer must be a value, a short phrase, a specific name, a label, or a list of values read directly from the figure
or caption.
- **For numerical values:** Read values as precisely as possible from the graph axes, data points, or labels. Include
units ONLY if they appear in the figure.
- **For non-numerical values:** Reproduce them EXACTLY as they appear in the figure or caption.
- Do NOT add any introductory phrases, explanations, or surrounding text.

- For 'unanswerable':
- Respond ONLY with the exact phrase: 'It is not possible to answer this question based only on the provided data.'
- Do NOT add any other text.

IMPORTANT: Your response should ONLY contain the answer in the correct format as specified above - nothing else.
Do NOT include any additional text, explanations, comments, or contextual information.
Your answer must be based solely on the information visible in the figure and its provided caption.

Below are examples of questions and answers similar to what you will receive. Study these examples carefully to understand
the expected answer format. Your question will be in the user message after these examples:

Example 1:
Figure Caption: {caption}
Figure Type: {figure type}
Question Type: {question type}
Question: {question}
Correct answer: {answer}

Example 2:
Figure Caption: {caption}
Figure Type: {figure type}
Question Type: {question type}
Question: {question}
Correct answer: {answer}

Example 3:
Figure Caption: {caption}
Figure Type: {figure type}
Question Type: {question type}
Question: {question}
Correct answer: {answer}

Example 4:
Figure Caption: {caption}
Figure Type: {figure type}
Question Type: {question type}
Question: {question}
Correct answer: {answer}

Example 5:
Figure Caption: {caption}
Figure Type: {figure type}
Question Type: {question type}
Question: {question}
Correct answer: {answer}

REMEMBER: {answer format instruction}.
```

Figure 8: System prompt used for the SciVQA baseline model, GPT-4.1-mini. For unanswerable questions, the metadata on their type is excluded since it directly reveals the answer.

```
Figure Caption: {caption}
Figure Type: {figure type}
Question Type: {question type}
Question: {question}
```

Figure 9: User prompt used for the SciVQA baseline model, GPT-4.1-mini. For unanswerable questions, the metadata on their type is excluded since it directly reveals the answer.

```
Analyse the incorrectly predicted answers and try to find common patterns.
Here are the evaluation scores for the predictions: {scores}
Here is the JSON string with the gold and predicted answers: {JSON string}
```

Figure 10: Prompt used for Gemini-2.5-Pro to summarise the common errors in the predictions from the SciVQA baseline. JSON string contains instance IDs, questions, gold answers, predictions, information on figure and question types.

C Label Studio configuration examples

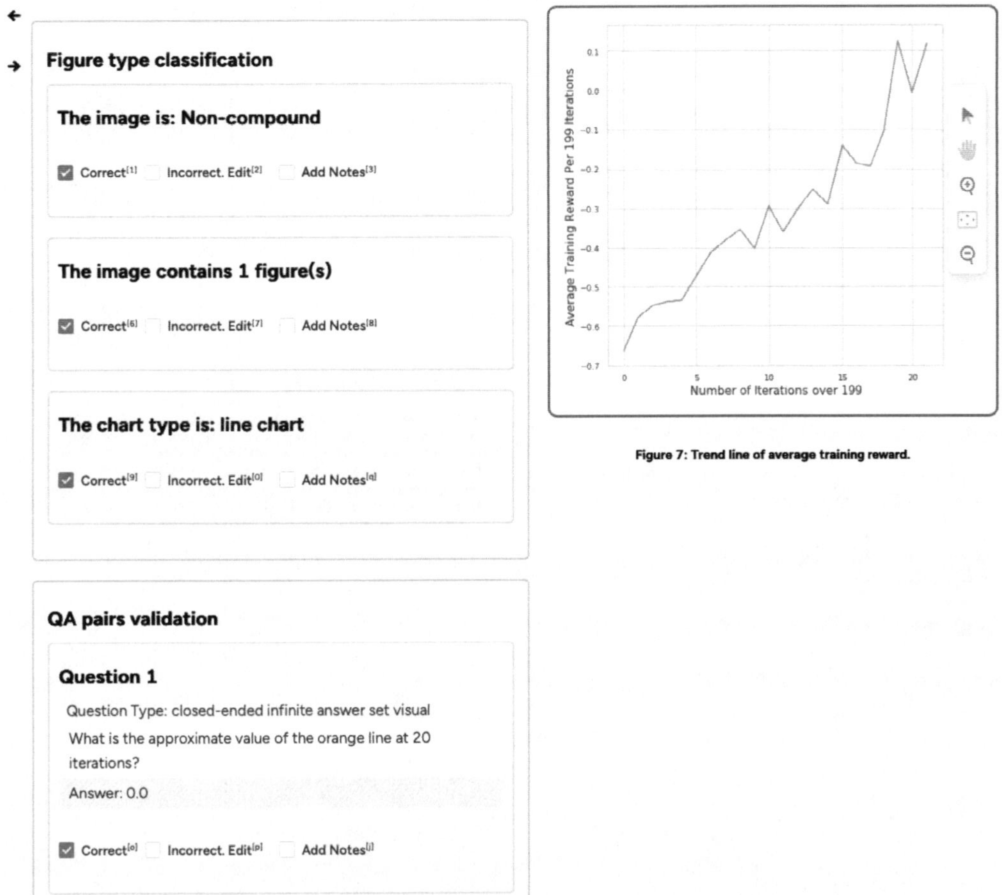

Figure 11: Example setup for the human validation phase in Label Studio (a snapshot).

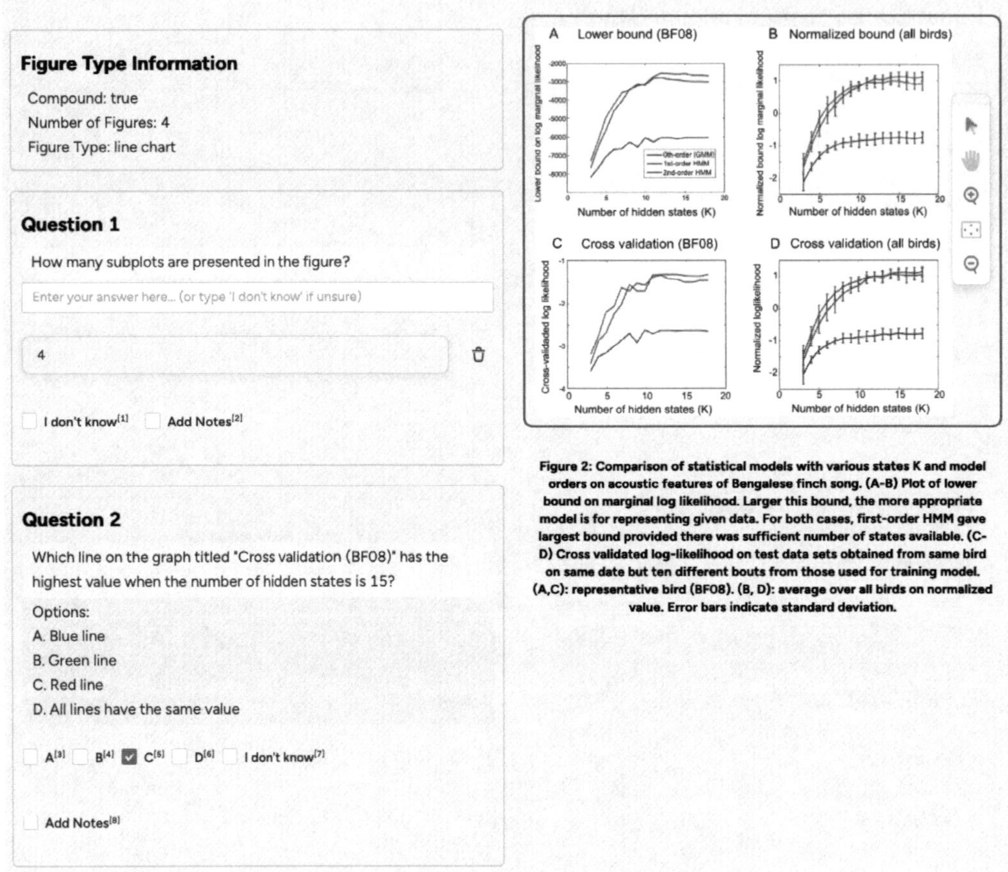

Figure 12: Example setup for the human performance evaluation in Label Studio (a snapshot).

D Data distribution in SciVQA

Split	Images	QA pairs
Train	2160	15120
Validation	240	1680
Test	600	4200
Total	**3000**	**21000**

Table 4: Distribution of figure images and QA pairs in SciVQA dataset across train, validation, and test splits.

E Figure types in SciVQA

The final list of figure types based on the stylistic features comprises 32 classes: *line chart, bar chart, box plot, confusion matrix, pie chart, scatter plot, pareto chart, venn diagram, architecture diagram, neural networks, tree, graph, other, histogram, heat map, illustrative diagram, flow chart, violin plot, vector plot, density plot, faceted dot plot, t-sne plot, word-alignment grid, tree set, target plot, bar chart with error, lex plot, contour, dendogram, speech balloons, surface plot,* and *parallel coordinates plot.* As can be seen from Figure 13, line charts are the most common overall.

Figures 14 shows that the majority of the figures in SciVQA are non-compound (60.53%). Compound figures constitute 39.47% of the dataset, with those containing two sub-figures being the most prevalent (see Figure 15).

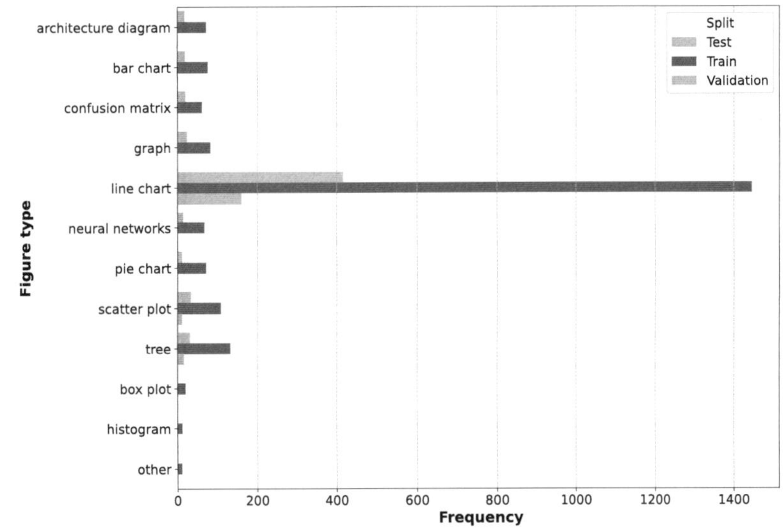

Figure 13: Distribution of figure types across train, validation, and test splits in the SciVQA dataset. Given the large number of classes (32), only those with the frequency of occurrence larger than 10 are shown.

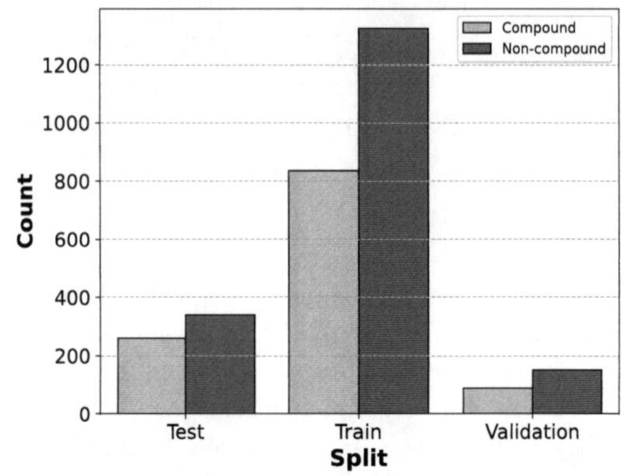

Figure 14: Distribution of compound and non-compound figures across train, validation, and test splits in the SciVQA dataset.

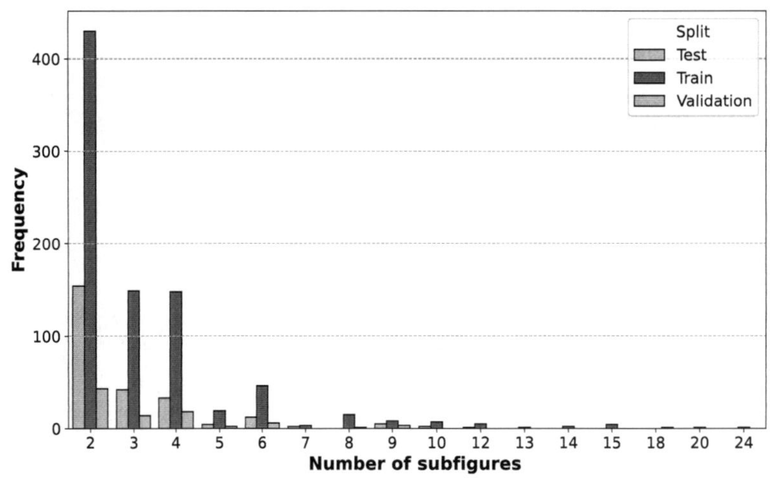

Figure 15: Distribution of the number of sub-figures in compound figures across train, validation, and test splits in the SciVQA dataset.

F Human performance

Annotator	ROUGE-1			ROUGE-L			BertScore			Avg. F1
	F1	Precision	Recall	F1	Precision	Recall	F1	Precision	Recall	
Annotator_1	0.8478	0.8437	0.8617	0.8464	0.8423	0.8603	0.9807	0.9791	0.9825	**0.8916**
Annotator_2	0.8420	0.8441	0.8501	0.8417	0.8439	0.8495	0.9809	0.9807	0.9813	**0.8882**
Annotator_3	0.8262	0.8322	0.8264	0.8256	0.8316	0.8258	0.9856	0.9860	0.9856	**0.8791**
Annotator_4	0.8218	0.8367	0.8225	0.8218	0.8367	0.8225	0.9799	0.9793	0.9807	**0.8745**
Annotator_5	0.8078	0.8170	0.8077	0.8073	0.8165	0.8070	0.9857	0.9859	0.9858	**0.8669**

Table 5: Evaluation results of the human performance on SciVQA for each annotator. "Avg." denotes average F1 score across ROUGE-1, ROUGE-L, and BertScore.

G Baseline performance

QA pair type	ROUGE-1			ROUGE-L			BERTScore			Avg. F1
	F1	Precision	Recall	F1	Precision	Recall	F1	Precision	Recall	
finite answer set binary non-visual	0.8317	0.8317	0.8317	0.8317	0.8317	0.8317	0.9999	0.9999	0.9999	**0.8877**
finite answer set binary visual	0.7683	0.7683	0.7683	0.7683	0.7683	0.7683	0.9998	0.9998	0.9998	**0.8455**
finite answer set non-binary non-visual	0.7316	0.7276	0.7571	0.7312	0.7272	0.7567	0.9814	0.9782	0.9853	**0.8148**
finite answer set non-binary visual	0.7089	0.7124	0.7143	0.7080	0.7115	0.7135	0.9921	0.9915	0.9929	**0.8030**
infinite answer set non-visual	0.7009	0.7211	0.6998	0.6985	0.7183	0.6977	0.9623	0.9646	0.9606	**0.7872**
infinite answer set visual	0.5329	0.5673	0.5237	0.5319	0.5659	0.5229	0.9524	0.9584	0.9470	**0.6724**
unanswerable	0.6689	0.6691	0.6700	0.6687	0.6689	0.6696	0.9412	0.9406	0.9420	**0.7596**

Table 6: Evaluation results of the SciVQA baseline model across different question answering (QA) pair types. "Avg." denotes average F1 score across ROUGE-1, ROUGE-L, and BertScore.

H Examples of errors

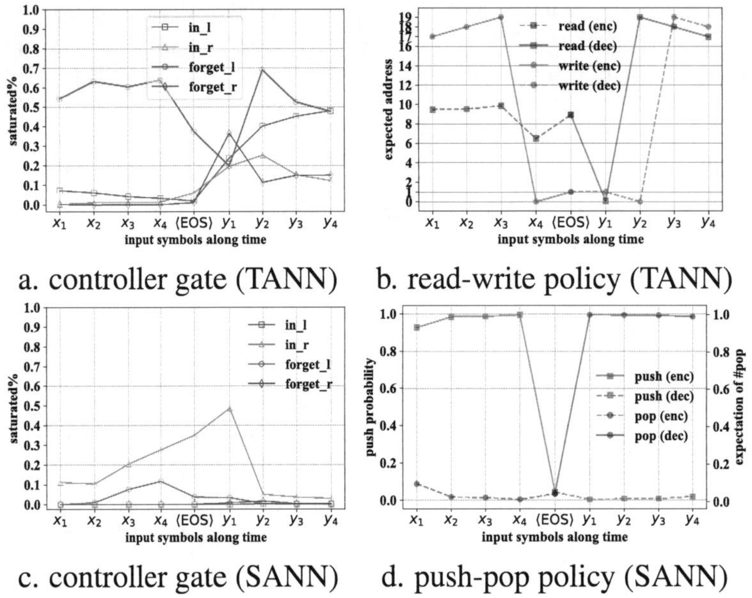

Figure Caption: Figure 3: Averaged visualization about (a and c) controller gate and (b and d) read-write policy for TANN and SANN on mirror task. Note that all the plots are derived from being averaging over 500 random samples. The x-axis shows each time step represented by input xi or output yi. The ⟨EOS⟩ represent the input delimiter.

Figure Type: line chart

Question Type: closed-ended finite answer set binary non-visual

Question: Does 'in_r' always have a higher saturated percentage compared to others in plot 'c'?

Gold answer: Yes

Predicted answer: No

Figure 16: An example of an incorrect prediction by the SciVQA baseline, categorised as containing visual attribute and arithmetic reasoning errors.

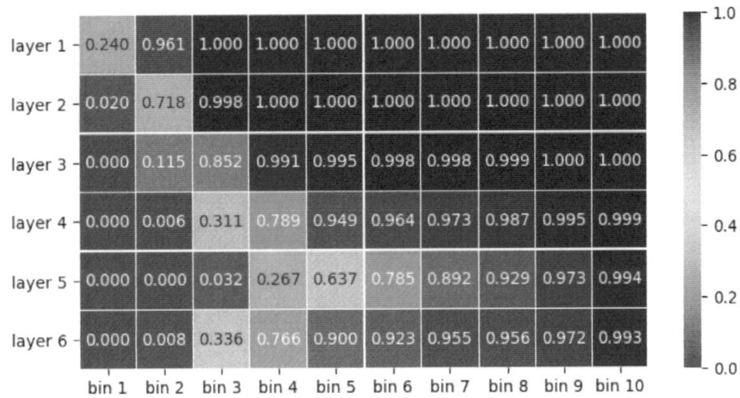

Figure Caption: Figure 9: Frequency-based classification accuracy on states from the ENDE encoder + lexical shortcuts.
Figure Type: heat map
Question Type: closed-ended infinite answer set visual
Question: What is the colour of the cell in the heatmap that is in the same row as 'layer 2' and the same column as 'bin 3'?

Gold answer: Red
Predicted answer: light orange

Figure 17: An example of an incorrect prediction by the SciVQA baseline, categorised as containing visual attribute reasoning error.

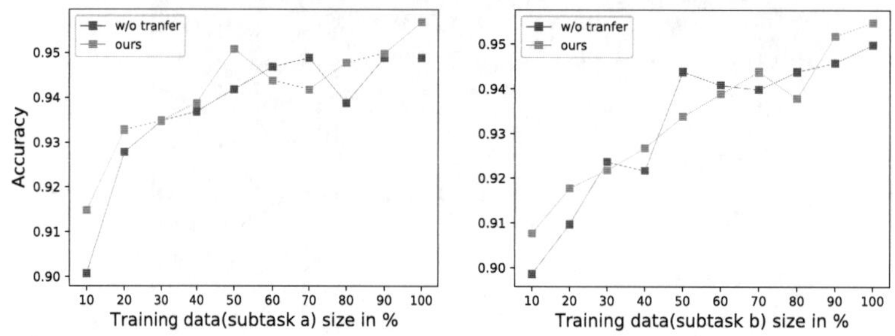

Figure Caption: Figure 4: Learning curve on the training dataset.
Figure Type: line chart
Question Type: closed-ended finite answer set non-binary non-visual
Question: Which of the following subtasks reach a value more than 0.93 at 20% training data for 'ours' methods?
Answer options: A: subtask a | B: subtask b | C: subtask c | D: All of the above

Gold answer: A
Predicted answer: A,B

Figure 18: An example of an incorrect prediction by the SciVQA baseline, categorised as containing incomplete/-partially correct list of items error.

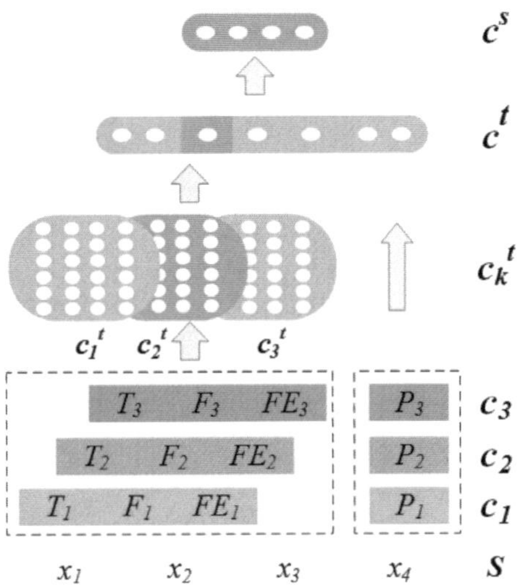

Figure Caption: Figure 4: Frame Integration Representation Model.
Figure Type: neural networks
Question Type: closed-ended infinite answer set non-visual
Question: What is the final vector c^s derived from?

Gold answer: c^t
Predicted answer: ct

Figure 19: An example of an incorrect prediction by the SciVQA baseline, categorised as containing text recognition and extraction error.

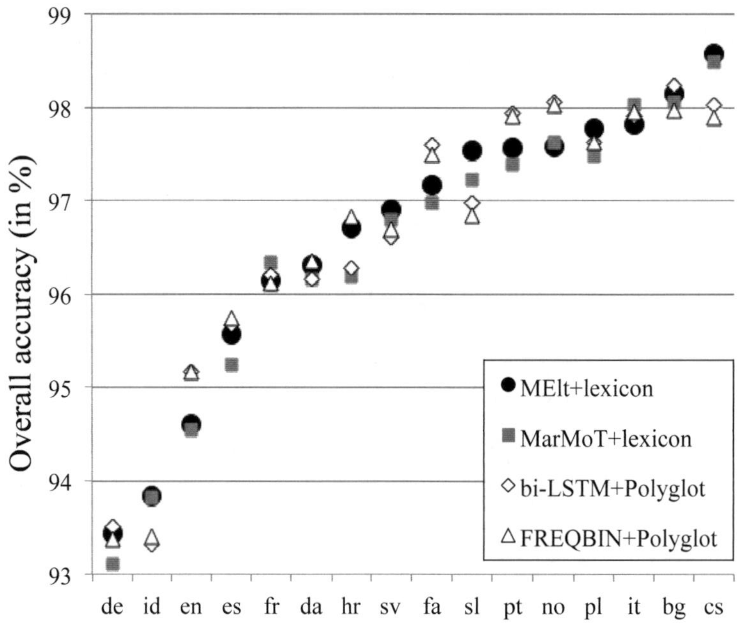

Figure Caption: Figure 1: Graphical visualisation of the overall tagging accuracies for all four types of enriched models. Detailed results are given in Table 4. Languages are sorted by increasing MElt's overall tagging scores.
Figure Type: scatter plot
Question Type: closed-ended infinite answer set visual
Question: What is the overall accuracy of the black circle marker for the language 'es'?

Gold answer: between 95 and 96
Predicted answer: 95.7

Figure 20: An example of an incorrect prediction by the SciVQA baseline, categorised as containing numerical value formatting error.

Visual Question Answering on Scientific Charts Using Fine-Tuned Vision-Language Models

Florian Schleid, Jan Strich, Chris Biemann

Language Technology Group, Universität Hamburg, Germany
florian.schleid@uni-hamburg.de

Abstract

Scientific charts often encapsulate the core findings of research papers, making the ability to answer questions about these charts highly valuable. This paper explores recent advancements in scientific chart visual question answering (VQA) enabled by large Vision Language Models (VLMs) and newly curated datasets. As part of the SciVQA shared task from the 5th Workshop on Scholarly Document Processing, we develop and evaluate multimodal systems capable of answering diverse question types - including multiple-choice, yes/no, unanswerable, and infinite answer set questions - based on chart images extracted from scientific literature. We investigate the effects of zero-shot and one-shot prompting, as well as supervised fine-tuning (SFT), on the performance of Qwen2.5-VL models (7B and 32B variants). We also tried to include more training data from domain-specific datasets (SpiQA and ArXivQA). Our fine-tuned Qwen2.5-VL 32B model achieves a substantial improvement over the GPT-4o mini baseline and reaches the 4th place in the shared task, highlighting the effectiveness of domain-specific fine-tuning. We published the code for the experiments[1].

1 Introduction

Figures are often the first thing that readers of scientific papers look at (Rolandi et al., 2011). Also, they frequently communicate the main results. Therefore, the ability to extract information from scientific chart images would be of great value. However, automatically interpreting charts poses challenges due to their detailed visual components and the complex spatial arrangements of elements. The process requires spatial reasoning and numerical understanding (Meng et al., 2024). New SOTA VLMs like Qwen2.5-VL (Bai et al., 2025) enable better results in the domain of chart VQA (Masry et al., 2025). Furthermore, recent datasets, like

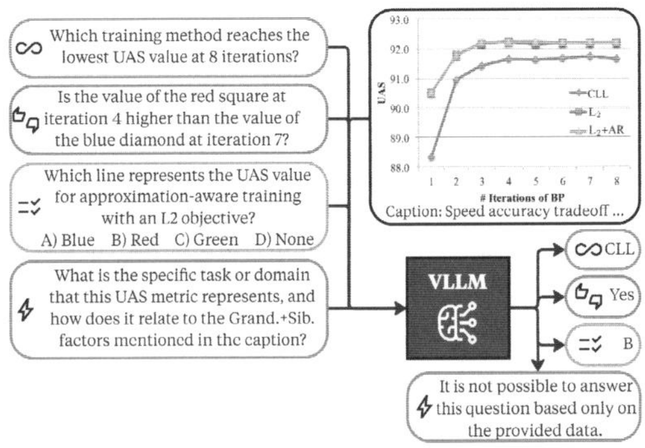

Figure 1: Overview of the system with the four question types: infinite answer set, yes/no, multiple-choice, and unanswerable.

SpiQA (Pramanick et al., 2024) and ArXivQA (Li et al., 2024), provide large amounts of data on scientific chart VQA. This paper intends to explore these new possibilities in the context of the SciVQA shared task (Borisova et al., 2025). It challenges participants to answer questions about scientific charts. An example of such questions can be seen in Figure 1.
The contributions of this paper are:

- **Fine-tuning Qwen2.5-VL models (Bai et al., 2025) for chart VQA:** The model size and the hyperparameters used for the fine-tuning have a strong impact on the results. This paper explores different configurations.

- **Testing prompt templates and one-shot prompting:** Prompt engineering is important to get the desired output format and can improve the results.

- **Exploring other datasets:** We investigate the influence of adding training data from similar-domain datasets.

[1] https://github.com/Flo0620/Scientific-Chart-QA

Proceedings of the Fifth Workshop on Scholarly Document Processing (SDP 2025), pages 211–220

2 Related Work

The SciVQA shared task invites participants to develop multimodal systems for VQA on scientific charts (Borisova et al., 2025). To support this, we use the SciVQA dataset[2], which contains 3,000 real-world chart images from scientific papers, each paired with seven questions. The dataset features four question types: multiple-choice, yes/no, unanswerable, and infinite answer set questions. These are further categorized into visual and non-visual questions, where visual questions refer to attributes such as size, height, color, direction, shape, or position. This task aligns with growing research interest in chart-based VQA, where existing benchmarks such as ChartQA have seen performance plateaus among large VLMs, largely due to limited data diversity (Masry et al., 2025). In response, new benchmarks such as SpiQA (Pramanick et al., 2024) and ArXivQA (Li et al., 2024) have been introduced to address this limitation by using more diverse scientific charts from the real world.

These new datasets provide additional training data to fine-tune VLMs. Li and Tajbakhsh (2023) found a positive correlation between the size of the training set and the model performance when fine-tuning a VLM for chart VQA. Furthermore, Wu et al. (2024) showed that the used prompt has a significant influence on the results of the task of VQA on charts, underlining the importance of prompt engineering.

Recent progress in the field of VLMs includes models such as Qwen2.5-VL (Bai et al., 2025), a successor to Qwen2-VL that has achieved SOTA results in chart VQA tasks (Li et al., 2025; Masry et al., 2025). There are also models specifically developed for chart-related tasks, such as ChartLlama, which performed fine-tuning on a curated dataset and reached good results on the ChartQA benchmark (Han et al., 2023). ChartAssistant (Meng et al., 2024) and ChartVLM (Xia et al., 2024) fine-tuned models to perform chart-to-table translation. The output of these models is then used as input to specialized models fine-tuned for VQA.

The fine-tuning of such models is possible through Low Rank Adaptation (LoRA) (Hu et al., 2022), which drastically reduces the memory and computation requirements for the training.

3 Experiments

To explore the influence of the prompting strategy, the effectiveness of domain-specific fine-tuning, and the importance of the training dataset size, we conducted four different experiments to tackle the task. Firstly, we tried zero-shot inference in combination with prompt engineering. Secondly, we performed one-shot prompting with one example. Third, the VLMs were fine-tuned on the dataset provided by the task[2]. Lastly, we expanded the fine-tuning by including the SpiQA (Pramanick et al., 2024) and ArXivQA (Li et al., 2024) datasets in the training data. All four approaches were tested on the 7B and 32B variants of the Qwen2.5-VL model (Bai et al., 2025) and the first two on GPT-4o mini[3] (OpenAI et al., 2024).

3.1 Zero-Shot

In the zero-shot prompt, the model is given clear instructions on how to respond to different types of questions, reducing hallucinations by providing a desired output if the question cannot be answered from the given information. Furthermore, it is provided with the caption of the chart as an additional information source. The prompt templates are given in the Appendix A.1.

3.2 One-Shot

The user prompt is expanded with an example. If the target question is a multiple-choice question, we align the example to the target by using a multiple-choice question as an example. Otherwise, an infinite answer set question is used. The complete one-shot prompt can be seen in the Appendix in Figure 4. The multiple-choice example question and the infinite answer set example question were selected from the training split of the SciVQA dataset to have one visual and one non-visual question.

3.3 LoRA Fine-Tuning

The SFT of the 7B and 32B variants of the Qwen2.5-VL model (Bai et al., 2025) was performed using LoRA (Hu et al., 2022) with the zero-shot prompt template (see Appendix A.1) on the SciVQA training data[2] (15K questions). The base models are loaded in 8-bit, the learning rate was set to 2×10^{-4} with a linear learning rate scheduler. Hyperparameter tuning determined the

[2] https://huggingface.co/datasets/katebor/SciVQA

[3] https://openai.com/index/GPT-4o-mini-advancing-cost-efficient-intelligence/

Models	Zero-Shot	One-Shot	LoRA Fine-tuning	Fine-tuning + other datasets
Qwen 7B	**0.5968**	0.5972	0.8128	0.7989
Qwen 32B	0.5188	0.5243	**0.8361**	**0.8176**
GPT-4o mini	0.5424	**0.6326**	-	-

Table 1: Performance comparison of the Qwen 7B, Qwen 32B, and GPT-4o mini models on the SciVQA test set (4,200 questions) across different learning paradigms: zero-shot, one-shot, LoRA fine-tuning, and fine-tuning with additional datasets. Reported values are the average of the F1-scores of ROUGE-1, ROUGE-L, and BERTScore. The best score in each setting is highlighted in bold.

LoRA parameters rank $= 64$, alpha $= 128$, and dropout $= 0.2$, since they led to the best average of the ROUGE-1, ROUGE-L, and BERTScore F1-scores (see Table 4 in Appendix). This average also determines the ranking in the competition. Fine-tuning the Qwen2.5-VL 32B model for four epochs with the described parameters led to the best results after two epochs (see Table 5 in Appendix). Therefore, the 7B and 32B models used in the evaluation were fine-tuned for two epochs. The GPUs used for the fine-tuning were one NVIDIA RTX A6000 (48GB VRAM) for the 7B model and one NVIDIA A100 (80GB VRAM, PCIe) for the 32B model.

3.4 LoRA Fine-tuning with other Datasets

To explore the effects of using more domain-specific data for fine-tuning, we sought datasets similar to SciVQA[2]. We therefore incorporated the SpiQA (Pramanick et al., 2024) and ArXivQA (Li et al., 2024) datasets as additional data sources, as they also use real-world scientific charts and primarily contain infinite answer set and multiple-choice questions, respectively. To avoid overlap, any questions from papers which were also scraped in the SciVQA dataset were excluded.

To align the filtered SpiQA questions closer to the SciVQA questions, only questions with answers that have at most 50 characters were retained, leaving 39K mostly infinite answer set questions. The resulting average answer length in the filtered SpiQA questions is with 15.3 characters, relatively close to the average answer length of 14.4 characters of the SciVQA train dataset.

From ArXivQA, only multiple-choice questions with 4 options were kept, as the multiple-choice questions in the SciVQA dataset also have 4 options. This yielded 61K questions. Images from both datasets were resized to a maximum of 500K pixels while preserving the aspect ratio. These filtered datasets, along with the SciVQA train dataset, were combined to 115K questions and used to fine-tune both the 7B and 32B Qwen2.5-VL models for one epoch each. Due to time constraints, no hyperparameter tuning could be performed for the training with this combined dataset. Therefore, except for the described changes in the data and the number of epochs, the other training parameters, as well as the GPUs used, were the same as described in Subsection 3.3.

4 Evaluation

This section presents the main experimental results and provides a detailed comparison between our models and the GPT-4o mini model, including a manual error analysis in the ablation study.

4.1 Main Results

The experiments were evaluated on the test split of the SciVQA dataset, which contains 4200 questions. As the main evaluation metric, the average of the F1-scores of ROUGE-1, ROUGE-L, and BERTScore was used. The results of the experiments are presented in Table 1.

For the zero-shot experiment, the fact that the 7B Qwen model received a significantly better score (0.597) than the 32B model (0.519) and GPT-4o mini (0.543) was unexpected. However, taking a closer look at the provided answers revealed that the answers given by the 32B model had an average length of 351.8 characters, while the 7B model had an average answer length of 57.3 characters, and the GPT-4o mini model of 64.9 characters. Though the test set answers are not public, the validation set has an average answer length of 14.4 characters. Since most of the ground-truth answers only contain a few words and often only one word, the precision of the ROUGE-1 and ROUGE-L metrics reduces for long answers, and the recall is capped at one. This explains why the F1-scores and therefore their average for the 32B model are poor.

Providing the model with a one-shot example works best on the GPT-4o mini model. It reached a

Model	Infinite		Yes/No		Multiple-Choice		Unans.	Overall
	v	n-v	v	n-v	v	n-v		
GPT-4o mini 0-shot	0.4500	0.6833	0.6625	0.7125	0.5042	0.5167	0.6250	**0.5935**
GPT-4o mini 1-shot	0.3875	0.6500	0.6458	0.7000	0.5042	0.5708	0.7708	**0.6042**
Ours	0.5458	0.7500	0.8000	0.8167	0.7583	0.6958	0.9792	**0.7637**

Table 2: Manual evaluation of results obtained for the Qwen2.5-VL 32B model, fine-tuned for two epochs (Ours), and GPT-4o mini. The table shows the fraction of correctly answered questions on the SciVQA validation dataset (1680 questions) per question type. Each question type contains 240 questions. The fine-tuning on the Qwen model was performed on the training split of the SciVQA dataset (15K questions). 'v' and 'n-v' indicate if the questions are visual or non-visual.

Model	Infinite		Yes/No		Multiple-Choice		Unans.	Overall
	v	n-v	v	n-v	v	n-v		
Combined	0.6342	0.7443	0.7971	0.8388	0.7694	0.7718	0.9546	**0.7872**
SciVQA	0.6878	0.7877	0.8527	0.8611	0.8227	0.7821	0.9669	**0.8230**

Table 3: Comparison of the average F1-scores of the ROUGE-1, ROUGE-L, and BERTScore metrics by question type between the Qwen2.5-VL 7B model that was fine-tuned on the combined dataset and the 7B model exclusively fine-tuned on the SciVQA dataset. 'v' and 'n-v' indicate if the questions are visual or non-visual. The evaluation was done on the SciVQA validation dataset (1680 questions). Each question type contains 240 questions.

score of 0.633, outperforming both the 7B and 32B Qwen models and improving greatly compared to the GPT-4o mini model with the zero-shot prompt. Surprisingly, adding a one-shot example does not lead to great improvements for the 7B and 32B models as compared to the zero-shot setting. An analysis of the 7B model's responses revealed that it marked over 2,200 out of 4,200 questions as unanswerable, despite only 600 questions being unanswerable. For the 32B model, the answers even got longer, with an average answer length of 433.3 characters. The average answer length of the GPT-4o mini model reduced to 40.6 characters. These results show that the GPT-4o mini model can leverage one-shot examples much better than the Qwen2.5-VL models and that one-shot prompting can be suitable for doing VQA on charts.

Fine-tuning led to the best result we could achieve across our experiments, with a score of 0.836 for the Qwen2.5-VL 32B model. The expected superiority of the 32B model is also evident here. It outperformed the fine-tuned 7B variant by 0.023, and the GPT-4o mini models, that did not receive fine-tuning, by 0.206. This shows the great potential of domain-specific fine-tuning.

Adding more training data from the SpiQA (Pramanick et al., 2024) and ArXivQA (Li et al., 2024) datasets, as described in Subsection 3.4 resulted in a score of 0.818 for the Qwen2.5-VL 32B model. It therefore reduced the performance in comparison to the model fine-tuned only on the SciVQA dataset. The reason for that is not clear, and further studies are needed to explain the performance drop. A starting point could be to perform dedicated hyperparameter tuning for the combined dataset, since the substantially larger number of training samples could require the hyperparameters to be adjusted. Also, the fact that especially ArXivQA covers a wider range of scientific fields than the SciVQA dataset[2] (Li et al., 2024; Li and Tajbakhsh, 2023; Karishma et al., 2023) should be further investigated as a possible problem source.

4.2 Ablation Studies

Although the F1-scores of ROUGE-1, ROUGE-L and BERTScore provide a useful estimate of the result quality, accurate evaluation, where the answer length does not influence the results, requires a more detailed analysis. Therefore, a manual error analysis was conducted on the SciVQA validation dataset (1680 questions) for the Qwen2.5-VL 32B model fine-tuned for two epochs on the SciVQA dataset, and the GPT-4o mini model using zero- and one-shot prompting. Each answer was manually checked by one annotator to determine whether it accurately answers the given question. The formulation was not taken into account. Table 2 shows the fractions of correctly answered questions.

These results show that our fine-tuned model outperformed the GPT-4o mini model by ~16%, demonstrating the effectiveness of domain-specific fine-tuning. A significant improvement was observed for multiple-choice and unanswerable questions, suggesting that fine-tuning may have reduced hallucinations and helped the model to estimate when not to answer. Additionally, there was a marked difference in performance between visual and non-visual infinite answer set questions for both models. Referencing visual elements appears to be considerably more challenging in the infinite answer set context. Interestingly, this difficulty was not as pronounced in other question types. Surprisingly, providing a one-shot prompt with a visual infinite answer set question led to even worse results for that question type.

To further investigate the poorer results of the fine-tuning on the combined dataset, we compare them with the scores of the 7B model fine-tuned solely on SciVQA in Table 3. Using only SciVQA as training data led to a better score across all question types. Even on multiple-choice questions the results of the model trained on the combined dataset are notably worse than those of the model fine-tuned exclusively on SciVQA. This is unexpected since more than half of the samples in the combined dataset were multiple-choice questions.

5 Conclusion

This paper explored the application of VLMs for scientific chart VQA in the context of the SciVQA shared task. We evaluated zero-shot and one-shot prompting alongside domain-specific fine-tuning using LoRA on Qwen2.5-VL models. Our experiments showed that fine-tuning, especially on the SciVQA dataset alone, led to the most significant performance gains, outperforming the GPT-4o mini baseline and reducing hallucinations. In contrast, incorporating external datasets offered limited benefits, possibly due to suboptimal training conditions or data mismatch. Overall, the results emphasize the value of targeted fine-tuning and careful dataset curation for improving VQA on scientific charts. Future work could include a more sophisticated, possibly manual, selection of training data to further improve the fine-tuning. Testing different hyperparameters for the fine-tuning with more data might also improve the results.

6 Limitations

A key limitation of the system lies in its performance on visual questions with an infinite answer set. For such questions the manual evaluation showed that the model frequently fails to return the exact value of a target datapoint, often producing approximate answers that are close, but fall outside the acceptable error margin to be considered correct. Moreover, the observation that fine-tuning with additional datasets from closely related domains led to a decline in performance suggests limited generalization capabilities. Despite the apparent similarity between the datasets, subtle domain shifts such as differences in the underlying research area or question phrasing, may hinder the model's ability to transfer learned concepts effectively. Potentially, the larger training dataset might also require more trainable parameters than our fine-tuned models had. This highlights potential challenges in developing robust, generalizable models for scientific chart understanding across diverse real-world sources.

References

Shuai Bai, Keqin Chen, Xuejing Liu, Jialin Wang, Wenbin Ge, Sibo Song, Kai Dang, Peng Wang, Shijie Wang, Jun Tang, Humen Zhong, Yuanzhi Zhu, Mingkun Yang, Zhaohai Li, Jianqiang Wan, Pengfei Wang, Wei Ding, Zheren Fu, Yiheng Xu, and 8 others. 2025. Qwen2.5-VL Technical Report. *arXiv preprint*. ArXiv:2502.13923.

Ekaterina Borisova, Nikolas Rauscher, and Georg Rehm. 2025. SciVQA 2025: Overview of the first scientific visual question answering shared task. In *Proceedings of the 5th Workshop on Scholarly Document Processing (SDP)*, Vienna, Austria.

Yucheng Han, Chi Zhang, Xin Chen, Xu Yang, Zhibin Wang, Gang Yu, Bin Fu, and Hanwang Zhang. 2023. ChartLlama: A Multimodal LLM for Chart Understanding and Generation. *arXiv preprint*. ArXiv:2311.16483.

Edward J. Hu, Yelong Shen, Phillip Wallis, Zeyuan Allen-Zhu, Yuanzhi Li, Shean Wang, Lu Wang, and Weizhu Chen. 2022. LoRA: Low-rank adaptation of large language models. In *The Tenth International Conference on Learning Representations*. ICLR 2022, April 25–29.

Zeba Karishma, Shaurya Rohatgi, Kavya Shrinivas Puranik, Jian Wu, and C. Lee Giles. 2023. Acl-fig: A Dataset for Scientific Figure Classification. In *Proceedings of the Workshop on Scientific Document Understanding co-located with 37th AAAI Conference on Artificial Inteligence (AAAI 2023)*, volume

3656 of *CEUR Workshop Proceedings*, Washington DC, USA. AAAI.

Lei Li, Yuqi Wang, Runxin Xu, Peiyi Wang, Xiachong Feng, Lingpeng Kong, and Qi Liu. 2024. Multimodal ArXiv: A Dataset for Improving Scientific Comprehension of Large Vision-Language Models. In *Proceedings of the 62nd Annual Meeting of the Association for Computational Linguistics (Volume 1: Long Papers)*, pages 14369–14387, Bangkok, Thailand. Association for Computational Linguistics.

Shengzhi Li and Nima Tajbakhsh. 2023. SciGraphQA: A Large-Scale Synthetic Multi-Turn Question-Answering Dataset for Scientific Graphs. *arXiv preprint*. ArXiv:2308.03349.

Zongxia Li, Xiyang Wu, Hongyang Du, Fuxiao Liu, Huy Nghiem, and Guangyao Shi. 2025. A Survey of State of the Art Large Vision Language Models: Alignment, Benchmark, Evaluations and Challenges. *arXiv preprint*. ArXiv:2501.02189.

Ahmed Masry, Mohammed Saidul Islam, Mahir Ahmed, Aayush Bajaj, Firoz Kabir, Aaryaman Kartha, Md Tahmid Rahman Laskar, Mizanur Rahman, Shadikur Rahman, Mehrad Shahmohammadi, Megh Thakkar, Md Rizwan Parvez, Enamul Hoque, and Shafiq Joty. 2025. ChartQAPro: A More Diverse and Challenging Benchmark for Chart Question Answering. *arXiv preprint*. ArXiv:2504.05506.

Fanqing Meng, Wenqi Shao, Quanfeng Lu, Peng Gao, Kaipeng Zhang, Yu Qiao, and Ping Luo. 2024. ChartAssistant: A Universal Chart Multimodal Language Model via Chart-to-Table Pre-training and Multitask Instruction Tuning. In *Findings of the Association for Computational Linguistics ACL 2024*, pages 7775–7803, Bangkok, Thailand and virtual meeting. Association for Computational Linguistics.

OpenAI, Josh Achiam, Steven Adler, Sandhini Agarwal, Lama Ahmad, Ilge Akkaya, Florencia Leoni Aleman, Diogo Almeida, Janko Altenschmidt, Sam Altman, Shyamal Anadkat, Red Avila, Igor Babuschkin, Suchir Balaji, Valerie Balcom, Paul Baltescu, Haiming Bao, Mohammad Bavarian, Jeff Belgum, and 262 others. 2024. GPT-4 Technical Report. *arXiv preprint*. ArXiv:2303.08774.

Shraman Pramanick, Rama Chellappa, and Subhashini Venugopalan. 2024. SPIQA: A Dataset for Multimodal Question Answering on Scientific Papers. In *Advances in Neural Information Processing Systems 38: Annual Conference on Neural Information Processing Systems 2024*. NeurIPS Vancouver, BC, Canada, December 10 - 15, 2024.

Marco Rolandi, Karen Cheng, and Sarah Pérez-Kriz. 2011. A Brief Guide to Designing Effective Figures for the Scientific Paper. *Advanced Materials volume 23*, pages 4343 – 4346.

Yifan Wu, Lutao Yan, Leixian Shen, Yunhai Wang, Nan Tang, and Yuyu Luo. 2024. ChartInsights: Evaluating Multimodal Large Language Models for Low-Level Chart Question Answering. In *Findings of the Association for Computational Linguistics: EMNLP 2024*, pages 12174–12200, Miami, Florida, USA. Association for Computational Linguistics.

Renqiu Xia, Bo Zhang, Hancheng Ye, Xiangchao Yan, Qi Liu, Hongbin Zhou, Zijun Chen, Min Dou, Botian Shi, Junchi Yan, and Yu Qiao. 2024. ChartX & ChartVLM: A Versatile Benchmark and Foundation Model for Complicated Chart Reasoning. *arXiv preprint*. ArXiv:2402.12185.

A Appendix

A.1 Prompt Templates

This section contains the final system prompt in Figure 2 and the user prompt used in the zero-shot experiment and to fine-tune the models in Figure 3. Figure 4 shows the user prompt with an example used for the one-shot experiment.

A.2 Hyperparameter Tuning

The correct hyperparameters are essential for good results of the fine-tuned model. This especially applies to the LoRA parameters rank and alpha as well as the dropout. Multiple combinations were tested by fine-tuning the Qwen2.5-7B model on the train split of the SciVQA dataset with 15K questions and evaluating the fine-tuned models on the validation split with 1680 questions. The learning rate used in the experiments was 2×10^{-4} together with a linear learning rate scheduler. Based on the results visible in Table 4 we used a rank of 64, an alpha of 128, and a dropout of 0.2 since it led to the best average of F1-scores, which determines the ranking in the SciVQA competition.

Another important hyperparameter is the number of training epochs. The Qwen2.5-VL 32B model was trained for 1 to 4 epochs on the training data of the SciVQA dataset with LoRA rank $= 64$, alpha $= 128$, and dropout $= 0.2$. To evaluate the training runs the validation split of the SciVQA dataset was again used. As visible in Table 5 the model performs best across all metrics after two training epochs. Therefore, we used two training epochs for the training on the SciVQA data (see Subsection 3.3).

System Prompt

You are an expert data analyst. You will be given an image of a chart and a question.
You will answer the question based on the image of the chart.
If you are sure that you do not have enough information to answer the question answer with: 'It is not possible to answer this question based only on the provided data.'

Figure 2: System Prompt used for fine-tuning the Qwen2.5-VL models, as well as for the zero-shot and one-shot inference.

User Prompt

Here is the caption of the image:
{{ caption }}
This is the Question:
{{ question }}
{% if answer_options %}
You have the following answer options to choose from. Multiple answers may be correct. List only the letter of the correct answers in the order they are given without spaces between them.
Answer Options:
{{answer_options}}
{%endif%}
Give a short and precise answer:

Figure 3: User Prompt for fine-tuning the Qwen2.5-VL models and for the zero-shot inference.

One Shot User Prompt

Here is an example:
The caption of the image is:
Figure 3. Annual frequency of USA being mentioned with Russia, Japan, and G20 countries
This is the Question:
{% if answer_options %}
The line of which color had highest annual mention frequency before 1925?
You have the following answer options to choose from. Multiple answers may be correct. List only the letters of the correct answers in the order they are given without spaces between them.
Answer Options:
A: Red line
B: Green line
C: Blue line
D: Yellow line
{% else %}
Which country, besides the USA, is mentioned the most frequently in the year 1990?
{%endif%}
Give a short and precise answer:

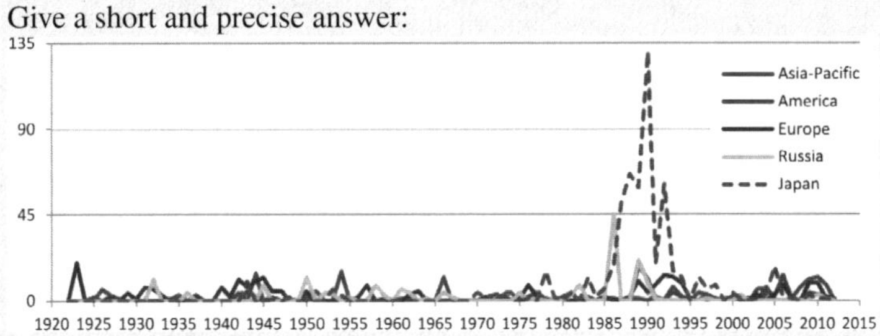

{% if answer_options %}
Answer: C
{% else %}
Answer: Japan
{%endif%}

This is the real query you should answer:
Here is the caption of the image:
{{ caption }}
This is the Question:
{{ question }}
{% if answer_options %}
You have the following answer options to choose from. Multiple answers may be correct. List only the letter of the correct answers in the order they are given without spaces between them.
Answer Options:
{{answer_options}}
{%endif%}
Give a short and precise answer:
<image>

Figure 4: User Prompt with one-shot example for the one-shot inference.

			Train Epochs: 1				Train Epochs: 2			
r	α	**d**	**BERT**	**R-1**	**R-L**	**Avg.**	**BERT**	**R-1**	**R-L**	**Avg.**
16	16	0.1	0.9814	0.7250	0.7242	0.8102	0.9810	0.7230	0.7219	0.8087
16	16	0.2	0.9810	0.7278	0.7268	0.8119	0.9806	0.7270	0.7262	0.8113
16	32	0.1	0.9815	0.7259	0.7250	0.8108	0.9825	0.7323	0.7313	0.8154
16	32	0.2	0.9811	0.7188	0.7178	0.8059	0.9817	0.7190	0.7183	0.8063
32	32	0.1	0.9811	0.7288	0.7281	0.8127	0.9810	0.7330	0.7323	0.8155
32	32	0.2	0.9821	0.7271	0.7267	0.8120	0.9822	0.7279	0.7271	0.8124
32	64	0.1	0.9816	0.7381	0.7374	0.8190	0.9819	0.7355	0.7346	0.8173
32	64	0.2	0.9808	0.7301	0.7288	0.8133	0.9810	0.7347	0.7337	0.8165
64	64	0.1	0.9817	0.7318	0.7310	0.8149	0.9828	0.7435	0.7425	0.8230
64	64	0.2	0.9823	0.7400	0.7391	0.8205	0.9819	0.7427	0.7420	0.8228
64	128	0.1	0.9805	0.7315	0.7307	0.8156	0.9811	0.7316	0.7304	0.8144
64	128	0.2	0.9826	0.7388	0.7378	0.8197	0.9822	0.7452	0.7437	0.8237
128	128	0.1	0.9823	0.7401	0.7392	0.8205	0.9827	0.7434	0.7425	0.8228
128	128	0.2	0.9821	0.7376	0.7367	0.8188	0.9819	0.7437	0.7427	0.8228
128	256	0.1	0.9803	0.7270	0.7260	0.8111	0.9815	0.7404	0.7395	0.8205
128	256	0.2	0.9821	0.7329	0.7318	0.8156	0.9823	0.7361	0.7352	0.8179
256	256	0.1	0.9799	0.7292	0.7279	0.8123	0.9808	0.7332	0.7320	0.8153
256	256	0.2	0.9804	0.7302	0.7291	0.8133	0.9808	0.7334	0.7320	0.8154
256	512	0.1	0.9809	0.7263	0.7251	0.8108	0.9813	0.7319	0.7306	0.8146
256	512	0.2	0.9825	0.7249	0.7236	0.8103	0.9818	0.7359	0.7348	0.8175

Table 4: Evaluation with the SciVQA validation dataset (1680 questions) on the fine-tuned Qwen2.5-VL 7B model for the different hyperparameters LoRA rank, alpha, and dropout. The learning rate was always 2×10^{-4}, and the learning rate scheduler was linear. The metrics are the F1-scores of BERTScore, ROUGE-1, ROUGE-L, and their average.

#epochs	BERT	ROUGE-1	ROUGE-L	Average
1	0.9836	0.7606	0.7591	0.8345
2	**0.9849**	**0.7723**	**0.7709**	**0.8427**
3	0.9848	0.7698	0.7683	0.8410
4	0.9844	0.7652	0.7637	0.8378

Table 5: F1-scores of BERTScore, ROUGE-1 and ROUGE-L with their average across one to four training epochs for fine-tuning Qwen2.5-VL 32B with LoRA rank = 64, LoRA alpha = 128, dropout = 0.2 and 8-bit quantization. The fine-tuning was performed on the SciVQA train split, and the evaluation was done on the SciVQA validation dataset (1680 questions).

ExpertNeurons at SciVQA-2025: Retrieval Augmented VQA with Vision Language Model (RAVQA-VLM)

Nagaraj Bhat
AI Researcher
nagbhat25@gmail.com

Joydeb Mondal
AI Researcher
joydeb28@gmail.com

Srijon Sarkar
AI Researcher
srijonsarkar41@gmail.com

Abstract

We introduce **RAVQA-VLM**, a Retrieval-Augmented Generation (RAG) architecture with Vision Language Model for the SciVQA challenge, which targets closed-ended visual and non-visual questions over scientific figures drawn from ACL Anthology and arXiv papers. Our system first encodes each input figure and its accompanying metadata (caption, figure ID, type) into dense embeddings, then retrieves context passages from the full PDF of the source paper via a Dense Passage Retriever. The extracted contexts are concatenated with the question and passed to a vision-capable generative backbone (e.g., Qwen-2.5, Pixtral-12B, Mistral-24B-small, InterVL-3-14B) fine-tuned on the 15.1K SciVQA training examples. We jointly optimize retrieval and generation end-to-end to minimize answer loss and mitigate hallucinations. On the SciVQA test set, RAVQA-VLM achieves significant improvements over parametric only baselines, with relative gains of +5% ROUGE1 and +5% ROUGE-L, demonstrating the efficacy of RAG for multimodal scientific QA. In this shared task, our **RAVQA-VLM** approach secured the top rank in the leaderboard with an F1 score of 0.8049 (ROUGE-1), 0.8043 (ROUGE-L), and 0.9849 (BERTScore).

1 Introduction

Scientific literature often conveys core findings through figures such as bar charts, line graphs, scatter plots, and compound diagrams. Understanding these figures requires interpreting both visual cues (e.g., color, shape, and size) and associated textual elements (e.g., captions, methodology descriptions, result interpretations) (Karishma et al., 2023; Li et al., 2024). This multimodal nature presents challenges for automated systems aiming to answer questions about scientific figures.

Traditional vision-only architectures such as standard convolutional neural networks (CNNs) and object detection models like Faster R-CNN (Ren et al., 2015) are limited to spatial and visual patterns and typically fail to reason over abstract visual encodings used in scientific plots. On the other hand, language-only models cannot perceive visual structure or layout, making them unsuitable for figure-centric reasoning tasks (Radford et al., 2021).

Recent advances in large vision-language models (LVLMs), such as InterVL-3-14B (Zhu et al., 2025), Qwen-2.5-VL (Bai et al., 2025), Phi-3.5 (Abdin et al., 2024), and Mistral-Small-24B (Mistral AI, 2025), have enabled more robust multimodal understanding. However, these models often produce hallucinated answers when key context is missing or ambiguous (Brown et al., 2020). Retrieval-Augmented Generation (RAG) offers a potential remedy by enriching model inputs with contextually relevant external passages at inference time (Lewis et al., 2020).

To accelerate research in this area, the SciVQA shared task (Borisova et al., 2025) provides a benchmark dataset of 3,000 figures from scientific documents, each accompanied by seven question-answer pairs and includes metadata such as caption, figure ID, figure type (e.g., compound, line graph, bar chart, scatter plot), QA pair type. The task emphasizes both visual and non-visual question types, facilitating comprehensive evaluation across multimodal reasoning skills (Borisova et al., 2025).

We build on these insights to propose Retrieval-Augmented Generation architecture with Vision Language Model (**RAVQA-VLM**), a unified framework that:

1. retrieves paragraph-level context from the source PDF,
2. fuses visual features with retrieved textual evidence, and
3. generates accurate, closed-ended answers.

Proceedings of the Fifth Workshop on Scholarly Document Processing (SDP 2025), pages 221–229
July 31, 2025 ©2025 Association for Computational Linguistics

Our code and implementation details are publicly available at GitHub[1] for reproducibility and further research.

2 Related Work

Multimodal Scientific Figure Understanding. Scientific visual question answering (VQA) and captioning require models to interpret domain-specific plots, charts, and diagrams that differ significantly from natural images. Early datasets such as ACL-Fig introduced a taxonomy for figure types from the ACL Anthology, enabling classification and captioning research on structured scientific visual content (Karishma et al., 2023). SciGraphQA (Shengzhi Li, 2023), a foundational dataset for SciVQA, focused on QA over scientific graphs by pairing structured visual content with underlying textual and symbolic metadata. SciCap+ demonstrated that incorporating contextual mention-paragraphs improves caption quality for scientific figures (Yang et al., 2023), while Multimodal ArXiv showed that domain-specific finetuning on scientific plots closes the generalization gap of large vision-language models (LVLMs) (Li et al., 2024). SPIQA introduced one of the first QA benchmarks over interleaved figures and texts from scientific papers, emphasizing the importance of cross-modal reasoning in retrieval-based QA systems (Pramanick et al., 2024).

Retrieval-Augmented Generation in QA. Retrieval-Augmented Generation (RAG) (Lewis et al., 2020) combines dense retrieval with sequence-to-sequence generation to improve factual correctness and grounding in QA tasks. While originally introduced for open-domain QA, subsequent works have adapted RAG to handle domain-specific documents, including scientific literature, by embedding long-form PDFs (Rujun Han and Castelli, 2024) and utilizing contrastive retrieval strategies such as Dense Passage Retrieval (DPR) (Karpukhin et al., 2020). Recent multimodal QA studies have integrated RAG with LVLMs to support visual reasoning over complex figures and tables.

Large Vision-Language Models. Early LVLMs like CLIP and ViLT excelled on natural image benchmarks but struggled with abstract scientific diagrams due to limited domain grounding (Radford et al., 2021; Kim et al., 2021). Recent advances, including InterVL3-14B and other 14B+ parameter models, demonstrate better cross-modal understanding through pretraining on multimodal documents and structured figures (Li et al., 2024). However, these models still benefit significantly from RAG pipelines, which inject external domain knowledge and context—especially for nuanced figure-based QA tasks, as explored in our work.

3 Dataset

The SciVQA dataset[2] comprises scientific figures extracted from papers in the ACL Anthology and arXiv, each annotated with question–answer (QA) pairs and associated metadata. The dataset is organized into three splits: a training set with approximately 15k instances, a validation set with 1.7k instances, and a test set containing 4.2k instances. An instance is one datapoint consisting of figure and its respective question answer pair.

Each QA pair in SciVQA is categorized along two key dimensions: answerability and visual grounding. Based on answerability, QA pairs are labeled as either closed-ended (answerable solely from the image or image+caption), unanswerable (not inferable from the given source), finite answer set (with binary or multiple-choice answers), or infinite answer set (requiring open-form answers, such as numerical sums). Based on visual grounding, QA pairs are classified as either visual—requiring interpretation of figure elements like shape, size, position, height, direction, or colour—or non-visual, which do not involve these aspects.

The dataset also provides annotations for figure types, distinguishing between compound figures—those composed of multiple subfigures—and non-compound figures, which depict a single visual element. Figure types span common scientific visualizations such as line charts, bar charts, box plots, confusion matrices, and pie charts. We perform all the evaluation on test set only.

Figure 1 presents a sample QA pair along with its corresponding figure from the test set. In the SciVQA dataset, each figure is accompanied by a caption and is paired with seven distinct QA pairs, each corresponding to a different QA pair type. The example shown illustrates one such QA pair, demonstrating the format of the image, caption, and

[1] https://github.com/joydeb28/ExpertNeurons-SciVQA_2025

[2] https://huggingface.co/datasets/katebor/SciVQA

associated multiple-choice question and answer.

> *"Figure 6: Number of documents with an 'attacking' country per 3-month period, and coreference posterior uncertainty for that quantity. The dark line is the posterior mean, and the shaded region is the 95% posterior credible interval. See appendix for more examples."*

and the associated figure, a representative question is:

> *"Which line represents the quantity of documents with an 'attacking' country for Serbia/Yugoslavia?"*

with answer choices such as: **A.** The blue line, **B.** The red line, **C.** The gray line, **D.** All of the above.

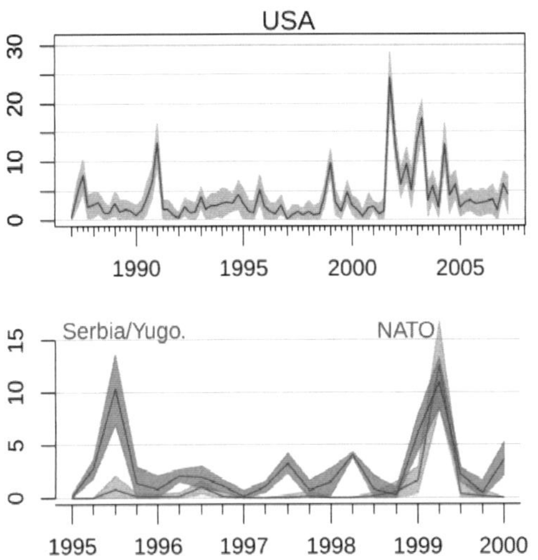

Figure 1: Example scientific figure from the SciVQA dataset showing temporal trends for different countries.

We also do preprocessing of images in the later step as mentioned in Setting C. Captions and questions are tokenized using the BERT tokenizer, with a maximum sequence length of 512 subword tokens. This preprocessing ensures a consistent input structure for our RAG-based architecture. The term subword tokens refers to the output units produced by the BERT tokenizer after applying WordPiece tokenization to the input text.

4 Methodology

The overall flow of our proposed approach is illustrated in Figure 2. We conducted experiments across multiple distinct configurations, each incrementally improving upon the last to evaluate model capabilities comprehensively. Below are details of input meta information across settings.

Setting A: For inference, the prompt includes `image_file`, `caption`, and `question`.

Setting B: During fine-tuning, only `image_file` is used. For inference, the prompt includes `image_file`, `caption`, and `question`.

Setting C: Fine-tuning uses `image_file` and the corresponding `PDF`. Inference is performed using `image_file`, `caption`, and `question`.

Setting D (Final Approach): Identical to Setting C, fine-tuning utilizes `image_file` and `PDF`, and inference uses `image_file`, `caption`, and `question`.

4.1 Setting A: Baseline Evaluation with Image-Only Inputs

In this preliminary evaluation, we assessed several state-of-the-art multimodal models based on Open VLM leaderboard (opencompass) to establish baseline performance on the SciVQA chart image question-answering task without additional training or context. Due to resource constraints for further finetuning, we limited our experiments to models up to 32 billion parameters only. Models evaluated included Pixtral-12B (Agrawal et al., 2024), Mistral-Small-24B (Mistral AI, 2025), InternVL3-14B (OpenGVLab), and Qwen-2.5-VL (Alibaba Group, 2024). The InternVL3-14B model demonstrated notably superior initial performance, as summarized in Table 1. Consequently, InternVL3-14B was selected as the foundational model for all subsequent experimental settings.

4.2 Setting B: Image-Only Finetuning (SciVQA Data)

Building upon our baseline, we finetuned the InternVL3 model using the official SciVQA training dataset. Finetuning employed a Low-Rank Adaptation (LoRA) (Hu et al., 2021) strategy with the following hyperparameters: rank = 64, epochs = 4, and a learning rate of 4×10^{-4}. The purpose was to specialize the model explicitly toward chart-based visual question-answering tasks. The models were finetuned on a single A100 GPU of 80 GB RAM.

4.3 Setting C: Enhanced Contextual Finetuning (Image Sharpening and RAG)

Analysis of results from Setting B via manual verification of 100+ random samples highlighted two prevalent challenges:

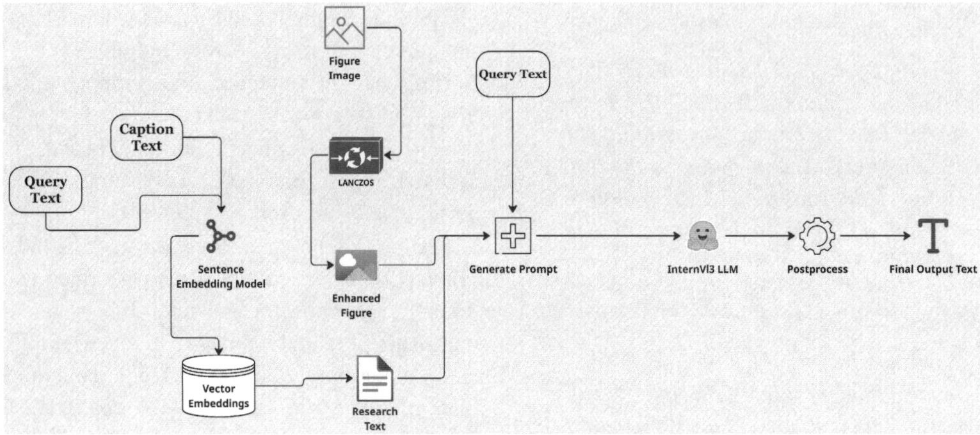

Figure 2: Overall Methodology

1. **Image Quality:** A significant portion of failed cases on the validation set were associated with poor image clarity, which hindered effective visual information extraction. To investigate this, we manually inspected 100 randomly sampled failure cases. Among these, approximately 20% (i.e., 20 samples) were found to exhibit image quality issues. These included low-resolution renders, blurry charts, and faint or unreadable axis labels and legends. The annotations were performed manually by the authors, who marked these images as visually noisy or difficult to interpret for tasks such as reading precise values or identifying attributes like bar height or line trends. Figure 3 in Appendix A shows one such sample image.

2. **Contextual Insufficiency:** Another source of model error stemmed from textual context. In certain cases, relying solely on the figure and its caption failed to provide sufficient cues such as variable definitions, experimental configurations, or axis descriptions needed to fully disambiguate the question. While the dataset formally categorizes most QA pairs as closed-ended (i.e., answerable from the image and caption), we found that in practice, additional context from the surrounding text could enhance answerability. During our manual analysis of 100 failed cases, we noticed around 7% of the samples which could have benefited by additional context provided in the caption or data from the paper. These were also verified by the authors through a qualitative assessment of whether access to more textual context (e.g., caption or the paragraph surrounding the figure in the paper) could plausibly improve performance. While the correct answer may not always be explicitly stated in the surrounding text, this additional context often reinforces key concepts, thereby supporting more accurate answer generation. Sample instances illustrating such contextual gaps are included in the Appendix A referred to in Figure 4 and Figure 5.

   Also note that these annotations were based on a limited, manually inspected subset (n=100) due to resource constraints. While the proportions reported here may not generalize to the entire dataset, our intent is to identify common failure modes rather than provide exact quantitative prevalence.

To address these issues, we adopted two significant improvements:

Image Upscaling and Sharpening: We applied a Lanczos resampling technique (Turkowski and Gabriel, 1990), which is renowned for effectively preserving edge sharpness, to enhance image clarity. Specifically, each image was resized by doubling its original dimensions uniformly to maintain aspect ratios while improving visual fidelity.

Retrieval-Augmented Generation (RAG): To incorporate broader textual context for scientific visual questions, we implemented a retrieval-augmented pipeline that extracts relevant text from the source papers associated with each figure in the SciVQA dataset.

For each figure instance, we first downloaded

the corresponding academic paper in PDF format using the metadata provided (e.g., arXiv or ACL Anthology identifiers). The full text of the PDF was segmented into semantically meaningful blocks—such as section titles, paragraphs, captions, and table/figure references—using PDF parsing tools like PDFMiner[3]. These blocks, separated based on structural whitespace in the document, were treated as retrieval units.

To locate the caption associated with each figure, we applied regular expressions to detect references such as "Figure X" in the parsed text. This enabled us to extract the specific caption block aligned with the figure metadata.

Next, we generated sentence embeddings (Reimers and Gurevych, 2019) for all textual blocks using a pre-trained Sentence-BERT model. An embedding was also computed for the extracted figure caption. To identify the most relevant textual context, we computed cosine similarity between the caption embedding and each block embedding within the same paper. The top two blocks with the highest similarity were selected—typically the caption itself and an adjacent explanatory section (e.g., description of results or methods).

To further enrich context, we also generated an embedding of the input question and used it to retrieve an additional textual block. This block often provided broader or complementary information from the paper, such as experimental setup, variable definitions, or related discussion, which might not be present near the figure.

Thus, each instance is paired with three retrieved text blocks: the caption block and two additional context blocks (one based on caption similarity, one on question similarity). These were concatenated and used as external context alongside the image during fine-tuning. We retained the LoRA-based fine-tuning strategy from Setting B.

4.4 Setting D: Augmented Dataset and Post-processing Refinement

To further enhance model robustness and generalization, we augmented the training data with additional samples from the ChartQA dataset (Masry et al., 2022), which features complex reasoning-based questions spanning diverse chart types. ChartQA was selected due to its structural and semantic alignment with SciVQA, particularly in its inclusion of real-world scientific plots, numeric reasoning, and visual attribute-based questions. From this dataset, we integrated approximately 2,500 samples into our training corpus. These samples were filtered to retain those that met two criteria: (i) the figure type was within the scope of our model (e.g., bar, line, or pie charts), and (ii) the questions were of high quality, which we ensured by selecting only those samples from the ChartQA dataset that were explicitly tagged as human authored. In ChartQA, each QA pair includes metadata indicating whether it was generated by a human or machine based method. We filtered out all machine generated questions and retained only those tagged as human annotated, as these are typically designed to be of higher semantic quality. The dataset filtering was done automatically solely based on the tags provided in the dataset without any manual inspection. The 2,500 sample limit was chosen to maintain a balanced distribution with the original SciVQA samples and to prevent the model from overfitting to the style or domain of a single dataset.

Despite accuracy improvements, we observed that the fine-tuned InternVL model occasionally generates a range of values (e.g., *"between 0.2 and 0.3"*) instead of a single numerical answer, particularly in cases where the model exhibits uncertainty. This behavior appears to stem from the model's tendency to express ambiguity when it is not confident about a precise value. We have included an example of such a case in the Appendix A. While such responses can be semantically reasonable (particularly when axis resolution is low or approximate visual estimation is needed), they pose challenges for automatic evaluation, which often relies on exact matching or scalar closeness to gold answers.

To address inconsistent range-based outputs in direct answer questions, we implemented a lightweight post-processing module using regular expressions and simple heuristics to detect numeric ranges and replace them with their arithmetic mean. This standardization improves alignment with expected ground truth formats and ensures more consistent scoring under numeric evaluation schemes. While this transformation may introduce minor inaccuracies when ranges are semantically justified, it generally enhances answer conformity and evaluation robustness.

This combined approach leveraging data set enhancement and output refinement further improved model precision and interpretability, as shown in Table 1.

[3]https://github.com/pdfminer/pdfminer.six

Setting	Model Settings	R-1 F1	R-L F1	BS F1
A	Pixtral-12B	0.6480	0.6480	0.9680
	Mistral-Small-24B	0.6787	0.6782	0.9742
	Qwen-2.5-VL	0.6780	0.6780	0.9610
	InternVL3-14B	0.7130	0.7130	0.9750
B	InternVL3-14B + Finetuning	0.7753	0.7750	0.9804
C	InternVL3-14B + Finetune + RAG	0.7986	0.7983	0.9846
D	InternVL3-14B + Finetune + RAG + Augmentation and Post Refinement	0.8049	0.8043	0.9849

Table 1: Evaluation metrics across multiple settings. Each row shows results using progressively advanced configurations for vision-language QA. Setting A includes baseline models; B-D represent stages of fine-tuning, RAG integration, and data augmentation. R-1: ROUGE-1, R-L: ROUGE-L, BS: BERTScore

Table 2 presents the leaderboard results for the SciVQA 2025 shared task. Our system, ExpertNeurons, achieved the highest performance across all evaluation metrics, demonstrating the effectiveness of our RAG-VLM architecture.

#	Team	R-1 F1	R-L F1	BS F1
1	ExpertNeurons	0.8049	0.8043	0.9849
2	THAii_LAB	0.7899	0.7892	0.9839
3	Coling_UniA	0.7862	0.7856	0.9817
4	florian	0.7631	0.7621	0.9831
5	Infyn	0.7350	0.7345	0.9787

Table 2: Leaderboard on SciVQA 2025 test set. R-1: ROUGE-1, R-L: ROUGE-L, BS: BERTScore. Baseline not ranked.

5 Discussion

Table 1 summarizes the performance of F1 for ROUGE-1, ROUGE-L and BERTScore in the four setting of methodology (A to D) on test set. Each stage demonstrates incremental improvements with better contextual modeling and data augmentation. Setting D secured the top rank in the leaderboard with 0.8049 (ROUGE-1 F1-score), 0.8043 (ROUGE-L F1-score), and 0.9849 (BERTScore F1-score).

Our experiments highlight several key insights into the performance and limitations of retrieval-augmented VQA systems in scientific domains.

Baseline models evaluated under Setting A (A1–A4) demonstrated limited ability to handle scientific chart-based questions. Among them, InternVL3-14B (A4) performed the best with ROUGE-1 and ROUGE-L scores of 0.7130, and a BERTScore F1 of 0.9750, indicating that even strong vision-language models struggle without task-specific adaptation. This highlights the inherent complexity of scientific figures, which often lack standalone semantics and require specialized training or contextual information.

With fine-tuning on the SciVQA dataset (Setting B), InternVL3-14B achieved a substantial performance boost—ROUGE-1 improved from 0.7130 to 0.7753 (+6.23%), and BERTScore rose to 0.9804. However, we observed a plateau on questions demanding deeper reasoning beyond surface-level visual cues, underscoring the need for additional context.

Setting C addressed these limitations by integrating high-resolution image sharpening and contextual grounding via our RAG pipeline. This led to a further increase in ROUGE-1 to 0.7986 and BERTScore to 0.9846, suggesting enhanced capacity for visual-textual reasoning through targeted retrieval from source PDFs.

Finally, Setting D yielded the highest performance: ROUGE-1 reached 0.8049, and BERTScore climbed to 0.9849. The 0.63% gain in ROUGE-1 and marginal BERTScore improvement over Setting C reflect the complementary benefits of including 2,500 reasoning-centric samples from ChartQA and the application of post-processing techniques to resolve answer ambiguity

6 Limitations

Although our approach demonstrates promising results, it still has several limitations stemming from two primary factors.

Firstly, certain challenges arise from the data itself. These include poor image quality, lack of contextual information, or missing visual elements. Additionally, in some instances, the correct answer is visually ambiguous or difficult to distinguish from the figure for example, differentiating between values such as 0.54 and 0.56 in a bar graph.

Secondly, while our method incorporates additional contextual information to support answer prediction, this context is not always sufficient or fully relevant. Although the inclusion of retrieved context generally improves performance, there are edge cases where questions originally labeled as unanswerable could become answerable with the added context potentially leading to inconsistencies in evaluation and lower performance. A systematic analysis of these cases is currently lacking and would require additional strategies to robustly identify and handle such cases. Furthermore, although the auxiliary dataset used to enhance model performance contributes positively, it does not comprehensively capture the full complexity and diversity of question types presented in the shared task.

7 Conclusion

We present a Retrieval-Augmented VQA pipeline that combines vision-language modeling with document-aware context retrieval to improve scientific chart understanding. Through progressive experimentation and enhancement, our method achieved significant gains in accuracy, reasoning depth, and answer quality.

By integrating image sharpening, textual retrieval, and dataset augmentation, the system successfully bridges the gap between purely visual inputs and the rich semantic context needed for effective scientific QA. Our approach demonstrates the potential of LLM enhanced vision-language systems in handling complex academic visual data.

Future work will explore multi-modal attention mechanisms across figure-caption-text triplets and generalize the framework to broader scientific domains, enabling more diverse and open-ended question answering capabilities.

References

Marah Abdin, Jyoti Aneja, Hany Awadalla, Ahmed Awadallah, Ammar Ahmad Awan, Nguyen Bach, Amit Bahree, Arash Bakhtiari, Jianmin Bao, Harkirat Behl, Alon Benhaim, Misha Bilenko, Johan Bjorck, Sébastien Bubeck, Martin Cai, Qin Cai, Vishrav Chaudhary, Dong Chen, Dongdong Chen, and 110 others. 2024. Phi-3 technical report: A highly capable language model locally on your phone. *arXiv preprint arXiv:2404.14219*.

Pravesh Agrawal, Szymon Antoniak, Emma Bou Hanna, Baptiste Bout, Devendra Chaplot, Jessica Chudnovsky, Diogo Costa, Baudouin De Monicault, Saurabh Garg, Theophile Gervet, Soham Ghosh, Amélie Héliou, Paul Jacob, Albert Q. Jiang, Kartik Khandelwal, Timothée Lacroix, Guillaume Lample, Diego Las Casas, Thibaut Lavril, and 23 others. 2024. Pixtral 12b. *arXiv preprint arXiv:2410.07073*.

Alibaba Group. 2024. Qwen2.5-VL. `https://huggingface.co/Qwen/Qwen2.5-VL-32B-Instruct`. Accessed: 2025-06-18.

Shuai Bai, Keqin Chen, Xuejing Liu, Jialin Wang, Wenbin Ge, Sibo Song, Kai Dang, Peng Wang, Shijie Wang, Jun Tang, and 1 others. 2025. Qwen2.5-vl technical report. *arXiv preprint arXiv:2502.13923*.

Ekaterina Borisova, Nikolas Rauscher, and Georg Rehm. 2025. SciVQA 2025: Overview of the first scientific visual question answering shared task. In *Proceedings of the 5th Workshop on Scholarly Document Processing (SDP)*, Vienna, Austria. Accepted.

Tom B. Brown, Benjamin Mann, Nick Ryder, Melanie Subbiah, Jared Kaplan, Prafulla Dhariwal, Arvind Neelakantan, Pranav Shyam, Girish Sastry, Amanda Askell, and 1 others. 2020. Language models are few-shot learners. *NeurIPS*.

Edward J. Hu, Yelong Shen, Phillip Wallis, Zeyuan Allen-Zhu, Yuanzhi Li, Shean Wang, Lu Wang, and Weizhu Chen. 2021. Lora: Low-rank adaptation of large language models. *arXiv preprint arXiv:2106.09685*.

Zeba Karishma, Shaurya Rohatgi, Kavya Puranik, Jian Wu, and C. Lee Giles. 2023. Acl-fig: A dataset for scientific figure classification. *arXiv preprint arXiv:2301.12293*.

Vladimir Karpukhin, Barlas Oguz, Sewon Min, Patrick Lewis, Wen-tau Yih, Tim Rockt"aschel, and Sebastian Riedel. 2020. Dense passage retrieval for open-domain question answering. *Proceedings of EMNLP*.

Wonjae Kim, Bokyung Cho, Sungdong Yoo, Jaewoo Choi, Jinyeong Kim, Taeuk Lee, Jaewook Kang, and Jaewhan Choi. 2021. Vilt: Vision-and-language transformer without convolution or region supervision. *ICML*.

Patrick Lewis, Ethan Perez, Aleksandra Piktus, Vladimir Karpukhin, Naman Goyal, Abdelrahman Mohamed, Tim Rockt"aschel, and Sebastian Riedel. 2020. Retrieval-augmented generation for knowledge-intensive nlp tasks. *NeurIPS*.

Lei Li, Yuqi Wang, Runxin Xu, Peiyi Wang, Xiachong Feng, Lingpeng Kong, and Qi Liu. 2024. Multimodal arxiv: A dataset for improving scientific comprehension of large vision-language models. *arXiv preprint arXiv:2403.00231*.

Ahmed Masry, Do Xuan Long, Jia Qing Tan, Shafiq Joty, and Enamul Hoque. 2022. Chartqa: A benchmark for question answering about charts with visual and logical reasoning. *arXiv preprint arXiv:2203.10244*.

Mistral AI. 2025. Mistral small 3.1. `https://mistral.ai/news/mistral-small-3-1`. Accessed: 2025-05-23.

opencompass. Open-vlm-leaderboard. `https://huggingface.co/spaces/opencompass/open_vlm_leaderboard`. Accessed: 2025-06-18.

OpenGVLab. InternVL3-14B. https://huggingface.co/OpenGVLab/InternVL3-14B. Accessed: 2025-06-18.

Shraman Pramanick, Rama Chellappa, and Subhashini Venugopalan. 2024. Spiqa: A dataset for multimodal question answering on scientific papers. *arXiv preprint arXiv:2407.09413.*

Alec Radford, Jong Wook Kim, Tao Xu, Greg Brockman, Christine McLeavey, and Ilya Sutskever. 2021. Learning transferable visual models from natural language supervision. *ICML.*

Nils Reimers and Iryna Gurevych. 2019. Sentence-bert: Sentence embeddings using siamese bert-networks. In *Proceedings of the 2019 Conference on Empirical Methods in Natural Language Processing (EMNLP).*

Shaoqing Ren, Kaiming He, Ross Girshick, and Jian Sun. 2015. Faster r-cnn: Towards real-time object detection with region proposal networks. *Advances in neural information processing systems*, 28.

Peng Qi Yumo Xu Jenyuan Wang Lan Liu William Yang Wang Bonan Min Rujun Han, Yuhao Zhang and Vittorio Castelli. 2024. Rag-qa arena: Evaluating domain robustness for long-form retrieval augmented question answering. *EMNLP.*

Nima Tajbakhsh Shengzhi Li. 2023. Scigraphqa: A large-scale synthetic multi-turn question-answering dataset for scientific graphs. *arXiv preprint arXiv:2308.03349.*

Ken Turkowski and Steve Gabriel. 1990. Filters for common resampling tasks. In Andrew Glassner, editor, *Graphics Gems I*, pages 147–165. Academic Press. Includes descriptions of Lanczos interpolation.

Zhishen Yang, Raj Dabre, Hideki Tanaka, and Naoaki Okazaki. 2023. Scicap+: A knowledge augmented dataset to study the challenges of scientific figure captioning. *arXiv preprint arXiv:2306.03491.*

Jinguo Zhu, Weiyun Wang, Zhe Chen, Zhaoyang Liu, Shenglong Ye, Lixin Gu, Hao Tian, Yuchen Duan, Weijie Su, Jie Shao, Zhangwei Gao, Erfei Cui, Xuehui Wang, Yue Cao, Yangzhou Liu, Xingguang Wei, Hongjie Zhang, Haomin Wang, Weiye Xu, and 32 others. 2025. Internvl3: Exploring advanced training and test-time recipes for open-source multimodal models. *arXiv preprint arXiv:2504.10479.*

A Error Analysis Examples

All the samples shown below are from validation set.

Case 1: Low Quality Image

Example 1: Figure 3 shows an image with low visual resolution. Such figures may hinder model comprehension of fine-grained visual details, including axis labels and line plots, impacting the model's accuracy in visual question answering.

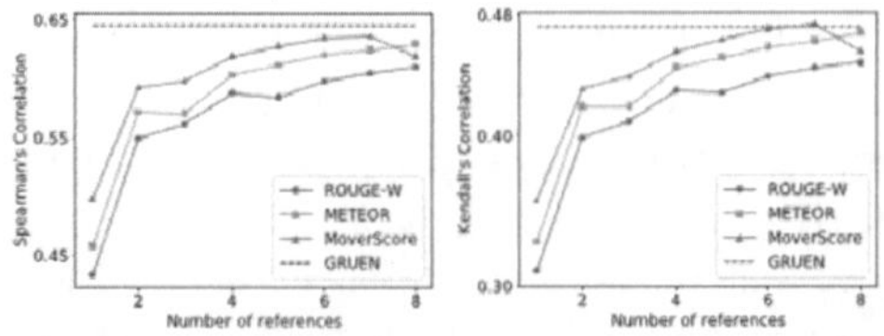

Figure 3: image_file : 2010.02498v1-Figure3-1.png

Case 2: Need for Additional Context Beyond Caption

Example 1: Figure 4 depicts a Q-network structure. The question requires reasoning beyond the figure and its caption. Without context, the model misinterprets the output of the Q-network.

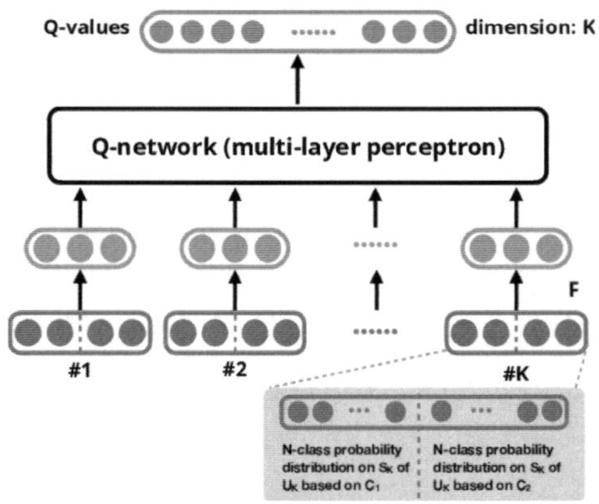

Figure 4: image_file : N18-1113.pdf-Figure3.png

Instance ID: `07a642e0d2e24761496b7e0a3b41d5fd`

Question: *Is 'Q-keys' the output of 'Q-network'?*

Caption: *Figure 3: The structure of Q-network. It chooses a unlabeled subset from U1, U2, ..., UK at each time step. The state representation is computed according to the two classifiers N -class probability distribution on the representative example Si of each subset Ui.*

Context Extracted from PDF: *The Q-value Q(st,a) is determined by a neural network as illustrated in Figure 3.*

Gold Answer: No

Model prediction without Context: Yes

Model prediction with Context: No

Explanation: In this example, the model initially struggled to produce the correct answer when relying solely on the image and its caption. The term "Q-keys" does not appear in the figure or caption, making it difficult to verify whether it is part of the Q-network's output. However, upon incorporating the additional textual context which explicitly states that "the Q-value Q(st, a) is determined by a neural network" the model is able to correctly infer that the Q-network's output is the Q-value, not "Q-keys". This additional information provides supporting clarification and helps leads to the correct answer.

Example 2: In Figure 5, the question requires semantic inference of correlation between social score and Airbnb penetration. The additional context helps the model to better comprehend this information.

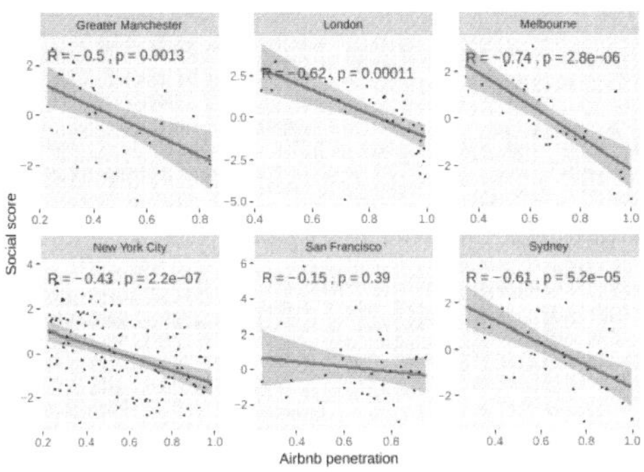

Figure 5: image_file : 2004.11604v1-Figure8-1.png

Instance ID: db801444b0b421e86bc07199fa465997

Question: *Is the social score negatively correlated with Airbnb penetration rate in every city?*

Caption: *Fig. 8: Social score against area Airbnb penetration rate (on a per city basis)*

Context Extracted from PDF: *Figure 8 shows the scatter plot (along with Pearson Correlation) between the Airbnb penetration rate and the social score for neighbourhoods in each city in our dataset. We observe that neighbourhoods with very high Airbnb adoption rates show lower social scores than those with lower penetration rates (Pearson correlation up to -0.74). Results are valid across all cities considered*

Gold Answer: Yes

Model prediction without Context: No

Model prediction with Context: Yes

Explanation: In this case, the model failed to produce the correct answer when limited to just the image and caption. The additional context, however, clearly asserts that the results are "valid across all cities considered" and quantifies the negative correlation (Pearson correlation up to -0.74). This reinforces the claim that high Airbnb penetration consistently corresponds to lower social scores in every city analyzed. With this information, the model is able to identify the presence of a negative correlation across all cities, showing that additional textual context can help the model in answering complex questions.

Case 3: Sample highlighting postprocessing module refinement
Example 1

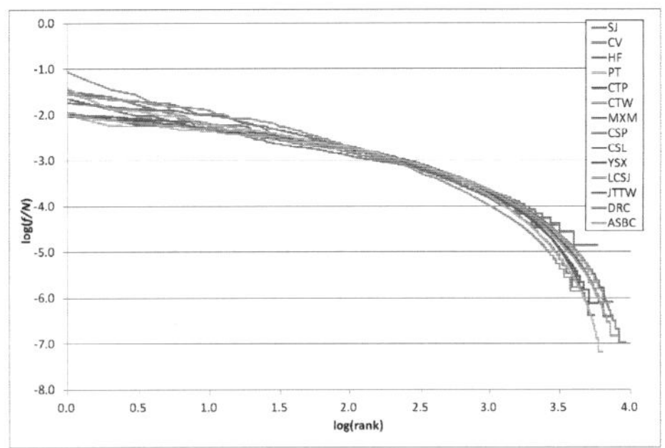

Figure 6: image_file : 1709.05587v1-Figure1-1.png

Instance ID: 6b81a93e1cce9b999b05564beda9ba52

Question: *What is the approximate value of log(f/N) for the blue line labeled 'DCR' at a log(rank) value of 3.5?*

reference figure: Figure 6

Gold Answer: -5

Model prediction before postprocessing step: between -4 and -6

Model prediction after postprocessing step: -5

Explanation: In this case, the model exhibited uncertainty regarding the exact answer and returned a range as output. Our heuristic based post processing module identified this pattern and replaced the range with a single scalar value, computing the mean of -4 and -6 to produce -5. The rationale behind this step is to standardize outputs and thereby improve the reliability and consistency of the evaluation process, which might benefit from precise answers for comparison against ground truth.

Coling-UniA at SciVQA 2025: Few-Shot Example Retrieval and Confidence-Informed Ensembling for Multimodal Large Language Models

Christian Jaumann **Annemarie Friedrich** **Rainer Lienhart**
University of Augsburg, Germany
{firstname.lastname}@uni-a.de

Abstract

This paper describes our system for the SciVQA 2025 Shared Task on Scientific Visual Question Answering. Our system employs an ensemble of two Multimodal Large Language Models and various few-shot example retrieval strategies. The model and few-shot setting are selected based on the figure and question type. We also select answers based on the models' confidence levels. On the blind test data, our system ranks third out of seven with an average F1 score of 85.12 across ROUGE-1, ROUGE-L, and BERTS. Our code is publicly available.[1]

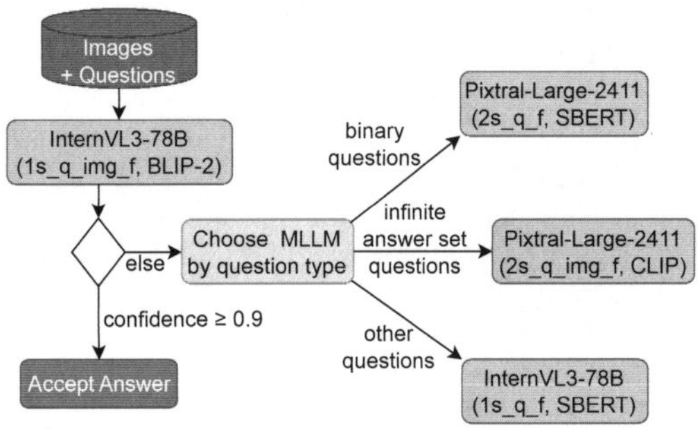

Figure 1: System overview. Abbreviations for few-shot example selection: #s = #-shot, q = question similarity, img = image similarity, f = filter for same figure type, nf = no filtering (search in entire train set).

1 Introduction

Visual Question Answering (VQA) requires systems to answer natural language questions about visual content. The complexity of these questions can range from binary questions to free-form and open-ended questions. Existing VQA datasets address various types of images, e.g., VQA v2 focuses on real-world photos (Goyal et al., 2017), DocVQA focuses on scanned documents (Mathew et al., 2021), while ChartQA (Masry et al., 2022) and PlotQA (Methani et al., 2020) focus on charts.

In this paper, we describe our system submission for the 2025 Shared Task on Scientific Visual Question Answering (SciVQA) (Borisova et al., 2025). The dataset[2] comprises 3000 real-world scientific figure images, which were collected from the ACL-Fig (Karishma et al., 2023) and SciGraphQA (Li and Tajbakhsh, 2023).

Most existing VQA approaches that focus on charts rely on models explicitly tuned for this domain (Liu et al., 2023; Han et al., 2023; Xia et al., 2024; Zhang et al., 2024). In contrast, our approach uses Multimodal Large Language Models (MLLMs) in a zero/few-shot setting without any fine-tuning. We test several strategies for retrieving few-shot examples from the training set based on question or question-and-image similarity. We find that performance varies widely by question/figure type and by MLLM. Our best-performing approach first selects highly confident answers from a configuration of an MLLM and a few-shot setting. For all remaining instances, the system configuration is varied by the instance's question type. In the official evaluation, our system ranks third.

2 Method

Our system is configurable to use different MLLMs in either a zero-shot or a few-shot setting. These settings are combined using an ensemble approach (see Figure 1) that first selects all high-confidence answers from a configuration that we find to be well-calibrated, i.e., the predicted confidence scores align well with the actual empirical accuracy on the development set. We approximate answer confidence by exponentiating the mean log-probability of all generated answer tokens. For the remaining instances, the model configuration is selected based on question type as identified on the development set. The MLLM is prompted with each image and the associated question (see Ap-

[1] https://github.com/coling-unia/few-shot-scivqa2025
[2] https://huggingface.co/datasets/katebor/SciVQA

Proceedings of the Fifth Workshop on Scholarly Document Processing (SDP 2025), pages 230–239
July 31, 2025

Rank	Submission	R1-F1	RL-F1	BS-F1	Avg.
1.	ExpertNeurons	80.49	80.43	98.49	86.47
2.	THAii_LAB	78.99	78.92	98.39	85.43
3.	**Coling-UniA**	78.62	78.56	98.17	85.12
	Median	75.83	75.75	98.36	83.31

Table 1: Overview of SciVQA@SDP 2025 results. Metrics: R1 = ROUGE-1, RL = ROUGE-L, BS = BERTS.

pendix A.2). Following the oracle-style setup of the Shared Task, we also provide the model with additional image metadata that is included in the dataset, i.e., the image caption, figure type, and whether the image contains multiple subfigures. The task description depends on whether there are pre-defined answer options for the questions. The model is instructed to answer and to determine whether it is possible to answer based solely on the provided information.

To enhance the reproducibility, our selection of MLLMs is constrained to open-weights models. We use InternVL3-78B (Zhu et al., 2025) and Pixtral-Large-Instruct-2411.[3] We run all models using 16-bit quantization and a temperature of 0.

Few-shot Example Retrieval. We evaluate different few-shot retrieval approaches. First, we use question similarity to select examples from the training data for the input instance. For ranking, we use the cosine similarities of the questions' SBERT embeddings (Reimers and Gurevych, 2019). Second, we select examples based on the question-image similarity using CLIP (Radford et al., 2021). We compute CLIP embeddings for each question and image, normalize them, compute the mean embedding of each image-question pair, normalize again, and determine the best-fit example using cosine similarity. We also experimented with computing similarities based on the image-question embeddings directly provided by BLIP-2 (Li et al., 2023). In case of similarity ties, we choose the first instance in the order as they are provided in the training set.

For both settings, we retrieve few-shot examples from the training set in two variants: (1) We consider only the subset of the training data that has the same figure type, and, if possible, the same number of sub-figures, as the input instance. (2) We search for few-shot examples in the entire training set. In both cases, we exclude all instances that use the input image from the set of few-shot candidates. We do not filter training data based on the question type. In the oracle-style setting of the Shared Task, it would have been possible to additionally filter based on question type. We do so only indirectly by searching for questions and images with high embedding similarity, which makes our approach more directly applicable to real-world scenarios, where the question type may not be provided. Moreover, the question type "unanswerable" directly reveals the gold answer.

Our retrieval method ranks instances. It can thus be used to retrieve an arbitrary number of few-shot examples. We evaluate the performance of these retrieval strategies in one-shot and two-shot settings. When using two examples, the model is given one answerable and one unanswerable example.

3 Development Results and Ablations

Since our approach does not require any fine-tuning, we combine the training and validation sets into one development set. This section describes our careful experimentation and ablation studies on the development set. For more information on the dataset, see Appendix A.3.

We rely on the metrics of the Shared Task, F1, Precision, and Recall of ROUGE-1, ROUGE-L (Lin, 2004), and BERTScore (BERTS, Zhang et al., 2020), respectively, to evaluate our approach. However, we focus on ROUGE-1 F1, as the BERTS scores are similar for all approaches, and the ROUGE-L scores are comparable to ROUGE-1.

We run our experiments on Nvidia A100 (80 GB) GPUs, using up to 4 GPUs in parallel. The total amount of GPU hours was about 3600h.

3.1 Retrieval of Few-Shot Examples

As shown in Figure 2, the degree to which the question type of the retrieved few-shot examples matches that of the input instance varies greatly by question type. Searching for examples using only question similarity leads to matching the input instance's question type far more often than searching using image and question similarity. However, this does not seem to make a marked difference in overall performance. We found BLIP-2's text-image embeddings to primarily reflect the image content, resulting in many ties.[4]

[3] https://huggingface.co/mistralai/Pixtral-Large-Instruct-2411

[4] Our tie-breaking strategy leads to instances of the question type "closed-ended infinite answer set visual" to be selected, which comes first in the training set ordering for each image.

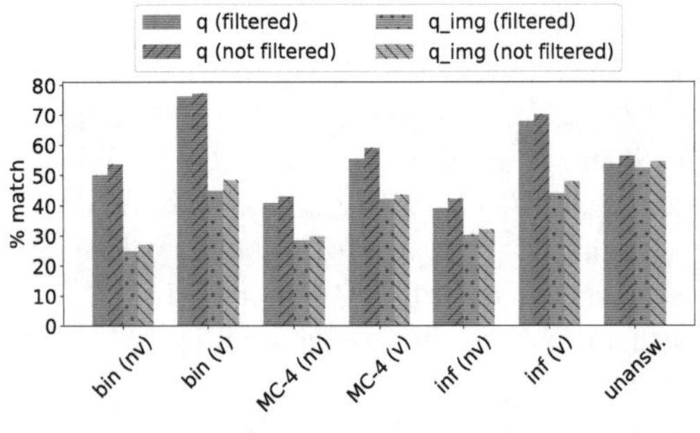

Figure 2: Percentage of selected one-shot example matching the question type of the input instance. bin = binary question, MC-4 = four answer options, inf = infinite answer set, unansw. = unanswerable, (v) = visual, (nv) = non-visual, filtered = filter for same figure type, not filtered = search in entire train set, q = question similarity, img = image similarity.

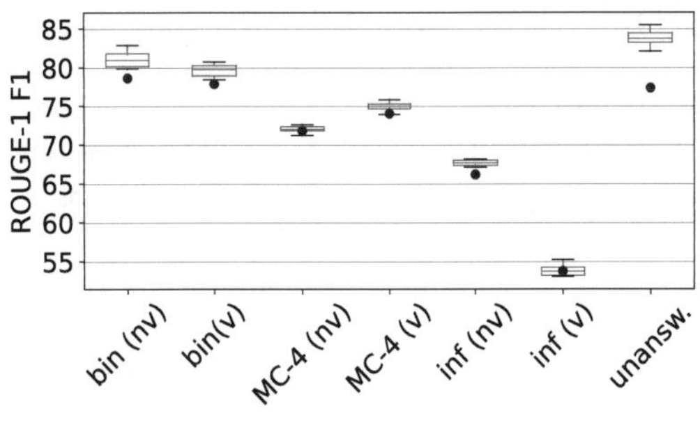

Figure 3: ROUGE-1 F1 scores per question type. Boxplot: 1-shot and 2-shot question and question+image similarity configurations of Pixtral-Large-2411. Blue dots = Pixtral-Large-2411 (0-shot).

3.2 Impact of Few-Shot Examples

Table 2 compares the effectiveness of InternVL3-78B and Pixtral-Large-2411 using various few-shot settings with that of our ensemble approaches. Adding few-shot examples generally improves performance. We cannot report 2-shot results for InternVL3-78B because its context window is too small to incorporate two examples. Comparing performance by question type reveals that adding examples can be highly beneficial, e.g., for recognizing unanswerable questions, though they can also be distracting (see Figure 3 or Appendix A.1). However, adding two examples is almost always beneficial. Furthermore, using one answerable and one unanswerable example helps the model to distinguish between these two types of instances, especially when compared to using only one example (see Table 3).

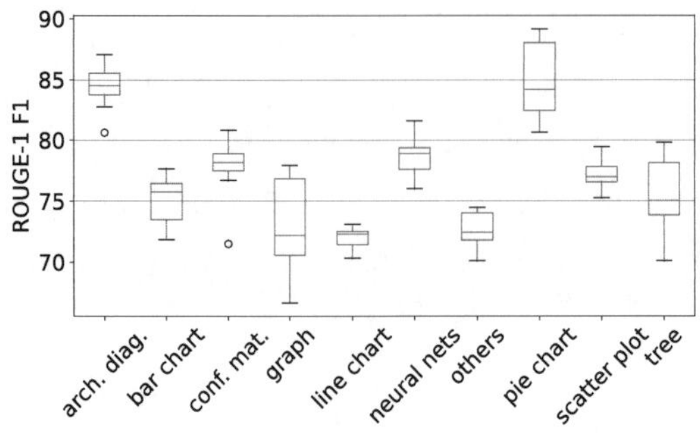

Figure 4: ROUGE-1 F1 scores per figure type of all configurations (zero- and few-shot) of both MLLMs visualized as boxplots.

3.3 Question/Figure Type Ensemble

To determine the best configuration of MLLM and few-shot strategy for each pair of question type and figure type, we systematically search for the optimal ensemble settings by obtaining and analyzing distributions of performance scores over subsets of the data similar to cross-validation.

While there appears to be a general trend of enhanced performance with the use of examples (see Table 2), our findings reveal considerable variations in the performance of our configurations across different question and figure types (see Figure 3 and Figure 4 or Appendix A.1). Therefore, we use the results on the development set to systematically identify the optimal combination of configurations that work well across as many subsets of the data as possible. The dataset consists of seven evenly represented question types and various figure types that are not evenly distributed. We record performance scores for each figure type separately. To avoid overfitting, we summarize all figure types that encompass less than two percent of the total number of figures into the figure type "others", which leads to nine groups with homogeneous figure types (line chart, tree, scatter plot, pie chart, bar chart, architecture diagram, neural networks, confusion matrix, graph) plus one group of the "others", i.e., 10 groups in total. For the largest figure type, i.e., line chart, we divide the data into seven groups by further dividing the data by question type. In total, we divide the data into 16 groups (8 homogeneous figure types, 1 "others", and 7 subsets with line charts).

We split the data of each group into 5 folds and compute performance scores. We repeat this process at least 10 times with different splits until the predicted best-performing configuration remains

Setting	Configuration	R1-F1	R1-P	R1-R	RL-F1	RL-P	RL-R	BS-F1	BS-P	BS-R
Individual runs (dev set)	InternVL (0s)	74.2	75.2	74.9	74.1	75.1	74.8	97.1	97.3	97.0
	InternVL (1s_q_f)	74.7	75.7	74.8	74.6	75.6	74.8	97.8	97.9	97.8
	InternVL (1s_q_nf)	74.5	75.5	74.6	74.4	75.4	74.6	97.8	97.8	97.7
	InternVL (1s_q_img_f)	74.8	75.6	**75.2**	74.7	75.6	**75.1**	97.8	97.8	97.8
	InternVL (1s_q_img_nf)	74.7	75.7	75.1	74.6	75.6	75.0	97.8	97.8	97.8
	InternVL (1s_q_img_f, BLIP2)	**75.0**	**76.0**	**75.2**	**74.9**	**76.0**	**75.1**	**97.9**	**98.0**	**97.9**
	Pixtral (0s)	71.4	72.5	72.4	71.2	72.4	72.2	96.3	96.6	96.0
	Pixtral (1s_q_f)	72.8	74.0	73.1	72.7	73.9	73.0	97.5	97.6	97.5
	Pixtral (1s_q_nf)	72.3	73.5	72.6	72.2	73.4	72.5	97.5	97.5	97.5
	Pixtral (1s_q_img_f)	72.8	74.1	73.1	72.7	74.0	73.0	97.4	97.5	97.3
	Pixtral (1s_q_img_nf)	72.8	74.0	73.2	72.7	73.9	73.1	97.4	97.5	97.3
	Pixtral (2s_q_f)	73.9	75.2	74.0	73.8	75.1	73.9	97.7	97.8	97.7
	Pixtral (2s_q_nf)	73.7	75.0	73.8	73.6	74.9	73.7	97.7	97.8	97.7
	Pixtral (2s_q_img_f)	74.1	75.5	74.2	74.0	75.4	74.1	97.7	97.8	97.6
	Pixtral (2s_q_img_nf)	73.8	75.2	73.9	73.7	75.1	73.8	97.6	97.8	97.6
Ensembles (dev set)	Question/Figure-Type Ensemble	76.6	78.0	76.5	76.5	77.8	76.4	97.9	98.0	**97.9**
	Confidence-Informed Ensemble	**76.9**	**78.2**	**76.8**	**76.8**	**78.1**	**76.8**	**98.0**	**98.1**	**97.9**
Results on test set	InvernVL (1s_q_img_f, BLIP2)	77.2	78.0	77.4	77.2	77.9	77.3	98.1	98.2	**98.1**
	Question/Figure-Type Ensemble	77.7	78.8	77.7	77.6	78.7	77.6	98.1	98.2	98.0
	Confidence-Informed Ensemble	**78.6**	**79.7**	**78.6**	**78.6**	**79.6**	**78.5**	**98.2**	**98.3**	**98.1**

Table 2: Results of individual runs vs. ensembles on development and test set. Abbreviations for few-shot example selection: #s = #-shot, q = question similarity, img = image similarity, f = filter for same figure type, nf = no filtering (search in entire train set). Metrics: R1 = ROUGE-1, RL = ROUGE-L, BS = BERTS, P = Precision, R = Recall. Question/Figure-Type Ensemble refers to the approach described in section 3.3 and Confidence-Informed Ensemble to that of section 3.4.

Approach	Precision
Pixtral (0s)	93.0
Pixtral (1s_q_f)	89.2
Pixtral (1s_q_img_f)	89.3
Pixtral (1s_q_img_nf)	90.3
Pixtral (1s_q_nf)	88.7
Pixtral (2s_q_f)	92.7
Pixtral (2s_q_img_f)	94.1
Pixtral (2s_q_img_nf)	93.7
Pixtral (2s_q_nf)	93.3

Table 3: Precision of instances predicted to be unanswerable.

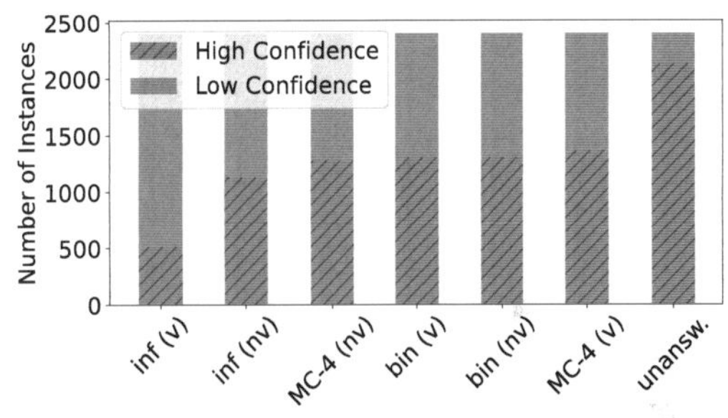

Figure 5: Number of instances having received high confidence answer of InternVL3-78B (1s_q_img_f, BLIP) by question type.

constant. In each fold, we calculate the ROUGE-1 F1 score for all configurations, then subtract the highest score achieved in that fold. For each configuration, we then compute the mean of these scores across all folds and all runs. The best-performing configuration is identified by the highest score. For the final chosen configuration of this ensemble, refer to Table 8 in Appendix A.1.

3.4 Confidence-Informed Ensemble

Figure 6 shows that InternVL3-78B (1s_q_img_f, BLIP2) with examples derived from BLIP-2, which focus primarily on image similarity as explained in Sec. 3.1, is meaningfully calibrated. This means that high confidence scores indicate highly likely correct instances (refer to Appendix A.1 for detailed results). Thus, for our final submission, we directly use all predictions from this model with a confidence score of at least 90%, which corresponds to approximately half of the instances, in the initial stage. As shown in Figure 5, the number of high-confidence instances varies by question type. The model is most confident on identifying unanswerable questions, while it is least sure about its answers for questions with infinite answers sets about the image's visual features. After removing high-confidence instances, the performance per question type varies widely between our configruations (see Appendix A.1 for detailed results). The best configuration per question type does not seem

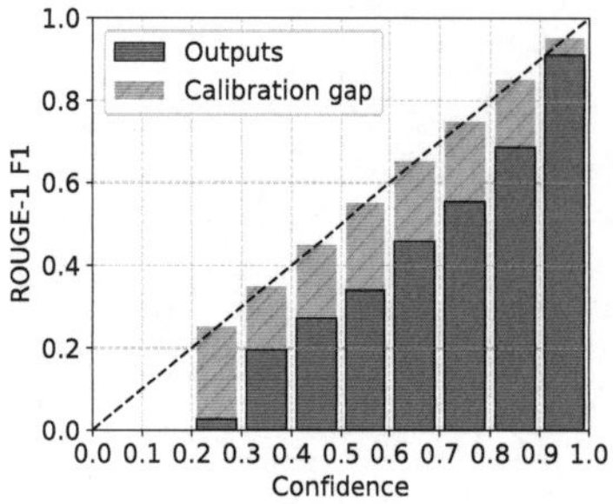

Figure 6: Calibration plot for InternVL3-78B (1s_q_img_f, BLIP) showing that instances with confidence score ≥ 0.9 have high expected accuracy.

to depend on whether the question incorporates visual or non-visual features. Since the vast majority of the remaining instances are of figure type *line chart*, we do not perform cross-validation to determine the optimal configuration of approaches. Instead, we select the best-performing approach for each question type, while also trying to reduce the number of approaches required.

As can be seen in Figure 1, we use the following models for the remaining instances: Pixtral-Large-2411 (2s_q_f) for binary questions, Pixtral-Large-2411 (2s_q_img_f) for questions with an infinite answer set, and InternVL3-78B (1s_q_f) for all others.

4 Results on Test Set

Table 2 also shows the results of our approaches on the test set, indicating that our ensembling strategies improve the performance compared to using only one approach to answer all questions. On the test set, we also find the confidence-informed ensemble to work best, while the question/figure type ensemble outperforms the simple InternVL model not as strongly as on the development set. The confidence-informed ensemble is the approach submitted for the leaderboard, ranking third in the official evaluation (almost on par with the second-ranking system) as shown in Table 1, and outperforming the baseline by about 4 percentage points.

5 Discussion and Conclusion

This paper described our submission to the SciVQA 2025 Shared Task. Our results show that MLLMs are highly effective at answering questions about scientific figures. However, performance varies greatly by question type. Results on finite answer sets are considerably better than on infinite ones. In particular, answering infinite answer set questions about visual features of images remains challenging, highlighting the need for a more sophisticated approach.

The use of few-shot examples improves performance. However, there are no major performance differences between retrieving the examples by question or question-image similarity.

Limitations

Since the ACL-Fig and SciGraphQA datasets, on which the figures in this Shared Task are based, rely on images published several years ago, some of these images may have already been exposed to MLLMs during training.

Another limitation is performance on unanswerable questions. Although our approach performed best on this question type, it is difficult to determine if it would perform equally well on real-world unanswerable questions. This is because the unanswerable questions in this dataset follow a different pattern than the answerable ones. For example, they mostly refer to material unavailable to the model and often do not focus on the images' visual/non-visual features.

Acknowledgments

The authors gratefully acknowledge the scientific support and HPC resources provided by the Erlangen National High Performance Computing Center (NHR@FAU) of the Friedrich-Alexander-Universität Erlangen-Nürnberg (FAU) under the BayernKI project v110ee. BayernKI funding is provided by Bavarian state authorities.

References

Ekaterina Borisova, Nikolas Rauscher, and Georg Rehm. 2025. SciVQA 2025: Overview of the first scientific visual question answering shared task. In *Proceedings of the 5th Workshop on Scholarly Document Processing (SDP)*, Vienna, Austria.

Yash Goyal, Tejas Khot, Douglas Summers-Stay, Dhruv Batra, and Devi Parikh. 2017. Making the V in VQA matter: Elevating the role of image understanding in visual question answering. In *2017 IEEE Conference on Computer Vision and Pattern Recognition, CVPR 2017, Honolulu, HI, USA, July 21-26, 2017*, pages 6325–6334. IEEE Computer Society.

Yucheng Han, Chi Zhang, Xin Chen, Xu Yang, Zhibin Wang, Gang Yu, Bin Fu, and Hanwang Zhang. 2023. Chartllama: A multimodal LLM for chart understanding and generation. *CoRR*, abs/2311.16483.

Zeba Karishma, Shaurya Rohatgi, Kavya Shrinivas Puranik, Jian Wu, and C. Lee Giles. 2023. Acl-fig: A dataset for scientific figure classification. In *Proceedings of the Workshop on Scientific Document Understanding co-located with 37th AAAI Conference on Artificial Inteligence (AAAI 2023), Remote, February 14, 2023*, volume 3656 of *CEUR Workshop Proceedings*. CEUR-WS.org.

Junnan Li, Dongxu Li, Silvio Savarese, and Steven C. H. Hoi. 2023. BLIP-2: bootstrapping language-image pre-training with frozen image encoders and large language models. In *International Conference on Machine Learning, ICML 2023, 23-29 July 2023, Honolulu, Hawaii, USA*, volume 202 of *Proceedings of Machine Learning Research*, pages 19730–19742. PMLR.

Shengzhi Li and Nima Tajbakhsh. 2023. Scigraphqa: A large-scale synthetic multi-turn question-answering dataset for scientific graphs. *CoRR*, abs/2308.03349.

Chin-Yew Lin. 2004. ROUGE: A package for automatic evaluation of summaries. In *Text Summarization Branches Out*, pages 74–81, Barcelona, Spain. Association for Computational Linguistics.

Fangyu Liu, Francesco Piccinno, Syrine Krichene, Chenxi Pang, Kenton Lee, Mandar Joshi, Yasemin Altun, Nigel Collier, and Julian Eisenschlos. 2023. MatCha: Enhancing visual language pretraining with math reasoning and chart derendering. In *Proceedings of the 61st Annual Meeting of the Association for Computational Linguistics (Volume 1: Long Papers)*, pages 12756–12770, Toronto, Canada. Association for Computational Linguistics.

Ahmed Masry, Xuan Long Do, Jia Qing Tan, Shafiq Joty, and Enamul Hoque. 2022. ChartQA: A benchmark for question answering about charts with visual and logical reasoning. In *Findings of the Association for Computational Linguistics: ACL 2022*, pages 2263–2279, Dublin, Ireland. Association for Computational Linguistics.

Minesh Mathew, Dimosthenis Karatzas, and C. V. Jawahar. 2021. Docvqa: A dataset for VQA on document images. In *IEEE Winter Conference on Applications of Computer Vision, WACV 2021, Waikoloa, HI, USA, January 3-8, 2021*, pages 2199–2208. IEEE.

Nitesh Methani, Pritha Ganguly, Mitesh M. Khapra, and Pratyush Kumar. 2020. Plotqa: Reasoning over scientific plots. In *IEEE Winter Conference on Applications of Computer Vision, WACV 2020, Snowmass Village, CO, USA, March 1-5, 2020*, pages 1516–1525. IEEE.

Alec Radford, Jong Wook Kim, Chris Hallacy, Aditya Ramesh, Gabriel Goh, Sandhini Agarwal, Girish Sastry, Amanda Askell, Pamela Mishkin, Jack Clark, Gretchen Krueger, and Ilya Sutskever. 2021. Learning transferable visual models from natural language supervision. In *Proceedings of the 38th International Conference on Machine Learning, ICML 2021, 18-24 July 2021, Virtual Event*, volume 139 of *Proceedings of Machine Learning Research*, pages 8748–8763. PMLR.

Nils Reimers and Iryna Gurevych. 2019. Sentence-bert: Sentence embeddings using siamese bert-networks. In *Proceedings of the 2019 Conference on Empirical Methods in Natural Language Processing*. Association for Computational Linguistics.

Renqiu Xia, Bo Zhang, Hancheng Ye, Xiangchao Yan, Qi Liu, Hongbin Zhou, Zijun Chen, Min Dou, Botian Shi, Junchi Yan, and Yu Qiao. 2024. Chartx & chartvlm: A versatile benchmark and foundation model for complicated chart reasoning. *CoRR*, abs/2402.12185.

Liang Zhang, Anwen Hu, Haiyang Xu, Ming Yan, Yichen Xu, Qin Jin, Ji Zhang, and Fei Huang. 2024. Tinychart: Efficient chart understanding with program-of-thoughts learning and visual token merging. In *Proceedings of the 2024 Conference on Empirical Methods in Natural Language Processing, EMNLP 2024, Miami, FL, USA, November 12-16, 2024*, pages 1882–1898. Association for Computational Linguistics.

Tianyi Zhang, Varsha Kishore, Felix Wu, Kilian Q. Weinberger, and Yoav Artzi. 2020. Bertscore: Evaluating text generation with BERT. In *8th International Conference on Learning Representations, ICLR 2020, Addis Ababa, Ethiopia, April 26-30, 2020*. OpenReview.net.

Jinguo Zhu, Weiyun Wang, Zhe Chen, Zhaoyang Liu, Shenglong Ye, Lixin Gu, Yuchen Duan, Hao Tian, Weijie Su, Jie Shao, and 1 others. 2025. Internvl3: Exploring advanced training and test-time recipes for open-source multimodal models. *arXiv preprint arXiv:2504.10479*.

A Appendix

A.1 Detailed Results on Development Set

Table 4 shows the detailed results of the different zero- and few-shot approaches on the development set, broken down by question type. Performance varies greatly between question types, indicating that questions with an infinite answer set are more difficult. Furthermore, performance depends on the MLLM and few-shot configuration used. Mostly, using examples is beneficial for performance.

As shown in Table 5, the performance of the different configurations also depends on the figure type of the image.

Table 6 reports the ROUGE-1 F1 score per confidence bin and the relative proportion of respective bin of the development set. Interestingly, the configuration that uses BLIP-2 to retrieve similar examples is well-calibrated for high confidence. In general, InternVL3-78B appears to be better calibrated than Pixtral-Large-2411 for our task.

The performance of different approaches per question type can be seen in Table 7 after having removed all instances of InternvL3-78B (1s_q_img_f, BLIP) with a confidence of $\geq 90\%$. Performance is worse compared to Table 4 since the high confidence answers are removed. Nevertheless, there are still large performance differences between the different approaches.

Table 8 shows the best configurations per figure and question type identified via cross-validation for the Question/Figure Type Ensemble.

A.2 Detailed Prompt

Figure 7 shows the prompt used in our approach. Its formatting depends on the annotated metadata, i.e., whether the instance has annotated answer options and whether the figure consists of multiple subfigures.

A.3 Dataset Characteristics

The dataset consists of 3000 real-world figures extracted from English scientific publications available in the ACL Anthology and arXiv. The figures can be categorized into different figure types such as *line chart*, *tree*, or *scatter plot*. These figure types are not evenly distributed. For example, *line chart* makes up 65% of all figures in the development set (see Figure 8).

Each figure is annotated with seven questions. Two binary questions (one focusing on visual features and one focusing on non-visual features), two questions with four answer options respectively (one visual and one non-visual), two questions with infinite answer sets (one visual and one non-visual), and one unanswerable question. The unanswerable questions are not subdivided into visual and non-visual questions, and they generally follow a different pattern than the answerable ones. For example, they mostly refer to material unavailable to the model and often do not focus on the images' visual/non-visual features.

Approach	binary (nv)	binary(v)	MC-4 (nv)	MC-4 (v)	inf (nv)	inf (v)	unanswerable
InternVL (0s)	78.9	80.9	76.6	79.3	66.4	51.2	86.2
InternVL (1s_q_f)	82.0	80.8	**76.9**	**79.9**	63.4	49.3	90.4
InternVL (1s_q_nf)	82.0	81.0	76.3	79.1	63.5	50.0	89.5
InternVL (1s_q_img_f)	80.4	**81.3**	76.3	79.3	65.3	49.5	**91.2**
InternVL (1s_q_img_nf)	80.6	80.8	76.3	78.6	65.7	50.1	91.0
InternVL (1s_q_img_f, BLIP)	82.7	80.6	76.7	79.0	67.4	51.8	87.0
Pixtral (0s)	78.6	77.9	71.8	74.0	66.2	53.8	77.4
Pixtral (1s_q_f)	80.2	79.5	71.7	73.9	67.4	53.4	83.4
Pixtral (1s_q_nf)	79.9	78.5	71.2	74.1	67.5	53.1	82.0
Pixtral (1s_q_img_f)	80.3	79.0	71.9	75.0	67.1	53.1	83.2
Pixtral (1s_q_img_nf)	79.9	79.0	72.3	75.1	67.3	53.2	83.0
Pixtral (2s_q_f)	**82.9**	80.7	72.1	74.9	**68.1**	54.0	84.4
Pixtral (2s_q_nf)	82.1	80.3	71.9	75.0	68.0	54.6	84.0
Pixtral (2s_q_img_f)	81.5	80.4	72.6	75.8	67.9	**55.2**	85.4
Pixtral (2s_q_img_nf)	81.6	80.0	72.4	75.9	**68.1**	54.1	84.5

Table 4: Results (ROUGE-1 F1 scores) on development set by question type. v=visual, nv= non-visual.

Approach	architecture diagram	bar chart	confusion matrix	graph	line chart	neural networks	others	pie chart	scatter plot	tree
InternVL (0s)	83.9	**77.7**	77.0	75.4	72.2	78.9	73.4	87.4	78.0	76.2
InternVL (1s_q_f)	86.2	77.3	76.7	76.8	72.5	79.2	**74.5**	**89.2**	75.6	78.6
InternVL (1s_q_nf)	85.0	76.4	78.6	77.4	72.5	79.2	73.4	88.0	76.2	77.8
InternVL (1s_q_img_f)	86.2	76.6	78.4	77.7	72.6	78.8	74.4	88.7	77.1	78.2
InternVL (1s_q_img_nf)	85.4	76.1	78.3	**78.0**	72.6	79.7	73.9	88.0	76.9	**79.2**
InternVL (1s_q_img_f, BLIP)	**87.0**	76.3	78.8	77.1	**72.8**	**81.6**	74.4	88.1	77.9	78.1
Pixtral (0s)	80.6	72.8	71.5	66.7	70.3	76.0	70.1	82.8	75.3	70.1
Pixtral (1s_q_f)	84.7	73.8	77.5	67.9	71.3	77.5	72.0	82.1	76.7	73.5
Pixtral (1s_q_nf)	83.3	73.4	77.7	69.8	71.0	77.1	70.3	81.6	75.7	72.6
Pixtral (1s_q_img_f)	82.8	73.3	78.1	70.7	71.4	77.7	71.4	80.9	76.9	73.9
Pixtral (1s_q_img_nf)	84.1	71.8	78.0	70.3	71.5	76.2	71.6	80.6	76.9	74.3
Pixtral (2s_q_f)	83.6	76.2	79.9	71.4	72.3	79.6	72.7	82.6	77.4	74.5
Pixtral (2s_q_nf)	83.9	73.5	77.4	72.6	72.3	78.6	72.3	83.7	77.8	74.2
Pixtral (2s_q_img_f)	85.2	75.4	80.4	71.7	72.5	78.9	71.9	84.4	**78.9**	75.7
Pixtral (2s_q_img_nf)	84.3	74.2	**80.8**	71.3	72.3	79.3	72.2	84.0	77.6	73.8

Table 5: Results (ROUGE-1 F1 scores) on development set by figure type.

Approach	0.3_0.4	0.4_0.5	0.5_0.6	0.6_0.7	0.7_0.8	0.8_0.9	0.9_1.0
InternVL (0s)	15.2 (0.1)	**34.5** (1.2)	**48.7** (5.3)	**55.4** (13.6)	**69.9** (21.2)	**73.3** (18.2)	87.9 (40.4)
InternVL (1s_q_f)	18.5 (0.1)	30.2 (0.8)	30.3 (2.9)	45.4 (7.4)	56.8 (14.1)	66.4 (16.2)	88.0 (58.5)
InternVL (1s_q_nf)	22.9 (0.1)	25.0 (0.9)	31.1 (3.1)	45.5 (7.2)	55.5 (14.1)	66.3 (16.2)	88.1 (58.4)
InternVL (1s_q_img_f)	21.2 (0.1)	30.9 (0.8)	37.6 (3.4)	48.8 (8.4)	57.6 (14.8)	68.6 (16.5)	88.1 (55.9)
InternVL (1s_q_img_nf)	15.9 (0.1)	28.3 (0.8)	38.7 (3.3)	48.1 (8.4)	56.1 (14.7)	69.2 (16.7)	88.3 (55.9)
InternVL (1s_q_img_f, BLIP)	19.6 (0.2)	27.3 (1.0)	34.0 (3.5)	45.8 (8.3)	55.4 (15.3)	68.6 (17.8)	**91.1** (53.9)
Pixtral (0s)	**25.0** (0.0)	24.7 (0.3)	34.6 (1.8)	45.4 (6.0)	61.2 (17.3)	64.5 (24.6)	83.0 (50.0)
Pixtral (1s_q_f)	0.0 (0.0)	31.1 (0.3)	33.7 (1.6)	43.3 (5.6)	54.6 (13.4)	61.8 (19.9)	84.7 (59.2)
Pixtral (1s_q_nf)	11.4 (0.0)	32.6 (0.3)	32.8 (1.6)	42.1 (5.6)	52.9 (13.5)	61.7 (19.9)	84.5 (59.1)
Pixtral (1s_q_img_f)	16.3 (0.0)	25.8 (0.3)	39.5 (1.8)	45.5 (6.2)	55.9 (13.8)	62.9 (20.8)	84.8 (57.1)
Pixtral (1s_q_img_nf)	19.0 (0.0)	23.5 (0.3)	40.0 (1.7)	46.9 (6.2)	54.3 (14.0)	63.2 (20.5)	85.0 (57.1)
Pixtral (2s_q_f)	0.0 (0.0)	24.1 (0.2)	37.8 (1.2)	40.8 (4.6)	52.8 (12.3)	62.1 (19.2)	84.9 (62.5)
Pixtral (2s_q_nf)	0.0 (0.0)	20.1 (0.2)	31.4 (1.2)	42.3 (4.6)	52.3 (11.8)	60.9 (19.6)	85.0 (62.6)
Pixtral (2s_q_img_f)	14.3 (0.0)	25.6 (0.1)	33.6 (1.4)	47.2 (5.2)	55.1 (12.6)	61.9 (20.3)	85.6 (60.4)
Pixtral (2s_q_img_nf)	0.0 (0.0)	28.8 (0.2)	34.2 (1.4)	42.8 (5.1)	52.6 (12.8)	63.1 (19.9)	85.4 (60.7)

Table 6: Results (ROUGE-1 F1 scores) per confidence bin. The values in brackets indicate the relative proportion of instances in each bin.

Approach	binary (nv)	binary(v)	MC-4 (nv)	MC-4 (v)	inf (nv)	inf (v)	unanswerable
InternVL (0s)	64.8	68.8	60.6	62.0	50.6	45.0	34.3
InternVL (1s_q_f)	70.7	68.3	**61.0**	**63.1**	46.9	42.0	48.6
InternVL (1s_q_img_f)	67.8	69.2	60.1	62.2	49.9	42.3	50.2
InternVL (1s_q_img_nf)	68.2	67.9	59.6	60.8	50.1	43.0	**50.8**
InternVL (1s_q_nf)	70.2	68.5	60.4	62.0	47.3	42.8	42.8
Pixtral (0s)	67.8	67.1	58.1	58.4	52.3	48.1	29.8
Pixtral (1s_q_f)	70.3	68.9	57.2	57.7	53.8	48.0	38.2
Pixtral (1s_q_img_f)	71.4	69.0	57.6	59.2	53.8	48.0	32.2
Pixtral (1s_q_img_nf)	70.3	68.0	58.8	59.3	53.8	48.1	33.1
Pixtral (1s_q_nf)	70.1	67.0	56.8	58.1	53.6	47.8	34.7
Pixtral (2s_q_f)	**74.0**	**70.8**	57.5	58.9	54.8	48.4	36.8
Pixtral (2s_q_img_f)	72.5	69.4	58.2	59.9	55.2	**49.5**	39.0
Pixtral (2s_q_img_nf)	72.7	69.0	58.4	60.0	**55.4**	48.4	35.8
Pixtral (2s_q_nf)	73.2	69.9	57.4	59.0	54.5	**49.5**	37.0

Table 7: Results (ROUGE-1 F1 scores) on development set by question type after removing high confidence instances of run with InternVL3-78B (1s_q_img_f with BLIP-2).

Figure Type	inf (v)	inf (nv)	bin (v)	bin (nv)	MC-4 (v)	MC-4 (nv)	unansw.
line chart	Pixtral (2s_q_img_f)	Pixtral (2s_q_nf)	Pixtral (2s_q_f)	Pixtral (2s_q_f)	InternVL (1s_q_f)	InternVL (1s_q_f)	InternVL (1s_q_img_f)
tree	InternVL (1s_q_img_nf)	InternVL (1s_q_img_nf)	InternVL (1s_q_img_nf)	InternVL (1s_q_img_nf)	InternVL (1s_q_img_nf)	InternVL (1s_q_img_nf)	InternVL (1s_q_img_nf)
scatter plot	Pixtral (2s_q_img_f)	Pixtral (2s_q_img_f)	Pixtral (2s_q_img_f)	Pixtral (2s_q_img_f)	Pixtral (2s_q_img_f)	Pixtral (2s_q_img_f)	Pixtral (2s_q_img_f)
pie chart	InternVL (1s_q_f)	InternVL (1s_q_f)	InternVL (1s_q_f)	InternVL (1s_q_f)	InternVL (1s_q_f)	InternVL (1s_q_f)	InternVL (1s_q_f)
bar chart	InternVL (0s)	InternVL (0s)	InternVL (0s)	InternVL (0s)	InternVL (0s)	InternVL (0s)	InternVL (0s)
architecture diagram	InternVL (1s_q_f)	InternVL (1s_q_f)	InternVL (1s_q_f)	InternVL (1s_q_f)	InternVL (1s_q_f)	InternVL (1s_q_f)	InternVL (1s_q_f)
neural networks	InternVL (1s_q_img_nf)	InternVL (1s_q_img_nf)	InternVL (1s_q_img_nf)	InternVL (1s_q_img_nf)	InternVL (1s_q_img_nf)	InternVL (1s_q_img_nf)	InternVL (1s_q_img_nf)
confusion matrix	Pixtral (2s_q_img_nf)	Pixtral (2s_q_img_nf)	Pixtral (2s_q_img_nf)	Pixtral (2s_q_img_nf)	Pixtral (2s_q_img_nf)	Pixtral (2s_q_img_nf)	Pixtral (2s_q_img_nf)
graph	InternVL (1s_q_img_nf)	InternVL (1s_q_img_nf)	InternVL (1s_q_img_nf)	InternVL (1s_q_img_nf)	InternVL (1s_q_img_nf)	InternVL (1s_q_img_nf)	InternVL (1s_q_img_nf)
others	InternVL (1s_q_f)	InternVL (1s_q_f)	InternVL (1s_q_f)	InternVL (1s_q_f)	InternVL (1s_q_f)	InternVL (1s_q_f)	InternVL (1s_q_f)

Table 8: Best configurations for combination of figure type and question type identified via cross-validation for Question/Figure Type Ensemble.

System Message: You are an assistant answering questions about (semi-)structured figures such as charts and diagrams. Answer the question as precisely as possible.
User Message: Image: {image}
Question: '{question}'

```
if image_metadata['answer_options']:
    Answer options: {answer_options}
```

Additional Information:

- The caption of the image is 'image_metadata['caption']'.

```
if image_metadata["compound"]:
    - The figure image contains {image_metadata['figs_numb']} (sub)figures which can be separated and constitute individual figures.
else:
    - The figure image contains a single figure object which cannot be decomposed into multiple subfigures.
```

- The figure type is '{image_metadata['figure_type']}'.

Task:
You are presented with a figure and an associated question.

```
if image_metadata['answer_options:']:
    Your task is to select the correct answer options based on the figure. One or more answer options are correct. Only respond with
    the key(s) of the correct answer option(s), so e.g., 'A,C' if answer options A and C are correct.
else:
    Your task is to answer the question based on the figure.
```

You should only use the information in the figure to answer the question. Do not use any external knowledge or information. If the figure does not provide enough information to answer the question, respond with 'It is not possible to answer this question based only on the provided data.'. If you can answer the question, simply provide the answer without further explanation and do not repeat the question.
Answer:

Figure 7: The zero-shot prompt is formatted based on the annotated metadata via conditional statements. The MLLM is not given the if-else logic; it is only given the indented text inside the block. Bold text is not part of the prompt for the LLM either; it only indicates which parts of the prompt belong to the system or user message. Values in brackets are placeholders for the respective instance's actual values.

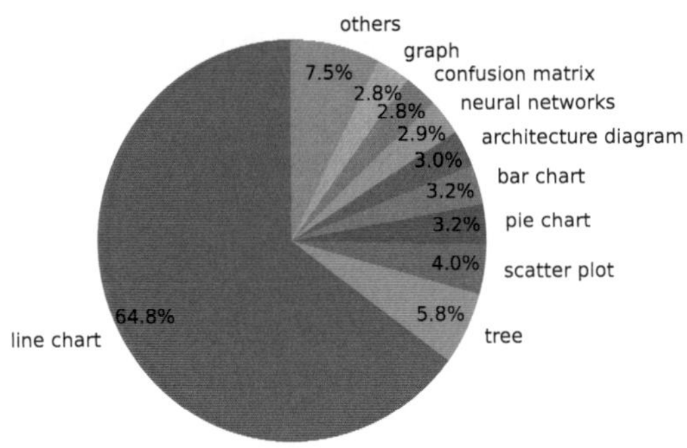

Figure 8: Figure type distribution on development set.

Instruction-tuned QwenChart for Chart Question Answering

Viviana Ventura, Lukas Kleybolte, Alessandra Zarcone
Technische Hochschule Augsburg
`viviana.ventura, lukas.kleybolte, alessandra.zarcone@tha.de`

Abstract

Charts, where information is delivered jointly by visual and textual features, represent a challenge when it comes to downstream tasks such as chart question answering, where both kinds of information contribute to the task. The standard approach is to decouple the task in two steps, first extracting information from the charts, or representing it as a table, text or code, and then a second reasoning step to output the answers. Today, the advancements in visual encoding of Visual Large Language Models (VLLM) have shown their capabilities to solve such complex tasks without using in-between representations of the charts or massive in-domain training. We propose a solution for the Scientific Visual Question Answering (SciVQA) Shared Task, on which our team THAii_LAB scored the second position in the final leaderboard. Our new instruction fine-tuned and Chain-of-Thought (CoT) model QwenChart-7B showed that even in a complex new benchmark general models can achieve great performances with low-cost training, matching the capabilities that LLMs have showed in unimodal downstream tasks. An out-of-domain evaluation showed satisfactory results, albeit with an expected drop in performance.

1 Introduction

Everything in a chart conveys information: besides labels such as numbers or text, they feature shapes, colors and complex visual elements such as bars, lines or points that contribute to the delivery of their meaning. Understanding complex texts such as scientific articles also requires chart comprehension, including answering questions about charts in natural language (QA over charts or chart QA). To tackle this task, previous work has focused on two main aspects: information extraction from charts and complex, often logical or arithmetic, reasoning over that information.

Early approaches would identify and extract information to feed into a classifier (Kafle et al., 2018; Chaudhry et al., 2020). Since the rise of Visual Large Language Models (VLLMs), many approaches convert charts into a format suitable for a language model, such as text descriptions, (Liu et al., 2023a), tables, or code (Lee et al., 2023; Liu et al., 2023b; He et al., 2025), due to the limited resolution capability of the visual encoders, and the conversely great capabilities of the LLMs. While using tables instead of images leads to some information loss, this approach still remains preferable.

Despite reaching satisfactory performance in general visual understanding tasks, VLLMs have struggled with downstream chart understanding tasks (Huang et al., 2024; Islam et al., 2024; Li et al., 2024a; Lu et al., 2024; Xu et al., 2025a,b). VLLMs usually consist of a visual encoder and a language decoder. The complexity of the visual features of charts represents a bottleneck for visual encoders, whereas the language decoder struggles to extract the necessary information from the visual representations due to the complexity of the relations between visual and linguistic elements (Liu et al., 2025). A common approach today involves augmenting data with task-specific instructions and fine-tuning a pre-trained model accordingly (Han et al., 2023; Islam et al., 2024; Liu et al., 2024; Masry et al., 2024, 2025). Some researchers have also opted to train the visual encoder using chart–table pairs to enhance its representational capabilities (Han et al., 2023; Islam et al., 2024; Liu et al., 2024; Masry et al., 2024, 2025; Xu et al., 2025b).

Borisova et al. (2025) introduced the Scientific Visual Question Answering (SciVQA) shared task[1], designed to evaluate multi-modal QA systems on real-world scientific figures through a diverse set of

[1] `https://www.codabench.org/competitions/5904/#/pages-tab`

Proceedings of the Fifth Workshop on Scholarly Document Processing (SDP 2025), pages 240–251
July 31, 2025 ©2025 Association for Computational Linguistics

both finite and infinite questions. The task emphasizes reasoning over complex visualizations and includes chart types rarely represented in earlier datasets, such as architecture diagrams, confusion matrices, and compound figures. In this context, we propose QwenChart-7B, a vision-language model specifically designed for the SciVQA task which achieved second place in the competition.

QwenChart-7B has been instruction-tuned with Low Rank Adaptation (LoRa, Hu et al. 2021) and exploits Chain-of-Thought (CoT, Wei et al., 2022) to improve its reasoning capabilities. We show that QwenChart-7B is capable of achieving good performance in chart QA without pretraining on domain data or using in-between representations of charts, such as tables. Furthermore, we show that scaling size of the model does not have a great impact on performance and identify what parameters mostly contribute to the performance of the model. Our model is one of the first visual models reaching high performance on a challenging benchmarks such as SciVQA without using intermediate representations of charts.

Our contributions are the following:

- a new instruction-tuned VLLM (QwenChart-7B) that achieves high scores in a challenging benchmark such as SciVQA, reaching the second place in the SciVQA shared task;
- several experiments, showing the influence of parameters, size of the model and additional information in the training data during fine-tuning.

2 Related work

2.1 Data and Benchmarks

Early benchmarks for chart QA included a limited variety of charts, more often synthetically generated than derived from real-world sources. DVQA (Kafle et al., 2018) and FigureQA (Kahou et al., 2018) are the first datasets for factoid QA over synthetically generated line, bar, and pie charts. Early datasets provided an alignment with structured auxiliary data such as numerical data or tables (Kahou et al., 2018; Masry et al., 2022), which was necessary to compensate for the lack of sufficiently robust methods to directly extract graph components (Luo et al., 2021; Rane et al., 2021; Kato et al., 2022).

ChartQA (Masry et al., 2022) is one of the most widely used benchmarks for chart understanding and features both synthetically generated and real-world graphs.

SciVQA[2] (Borisova et al., 2025) is a new chart corpus built from two pre-existing datasets, ACL-Fig (Karishma et al., 2023) and SciGraphQA (Li and Tajbakhsh, 2023). The 3000 figures are from English scientific publications from the ACL Anthology[3] and arXiv[4]. Unlike other datasets, it is composed exclusively of real-world figures, rather than synthetic data and features a wide variety of figure types, including trees, architecture diagrams, neural networks, confusion matrices, scatter plots, and box plots. In addition, it is annotated both with finite and infinite questions, as well as unanswerable questions. The figures are paired with captions and chart types as additional metadata. An additional challenge in SciVQA are figures with more than one chart.

2.2 Limitations of VLLMs in chart QA

Despite recent advancements in tasks such as image understanding brought forward by the emergence of VLLMs, QA over charts remains challenging. Typical approaches focus on two different aspects: (1) understanding the chart, that is extracting its meaningful components, such as numbers, labels but also shape, colors and position of points and (2) reasoning over the extracted information, for example, to compute mathematical operations based on numbers extracted from the figures.

Early approaches used encoder-only classification-based models to encode chart and question separately, and combining them later with attention blocks (Kafle et al., 2018; Chaudhry et al., 2020; Singh and Shekhar, 2020), but were often limited as they had a fixed output vocabulary (Santoro et al., 2017; Kafle et al., 2018; Kahou et al., 2018).

Recently, VLLMs have demonstrated remarkable capabilities in various chart comprehension tasks, outperforming specialized models (Huang et al., 2024), such as ChartBERT (Akhtar et al., 2023), MatCha (Liu et al., 2023b) or UniChart (Masry et al., 2023). However, VLLMs are not as good at chart understanding as they are in other visual tasks (Huang et al., 2024; Islam et al., 2024; Li et al., 2024a; Lu et al., 2024; Xu et al., 2025a,b).

[2] https://huggingface.co/datasets/katebor/SciVQA

[3] https://aclanthology.org

[4] https://arxiv.org

Proprietary models such as GPT-V[5], Gemini (Team et al., 2025) and Claude[6] currently achieve the best results in zero-shot scenarios in most of vision-language benchmarks, showing strong zero/few shot inference capabilities. Models such as GPT-4o[7] have shown unprecedented performance in chart understanding compared to open-source models (Islam et al., 2024; Wang et al., 2024), such as Phi-3 (Abdin et al., 2024) or LlaVA (Liu et al., 2023c). However, the performance is not comparable to that achieved in non-visual tasks.

There are two major bottlenecks in chart understanding: the perception capabilities of existing VLLMs are limited (Razeghi et al., 2024; Zhang et al., 2024b), and they fail in extracting the necessary information from the provided visual representations (Liu et al., 2025). Therefore, the state of the art approach separate a vision encoder and a text decoder stage, with a stronger focus on the former or the latter. Common approaches are to transform charts into structured formats, such as tables, code, and text (Lee et al., 2023; Liu et al., 2023a,b; Zhou et al., 2023), as a bridge to a text decoder to leverage the power of LLM in reasoning.

Some authors have stressed the impact of input resolution on pre-training and fine-tuning (Zhang et al., 2024a). The standard procedure would be to resize images into fixed resolution to reduce the length of the visual feature sequence. However, high and native resolution are essentials for chart understanding. Models such as Tinychart (Zhang et al., 2024a) tried to solve this issue merging visual tokens inside each vision transformer layer.

2.3 Instruction-tuned VLLMs

Some authors point out that VLLMs still struggle in analyzing charts due to the weak alignment between vision and language caused by the lack of charts in pre-trained model data (Xu et al., 2025b).

Recently, many VLLMs models have been trained on charts to improve their representations including ChartLLaMa (Han et al., 2023), ChartAssistant (Islam et al., 2024), MMC (Liu et al., 2024), ChartInstruct (Masry et al., 2024), and ChartGemma (Masry et al., 2025).

Besides being trained on charts, all these models follow the same methodology: they use chart-specific instruction tuning[8] to enhance the extraction capability of the language decoder (Liu et al., 2023c; Islam et al., 2024; Liu et al., 2024; Masry et al., 2024, 2025). With instruction tuning the model should learn to understand and internally represent the components of a chart, such as axes, labels, bars, trends. Hence, the first step is to augment dataset of charts with instructions, rationales or CoT data (Wang et al., 2023; Carbune et al., 2024; Huang et al., 2024; Jia et al., 2024; Li et al., 2024b; Kim et al., 2025; Wang et al., 2025).

While showing promising results, models which are fine-tuned on task-specific datasets show their limits when it comes to generalizing on unseen data.

3 QwenChart

3.1 Model Architecture

To develop our model[9], **QwenChart**, we fine-tuned Qwen2.5-VL (Bai et al., 2025) using LoRa (Hu et al., 2021) on an instruction-based chart dataset generated via dynamic CoT prompting (Wei et al., 2022). With LoRa, the original model weights are frozen and only a few new parameters are trained. Instead of updating all the weights in a large matrix, LoRa inserts small trainable matrices that approximate the change, thus maintaining the capabilities of the original model intact while reducing the computational cost. Our dataset comprises chart images and associated metadata from the SciVQA dataset (Borisova et al., 2025). Section 3.2 describes the process we followed to augment SciVQA.

Our model is particularly suited for chart tasks thanks to the dynamic encoding, i.e., the ability to receive images with different sizes as input without the need for normalization. As discussed in Section 2.2, native and high resolution are two important features for chart understanding. Bai et al. (2025) trained a Vision Transformer (ViT, Dosovitskiy et al. 2021) from scratch with native dynamic encoding to maintain images (or videos) with native resolution. They also incorporate a Window Attention in the ViT. The model comes in 4 sizes: 3B, 7B, 32B and 72B. We used the 7B model and compared it with the 72B. The model is composed by a visual encoder, a cross-modal projector and a text decoder.

[5]https://openai.com/index/gpt-4v-system-card/

[6]https://www.anthropic.com/news/claude-3-family

[7]https://openai.com/index/hello-gpt-4o/

[8]Llava (Liu et al., 2023c) is the first attempt to use instruction tuning with multi-modal models.

[9]https://github.com/tha-atlas/QwenChart

3.2 Pre-Processing

3.2.1 Data augmentation with dynamic prompting and Chain-of-Thought

To prepare the SciVQA dataset for fine-tuning we built a dynamic prompting pipeline with instructions and CoT.

For each question-chart pair a different prompt was generated. Figure 2 (in the Appendix A.1), presents two example prompts for a single question–chart pair. The first prompt is specifically designed to match the format of questions found in the SciVQA dataset. The second is a more generic prompt we developed to facilitate experiments on other benchmarks, allowing for prompt adaptation based on the target dataset.

The prompt is built using the metadata from SciVQA. The first information provided in the prompt is the type of chart, then the caption. Then the question is provided, followed by some clues about the information the model should focus on. This can change based on the type of question that is provided. The model was instructed to provide concise answers, as Qwen2.5-VL tends to generate overly verbose responses.

To support this claim, we conducted a controlled comparison using two prompting strategies:

Simple Question Prompt: the prompt contains only the question;

Dynamic Prompt (ours): a structured prompt instructing the model to provide a concise answer.

We observed a significant difference in response length. On average, answers generated using the Simple Question Prompt were approximately 31.18 words, while responses using our Dynamic Prompt averaged just 1.35 words, closely aligning with the gold standard answers (1.32 words on average). An example of answers generated by the model with the two different prompts can be found in Appendix A.2. This experiment confirms that explicit prompting for brevity is essential to prevent unnecessarily long and redundant answers from Qwen2.5-VL. Given that we use ROUGE-1 and ROUGE-L metrics (Lin, 2004) for evaluation, it was essential to produce outputs that closely matched the gold standard. For this reason, we also specified the use of digits only and the inclusion of appropriate suffixes. Moreover, the instruction on how to respond when a question was unanswerable was included to ensure consistency with the format of the gold standard. Additional instructions were adapted based on the nature of the question. For example, whether it involved multiple-choice or binary-choice formats, or if addressed six visual attributes or not (shape, size, position, height, direction or colour). The final section of the prompt, labeled <thinking>, represents the CoT component. We observed that including this step encourages the model to engage in self-reflection, resulting in more reasoned and coherent responses. The CoT prompting leads to a substantial improvement across all evaluated metrics, with ROUGE-1 F1 increasing from 72.41% to 79.23% and ROUGE-L F1 from 72.30% to 79.06% - reflecting a gain of nearly 7 points in both cases.

3.2.2 Image Pre-processing

As an additional preprocessing step prior to fine-tuning, we applied a 10% white padding uniformly around each image in the dataset. This modification was introduced after observing that the model exhibited difficulties in accurately recognizing objects located near the image boundaries. Two human annotators manually checked the results from first experiments on 100 QA pairs and identify this tendency in the model.

3.2.3 Conversation-Based Queries

We converted every dataset entry from SciVQA in conversation-based queries that contained the prompt as described in Section 3.2.1, with the goal of using the queries as training data. Each entry in the SciVQA dataset consists of an image paired with a corresponding question, along with additional metadata (figure type, figure caption, and question category). The question type is classified as unanswerable, infinite, or finite (e.g., multiple choice or binary), and is further annotated as either visual or non-visual depending on whether it involves any of six predefined visual attributes: shape, size, position, height, direction, or color. In the conversation query we added this system message: "You are a Vision Language Model specialized in interpreting visual data from chart images. Your task is to analyze the provided chart image and respond to queries with concise answers, usually a single word, number, or short phrase. The charts include a variety of types (e.g., line charts, bar charts) and contain colors, labels, and text. Focus on delivering accurate, succinct answers based on the visual information. Avoid additional explanation unless absolutely necessary".

During the fine-tuning process, the gold (ground-truth) answer was included at the end of each conversational query, in order to provide the model with supervised learning signals. This information was excluded in the testing phase.

4 Experimental setup

4.1 Instruction-tuned QwenChart with dynamic prompting

We performed supervised fine-tuning of Qwen2.5-VL (Bai et al., 2025) on the training set of SciVQA prepared as described in Section 3.2. Specifically, we set up a rank of r = 64, an alpha (scaling factor) of 32. The dropout rate is set to 5%. We applied LoRA to the query, key, value and output projection layers of the attention modules of the text decoder and to the gate, up, down projectors of the Multi-Layer Perceptron. All other parameters, including the visual encoder, remained frozen during fine-tuning.

The total number of Qwen2.5-VL is 9,537,950,720, we trained the 13.0912% of them. Training was conducted for 2 epochs with an effective batch size of 24 (batch size = 6, gradient accumulation = 4), using a learning rate of 2e-4 and bfloat16 precision. Experiments were run on 8× H100 (80GB) GPUs. This version of the model, called **QwenChart-7B**, is the one used for the final submission on the leaderboard of the SciVQA shared task (Borisova et al., 2025). Furthermore, we fine-tuned the 72B Qwen2.5-VL version following the same configuration to see how it copes with the scaling up of the model. This version is called **QwenChart-72B**.

4.2 Instruction-tuned QwenChart with general prompting

We developed a different version of the prompt that can be adapted to other datasets, as illustrated in Section 3.2.1 and in Figure 2 in Appendix A.1. We fine-tuned Qwen2.5-VL on the the training set of SciVQA, prepared as discussed in Section 3.2, but using the adapted prompt version. For this model, we use the same configuration detailed in Section 4.1. This version of the model, **QwenChart2-7B**, does not include captions in the training data.

4.3 Evaluation

We evaluate the performance of our proposed models —**QwenChart-7B**, **QwenChart2-7B**, and **QwenChart-72B**— on both the development and test sets of the SciVQA benchmark (Table 1). To assess generalization capabilities, we also evaluate QwenChart-7B on ChartQA (Masry et al., 2022) (Table 1, last row), a widely adopted benchmark for chart question answering.

For comparison, we report zero-shot performance of two strong baseline models: the original **Qwen2.5-VL** and **Gemma3-12B-IT**[10]. For this results we used the dynamic prompt as in Section 3.2.1. These results, presented in Table 1, serve as a reference point to quantify the impact of fine-tuning and instruction design in our models.

We conduct our evaluation across different scenarios using ROUGE-1, ROUGE-L, and BERTScore (Zhang et al., 2020).

5 Analysis and Discussions

Table 1 shows that QwenChart-7B is the top performer on SciVQA across all metrics (highest ROUGE-1, ROUGE-L and BERTScore), indicating both lexical and semantic closeness to the ground truth. It slightly outperforms the larger QwenChart-72B, suggesting size alone does not guarantee better performance. QwenChart2-7B shows a performance drop on ChartQA. This implies that our model is not robust enough for generalization on out-of-domain data. Qwen2.5-VL on zero-shot performs well on SciVQA especially if compared to Gemma3.12b-it. The QwenChart models (7B, 72B, and 2-7B) show consistently high performance, but we notice a significant increase in performance with version QwenChart-7B. We also observe that figure captions have limited impact on results, as QwenChart2-7B achieves strong performance despite not being trained with caption information.

One of the key contributions of this work is the demonstration that high performance on chart understanding can be achieved using a visual model that does not rely on intermediate representations such as tables or code. This is particularly significant in the context of the SciVQA benchmark, which features a diverse set of real-world charts. The strong performance of QwenChart-7B, which surpasses even its larger counterpart (QwenChart-72B), suggests that model architecture and prompt engineering may have a more substantial impact on downstream performance than model size.

Another advantage lies in the efficient training process enabled by LoRA. By fine-tuning only 13% of the model's parameters, we achieve competitive results while significantly reducing computational cost and preserving the core capabilities of the pre-

[10]https://huggingface.co/google/gemma-3-12b-it

	ROUGE-1			ROUGE-L			BERTScore		
Model	F1	Precision	Recall	F1	Precision	Recall	F1	Precision	Recall
Qwen2.5-VL (dev set)	71.57%	72.96%	71.72%	71.52%	72.88%	71.67%	97.29%	97.38%	97.25%
Gemma3-12b-it (dev set)	60.96%	62.83%	60.43%	60.92%	62.78%	60.41%	96.61%	96.75%	96.52%
QwenChart-7B (test set)	78.99%	79.60%	79.49%	78.92%	79.53%	79.42%	98.39%	98.41%	98.40%
QwenChart-7B (dev set)	79.23%	80.24%	79.25%	79.06%	80.05%	79.08%	98.40%	98.50%	98.33%
QwenChart-72B (dev set)	77.54%	78.29%	77.93%	77.40%	78.16%	77.79%	98.23%	98.29%	98.19%
QwenChart2-7B (dev set)	76.62%	77.25%	77.16%	76.50%	77.13%	77.03%	98.19%	98.22%	98.19%
QwenChart2-7B (ChartQA)	66.38%	66.46%	67.20%	66.28%	66.27%	67.10%	94.69%	94.19%	95.23%

Table 1: Evaluation metrics across models on development and test set of SciVQA and ChartQA (validation set) (last row).

	ROUGE-1			ROUGE-L			BERTScore		
QA type	F1	Precision	Recall	F1	Precision	Recall	F1	Precision	Recall
finite binary non-visual	79.86%	79.86%	79.86%	79.86%	79.86%	79.86%	100.0%	100.0%	100.0%
finite binary visual	78.93%	78.93%	78.93%	78.93%	78.93%	78.93%	100.0%	100.0%	100.0%
finite non-binary non-visual	75.68%	75.79%	77.96%	74.5%	74.61%	76.79%	98.25%	98.07%	98.43%
finite non-binary visual	65.36%	65.0%	67.0%	65.36%	65.0%	67.0%	98.5%	98.21%	98.79%
infinite non-visual	74.46%	76.0%	75.5%	74.43%	75.96%	75.5%	96.39%	96.43%	96.54%
infinite visual	62.36%	63.36%	62.57%	62.04%	62.96%	62.21%	96.79%	96.82%	96.86%
unanswerable	95.0%	95.0%	95.0%	95.0%	95.0%	95.0%	99.11%	99.14%	99.07%

Table 2: Evaluation metrics of QwenChart-7B on the development set of SciVQA by QA type.

trained model. Dynamic prompting, combined with CoT rationales, further enhances the model's reasoning capabilities. This strategy allows the model to decompose complex questions into intermediate logical steps, resulting in more coherent and contextually accurate responses.

Despite promising results on SciVQA, our experiments reveal a performance drop on the ChartQA benchmark, indicating that the model's generalization capability to out-of-domain data is limited. This suggests potential overfitting to the prompt format or chart types seen during fine-tuning. Further efforts are needed to enhance the robustness of instruction-tuned models across datasets.

We observed that the ROUGE-1, ROUGE-L, and BERTScore metrics exhibit certain limitations when applied to this type of task. Compared to BERTScore, ROUGE proves to be more sensitive, as it is better able to highlight performance differences. ROUGE, in fact, imposes a heavier penalty on responses that do not exactly match the gold standard, making it more suitable for this task. However, this can also lead to an underestimation of model performance when responses are correct but differ in form from the reference answers. Table 3 shows some illustrative examples.

Answer	**Gold Answer**
RANDOM, SSID	RANDOM and SSID
0.4	0.32–0.52
Three	3
IT	Italian
A B C D	A,B,C,D

Table 3: Examples of QwenChart-7B answers vs gold answers from SciVQA development set.

5.1 Error Analysis

To gain deeper insights into model performance across different chart and question types, we conducted a quantitative analysis of the performance of QwenChart-7B on the development set of SciVQA (Table 2 and Table 4). The results reveal several notable patterns in how QwenChart-7B handles various categories of questions within the figure type.

First, we observe that binary (yes/no, true/false) answer set questions—both visual[11] and non-visual —yield the highest performance across all metrics. This suggests that the model excels when the answer space is limited and well-structured. Similarly, multiple choice visual questions also perform

[11]A visual question in SciVQA dataset is a question that addresses six designated features of the image: shape, size, position, height, direction or color.

Figure Type	ROUGE-1 F1	ROUGE-1 Precision	ROUGE-1 Recall	ROUGE-L F1	ROUGE-L Precision	ROUGE-L Recall	BERTScore F1	BERTScore Precision	BERTScore Recall
Line Chart	68.79%	69.78%	68.86%	68.72%	69.72%	68.86%	97.64%	97.5%	97.57%
Line Chart, Table	85.71%	85.71%	85.71%	85.71%	85.71%	85.71%	98.29%	98.14%	98.57%
Tree	71.28%	72.57%	70.72%	71.28%	72.57%	70.72%	98.42%	98.58%	98.5%
Scatter Plot	71.5%	71.79%	71.36%	71.5%	71.79%	71.36%	98.42%	98.78%	98.15%
Pie Chart	84.29%	83.71%	85.71%	84.29%	83.71%	85.71%	99.29%	99.14%	99.43%
Architecture Diagram	91.15%	91.5%	90.93%	90.93%	91.22%	90.72%	99.57%	99.65%	99.5%
Box Plot	79.71%	78.57%	82.14%	79.71%	78.57%	82.14%	98.71%	98.43%	99.14%
Neural Networks	83.14%	83.14%	83.28%	83.14%	83.14%	83.28%	99.5%	99.57%	99.65%
Confusion Matrix	81.71%	81.43%	83.57%	81.71%	81.43%	83.57%	97.57%	97.29%	97.43%
Graph	76.5%	76.86%	77.85%	76.07%	76.36%	77.35%	98.15%	98.08%	98.28%
Bar Chart	73.0%	73.86%	73.43%	73.0%	73.86%	73.43%	97.71%	97.57%	98.0%
Histogram	83.35%	85.71%	82.14%	83.35%	85.71%	82.14%	99.35%	99.5%	99.22%
Venn Diagram	85.71%	85.71%	85.71%	85.71%	85.71%	85.71%	100.0%	100.0%	100.0%
Vector Plot	95.29%	100.0%	92.86%	95.29%	100.0%	92.86%	97.86%	98.0%	97.71%
Other	35.14%	32.86%	42.86%	35.14%	32.86%	42.86%	98.29%	97.71%	98.86%
Line Chart, Bar Chart	42.86%	42.86%	42.86%	42.86%	42.86%	42.86%	97.29%	97.43%	97.14%
Flow Chart	85.71%	85.71%	85.71%	85.71%	85.71%	85.71%	98.0%	98.57%	97.57%
Tree, Graph	62.86%	61.86%	64.29%	58.14%	57.14%	59.57%	95.57%	94.86%	96.57%
Illustrative Diagram	74.57%	74.29%	75.0%	74.57%	74.29%	75.0%	98.14%	97.86%	98.29%
Line Chart, Scatter Plot	71.43%	71.43%	71.43%	71.43%	71.43%	71.43%	100.0%	100.0%	100.0%
Heat Map	77.14%	75.0%	85.71%	77.14%	75.0%	85.71%	97.29%	96.43%	98.29%

Table 4: Evaluation metrics of QwenChart-7B on the development set of SciVQA by figure type.

strongly, indicating that the model handles moderate complexity well.

On the other hand, performance drops for visually-anchored queries. Specifically, infinite visual questions scored the lowest. This may be due to the model's difficulty in generating precise free-form answers from ambiguous or densely visual inputs without clearly bounded outputs.

Table 4 demonstrates that the type of figure significantly impacts model performance. "Vector Plot" yielded the highest overall performance with scores of 95.29% ROUGE-1 F1 and 97.86% BERTScore F1, indicating the model's strong ability to extract and interpret information from this format. "Pie Chart", "Architecture Diagram", and "Neural Networks" also demonstrated consistently strong results, suggesting that these figure types offer more visually consistent and interpretable structures for the model. In contrast, "Other" and hybrid types like "Line Chart, Bar Chart" significantly underperformed, with ROUGE-1 F1 scores as low as 35.14% and 42.86%, respectively. This disparity indicates that composite visualizations or less conventional diagrams introduce ambiguity or complexity that current models struggle to resolve effectively. This aligns with findings by Zhu et al. (2025), who highlight that VLMMs are still not robust when it comes to multi-chart reasoning. Conversely, we observed that other multi-chart figures, such as "Line Chart, Table", or "Line Chart, Scatter Plot" yield acceptable scores (85.71% and 71.43% with ROUGE-1 F1). Overall, these results underscore the importance of figure type in influencing model performance and reveal that chart complexity and visual composition remain critical challenges for VLMMs.

Notably, the model performs almost perfectly on unanswerable questions, indicating that it reliably recognizes when the provided visual information is insufficient to answer the question.

These findings support the broader observation that structured question formats (e.g., yes/no answers) better align with the model's reasoning capabilities, while open or unconstrained queries involving visual reasoning are more challenging. It should also be noted that the proportion of chart types and questions in the training dataset was not balanced. Future improvements may involve training on more varied chart types to improve generalization.

6 Conclusions

In this work, we introduced QwenChart-7B, an instruction-tuned VLLM built on Qwen2.5-VL for the shared task SciVQA. Our approach leverages dynamic CoT prompting and LoRA-based parameter-efficient fine-tuning. Despite its relatively small size, QwenChart-7B demonstrates state-of-the-art performance on the challenging SciVQA benchmark, outperforming even larger models like QwenChart-72B. This suggests that architecture-specific optimization and well-designed prompts can surpass gains from model scaling alone. However, we also observed limitations in out-of-domain generalization, particularly on the ChartQA benchmark, indicating room for improvement. Future work will explore richer multimodal alignment, broader datasets, and more generalized instruction strategies to address these challenges and further improve performance across diverse chart types and QA formats.

Limitations

Despite the strong performance of QwenChart-7B on SciVQA, several limitations remain. First, the model struggles with generalization when evaluated on out-of-domain benchmarks such as ChartQA. This suggests a sensitivity to dataset-specific features and prompt formulations, potentially limiting its broader applicability without additional fine-tuning. Second, the relatively small amount of fine-tuning data used may not adequately capture the diversity of real-world chart formats and question styles, further constraining generalization in unseen tasks and out-of-domain data. Another limitation concerns the evaluation methodology. While automatic metrics such as ROUGE-1, ROUGE-L, and BERTScore are standard in natural language generation tasks, they are not ideally suited for assessing short, factual responses typical in chart QA. These metrics may fail to penalize near-miss answers or reward semantically correct but lexically mismatched outputs, thus potentially misrepresenting true model performance. We notice that sometimes the result is evaluated as wrong even if it is correct. A human evaluation could solve this issue. Furthermore, the work is limited in providing evaluations with other models or benchmarks.

Acknowledgments

This research was funded by the Bavarian State Ministry for Science and the Arts (StMWK: Bayerische Staatsministerium für Wissenschaft und Kunst - StMWK) as part of the Project "CHIASM" (Changenreiche industrielle Anwendungen für vortrainierte Sprachmodelle) and as part the High Tech Agenda of the Free State of Bavaria.

References

Marah Abdin, Jyoti Aneja, Hany Awadalla, Ahmed Awadallah, Ammar Ahmad Awan, Nguyen Bach, Amit Bahree, Arash Bakhtiari, Jianmin Bao, Harkirat Behl, Alon Benhaim, Misha Bilenko, Johan Bjorck, Sébastien Bubeck, Martin Cai, Qin Cai, Vishrav Chaudhary, Dong Chen, Dongdong Chen, and 110 others. 2024. Phi-3 technical report: A highly capable language model locally on your phone. *Preprint*, arXiv:2404.14219.

Mubashara Akhtar, Oana Cocarascu, and Elena Simperl. 2023. Reading and reasoning over chart images for evidence-based automated fact-checking. In *Findings of the Association for Computational Linguistics: EACL 2023*, pages 399–414, Dubrovnik, Croatia. Association for Computational Linguistics.

Shuai Bai, Keqin Chen, Xuejing Liu, Jialin Wang, Wenbin Ge, Sibo Song, Kai Dang, Peng Wang, Shijie Wang, Jun Tang, Humen Zhong, Yuanzhi Zhu, Mingkun Yang, Zhaohai Li, Jianqiang Wan, Pengfei Wang, Wei Ding, Zheren Fu, Yiheng Xu, and 8 others. 2025. Qwen2.5-vl technical report. *Preprint*, arXiv:2502.13923.

Ekaterina Borisova, Nikolas Rauscher, and Georg Rehm. 2025. SciVQA 2025: Overview of the first scientific visual question answering shared task. In *Proceedings of the 5th Workshop on Scholarly Document Processing (SDP)*, Vienna, Austria.

Victor Carbune, Hassan Mansoor, Fangyu Liu, Rahul Aralikatte, Gilles Baechler, Jindong Chen, and Abhanshu Sharma. 2024. Chart-based reasoning: Transferring capabilities from LLMs to VLMs. In *Findings of the Association for Computational Linguistics: NAACL 2024*, pages 989–1004, Mexico City, Mexico. Association for Computational Linguistics.

Ritwick Chaudhry, Sumit Shekhar, Utkarsh Gupta, Pranav Maneriker, Prann Bansal, and Ajay Joshi. 2020. LEAF-QA: Locate, Encode Attend for Figure Question Answering . In *2020 IEEE Winter Conference on Applications of Computer Vision (WACV)*, pages 3501–3510, Los Alamitos, CA, USA. IEEE Computer Society.

Alexey Dosovitskiy, Lucas Beyer, Alexander Kolesnikov, Dirk Weissenborn, Xiaohua Zhai, Thomas Unterthiner, Mostafa Dehghani, Matthias Minderer, Georg Heigold, Sylvain Gelly, Jakob Uszkoreit, and Neil Houlsby. 2021. An image is worth 16x16 words: Transformers for image recognition at scale. In *International Conference on Learning Representations*.

Yucheng Han, Chi Zhang, Xin Chen, Xu Yang, Zhibin Wang, Gang Yu, Bin Fu, and Hanwang Zhang. 2023. Chartllama: A multimodal llm for chart understanding and generation. *Preprint*, arXiv:2311.16483.

Wei He, Zhiheng Xi, Wanxu Zhao, Xiaoran Fan, Yiwen Ding, Zifei Shan, Tao Gui, Qi Zhang, and Xuanjing Huang. 2025. Distill visual chart reasoning ability from LLMs to MLLMs.

Edward J. Hu, Yelong Shen, Phillip Wallis, Zeyuan Allen-Zhu, Yuanzhi Li, Shean Wang, and Weizhu Chen. 2021. Lora: Low-rank adaptation of large language models. *CoRR*, abs/2106.09685.

Kung-Hsiang Huang, Mingyang Zhou, Hou Pong Chan, Yi Fung, Zhenhailong Wang, Lingyu Zhang, Shih-Fu Chang, and Heng Ji. 2024. Do LVLMs understand charts? analyzing and correcting factual errors in chart captioning. In *Findings of the Association for Computational Linguistics: ACL 2024*, pages 730–749, Bangkok, Thailand. Association for Computational Linguistics.

Mohammed Saidul Islam, Raian Rahman, Ahmed Masry, Md Tahmid Rahman Laskar, Mir Tafseer Nayeem, and Enamul Hoque. 2024. Are large vision language models up to the challenge of chart comprehension and reasoning. In *Findings of the Association for Computational Linguistics: EMNLP 2024*, pages 3334–3368, Miami, Florida, USA. Association for Computational Linguistics.

Mengzhao Jia, Zhihan Zhang, Wenhao Yu, Fangkai Jiao, and Meng Jiang. 2024. Describe-then-reason: Improving multimodal mathematical reasoning through visual comprehension training. *Preprint*, arXiv:2404.14604.

Kushal Kafle, Brian Price, Scott Cohen, and Christopher Kanan. 2018. DVQA: Understanding Data Visualizations via Question Answering . In *2018 IEEE/CVF Conference on Computer Vision and Pattern Recognition (CVPR)*, pages 5648–5656, Los Alamitos, CA, USA. IEEE Computer Society.

Samira Ebrahimi Kahou, Adam Atkinson, Vincent Michalski, Ákos Kádár, Adam Trischler, and Yoshua Bengio. 2018. FigureQA: An annotated figure dataset for visual reasoning.

Zeba Karishma, Shaurya Rohatgi, Kavya Shrinivas Puranik, Jian Wu, and C. Lee Giles. 2023. Acl-fig: A dataset for scientific figure classification. In *Proceedings of the 2023 Workshop on Scientific Document Understanding (SDU)*, volume 3656, pages 1–12. CEUR-WS. Presented at the 2023 Workshop on Scientific Document Understanding (SDU 2023).

Hajime Kato, Mitsuru Nakazawa, Hsuan-Kung Yang, Mark Chen, and Björn Stenger. 2022. Parsing line chart images using linear programming. In *2022 IEEE/CVF Winter Conference on Applications of Computer Vision (WACV)*, pages 2553–2562.

Wonjoong Kim, Sangwu Park, Yeonjun In, Seokwon Han, and Chanyoung Park. 2025. SIMPLOT: Enhancing chart question answering by distilling essentials. In *Findings of the Association for Computational Linguistics: NAACL 2025*, pages 573–593, Albuquerque, New Mexico. Association for Computational Linguistics.

Kenton Lee, Mandar Joshi, Iulia Turc, Hexiang Hu, Fangyu Liu, Julian Eisenschlos, Urvashi Khandelwal, Peter Shaw, Ming-Wei Chang, and Kristina Toutanova. 2023. Pix2struct: screenshot parsing as pretraining for visual language understanding. In *Proceedings of the 40th International Conference on Machine Learning*, ICML'23. JMLR.org.

Lei Li, Yuqi Wang, Runxin Xu, Peiyi Wang, Xiachong Feng, Lingpeng Kong, and Qi Liu. 2024a. Multimodal ArXiv: A dataset for improving scientific comprehension of large vision-language models. In *Proceedings of the 62nd Annual Meeting of the Association for Computational Linguistics (Volume 1: Long Papers)*, pages 14369–14387, Bangkok, Thailand. Association for Computational Linguistics.

Shengzhi Li and Nima Tajbakhsh. 2023. Scigraphqa: A large-scale synthetic multi-turn question-answering dataset for scientific graphs. *Preprint*, arXiv:2308.03349.

Zhuowan Li, Bhavan Jasani, Peng Tang, and Shabnam Ghadar. 2024b. Synthesize Step-by-Step: Tools, Templates and LLMs as Data Generators for Reasoning-Based Chart VQA . In *2024 IEEE/CVF Conference on Computer Vision and Pattern Recognition (CVPR)*, pages 13613–13623, Los Alamitos, CA, USA. IEEE Computer Society.

Chin-Yew Lin. 2004. ROUGE: A package for automatic evaluation of summaries. In *Text Summarization Branches Out*, pages 74–81, Barcelona, Spain. Association for Computational Linguistics.

Fangyu Liu, Julian Eisenschlos, Francesco Piccinno, Syrine Krichene, Chenxi Pang, Kenton Lee, Mandar Joshi, Wenhu Chen, Nigel Collier, and Yasemin Altun. 2023a. DePlot: One-shot visual language reasoning by plot-to-table translation. In *Findings of the Association for Computational Linguistics: ACL 2023*, pages 10381–10399, Toronto, Canada. Association for Computational Linguistics.

Fangyu Liu, Francesco Piccinno, Syrine Krichene, Chenxi Pang, Kenton Lee, Mandar Joshi, Yasemin Altun, Nigel Collier, and Julian Eisenschlos. 2023b. MatCha: Enhancing visual language pretraining with math reasoning and chart derendering. In *Proceedings of the 61st Annual Meeting of the Association for Computational Linguistics (Volume 1: Long Papers)*, pages 12756–12770, Toronto, Canada. Association for Computational Linguistics.

Fuxiao Liu, Xiaoyang Wang, Wenlin Yao, Jianshu Chen, Kaiqiang Song, Sangwoo Cho, Yaser Yacoob, and Dong Yu. 2024. MMC: Advancing multimodal chart understanding with large-scale instruction tuning. In *Proceedings of the 2024 Conference of the North American Chapter of the Association for Computational Linguistics: Human Language Technologies (Volume 1: Long Papers)*, pages 1287–1310, Mexico City, Mexico. Association for Computational Linguistics.

Haotian Liu, Chunyuan Li, Qingyang Wu, and Yong Jae Lee. 2023c. Visual instruction tuning. In *Advances in Neural Information Processing Systems*, volume 36, pages 34892–34916. Curran Associates, Inc.

Junteng Liu, Weihao Zeng, Xiwen Zhang, Yijun Wang, Zifei Shan, and Junxian He. 2025. On the perception bottleneck of vlms for chart understanding. *Preprint*, arXiv:2503.18435.

Pan Lu, Hritik Bansal, Tony Xia, Jiacheng Liu, Chunyuan Li, Hannaneh Hajishirzi, Hao Cheng, Kai-Wei Chang, Michel Galley, and Jianfeng Gao. 2024. Mathvista: Evaluating mathematical reasoning of foundation models in visual contexts. In *The Twelfth International Conference on Learning Representations*.

Junyu Luo, Zekun Li, Jinpeng Wang, and Chin-Yew Lin. 2021. Chartocr: Data extraction from charts images via a deep hybrid framework. In *2021 IEEE Winter Conference on Applications of Computer Vision (WACV)*, pages 1916–1924.

Ahmed Masry, Parsa Kavehzadeh, Xuan Long Do, Enamul Hoque, and Shafiq Joty. 2023. UniChart: A universal vision-language pretrained model for chart comprehension and reasoning. In *Proceedings of the 2023 Conference on Empirical Methods in Natural Language Processing*, pages 14662–14684, Singapore. Association for Computational Linguistics.

Ahmed Masry, Do Xuan Long, Jia Qing Tan, Shafiq Joty, and Enamul Hoque. 2022. ChartQA: A benchmark for question answering about charts with visual and logical reasoning. In *Findings of the Association for Computational Linguistics: ACL 2022*, pages 2263–2279, Dublin, Ireland. Association for Computational Linguistics.

Ahmed Masry, Mehrad Shahmohammadi, Md Rizwan Parvez, Enamul Hoque, and Shafiq Joty. 2024. ChartInstruct: Instruction tuning for chart comprehension and reasoning. In *Findings of the Association for Computational Linguistics: ACL 2024*, pages 10387–10409, Bangkok, Thailand. Association for Computational Linguistics.

Ahmed Masry, Megh Thakkar, Aayush Bajaj, Aaryaman Kartha, Enamul Hoque, and Shafiq Joty. 2025. ChartGemma: Visual instruction-tuning for chart reasoning in the wild. In *Proceedings of the 31st International Conference on Computational Linguistics: Industry Track*, pages 625–643, Abu Dhabi, UAE. Association for Computational Linguistics.

Chinmayee Rane, Seshasayee Mahadevan Subramanya, Devi Sandeep Endluri, Jian Wu, and C. Lee Giles. 2021. Chartreader: Automatic parsing of bar-plots. In *2021 IEEE 22nd International Conference on Information Reuse and Integration for Data Science (IRI)*, pages 318–325.

Yasaman Razeghi, Ishita Dasgupta, Fangyu Liu, Vinay Venkatesh Ramasesh, and Sameer Singh. 2024. Plot twist: Multimodal models don't comprehend simple chart details. In *Findings of the Association for Computational Linguistics: EMNLP 2024*, pages 5922–5937, Miami, Florida, USA. Association for Computational Linguistics.

Adam Santoro, David Raposo, David G Barrett, Mateusz Malinowski, Razvan Pascanu, Peter Battaglia, and Timothy Lillicrap. 2017. A simple neural network module for relational reasoning. In *Advances in Neural Information Processing Systems*, volume 30. Curran Associates, Inc.

Hrituraj Singh and Sumit Shekhar. 2020. STL-CQA: Structure-based transformers with localization and encoding for chart question answering. In *Proceedings of the 2020 Conference on Empirical Methods in Natural Language Processing (EMNLP)*, pages 3275–3284, Online. Association for Computational Linguistics.

Gemini Team, Rohan Anil, Sebastian Borgeaud, Jean-Baptiste Alayrac, Jiahui Yu, Radu Soricut, Johan Schalkwyk, Andrew M. Dai, Anja Hauth, Katie Millican, David Silver, Melvin Johnson, Ioannis Antonoglou, Julian Schrittwieser, Amelia Glaese, Jilin Chen, Emily Pitler, Timothy Lillicrap, Angeliki Lazaridou, and 1332 others. 2025. Gemini: A family of highly capable multimodal models. *Preprint*, arXiv:2312.11805.

Peifang Wang, Olga Golovneva, Armen Aghajanyan, Xiang Ren, Muhao Chen, Asli Celikyilmaz, and Maryam Fazel-Zarandi. 2023. Domino: A dual-system for multi-step visual language reasoning. *Preprint*, arXiv:2310.02804.

Shulei Wang, Shuai Yang, Wang Lin, Zirun Guo, Sihang Cai, Hai Huang, Ye Wang, Jingyuan Chen, and Tao Jin. 2025. Omni-chart-600K: A comprehensive dataset of chart types for chart understanding. In *Findings of the Association for Computational Linguistics: NAACL 2025*, pages 4051–4069, Albuquerque, New Mexico. Association for Computational Linguistics.

Zirui Wang, Mengzhou Xia, Luxi He, Howard Chen, Yitao Liu, Richard Zhu, Kaiqu Liang, Xindi Wu, Haotian Liu, Sadhika Malladi, Alexis Chevalier, Sanjeev Arora, and Danqi Chen. 2024. Charxiv: Charting gaps in realistic chart understanding in multimodal llms. In *Advances in Neural Information Processing Systems*, volume 37, pages 113569–113697. Curran Associates, Inc.

Jason Wei, Xuezhi Wang, Dale Schuurmans, Maarten Bosma, Brian Ichter, Fei Xia, Ed H. Chi, Quoc V. Le, and Denny Zhou. 2022. Chain-of-thought prompting elicits reasoning in large language models. In *Proceedings of the 36th International Conference on Neural Information Processing Systems*, NIPS '22, Red Hook, NY, USA. Curran Associates Inc.

Zhengzhuo Xu, SiNan Du, Yiyan Qi, Chengjin Xu, Chun Yuan, and Jian Guo. 2025a. Chartbench: A benchmark for complex visual reasoning in charts.

Zhengzhuo Xu, Bowen Qu, Yiyan Qi, SiNan Du, Chengjin Xu, Chun Yuan, and Jian Guo. 2025b. Chartmoe: Mixture of diversely aligned expert connector for chart understanding. In *The Thirteenth International Conference on Learning Representations*.

Liang Zhang, Anwen Hu, Haiyang Xu, Ming Yan, Yichen Xu, Qin Jin, Ji Zhang, and Fei Huang. 2024a. TinyChart: Efficient chart understanding with program-of-thoughts learning and visual token merging. In *Proceedings of the 2024 Conference on Empirical Methods in Natural Language Processing*, pages 1882–1898, Miami, Florida, USA. Association for Computational Linguistics.

Tianyi Zhang, Varsha Kishore, Felix Wu, Kilian Q. Weinberger, and Yoav Artzi. 2020. Bertscore: Evaluating text generation with bert. In *International Conference on Learning Representations*.

Wenqi Zhang, Zhenglin Cheng, Yuanyu He, Mengna Wang, Yongliang Shen, Zeqi Tan, Guiyang Hou, Mingqian He, Yanna Ma, Weiming Lu, and Yueting Zhuang. 2024b. Multimodal self-instruct: Synthetic abstract image and visual reasoning instruction using language model. In *Proceedings of the 2024 Conference on Empirical Methods in Natural Language Processing*, pages 19228–19252, Miami, Florida, USA. Association for Computational Linguistics.

Mingyang Zhou, Yi Fung, Long Chen, Christopher Thomas, Heng Ji, and Shih-Fu Chang. 2023. Enhanced chart understanding via visual language pretraining on plot table pairs. In *Findings of the Association for Computational Linguistics: ACL 2023*, pages 1314–1326, Toronto, Canada. Association for Computational Linguistics.

Zifeng Zhu, Mengzhao Jia, Zhihan Zhang, Lang Li, and Meng Jiang. 2025. MultiChartQA: Benchmarking vision-language models on multi-chart problems. In *Proceedings of the 2025 Conference of the Nations of the Americas Chapter of the Association for Computational Linguistics: Human Language Technologies (Volume 1: Long Papers)*, pages 11341–11359, Albuquerque, New Mexico. Association for Computational Linguistics.

A Appendix

A.1 Example of chart and corresponding prompts

We show here an example of a chart from the SciVQA dataset (Figure 1) and two different prompts (Figure 2), used as described in Section 3.2.

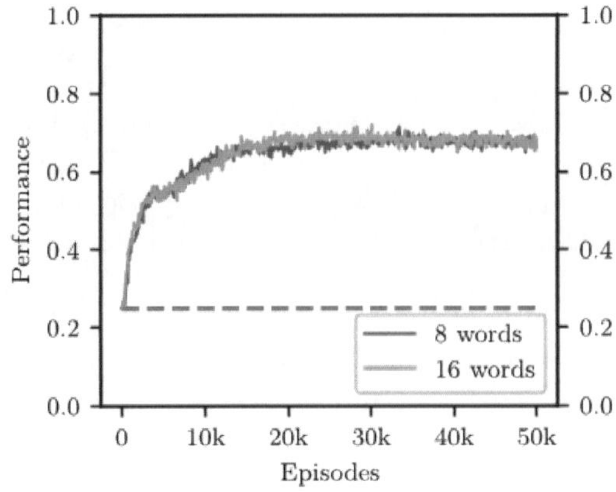

Figure 1: Chart paired with the prompts shown in Figure 2.

```
You are looking at a line chart.
The caption is: 'Figure 5: Performance of the model on images from the
CelebA dataset when the asking-agent has four images, two rounds of
question-answer are performed and with a vocabulary of eight and sixteen
words available. The dashed grey lines represents the baseline performance
where the asking-agent guesses randomly.'.
Question: What is the range of episodes?
[Data-only cue] Focus your response more on numeric or textual values.
Please also consider the caption of the figure to respond to the question.
Respond with a concise, one-word or very short phrase. No full sentences,
no explanations.
If the response is numeric, use digits only and include any units or
suffixes (e.g., %, kg, $).
If the answer cannot be inferred from the figure and caption, please reply
with the sentence: 'It is not possible to answer this question based only
on the provided data.'
---
<thinking> Reasoning (do NOT respond yet)
Step 1 Identify the figure type and its axes / legend.
Step 2 Locate the graphical elements relevant to the question.
Step 3 Extract the key-value information.
Step 4 Read the required values or qualitative trends.
Step 5 Form the short response requested above.
---
Final respond:
<answer>
```

```
Prompt: You are looking at one or more charts or graphs.
While inspecting the visual, pay attention to: color, position, shape,
size, height, direction, and any numeric values on axes, legends, or
labels.
Use the caption only if it clarifies the figure; otherwise rely on the
visual itself.

Answer format:
- Yes/No question -> reply 'Yes' or 'No' only.
- Multiple-choice question -> reply with the capital letter(s) of the
chosen option(s) (e.g. `A` or `A,B`, no spaces).
- Numeric answer -> digits only, include any units or symbols (e.g., %, kg,
$).
- If the answer cannot be inferred -> reply exactly: 'It is not possible to
answer this question based only on the provided data.'
- Please be concise and avoide explenations or reasoning in your final
answer.


Question: What is the range of episodes?


---
<thinking> Reasoning (do NOT respond yet)
1. Identify the chart type, axes, and legend.
2. Locate the graphical elements relevant to the question.
3. Extract the key values or qualitative trends.
4. Integrate helpful details from the caption (if any).
5. If multiple choice, match your finding to the option(s); if yes/no,
decide 'Yes' or 'No'.
6. Produce the concise answer following the formatting rules above.
---
Final respond:
<answer>
```

Figure 2: Examples of prompts for image-question pair. The image is shown in Figure 1.

A.2 Simple Question Prompt vs. Dynamic Prompt

The following example shows the answers generated with Qwen2.5-VL with Simple Question Prompt and with our Dynamic Prompt, as described in Section 3.2.1. The question is taken from the SciVQA dataset.

Question: "Does the accuracy of the red line decrease as the percentage of tokens selected increases?"

Simple Question Prompt Answer: “No, the accuracy of the red line does not decrease as the percentage of tokens selected increases. The red line remains relatively flat and stable across the range of percentages shown in the figure, indicating that the accuracy is consistent regardless of the number of tokens selected”. (Length: 47 words)

Dynamic Prompt Answer: "No".

Gold Answer: "No".

Enhancing Scientific Visual Question Answering through Multimodal Reasoning and Ensemble Modeling

Prahitha Movva
University of Massachusetts Amherst
Amherst, MA, USA
prahitha.movva03@gmail.com

Naga Harshita Marupaka
University of Southern California
Los Angeles, CA, USA
nagaharshitamarupaka@gmail.com

Abstract

Technical reports and articles often contain valuable information in the form of semi-structured data like charts, and figures. Interpreting these and using the information from them is essential for downstream tasks such as question answering (QA). Current approaches to visual question answering often struggle with the precision required for scientific data interpretation, particularly in handling numerical values, multi-step reasoning over visual elements, and maintaining consistency between visual observation and textual reasoning. We present our approach to the SciVQA 2025 shared task, focusing on answering visual and non-visual questions grounded in scientific figures from scholarly articles.

We conducted a series of experiments using models with 5B to 8B parameters. Our strongest individual model, InternVL3, achieved ROUGE-1 and ROUGE-L F1 scores of **0.740** and a BERTScore of **0.983** on the SciVQA test split. We also developed an ensemble model with multiple vision language models (VLMs). Through error analysis on the validation split, our ensemble approach improved performance compared to most individual models, though InternVL3 remained the strongest standalone performer. Our findings underscore the effectiveness of prompt optimization, chain-of-thought reasoning and ensemble modeling in improving the model's ability in visual question answering.

1 Introduction

Scientific literature communicates complex ideas not only through text but also through carefully designed visual elements including charts, graphs, diagrams, and technical illustrations. These visualizations serve as dense information carriers, encoding quantitative relationships, experimental results, architectural designs, and conceptual frameworks that are essential for scientific understanding. The ability to automatically interpret and reason about these visual elements represents a critical challenge in advancing scientific AI systems.

The task of Visual Question Answering (VQA) over scientific figures presents unique challenges that distinguish it from general-domain VQA. Scientific visualizations demand mathematical precision, often requiring exact numerical extraction and calculation. They involve complex compositional reasoning across multiple visual elements, and frequently contain domain-specific conventions, symbols, and representations that require specialized understanding (Ishmam et al., 2024). Furthermore, scientific figures often embed multiple layers of information, including raw data points, derived trends, statistical relationships, and comparative analyses.

Current VQA models, while showing impressive performance on general datasets, often struggle with the precision and reasoning depth required for scientific applications (Kabir et al., 2024). Common failure modes include visual grounding errors, where models misinterpret chart elements or scales; compositional reasoning failures, where multi-step logical processes break down; and consistency issues between visual observations and textual explanations (Tanjim et al., 2025; Thawakar et al., 2025).

This paper presents our approach to the SciVQA Shared Task[1] [2] (Borisova et al., 2025), focusing on QA over scientific visualizations. The task involves answering closed-ended visual (i.e., addressing visual attributes such as colour, shape, size, height, etc.) and non-visual (not addressing figure visual attributes) questions. We leverage the reasoning and visual understanding capabilities of VLMs, and employ task-specific Chain-of-Thought (CoT) (Wei et al., 2023) prompting techniques to retrieve and summarize relevant information from the visual-

[1] https://sdproc.org/2025/scivqa.html
[2] https://huggingface.co/datasets/katebor/SciVQA

Proceedings of the Fifth Workshop on Scholarly Document Processing (SDP 2025), pages 252–262
July 31, 2025 ©2025 Association for Computational Linguistics

izations. Our approach involved testing multiple prompt variants and selecting optimal configurations based on validation performance. To support reproducibility and future research, we make the code publicly available on GitHub[3].

Our main contributions are:

- A systematic ensemble strategy with figure type specific model selection based on comprehensive validation analysis.
- Optimized prompt engineering templates tailored to different question answer pair and figure type combinations.

2 Related Work

Recent advancements in chart-based QA have focused on various approaches to understanding and generating responses about visualizations. ChartLlama (Han et al., 2023) and UniChart (Masry et al., 2023) demonstrate the benefits of chart-specialized language models, showing improved performance in both chart captioning and QA tasks. These works often rely on explicit chart structure parsing as a preprocessing step, achieving strong results on synthetic chart datasets.

Chart-based Reasoning (Carbune et al., 2024) and LlamaV-o1 (Thawakar et al., 2025) propose decomposed reasoning traces and transfer of LLM capabilities to visual settings. Our work builds on these insights by emphasizing structured reasoning and adopt step-level supervision to encourage coherent and faithful intermediate reasoning in visual contexts.

Other relevant works include SPIQA (Pramanick et al., 2025) and MathVista (Lu et al., 2024), which evaluate visual reasoning in scientific domains. MathVista particularly focuses on precise numerical and symbolic interpretation in mathematical visualizations, similar to our emphasis on scientific accuracy.

In the realm of prompt engineering and model alignment, (Zhan et al., 2025) proposed SPRI (Situated-PRInciples), a framework that automatically generates context-specific guiding principles for each input query to improve model alignment. Their approach demonstrates that instance-specific principles can outperform generic ones, which informs our ensemble methodology that combines prompt engineering with multiple VLMs.

Motivated by recent advances in prompt rewriting (Tanjim et al., 2025), we explore instruction tuning and prompt optimization to enhance model adherence to scientific QA formats. Unlike previous work that focuses on architectural innovations requiring additional training, our approach focuses on ensemble strategies and prompt optimization for maximum performance on scientific VQA tasks.

3 Dataset

The SciVQA dataset comprises scientific figures from ACL Anthology and arXiv papers. Each figure is annotated with seven question-answer pairs and associated metadata including captions, figure IDs, figure types (e.g., compound, line graph, bar chart, scatter plot), and QA pair types, with dataset splits and distributions detailed in Section A and Tables 3, 4, and 5.

4 Methodology

Our system integrates three key components:

- systematic prompt optimization for different figure types
- strategic ensemble modeling, and
- post-processing for answer standardization.

We utilized the vLLM (Kwon et al., 2023) engine for maximum compute utilization during inference. A40 instances were sufficient for 7B models, while 8B models required A100 GPUs. CoT inference required approximately twice the computation time due to the two-level reasoning process, but provided significant quality improvements.

4.1 Model Selection

To inform model selection and ensure alignment with the target domain, we referred to the performance of recent models on established multimodal QA benchmarks analogous to SciVQA (Borisova et al., 2025), including ChartQA (Masry et al., 2022), MathVista (Lu et al., 2024), ChartXiv (Wang et al., 2024). VLMs in the 5–8B parameter range demonstrated competitive performance on these leaderboards, achieving results comparable to significantly larger models with 32–72B parameters.

According to the InternVL3 technical report (Zhu et al., 2025), the models InternVL3-8B and Qwen2.5-VL-7B performed well on tasks such as OCR, chart, and document understanding, specifically on datasets like ChartXiv and ChartQA. Additionally, a fine-tuned version of the Qwen2.5-VL-7B Instruct model (Bai et al.,

[3] `https://github.com/NagaHarshita/Infyn-SciVQA`

2025), as reported in the Bespoke technical report [4], demonstrates competitive performance on ChartXiv, ChartQA, and EvoChart, achieving results comparable to InternVL3-8B. Based on these observations, we chose the following four VLMs, namely, InternVL3-8B, Qwen2.5-VL-7B Instruct, Bespoke MiniChart 7B, and Phi-4 Multimodal Instruct for our task.

InternVL3-8B (Zhu et al., 2025) features an advanced vision encoder architecture tailored for complex visual understanding, unlike Qwen2.5-VL which uses a standard ViT encoder (Zhu et al., 2025). The model supports high-resolution image processing capabilities essential for interpreting detailed charts, and incorporates multi-scale feature extraction to enable both global comprehension and fine-grained numerical reading. It is particularly robust when handling overlapping text and visually dense layouts commonly found in scientific figures.

Qwen2.5-VL-7B Instruct (Bai et al., 2025) exhibits strong mathematical reasoning, although its performance is limited by the underlying vision encoder. **Bespoke MiniChart 7B**, trained with DPO (Rafailov et al., 2024), benefits from improved chain-of-thought reasoning for chart understanding tasks, but lacks architectural features suited for complex scientific visualizations. Finally, **Phi-4 Multimodal Instruct** (5.6B) (Microsoft et al., 2025) offers general multimodal capabilities but is not specifically optimized for scientific content.

4.2 Prompt Optimization

We crafted task-specific prompts that incorporate captions, figure types, and QA pair types. Prompt variants included explicit CoT cues, multiple correct answer hints, and image-caption-context fusion, with performance differences noted across QA pair types. Additionally, we set two baseline models (both using InternVL3): one using a general prompt without specifying the expected output format, and another with explicit formatting instructions stating that the output should be either a number or a single sentence. Baseline 1 refers to a general prompt without formatting constraints, while Baseline 2 uses explicit answer formatting instructions (exact prompts provided in the Appendix in Table 6). The structured format ensures consistency and enables automated evaluation of both reasoning quality and final answers. All the components described below (e.g., Base Prompt, Compound Images Prompt, Figure Type Prompt, etc.), and in the Tables 7 and 8 are combined into a single, composite prompt to ensure that all possible aspects of the task are considered.

4.2.1 Single Prompt

We developed an initial prompt that includes the figure caption, question-answer pair type classification, and task-specific instructions that elicit reasoning, with exact prompts detailed in Table 7.

Prompt Used: *Base Prompt + Compound Images Prompt + Figure Type Prompt + Question + Binary Prompt + Choice Prompt*

4.2.2 CoT and Rethink

Incorporating Chain-of-Thought (CoT) (Wei et al., 2023) and Rethink mechanisms (Wang et al., 2025) where models regenerate answers with self-correction significantly enhances performance, particularly for math-intensive and ambiguous examples. Prompts are designed to elicit reflective thinking, with final answers distinctly highlighted using structured XML tags ($< reasoning >$ and $< answer >$), as detailed in Table 8.

Step 1 Prompt Used: *Step 1 Base Prompt + Compound Images Prompt*

Step 2 Prompt Used: *Step 2 Base Prompt + Figure Type Prompt + Binary Prompt + Choice Prompt*

4.3 Ensemble

Based on a comprehensive validation analysis (see Section B and Table 9 in Appendix for detailed model performance across figure types), we implemented a figure-type-aware ensemble approach in which each model was assigned to chart types aligned with its demonstrated strengths. Specifically, Qwen2.5-VL was selected for scatter plots, confusion matrices, trees, and graphs, given its relative effectiveness on relational and structural visualizations. Bespoke MiniChart was applied to pie charts, bar charts, architecture diagrams, neural networks, and box plots, leveraging its finetuning for specialized chart comprehension. Meanwhile, Phi-4 was assigned to line charts, tables, histograms, vector plots, and illustrative diagrams, where it showed comparatively better performance. Although this targeted ensemble method yielded competitive results, it was ultimately outperformed by InternVL3, which demonstrated robust and consistent accuracy across all figure types.

[4] https://www.bespokelabs.ai/blog/bespoke-minichart-7b

Model	R1-F1	R1-P	R1-R	RL-F1	RL-P	RL-R	BS-F1	BS-P	BS-R
InternVL3	**0.730**	**0.744**	**0.732**	**0.729**	**0.743**	**0.731**	**0.981**	**0.983**	**0.980**
Qwen2.5-VL	0.619	0.621	0.641	0.618	0.620	0.641	0.970	0.967	0.973
Bespoke	0.636	0.641	0.647	0.634	0.640	0.645	0.975	0.975	0.976
Phi-4	0.532	0.531	0.596	0.531	0.529	0.595	0.950	0.944	0.956
Ensemble	0.646	0.651	0.660	0.645	0.650	0.658	0.974	0.974	0.976

Table 1: Comparison across ROUGE (R1, RL) and BERTScore (BS) metrics (F1, Precision, Recall) on **validation (without CoT)** after applying post-processing.

Model	R1-F1	R1-P	R1-R	RL-F1	RL-P	RL-R	BS-F1	BS-P	BS-R
InternVL3	**0.740**	**0.754**	**0.739**	**0.740**	**0.754**	**0.738**	**0.983**	**0.985**	**0.982**
Qwen2.5-VL	0.695	0.699	0.714	0.694	0.698	0.713	0.975	0.973	0.977
Bespoke	0.709	0.716	0.716	0.708	0.715	0.715	0.979	0.979	0.979
Phi-4	0.562	0.566	0.578	0.561	0.565	0.578	0.969	0.966	0.970
Ensemble	0.735	0.744	0.744	0.734	0.743	0.743	0.979	0.978	0.980
InternVL3	0.727	0.739	0.728	0.727	0.738	0.727	0.982	0.983	0.981
Qwen2.5-VL	0.633	0.633	0.658	0.633	0.632	0.658	0.972	0.969	0.975
Bespoke	0.652	0.657	0.664	0.651	0.656	0.663	0.976	0.976	0.977
Phi-4	0.544	0.540	0.600	0.543	0.540	0.600	0.954	0.948	0.960
Ensemble	0.705	0.714	0.710	0.704	0.713	0.709	0.979	0.979	0.979
Baseline 1	0.180	0.164	0.498	0.180	0.163	0.496	0.834	0.812	0.857
Baseline 2	0.700	0.707	0.710	0.699	0.707	0.710	0.977	0.977	0.978

Table 2: Comparison across ROUGE (R1, RL) and BERTScore (BS) metrics (F1, Precision, Recall) on **test with CoT (top) and without CoT (bottom)** after applying post-processing.

4.4 Postprocessing

Our post-processing pipeline involved two key modifications to improve answer quality and evaluation metrics. First, all $|end|$ tags were removed from generated responses to ensure clean output format. Then, for questions where the reasoning process determined insufficient information to give a valid response, outputs were standardized to "It is not possible to answer this question based only on the provided data." regardless of the initial model output. Model outputs, after applying post-processing, were evaluated on both the test set (Table 2) and validation set (Table 1) using BERTScore and ROUGE metrics.

4.5 Results

Our final system, based on an ensemble approach, was submitted to the challenge leaderboard and ranked 5th. Table 10 in Appendix shows the top-7 rankings as on the leaderboard.

Chain-of-Thought Performance: CoT prompting achieved consistent improvements across all VLMs on the test set, with gain in scores for complex multi-step reasoning questions. CoT with rethinking mechanisms demonstrated the most stable performance across different question types.

Model Scale Impact: Larger parameter models consistently outperformed smaller variants on the test set, confirming the correlation between model capacity and reasoning quality in scientific visual question answering.

Comparative Performance: InternVL3 achieved the highest individual model performance, outperforming other individual models by at least +0.30 ROUGE-1 F1 score on the test split.

5 Conclusion and Future Work

This work demonstrates that advanced vision encoding architecture, combined with systematic prompt engineering, provides a highly effective approach to scientific visual question answering. High-quality visual understanding is critical for strong performance. Our approach establishes a strong baseline for the SciVQA dataset with a ROUGE-1 and ROUGE-L F1 score of 0.740.

5.1 Future Directions

Advanced Reasoning Techniques: Exploring advanced prompting techniques such as Tree-of-Thought (Yao et al., 2023), leveraging Mixture-of-Experts (MoE) (Shazeer et al., 2017) models tailored to different question-answer pairs, and incorporating expert-critic ensembles for answer re-ranking holds significant potential for enhancing overall performance.

Scalability and Model Improvements: Running inference using larger models or fine-tuning the current models on this dataset, enabled by increased computational resources, is expected to yield substantial performance gains.

Quality of the Dataset: Addressing the identified dataset quality issues from Appendix C by standardizing data formatting (e.g., multi-correct answers, numerical representations, and answer formatting) and conducting a comprehensive review of the gold standard annotations, to ensure more accurate evaluations. These improvements will enhance dataset accuracy, provide fairer evaluations, and help ensure more reliable model performance comparisons in subsequent iterations of this task.

Limitations

Due to computational resource constraints, experiments were primarily limited to 7B model variants. Larger model variants and fine-tuning using the entire train split would most definitely yield superior results.

References

Shuai Bai, Keqin Chen, Xuejing Liu, Jialin Wang, Wenbin Ge, Sibo Song, Kai Dang, Peng Wang, Shijie Wang, Jun Tang, Humen Zhong, Yuanzhi Zhu, Mingkun Yang, Zhaohai Li, Jianqiang Wan, Pengfei Wang, Wei Ding, Zheren Fu, Yiheng Xu, Jiabo Ye, Xi Zhang, Tianbao Xie, Zesen Cheng, Hang Zhang, Zhibo Yang, Haiyang Xu, and Junyang Lin. 2025. Qwen2.5-vl technical report.

Ekaterina Borisova, Nikolas Rauscher, and Georg Rehm. 2025. SciVQA 2025: Overview of the first scientific visual question answering shared task. In *Proceedings of the 5th Workshop on Scholarly Document Processing (SDP)*, Vienna, Austria.

Victor Carbune, Hassan Mansoor, Fangyu Liu, Rahul Aralikatte, Gilles Baechler, Jindong Chen, and Abhanshu Sharma. 2024. Chart-based reasoning: Transferring capabilities from llms to vlms.

Yucheng Han, Chi Zhang, Xin Chen, Xu Yang, Zhibin Wang, Gang Yu, Bin Fu, and Hanwang Zhang. 2023. Chartllama: A multimodal llm for chart understanding and generation.

Edward J. Hu, Yelong Shen, Phillip Wallis, Zeyuan Allen-Zhu, Yuanzhi Li, Shean Wang, Lu Wang, and Weizhu Chen. 2021. Lora: Low-rank adaptation of large language models.

Md. Farhan Ishmam, Md. Sakib Hossain Shovon, M.F. Mridha, and Nilanjan Dey. 2024. From image to language: A critical analysis of visual question answering (vqa) approaches, challenges, and opportunities. *Information Fusion*, 106:102270.

Raihan Kabir, Naznin Haque, Md Saiful Islam, and Marium-E-Jannat. 2024. A comprehensive survey on visual question answering datasets and algorithms.

Woosuk Kwon, Zhuohan Li, Siyuan Zhuang, Ying Sheng, Lianmin Zheng, Cody Hao Yu, Joseph E. Gonzalez, Hao Zhang, and Ion Stoica. 2023. Efficient memory management for large language model serving with pagedattention.

Pan Lu, Hritik Bansal, Tony Xia, Jiacheng Liu, Chunyuan Li, Hannaneh Hajishirzi, Hao Cheng, Kai-Wei Chang, Michel Galley, and Jianfeng Gao. 2024. Mathvista: Evaluating mathematical reasoning of foundation models in visual contexts.

Ahmed Masry, Parsa Kavehzadeh, Xuan Long Do, Enamul Hoque, and Shafiq Joty. 2023. Unichart: A universal vision-language pretrained model for chart comprehension and reasoning.

Ahmed Masry, Do Xuan Long, Jia Qing Tan, Shafiq Joty, and Enamul Hoque. 2022. Chartqa: A benchmark for question answering about charts with visual and logical reasoning. *arXiv preprint arXiv:2203.10244*.

Microsoft, :, Abdelrahman Abouelenin, Atabak Ashfaq, Adam Atkinson, Hany Awadalla, Nguyen Bach, Jianmin Bao, Alon Benhaim, Martin Cai, Vishrav Chaudhary, Congcong Chen, Dong Chen, Dongdong Chen, Junkun Chen, Weizhu Chen, Yen-Chun Chen, Yi ling Chen, Qi Dai, Xiyang Dai, Ruchao Fan, Mei Gao, Min Gao, Amit Garg, Abhishek Goswami, Junheng Hao, Amr Hendy, Yuxuan Hu, Xin Jin, Mahmoud Khademi, Dongwoo Kim, Young Jin Kim, Gina Lee, Jinyu Li, Yunsheng Li, Chen Liang, Xihui Lin, Zeqi Lin, Mengchen Liu, Yang Liu, Gilsinia Lopez, Chong Luo, Piyush Madan, Vadim Mazalov, Arindam Mitra, Ali Mousavi, Anh Nguyen, Jing Pan, Daniel Perez-Becker, Jacob Platin, Thomas Portet, Kai Qiu, Bo Ren, Liliang Ren, Sambuddha Roy, Ning Shang, Yelong Shen, Saksham Singhal, Subhojit Som, Xia Song, Tetyana Sych, Praneetha Vaddamanu, Shuohang Wang, Yiming Wang, Zhenghao Wang, Haibin Wu, Haoran Xu, Weijian Xu, Yifan Yang, Ziyi Yang, Donghan Yu, Ishmam Zabir, Jianwen Zhang, Li Lyna Zhang, Yunan Zhang, and Xiren Zhou. 2025. Phi-4-mini technical report: Compact yet powerful multimodal language models via mixture-of-loras.

Shraman Pramanick, Rama Chellappa, and Subhashini Venugopalan. 2025. Spiqa: A dataset for multimodal question answering on scientific papers.

Rafael Rafailov, Archit Sharma, Eric Mitchell, Stefano Ermon, Christopher D. Manning, and Chelsea Finn. 2024. Direct preference optimization: Your language model is secretly a reward model.

Noam Shazeer, Azalia Mirhoseini, Krzysztof Maziarz, Andy Davis, Quoc Le, Geoffrey Hinton, and Jeff Dean. 2017. Outrageously large neural networks: The sparsely-gated mixture-of-experts layer.

Md Mehrab Tanjim, Ryan A. Rossi, Mike Rimer, Xiang Chen, Sungchul Kim, Vaishnavi Muppala, Tong Yu, Zhengmian Hu, Ritwik Sinha, Wei Zhang, Iftikhar Ahamath Burhanuddin, and Franck Dernoncourt. 2025. Exploring rewriting approaches for different conversational tasks.

Omkar Thawakar, Dinura Dissanayake, Ketan More, Ritesh Thawkar, Ahmed Heakl, Noor Ahsan, Yuhao Li, Mohammed Zumri, Jean Lahoud, Rao Muhammad Anwer, Hisham Cholakkal, Ivan Laptev, Mubarak Shah, Fahad Shahbaz Khan, and Salman Khan. 2025. Llamav-o1: Rethinking step-by-step visual reasoning in llms.

Haozhe Wang, Chao Qu, Zuming Huang, Wei Chu, Fangzhen Lin, and Wenhu Chen. 2025. Vl-rethinker: Incentivizing self-reflection of vision-language models with reinforcement learning.

Zirui Wang, Mengzhou Xia, Luxi He, Howard Chen, Yitao Liu, Richard Zhu, Kaiqu Liang, Xindi Wu, Haotian Liu, Sadhika Malladi, et al. 2024. Charxiv: Charting gaps in realistic chart understanding in multimodal llms. *Advances in Neural Information Processing Systems*, 37:113569–113697.

Jason Wei, Xuezhi Wang, Dale Schuurmans, Maarten Bosma, Brian Ichter, Fei Xia, Ed Chi, Quoc Le, and Denny Zhou. 2023. Chain-of-thought prompting elicits reasoning in large language models.

Shunyu Yao, Dian Yu, Jeffrey Zhao, Izhak Shafran, Thomas L. Griffiths, Yuan Cao, and Karthik Narasimhan. 2023. Tree of thoughts: Deliberate problem solving with large language models.

Hongli Zhan, Muneeza Azmat, Raya Horesh, Junyi Jessy Li, and Mikhail Yurochkin. 2025. Spri: Aligning large language models with context-situated principles.

Qihao Zhu Runxin Xu Junxiao Song Mingchuan Zhang Y.K. Li Y. Wu Daya Guo Zhihong Shao, Peiyi Wang. 2024. Deepseekmath: Pushing the limits of mathematical reasoning in open language models.

Jinguo Zhu, Weiyun Wang, Zhe Chen, Zhaoyang Liu, Shenglong Ye, Lixin Gu, Hao Tian, Yuchen Duan, Weijie Su, Jie Shao, Zhangwei Gao, Erfei Cui, Xuehui Wang, Yue Cao, Yangzhou Liu, Xingguang Wei, Hongjie Zhang, Haomin Wang, Weiye Xu, Hao Li, Jiahao Wang, Nianchen Deng, Songze Li, Yinan He, Tan Jiang, Jiapeng Luo, Yi Wang, Conghui He, Botian Shi, Xingcheng Zhang, Wenqi Shao, Junjun He, Yingtong Xiong, Wenwen Qu, Peng Sun, Penglong Jiao, Han Lv, Lijun Wu, Kaipeng Zhang, Huipeng Deng, Jiaye Ge, Kai Chen, Limin Wang, Min Dou, Lewei Lu, Xizhou Zhu, Tong Lu, Dahua Lin, Yu Qiao, Jifeng Dai, and Wenhai Wang. 2025. Internvl3: Exploring advanced training and test-time recipes for open-source multimodal models.

Appendix

A Dataset Distribution

The dataset is biased toward line charts (66%), requiring strong numerical reading capabilities. Additionally, a high percentage of non-visual questions (around 60%) highlights the need for reasoning that goes beyond visual features.

Dataset Split	Samples
Train	15,120
Validation	1,680
Test	4,200

Table 3: Dataset split with number of samples.

QA Type	Answer Set		Samples
Closed -ended	Infinite	Visual	1,079
		Non-visual	2,172
	Finite	Binary & Visual	1,124
		Binary & Non-visual	3,219
		Non-binary & Visual	1,751
		Non-binary & Non-visual	3,615
Unanswerable			2,160

Table 4: QA Pair Type Categorization in the Train split.

Figure Type	Samples
Line Chart	10,007
Tree	924
Scatter Plot	735
Graph	553
Bar Chart	525
Architecture Diagram	504
Pie Chart	497
Neural Networks	462
Confusion Matrix	427
Box Plot	133
Histogram	77
Other	77

Table 5: Figure Type Distribution in the Train split.

B Error Analysis

We conducted error analysis manually on the validation dataset because gold answers are available for it. We only selected incorrect predictions and categorized them into three primary types:

Visual Misinterpretations: Issues with feature extraction from images, including:

- Comparing sub-figures on different scales
- Misunderstanding axis starting points
- Difficulties with overlapping text
- Challenges with low-resolution images

Numerical Misalignments: Precision issues in numerical extraction and calculation, often stemming from visual ambiguity in chart elements.

Flawed Reasoning: Instances where logical progression was incorrect despite proper visual observation, or cases where correct reasoning led to incorrect answers due to misalignment with reference answer formats.

Notably, some failures occurred in compound charts and arose from misinterpreted visual cues or insufficient numerical precision. The use of more powerful vision encoders could address many of these issues and further improve performance.

C Dataset Quality Issues

During our validation analysis, we identified several systematic inconsistencies in the gold standard annotations that may impact evaluation reliability:

Format Inconsistencies:

- Multi-correct answers appear in inconsistent formats: ["A", "B"] instead of the expected A,B format
- Numerical representations vary between word form ("three") and digit form ("3") within similar contexts
- Answer formatting lacks standardization across question types

Annotation Errors: We identified potential annotation errors through manual inspection. For example: instance_id 09dab5a715034cebb2a62f0f1c2a75c9 gold answer is "52,3%" but visual inspection suggests that the correct answer should be "3%" or "3", which our models corrects predict.

These inconsistencies suggest that reported performance metrics may underestimate true model capabilities, as models may be penalized for providing correct answers that don't match inconsistent gold standards. A comprehensive gold standard review and standardization would benefit future iterations of this shared task.

D Alternative Approaches Evaluated

Majority Voting: Simple majority voting across models showed minimal improvement over InternVL3 alone, confirming the quality-over-quantity principle.
Fine-tuning: Limited computational resources prevented extensive fine-tuning, but initial experiments suggested that InternVL3's pre-trained capabilities were already well-suited for the task. To enhance performance, we performed supervised fine-tuning (SFT) using LoRA (Hu et al., 2021), targeting all linear layers and the vision encoder, on a subset of 5,000 training samples for the Bespoke MiniChart model, which yielded a slight performance improvement. We are currently extending this approach by applying Group Relative Policy Optimization (GRPO)-based (Zhihong Shao, 2024) fine-tuning in a similar fashion.

E Tables

Baseline	Prompt Content
1	You are a helpful assistant. Give the concise answer for the context given below. The caption of the figure is mentioned as, [caption]. The question for the figure is, [question]
2	Answer the question with only the raw numerical value or single word/phrase, omitting all units, context words, and explanatory text. The caption of the figure is mentioned as, [caption]. The question for the figure is, [question]

Table 6: Baseline Prompts

Prompt Type	Prompt Content
Base	Answer the question with only the raw numerical value or single word/phrase, omitting all units, context words, and explanatory text. The caption of the figure is mentioned as, [caption].
Compound Images	This is a compound figure containing multiple subfigures. Navigate to [fig_numb] graph in the compound figure to answer the question.
Figure Type	**Line Chart:** Focus on the following aspects of the line chart: • Colors of different lines and their meanings • X and Y axis labels and their units • Scale and range of values • Trends and patterns in the lines **Bar Chart:** Focus on the following aspects of the bar chart: • Colors of different bars and their meanings • X and Y axis labels and their units • Scale and range of values • Height and position of bars **Box Plot:** Focus on the following aspects of the box plot: • Median line position • Box boundaries (Q1 and Q3) • Whisker extent • Outliers if present **Confusion Matrix:** Focus on the following aspects of the confusion matrix: • Row and column labels • Numerical values in each cell • Color intensity if present • Overall distribution of values **Pie Chart:** Focus on the following aspects of the pie chart: • Segments and their labels • Percentage or proportion values • Colors of different segments • Size of each segment relative to others **Others:** Focus on the following aspects of the figure: • Colors and the labels present in the figure • Any other relevant information present in the figure
Binary	This is a binary question. Answer with 'Yes' or 'No' based on [visual/textual] evidence. Respond affirmatively only if supported.
Choice	Return only the corresponding letter(s) of the correct answer(s). Only output the letter(s) corresponding to the correct choice. [answer_choices]

Table 7: Instruction Prompts for Single Prompt

Prompt Type	Prompt Content
Step 1 Base Prompt	STEP 1: INITIAL ANALYSIS Given the figure, caption, and question, analyze and answer step by step. Regularly perform self-questioning, self-verification, self-correction to check your ongoing reasoning, using connectives such as "Wait a moment", "Wait, does it seem right?" etc. Caption: [caption] Question: [question] Analyse the key visual elements (lines, shapes, colors) that address the question and analyze the relationships between elements. Then, extract the specific numerical/positional information from the figure and caption to answer the question.
Compound Images Prompt	Same as single prompt
Step 2 Base Prompt	STEP 2: COT INFERENCE Answer the question with only the raw numerical value or single word/phrase, omitting all units, context words, and explanatory text. Approximations in the scale are allowed.
Figure Type Prompt	Same as single prompt
Binary Prompt	Same as single prompt
Choice Prompt	*(For non-binary finite answer sets)*: Based on the reasoning above, match it to one or more of the provided answer options: [answer_choices] Return only the corresponding letter(s) of the correct answer(s). Do not explain your choice, do not rephrase the answer, and do not repeat the option text. Only output the letter(s) corresponding to the correct choice. If multiple letters are correct, separate them by commas without spaces (for example: B,C). If all options are correct, return A,B,C,D. Do not add anything else.

Table 8: Instruction Prompts for CoT

Chart Type	Bespoke		InternVL3		Qwen2.5-VL		Phi-4	
	Acc. (mean)	Std. Dev.	Acc. (mean)	Std. Dev.	Acc. (mean)	Std. Dev.	Acc. (mean)	Std. Dev.
line_chart	54.23	49.82	63.97	48.01	50.68	50.00	42.40	49.42
line_chart,table	42.86	49.49	85.71	34.99	42.86	49.49	57.14	49.49
tree	56.19	49.62	61.90	48.56	53.33	49.89	44.76	49.72
scatter_plot	55.71	49.67	70.00	45.83	57.14	49.49	40.00	48.99
pie_chart	67.35	46.89	73.47	44.15	67.35	46.89	44.90	49.74
architecture_diagram	67.86	46.70	76.79	42.22	55.36	49.71	28.57	45.18
box_plot	50.00	50.00	50.00	50.00	50.00	50.00	35.71	47.92
neural_networks	62.50	48.41	71.43	45.18	58.93	49.20	32.14	46.70
confusion_matrix	54.76	49.77	64.29	47.92	57.14	49.49	40.48	49.08
graph	57.14	49.97	60.71	48.84	46.43	49.87	41.07	49.20
bar_chart	53.06	49.91	69.39	46.09	51.02	49.99	40.82	49.15
histogram	35.71	47.92	71.43	45.18	35.71	47.92	50.00	50.00
venn_diagram	57.14	49.49	85.71	34.99	57.14	49.49	57.14	49.49
vector_plot	71.43	45.18	100.00	0.00	85.71	34.99	85.71	34.99
other	42.86	49.49	57.14	49.49	42.86	49.49	42.86	49.49
line_chart,bar_chart	28.57	45.18	71.43	45.18	14.29	34.99	28.57	45.18
flow_chart	85.71	34.99	85.71	34.99	71.43	45.18	42.86	49.49
tree,graph	28.57	45.18	42.86	49.49	42.86	49.49	14.29	34.99
illustrative_diagram	28.57	45.18	71.43	45.18	28.57	45.18	57.14	49.49
line_chart,scatter_plot	71.43	45.18	71.43	45.18	42.86	49.49	42.86	49.49
heat_map	57.14	49.49	71.43	45.18	28.57	45.18	57.14	49.49

Table 9: Scores for exact match across models for various chart types. Accuracy and standard deviation (both in %) are shown.

Rank	Team	R1-F1	R1-P	R1-R	RL-F1	RL-P	RL-R	BS-F1	BS-P	BS-R
1	ExpertNeurons	0.805	0.809	0.811	0.804	0.808	0.810	0.985	0.985	0.985
2	THAii_LAB	0.790	0.796	0.795	0.789	0.795	0.794	0.984	0.984	0.984
3	Coling_UniA	0.786	0.798	0.786	0.786	0.796	0.785	0.982	0.983	0.981
4	florian	0.763	0.766	0.770	0.762	0.765	0.769	0.983	0.983	0.984
5	Infyn	0.735	0.744	0.744	0.734	0.743	0.743	0.979	0.978	0.980
6	Soham Chitnis	0.706	0.719	0.705	0.705	0.719	0.704	0.980	0.982	0.979
7	psr123	0.607	0.609	0.617	0.606	0.608	0.616	0.959	0.959	0.959

Table 10: Top-7 leaderboard rankings

The ClimateCheck Shared Task: Scientific Fact-Checking of Social Media Claims about Climate Change

Raia Abu Ahmad[1,2], **Aida Usmanova**[3], **Georg Rehm**[1,4]

[1]Deutsches Forschungszentrum für Künstliche Intelligenz GmbH (DFKI), Berlin, Germany
[2]Technische Universität Berlin, Germany [3]Leuphana Universität Lüneburg, Germany
[4]Humboldt-Universität zu Berlin, Germany

Corresponding author: raia.abu_ahmad@dfki.de

Abstract

Misinformation in public discourse on global and significant issues like climate change is often facilitated through social media. However, current systems do not address fact-checking climate-related claims against trustworthy, evidence-based sources, such as scientific publications. To address this, we organised the ClimateCheck shared task at the 5th Scholarly Document Processing (SDP) Workshop, co-located with ACL 2025 in Vienna, Austria. The task featured two subtasks: I. Abstracts retrieval given a claim, and II. Claim verification based on the retrieved abstract. ClimateCheck had 27 registered users with active participation from 13 teams, ten of which submitted results for the first subtask and three for the second. The winning team achieved a Recall@10 score of 0.66 and a Binary Preference score of 0.49 for subtask I, and an F1 score of 0.73 for subtask II. Their method combined sparse retrieval using BM25, an ensemble of fine-tuned cross-encoder models using BGE-rerankers, and LLMs for classification.

1 Introduction

The widespread use of social media has transformed the way people engage with crucial global challenges such as climate change. While these platforms enable a public dialogue, they also fast-track the spread of inaccurate and misleading information (Fownes et al., 2018; Al-Rawi et al., 2021).

Recent work in natural language processing (NLP) offers promising advances in decoding and analysing complex discourse online (Stede and Patz, 2021). Researchers have used methods to detect misinformation (Aldwairi and Alwahedi, 2018; Aïmeur et al., 2023), extract scientific claims and entities (Hafid et al., 2022; Hughes and Song, 2024), and fact-check statements (Guo et al., 2022; Diggelmann et al., 2020). At the same time, work on scholarly document processing has advanced methods for extracting and structuring scientific knowledge (Dagdelen et al., 2024), making it easier to link it to public discourse.

Shared tasks are effective tools for mobilising the research community around challenging tasks, driving innovation and the development of state-of-the-art methods (Filannino and Uzuner, 2018). Previous shared tasks targeted fact-checking by retrieving relevant evidence for a given claim and classifying their relation. However, they mainly focused on non-scientific evidence corpora, e. g., Wikipedia (Thorne et al., 2018; Aly et al., 2021), or were limited to the biomedical domain (Wadden and Lo, 2021). To the best of our knowledge, no previous effort has tackled the challenge of connecting claims posted online about climate change to credible scientific sources.

To address this, we present **the ClimateCheck shared task**, focusing on automatic fact-checking of climate-related claims from social media against scientific publications. The task was hosted at the 5th Scholarly Document Processing (SDP) Workshop[1] and consisted of two subtasks: (I) Retrieving relevant scientific documents for a given claim, and (II) Classifying the claim's veracity based on the retrieved evidence. Subtask I was evaluated using the average scores of Recall@K ($K = 2, 5, 10$) and Binary Preference (Bpref, Buckley and Voorhees, 2004), and subtask II was evaluated using the F1 score in addition to Recall@10 from subtask I.

We used the Codabench platform to host the task (Xu et al., 2022), attracting registrations from 27 users and 13 active teams, ten of which submitted results to the leaderboard.[2] The competition followed the timeline below:

- Training set release: April 1, 2025
- Test set release: April 15, 2025
- Systems submissions deadline: May 16, 2025

[1]https://sdproc.org/2025/
[2]https://www.codabench.org/competitions/6639/

Proceedings of the Fifth Workshop on Scholarly Document Processing (SDP 2025), pages 263–275
July 31, 2025 ©2025 Association for Computational Linguistics

- Paper submission deadline: May 23, 2025
- Notification of acceptance: June 13, 2025
- Camera-ready paper due: June 20, 2025
- Workshop date: July 31, 2025

This paper presents an overview of the shared task and summarises the task design (§3), evaluation strategies (§4), dataset preparation (§5), our baselines (§6), approaches of submitted systems (§7), and lessons learned throughout (§8), aiming to inform and encourage future efforts in NLP for mitigating climate change misinformation online.

2 Related Shared Tasks

Several shared tasks have been introduced to support research on automatic evidence retrieval and claim verification. These tasks differ in the domain of claims, the type of evidence corpora, and the complexity of the verification process.

Fact Extraction and VERification (FEVER, Thorne et al., 2018) and its extension, FEVER Over Unstructured and Structured information (FEVEROUS, Aly et al., 2021), were tasks focused on claim verification against Wikipedia articles, the latter expanding into structured evidence such as tables and lists. FEVER established the widely adopted three-stage pipeline of document retrieval, sentence selection, and natural language inference (NLI). However, despite their scale and influence, FEVER and FEVEROUS differ from our effort in their evidence domain, which is encyclopedic rather than scientific, potentially affecting the applicability of certain retrieval methods.

The Automated Verification of Textual Claims (AVeriTeC) shared task was a recent effort presented at the FEVER 2024 Workshop (Schlichtkrull et al., 2024). The task focused on evidence retrieval and veracity prediction of general real-world claims with linked evidence from the web using search engines. This task differs from ours in two main aspects: claims are not domain-specific, and the evidence is retrieved from the web rather than the more trustworthy scientific literature.

The SCIVER shared task was organised at the SDP 2021 workshop, aiming to verify scientific claims extracted from research articles against a given corpus of publications (Wadden and Lo, 2021). Although the task is similar in its focus on scientific evidence, SCIVER's claims originate from research papers and are limited to the biomedical domain, in contrast to our task, which focuses on climate-related claims from public discourse.

Finally, CheckThat!, organised annually as a CLEF lab since 2018 (Nakov et al., 2018), focuses on mitigating misinformation online across different platforms and several languages. Previous editions have addressed claim detection, stance verification, and evidence retrieval, focusing primarily on political and journalistic content. Most recently, the 2025 edition included the Scientific Web Discourse task (Alam et al., 2025), focusing on 1. Detecting whether a post contains references to scientific entities, and 2. Linking posts with implicit references of studies to their relevant publications. These tasks are similar to our work in their objective of connecting public discourse to scientific publications, with task 1 being especially relevant to the pre-processing steps of preparing the ClimateCheck dataset. However, unlike task 2, our work does not assume any mention of a study in a post, rather processing general claims.

3 Task Description

ClimateCheck consisted of two subtasks:

1. **Subtask I – Abstracts Retrieval:** Given a claim from social media about climate change and a corpus of abstracts, retrieve the top 10 most relevant abstracts to the claim.
2. **Subtask II – Claim Verification:** Given the claim-abstract pair received from the previous subtask, classify their relation as 'supports', 'refutes', or 'not enough information (NEI)'.

Participants were allowed to take part either in subtask I only or in both subtasks. The testing dataset consisted of 176 unique claims along with a corpus of 394,269 abstracts from climate-related publications. For the first subtask, the participants were asked to upload a CSV file that includes rows of unique claim-abstract pairs, where each claim was linked to 10 relevant abstracts. If they wished to participate in subtask II, they were asked to add a column denoting the label of the pair. Samples of five claims from the test set along with connected abstracts retrieved by three teams in the competition are available in Appendix A.

4 Evaluation

Subtask I: Abstracts Retrieval

As an information retrieval (IR) task, subtask I tackles identifying relevant pieces of information from large corpora based on a user query. Evaluating IR is an inherently difficult task due to the problem of incomplete relevance annotations when the evidence corpus contains a large number of documents (Buckley and Voorhees, 2004). That is because not all potentially relevant documents can be annotated, making it hard to know whether a system truly failed to retrieve relevant items or simply retrieved items that were never judged.

Various metrics are employed to evaluate IR based on rankings (Buckley and Voorhees, 2004; Järvelin and Kekäläinen, 2002), including Mean Average Precision, Mean Reciprocal Rank, and normalised Discounted Cumulative Gain (Järvelin and Kekäläinen, 2002). However, in our specific task, we faced two primary challenges: the absence of annotated ranking information and the problem of incomplete relevance judgements. Given these constraints, we selected Recall@K and Bpref as our evaluation metrics.

Recall@K measures the proportion of relevant documents retrieved in the top K results. It does not consider the order of the retrieved documents, making it suitable for scenarios where gold ranking information is unavailable. The metric has been widely used to evaluate dense retrieval systems (Karpukhin et al., 2020). In subtask I, we ask participants to retrieve the top 10 abstracts per claim, hence we use $K = 2, 5, 10$ to compare systems on different levels. Bpref is a score designed to handle situations with incomplete relevant judgements. It evaluates how many judged non-relevant documents are retrieved before judged relevant ones, mitigating potential bias introduced by unjudged documents (Buckley and Voorhees, 2004).

The final evaluation of subtask I, which decides the rankings, is the average of the four scores mentioned above. We considered a retrieved abstract to be relevant if it was annotated as evidentiary (i. e., supports or refutes) in our gold data. However, this data was bound to be biased towards our own retrieval method used to create the annotation corpus. Thus, to ensure a fair evaluation, we collected participants' outputs weekly during the test phase, subsequently adding more human-annotated instances to the gold data (see Section 5).

Subtask II: Claim Verification

Claim verification is a classification task, where the system labels each claim-abstract pair retrieved in subtask I as *supports*, *refutes*, or *NEI*, indicating the relation of the abstract to the claim. To evaluate it, we used standard weighted metrics: Precision, Recall, and F1.

Only claim-abstract pairs that have been manually annotated in the gold data were used for evaluation, meaning that unjudged ones were excluded. To ensure a fair comparison across systems, especially since the number of predicted labels varied, the final ranking consisted of the sum of the F1-score and the Recall@10 score from subtask I. This approach rewards systems that not only made accurate classifications, but also retrieved more relevant abstracts, penalising those that have a high F1 score based on only a few examples.

5 Dataset

The foundation of the shared task is the ClimateCheck dataset (Abu Ahmad et al., 2025),[3] consisting of 435 unique English climate-related claims in lay language linked to scientific abstracts, resulting in 1,815 claim-abstract pairs. Each pair was reviewed by two graduate students in climate sciences and annotated as *supports*, *refutes*, or *NEI*. In cases of disagreements, a third student curated the claim-abstract pair, deciding its final label.

Claims were collected from available datasets (Diggelmann et al., 2020; Pougué-Biyong et al., 2021; Shiwakoti et al., 2024; Augenstein et al., 2019), and underwent several pre-processing steps: scientific check-worthiness detection, atomic claim generation, and text style transfer, the latter for those not originating directly from social media. The abstracts were collected from OpenAlex (Priem et al., 2022) and S2ORC (Lo et al., 2020), resulting in a corpus of 394,269 climate-related publications.[4] Claims and abstracts were then linked using BM25 (Robertson and Zaragoza, 2009) followed by a cross-encoder trained on the MS-MARCO data and a TREC-like pooling approach using six models to create the annotation corpus. In Abu Ahmad et al. (2025), we describe the development of the dataset in more detail.

The available data was split into training and test-

[3] https://huggingface.co/datasets/rabuahmad/climatecheck

[4] https://huggingface.co/datasets/rabuahmad/climatecheck_publications_corpus

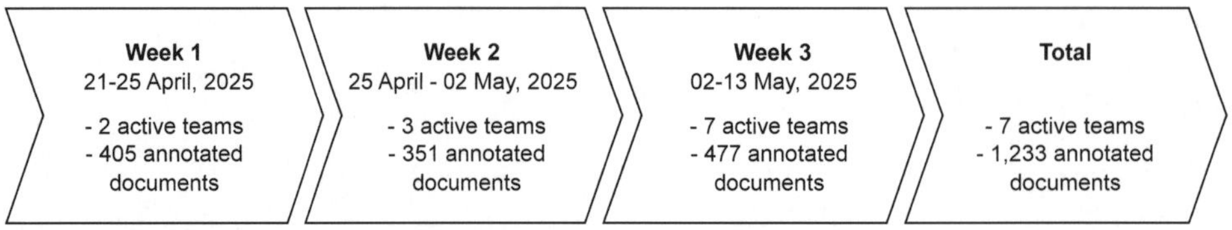

Figure 1: The timeline of our dynamic human annotation process during the testing phase of the ClimateCheck shared task. The process resulted in 1,233 additional claim-abstract pairs added to the gold test data.

ing sets, the former consisting of 259 unique claims and a total of 1,144 claim-abstract pairs, while the latter 176 unique claims and 671 claim-abstract pairs. The annotated pairs of the test set were not released publicly for participants, since they were used as the reference test set for evaluation.

In an attempt to make the evaluation less biased towards the gold test set, which is based on our own linking approach, we annotated more documents on a weekly basis as the task was running. These were based on participants' submissions using the following approach:

1. Every week, we combined the highest-scoring submissions from each active team.
2. For each unique claim-abstract pair, we assessed the agreement among the participating teams (i. e., how many systems retrieved this pair).
3. We annotated pairs with a specific agreement threshold so that as many teams as possible benefit from the new annotations.
4. We updated the gold data with the additional annotations a week later.

The agreement threshold was decided each week depending on the number of submitting teams, taking into account our limited human annotation capacity (four student annotators). If needed, we filtered further based on the rankings of claim-abstract pairs across submitted systems. We summarise the result of this process in Figure 1, and report more details in Appendix B.

To accommodate the timeline of the SDP 2025 workshop and the pace of the annotators, we were able to gather new documents from runs submitted until May 13, 2025, one week before the competition deadline. This process resulted in the addition of 1,233 new claim-abstract pairs added to the gold testing data, with an overall number of 1,904 manually annotated pairs in the gold test set.

6 Baselines

For subtask I, we developed a multi-stage retrieval approach as a baseline, combining sparse and dense retrieval with a neural reranker. BM25 has proven to be a fast and efficient method for initial retrieval (Chen et al., 2017; Nie et al., 2019). We used it as a sparse retrieval step to get an initial set of the top 1000 relevant abstracts per claim. Next, we computed embeddings for each claim and abstract using the msmarco-MiniLM-L-12-v3 sentence transformer,[5] and calculated the cosine similarity for each claim-abstract pair. We selected the top 20 ranked abstracts per claim, filtering out lexically relevant but semantically irrelevant candidates. Finally, a neural reranker, ms-marco-MiniLM-L6-v2,[6] provided cross-encoder scores, resulting in the final candidate pool of the top 10 abstracts per claim.

To obtain labels for each claim-abstract pair as a baseline for subtask II, we used the open source Yi-1.5-9B-Chat-16K model (Young et al., 2024), selected based on our experiments with several models when creating the dataset (Abu Ahmad et al., 2025). The model was prompted in a zero-shot manner with the following prompt:

```
You are an expert claim verification
assistant  with vast knowledge of
climate change , climate science ,
environmental science , physics ,
and energy science.
Your task is to check if the claim is
correct according to the evidence.
Generate 'Supports' if the claim is
correct according to the evidence,
'Refutes' if the claim is incorrect or
cannot be verified, or 'Not enough
information' if you there is not enough
information in the evidence to make an
informed decision.
Only return the verification verdict.
```

[5]https://huggingface.co/sentence-transformers/msmarco-MiniLM-L12-v3

[6]https://huggingface.co/cross-encoder/ms-marco-MiniLM-L6-v2

7 Submitted Systems and Results

A total of ten teams participated in the ClimateCheck shared task, three of which took part in both abstract retrieval and claim verification tasks. Table 1 summarises the submission statistics and Figure 2 illustrates the amount of submissions throughout the one month testing phase of the task.

Number of registered users	27
Number of active users	13
Number of final submissions (subtask I)	10
Number of final submissions (subtask II)	3
Number of total submissions	613
avg. number of submissions per user	43.64
max. number of submissions by a single user	182

Table 1: ClimateCheck submission statistics.

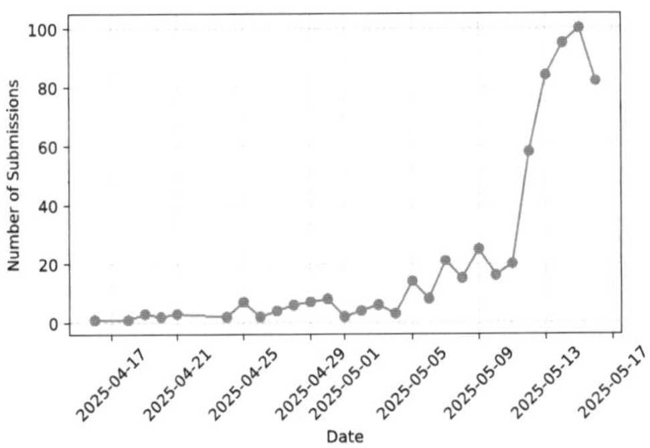

Figure 2: Number of submissions over the one month timeline of the task.

We present the results of subtasks I and II in Tables 2 and 3, respectively. Notably, six teams outperformed our baseline in subtask I, while all of them outperformed it in subtask II. For both subtasks, the winning team is **Ant Bridge**, followed by **akiepura_jlam** in 2nd place, while team **AlexUNLP-FMT** achieves 3rd place in subtask I, and team **EFC** in subtask II. We received system descriptions from the aforementioned top four teams and team **Pranav**, which we briefly summarise below.

7.1 Team Ant Bridge

Team Ant Bridge (Wang et al., 2025) developed a hybrid three-stage approach, combining sparse retrieval, fine-grained reranking, and large language models (LLMs) for claim-abstract classification. As a first step, the team pre-processed all abstract and claim texts to be lowercase, additionally tokenizing and removing punctuation and stopwords. Then, they used BM25 to get the top 5000 abstracts per claim, chosen to maximise recall for the reranking step. In the second stage, they fine-tuned several cross-encoder models based on the BGE-Reranker architecture (Chen et al., 2024a). Training data was constructed as triples of (claim, relevant abstract, irrelevant abstract), with negatives drawn either randomly or as hard negatives, which are abstracts ranked highly by BM25 or semantically close to the claim but not evidentiary. Rerankers were trained using a marginal ranking loss, and their outputs were aggregated using Reciprocal Rank Fusion (RRF, Cormack et al., 2009) to produce the top 10 abstracts per claim.

For subtask II, the team used Gemini 2.5 Pro (Gemini Team et al., 2023) to perform claim-abstract relation classification. Their prompting strategy included persona and task definitions, and supported batch processing of multiple claim-abstract pairs. Additionally, they included distribution guidelines in the prompt to steer the model toward a more balanced output, explicitly instructing it to ensure that the proportion of NEI labels remained at or above 30%. This soft calibration approach helped mitigate bias in label distribution and improved robustness in classification.

7.2 Team akiepura_jlam

The akiepura_jlam team (Kiepura and Lam, 2025) employed a three-stage retrieval and reranking pipeline for subtask I, starting with a hybrid retrieval system that fused BM25, dense and sparse neural retrieval methods using RRF. Their dense model was based on a fine-tuned BGE-M3 encoder (Chen et al., 2024b) trained using triples of (claim, relevant abstract, irrelevant abstract), where NEI-labelled abstracts from the training data served as the negative samples. Dense embeddings were computed for all abstracts, and claim-abstract similarity scores were obtained via dot products. For sparse retrieval, they used SPLADE-v3 (Lassance et al., 2024) to generate high-dimensional vectors for claims and abstracts. The retrieval results from all three methods, BM25, SPLADE, and BGE-M3, were combined with RRF, and the top 600 abstracts per claim were selected for further reranking.

Their second stage comprised of a cross-encoder reranker based on ms-marco-MiniLM-L-6-v2[7] (Wang et al., 2020), which was fine-tuned on the ClimateCheck data using the top 200 candidates

[7] https://huggingface.co/cross-encoder/ms-marco-MiniLM-L6-v2

Rank	Team	Recall@2	Recall@5	Recall@10	Bpref	Subtask I Score
1	Ant Bridge	*0.21848*	**0.45112**	**0.66476**	**0.49470**	**0.45727**
2	akiepura_jlam	**0.23085**	*0.44128*	*0.60061*	*0.48179*	*0.43863*
3	AlexUNLP-FMT	0.20997	0.39627	0.59112	0.46348	0.41521
4	EFC	0.21769	0.40582	0.57411	0.44952	0.41178
5	gmguarino	0.18064	0.3386	0.47696	0.38678	0.34574
6	Pranav	0.17988	0.31059	0.44038	0.37614	0.32675
–	Our baseline	0.1947	0.30468	0.34359	0.29803	0.28525
7	vanguard	0.1065	0.18062	0.27069	0.243	0.2002
8	nakrayko	0.11499	0.16868	0.27069	0.24266	0.19926
9	lephuquy	0.11101	0.15483	0.15759	0.14953	0.14324
10	seniichev	0.07889	0.12156	0.17622	0.14888	0.13139

Table 2: Results of Subtask I: Abstracts Retrieval; top result in bold, runner-up italicised, third place underlined.

Rank	Team	Precision	Recall	F1	Subtask II Score
1	Ant Bridge	**0.72905**	**0.72644**	**0.72528**	**1.39004**
2	akiepura_jlam	0.69496	0.69726	0.69573	*1.29634*
3	EFC	*0.71676*	*0.71746*	*0.71696*	1.29107
–	Our baseline	0.65448	0.62603	0.63148	0.97507

Table 3: Results of Subtask II: Claim Verification; top result in bold, runner-up italicised, third place underlined.

from Stage 1. Training again involved both positive (evidentiary) and negative (NEI and random) examples. The top 20 reranked abstracts were passed to Stage 3, where a few-shot LLM-based reranker was used, namely RankGPT (Sun et al., 2023) using GPT-4.1[8]. RankGPT treated reranking as a permutation task, reasoning over the full set of abstracts per claim to produce a final ordering. Their final ranking combined the LLM's output with the semantic precision score from the cross-encoder. An ablation study demonstrated the incremental benefits of each stage, showcasing the effectiveness of the entire pipeline.

For subtask II, team akiepura_jlam experimented with both zero- and few-shot prompting, as well as fine-tuned transformer classifiers, with their best performance coming from a hybrid zero-shot prompt that first asked the LLM to determine whether an abstract was evidentiary and if so, to assess whether it supported or refuted the claim.

7.3 Team AlexUNLP-FMT

Team AlexUNLP-FMT (Fathallah et al., 2025) participated only in subtask I, proposing a hybrid retrieval and adaptive reranking strategy to address the limitation of excluding relevant documents in the initial retrieval step. The team combined sparse retrieval, using BM25, with dense retrieval, using a fine-tuned Stella-en-400M-v5 (Zhang et al., 2024) in a contrastive learning approach. From each retrieval method, they extracted the top 50 abstract candidates from the original set of publications. The candidates from both methods were combined, deduplicated, and an initial reranking set was formed. This was followed by the ms-marco-MiniLM-L12-v2 reranker[9] obtaining the top 30 abstracts from the initial reranking set.

For each of the 30 abstracts, the top 10 were selected by choosing the closest neighbours from a similarity graph. The graph was constructed from the entire abstract corpus using the all-MiniLM-L6-v2 bi-encoder model[10]. Each abstract in the graph was connected to the top 10 most semantically similar abstracts, and an iterative process of augmenting candidate sets with semantic neighbours was repeated 20 times. In the last iteration, the top 10 most relevant abstracts with respect to a given claim were selected.

7.4 Team EFC

Similar to other teams, EFC's pipeline included sparse and dense retrieval stages followed by a reranker (Upravitelev et al., 2025). First, 1,500 abstracts were retrieved via BM25, further reduced using a fine-tuned e5-large-v2 model[11] to 150 ab-

[8] https://openai.com/index/gpt-4-1/

[9] https://huggingface.co/cross-encoder/ms-marco-MiniLM-L12-v2

[10] https://huggingface.co/sentence-transformers/all-MiniLM-L6-v2

[11] https://huggingface.co/intfloat/e5-large-v2

Team	Sparse Retrieval	Dense Retrieval	Cross-Encoder	LLM	Graph
Ant Bridge	BM25	✗	BGE-reranker*	✗	✗
akiepura_jlam	BM25, SPLADE	BGE-M3*	MiniLM*	GPT-4.1	✗
AlexUNLP-FMT	BM25	Stella*	MiniLM	✗	MiniLM
EFC	BM25	E5*	MiniLM	✗	✗
Pranav	SPLADE	✗	✗	Gemini-2.0-Flash	✗
Our baseline	BM25	MiniLM	MiniLM	✗	✗

Table 4: Summary of retrieval systems used for subtask I; * indicates fine-tuning with contrastive learning.

Team	LLM	Classification Setup
Ant Bridge	Gemini 2.5	ZS + distribution guidelines
akiepura_jlam	GPT-4.1	Hybrid ZS
EFC	Qwen 14B	ZS w/ reasoning
Our baseline	Yi-1.5-9B-Chat-16K	ZS

Table 5: Summary of classification models used for subtask II (ZS = zero-shot).

stracts. The model was fine-tuned on the entire ClimateCheck training set for three epochs, utilising a contrastive learning approach with positive and negative samples, the latter mined by retrieving the three least relevant publications using their dense retrieval method. Finally, the ms-marco-MiniLM-L12-v2 reranker, also used by Team AlexUNLP-FMT, was applied to get the top 10 relevant abstracts per claim.

To minimise computational inference cost, the team chose to compare smaller encoder-only architectures with larger decoder-only LLMs for subtask II. Their best-performing encoder only model was DeBERTa-v3-large[12], fine-tuned on several NLI datasets as well as the ClimateCheck dataset, while the best LLM was Qwen3 with 14B parameters (Yang et al., 2025). Their best results, those submitted to the leaderboard, were achieved using the Qwen model. However, the team demonstrated that the fine-tuned DeBERTa is not far behind, with a total score of 1.257 in subtask II, while requiring about 0.0026 of the runtime that Qwen needs.

7.5 Team Pranav

Team Pranav participated only in subtask I, utilising a two-stage retrieve-and-rerank approach. They start with sparse retrieval using SPLADE-v3[13] by indexing the entire publications corpus with sparse vector representations. Then, for each claim, they calculate the dot product similarity to retrieve the top 40 abstracts. The second stage of the approach is based on LLM reranking using the Gemini-2.0-Flash[14] model with a list-wise strategy. The LLM is presented with all 40 candidates simultaneously, prompting it to rerank and output the top 10 abstracts that provide evidence to the claim.

8 Discussion

The submissions to ClimateCheck reveal key design patterns and trade-offs in building claim verification pipelines grounded in scientific literature. Although architecture choices varied, several common effective strategies emerged across top-performing teams. We summarise the approaches for subtasks I and II in Tables 4 and 5, respectively, and compare their results visually in Figure 3.

A clear pattern from subtask I is the use of hybrid pipelines, combining sparse retrievers (e.g., BM25 and SPLADE) with different dense retrievers, as well as cross-encoder rerankers (e.g., BGE and MiniLM). Three teams extended this by utilising more advanced components: LLM-based reranking (akiepura_jlam and Pranav) and graph-based reranking (AlexUNLP-FMT). Although the teams achieved competitive scores, they were still outperformed by the relatively simpler ensemble of fine-tuned cross-encoders using RRF presented by Ant Bridge.

Despite variations in retrieval strategies, all teams, except Pranav, followed a similar paradigm of fine-tuning models with the available training data in a contrastive learning approach. The main difference in their approaches was the way negative samples were selected, with some incorporating NEI-labelled abstracts, while others using the

[12] https://huggingface.co/MoritzLaurer/DeBERTa-v3-large-mnli-fever-anli-ling-wanli

[13] https://huggingface.co/naver/splade-v3

[14] https://deepmind.google/models/gemini/flash/

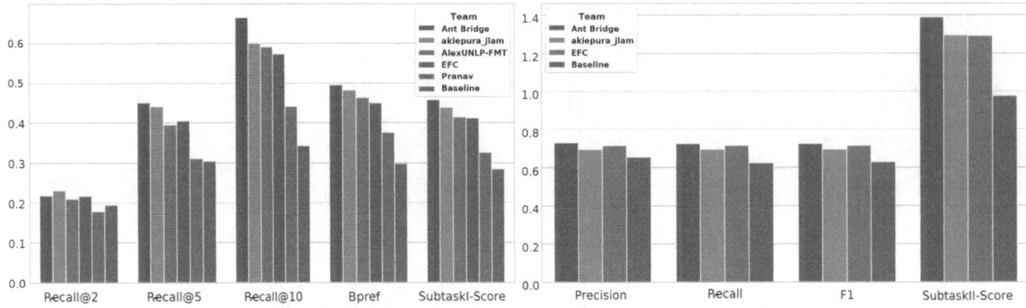

(a) Subtask I Scores **(b) Subtask II Scores**

Figure 3: Results of participants who submitted system descriptions compared to our baselines for subtask I (left) and subtask II (right). Subtask I scores are reported using Recall@K ($K = 2, 5, 10$), Bpref, and the average-based SubtaskI-Score. Subtask II scores are reported using weighted metrics of Precision, Recall, and F1, along with SubtaskII-Score which is the sum of Recall@10 from subtask I and F1 from subtask II.

least relevant abstracts from their own retrieval approach. We hypothesise that this enabled models to distinguish subtle semantic differences in scientific discourse (Zhan et al., 2021). Notably, the top two systems fine-tuned the cross-encoders, while the others did so on their dense retrieval models.

When comparing systems, we additionally note the impact of retrieval depth and recall preservation. The top-ranked system retrieved up to 5000 abstracts per claim before reranking, enabling a high coverage of potentially relevant documents. In contrast, systems that retrieved a limited number of abstracts early on could have missed documents, impacting the effectiveness of reranking. This highlights that in tasks where relevant evidence is sparse and semantically complex, such as scientific abstracts, high recall in retrieval is effective.

For subtask II, all leaderboard results employed an LLM classification approach, resulting in relatively small margins in their scores. Notably, the top two teams used closed-source, commercial LLMs, while the third ranked team and the baseline employed open-source models. That being said, team EFC showed that a more lightweight architecture, fine-tuned correctly, can still yield competitive results, highlighted by the results they achieved using DeBERTa. This emphasises the practical trade-off between performance and efficiency, which is an important consideration for real-world applications such as content moderation or misinformation detection. In such scenarios, latency, scalability, and interpretability matter. Thus, systems optimised for low-resource settings remain very relevant, while other systems that employ commercial LLMs might be less useful.

9 Conclusion

This paper presented the ClimateCheck shared task, which focused on fact-checking claims from social media about climate change against scholarly articles. The task ran during April/May 2025 and was hosted as part of the 5th SDP Workshop in 2025. Given a claim, two subtasks were available: (I) Retrieving the top 10 most relevant (i. e., evidentiary) abstracts, and (II) Classifying the veracity of the claim given the abstract. The first subtask was evaluated using Recall@K ($K = 2, 5, 10$) and Bpref, while the second using F1 with additional scaling based on correctly retrieved abstracts. The task received ten leaderboard submissions, three of which for both subtasks. Participants explored a wide range of retrieval and classification strategies, including sparse and dense retrieval fusion, supervised reranking with cross-encoders, prompt-based classification with LLMs, and fine-tuned transformer classifiers. Despite methodological differences, the most effective systems shared an emphasis on high-recall retrieval, robust reranking, and careful label calibration. The ClimateCheck datasets are publicly available,[15,16] and a test suite can be accessed for further submissions by the community.[17] While the task results are encouraging, it remains an open question whether these systems are reliable enough for practical deployment. Key open challenges include ensuring system robustness under noisy or multilingual in-

[15]https://huggingface.co/datasets/rabuahmad/climatecheck

[16]https://huggingface.co/datasets/rabuahmad/climatecheck_publications_corpus

[17]https://www.codabench.org/competitions/8304/

put, reducing inference latency for real-time use, and scaling evidence retrieval across large scholarly corpora. Addressing these challenges will be essential to transition from prototype systems to real-world fact-checking tools that can support climate literacy and policy discourse.

Limitations

Although the ClimateCheck task provides a valuable benchmark for evaluating retrieval-augmented fact-checking systems in the climate science domain, several limitations should be noted. First, the evaluation was conducted at the abstract level, which may not fully capture the granularity needed for real-world scientific fact-checking, where evidence often resides at the sentence or paragraph level. This limited both the precision of retrieval and the interpretability of classification outputs.

Moreover, although the task focused on social media claims, the claims were presented in isolation, without access to contextual metadata (such as source, post history, or surrounding discourse). As a result, systems could not leverage pragmatic or contextual cues that are often important in assessing claim intent or credibility in practice.

While the task encouraged participation in both subtasks, only a small subset of teams did so, limiting the ability to assess full-pipeline performance across systems. Additionally, some systems relied on commercial LLMs, which, while effective, reduce reproducibility and raise concerns around fairness in evaluation due to their proprietary nature and limited accessibility.

The annotated training data is relatively limited in size and scope, covering a restricted set of claims and evidence pairs. Although sufficient to train and evaluate retrieval and classification models, further scaling is needed to support generalisation across claim types and evidence complexity. More training data is planned to be annotated in the next months and released as an updated version of the ClimateCheck dataset.

Finally, a notable limitation in the evaluation setup stems from the iterative annotation process, which introduced an inherent bias toward teams that submitted results early and consistently. Throughout the competition, additional evidence annotations were guided by intermediate system outputs, meaning that teams whose systems were included in early and repeated annotation rounds had the advantage of gold testing data that better reflected their own retrieval outputs. Unsurprisingly, the top four teams participated from the beginning and were included in nearly all annotation iterations. In contrast, team Pranav stands out as the only team to outperform the baseline without ever being included in the additional annotation cycles. This highlights how annotation strategies can unintentionally reinforce system-specific retrieval patterns, favouring early participants and potentially underestimating the performance of latecomers.

Ethical Statement

Our annotators were compensated through a typical payment scheme and have been informed about the further use of their annotations. The claims used in the task do not contain sensitive or personal information and are collected from open-source datasets. Due to preprocessing, real claims from social media cannot be traced back to their original posts. We additionally emphasise that automated fact-checking systems are not a substitute for expert judgement and should be deployed with appropriate human oversight.

Acknowledgements

This work was supported by the consortium NFDI for Data Science and Artificial Intelligence (NFDI4DS)[18] as part of the non-profit association National Research Data Infrastructure (NFDI e. V.). The consortium is funded by the Federal Republic of Germany and its states through the German Research Foundation (DFG) project NFDI4DS (no. 460234259). We thank the annotators: Emmanuella Asante, Farzaneh Hafezi, Senuri Jayawardena, and Shuyue Qu for their work.

References

Raia Abu Ahmad, Aida Usmanova, and Georg Rehm. 2025. The ClimateCheck dataset: Mapping social media claims about climate change to corresponding scholarly articles. In *Proceedings of the 5th Workshop on Scholarly Document Processing (SDP)*, Vienna, Austria.

Esma Aïmeur, Sabrine Amri, and Gilles Brassard. 2023. Fake news, disinformation and misinformation in social media: a review. *Social Network Analysis and Mining*, 13(1):30.

Ahmed Al-Rawi, Derrick O'Keefe, Oumar Kane, and Aimé-Jules Bizimana. 2021. Twitter's fake news dis-

[18]https://www.nfdi4datascience.de

courses around climate change and global warming. *Frontiers in Communication*, 6:729818.

Firoj Alam, Julia Maria Struß, Tanmoy Chakraborty, Stefan Dietze, Salim Hafid, Katerina Korre, Arianna Muti, Preslav Nakov, Federico Ruggeri, Sebastian Schellhammer, and 1 others. 2025. The clef-2025 checkthat! lab: Subjectivity, fact-checking, claim normalization, and retrieval. In *European Conference on Information Retrieval*, pages 467–478. Springer.

Monther Aldwairi and Ali Alwahedi. 2018. Detecting fake news in social media networks. *Procedia Computer Science*, 141:215–222.

Rami Aly, Zhijiang Guo, Michael Sejr Schlichtkrull, James Thorne, Andreas Vlachos, Christos Christodoulopoulos, Oana Cocarascu, and Arpit Mittal. 2021. The fact extraction and VERification over unstructured and structured information (FEVEROUS) shared task. In *Proceedings of the Fourth Workshop on Fact Extraction and VERification (FEVER)*, pages 1–13, Dominican Republic. Association for Computational Linguistics.

Isabelle Augenstein, Christina Lioma, Dongsheng Wang, Lucas Chaves Lima, Casper Hansen, Christian Hansen, and Jakob Grue Simonsen. 2019. MultiFC: A real-world multi-domain dataset for evidence-based fact checking of claims. In *Proceedings of the 2019 Conference on Empirical Methods in Natural Language Processing and the 9th International Joint Conference on Natural Language Processing (EMNLP-IJCNLP)*, pages 4685–4697, Hong Kong, China. Association for Computational Linguistics.

Chris Buckley and Ellen M Voorhees. 2004. Retrieval evaluation with incomplete information. In *Proceedings of the 27th annual international ACM SIGIR conference on Research and development in information retrieval*, pages 25–32.

Danqi Chen, Adam Fisch, Jason Weston, and Antoine Bordes. 2017. Reading wikipedia to answer open-domain questions. In *Proceedings of the 55th Annual Meeting of the Association for Computational Linguistics, ACL 2017, Vancouver, Canada, July 30 - August 4, Volume 1: Long Papers*, pages 1870–1879. Association for Computational Linguistics.

Jianlv Chen, Shitao Xiao, Peitian Zhang, Kun Luo, Defu Lian, and Zheng Liu. 2024a. BGE M3-embedding: Multi-lingual, multi-functionality, multi-granularity text embeddings through self-knowledge distillation. *arXiv preprint arXiv:2402.03216*.

Jianlv Chen, Shitao Xiao, Peitian Zhang, Kun Luo, Defu Lian, and Zheng Liu. 2024b. Bge m3-embedding: Multi-lingual, multi-functionality, multi-granularity text embeddings through self-knowledge distillation. *Preprint*, arXiv:2402.03216.

Gordon V Cormack, Charles LA Clarke, and Stefan Buettcher. 2009. Reciprocal rank fusion outperforms condorcet and individual rank learning methods. In *Proceedings of the 32nd international ACM SIGIR conference on Research and development in information retrieval*, pages 758–759.

John Dagdelen, Alexander Dunn, Sanghoon Lee, Nicholas Walker, Andrew S Rosen, Gerbrand Ceder, Kristin A Persson, and Anubhav Jain. 2024. Structured information extraction from scientific text with large language models. *Nature Communications*, 15(1):1418.

Thomas Diggelmann, Jordan Boyd-Graber, Jannis Bulian, Massimiliano Ciaramita, and Markus Leippold. 2020. Climate-fever: A dataset for verification of real-world climate claims. *arXiv preprint arXiv:2012.00614*.

Mahmoud Fathallah, Nagwa El-Makky, and Marwan Torki. 2025. AlexUNLP-FMT at ClimateCheck shared task: Hybrid retrieval with adaptive similarity graph-based reranking for climate-related social media claims fact checking. In *Proceedings of the 5th Workshop on Scholarly Document Processing (SDP)*, Vienna, Austria.

Michele Filannino and Özlem Uzuner. 2018. Advancing the state of the art in clinical natural language processing through shared tasks. *Yearbook of medical informatics*, 27(1):184–192.

Jennifer R Fownes, Chao Yu, and Drew B Margolin. 2018. Twitter and climate change. *Sociology Compass*, 12(6):e12587.

Google Gemini Team, Rohan Anil, Sebastian Borgeaud, Jean-Baptiste Alayrac, Jiahui Yu, Radu Soricut, Johan Schalkwyk, Andrew M Dai, Anja Hauth, Katie Millican, and 1 others. 2023. Gemini: a family of highly capable multimodal models. *arXiv preprint arXiv:2312.11805*.

Zhijiang Guo, Michael Schlichtkrull, and Andreas Vlachos. 2022. A survey on automated fact-checking. *Transactions of the Association for Computational Linguistics*, 10:178–206.

Salim Hafid, Sebastian Schellhammer, Sandra Bringay, Konstantin Todorov, and Stefan Dietze. 2022. Scitweets-a dataset and annotation framework for detecting scientific online discourse. In *Proceedings of the 31st ACM International Conference on Information & Knowledge Management*, pages 3988–3992.

Anthony James Hughes and Xingyi Song. 2024. Identifying and aligning medical claims made on social media with medical evidence. In *Proceedings of the 2024 Joint International Conference on Computational Linguistics, Language Resources and Evaluation (LREC-COLING 2024)*, pages 8580–8593, Torino, Italia. ELRA and ICCL.

Kalervo Järvelin and Jaana Kekäläinen. 2002. Cumulated gain-based evaluation of ir techniques. *ACM Transactions on Information Systems (TOIS)*, 20(4):422–446.

Vladimir Karpukhin, Barlas Oguz, Sewon Min, Patrick Lewis, Ledell Wu, Sergey Edunov, Danqi Chen, and Wen-tau Yih. 2020. Dense passage retrieval for open-domain question answering. In *Proceedings of the 2020 Conference on Empirical Methods in Natural Language Processing, EMNLP 2020, Online, November 16-20, 2020*, pages 6769–6781. Association for Computational Linguistics.

Anna Kiepura and Jessica Lam. 2025. Climate-Check2025: Multi-stage retrieval meets llms for automated scientfic fact-checking. In *Proceedings of the 5th Workshop on Scholarly Document Processing (SDP)*, Vienna, Austria.

Carlos Lassance, Hervé Déjean, Thibault Formal, and Stéphane Clinchant. 2024. SPLADE-v3: New baselines for SPLADE. *arXiv preprint arXiv:2403.06789*.

Kyle Lo, Lucy Lu Wang, Mark Neumann, Rodney Kinney, and Daniel Weld. 2020. S2ORC: The semantic scholar open research corpus. In *Proceedings of the 58th Annual Meeting of the Association for Computational Linguistics*, pages 4969–4983, Online. Association for Computational Linguistics.

Preslav Nakov, Alberto Barrón-Cedeno, Tamer Elsayed, Reem Suwaileh, Lluís Màrquez, Wajdi Zaghouani, Pepa Atanasova, Spas Kyuchukov, and Giovanni Da San Martino. 2018. Overview of the CLEF-2018 CheckThat! lab on automatic identification and verification of political claims. In *Experimental IR Meets Multilinguality, Multimodality, and Interaction: 9th International Conference of the CLEF Association, CLEF 2018, Avignon, France, September 10-14, 2018, Proceedings 9*, pages 372–387. Springer.

Yixin Nie, Haonan Chen, and Mohit Bansal. 2019. Combining fact extraction and verification with neural semantic matching networks. In *The Thirty-Third AAAI Conference on Artificial Intelligence, AAAI 2019, The Thirty-First Innovative Applications of Artificial Intelligence Conference, IAAI 2019, The Ninth AAAI Symposium on Educational Advances in Artificial Intelligence, EAAI 2019, Honolulu, Hawaii, USA, January 27 - February 1, 2019*, pages 6859–6866. AAAI Press.

John Pougué-Biyong, Valentina Semenova, Alexandre Matton, Rachel Han, Aerin Kim, Renaud Lambiotte, and Doyne Farmer. 2021. DEBAGREEMENT: A comment-reply dataset for (dis)agreement detection in online debates. In *Thirty-fifth Conference on Neural Information Processing Systems Datasets and Benchmarks Track (Round 2)*.

Jason Priem, Heather Piwowar, and Richard Orr. 2022. OpenAlex: A fully-open index of scholarly works, authors, venues, institutions, and concepts. *arXiv preprint arXiv:2205.01833*.

Stephen Robertson and Hugo Zaragoza. 2009. The probabilistic relevance framework: BM25 and beyond. *Foundations and Trends in Information Retrieval*, 3(4):333–389.

Michael Schlichtkrull, Yulong Chen, Chenxi Whitehouse, Zhenyun Deng, Mubashara Akhtar, Rami Aly, Zhijiang Guo, Christos Christodoulopoulos, Oana Cocarascu, Arpit Mittal, James Thorne, and Andreas Vlachos. 2024. The automated verification of textual claims (AVeriTeC) shared task. In *Proceedings of the Seventh Fact Extraction and VERification Workshop (FEVER)*.

Shuvam Shiwakoti, Surendrabikram Thapa, Kritesh Rauniyar, Akshyat Shah, Aashish Bhandari, and Usman Naseem. 2024. Analyzing the dynamics of climate change discourse on Twitter: A new annotated corpus and multi-aspect classification. In *Proceedings of the 2024 Joint International Conference on Computational Linguistics, Language Resources and Evaluation (LREC-COLING 2024)*, pages 984–994, Torino, Italia. ELRA and ICCL.

Manfred Stede and Ronny Patz. 2021. The climate change debate and natural language processing. In *Proceedings of the 1st Workshop on NLP for Positive Impact*, pages 8–18, Online. Association for Computational Linguistics.

Weiwei Sun, Lingyong Yan, Xinyu Ma, Shuaiqiang Wang, Pengjie Ren, Zhumin Chen, Dawei Yin, and Zhaochun Ren. 2023. Is ChatGPT good at search? investigating large language models as re-ranking agents. In *Proceedings of the 2023 Conference on Empirical Methods in Natural Language Processing*, pages 14918–14937, Singapore. Association for Computational Linguistics.

James Thorne, Andreas Vlachos, Oana Cocarascu, Christos Christodoulopoulos, and Arpit Mittal. 2018. The fact extraction and VERification (FEVER) shared task. In *Proceedings of the First Workshop on Fact Extraction and VERification (FEVER)*, pages 1–9, Brussels, Belgium. Association for Computational Linguistics.

Max Upravitelev, Nicolau Duran-Silva, Christian Woerle, Giuseppe Guarino, Jing Yang Salar Mohtaj, Veronika Solopova, and Vera Schmitt. 2025. Comparing LLMs and BERT-based classifiers for resource-sensitive claim verification in social media. In *Proceedings of the 5th Workshop on Scholarly Document Processing (SDP)*, Vienna, Austria.

David Wadden and Kyle Lo. 2021. Overview and insights from the SCIVER shared task on scientific claim verification. In *Proceedings of the Second Workshop on Scholarly Document Processing*, pages 124–129, Online. Association for Computational Linguistics.

Junjun Wang, Kunlong Chen, Zhaoqun Chen, Peng He, and Wenlu Zheng. 2025. Winning ClimateCheck: A multi-stage system with BM25, BGE-reranker ensembles, and LLM-based analysis for scientific abstract retrieval. In *Proceedings of the 5th Workshop on Scholarly Document Processing (SDP)*, Vienna, Austria.

Wenhui Wang, Furu Wei, Li Dong, Hangbo Bao, Nan Yang, and Ming Zhou. 2020. Minilm: Deep self-attention distillation for task-agnostic compression of pre-trained transformers. In *Advances in Neural Information Processing Systems 33: Annual Conference on Neural Information Processing Systems 2020, NeurIPS 2020, December 6-12, 2020, virtual.*

Zhen Xu, Sergio Escalera, Adrien Pavão, Magali Richard, Wei-Wei Tu, Quanming Yao, Huan Zhao, and Isabelle Guyon. 2022. Codabench: Flexible, easy-to-use, and reproducible meta-benchmark platform. *Patterns*, 3(7):100543.

An Yang, Anfeng Li, Baosong Yang, Beichen Zhang, Binyuan Hui, Bo Zheng, Bowen Yu, Chang Gao, Chengen Huang, Chenxu Lv, and 1 others. 2025. Qwen3 technical report. *arXiv preprint arXiv:2505.09388.*

Alex Young, Bei Chen, Chao Li, Chengen Huang, Ge Zhang, Guanwei Zhang, Guoyin Wang, Heng Li, Jiangcheng Zhu, Jianqun Chen, and 1 others. 2024. Yi: Open foundation models by 01.ai. *arXiv preprint arXiv:2403.04652.*

Jingtao Zhan, Jiaxin Mao, Yiqun Liu, Jiafeng Guo, Min Zhang, and Shaoping Ma. 2021. Optimizing dense retrieval model training with hard negatives. In *SIGIR '21: The 44th International ACM SIGIR Conference on Research and Development in Information Retrieval, Virtual Event, Canada, July 11-15, 2021*, pages 1503–1512. ACM.

Dun Zhang, Jiacheng Li, Ziyang Zeng, and Fulong Wang. 2024. Jasper and Stella: distillation of SOTA embedding models. *arXiv preprint arXiv:2412.19048.*

A Dataset Samples

Table 6 presents five random claims extracted from the test set of the ClimateCheck dataset. Each claim is presented with the top five abstracts retrieved by the three teams that participated in the two shared task subtasks: Ant Bridge, akiepura_ljam, and EFC. Each abstract is followed by a symbol indicating whether it supports, refutes, or does not have enough information about the claim, according to the results of the team's subtask II labels.

B Iterative Human Annotation Process

During the testing phase of the competition, additional documents were collected based on submissions to mitigate bias in the gold testing data. We did so using the following timeline:

- **Week 1, submissions until April 25, 2025**: we had two active teams: Ant Bridge and AlexUNLP-FMT, thus filtering based on an agreement threshold of 2 without further filtering based on ranking. We extracted the following runs: 275408 and 272964, resulting in 405 additional annotated documents.
- **Week 2, submissions until May 2, 2025**: we received submissions from 3 active participants: Ant Bridge, AlexUNLP-FMT, and akiepura_jlam. We filtered pairs for annotation with an agreement between at least two teams and a minimum rank of 8 across all teams. This helped us manage the annotation workload while still maintaining a fairer evaluation strategy, taking into account all active teams. The following runs were extracted: 279364, 280185, and 280233. As a result, 351 additional pairs were annotated.
- **Week 3, submissions until May 13, 2025**: seven users were active: Ant Bridge, AlexUNLP-FMT, akiepura_jlam, gmguarino, salarmohtaj, nicolauduran45, and EFC, from which we filtered based on an agreement of at least three systems with no further ranking filtering. The following runs were extracted: 285646, 285887, 286061, 286273, 286663, 286806, 286836. This resulted in 477 new annotated claim-abstract pairs.

Overall, the full process resulted in 1,233 additional human-annotate claim-abstract pairs for the 176 unique claims in the test set.

Input (Claim)	Output (Publications)		
	Ant Bridge	**akiepura_jlam**	**EFC**
People make it seem like we can change our energy habits, which is quite difficult.	1. Maréchal, 2014 ✓ 2. Jaccard, 2020 ✓ 3. De Vries et al., 2011 ○ 4. Jans et al., 2018 ✓ 5. Malott, 2017 ○	1. Jaccard, 2020 ✗ 2. Maréchal, 2014 ✓ 3. Horgan et al. 2016 ✓ 4. De Vries et al., 2011 ✓ 5. Bloodhart et al., 2013 ✗	1. Maréchal, 2014 ✓ 2. Jaccard, 2020 ✓ 3. Horgan et al. 2016 ✓ 4. Viguié et al., 2020 ✓ 5. Welton, 2018 ○
Greenhouse gases from our actions are a major factor in warming our planet.	1. Nadeau et al., 2021 ✓ 2. Simkins, 1991 ✓ 3. Feely et al., 2015 ✓ 4. Verma, 2021 ✓ 5. Solomon et al., 2010 ✓	1. Al-Ghussain, 2018 ✓ 2. Simkins, 1991 ✓ 3. Haines & Patz, 2004 ✓ 4. Nadeau et al., 2021 ✓ 5. Miller et al., 2008 ✓	1. Nadeau et al., 2021 ✓ 2. Simkins, 1991 ✓ 3. Gadani & Vyas, 2011 ✓ 4. Haines & Patz, 2004 ✓ 5. Giudice et al., 2021 ✓
Burning biomass is a source of air pollution.	1. Rogers et al., 2020 ✓ 2. Huang et al., 2016 ✓ 3. Naik et al., 2007 ✓ 4. Corsini et al., 2019 ✓ 5. Sigsgaard et al., 2015 ✓	1. Rogers et al., 2020 ✓ 2. Corsini et al., 2019 ✓ 3. Naik et al., 2007 ✓ 4. Sigsgaard et al., 2015 ✓ 5. Unosson et al., 2013 ✓	1. Naik et al., 2007 ✓ 2. Corsini et al., 2019 ✓ 3. Rogers et al., 2020 ✓ 4. Li et al., 2019 ✓ 5. Huang et al., 2016 ✓
heat waves have been on a downward trend both in the US and globally #ClimateChangeFacts	1. Peterson et al., 2013 ✗ 2. Ceccherini et al., 2016 ✗ 3. Bumbaco et al., 2013 ✗ 4. Cao et al., 2021 ○ 5. Li & Amatus., 2020 ✗	1. Peterson et al., 2013 ✗ 2. Ceccherini et al., 2016 ✗ 3. Bumbaco et al., 2013 ✗ 4. Chase et al., 2006 ✗ 5. Mo & Lettenmaier, 2015 ○	1.Peterson et al., 2013 ✗ 2. Huang et al., 2021 ✗ 3. Ceccherini et al., 2016 ✗ 4. Bumbaco et al., 2013 ✗ 5. Mo & Lettenmaier, 2015 ○
Apparently, ice caps are at record levels now, despite predictions of melting.	1. Thompson, 2017 ✗ 2. Anderson et al., 2008 ✗ 3. Isaksson et al., 2005 ○ 4. NEEM community members, 2013 ✗ 5. Thompson et al., 2021 ✗	1. Devasthale et al., 2013 ✗ 2. Taranczewski et al., 2019 ✗ 3. Graeter et al., 2018 ✗ 4. Thompson, 2017 ✗ 5. Massonnet et al., 2023 ✗	1. Edwards et al., 2019 ○ 2. Taranczewski et al., 2019 ✗ 3. Hanna et al., 2013 ○ 4. Devasthale et al., 2013 ✗ 5. Graeter et al., 2018 ✗

Table 6: Sample of five random claims from the test set along with the top five retrieved abstracts from each one of the three teams that participated in both subtasks. Each abstract is followed by a symbol denoting the annotation label given to the claim-abstract pair: ✓ = Supports, ✗ = Refutes, ○= NEI.

Winning ClimateCheck: A Multi-Stage System with BM25, BGE-Reranker Ensembles, and LLM-based Analysis for Scientific Abstract Retrieval

Wang Junjun, Chen Kunlong, Chen Zhaoqun, He Peng, Zheng Wenlu
Ant Group
xingruo.wjj@antgroup.com, cklwanfifa@gmail.com,
zhaoqun.czq@antgroup.com, penghe.hp@antgroup.com, zhengwenlu1@126.com

Abstract

The ClimateCheck shared task addresses the critical challenge of grounding social media claims about climate change in scientific literature. This paper details our winning approach for solving two subtasks. For abstract retrieval, we propose a multi-stage pipeline: (1) initial candidate generation from a corpus of ∼400,000 abstracts using BM25; (2) fine-grained reranking of these candidates using an ensemble of BGE-Reranker cross-encoder models, fine-tuned with a specialized training set incorporating both random and hard negative samples; and (3) final list selection based on an RRF-ensembled score. For the verification aspect, we leverage Gemini 2.5 Pro to classify the relationship between claims and the retrieved abstracts. Our system achieved first place in both subtasks. Part of the example code: `https://github.com/cklcklcklckl/climatecheck_1st_solution`.

1 Introduction

The widespread dissemination of misinformation on social media platforms represents a serious threat to informed public discourse (Wu et al., 2019), particularly regarding critical global issues such as climate change (Treen et al., 2020).

Addressing this challenge, the ClimateCheck shared task at the Fifth Workshop on Scholarly Document Processing (Abu Ahmad et al., 2025b) aims to bridge the gap between social media discourse on climate change and scientific literature. The ClimateCheck Dataset (Abu Ahmad et al., 2025a) is also provided in this shared task for model training and evaluation. Participants develop systems to: (1) Retrieve relevant scholarly abstracts for social media claims (Subtask I: Abstract Retrieval), and (2) Verify claims against these abstracts (Subtask II: Claim Verification).

2 Task Description

2.1 Subtask I: Abstract Retrieval

Given a claim c and a corpus of scientific abstracts $\mathcal{A}$ ($N \approx 400,000$), the goal is to retrieve a ranked list L_c of the top-K (here $K = 10$) most relevant abstracts. Formally, given a scoring function $s(c, a_i)$, $L_c = (a'_1, \ldots, a'_K)$ such that $a'_j \in \mathcal{A}$, $s(c, a'_j) \geq s(c, a'_{j+1})$, and L_c contains the K highest-scoring abstracts. Evaluation uses Recall@k ($k \in \{2, 5, 10\}$) and B-Pref.

2.2 Subtask II: Claim Verification

Given a claim-abstract pair (c, a), the task is to classify their relationship as 'support', 'refutes', or 'not enough information'. Evaluation uses precision, recall, and F1-score, scaled by Subtask I retrieval performance if applicable.

3 Method

Our winning solution employs a multi-stage process designed to maximize both recall and precision as illustrated in Figure 1. This approach for Subtask I involves: (1) coarse retrieval with BM25 (Robertson et al., 2009) for top 5,000 abstracts; (2) fine-grained reranking using an ensemble of fine-tuned BGE-Reranker models; and (3) final list selection using Reciprocal Rank Fusion (RRF). For Subtask II, we integrate a large language model (LLM), Gemini 2.5 Pro (Team et al., 2023), for claim-abstract relationship classification.

3.1 BM25 for Initial Retrieval

BM25 (Robertson et al., 2009) was chosen for the initial retrieval stage due to its proven effectiveness in lexical matching and its computational efficiency for large corpora.

3.1.1 Preprocessing

Our preprocessing pipeline consists of the following steps:

Proceedings of the Fifth Workshop on Scholarly Document Processing (SDP 2025), pages 276–280
July 31, 2025 ©2025 Association for Computational Linguistics

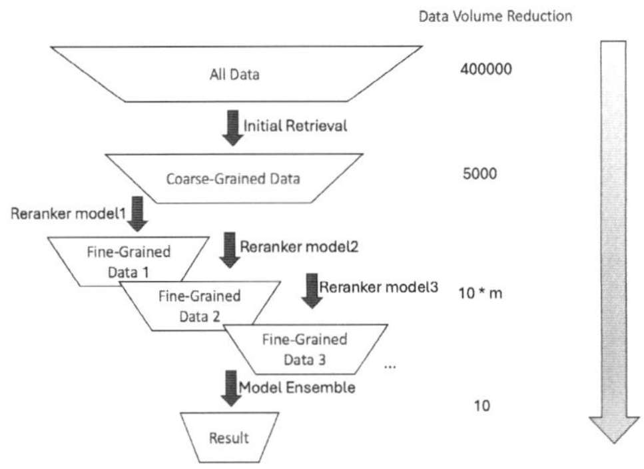

Figure 1: The Multi-Stage Text Retrieval Process with Ensemble Learning for solving subtask I. This diagram illustrates a three-stage text retrieval pipeline combining initial retrieval, multi-model reranking, and ensemble learning. Starting from 400,000 documents, the system first performs coarse-grained filtering (reducing to 5,000 candidates) through Initial Retrieval. The top results then undergo fine-grained ranking by multiple BGE-based reranker models, generating m candidate sets. Finally, an ensemble method combines outputs from all models to produce the final 10 results. The orange arrow emphasizes the progressive data volume reduction across stages

1. **Lowercasing:** All text is converted to lowercase to ensure case-insensitive matching.

2. **Punctuation Removal:** Punctuation marks are removed to focus on the textual content.

3. **Tokenization:** Text is split into individual words or tokens.

4. **Stopword Removal:** Common English stopwords (e.g., "the", "is", "in") are removed as they typically do not contribute significantly to relevance scoring (Manning, 2009). We use a standard list of English stopwords, specifically the one provided by the NLTK library.

This preprocessing pipeline was applied to all abstracts in the corpus to create a tokenized representation for BM25 indexing.

3.1.2 Retrieval Process

For each preprocessed claim, BM25 scores against all indexed abstracts are computed and sorted. The top $N_{BM25} = 5,000$ abstracts are selected as candidates. This large candidate pool size is chosen to maximize the likelihood of including true relevant documents, ensuring high recall for the subsequent reranking stage.

3.2 BGE-Reranker for Fine-Grained Ranking

For each claim, we aggregate the top 5,000 BM25-retrieved abstracts to generate a candidate pool that undergoes fine-grained reranking through our proposed method. We fine-tune multiple BGE-Reranker cross-encoders (Xiao et al., 2023), which excel at reranking through deep token-level interactions between claims and documents, yielding superior relevance judgments over bi-encoders.

3.2.1 Training Data with Hard Negatives

We trained the reranker using triplets (q, d^+, d^-) where q is a claim, d^+ a relevant abstract, and d^- an irrelevant abstract. For each positive pair:

- **Random Negatives:** Abstracts sampled uniformly from the corpus to teach broad distinctions.

- **Hard Negatives:** We generated hard negatives through a two-stage retrieval process:
  1. *BM25 Retrieval:* For each claim, we retrieved 1000 candidate abstracts using BM25.
  2. *BGE Re-ranking:* We re-ranked candidates using original BGE-Reranker.
  3. *Selection:* From the top-1000 re-ranked results, we excluded positive abstracts and selected the top-500 non-relevant abstracts as hard negative candidates.

  During training, hard negatives were randomly sampled from this candidate pool.

Combining both negative types (10 random + 5 hard negatives per positive example) created a robust training set for nuanced relevance learning.

3.2.2 Model Fine-tuning

We fine-tuned two pre-trained Transformer models, `BAAI/bge-reranker-large`[1] and `BAAI/bge-reranker-v2-m3`[2] to act as a cross-encoder. The model takes a claim and an abstract, tokenized together, as input and outputs a single relevance score. The fine-tuning process involved the following:

- **Input Representation:** Claims and abstracts were concatenated and tokenized using the model's specific tokenizer. Inputs were padded or truncated.

[1] https://huggingface.co/BAAI/bge-reranker-large
[2] https://huggingface.co/BAAI/bge-reranker-v2-m3

- **Triplet Loss Objective:** We employed a margin ranking loss. For each triplet (q, d^+, d^-), the model computes scores $s(q, d^+)$ and $s(q, d^-)$. The loss encourages $s(q, d^+) > s(q, d^-)$ plus a margin value.

We trained multiple reranker models by varying hyperparameters such as the margin value, learning rate, and batch size to encourage diversity in their predictions for later ensembling.

3.2.3 Ensemble of Reranked Lists

To leverage the strengths of different reranker models (each fine-tuned with slightly different hyperparameters or on different data shuffles, as shown in table 1), we ensembled their outputs. Our ensembling strategy, implemented in the function, is based on a variation of Reciprocal Rank Fusion (RRF) (Cormack et al., 2009). The core design principle is: *higher-ranked items should receive exponentially more weight, while maintaining balanced influence across different ranking systems.* For each claim:

1. Each of the M fine-tuned reranker models processed the top 5,000 candidates from BM25 and produced a ranked list of abstracts.
2. For each abstract a_j in the ranked list from model m_i, its rank r_{ij} was converted into a score s_{ij} using the formula: $s_{ij} = \frac{1}{k+r_{ij}}$.
3. The scores for each unique abstract a_j were then summed across all M models: $S_j = \sum_{i=1}^{M} s_{ij}$.
4. The abstracts were then re-ranked based on their aggregated scores S_j in descending order.

The final top-10 abstracts according to this ensembled ranking were selected as our submission for Subtask I. This ensemble approach helps to improve robustness and often yields better performance than any single model.

3.3 Claim-Abstract Relationship Classification with Gemini 2.5 Pro

The final component of our system, primarily designed to support downstream claim verification (akin to Subtask II), involves classifying the relationship between a given claim and each of its top-k retrieved abstracts. For this task, we leveraged the

Base model	batch size	margin
BGE-Reranker-large	8	0.2
BGE-Reranker-large	16	0.2
BGE-Reranker-large	8	0.25
BGE-Reranker-large	16	0.25
BGE-Reranker-v2-m3	16	0.2

Table 1: The different fine-tuned configurations used for model ensemble.

capabilities of a large language model, specifically Gemini 2.5 Pro.

The objective was to categorize each claim-abstract pair into one of three predefined labels:

1. **Supports:** The abstract contains information that supports the assertion made in the claim.
2. **Refutes:** The abstract contains information that contradicts or refutes the assertion made in the claim.
3. **Not Enough Information (NEI):** The abstract does not provide sufficient information to either support or refute the claim.

To achieve this, we designed a specific prompt for Gemini 2.5 Pro (Team et al., 2023). The core elements of this prompt were:

- **Persona Setting:** The LLM was instructed to act as a "climate change expert."
- **Task Definition:** The model was tasked to analyze a given claim and a potentially related scientific abstract, identify relevant content within the abstract, and determine the relationship between the two.
- **Input Structure:** The prompt was designed to accept a list of claims and a corresponding list of abstracts, enabling batch processing.
- **Output Format Constraint:** A critical instruction was for the LLM to return only a numerical digit (1 for 'Not Enough Information', 2 for 'Supports', 3 for 'Refutes') for each pair, without any additional text or explanation. For batch inputs, a list of these digits was expected.
- **Output Distribution Guideline:** An explicit instruction was included to guide the model's output distribution: (Try to ensure that the proportion of '1' (Not Enough Information)

in your overall results is not less than 30%). This was intended to encourage the model to be conservative when explicit evidence was lacking, potentially mitigating over-confident "Supports" or "Refutes" classifications on ambiguous or tangentially related abstracts.

The process of generating this prompt is shown in Apprendix A.

For each claim from the dataset, its top-10 retrieved abstracts (from the ensemble reranking stage described in Section 3.2.3) were paired with the claim and fed to the Gemini 2.5 Pro model using this prompt structure. The resulting classification (Supports, Refutes, NEI) for each claim-abstract pair provides an additional layer of analysis. While our primary submission for Subtask I focused on the retrieval ranking, these LLM-derived relationship labels offer valuable insights for subsequent fact-checking efforts and could be directly utilized in a Subtask II system. The pipeline is shown in figure 2.

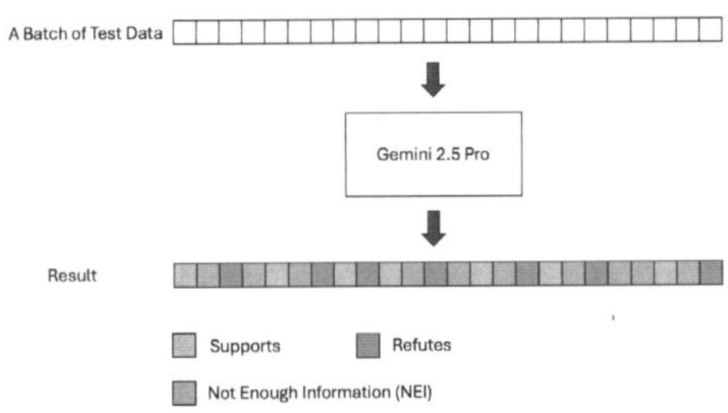

Figure 2: The pipeline of solving subtask II. Note that we input a batch of data (around 50 samples) at once in the prompt. The purpose of this approach is to ensure the model has a significantly higher probability of outputting "NEI". In the author's practice, when feeding individual data points separately, it becomes difficult to elicit "NEI" outputs from the model, with a probability of less than 1%.

4 Discussion

In this section, we discuss why we chose this cascaded architecture to solve the problem. For algorithm competitions, practicality in solving problems within limited timeframes needs consideration. Since we needed to iteratively submit results and receive feedback to refine our models, an efficient and accurate coarse-ranking solution became essential. We ultimately selected BM25 for recall because it could rapidly screen 5,000 candidate samples within a short time frame. In the subsequent second stage, we experimented with various models repeatedly and finally chose the BGE-reranker through offline evaluation. Ensemble learning effectively improved model accuracy, as demonstrated in our previous practice at KDD Cup 2024 (Chen et al., 2024). For Task II, we directly used Gemini Pro 2.5 for reasoning to obtain final results. This was because we believed that large-parameter closed-source LLM would achieve better performance in deep semantic understanding tasks compared to fine-tuned smaller-parameter models. However, resource constraints prevented us from conducting more sophisticated experiments.

Another benefit of our approach is that for Subtask I, the time required to process the data does not increase significantly when the data volume grows. This is because the first step, BM25, will only retain a fixed set of 5,000 entries. Naturally, for Subtask II, the processing time will increase linearly with the amount of data.

5 Conclusion

This paper describes our ClimateCheck shared task system, which won first place in both Subtasks. Our approach combines a BM25 sparse retriever for candidate pooling with an ensemble of fine-tuned BGE-Reranker models for semantic reranking. Training the rerankers on a dataset incorporating hard negative mining significantly improved their performance. For claim verification, Gemini 2.5 Pro effectively classified claim-abstract relationships. This hybrid pipeline demonstrates the efficacy of combining optimized retrieval with large language models.

Limitations

One practical drawback of our solution is that during the re-ranking phase for subtask I, we fine-tuned several different models using various parameters and combined them via ensemble learning. Although this is a common technique to boost rankings in data science competitions, it often proves impractical in real-world industrial applications due to its excessive complexity. Additionally, despite significant efforts, we failed to identify a practical method for effectively utilizing large language models in subtask I, even though we firmly believe LLM would raise the performance ceiling for this subtask. We believe that the recently studied large language model-based text retrieval methods (such as qwen3-embedding [3]) can likely improve performance in subtask I without the need for ensemble learning. We will conduct further exploratory work on this subsequently.

References

Raia Abu Ahmad, Aida Usmanova, and Georg Rehm. 2025a. The ClimateCheck dataset: Mapping social media claims about climate change to corresponding scholarly articles. In *Proceedings of the 5th Workshop on Scholarly Document Processing (SDP)*, Vienna, Austria.

Raia Abu Ahmad, Aida Usmanova, and Georg Rehm. 2025b. The ClimateCheck shared task: Scientific fact-checking of social media claims about climate change. In *Proceedings of the 5th Workshop on Scholarly Document Processing (SDP)*, Vienna, Austria.

Kunlong Chen, Junjun Wang, Zhaoqun Chen, Kunjin Chen, and Yitian Chen. 2024. Llm-powered ensemble learning for paper source tracing: A gpu-free approach. *arXiv preprint arXiv:2409.09383*.

Gordon V Cormack, Charles LA Clarke, and Stefan Buettcher. 2009. Reciprocal rank fusion outperforms condorcet and individual rank learning methods. In *Proceedings of the 32nd international ACM SIGIR conference on Research and development in information retrieval*, pages 758–759.

Christopher D Manning. 2009. *An introduction to information retrieval.*

Stephen Robertson, Hugo Zaragoza, et al. 2009. The probabilistic relevance framework: Bm25 and beyond. *Foundations and Trends® in Information Retrieval*, 3(4):333–389.

Gemini Team, Rohan Anil, Sebastian Borgeaud, Jean-Baptiste Alayrac, Jiahui Yu, Radu Soricut, Johan Schalkwyk, Andrew M Dai, Anja Hauth, Katie Millican, et al. 2023. Gemini: a family of highly capable multimodal models. *arXiv preprint arXiv:2312.11805*.

Kathie M d'I Treen, Hywel TP Williams, and Saffron J O'Neill. 2020. Online misinformation about climate change. *Wiley Interdisciplinary Reviews: Climate Change*, 11(5):e665.

Liang Wu, Fred Morstatter, Kathleen M Carley, and Huan Liu. 2019. Misinformation in social media: definition, manipulation, and detection. *ACM SIGKDD explorations newsletter*, 21(2):80–90.

Shitao Xiao, Zheng Liu, Peitian Zhang, and Niklas Muennighoff. 2023. C-pack: Packaged resources to advance general chinese embedding.

[3]https://github.com/QwenLM/Qwen3-Embedding

A Prompt Implementation for Gemini 2.5 pro

In this section, we introduce how to generate prompts mentioned in section 3.3. Note that this prompt is written in Chinese in the competition.

```
def get_prompt(claims, abstracts):
    return f"""You are an expert in
    climate change. I will provide you
    with a claim and an abstract.
            A claim typically
    represents an assertion about
    climate change, while an abstract is
     a paper abstract potentially
    related to that claim.
            Your task is to identify
     content in the abstract relevant to
     the claim and analyze the
    relationship between the abstract
    and the claim.
            There are three possible
     relationship categories:
            1. 'Not Enough
    Information': Indicates the abstract
     neither supports nor refutes the
    claim;
            2. 'Supports': Indicates
     the abstract provides evidence
    supporting the claim;
            3. 'Refutes': Indicates
    the abstract provides evidence
    refuting the claim.

            Your response must
    consist ONLY of a single number
    between 1 and 3, representing the
    relationship category. Return ONLY
    the number, without any additional
    text.
            I will provide N claims
    and N abstracts simultaneously. You
    should return a list of N numbers.
            Important Notes:
            1. Ensure the returned
    numbers are strictly between 1 and
    3.
            2. Aim for the overall
    proportion of '1' (Not Enough
    Information) responses in your
    results to be at least 30%.

            Claims list: {claims}
            Abstracts list: {
    abstracts}
            """
```

Listing 1: Prompt generation function

Comparing LLMs and BERT-based Classifiers for Resource-Sensitive Claim Verification in Social Media

Max Upravitelev[1], Nicolau Duran-Silva[2,3], Christian Woerle[4], Giuseppe Guarino[5], Salar Mohtaj[6], Jing Yang[1,7], Veronika Solopova[7], and Vera Schmitt[1,6,7,8]

[1]Technische Universität Berlin [2]SIRIS Lab, Research Division of SIRIS Academic
[3]LaSTUS Lab, TALN, Universitat Pompeu Fabra [4]Climate+Tech AI Think-tank [5]Data for good
[6]German Research Center for Artificial Intelligence (DFKI)
[7]BIFOLD – Berlin Institute for the Foundations of Learning and Data
[8]Centre for European Research in Trusted AI (CERTAIN)

Abstract

The overwhelming volume of content being published at any given moment poses a significant challenge for the design of automated fact-checking (AFC) systems on social media, requiring an emphasized consideration of efficiency aspects. As in other fields, systems built upon zero-shot LLMs have achieved good results on different AFC benchmarks. The application of LLMs, however, is accompanied by high resource requirements. The energy consumption of LLMs poses a significant challenge from an ecological perspective, while remaining a bottleneck in latency-sensitive scenarios like AFC within social media. Therefore, we propose a system built upon fine-tuned smaller BERT-based models and comprised of components for abstract retrieval and claim verification. When evaluated on the ClimateCheck dataset against decoder-only LLMs, our best fine-tuned model outperforms Phi 4 14B and approaches Qwen3 14B in reasoning mode — while significantly reducing runtime per claim. Our findings demonstrate that small encoder-only models fine-tuned for specific tasks can still provide a substantive alternative to large decoder-only LLMs, especially in efficiency-concerned settings.

1 Introduction

While social media can be a space for public discourse, it can also be a place where misinformation and disinformation claims become dominant. In real-life claim verification, fast response times could be decisive in regard to the impact of harmful claims, such as providing verdicts before the claims start to spread. In the context of climate-related topics, where claims can be verified by a large amount of research, an opportunity is provided to combat misinformation by retrieving relevant research to verify said claims.

Like many other tasks in the natural language processing (NLP) domain, automated fact-checking systems are gaining significant performance boosts with the rise of large language models (LLMs). In the context of social media, however, the application of LLMs for tasks such as claim verification is greatly hindered by their high computational costs and latency. Which, on a large scale, is problematic from an ecological point of view (Jegham et al., 2025), as well as when considered from a latency-sensitive system design perspective (Wang et al., 2025).

Moreover, recent research indicates that BERT-based models fine-tuned for specific tasks can still be competitive with zero-shot LLMs in text classification (Kostina et al., 2025), or even outperform LLMs as shown in Bucher and Martini (2024) while also outperforming other classifiers in related challenging tasks like propaganda detection (Solopova et al., 2024). As discussed in related studies such as Li (2025), many encoder-only BERT-based models like deberta-v3 (He et al., 2023) are accompanied by significantly lower computational costs and therefore have a lower ecological impact due to a smaller number of parameters than many of their recent decoder-only counterparts like Qwen3 (Yang et al., 2025) or Phi 4 (Abdin et al., 2024). Thus, we want to explore how both model classes perform on the ClimateCheck dataset (Abu Ahmad et al., 2025a) – which was released in the context of the ClimateCheck@SDP 2025 Shared Task (Abu Ahmad et al., 2025b) – with respect to veracity prediction. In both cases, the input for prediction is acquired by an abstract retrieval pipeline, which we propose in this paper, and which also does not rely on LLMs.

The main contributions of this paper can be summarized as follows:

1. Proposing a new pipeline for retrieving abstracts from the ClimateCheck dataset corpus;
2. Exploring the fine-tuning of BERT-based models on the ClimateCheck dataset;

Proceedings of the Fifth Workshop on Scholarly Document Processing (SDP 2025), pages 281–287
July 31, 2025 ©2025 Association for Computational Linguistics

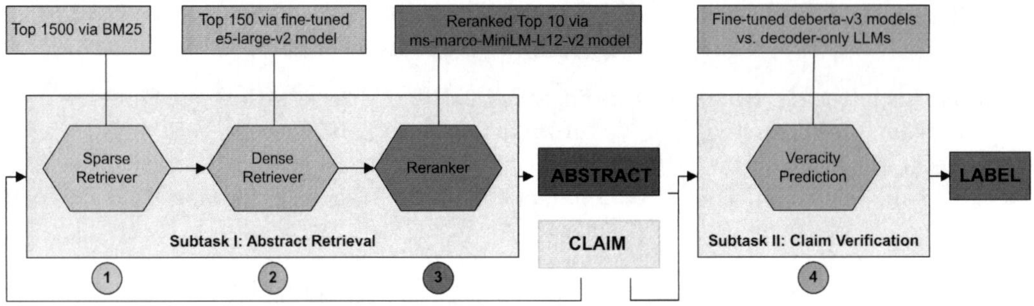

Figure 1: Architecture of the proposed system

3. Evaluating the claim verification results of fine-tuned BERT-based models against LLMs on runtime and the official ClimateCheck scores.

We have released our code[1] and the models[2,3] we fine-tuned in the context of this paper.

2 Related Work

In recent studies on the verification of climate claims (Leippold et al., 2024), agent-based LLM systems have been shown to achieve promising results when verifying claims based on retrieved knowledge from a corpus such as provided by the Intergovernmental Panel on Climate Change (IPCC). However, in a dynamic situation with a large unfiltered corpus of scientific papers and the frequency of social media claims, the cost and latency may limit the applicability of such a pipeline alone.

At the same time, several datasets were published for the verification of claims outside of the climate domain. For example, PubHealth (Kotonya and Toni, 2020) focuses on public health-related claims, which are accompanied by claims labeled with "true", "false", "mixture" and "unproven". The FEVER (Fact Extraction and VERification) dataset (Thorne et al., 2018) aims at the development of systems for the verification of claims on different topics against textual sources, using the labels "Supported", "Refuted" or "NotEnoughInfo" – a label scheme similar to the labels in ClimateCheck. AVeriTeC (Automated Verification of Textual Claims) (Schlichtkrull et al., 2023) focuses on retrieved evidence from the open web to verify claims, also providing samples with the additional label "Conflicting Evidence/Cherrypicking". In Yang and Rocha (2024), the AVeriTeC task is understood as related to natural language inference (NLI) tasks, which focus on logical inference based on free-text data. In this paper, the authors proposed a label mapping scheme for PubHealth and AVeriTeC and fine-tuned a T5-3B model (Raffel et al., 2023), whose initial training included data from NLI datasets. This strategy inspired us to explore models beyond decoder-only architectures that were fine-tuned on NLI datasets and to fine-tune them further in the context of ClimateCheck.

3 Methodology

Subtask I: Abstract Retrieval The first subtask focuses on the retrieval of relevant abstracts from a corpus of around 400K abstracts of publications from the climate science domains. We propose the following pipeline for this subtask, also illustrated in Figure 1:

1. Sparse retrieval: Get the top 1500 most relevant abstracts from the corpus using each claim as the query via BM25
2. Dense retrieval: Get the most relevant top 150 results from (1)
3. Rerank the results from (2) with a reranking model and return the final top 10 results

The inclusion of step (1) was the result of preliminary experiments, where we first explored the strategy of running dense retrieval on the full set of the embeddings of all 400k abstracts. Since this strategy yielded subpar results, we opted for a hybrid search approach by including sparse retrieval, which is a frequent approach in retrieval tasks to improve retrieval scores (as shown in Sawarkar et al.

[1] https://github.com/XplaiNLP/climatecheck-submission
[2] https://huggingface.co/xplainlp/e5-large-v2-climatecheck
[3] https://huggingface.co/xplainlp/DeBERTa-v3-large-mnli-fever-anli-ling-wanli-climatecheck

#	Embedding Model	Reranking Model	R@2	R@5	R@10	B-Pref	Score
1	e5-large-v2-climatecheck	ms-marco-MiniLM-L12-v2	0.217	0.405	0.574	0.449	0.411
2	e5-large-v2	ms-marco-MiniLM-L12-v2	0.208	0.399	0.560	0.437	0.401
3	e5-large-v2-climatecheck	bge-reranker-large	0.176	0.348	0.502	0.414	0.360
4	e5-large-v2-climatecheck	jina	0.193	0.328	0.464	0.398	0.346
5	#1 w/o bm25	ms-marco-MiniLM-L12-v2	0.197	0.365	0.521	0.397	0.370
6	e5-large-v2-climatecheck	-	0.151	0.257	0.375	0.311	0.273

Table 1: Evaluation on the abstract retrieval subtask. "R" refers to Recall and "Score" to the final ClimateCheck Subtask I Score. "jina" in Configuration #4 refers to jina-reranker-v2-base-multilingual.

(2024), for example). The top k value of 1500 retrieved abstracts was another result of preliminary testing, where we tried different values and chose the one with the best scores on the ClimateCheck dataset.

The results of step (2) are dependent on the embedding model. Here, we experimented with different fine-tuning strategies on e5-large-v2 (introduced in Wang et al. (2022a)). Finally, we fine-tuned the model for three epochs on the entire dataset while incorporating positive and negative examples into the training process. The related claims and abstracts in the ClimateCheck dataset can be seen as sets of positive pairs that map semantically close pairs of texts to each other, which can can be used as positive examples during fine-tuning. As shown in studies like Zhan et al. (2021), the performance in retrieval tasks can be further improved by expending such sets with negative examples. We mined three negative examples by retrieving the three least relevant abstracts via dense retrieval-based ranking.

Finally, we refined the ranking of the result from step (2) with a reranker model in step (3), which was chosen by comparing which model yielded the best results.

Subtask II: Claim Verification The second subtask focuses on the prediction of veracity labels based on the claims and abstracts retrieved in subtask I.

Inspired by Yang and Rocha (2024), our strategy was to fine-tune a BERT-based model previously fine-tuned on related NLI tasks to predict the veracity on the ClimateCheck dataset. This strategy deviates from Yang and Rocha (2024), in which a T5-3B model with an encoder-decoder architecture was used. Since our goal was to achieve good results while minimizing computational inference cost, we opted to work with smaller, encoder-only architectures. Finally, we explored publicly available options of models fine-tuned for NLI tasks and decided to compare two fined-tuned versions of deberta-v3 (He et al., 2023), which allowed for better comparison of the fine-tuning effects due to the same base model:

1. nli-deberta-v3-large from the cross-encoders series by Sentence Transformers[4] fine-tuned on SNLI (Bowman et al., 2015) and MultiNLI (Williams et al., 2018).

2. DeBERTa-v3-large-mnli-fever-anli-ling-wanli (Laurer et al., 2022), which was fine-tuned on five NLI-related datasets including MultiNLI, ANLI (Nie et al., 2020), LingNLI (Parrish et al., 2021), WANLI (Liu et al., 2022) and FEVER NLI, which is a FEVER variant transposed into the NLI schema (Nie et al., 2019). Unlike the model in (1), it is also explicitly not fine-tuned on SNLI.

We fine-tuned the models as follows:

1. Each input consisted of a claim and abstract concatenated with a `[SEP]` token.

2. Training was stopped when the evaluation metric failed to improve over successive epochs, resulting in 8 epochs in total.

3. We computed class-wise accuracies SUP_{acc}, REF_{acc} and NEI_{acc} and used $Acc_{min} = min(SUP_{acc}, REF_{acc}, NEI_{acc})$ as the optimization target to penalize imbalance.

4. To account for randomized factors (data split, model initialization), we ran the training procedure multiple times and selected the model with the highest Acc_{min} score.

[4]https://huggingface.co/cross-encoder/nli-deberta-v3-large

#	Model	s/claim	Precision	Recall	F1	Score
1	DeBERTa-v3-large-climatecheck	**0.032**	0.686	0.683	0.683	1.257
2	DeBERTa-v3-large-mnli-fever-anli-ling-wanli	0.032	0.261	0.154	0.104	0.678
3	nli-deberta-v3-large-climatecheck	0.032	0.604	0.607	0.602	1.176
4	nli-deberta-v3-large	0.032	0.413	0.418	0.289	0.863
5	Phi 4 14B	0.729	0.668	0.662	0.660	1.234
6	Qwen3 14B	12.229	**0.716**	**0.717**	**0.716**	**1.291**
7	Qwen3 14B w/o reasoning	0.363	0.690	0.629	0.597	1.171
8	Qwen3 1.7B	9.176	0.697	0.661	0.646	1.242

Table 2: Evaluation of subtask II concerning claim verification. The full name of our fine-tuned model in #1 is "DeBERTa-v3-large-mnli-fever-anli-ling-wanli-climatecheck". "Score" refers to the final ClimateCheck Subtask II score.

4 Evaluation

Subtask I The first subtask is evaluated on Recall@k, where $k = [2, 5, 10]$, and Binary Preference (B-Pref). All 4 scores are averaged into a final Subtask I score. Our pipeline achieved 4th place out of 10 on the subtask. Our evaluation results are documented in Table 1.

The first two results highlight the influence of our fine-tuning strategy by ablating it, resulting in worse performance. Next, we evaluate the influence of the reranking model by running bge-large-rerank (Xiao et al., 2023), a jina model[5], and a model from the Sentence Transformers Cross-Encoder series[6] against each other. For our final pipeline, we choose the highest scoring model, which was also explicitly fine-tuned on the information retrieval MS MARCO dataset (Bajaj et al., 2018). In the last section of Table 1 we assess the influence of retrieval components by ablating them. Setting (S) #5 documents our best performing configuration from S#1 without the BM25 step, indicating its importance due to a performance drop. Similarly, another drop is shown by S#6, where reranking was removed from the pipeline.

Subtask II The second subtask is evaluated on Precision, Recall, and the weighted F1-score. The final Subtask II score is the F1-score scaled by the number of claim-abstract pairs that were retrieved correctly, represented by the Recall@10 score of Subtask I. Since runtime was an important factor in our system design, we also included the processing time per claim in our evaluation. All experiments were run on a system with one NVIDIA H100 80 GB GPU. Table 2 documents our results.

S#1 achieves competitive results against our LLM configurations, while processing claims at only 0.032 seconds on average, outperforming LLMs on this metric by a margin. The other NLI-fine-tuned model in S#3 performed worse, which could be related to the selection of the datasets both were fine-tuned on, respectively. Both models perform worse without our fine-tuning strategy, as documented by S#2 and S#4. Surprisingly, there is also a large performance gap between both, where S#4 outperforms S#2 despite S#2 being more successful with our fine-tuning strategy.

For the comparison with current decoder-only LLMs, we start by evaluating against Phi 4 (Abdin et al., 2024), which is a recent model with 14B parameters and good performance results on many benchmarks. It is outperformed by S#1 across all metrics, most notably on the runtime. For better comparison, we also evaluate against members of the Qwen3 (Yang et al., 2025) series. S#6 was our final submission in the shared task, achieving 3rd place in the Subtask II score and 2nd place in Recall, Precision and F1.

Compared to our other settings, it has the best results in all metrics – except on runtime, yielding 12.229 seconds per claim. Turning off the reasoning in S#7 greatly improved the runtime while still achieving competitive results. However, this configuration was outperformed by S#1 and S#2 on the final Subtask II score while being around 14.4 times slower. In S#8 we replaced the Qwen 14B model with the 1.7B variant. Although still slower compared to S#1, it outperformed Phi 4 and S#7 on the Subtask II metric.

[5] https://huggingface.co/jinaai/jina-reranker-v2-base-multilingual

[6] https://huggingface.co/cross-encoder/ms-marco-MiniLM-L12-v2

To further evaluate runtime differences, we perform a paired t-test over the test set (N = 1760) on per-claim runtimes. The BERT-based model in S#1 (mean = 0.032 s, std = 0.002 s) is significantly faster than the fastest decoder-only LLM in S#7 (mean = 0.363 s, std = 0.133 s) with $t(1759) = -104.541$, $p < 0.001$, Cohen's $d = 2.49$.

5 Discussion

Our results indicate that while recent decoder-only zero-shot LLMs such as Qwen3 are able to receive impressive results on datasets like ClimateCheck just by prompting them without applying any fine-tuning strategies, fine-tuned encoder-only BERT-based models can achieve comparable results at a fraction of the runtime. In conclusion, the smaller model class can still be a valid choice, particularly in scenarios where low latency is a critical factor.

Limitations

This study focuses on the comparison between fine-tuned encoder-only BERT models and decoder-only zero-shot LLMs in task-specific performance and runtime. While our results align with prior work (e.g., Bucher and Martini (2024)), they are limited to the described settings and the dataset used. Our system is tailored to the current iteration of the ClimateCheck dataset, and evaluating it on other datasets is necessary to assess generalizability. This is particularly relevant for the comparison of the two model families: Studies such as Wang et al. (2022b) indicate that decoder-only zero-shot LLMs generalize better than their fine-tuned encoder-only counterparts and therefore are less sensitive to changes in data.

The competitive results of BERT-based models as shown here are limited to the comparison against LLMs in a zero-shot setting. The performance of decoder-only LLMs could be further improved, for example, by prompting strategies such as few-shot learning (adding examples to prompts). Although this could further slow down the inference time due to increased length of input context that needs to be processed, it could also lead to a more consequential performance gap.

Finally, while the reported runtime performance at 0.032 seconds per claim on average can be considered as approaching real-time latency requirements, this results was achieved on a high-end GPU (NVIDIA H100). For real-life deployment, more optimization like quantization and parallelization techniques are needed to enable similar runtime on lower-end devices.

Acknowledgments

The work on this paper is performed in the scope of the projects "VeraExtract" (01IS24066) and "news-polygraph" (reference: 03RU2U151C) funded by the German Federal Ministry for Research, Technology and Aeronautics (BMFTR).

References

Marah Abdin, Jyoti Aneja, Harkirat Behl, Sébastien Bubeck, Ronen Eldan, Suriya Gunasekar, Michael Harrison, Russell J. Hewett, Mojan Javaheripi, Piero Kauffmann, James R. Lee, Yin Tat Lee, Yuanzhi Li, Weishung Liu, Caio C. T. Mendes, Anh Nguyen, Eric Price, Gustavo de Rosa, Olli Saarikivi, and 8 others. 2024. Phi-4 Technical Report. *arXiv preprint*. ArXiv:2412.08905 [cs].

Raia Abu Ahmad, Aida Usmanova, and Georg Rehm. 2025a. The ClimateCheck dataset: Mapping social media claims about climate change to corresponding scholarly articles. In *Proceedings of the 5th Workshop on Scholarly Document Processing (SDP)*, Vienna, Austria.

Raia Abu Ahmad, Aida Usmanova, and Georg Rehm. 2025b. The ClimateCheck shared task: Scientific fact-checking of social media claims about climate change. In *Proceedings of the 5th Workshop on Scholarly Document Processing (SDP)*, Vienna, Austria.

Payal Bajaj, Daniel Campos, Nick Craswell, Li Deng, Jianfeng Gao, Xiaodong Liu, Rangan Majumder, Andrew McNamara, Bhaskar Mitra, Tri Nguyen, Mir Rosenberg, Xia Song, Alina Stoica, Saurabh Tiwary, and Tong Wang. 2018. Ms marco: A human generated machine reading comprehension dataset. *Preprint*, arXiv:1611.09268.

Samuel R. Bowman, Gabor Angeli, Christopher Potts, and Christopher D. Manning. 2015. A large annotated corpus for learning natural language inference. In *Proceedings of the 2015 Conference on Empirical Methods in Natural Language Processing*, pages 632–642, Lisbon, Portugal. Association for Computational Linguistics.

Martin Juan José Bucher and Marco Martini. 2024. Fine-tuned 'small' llms (still) significantly outperform zero-shot generative ai models in text classification. *Preprint*, arXiv:2406.08660.

Pengcheng He, Jianfeng Gao, and Weizhu Chen. 2023. Debertav3: Improving deberta using electra-style pre-training with gradient-disentangled embedding sharing. *Preprint*, arXiv:2111.09543.

Nidhal Jegham, Marwen Abdelatti, Lassad Elmoubarki, and Abdeltawab Hendawi. 2025. How hungry is ai?

benchmarking energy, water, and carbon footprint of llm inference. *Preprint*, arXiv:2505.09598.

Arina Kostina, Marios D. Dikaiakos, Dimosthenis Stefanidis, and George Pallis. 2025. Large language models for text classification: Case study and comprehensive review. *Preprint*, arXiv:2501.08457.

Neema Kotonya and Francesca Toni. 2020. Explainable automated fact-checking for public health claims. *arXiv preprint arXiv:2010.09926*.

Moritz Laurer, Wouter van Atteveldt, Andreu Casas, and Kasper Welbers. 2022. BERT-NLI-transfer-learn-laurer.pdf. Publisher: Open Science Framework.

Markus Leippold, Saeid Ashraf Vaghefi, Dominik Stammbach, Veruska Muccione, Julia Bingler, Jingwei Ni, Chiara Colesanti-Senni, Tobias Wekhof, Tobias Schimanski, Glen Gostlow, Tingyu Yu, Juerg Luterbacher, and Christian Huggel. 2024. Automated fact-checking of climate change claims with large language models. *Preprint*, arXiv:2401.12566.

Andrew Li. 2025. A Case Study of Sentiment Analysis on Survey Data Using LLMs versus Dedicated Neural Networks.

Alisa Liu, Swabha Swayamdipta, Noah A. Smith, and Yejin Choi. 2022. Wanli: Worker and ai collaboration for natural language inference dataset creation.

Yixin Nie, Haonan Chen, and Mohit Bansal. 2019. Combining fact extraction and verification with neural semantic matching networks. In *Association for the Advancement of Artificial Intelligence (AAAI)*.

Yixin Nie, Adina Williams, Emily Dinan, Mohit Bansal, Jason Weston, and Douwe Kiela. 2020. Adversarial NLI: A new benchmark for natural language understanding. In *Proceedings of the 58th Annual Meeting of the Association for Computational Linguistics*, pages 4885–4901, Online. Association for Computational Linguistics.

Alicia Parrish, William Huang, Omar Agha, Soo-Hwan Lee, Nikita Nangia, Alex Warstadt, Karmanya Aggarwal, Emily Allaway, Tal Linzen, and Samuel R. Bowman. 2021. Does putting a linguist in the loop improve nlu data collection? *Preprint*, arXiv:2104.07179.

Colin Raffel, Noam Shazeer, Adam Roberts, Katherine Lee, Sharan Narang, Michael Matena, Yanqi Zhou, Wei Li, and Peter J. Liu. 2023. Exploring the limits of transfer learning with a unified text-to-text transformer. *Preprint*, arXiv:1910.10683.

Kunal Sawarkar, Abhilasha Mangal, and Shivam Raj Solanki. 2024. Blended rag: Improving rag (retriever-augmented generation) accuracy with semantic search and hybrid query-based retrievers. In *2024 IEEE 7th International Conference on Multimedia Information Processing and Retrieval (MIPR)*, volume 24, page 155–161. IEEE.

Michael Sejr Schlichtkrull, Zhijiang Guo, and Andreas Vlachos. 2023. Averitec: A dataset for real-world claim verification with evidence from the web. In *Thirty-thh Conference on Neural Information Processing Systems Datasets and Benchmarks Track*.

Veronika Solopova, Viktoriia Herman, Christoph Benzmüller, and Tim Landgraf. 2024. Check news in one click: NLP-empowered pro-kremlin propaganda detection. In *Proceedings of the 18th Conference of the European Chapter of the Association for Computational Linguistics: System Demonstrations*, pages 44–51, St. Julians, Malta. Association for Computational Linguistics.

James Thorne, Andreas Vlachos, Christos Christodoulopoulos, and Arpit Mittal. 2018. FEVER: a large-scale dataset for fact extraction and VERification. In *NAACL-HLT*.

Liang Wang, Nan Yang, Xiaolong Huang, Binxing Jiao, Linjun Yang, Daxin Jiang, Rangan Majumder, and Furu Wei. 2022a. Text embeddings by weakly-supervised contrastive pre-training. *arXiv preprint arXiv:2212.03533*.

Rui Wang, Zhiyong Gao, Liuyang Zhang, Shuaibing Yue, and Ziyi Gao. 2025. Empowering large language models to edge intelligence: A survey of edge efficient llms and techniques. *Computer Science Review*, 57:100755.

Thomas Wang, Adam Roberts, Daniel Hesslow, Teven Le Scao, Hyung Won Chung, Iz Beltagy, Julien Launay, and Colin Raffel. 2022b. What language model architecture and pretraining objective works best for zero-shot generalization? In *International Conference on Machine Learning*, pages 22964–22984. PMLR.

Adina Williams, Nikita Nangia, and Samuel Bowman. 2018. A broad-coverage challenge corpus for sentence understanding through inference. In *Proceedings of the 2018 Conference of the North American Chapter of the Association for Computational Linguistics: Human Language Technologies, Volume 1 (Long Papers)*, pages 1112–1122. Association for Computational Linguistics.

Shitao Xiao, Zheng Liu, Peitian Zhang, and Niklas Muennighoff. 2023. C-pack: Packaged resources to advance general chinese embedding. *Preprint*, arXiv:2309.07597.

An Yang, Anfeng Li, Baosong Yang, Beichen Zhang, Binyuan Hui, Bo Zheng, Bowen Yu, Chang Gao, Chengen Huang, Chenxu Lv, Chujie Zheng, Dayiheng Liu, Fan Zhou, Fei Huang, Feng Hu, Hao Ge, Haoran Wei, Huan Lin, Jialong Tang, and 41 others. 2025. Qwen3 technical report. *Preprint*, arXiv:2505.09388.

Jing Yang and Anderson Rocha. 2024. Take it easy: Label-adaptive self-rationalization for fact verification and explanation generation. *Preprint*, arXiv:2410.04002.

Jingtao Zhan, Jiaxin Mao, Yiqun Liu, Jiafeng Guo, Min Zhang, and Shaoping Ma. 2021. Optimizing dense retrieval model training with hard negatives. In *Proceedings of the 44th International ACM SIGIR Conference on Research and Development in Information Retrieval*, SIGIR '21, page 1503–1512, New York, NY, USA. Association for Computing Machinery.

A Appendix

A.1 Prompts Collection

For predicting veracity labels with LLMs, we used:

> f"<sys>You are a professional fact checker. You get a claim and an abstract of a scientific paper. Assess if the claim is supported or refuted by the abstract! Return only your verdict! Either 'Supports', 'Refutes' or 'Not Enough Information'.</sys><user>The claim: {claim}\n {abstract}\n Your verdict: "</user>

In all cases, the task description was used as the system prompt (indicated by the <sys>-tags), while the actual values of the variables where used within user prompts (indicated by the <user>-tags).

AlexUNLP-FMT at ClimateCheck Shared Task: Hybrid Retrieval with Adaptive Similarity Graph-based Reranking for Climate-related Social Media Claims Fact Checking

Mahmoud Fathallah, Nagwa ElMakky, Marwan Torki
Department of Computer and Systems Engineering
Alexandria University, Egypt
{es-mahmodfath96, nagwamakky, mtorki}@alexu.edu.eg

Abstract

In this paper, we describe our work for the ClimateCheck shared task at the Scholarly Document Processing (SDP) workshop, ACL 2025. We focus on Subtask 1: Abstracts retrieval. The task involves retrieving relevant abstracts from a large corpus to verify claims made on social media about climate change. We explore various retrieval and reranking techniques, including fine-tuning transformer-based dense retrievers, sparse retrieval methods, and reranking using cross-encoder models. Our final and best-performing system utilizes a hybrid retrieval approach combining BM25 sparse retrieval with a fine-tuned Stella model for dense retrieval, followed by an MSMARCO-trained MiniLM cross-encoder model for reranking. We adapt an iterative graph-based reranking approach that leverages a document similarity graph built over the document corpus to update the candidate pool for reranking dynamically. Our system achieved a score of 0.415 on the final test set for Subtask 1, securing third place on the final leaderboard.

Our code is available on GitHub[1].

1 Introduction

Misinformation spreading on social media poses a significant threat to public understanding of scientific issues, particularly in domains such as climate change, where accurate information is needed to raise awareness and create evidence-based policies.

Social media platforms are often the first point of exposure to climate-related content for the general public, making it easy for misleading claims and information to spread. Therefore, there is a need for automated fact-checking systems that can assess the veracity of such claims in real time.

Automated evidence-based fact-checking remains a challenging task (Glockner et al., 2022). Highly effective retrieval module that can retrieve relevant evidence to support or refute a given claim is a necessary component of the evidence-based fact-checking system (Zheng et al., 2024).

This paper presents our approach for Subtask 1 of the ClimateCheck shared task (Abu Ahmad et al., 2025b), held at the Scholarly Document Processing (SDP) workshop at ACL 2025. The Subtask focuses on retrieving relevant scientific abstracts from a large corpus in response to climate-related claims made on social media.

We experiment with dense and sparse retrieval models and employ a retrieval-reranking pipeline. We fine-tune models using supervised contrastive learning and evaluate the effectiveness of hybrid retrieval pipelines that combine sparse and dense approaches. We adapt a graph-based reranking approach inspired by prior work on corpus graph expansion (MacAvaney et al., 2022), where the reranking pool is iteratively enriched using neighbors of top-ranked documents.

2 Related Work

Information retrieval (IR) pipelines generally rely on sparse or dense retrieval techniques.

Sparse retrieval Sparse retrieval methods, such as BM25 (Robertson and Zaragoza, 2009), represent queries and documents as high-dimensional sparse vectors based on term frequency-inverse document frequency statistics (TF-IDF). While effective in capturing lexical similarity, these models often struggle to capture semantic similarity.

Dense Retrieval Dense retrieval models (Karpukhin et al., 2020; Xiao et al., 2023; Zhang et al., 2025) address the problem of semantic similarity faced by sparse retrieval models. They embed both queries and documents to obtain dense vector representations that allow similarity-based search through vector similarity.

Reranking Reranking is a critical step in IR

[1]`https://github.com/Mahmoud-Mohammed-Fathallah/climatecheck-shared-task`

Proceedings of the Fifth Workshop on Scholarly Document Processing (SDP 2025), pages 288–292
July 31, 2025 ©2025 Association for Computational Linguistics

Label	Training
Supports	446
Refutes	241
Not enough info.	457
Total	1144

Table 1: Distribution of labels in the provided training set.

Label	Training	Validation
Supports	360	86
Refutes	196	45
Not enough info.	361	96
Total	917	227

Table 2: Distribution of labels in our training and validation sets.

pipelines (Liu et al., 2025). Bi-encoder models enable efficient and fast retrieval but require reranking to enhance performance by utilizing a cross-encoder model to jointly encode query-document pairs and output a similarity score (Nogueira and Cho, 2020). This allows for deeper interaction between queries and documents, further enhancing the performance.

Adaptive reranking Adaptive reranking techniques that utilize similarity graphs (MacAvaney et al., 2022; Rathee et al., 2025) have been developed to overcome the limitations of standard retrieval-reranking pipelines, where the reranking performance is limited by the set initially retrieved by the retriever (MacAvaney et al., 2022). In the adaptive reranking approach, a similarity graph is used to retrieve documents related to the top-ranked ones, enabling richer reranking candidates.

3 Data

The shared task provided a training set, a test set, and a document corpus (Abu Ahmad et al., 2025a). The training set included 1,144 claim–abstract pairs labeled as supports, refutes, or not enough information; the label distribution is shown in Table 1. The retrieval corpus contained 394,269 paper abstracts. The test set consisted of 176 unlabeled claims.

Since the shared task initially provided only a training set, we created our own validation set by randomly sampling 50 unique claims and their associated data points from the original training set. The remaining samples formed our training set. Distributions for both sets are shown in Table 2.

4 Methodology

In this section, we outline our approach and the final submitted system.

4.1 Retrieval models

We first explored different bi-encoder models for dense retrieval, such as bge-large-en[2] (Xiao et al., 2023), stella-en-400M-v5[3] (Zhang et al., 2025), and inf-retriever-v1-1.5b[4] (Junhan Yang, 2025). We fine-tuned the first two using contrastive learning (Qiu et al., 2021) utilizing Multiple Negatives Ranking Loss to bring embeddings of related query-abstract pairs closer together and separate unrelated ones. We also experimented with BM25 (Robertson and Zaragoza, 2009), a traditional lexical search algorithm used as a strong baseline and in hybrid approaches.

4.2 Reranking models

We experimented with different cross-encoder models for reranking, comparing the powerful fine-tuned model bge-reranker-v2-m3[5] (Chen et al., 2024) to other models trained on the MS-MARCO dataset (Nguyen et al., 2016), such as ms-marco-MiniLM-L12-v2[6] (Wang et al., 2020), ms-marco-electra-base[7] (Clark et al., 2020), and reranker-msmarco-ModernBERT-base-lambdaloss[8] (Warner et al., 2024).

4.3 Hybrid retrieval

To enhance retrieval performance, we integrated dense retrieval with sparse retrieval, leveraging the strong lexical matching capabilities of methods like BM25(Robertson and Zaragoza, 2009) alongside the powerful semantic search capabilities of dense models such as Stella bi-encoder model (Zhang et al., 2025) to enhance retrieval performance. The top-k documents from both models were combined, with duplicates removed.

[2]https://huggingface.co/BAAI/bge-large-en
[3]https://huggingface.co/NovaSearch/stella_en_400M_v5
[4]https://huggingface.co/infly/inf-retriever-v1-1.5b
[5]https://huggingface.co/BAAI/bge-reranker-v2-m3
[6]https://huggingface.co/cross-encoder/ms-marco-MiniLM-L12-v2
[7]https://huggingface.co/cross-encoder/ms-marco-electra-base
[8]https://huggingface.co/tomaarsen/reranker-msmarco-ModernBERT-base-lambdaloss

4.4 Similarity graph-based reranking

To address the limitations of the initial retrieval stage, where highly relevant documents may be missing from the retrieved set, we implemented an adaptive retrieval and reranking strategy.

We first constructed a similarity graph over the entire corpus, connecting each document to its top-k semantically similar neighbors. The adaptive reranking strategy proceeds as follows: an initial set of documents is retrieved using a retriever, and the top-n candidates are ranked by a cross-encoder reranker. The top-p documents (p < n) are selected and expanded by including their neighbors from the similarity graph. This augmented set is reranked, and the process is repeated for a fixed number of iterations.

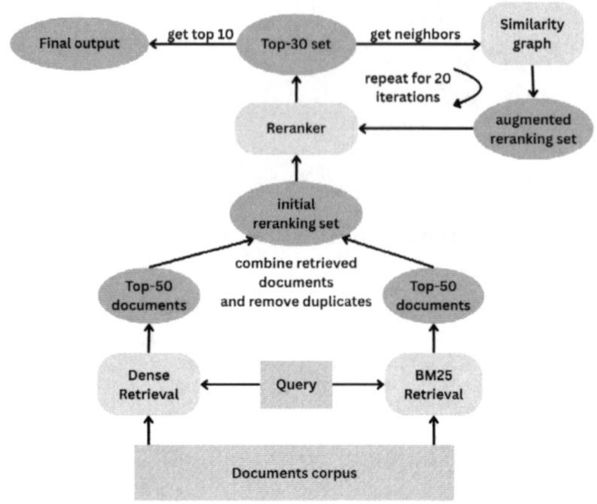

Figure 1: Our final system that utilizes hybrid retrieval with adaptive reranking.

4.5 Final system

Our final system used a graph built with all-MiniLM-L6-v2 bi-encoder model[9] with k=10 nearest neighbors per document and n=20 iterations for the adaptive reranking step. These values were selected after experimenting with different parameters to balance retrieval performance with computational efficiency, allowing the system to explore a broader set of relevant documents through multiple reranking iterations while keeping the runtime feasible. For reranking, we used "ms-marco-MiniLM-L12-v2" cross-encoder model. The initial retrieval stage combined the top 50 documents retrieved by BM25 sparse retrieval and the fine-tuned stella-en-400M-v5 dense retriever. The value 50 is chosen as a reasonable default, as we were unable to perform extensive hyperparameter tuning due to time limitations. The full system architecture is illustrated in Figure 1.

5 Experiments and Results

Evaluation on the validation and test sets was performed using the official shared task metrics: Recall@k (R@k for k=2, 5, 10), B-pref, and the overall SubtaskI-Score, defined as the average of the other metrics.

5.1 Training details

All experiments were conducted on a single NVIDIA V100 GPU. During training, we used batch sizes of 8 and 16, and optimized the models using the Adam optimizer with learning rates of 1e-5, 1e-6, and 4e-6.

5.2 Retrieval models

We compared BM25 (Robertson and Zaragoza, 2009), bge-large-en (Xiao et al., 2023), stella-en-400M-v5 (Zhang et al., 2025) and inf-retriever-v1-1.5b (Junhan Yang, 2025), both with and without fine-tuning on the training set using Multiple Negatives Ranking Loss. The fine-tuned stella model outperformed the other retrieval models. Results on the validation set are shown in Table 3.

5.3 Reranking models

To choose a reranking model, we compared several cross-encoder models: bge-reranker-v2-m3 (Chen et al., 2024), ms-marco-MiniLM-L12-v2 (Wang et al., 2020), ms-marco-electra-base (Clark et al., 2020), and reranker-msmarco-ModernBERT-base-lambdaloss (Warner et al., 2024). The bge-reranker model was fine-tuned on the training set using Multiple Negatives Ranking Loss, while the other models, trained on MS-MARCO dataset (Nguyen et al., 2016), were used without fine-tuning. For a fair comparison, we fixed BM25 as the initial retriever and applied each reranker to the same retrieved set. Results showed that the ms-marco-MiniLM-L12-v2 model outperformed the other models. Validation set results are presented in Table 4.

5.4 Hybrid retrieval

For the hybrid retrieval experiment, we combined the top 50 retrieved documents from BM25 and our best dense retrieval model, the fine-tuned stella-400M. We then rerank this initial set using our best

[9]https://huggingface.co/sentence-transformers/all-MiniLM-L6-v2

Model	R@2	R@5	R@10	B-pref	score
BM25	0.0977	0.1407	0.2051	0.1363	0.1450
bge-large	0.0255	0.1122	0.1422	0.1515	0.1078
bge-large*	**0.1351**	0.1840	0.2414	0.2112	0.1930
inf-retriever	0.0633	0.1774	0.2670	0.2676	0.1938
inf-retriever*	0.0785	**0.2044**	0.2862	0.2441	0.2033
stella*	0.1218	0.1851	**0.2911**	**0.2777**	**0.2189**

Table 3: Comparing different retrieval models on the validation set. The * in the model name means that it is fine-tuned on the training set. The best results are in bold.

Model	R@2	R@5	R@10	B-pref	Score
bge-reranker*	0.1440	0.2722	0.3570	0.2840	0.2643
ModernBERT	0.1807	0.2981	0.3918	0.3249	0.2989
electra-base	0.1381	0.3003	0.3644	0.2954	0.2746
MiniLM-L12	**0.1918**	**0.4144**	**0.6281**	**0.4053**	**0.4099**

Table 4: Comparing different Reranking models on the validation set. The * in the model name means that it is fine-tuned on the training set. The best results are in bold.

Metric	BM25	Stella*	Hybrid
R@2	0.1918	0.2303	**0.2344**
R@5	**0.4144**	0.4059	0.3933
R@10	0.6281	0.5640	**0.6466**
B-pref	0.4053	0.4259	**0.4297**
score	0.4099	0.4065	**0.4260**

Table 5: Results of Hybrid retrieval (BM25 + fine-tuned Stella) compared to each model alone with reranking using MiniLM-L12 on the validation set.

Metric	Validation	Test
R@2	0.2225	0.2099
R@5	0.4155	0.3962
R@10	0.6533	0.5911
B-pref	0.5162	0.4634
Score	0.4519	0.4152

Table 6: Results of our final system on the validation and test sets.

reranking model, ms-marco-MiniLM-L12-v2. To demonstrate the value of hybrid retrieval, we compared its results to those of each individual model. Results show that hybrid retrieval outperforms both models. Validation set results are shown in Table 5.

5.5 Graph-based adaptive reranking

For the final submission, we used the graph-based adaptive reranking approach, as illustrated in section 4.5. Results on the validation set showed that this adaptive reranking method improved the overall score by approximately 2.6% compared to the hybrid retrieval approach alone. The system's results on both the validation and test sets are shown in Table 6.

6 Conclusion

In this paper, we presented a hybrid retrieval system with adaptive reranking for evidence retrieval for climate-related social media claims, developed for Subtask 1 of the ClimateCheck shared task. Our system combined BM25-based sparse retrieval with a fine-tuned dense retriever, followed by a graph-based adaptive reranking approach utilizing a document similarity graph. We demonstrated that hybrid retrieval paired with iterative reranking significantly improved retrieval effectiveness, achieving third place in the final leaderboard.

Our findings emphasize the importance of combining hybrid retrieval with adaptive reranking to enhance the performance of scientific evidence retrieval systems. The use of graph-based expansion enabled the discovery of relevant abstracts that were missed by standard top-k methods.

Limitations

Despite the competitive performance of our adaptive reranking approach, several limitations remain. We did not explore careful tuning of hyperparameters, such as the number of neighbors in the similarity graph or the number of reranking iterations. Additionally, we did not explore the use of different models for constructing the similarity graph.

References

Raia Abu Ahmad, Aida Usmanova, and Georg Rehm. 2025a. The ClimateCheck dataset: Mapping social media claims about climate change to corresponding scholarly articles. In *Proceedings of the 5th Workshop on Scholarly Document Processing (SDP)*, Vienna, Austria.

Raia Abu Ahmad, Aida Usmanova, and Georg Rehm. 2025b. The ClimateCheck shared task: Scientific fact-checking of social media claims about climate change. In *Proceedings of the 5th Workshop on Scholarly Document Processing (SDP)*, Vienna, Austria.

Jianlv Chen, Shitao Xiao, Peitian Zhang, Kun Luo, Defu Lian, and Zheng Liu. 2024. Bge m3-embedding: Multi-lingual, multi-functionality, multi-granularity text embeddings through self-knowledge distillation. *Preprint*, arXiv:2402.03216.

Kevin Clark, Minh-Thang Luong, Quoc V. Le, and Christopher D. Manning. 2020. Electra: Pre-training text encoders as discriminators rather than generators. *Preprint*, arXiv:2003.10555.

Max Glockner, Yufang Hou, and Iryna Gurevych. 2022. Missing counter-evidence renders nlp fact-checking unrealistic for misinformation. *Preprint*, arXiv:2210.13865.

Yichen Yao Wei Chu Yinghui Xu Yuan Qi Junhan Yang, Jiahe Wan. 2025. inf-retriever-v1 (revision 5f469d7).

Vladimir Karpukhin, Barlas Oguz, Sewon Min, Patrick Lewis, Ledell Wu, Sergey Edunov, Danqi Chen, and Wen-tau Yih. 2020. Dense passage retrieval for open-domain question answering. In *Proceedings of the 2020 Conference on Empirical Methods in Natural Language Processing (EMNLP)*, pages 6769–6781, Online. Association for Computational Linguistics.

Qi Liu, Haozhe Duan, Yiqun Chen, Quanfeng Lu, Weiwei Sun, and Jiaxin Mao. 2025. Llm4ranking: An easy-to-use framework of utilizing large language models for document reranking. *Preprint*, arXiv:2504.07439.

Sean MacAvaney, Nicola Tonellotto, and Craig Macdonald. 2022. Adaptive re-ranking with a corpus graph. In *Proceedings of the 31st ACM International Conference on Information amp; Knowledge Management*, CIKM '22, page 1491–1500. ACM.

Tri Nguyen, Mir Rosenberg, Xia Song, Jianfeng Gao, Saurabh Tiwary, Rangan Majumder, and Li Deng. 2016. MS MARCO: A human generated machine reading comprehension dataset. *CoRR*, abs/1611.09268.

Rodrigo Nogueira and Kyunghyun Cho. 2020. Passage re-ranking with bert. *Preprint*, arXiv:1901.04085.

Hefei Qiu, Wei Ding, and Ping Chen. 2021. Contrastive learning of sentence representations. In *Proceedings of the 18th International Conference on Natural Language Processing (ICON)*, pages 277–283, National Institute of Technology Silchar, Silchar, India. NLP Association of India (NLPAI).

Mandeep Rathee, Sean MacAvaney, and Avishek Anand. 2025. Quam: Adaptive retrieval through lt;ugt;qult;/ugt;ery lt;ugt;alt;/ugt;ffinity lt;ugt;mlt;/ugt;odelling. In *Proceedings of the Eighteenth ACM International Conference on Web Search and Data Mining*, WSDM '25, page 954–962. ACM.

Stephen Robertson and Hugo Zaragoza. 2009. The probabilistic relevance framework: Bm25 and beyond. *Foundations and Trends in Information Retrieval*, 3:333–389.

Wenhui Wang, Furu Wei, Li Dong, Hangbo Bao, Nan Yang, and Ming Zhou. 2020. Minilm: Deep self-attention distillation for task-agnostic compression of pre-trained transformers. *Preprint*, arXiv:2002.10957.

Benjamin Warner, Antoine Chaffin, Benjamin Clavié, Orion Weller, Oskar Hallström, Said Taghadouini, Alexis Gallagher, Raja Biswas, Faisal Ladhak, Tom Aarsen, Nathan Cooper, Griffin Adams, Jeremy Howard, and Iacopo Poli. 2024. Smarter, better, faster, longer: A modern bidirectional encoder for fast, memory efficient, and long context finetuning and inference. *Preprint*, arXiv:2412.13663.

Shitao Xiao, Zheng Liu, Peitian Zhang, and Niklas Muennighoff. 2023. C-pack: Packaged resources to advance general chinese embedding. *Preprint*, arXiv:2309.07597.

Dun Zhang, Jiacheng Li, Ziyang Zeng, and Fulong Wang. 2025. Jasper and stella: distillation of sota embedding models. *Preprint*, arXiv:2412.19048.

Liwen Zheng, Chaozhuo Li, Xi Zhang, Yu-Ming Shang, Feiran Huang, and Haoran Jia. 2024. Evidence retrieval is almost all you need for fact verification. In *Findings of the Association for Computational Linguistics: ACL 2024*, pages 9274–9281, Bangkok, Thailand. Association for Computational Linguistics.

ClimateCheck2025: Multi-Stage Retrieval Meets LLMs for Automated Scientific Fact-Checking

Anna Kiepura[†], **Jessica Lam**[†]
[†]Institute of Neuroinformatics, University of Zurich and ETH Zurich, Switzerland
{akiepura, lamjessica}@ini.ethz.ch

Abstract

Misinformation on social media poses significant risks, particularly when it concerns critical scientific issues such as climate change. One promising direction for mitigation is the development of automated fact-checking systems that verify claims against authoritative scientific sources. In this work, we present our solution[1] to the ClimateCheck2025 shared task, which involves retrieving and classifying scientific abstracts as evidence for or against given claims. Our system is built around a multi-stage hybrid retrieval pipeline that integrates lexical, sparse neural, and dense neural retrievers, followed by cross-encoder and large language model (LLM)-based reranking stages. For stance classification, we employ prompting strategies with LLMs to determine whether a retrieved abstract supports, refutes, or provides no evidence for a given claim. Our approach achieves the second-highest overall score across both subtasks of the benchmark and significantly surpasses the final baseline by 53.76% on Subtask I score (defined as an average across Recall@2, Recall@5, Recall@10, and B-Pref). Notably, we achieve state-of-the-art performance in Recall@2. These results highlight the effectiveness of combining structured retrieval architectures with the emergent reasoning capabilities of LLMs for scientific fact verification, especially in domains where reliable human annotation is scarce and timely intervention is essential.

1 Introduction

The rapid proliferation of online misinformation, particularly in scientific, health, and policy contexts, has intensified the demand for reliable automated fact-checking systems (Li and Chang, 2022; Schlicht et al., 2023). These systems aim to assess the veracity of natural language claims by retrieving and evaluating relevant evidence from large text corpora. This process hinges on two core challenges: (**1**) retrieving relevant information from vast knowledge sources, and (**2**) determining whether the retrieved content supports, refutes, or fails to inform the claim.

Traditional keyword-based retrieval methods often struggle with these tasks, especially in domains requiring deep semantic understanding or domain-specific reasoning (Urbani et al., 2024; Devasier et al., 2025). Recent advances in neural retrievers and large language models (LLMs) have improved retrieval and reasoning capabilities across diverse topics (Vykopal et al., 2024; Quelle and Bovet, 2024; Ou et al., 2025). Nonetheless, integrating high-recall retrieval with robust, claim-sensitive reasoning remains a key bottleneck - particularly in scientific domains, where evidence is often sparse, nuanced, and hedged (Hyland, 1996).

In this paper, we present our system for the ClimateCheck2025 shared task (Abu Ahmad et al., 2025b), which consists of two subtasks: (**1**) for each climate-related claim extracted from social media, retrieve the top-10 most relevant abstracts from a corpus of nearly 400,000 scientific abstracts, and (**2**) classify each claim-abstract pair as `SUPPORTS`, `REFUTES`, or `NOT ENOUGH INFORMATION (NEI)`.

Our retrieval pipeline (**Subtask 1**) is a three-stage architecture. First, we combine BM25 (Robertson and Zaragoza, 2009), a fine-tuned dense retriever, and a sparse neural retriever using Reciprocal Rank Fusion (RRF) (Cormack et al., 2009). Second, we train a cross-encoder reranker with a two-phase hard negative mining strategy, leveraging both model uncertainty and relevance judgments. Finally, we apply an adapted RankGPT (Sun et al., 2023), prompting an LLM in a few-shot setting to rerank the top candidates using permutation-based generation informed by cross-encoder scores.

For evidence classification (**Subtask 2**), we eval-

[1]https://github.com/annamkiepura/ClimateCheck

Proceedings of the Fifth Workshop on Scholarly Document Processing (SDP 2025), pages 293–306
July 31, 2025

uate zero- and few-shot LLM prompting, and fine-tune transformer-based models for multi-class classification of claim-abstract pairs.

Our key contributions are:

- We propose a hybrid multi-stage retrieval framework, incorporating LLM-based permutation generation for reranking, to enhance retrieval effectiveness for automated fact-checking.

- We conduct an evaluation of evidence classification approaches, comparing LLMs under various prompting paradigms against supervised BERT-based classifiers.

- Our system achieves the second-highest performance across both subtasks of the ClimateCheck2025 benchmark, surpassing the official baseline by 53.76% on average across Recall@2, Recall@5, Recall@10, and B-pref.

- We set a new state-of-the-art on the ClimateCheck2025 benchmark in terms of Recall@2.

2 Related Work

Automated fact-checking aims to assess the veracity of claims using evidence, a task traditionally performed by human experts but increasingly addressed with automated methods due to scalability concerns (Nakov et al., 2021). Numerous datasets have been developed to support this research. General-domain resources include FEVER (Wikipedia-based claims) (Thorne et al., 2018), VitaminC (contrastive evidence) (Schuster et al., 2021), LIAR (Wang, 2017), and MultiFC (real-world political/media claims) (Augenstein et al., 2019a). MuMiN further expands this scope to multilingual, multimodal misinformation on social media (Nielsen and McConville, 2022).

Scientific fact-checking, a more specialized subfield, introduces challenges such as complex language, evolving knowledge, and domain-specific reasoning. Key datasets include SciFact (Wadden et al., 2020) (scientific claims and abstracts), HealthVer (Sarrouti et al., 2021) and COVID-Fact (Saakyan et al., 2021) (biomedical), and ClimateViz (climate science) (Su et al., 2025). These corpora underscore the risks of domain-specific misinformation, from harmful medical decisions (Wang et al., 2019) to distorted climate discourse (van der Linden et al., 2017).

The fact-checking process is typically modeled as a pipeline: (1) claim detection (Panchendrarajan and Zubiaga, 2024), (2) check worthiness estimation (Yu et al., 2025), (3) document retrieval (Dey et al., 2025), (4) claim verification via natural language inference (NLI) (Dammu et al., 2024). Some systems also generate explanations, though these face challenges with hallucination (Atanasova et al., 2020). Our work focuses on document retrieval and claim verification.

For retrieval, sparse methods such as BM25 use lexical matching, while dense methods, such as Dense Passage Retrieval (Karpukhin et al., 2020), leverage neural encoders for semantic similarity. Hybrid systems combining both have shown improved performance (Zhang et al., 2024), and retrieval-augmented generation (RAG) models further integrate retrieval with generation for grounded responses (Khaliq et al., 2024).

Claim verification is often framed as an entailment task, with transformer-based models, such as BERT (Devlin et al., 2019), fine-tuned to classify claim-evidence pairs as support, refute, or neutral (Wadden et al., 2022). Prompt-based methods using LLMs offer zero-shot alternatives, though performance varies across models and prompt designs (Chen et al., 2024a).

Despite advances, scientific fact-checking remains challenging due to long-context reasoning, subtle hedging, contradictory evidence, and the need for up-to-date knowledge. LLMs have shown promise as rerankers or classifiers, but often lag behind supervised models in consistency and interpretability (Ghosh et al., 2025). In this work, we investigate how traditional retrieval methods can be effectively integrated with LLMs to leverage their complementary strengths.

3 Dataset

The ClimateCheck dataset (Abu Ahmad et al., 2025a) was prepared by the task's organizers and comprises (i) claims sourced from ClimaConvo (Shiwakoti et al., 2024), DEBAGREEMENT (Pougué-Biyong et al., 2021), Climate-Fever (Diggelmann et al., 2021), MultiFC (Augenstein et al., 2019b), and ClimateFeedback[2], including both real and synthetically generated social media-style content, (ii) a corpus of scientific abstracts from OpenAlex[3] and S2ORC (Lo

[2] https://science.feedback.org/process/

[3] https://openalex.org/

et al., 2020), and (iii) annotated claim-abstract pairs labeled as SUPPORTS, REFUTES, or NOT ENOUGH INFORMATION (NEI). Annotations were produced via TREC-style pooling and reviewed by graduate-level domain experts. Key dataset statistics are summarized in Table 1.

Statistic	Value
Abstract Corpus	
Total # of abstracts	394,269
Mean length (words)	240.93
Min length (words)	1
Max length (words)	6,818
Std dev. of length	232.46
Claims (Train Split)	
Total # of unique claims	252
Mean length (words)	17.76
Min length (words)	3
Max length (words)	43
Std dev. of length	7.50
Claim-Abstract Pairs	
Total # of labeled claim-abstract pairs	1,144
SUPPORT instances	446 (38.99%)
REFUTES instances	241 (21.07%)
NEI instances	457 (39.95%)
Positive instances (SUPPORT + REFUTES)	687 (60.05%)
Relevant Abstracts per Claim	
Mean # of relevant abstracts/claim	2.73
Min # of relevant abstracts/claim	0
Max # of relevant abstracts/claim	5
Std dev. of the # of relevant abstracts/claim	1.68
Claim Relevance Distribution	
# of claims with $\geq$1 supporting abstract	150
# of claims $\geq$1 refuting abstract	101
# of claims with only NEI abstracts	27

Table 1: ClimateCheck dataset statistics.

4 Methodology

Below, we describe our multi-stage pipeline for scientific fact-checking, summarized in Figure 1, and our technical implementation details.

4.1 Subtask 1: Abstract Retrieval

Our approach to **Subtask 1** adopts a retrieve-then-rerank paradigm, inspired by prior multi-stage retrieval systems such as HLART (Zhang et al., 2022), Re2G (Glass et al., 2022), and MST-R (Malviya et al., 2024). In **Stage 1**, we employ a hybrid retrieval setup that combines lexical and neural methods, leveraging their complementary

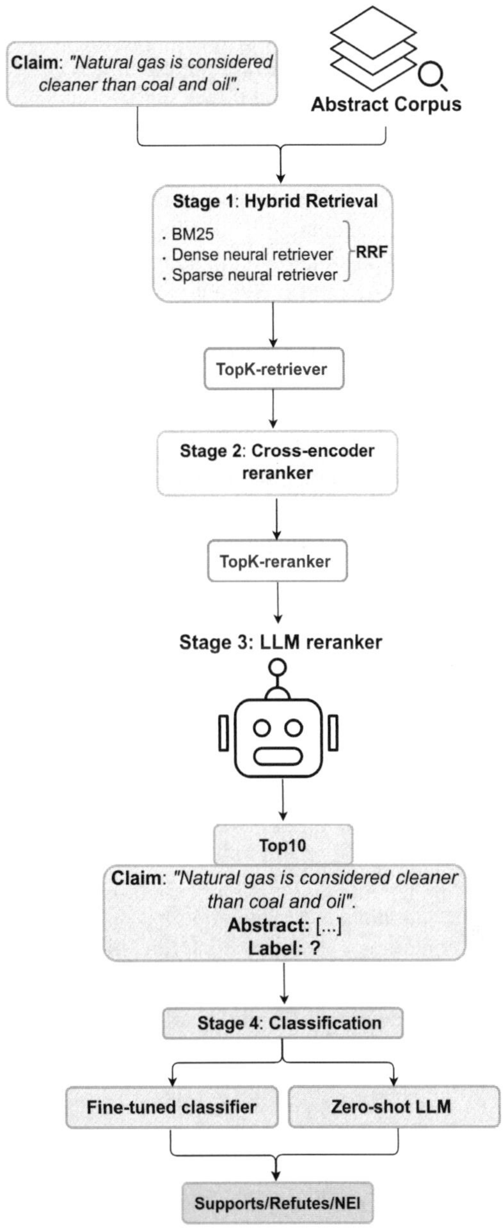

Figure 1: Overview of our fact-checking pipeline. A given claim is matched against an abstract corpus using a hybrid retrieval system (**Stage 1**) composed of BM25, dense, and sparse retrievers, fused via Reciprocal Rank Fusion (RRF). Top-ranked abstracts are reranked using a cross-encoder (**Stage 2**), followed by a few-shot LLM-based reranker (**Stage 3**). The final top 10 abstracts are passed to a classification stage (**Stage 4**), where each claim-abstract pair is labeled as SUPPORTS, REFUTES, or NEI using either a fine-tuned classifier or a zero-shot LLM.

strengths: lexical models excel at exact-match precision, while neural models capture semantic similarity. This integration improves overall recall and yields a more diverse set of candidate abstracts, increasing the chances of retrieving relevant evidence that might be overlooked by any single method. Since the combined results originate from heterogeneous retrieval models with non-comparable scoring functions, **Stages 2 and 3** introduce rerankers to normalize and refine the candidate list, enabling coherent and consistent ranking across sources.

4.1.1 Stage 1 - Hybrid Retrieval System

Dense Neural Retriever We fine-tune the BGE-M3 dense retriever model (Chen et al., 2024b) using a triplet loss objective with cosine distance and a margin of 0.3. Each training instance is a triplet consisting of an anchor (the claim), a positive abstract (labeled as `SUPPORTS` or `REFUTES`), and a negative abstract (labeled as `NEI`). The training objective encourages the model to embed the claim closer to the positive abstract than to the negative by a fixed margin in cosine space. Formally, the loss is defined as:

$$\mathcal{L}_{\text{triplet}} = \max\left(0, \cos(\mathbf{q}, \mathbf{d}^-) - \cos(\mathbf{q}, \mathbf{d}^+) + \gamma\right) \quad (1)$$

where $\mathbf{q}$ is the embedding of the claim, $\mathbf{d}^+$ is the embedding of the positive abstract, $\mathbf{d}^-$ is the embedding of the negative abstract, $\cos(\cdot, \cdot)$ denotes cosine similarity, and $\gamma = 0.3$ is the margin.

The model is fine-tuned for 3 epochs with a learning rate of 5×10^{-5}, using a warm-up schedule over the first 10% of training steps. All layers are updated during training, and mixed-precision computation is employed to improve training efficiency. We use a per-device batch size of 2 with gradient accumulation over 32 steps, yielding an effective batch size of 64. Fine-tuning enables the model to better adapt to the scientific domain and capture semantic relationships between claims and evidentiary abstracts more effectively.

After fine-tuning, we precompute dense embeddings for all abstracts in the corpus. At inference time, an input claim is encoded into a dense vector, and similarity scores are computed via the dot product between the claim vector and each abstract embedding. These scores are then used to directly rank the abstracts by relevance.

Sparse Lexical Retriever BM25 is a sparse lexical retriever model based on TF-IDF (Jones, 1972). We build a BM25 index over all corpus abstracts and use it to retrieve most relevant candidates by computing relevance scores between the tokenized claim and each abstract.

Sparse Neural Retriever We utilize a sparse neural retriever based on the pretrained SPLADE-v3 model (Lassance et al., 2024), which encodes queries into high-dimensional sparse vectors by applying a ReLU-activated max pooling over contextualized token logits. Specifically, given contextualized logits $\mathbf{L} \in \mathbb{R}^{T \times V}$ for a query of length T and vocabulary size V, the sparse representation $\mathbf{q} \in \mathbb{R}^V$ is computed as:

$$\mathbf{q}_v = \max_{t=1,\ldots,T} \text{ReLU}(\mathbf{L}_{t,v}) \quad (2)$$

This allows SPLADE to retain the efficiency of inverted index retrieval while incorporating semantic signals from deep transformer architecture. For each input claim, we compute a sparse claim representation and perform retrieval via a sparse dot product against precomputed document vectors of all abstracts.

RRF We combine the ranked outputs of BM25 (Robertson and Zaragoza, 2009), dense, and sparse neural retrievers using Reciprocal Rank Fusion (RRF), a method introduced by Cormack et al. (2009). In RRF, given the rank $r_i(d)$ of document d from retriever i, the final score is computed as:

$$S(d) = \sum_{i=1}^{n} \frac{1}{k_{\text{rrf}} + r_i(d)} \quad (3)$$

where k_{rrf} is a fixed hyperparameter that we set to 60, following the recommendation in Yang et al. (2017). RRF enables effective aggregation of retrieval results from heterogeneous models with non-comparable scoring scales. We apply this hybrid retrieval strategy to select the top-600 candidate abstracts for each claim (see Appendix B for discussion of the top-k choice).

4.1.2 Stage 2 - Cross-Encoder Reranker

At the first reranking stage, we use a cross-encoder model ms-marco-MiniLM-L-6-v2 (Reimers and Gurevych, 2021; Bajaj et al., 2018) trained on the MSMARCO dataset (Wang et al., 2020). Unlike bi-encoders used in **Stage 1**, the cross-encoder jointly encodes the claim and abstract, allowing for richer interaction and more accurate relevance estimation.

Fine-tuning We fine-tune the cross-encoder reranker in two phases using the ClimateCheck annotated dataset, following a curriculum-based learning strategy (Bengio et al., 2009). In the first phase, training examples are constructed by retrieving the top-k candidates (k=200) using the hybrid retrieval system. All truly relevant abstracts (labeled as `SUPPORTS` or `REFUTES` in the ground truth) are treated as positive examples. Hard negatives are selected from top-ranked abstracts that are labeled as `NEI`, while easy negatives are randomly sampled from the remaining `NEI` abstracts. In the second phase, we use the model trained in the first phase to re-mine more challenging hard negatives. The reranker is then further fine-tuned on this harder set, enabling progressive refinement of its discrimination ability.

We train the model using binary cross-entropy loss, inferred from the scalar output with sigmoid activation and threshold-based label prediction. We use a batch size of 16, a learning rate of 2×10^{-5}, and weight decay of 0.01. Phase 1 includes 3 epochs, followed by 2 additional epochs in phase 2. All experiments are conducted with mixed precision (FP16) (Micikevicius et al., 2018) training enabled for improved efficiency.

Inference At inference time, we retrieve the top-k = 600 candidate abstracts for each test claim using the hybrid retrieval system. The choice of the top-k parameter value used in **Stage 1** is further discussed in Appendix B. These candidates are then reranked using the fine-tuned cross-encoder, and the top-k = 20 are then passed to the **Stage 3** reranker. Different numbers of candidates passed on to the **Stage 3** reranker were not evaluated due to limited resources.

4.1.3 Stage 3 - LLM-based Reranker

The third stage of our pipeline applies an instruction-tuned LLM to rerank the top 20 abstracts produced by the cross-encoder. We use **RankGPT** (Sun et al., 2023) adapted from the official implementation[4], which formulates reranking as a *permutation generation task.* Rather than assigning independent relevance scores (pointwise) or comparing abstract pairs in isolation (pairwise), the model reasons over the entire candidate set holistically and outputs a single ranked list. Given a claim and 20 candidate abstracts, the LLM is prompted in a few-shot setting to generate a permutation $\pi \in \mathbb{S}_N$, where $\pi(i)$ denotes the rank assigned to the i-th abstract. The model is explicitly instructed to order the abstracts from most to least evidentiary, regardless of stance polarity (`SUPPORTS` or `REFUTES`). This enables the LLM to model complex interdependencies such as redundancy, diversity, and relative informativeness - capabilities not easily captured by pointwise or pairwise architectures. The resulting LLM-based ranks are converted into normalized scores using:

$$\text{LLM}_{\text{norm}}(d_i) = 1 - \frac{\pi(i) - 1}{N - 1} \tag{4}$$

where N is the number of candidates to rerank and a higher score corresponds to a more evidentiary abstract.

To integrate the LLM's global reasoning with the semantic precision of the cross-encoder, we compute a fused score for each document as:

$$\begin{aligned} \text{score}_{\text{fused}}(d_i) &= \alpha \cdot \text{CE}_{\text{norm}}(d_i) \\ &+ (1 - \alpha) \cdot \text{LLM}_{\text{norm}}(d_i) \end{aligned} \tag{5}$$

where the α parameter balances the contributions of the normalized cross-encoder score $\text{CE}_{\text{norm}}(d_i)$ and the normalized LLM-based score $\text{LLM}_{\text{norm}}(d_i)$. We used $\alpha = 0.4$ as it yielded the best performance. Full ablation results of the value of the α parameter are available in Appendix A. The top 10 abstracts based on the fused scores are then selected as the final ranked evidence set for each claim.

As the LLM, we used GPT-4.1[5] through OpenAI API, with temperature set to 0. Prompting details and the comparison between the zero- and few-shot settings are included in Appendix A.

4.1.4 Retrieval evaluation metrics

We evaluate retrieval performance using several standard metrics: Recall@2, Recall@5, and Recall@10 measure the proportion of relevant abstracts retrieved in the top 2, 5, and 10 positions, respectively. B-Pref (Binary Preference) (Buckley and Voorhees, 2004) quantifies how many relevant items are ranked ahead of non-relevant ones, accounting for incomplete relevance judgments. We also report a composite Retrieval Score, computed as the arithmetic mean of the four preceding metrics.

[4] `https://github.com/sunnweiwei/RankGPT`

[5] `https://https://openai.com/index/gpt-4-1/`

4.2 Subtask 2: Stance Classification

To classify the stance of retrieved abstracts (SUPPORTS, REFUTES, or NEI) with respect to the retrieved claims, we explore two approaches: (a) using LLMs in various prompting settings, and (b) training supervised classifiers based on DeBERTa (He et al., 2021) and RoBERTa (Liu et al., 2019), using human-annotated examples in the Climate-Check dataset.

4.2.1 LLM

We experiment with prompting LLMs to classify claim-abstract pairs using both zero-shot and few-shot settings. In the zero-shot setup, the model is directly instructed to assign labels, without any examples provided. In the few-shot variant, we provide examples of annotated pairs to guide the model's reasoning. Additionally, we investigate a two-step classification approach: first, the model predicts whether a given abstract is *evidentiary* (i.e., SUPPORTS or REFUTES) versus *non-evidentiary* (NEI); second, only for the evidentiary stances, a separate model instance predicts the polarity (SUPPORTS vs REFUTES). In the one-step approach, the model is directly prompted to assign one of the three possible labels. In the hybrid approach, a single model instance is instructed to first predict the relevance (evidentiary vs. non-evidentiary), and then the polarity. Full details regarding prompting are available in Appendix C. As the LLM, we used GPT-4.1[6] through OpenAI API, with temperature set to 0.

4.2.2 Supervised fine-tuning

We fine-tune three models, initializing from the following checkpoints: DeBERTa-v3-base-mnli[7], which was trained on the MultiNLI dataset (Williams et al., 2018) consisting of 392,702 NLI hypothesis-premise pairs, DeBERTa-v3-base-scifact[8] and RoBERTa-large-scifact[9], both fine-tuned on the SciFact dataset.

The human-labeled instances were stratified 90/10 into training and validation splits. We freeze the encoder layers, so that only the pooler and classifier layers are updated. To mitigate the mild class imbalance, we employ a custom `Trainer` that (i) inserts a `WeightedRandomSampler` so each mini-batch is class-balanced and (ii) replaces the standard cross-entropy with a class-weighted focal loss:

$$\mathcal{L}_{\text{focal}} = -\,\alpha_y\left(1 - p_y\right)^{\gamma}\,\log p_y \qquad (6)$$

where p_y is the softmax probability of the gold label y, $\alpha_y = 1/f_y$ is the inverse class frequency (normalized so $\sum_c \alpha_c = C$), and $\gamma = 2$ focuses the gradient on hard or minority examples. Training runs for 10 epochs with an effective batch of 32 and a flat learning rate 5×10^{-5}.

4.2.3 Classification evaluation metrics

We report weighted-averaged precision (P), recall (R), and F1-score, which compute metrics for each class and average them according to the number of true instances for the SUPPORTS, REFUTES, and NEI labels. This approach accounts for class imbalance while providing a comprehensive measure of overall system performance.

4.3 Hardware details

All fine-tuning and inference experiments were carried out on the A100 40 GB RAM NVIDIA GPU.

5 Results and Discussion

5.1 Subtask 1: Abstract Retrieval

Alg.	R@2	R@5	R@10	B-Pref	R. Score
B+S+D	0.1447	0.2693	0.3840	0.3102	0.2771
B+S+D+C	0.1882	0.3884	0.5643	0.4270	0.3920
B+S+D+C+L	**0.2309**	**0.4413**	**0.6006**	**0.4818**	**0.4386**
Final baseline	0.1947	0.3047	0.3436	0.2980	0.2853

Table 2: Retrieval results (B=BM25, S=SPLADE, D=Dense, C=Cross-encoder, L=LLM) across retrieval system variants on test dataset. Final baseline refers to the baseline results provided by the task's organizers. Full ablation available in Appendix A.

Retrieval results are shown in Table 2. The initial hybrid retriever, which combines lexical (BM25), sparse neural (SPLADE), and dense (BGE-M3) retrieval methods, achieves a Recall@10 of 0.3840 and a retrieval score of 0.2771. While this baseline benefits from diverse retrieval signals, its ability to rank truly relevant evidence is still limited by the heterogeneous scoring outputs and lack of deeper semantic matching.

Introducing the cross-encoder reranker (B+S+D+C) yields substantial gains across all evaluation metrics. Notably, Recall@10 increases

[6] https://https://openai.com/index/gpt-4-1/

[7] https://huggingface.co/MoritzLaurer/DeBERTa-v3-base-mnli

[8] https://huggingface.co/jedick/DeBERTa-v3-base-mnli-fever-anli-scifact-citint

[9] https://huggingface.co/nikolamilosevic/SCIFACT_xlm_roberta_large

by over 47% (from 0.3840 to 0.5643), while B-Pref improves from 0.3102 to 0.4270. This confirms the effectiveness of cross-encoders in modeling fine-grained semantic relationships between claims and abstracts, particularly in reordering high-recall but noisy candidate sets.

The full pipeline (B+S+D+C+L), which integrates an LLM-based permutation reranker as a final stage, achieves the strongest performance across all metrics. It reaches a Recall@10 of 0.6006 and a B-Pref of 0.4818, corresponding to a final retrieval score of 0.4386. This indicates that the LLM-based reranker provides complementary refinement, likely capturing subtle discourse cues and context-aware relevance signals missed by earlier stages. Improvements are consistent not only in recall-based metrics but also in B-Pref, suggesting that the model is not just retrieving more relevant documents, but also ranking them more coherently with respect to ground truth preferences. Overall, our approach yields an improvement of 53.76% in Retrieval Score over the final baseline published by the shared task's organizers[10].

5.2 Subtask 2: Stance Classification

Version	P	R	F1
LLM prompting			
Few-shots-hybrid	0.6811	0.6835	0.6811
Zero-shot-hybrid	**0.6950**	**0.6973**	**0.6957**
Zero-shot-two-step	0.6780	0.6835	0.6788
Zero-shot-one-step	0.6874	0.6909	0.6842
Supervised fine-tuning			
DeBERTa-v3-base-mnli	0.5468	0.5348	0.5176
DeBERTa-v3-base-scifact	0.5774	0.5285	0.5365
RoBERTa-large-scifact	0.5637	0.5032	0.5098
Final baseline	0.65448	0.62603	0.63148

Table 3: Classification performance across LLM prompting and supervised fine-tuning strategies on the test dataset. Final baseline refers to the baseline results provided by the task's organizers.

Classification results are summarized in Table 3. Among LLM-based strategies, the zero-shot hybrid prompt achieves the highest F1 score of 0.6957, slightly outperforming the few-shot variant (0.6811) and both the one-step and two-step zero-shot setups. This suggests that carefully crafted zero-shot prompts can be as effective - or even more so - than few-shot examples, likely due to reduced prompt length and reduced token-level noise from poorly aligned demonstrations.

The hybrid prompting format, which combines structured instruction with explicit claim-evidence formatting, proves consistently effective across setups. Compared to the two-step approach, where the stance is inferred via intermediate entailment, the one-step and hybrid strategies demonstrate better alignment with the task's categorical stance labels, yielding higher precision and recall. This suggests that direct classification is more robust for LLMs than compositional reasoning pipelines in this context.

Notably, all LLM-based approaches outperform the supervised baselines. The best supervised model (DeBERTa-v3-base fine-tuned on SciFact) achieves an F1 score of 0.5365 - substantially lower than any LLM-based method. This performance gap highlights the limitations of traditional fine-tuning approaches, even when trained on in-domain annotations, and underscores the strength of instruction-tuned LLMs in performing complex stance classification in few- or zero-shot settings.

6 Conclusion

Scientific fact verification poses unique challenges due to complex domain language and the need for precise evidence interpretation. In this work, we introduced a multi-stage retrieval and classification pipeline tailored to these challenges, integrating hybrid retrieval methods, cross-encoder reranking, and LLM-based reasoning modules.

Our experiments on the ClimateCheck benchmark demonstrate consistent improvements across all retrieval metrics, with each additional component - especially LLM-based reranking - contributing meaningfully to performance. In the classification subtask, prompting strategies based on LLMs outperformed traditional fine-tuned models, even when the latter were trained on task-specific human annotations. These findings highlight the flexibility and effectiveness of instruction-tuned LLMs for complex scientific reasoning tasks, especially in data-scarce or rapidly evolving domains.

Overall, our work underscores the importance of combining structured retrieval pipelines with the emergent reasoning abilities of LLMs. Future work could explore more tightly integrated retrieval-generation models, few-shot active learning for stance classification, and methods for im-

[10]The percentage change is calculated as $\left(\frac{0.4386-0.2853}{0.2853}\right) \times 100\% = \left(\frac{0.1533}{0.2853}\right) \times 100\% = 0.5373 \times 100\% = 53.73\%$.

proving the interpretability and trustworthiness of LLM-based decisions in scientific verification contexts.

Limitations

While our system demonstrates strong performance on both retrieval and classification for scientific fact verification, several limitations remain.

First, our retrieval pipeline relies on precomputed document embeddings and staged reranking, which - although effective - can be computationally expensive and may not scale efficiently to real-time or large-scale applications. The use of LLM-based reranking, in particular, introduces latency and resource demands that may be prohibitive in deployment scenarios without high-performance infrastructure.

Second, while prompting-based approaches outperform supervised baselines in our setting, they are sensitive to prompt design and require manual tuning. Our evaluation does not fully explore the robustness of these prompts to variation in phrasing, order, or input format, nor does it address the interpretability of the model's reasoning process.

References

Raia Abu Ahmad, Aida Usmanova, and Georg Rehm. 2025a. The ClimateCheck dataset: Mapping social media claims about climate change to corresponding scholarly articles. In *Proceedings of the 5th Workshop on Scholarly Document Processing (SDP)*, Vienna, Austria.

Raia Abu Ahmad, Aida Usmanova, and Georg Rehm. 2025b. The ClimateCheck shared task: Scientific fact-checking of social media claims about climate change. In *Proceedings of the 5th Workshop on Scholarly Document Processing (SDP)*, Vienna, Austria.

Pepa Atanasova, Jakob Grue Simonsen, Christina Lioma, and Isabelle Augenstein. 2020. Generating fact checking explanations. In *Proceedings of the 58th Annual Meeting of the Association for Computational Linguistics*, pages 7352–7364, Online. Association for Computational Linguistics.

Isabelle Augenstein, Christina Lioma, Dongsheng Wang, Lucas Chaves Lima, Casper Hansen, Christian Hansen, and Jakob Grue Simonsen. 2019a. MultiFC: A real-world multi-domain dataset for evidence-based fact checking of claims. In *Proceedings of the 2019 Conference on Empirical Methods in Natural Language Processing and the 9th International Joint Conference on Natural Language Processing (EMNLP-IJCNLP)*, pages 4685–4697, Hong Kong, China. Association for Computational Linguistics.

Isabelle Augenstein, Christina Lioma, Dongsheng Wang, Lucas Chaves Lima, Casper Hansen, Christian Hansen, and Jakob Grue Simonsen. 2019b. Multifc: A real-world multi-domain dataset for evidence-based fact checking of claims. *Preprint*, arXiv:1909.03242.

Payal Bajaj, Daniel Campos, Nick Craswell, Li Deng, Jianfeng Gao, Xiaodong Liu, Rangan Majumder, Andrew McNamara, Bhaskar Mitra, Tri Nguyen, Mir Rosenberg, Xia Song, Alina Stoica, Saurabh Tiwary, and Tong Wang. 2018. Ms marco: A human generated machine reading comprehension dataset. *Preprint*, arXiv:1611.09268.

Yoshua Bengio, Jérôme Louradour, Ronan Collobert, and Jason Weston. 2009. Curriculum learning. In *Proceedings of the 26th Annual International Conference on Machine Learning*, ICML '09, page 41–48, New York, NY, USA. Association for Computing Machinery.

Chris Buckley and Ellen M. Voorhees. 2004. Retrieval evaluation with incomplete information. In *Proceedings of the 27th annual international ACM SIGIR conference on Research and development in information retrieval*, pages 25–32. ACM.

Beiduo Chen, Xinpeng Wang, Siyao Peng, Robert Litschko, Anna Korhonen, and Barbara Plank. 2024a. "seeing the big through the small": Can llms approximate human judgment distributions on nli from a few explanations? *Preprint*, arXiv:2406.17600.

Jianlv Chen, Shitao Xiao, Peitian Zhang, Kun Luo, Defu Lian, and Zheng Liu. 2024b. Bge m3-embedding: Multi-lingual, multi-functionality, multi-granularity text embeddings through self-knowledge distillation. *Preprint*, arXiv:2402.03216.

Gordon V. Cormack, Charles L A Clarke, and Stefan Buettcher. 2009. Reciprocal rank fusion outperforms condorcet and individual rank learning methods. In *Proceedings of the 32nd International ACM SIGIR Conference on Research and Development in Information Retrieval*, SIGIR '09, page 758–759, New York, NY, USA. Association for Computing Machinery.

Preetam Prabhu Srikar Dammu, Himanshu Naidu, Mouly Dewan, YoungMin Kim, Tanya Roosta, Aman Chadha, and Chirag Shah. 2024. ClaimVer: Explainable claim-level verification and evidence attribution of text through knowledge graphs. In *Findings of the Association for Computational Linguistics: EMNLP 2024*, pages 13613–13627, Miami, Florida, USA. Association for Computational Linguistics.

Jacob Devasier, Rishabh Mediratta, Akshith Putta, and Chengkai Li. 2025. Task-oriented automatic fact-checking with frame-semantics. *Preprint*, arXiv:2501.13288.

Jacob Devlin, Ming-Wei Chang, Kenton Lee, and Kristina Toutanova. 2019. Bert: Pre-training of deep bidirectional transformers for language understanding. *Preprint*, arXiv:1810.04805.

Arka Ujjal Dey, Muhammad Junaid Awan, Georgia Channing, Christian Schroeder de Witt, and John Collomosse. 2025. Fact-checking with contextual narratives: Leveraging retrieval-augmented llms for social media analysis. *Preprint*, arXiv:2504.10166.

Thomas Diggelmann, Jordan Boyd-Graber, Jannis Bulian, Massimiliano Ciaramita, and Markus Leippold. 2021. Climate-fever: A dataset for verification of real-world climate claims. *Preprint*, arXiv:2012.00614.

Bishwamittra Ghosh, Sarah Hasan, Naheed Anjum Arafat, and Arijit Khan. 2025. Logical consistency of large language models in fact-checking. *Preprint*, arXiv:2412.16100.

Michael Glass, Gaetano Rossiello, Md Faisal Mahbub Chowdhury, Ankita Rajaram Naik, Pengshan Cai, and Alfio Gliozzo. 2022. Re2g: Retrieve, rerank, generate. *Preprint*, arXiv:2207.06300.

Pengcheng He, Xiaodong Liu, Jianfeng Gao, and Weizhu Chen. 2021. Deberta: Decoding-enhanced bert with disentangled attention. *Preprint*, arXiv:2006.03654.

Ken Hyland. 1996. Writing without conviction? hedging in science research articles. *Applied Linguistics*, 17(4):433–454.

K. Sparck Jones. 1972. A statistical interpretation of term specificity and its application in retrieval. *Journal of Documentation*, 28(1):11–21.

Vladimir Karpukhin, Barlas Oğuz, Sewon Min, Patrick Lewis, Ledell Wu, Sergey Edunov, Danqi Chen, and Wen tau Yih. 2020. Dense passage retrieval for open-domain question answering. *Preprint*, arXiv:2004.04906.

M. Abdul Khaliq, P. Chang, M. Ma, B. Pflugfelder, and F. Miletić. 2024. Ragar, your falsehood radar: Rag-augmented reasoning for political fact-checking using multimodal large language models. *Preprint*, arXiv:2404.12065.

Carlos Lassance, Hervé Déjean, Thibault Formal, and Stéphane Clinchant. 2024. Splade-v3: New baselines for splade. *Preprint*, arXiv:2403.06789.

Jiaxin Li and Xiaojun Chang. 2022. Combating misinformation by sharing the truth: a study on the spread of fact-checks on social media. *Information Systems Frontiers*, pages 1–15. Epub ahead of print.

Yinhan Liu, Myle Ott, Naman Goyal, Jingfei Du, Mandar Joshi, Danqi Chen, Omer Levy, Mike Lewis, Luke Zettlemoyer, and Veselin Stoyanov. 2019. Roberta: A robustly optimized bert pretraining approach. *Preprint*, arXiv:1907.11692.

Kyle Lo, Lucy Lu Wang, Mark Neumann, Rodney Kinney, and Daniel Weld. 2020. S2ORC: The semantic scholar open research corpus. In *Proceedings of the 58th Annual Meeting of the Association for Computational Linguistics*, pages 4969–4983, Online. Association for Computational Linguistics.

Yash Malviya, Karan Dhingra, and Maneesh Singh. 2024. Mst-r: Multi-stage tuning for retrieval systems and metric evaluation. *Preprint*, arXiv:2412.10313.

Paulius Micikevicius, Sharan Narang, Jonah Alben, Gregory Diamos, Erich Elsen, David Garcia, Boris Ginsburg, Michael Houston, Oleksii Kuchaiev, Ganesh Venkatesh, and Hao Wu. 2018. Mixed precision training. *Preprint*, arXiv:1710.03740.

Preslav Nakov, David Corney, Maram Hasanain, Firoj Alam, Tamer Elsayed, Alberto Barrón-Cedeño, Paolo Papotti, Shaden Shaar, and Giovanni Da San Martino. 2021. Automated fact-checking for assisting human fact-checkers. *Preprint*, arXiv:2103.07769.

Dan Saattrup Nielsen and Ryan McConville. 2022. Mumin: A large-scale multilingual multimodal fact-checked misinformation social network dataset. *Preprint*, arXiv:2202.11684.

Haoran Ou, Gelei Deng, Xingshuo Han, Jie Zhang, Xinlei He, Han Qiu, Shangwei Guo, and Tianwei Zhang. 2025. Holmes: Automated fact check with large language models. *Preprint*, arXiv:2505.03135.

Rrubaa Panchendrarajan and Arkaitz Zubiaga. 2024. Claim detection for automated fact-checking: A survey on monolingual, multilingual and cross-lingual research. *Natural Language Processing Journal*, 7:100066.

John Pougué-Biyong, Valentina Semenova, Alexandre Matton, Rachel Han, Aerin Kim, Renaud Lambiotte, and J Doyne Farmer. 2021. Debagreement: A comment-reply dataset for (dis)agreement detection in online debates. In *NeurIPS Datasets and Benchmarks Track (Round 2)*.

Dorian Quelle and Alexandre Bovet. 2024. The perils and promises of fact-checking with large language models. *Frontiers in Artificial Intelligence*, 7.

Nils Reimers and Iryna Gurevych. 2021. The curse of dense low-dimensional information retrieval for large index sizes. *Preprint*, arXiv:2012.14210.

Stephen Robertson and Hugo Zaragoza. 2009. The probabilistic relevance framework: Bm25 and beyond. *Found. Trends Inf. Retr.*, 3(4):333–389.

Arkadiy Saakyan, Tuhin Chakrabarty, and Smaranda Muresan. 2021. COVID-fact: Fact extraction and verification of real-world claims on COVID-19 pandemic. In *Proceedings of the 59th Annual Meeting of the Association for Computational Linguistics and the 11th International Joint Conference on Natural Language Processing (Volume 1: Long Papers)*, pages 2116–2129, Online. Association for Computational Linguistics.

Mourad Sarrouti, Asma Ben Abacha, Yassine Mrabet, and Dina Demner-Fushman. 2021. Evidence-based fact-checking of health-related claims. In *Findings of the Association for Computational Linguistics:*

EMNLP 2021, pages 3499–3512, Punta Cana, Dominican Republic. Association for Computational Linguistics.

Ipek Baris Schlicht, Eugenia Fernandez, Berta Chulvi, and Paolo Rosso. 2023. Automatic detection of health misinformation: a systematic review. *Journal of Ambient Intelligence and Humanized Computing*, pages 1–13. Advance online publication.

Tal Schuster, Adam Fisch, and Regina Barzilay. 2021. Get your vitamin c! robust fact verification with contrastive evidence. *Preprint*, arXiv:2103.08541.

Shuvam Shiwakoti, Surendrabikram Thapa, Kritesh Rauniyar, Akshyat Shah, Aashish Bhandari, and Usman Naseem. 2024. Analyzing the dynamics of climate change discourse on Twitter: A new annotated corpus and multi-aspect classification. In *Proceedings of the 2024 Joint International Conference on Computational Linguistics, Language Resources and Evaluation (LREC-COLING 2024)*, pages 984–994, Torino, Italia. ELRA and ICCL.

Ruiran Su, Jiasheng Si, Zhijiang Guo, and Janet B. Pierrehumbert. 2025. Climateviz: A benchmark for statistical reasoning and fact verification on scientific charts. *Preprint*, arXiv:2506.08700.

Weiwei Sun, Lingyong Yan, Xinyu Ma, Pengjie Ren, Dawei Yin, and Zhaochun Ren. 2023. Is chatgpt good at search? investigating large language models as re-ranking agent. *ArXiv*, abs/2304.09542.

James Thorne, Andreas Vlachos, Christos Christodoulopoulos, and Arpit Mittal. 2018. FEVER: a large-scale dataset for fact extraction and VERification. In *Proceedings of the 2018 Conference of the North American Chapter of the Association for Computational Linguistics: Human Language Technologies, Volume 1 (Long Papers)*, pages 809–819, New Orleans, Louisiana. Association for Computational Linguistics.

Nicolò Urbani, Sandip Modha, and Gabriella Pasi. 2024. Retrieving semantics for fact-checking: A comparative approach using CQ (claim to question) & AQ (answer to question). In *Proceedings of the Seventh Fact Extraction and VERification Workshop (FEVER)*, pages 37–46, Miami, Florida, USA. Association for Computational Linguistics.

Sander van der Linden, Anthony Leiserowitz, Seth Rosenthal, and Edward Maibach. 2017. Inoculating the public against misinformation about climate change. *Global Challenges*, 1(2):1600008.

Ivan Vykopal, Matúš Pikuliak, Simon Ostermann, and Marián Šimko. 2024. Generative large language models in automated fact-checking: A survey. *Preprint*, arXiv:2407.02351.

David Wadden, Shanchuan Lin, Kyle Lo, Lucy Lu Wang, Madeleine van Zuylen, Arman Cohan, and Hannaneh Hajishirzi. 2020. Fact or fiction: Verifying scientific claims. In *Proceedings of the 2020 Conference on Empirical Methods in Natural Language Processing (EMNLP)*, pages 7534–7550, Online. Association for Computational Linguistics.

David Wadden, Kyle Lo, Lucy Lu Wang, Arman Cohan, Iz Beltagy, and Hannaneh Hajishirzi. 2022. MultiVerS: Improving scientific claim verification with weak supervision and full-document context. In *Findings of the Association for Computational Linguistics: NAACL 2022*, pages 61–76, Seattle, United States. Association for Computational Linguistics.

Wenhui Wang, Furu Wei, Li Dong, Hangbo Bao, Nan Yang, and Ming Zhou. 2020. Minilm: Deep self-attention distillation for task-agnostic compression of pre-trained transformers. *Preprint*, arXiv:2002.10957.

William Yang Wang. 2017. "liar, liar pants on fire": A new benchmark dataset for fake news detection. In *Proceedings of the 55th Annual Meeting of the Association for Computational Linguistics (Volume 2: Short Papers)*, pages 422–426, Vancouver, Canada. Association for Computational Linguistics.

Yuxi Wang, Martin McKee, Aleksandra Torbica, and David Stuckler. 2019. Systematic literature review on the spread of health-related misinformation on social media. *Social Science Medicine*, 240:112552.

Adina Williams, Nikita Nangia, and Samuel Bowman. 2018. A broad-coverage challenge corpus for sentence understanding through inference. In *Proceedings of the 2018 Conference of the North American Chapter of the Association for Computational Linguistics: Human Language Technologies, Volume 1 (Long Papers)*, pages 1112–1122, New Orleans, Louisiana. Association for Computational Linguistics.

Peilin Yang, Hui Fang, and Jimmy Lin. 2017. Anserini: Enabling the use of lucene for information retrieval research. In *Proceedings of the 40th International ACM SIGIR Conference on Research and Development in Information Retrieval*, SIGIR '17, page 1253–1256, New York, NY, USA. Association for Computing Machinery.

Yinglong Yu, Hao Shen, Zhengyi Lyu, and Qi He. 2025. Application and optimization of large models based on prompt tuning for fact-check-worthiness estimation. *Preprint*, arXiv:2504.18104.

Haoyu Zhang, Jun Liu, Zhenhua Zhu, Shulin Zeng, Maojia Sheng, Tao Yang, Guohao Dai, and Yu Wang. 2024. Efficient and effective retrieval of dense-sparse hybrid vectors using graph-based approximate nearest neighbor search. *Preprint*, arXiv:2410.20381.

Yanzhao Zhang, Dingkun Long, Guangwei Xu, and Pengjun Xie. 2022. Hlatr: Enhance multi-stage text retrieval with hybrid list aware transformer reranking. *Preprint*, arXiv:2205.10569.

Version	R@2	R@5	R@10	B-Pref	R. Score
Zero-Shot LLM	0.2285	0.4398	0.5961	0.4692	0.4334
Few-Shot LLM	**0.2309**	**0.4413**	**0.6006**	**0.4818**	**0.4387**

Table 4: Comparison of zero-shot and few-shot prompting strategies results for the LLM-based reranker.

LLM Prompting Strategy for Passage Ranking (Zero-Shot)
System Prompt:
You are given a **CLAIM** and **N PASSAGES**. A passage is *evidentiary* with respect to a claim if it contains information that could either `SUPPORT` or `REFUTE` the claim. Whether it supports or refutes does not matter. Return exactly one line with the passage numbers, most evidentiary first, least evidentiary last. **Output numbers only**.

Figure 2: Prompting strategy for LLM-based passage ranking. Given a claim and a set of passages, the model is instructed to output a permutation of passage indices in decreasing order of evidentiary relevance.

A RankGPT prompting details

To use an LLM as the final reranking stage, we adopt the permutation generation approach (as introduced in RankGPT). It involves instructing an LLM to directly output the permutations of a group of passages. This method ranks passages directly without an intermediate relevance score. To combine the LLM output with the cross-encoder score, we convert the LLM-based ranks into normalized scores, and then compute a fused score incorporating the cross-encoder score for each document, as described in subsection 4.1.3.

The prompt to the LLM is depicted in Figure 2. For each claim, we include the top 20 abstracts retrieved by the cross-encoder. In a few-shots scenario, we additionally incorporate the examples shown in Figure 3. We then produce gold permutations as follows: all evidentiary abstracts (`SUPPORTS` or `REFUTES`) must be ranked higher than any `NEI` abstracts. Except for this rule, the relative order of abstracts is random.

We include the few-shot setting in our final results, as it was demonstrated to yield slightly higher results than the zero-shot setting, as shown in Table 4.

Table 5 contains the results of ablations for the fusion parameter α. As $\alpha = 0.4$ yielded the best overall retrieval performance (as defined by the R. Score), it was included in the final results.

B Full retrieval ablations

Table 6 presents a comprehensive ablation study evaluating different retrieval configurations. Among individual retrievers, SPLADE outperforms BM25 and Dense, particularly in Recall@10 and B-Pref. Adding a cross-encoder (CE) reranker consistently boosts performance across all settings, with SPLADE+CE achieving the best single-retriever reranking results. Combinations of multiple retrievers further improve performance, particularly when fused with the cross-encoder. The best performance is achieved with the full pipeline—BM25 + SPLADE + Dense + CE + LLM—which yields the highest Recall@2, Recall@5, Recall@10, and overall retrieval score.

Table 7 presents additional ablation results focusing on the first-stage retrieval component, comparing different combinations of BM25, Dense, and SPLADE retrievers across varying top-k cutoffs. Individually, SPLADE consistently outperforms BM25 and Dense, especially at lower k, but all three benefit significantly from hybridization. Notably, combining any two retrievers yields substantial gains over individual models. The best overall performance is achieved by the full hybrid—SPLADE + BM25 + Dense—which achieves the highest recall across all k values. These results confirm that hybrid retrieval setups provide more comprehensive and diverse evidence coverage than any single retriever alone. As R@600 is much higher than recall at lower values of k, top 600 abstracts retrieved by the first-stage retrieval component were passed on further to the reranker. Due to time constraints, the effect of setting the value of k for the first-stage retrieval component to 800 and higher on the overall system performance was not evaluated.

C Classification prompting details

For **Subtask 2** (Stance Classification), we tested four different prompting settings.

Few-shots-hybrid involves splitting the classification task into two stages within one prompt. The model is asked to first distinguish between the evidentiary (`SUPPORTS` or `REFUTES`) and non-

Alpha	R@2	R@5	R@10	B-Pref	R. Score
0.0	0.2280	0.3919	0.5728	**0.5016**	0.4236
0.2	**0.2375**	0.4069	0.5884	0.4826	0.4288
0.4	0.2309	**0.4413**	0.6006	0.4818	**0.4386**
0.6	0.1960	0.4151	**0.6044**	0.4521	0.4169
0.8	0.1837	0.3726	0.5795	0.4315	0.3918
1.0	0.1882	0.3884	0.5643	0.4270	0.3920

Table 5: Ablation results for different values of the fusion parameter α, which controls the weighting between LLM-based and cross-encoder (CE) scores in the final reranking step. $\alpha = 0.0$ corresponds to using only the LLM (RankGPT) scores, while $\alpha = 1.0$ corresponds to using only the CE scores.

Algorithm	R@2	R@5	R@10	B-Pref	R. Score
BM25	0.0717	0.1233	0.1803	0.1481	0.1309
Dense	0.0638	0.1123	0.1660	0.1591	0.1253
SPLADE	0.0647	0.1452	0.2190	0.1909	0.1550
BM25 + CE	0.0647	0.1452	0.2190	**0.5044**	0.2333
Dense + CE	0.2001	0.3251	0.4590	0.3715	0.3389
SPLADE + CE	0.1882	0.3511	0.5336	0.4014	0.3686
BM25 + Dense	0.1115	0.2204	0.3080	0.2509	0.2227
SPLADE + Dense	0.1006	0.1796	0.2821	0.2305	0.1982
BM25 + SPLADE	0.1412	0.2522	0.3476	0.2707	0.2529
BM25 + Dense + CE	0.2075	0.3743	0.5493	0.4246	0.3889
SPLADE + Dense + CE	0.1954	0.3683	0.5429	0.4177	0.3811
BM25 + SPLADE + CE	0.1993	0.3639	0.5455	0.4172	0.3815
BM25 + SPLADE + Dense	0.1447	0.2693	0.3840	0.3102	0.2771
BM25 + SPLADE + Dense + CE	0.1882	0.3884	0.5643	0.4270	0.3920
BM25 + SPLADE + Dense + CE + LLM	**0.2309**	**0.4413**	**0.6006**	0.4818	**0.4386**

Table 6: Retrieval performance for various ablation settings. We use RRF to combine the results of multiple models. CE = Cross-Encoder, Dense = dense retriever model.

evidentiary (NEI) abstracts, and then decide if the evidentiary abstracts should be labeled as SUPPORTS or REFUTES. We also provide six examples of claims + three abstracts labeled with respect to their relationship to the corresponding claim. The samples were selected such that each example claim has one supporting, one refuting, and one NEI abstract.

Zero-shot-hybrid involves using the prompt from Figure 2, but without the few-shot examples.

Zero-shot-one-step involves directly asking the model to assign one of the three labels to each claim-abstract pair, as shown in Figure 5.

Zero-shot-two-step involves splitting the classification task into two stages, similarly to **Zero-shot-hybrid**, but using a separate prompt and model instance for each stage, shown in Figure 4.

Algorithm	R@100	R@200	R@400	R@600	R@800
Dense	0.6000	0.6667	0.7333	0.7667	0.7833
BM25	0.3583	0.5083	0.7167	0.8000	0.8667
SPLADE	0.6250	0.7583	0.8083	0.8333	0.8667
BM25 + Dense	0.7000	0.8000	0.8333	0.9083	0.9333
SPLADE + Dense	0.7583	0.7833	0.8833	0.9000	0.9083
SPLADE + BM25	0.7083	0.8167	0.8833	0.9333	0.9500
SPLADE + BM25 + Dense	**0.8417**	**0.8667**	**0.9250**	**0.9583**	**0.9667**

Table 7: Additional ablation results for Stage 1 hybrid retrieval. Dense = dense retriever model.

System Prompt (LLM Instruction)
You are an expert scientific fact-checker.
Task
For a given claim and one paper abstract, reason internally in two steps:
1. Decide if the abstract contains evidence that directly supports OR directly refutes the claim.
2. If evidence exists, decide whether it `SUPPORTS` or `REFUTES`.

Output Rules

- Think silently; do NOT reveal your reasoning.
- Then output **exactly one** of these uppercase tokens with nothing else:
  - `SUPPORTS` (evidence backs the claim)
  - `REFUTES` (evidence contradicts the claim)
  - `NEI` (Not Enough Information – no evidence)
- If the input is malformed, your output is irrelevant because the client will never ask you (inputs are pre-validated).

Few-shot Example 1:

Claim: Looks like climate models might be overestimating the warming trend. #ClimateAction #ClimateData
Abstracts:

- **(Refutes)** Most present-generation climate models simulate an increase [...].
- **(Supports)** Multi-model climate experiments carried out as part of [...].
- **(NEI)** Air pressure at sea level during winter has decreased over [...].

Few-shot Example 2:
Claim: 'Natural gas' is considered cleaner than coal and oil
Abstracts:

- **(Refutes)** In April 2011, we published the first peer-reviewed analysis of [...].
- **(Supports)** A well-known theorem by Herfindahl states that the low-cost [...].
- **(NEI)** Shale gas proponents argue this unconventional fossil fuel offers [...].

[Four more examples were included in the real prompt]

Figure 3: Prompt diagram for the **"few-shots hybrid"** classification configuration. Full prompt included additional four examples, each with one `SUPPORTS`, one `REFUTES`, and one `NEI` abstract.

Two-Step LLM Prompting Strategy for Claim Verification (Zero-Shot)

Step 1: Evidence Detection
System Prompt:

You are an expert scientific fact-checker.

Task Given one claim and one scientific-paper abstract, decide whether the abstract contains evidence that directly supports *or* directly refutes the claim.

Label Definitions
• EVIDENCE – The abstract presents data, observations, arguments, or findings that clearly support *or* contradict the claim. Mere topical overlap is insufficient; there must be an evidentiary link.

• UNKNOWN – Not enough information. The abstract is off-topic, only tangentially related, or lacks evidence about the claim's truth value.

Output Rules 1. Think silently before answering. 2. Output exactly one of the two uppercase tokens, with no extra words, punctuation, or whitespace: EVIDENCE or UNKNOWN 3. If input is malformed, output UNKNOWN. **You must never reveal your reasoning—only the single label.**

Step 2: Polarity Classification
System Prompt:

You are an expert scientific fact-checker.

Task Given one claim and one scientific-paper abstract, decide whether the abstract contains evidence that directly supports OR directly refutes the claim.

Label Definitions
• SUPPORTS – The abstract presents data, observations, arguments, or findings that clearly support the claim.
• REFUTES – The abstract presents data, observations, arguments, or findings that clearly contradict the claim.
(Mere topical overlap is insufficient; there must be an evidentiary link.)

Output Rules 1. Think silently before answering. 2. Then output exactly one of the two lowercase tokens, with no extra words,

punctuation, or whitespace: SUPPORTS or REFUTES 3. If the inputs are missing or malformed, output UNKNOWN. **You must never reveal your reasoning—only the single label.**

Note: Abstracts labeled as UNKNOWN in Step 1 are not passed to Step 2.

Figure 4: Two-step prompting strategy used for **"zero-shot-two-step"** classification configuration. Step 1 filters out non-evidentiary abstracts, and Step 2 assigns polarity labels (SUPPORTS or REFUTES) to the evidentiary ones.

One-Step LLM Prompting Strategy for Claim Verification (Zero-Shot)

System Prompt:

You are an expert scientific fact-checker.
Given a claim and a paper abstract, reply with exactly one of: `supports | refutes | not enough information`

Figure 5: Prompt for the **"zero-shot-one-step"** classification configuration.

Overview of the SciHal25 Shared Task on Hallucination Detection for Scientific Content

Dan Li Bogdan Palfi Colin Kehang Zhang Jaiganesh Subramanian
Adrian Raudaschl Yoshiko Kakita
Anita De Waard Zubair Afzal Georgios Tsatsaronis
Elsevier
{d.li1, b.palfi, c.zhang.3, j.subramanian1, a.raudaschl, y.kakita,
a.dewaard, zubair.afzal, g.tsatsaronis}@elsevier.com

Abstract

This paper provides an overview of the Hallucination Detection for Scientific Content (SciHal) shared task held in the 2025 ACL Scholarly Document Processing workshop. The task invites participants to detect hallucinated claims in answers to research-oriented questions generated by real-world GenAI-powered research assistants. This task is formulated as a multi-label classification problem, each instance consists of a question, an answer, an extracted claim, and supporting reference abstracts. Participants are asked to label claims under two subtasks: (1) coarse-grained detection with labels Entailment, Contradiction, or Unverifiable; and (2) fine-grained detection with a more detailed taxonomy including 8 types. The dataset consists of 488 research-oriented questions collected over one week from a generative assistant tool. These questions were rewritten using GPT-4o and manually reviewed to address potential privacy or commercial concerns. In total, approximately 10,000 reference abstracts were retrieved, and 4,592 claims were extracted from the assistant's answers. Each claim is annotated with hallucination labels. The dataset is divided into 3,592 training, 500 validation, and 500 test instances. Subtask 1 saw 109 submissions across 11 teams while subtask 2 saw 43 submissions across 7 teams, resulting in a total of 5 published technical reports. This paper summarizes the task design, dataset, participation, and key findings.

1 Introduction

Generative AI-powered academic research assistants are transforming how research is conducted. These systems enable users to pose research-related questions in natural language and receive structured, concise summaries supported by relevant references. However, hallucinations pose a significant challenge to fully trusting these automatically generated scientific answers.

Recent shared tasks have begun to address hallucination detection across domains such as biomedical summarization (Gupta et al., 2024) and scientific content (Mickus et al., 2024). While these efforts have advanced benchmarking in specific settings, they are often limited to binary classification or constrained domains. Broader benchmarks like Hal-Eval (Jiang et al., 2024) provide general-purpose evaluation but lack task grounding.

To fill this gap, SciHal introduces a multi-label hallucination detection task grounded in real-world scientific question answering. The task invites participants to detect hallucinated claims in answers to research-oriented questions generated by a real-world GenAI-powered research assistant. This task is formulated as a multi-label classification problem, each instance consists of a question, an answer, an extracted claim, and supporting reference abstracts. The shared task is hosted on Kaggle[1].

Weighted F1 score is used as the primary evaluation metric to account for class imbalance. Subtask 1 attracted 109 submissions from 11 participating teams. On the public leaderboard (validation set), the top three teams were Schopf et al. (2025), Cao et al. (2025), and Le and Thin (2025), achieving weighted F1 scores of 0.60, 0.59, and 0.59, respectively. On the private leaderboard (test set), the top three teams were Schopf et al. (2025), Cao et al. (2025), and Galimzianova et al. (2025), with scores of 0.62, 0.60, and 0.59.

Subtask 2 attracted 43 submissions from 7 participating teams. On the public leaderboard (validation set), the top three teams were Cao et al. (2025), Schopf et al. (2025), and JB, achieving weighted F1 scores of 0.51, 0.50, and 0.49. On the private leaderboard (test set), the top teams were Schopf et al. (2025), Cao et al. (2025), Le and Thin (2025), JB, Carla and Uban (2025), achieving weighted F1

[1] https://www.kaggle.com/competitions/hallucination-detection-scientific-content-2025

Proceedings of the Fifth Workshop on Scholarly Document Processing (SDP 2025), pages 307–315
July 31, 2025

scores of 0.47, 0.47, 0.47, 0.47, 0.46.

These results highlight the difficulty and complexity of the task. Participating teams employed a diverse range of approaches, including fine-tuning transformer-based encoders, prompting large language models (LLMs), and hybrid methods using internal state representations. Additionally, the subjective nature of hallucination detection, particularly in edge cases, introduces annotation challenges and potential label noise. Improving annotation consistency remains an important direction for future work.

2 Related Work

Recent years have seen a growing interest in shared tasks on hallucination detection in the context of text generation by LLMs. One of the earliest domain-specific efforts is the TREC BioGen task, which evaluates the factual consistency of biomedical answers and summaries, using sentence-level labels over content generated from PubMed articles (Gupta et al., 2024). In the scientific domain, the SHROOM shared task (Mickus et al., 2024) introduced hallucination detection and mitigation challenges for scientific abstracts and question answering, incorporating both binary and fine-grained classifications. The SHROOM dataset includes human-annotated claims with hallucination labels grounded in scientific references, offering valuable insights but remaining limited in scale and question diversity. Beyond biomedical and scientific settings, the Hal-Eval benchmark (Jiang et al., 2024) provides a multi-domain benchmark covering summarization, question answering, and data-to-text generation, annotated with fine-grained hallucination spans.

Although these efforts contribute valuable datasets and evaluation protocols, they often focus on either general-purpose outputs, a single domain, or a binary classification setup. In contrast, SciHal is specifically designed for hallucination detection in academic research assistants. It introduces a two-tiered taxonomy (coarse- and fine-grained), grounded in real-world user queries and scientific reference abstracts, with large-scale expert annotations across five scientific domains. This makes SciHal the first shared task to target hallucination detection in the context of retrieval-augmented question answering for scholarly research.

3 Hallucination Taxonomy Creation

There is currently no established taxonomy for hallucination types specific to scientific content. Our goal is to develop one that (1) reflects real-world error patterns, (2) remains manageable for human annotators, and (3) ensures high label quality.

Existing work has developed detailed taxonomies to characterize hallucinations in large language models (LLMs). Early studies often framed hallucinations as a binary phenomenon, i.e. factual versus non-factual, but more recent work proposes nuanced classifications. A common distinction is between *intrinsic* hallucinations, which contradict the input or reference, and *extrinsic* hallucinations, which introduce unsupported content (Huang et al., 2023; Zhang et al., 2023). Other taxonomies categorize hallucinations based on the nature of the error, such as entity-level, numeric, or reasoning-based inconsistencies (Mishra et al., 2024; Li et al., 2024). Some frameworks adopt a multi-dimensional view; for example, Rawte et al. (2023) organize hallucinations by orientation (harmful vs. benign), grounding (intrinsic vs. extrinsic), and fine-grained types, including acronym misuse, quantitative errors, and temporal inaccuracies. These efforts provide a foundation for designing task-specific taxonomies in domains like scientific content generation (Hu et al., 2024).

Drawing from a small-scale analysis of 136 user feedback responses, we identified the most frequent error types: missing the main concept (34.6%), factually incorrect (21.3%), too general (21.3%), and unrelated references (11.8%). These findings highlight recurring issues in generative AI outputs.

Our final taxonomy is informed by both in-house analysis of GenAI-powered research assistant outputs and broader studies of hallucination patterns in general-purpose GenAI systems. Figure 1 presents the decision tree that underpins our taxonomy, which was included in the annotation guidelines provided to subject-matter experts (SMEs). Definitions and examples for each hallucination type are listed in Table 1.

4 Data Creation

The dataset consists of claim-level annotations designed to evaluate the factual consistency between claims in generated answers and their cited references within scientific retrieval-augmented generation (RAG) systems. The data are primarily derived

T1 label	T2 label	Definition	Examples
entail	entail	The claim is explicitly and clearly supported by at least one passage in the reference abstracts, while not being contradicted by any other passage from the reference.	*Reference: The weather is rainy and the wind is blowing. Claim: The weather is rainy.*
unver	unrelunvef	The claim and the abstracts address different topics, therefore making the claim unverifiable.	*Reference: The weather is rainy and the wind is blowing. Claim 1: He was born in the Netherlands. → The reference addresses the weather but the claim mentions where a person was born, being unrelated so unverifiable.*
unver	relunvef	The claim and all abstracts address the same broad topic, but the specific idea presented in the claim or any of its sub-parts is not covered, making the claim unverifiable.	*Reference: The weather is rainy and the wind is blowing. Claim 1: The rainy weather is causing widespread flooding in the region. → Both the reference and the claim address the weather, but nothing is mentioned about flooding.*
contra	entierr	The claim contains an erroneous entity that contradicts what is stated in the reference. A named entity is a real-world object, such as a person, location, organization, product, etc., that can be denoted with a proper name.	*Reference: The weather is rainy, as forecasted by BBC. Claim: The weather is rainy, as forecasted by The Weather Channel.*
contra	numerr	The claim contains an erroneous numeric value that contradicts the reference.	*Reference: The concentration was 80%. Claim: The concentration was 90%.*
contra	negat	The claim negates parts of the reference or replaces terms with their antonyms, therefore stating the opposite to what appears in the reference.	*Reference: It is windy and the temperature is increasing. Claim: It is not windy and the temperature is decreasing.*
contra	missinfo	The claim omits critical information from the reference, leading to an incorrect or incomplete understanding of the reference. This can occur when the reference abstract makes a conditional statement like: "when / if / by X then Y", but the condition is missing.	*Reference: Regular exercise, when performed consistently and in combination with a balanced diet and healthy lifestyle, can reduce the risk of heart disease by 30% and also improve mental health. Claim: Regular exercise mainly enhances mental well-being. → Missing critical info: omits the condition "when performed consistently and in combination with... ."*
contra	misinter	The claim presents logical fallacies, flawed reasoning or illogical conclusions through over-claiming, under-claiming, ambiguity, inconsistency or implying a consensus among references when there are disagreements.	*Reference: Regular exercise can reduce the risk of heart disease by 30% and also improve mental health. Claim 1: Regular exercise eliminates the risk of heart disease. → Overstatement. Claim 2: Only regular exercise is required for improved mental health. → Logical fallacy.*

Table 1: The definitions of hallucination types.

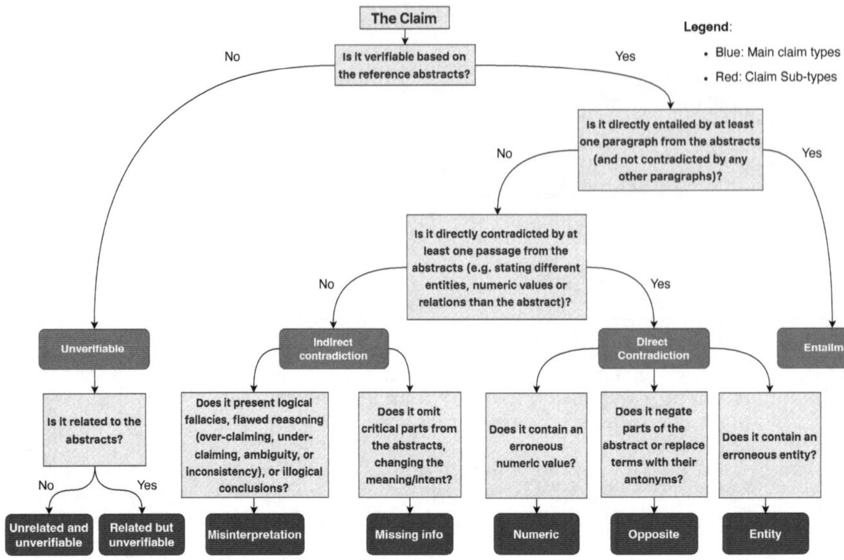

Figure 1: The hallucination taxonomy.

from Scopus AI[2], an in-house research assistant tool powered by a RAG system indexing millions of scientific abstracts.

4.1 Question, Answer, and Claim Collection

We first collected over 50,000 real-user questions from Scopus AI. Using a large language model (LLM), we classified each question by domain and verified its correctness, completeness, and language. Only English questions that were correct and complete were retained. Considering the popularity and availability of SMEs, we keep questions in the five domains – Engineering, Environmental Science, Medicine, Agricultural and Biological Sciences, and Computer Science. We then used an LLM to rewrite the queries, manually spot-checking them to remove privacy or commercial concerns, resulting in 500 questions for hallucination label annotation.

Next, we used the Scopus AI endpoint service to generate answers for the questions. Each answer was supported by up to 20 reference abstracts. We then extracted claims from each answer along with their corresponding references.

4.2 Inducing Hallucinations into Claims

To balance the class distribution, we introduced synthetic hallucinations into the claims via LLM prompting. An in-house annotator processed the original data, and 65% of the claims were randomly selected for modification, where an LLM induced hallucinations based on predefined types (Sub-task 2) while maintaining type balance. The dataset, comprising 35% original claims and 65% error-induced claims, was then sent to subject matter experts (SMEs) for annotation. This approach allows us to estimate the hallucination rate of the in-house research assistant using the original claims while ensuring a balanced dataset, where entailment accounts for less than 35% and other types each account for under 10%.

4.3 SME Annotation Process

SME annotation was conducted via external vendors. Annotators were provided with the data to be labeled, including the question, generated answer, extracted claim, and list of reference abstracts, as well as detailed annotation guidelines. These guidelines included definitions of hallucination types and a decision tree to support consistent labeling. A trial phase was conducted to ensure alignment with the guidelines before full-scale annotation.

To balance annotation quality and cost, we adopted a hybrid strategy that combined human SME labels with predictions from an internal LLM-based hallucination detection model. In the initial annotation phase, each instance was labeled by one domain-specific SME, who provided both a

[2]https://www.elsevier.com/products/scopus/scopus-ai

hallucination label and a brief textual justification (1 – 3 sentences). We then compared the SME-provided label with the LLM-generated prediction. Instances where both sources agreed were grouped into Batches 1 and 2, which we consider to be consistent and cost-effective, as they rely on a single SME confirmation.[3]

In the final annotation phase, instances where the SME and LLM disagreed were re-labeled by a second SME. A third SME then adjudicated, having access to both prior labels and their justifications. This adjudication step ensures high-quality, consensus-based annotations. The resulting data were split into Batch 3 (training), validation, and test sets. These subsets are particularly valuable: they are both challenging as they are derived from disagreement cases between humans and LLM, and they are reliable as they reflect consensus among two or three SMEs. Note that a few invalid instances were removed and this resulted in 488 questions in the final release data.

5 Analysis of Label Quality

The following sections will present an analysis of the label distribution and quality. To this end, it is important to note that a second SME was consulted only for claims where there was disagreement between the LLM judge and the first SME. As a result, the comparisons between SME 1 and SME 2 in the following analysis relate specifically to claims that are potentially more difficult to label or more subjective. These challenging claims constitute approximately 50% of the entire dataset. Consequently, the observed agreement rate between the two SMEs may be lower than if the comparison were conducted on the entire dataset. The third SME was excluded from this analysis because they were not independent, having had access to both the labels and justifications provided by the first two SMEs.

Overall, the agreement rates (accuracy) between the two SMEs on the **difficult** part of the entire dataset are **0.55** for Subtask 1 and **0.44** for Subtask 2, respectively.

5.1 Subtask 1

Table 2 shows that subtask 1 exhibits a relatively balanced distribution of labels, with Entailment and Contradiction accounting for approximately 38.71% and 36.89%, respectively, while Unverifiable claims are less frequent at 24.4%. Comparing the agreement between the two SMEs, Figure 2 and Table 3 reveal that the SMEs tend to agree more often when labeling claims as Entailment, while showing the highest disagreement when classifying Unverifiable claims. This may suggest that some SMEs are more strict when assigning the Entailment label. Overall, the agreement rate (accuracy) is 0.55, indicating that the SMEs concur in more than half of the cases. The Cohen's Kappa coefficient of 0.297 further reflects this trend, signifying a fair level of agreement where disagreements still occur between the raters. These results highlight the necessity of, and motivate our decision to, involve a third SME to adjudicate disagreements and aggregate the labels, thereby ensuring higher data quality.

Label	Count	Percentage
entail	1762	38.71%
unver	1111	24.40%
contra	1677	36.89%

Table 2: Claim distribution for the full Subtask 1 dataset.

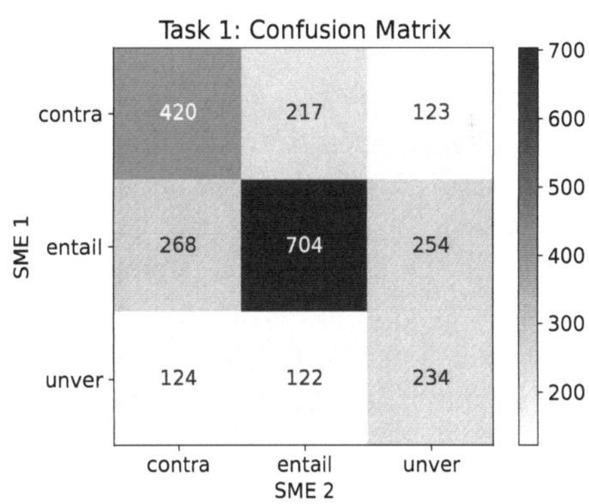

Figure 2: Confusion matrix comparing the predictions of two independent SMEs for Subtask 1. This figure is based solely on a more challenging subset of the data, comprising approximately 50% of the entire dataset, for which labels from the second SME are available.

5.2 Subtask 2

The second task involves a finer-grained classification, further subdividing the unverifiable and contradicted claims into multiple sub-types. The distribution of these sub-types is presented in Table 4. Notably, the majority of unverifiable claims

[3]Batch 1 is a subset of Batch 2 and will be deprecated in future updates. We recommend using Batches 2 and 3 for training.

	Precision	Recall	F1	Support
contra	0.55	0.52	0.53	812
entail	0.57	0.67	0.62	1043
unver	0.49	0.38	0.43	611

Table 3: Classification report comparing the predictions of two independent SMEs for Subtask 1. This report is based solely on a more challenging subset of the data, comprising approximately 50% of the entire dataset, for which labels from the second SME are available.

are related to the reference, comprising approximately 20.34% of the total, whereas only 4.07% are unrelated. Among contradicted claims, the most frequent sub-types are negations or opposite statements (15.4%) and misinterpretations (10.83%), while the remaining sub-types each account for less than 6% of cases.

Inter-annotator agreement between the two SMEs is showed in Figure 3 and Table 5. The SMEs demonstrate the highest levels of agreement on entailment claims, followed by numeric errors and opposite statements. In contrast, higher rates of disagreement are observed for other claim types, particularly for missing information as well as unrelated claims. The overall agreement rate for this subtask is 0.44, which is lower than the rate observed in subtask 1, indicating the increased complexity of the classification. Similarly, the Cohen's Kappa coefficient is 0.23, reflecting a fair but lower level of agreement compared to subtask 1. As mentioned previously, a third SME was included to account for the agreement rate and to adjudicate disagreements and aggregate labels for these results, therefore ensure a higher label quality.

Label	Count	Percentage
entail	1762	38.74%
relunvef	926	20.34%
negat	701	15.40%
misinter	493	10.83%
entierr	256	5.63%
unrelunvef	185	4.07%
numerr	132	2.90%
missinfo	95	2.09%

Table 4: Claim distribution for the full Subtask 2 dataset.

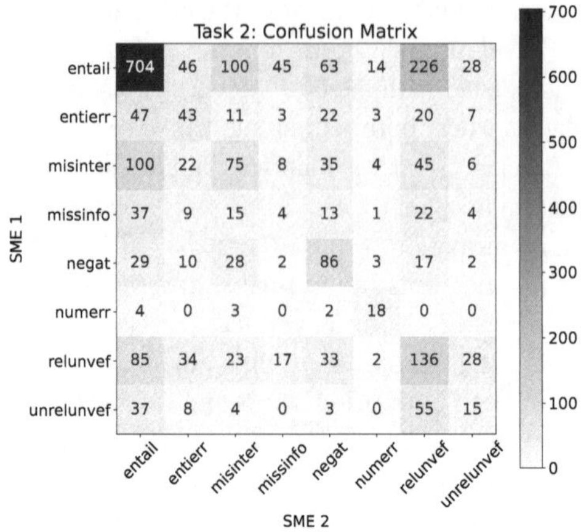

Figure 3: Confusion matrix comparing the predictions of two independent SMEs for Subtask 2. This figure is based solely on a more challenging subset of the data, comprising approximately 50% of the entire dataset, for which labels from the second SME are available.

	Precision	Recall	F1	Support
entail	0.57	0.67	0.62	1043
entierr	0.28	0.25	0.26	172
misinter	0.25	0.29	0.27	259
missinfo	0.04	0.05	0.04	79
negat	0.49	0.33	0.40	257
numerr	0.67	0.40	0.50	45
relunvef	0.38	0.26	0.31	521
unrelunvef	0.12	0.17	0.14	90

Table 5: Classification report comparing the predictions of two independent SMEs for Subtask 2. This report is based solely on a more challenging subset of the data, comprising approximately 50% of the entire dataset, for which labels from the second SME are available.

6 Competition Setup

6.1 Task

The Hallucination Detection for Scientific Content (SciHal) task challenges participants to identify hallucinated claims within answers generated by GenAI-powered research assistants in response to research-oriented questions. Formulated as a multi-label classification problem, each instance includes a question, a generated answer, an extracted claim, and a set of reference abstracts. The objective is to classify each claim based on its alignment with the reference abstracts, using a predefined set of hallucination types.

The task consists of two subtasks. **Subtask 1:**

Coarse-grained Hallucination Detection requires classifying each claim into one of three categories: *Entailment*, *Contradiction*, or *Unverifiable*. **Sub-task 2: Fine-grained Hallucination Detection** extends this framework by introducing a more detailed taxonomy, including the following labels: *Entailment*, *Unrelated and Unverifiable*, *Related but Verifiable*, *Misrepresentation*, *Missing Information*, *Numeric Error*, *Entity Error*, and *Opposite Meaning*.

6.2 Data

Table 6 lists data splits. Each data instance includes the following fields:

- `ID` – Unique identifier.
- `question` – The research-oriented question.
- `answer` – The answer generated by a GenAI-powered research assistant.
- `claim` – One or more sentences extracted from the generated answer.
- `reference` – One or more reference abstracts retrieved for grounding.
- `label` – The classification label (available only in training sets). Labels follow a three-class scheme for Sub-task 1 and an eight-class scheme for Sub-task 2.
- `justification` – The reasoning provided by subject-matter experts (SMEs) for assigning the label (available only in training sets).

Dataset	# Claim
training	3592
validation	500
test	500

Table 6: The statistics of the training, validation, and test set.

6.3 Evaluaiton Metrics

The competition will use one of the default classification metrics on Kaggle - the weighted F1 score as the major evaluation metric. Weighted F1 calculates metrics for each label, and finds their average weighted by support (the number of true instances for each label). This alters 'macro' to account for label imbalance; it can result in an F-score that is not between precision and recall.

Team	Wt F1
ScaDS.AI x sebis (Schopf et al., 2025)	0.62
YupengCao (Cao et al., 2025)	0.60
Daria Galimzianova (Galimzianova et al., 2025)	0.59
A.M.P (Le and Thin, 2025)	0.58
Crivoi Carla (Carla and Uban, 2025)	0.56
Ioan-Cristian Cordos	0.47
sasha boriskin	0.46
Andreea Brandiburu	0.44
e0nia	0.43
JB	0.27

Table 7: Performance of participants on the test set on Subtask 1.

Team	Wt F1
ScaDS.AI x sebis (Schopf et al., 2025)	0.47
A.M.P (Le and Thin, 2025)	0.47
JB	0.47
YupengCao (Cao et al., 2025)	0.47
Crivoi Carla (Carla and Uban, 2025)	0.46

Table 8: Performance of participants on the test set on Subtask 2.

7 Result

Tables 7, 8, 9, and 10 list the results of participants on the validation and test sets. lists the results of participants on the test set.

5 papers got accepted at the Fifth Scholarly Document Processing workshop(Ghosal et al., 2025). In Schopf et al. (2025), the team framed hallucination detection as a Natural Language Inference (NLI) problem. Their approach leveraged fine-tuned transformer models—specifically ModernBERT and DeBERTa-v3-large, and combined them using a weighted ensemble. Their results demonstrate that fine-tuned NLI models can outperform prompting-based approaches. They also highlight the importance of training on data that closely resembles the target task.

Cao et al. (2025) proposed a hybrid hallucination detection system combining prompting strategies with internal state classification. They benchmarked LLMs using zero-shot and few-shot prompts with Chain-of-Thought reasoning, and found that instruction-tuned, larger models per-

Team	Wt F1
ScaDS.AI x sebis (Schopf et al., 2025)	0.60
YupengCao (Cao et al., 2025)	0.59
A.M.P (Le and Thin, 2025)	0.59
Daria Galimzianova (Galimzianova et al., 2025)	0.58
Crivoi Carla (Carla and Uban, 2025)	0.51
Andreea Brandiburu	0.46
Ioan-Cristian Cordos	0.46
sasha boriskin	0.45
e0nia	0.42
JB	0.25

Table 9: Performance of participants on the validation set on Subtask 1.

Team	Wt F1
YupengCao (Cao et al., 2025)	0.51
ScaDS.AI x sebis (Schopf et al., 2025)	0.50
JB	0.49
A.M.P (Le and Thin, 2025)	0.48
Crivoi Carla (Carla and Uban, 2025)	0.43

Table 10: Performance of participants on the validation set on Subtask 2.

formed best. To further enhance detection, they extracted LLM hidden states and trained a logistic regression classifier without fine-tuning the models. This approach achieved top leaderboard scores (0.59 on subtask 1, 0.51 on subtask 2), demonstrating the effectiveness of integrating prompt reasoning with representation learning.

Le and Thin (2025) proposed a hallucination detection system using prompt-engineered LLMs. They designed structured prompts with role definitions, label explanations, and few-shot examples, and introduced a two-step method that predicts fine-grained labels before mapping to coarse ones. This approach outperformed direct prediction, with their best model (gemini-2.5-flash) achieving weighted F1-scores of 0.56 (subtask 1) and 0.44 (subtask 2).

Galimzianova et al. (2025) approached coarse-grained hallucination detection as an NLI task. They found that simply fine-tuning NLI-pretrained encoders like DeBERTa-v3 on the task dataset outperformed more complex pipelines and prompting-based methods. The study reaffirms that, for small-scale, domain-specific scientific data, targeted encoder fine-tuning remains both effective and efficient.

Carla and Uban (2025) combined SciBERT with contrastive learning techniques to improve hallucination detection. They applied a dual-head architecture with classification and contrastive objectives, using both Triplet and InfoNCE losses alongside standard cross-entropy. Their method aimed to enhance semantic alignment between claims and references, especially when surface wording differs.

8 Discussion

The SciHal shared task attracted a wide range of approaches to hallucination detection in scientific content. The participating teams explored diverse techniques including prompt-based LLMs, fine-tuned encoders, hybrid fusion strategies, and internal state modeling. Top-performing systems consistently relied on fine-tuning transformer models. This outcome suggests that supervised adaptation remains effective in domains with limited training data and high factual precision requirements.

Annotation quality remains a key challenge. Despite expert annotators and adjudication, hallucination labeling involves subjectivity and is time-intensive — each claim required an average of 7 minutes to annotate. This underscores the need for more scalable and consistent annotation protocols.

Although fine-grained hallucination types are difficult to annotate, they are particularly valuable for real-world applications, as they reflect common failure modes observed in practical GenAI systems. These include, but are not limited to: non-synonymous term substitutions, suboptimal grounding, direct copying instead of summarization, overgeneralization from a single source, tangential continuations, avoidance of direct answers, conceptual conflation, evidence overstatement. Capturing these phenomena offers critical insights into model behavior. However, such cases are relatively rare, making it challenging to collect sufficient labeled instances. This rarity, combined with the nuanced nature of these errors, also poses significant challenges for future work.

Another limitation lies in the data split strategy. The train/val/test sets were divided by claim rather than by question, resulting in all test questions being seen during training. However, the claims in train are very different than test: less than 1.5%

of test claims showed high similarity to training claims. Repeated exposure to identical questions and answer contexts may still favor memorization, particularly for fine-tuned models. Future iterations should ensure both question- and context-disjoint splits to better assess generalization.

In future work, we aim to expand hallucination type coverage, improve annotation consistency, and adopt stricter data partitioning to enable more robust benchmarking.

Acknowledgments

We thank the following individuals for their valuable contributions: Johanna Sergent, Joo Sic Choi, and Jaiganesh Subramanian for coordinating data annotation; Poonam Pandey, Akila Chandrasekhar, Veronique Moore, and Alamelu Mangai Krishnamurthy for reviewing the annotation guidelines and conducting trial annotations; Maya Oded, Alex Riemer for early discussions on the hallucination taxonomy; Jan Bij de Weg, Debarati Banerjee, and Ben Buckley for supporting the legal coordination of data release.

References

Yupeng Cao, Chun-Nam Yu, and K.P. Subbalakshmi. 2025. Detecting hallucinations in scientific claims by combining prompting strategies and internal state classification. In *Proceedings of the Fifth Workshop on Scholarly Document Processing (SDP 2025)*.

Crivoi Carla and Ana Sabina Uban. 2025. Scibert meets contrastive learning: A solution for scientific hallucination detection. In *Proceedings of the Fifth Workshop on Scholarly Document Processing (SDP 2025)*.

Daria Galimzianova, Aleksandr Boriskin, and Grigory Arshinov. 2025. From rag to reality: Coarse-grained hallucination detection via nli fine-tuning. In *Proceedings of the Fifth Workshop on Scholarly Document Processing (SDP 2025)*.

Tirthankar Ghosal, Philipp Mayr, Anita de Waard, Aakanksha Naik, Amanpreet Singh, Dayne Freitage, Georg Rehmf, Sonja Schimmlerh, and Dan Li. 2025. Overview of the fifth workshop on scholarly document processing. In *Proceedings of the Fifth Workshop on Scholarly Document Processing (SDP 2025)*.

Deepak Gupta, Dina Demner-Fushman, William Hersh, Steven Bedrick, and Kirk Roberts. 2024. Overview of trec 2024 biomedical generative retrieval (biogen) track. *arXiv preprint arXiv:2411.18069*.

Mengya Hu, Rui Xu, Deren Lei, Yaxi Li, Mingyu Wang, Emily Ching, Eslam Kamal, and Alex Deng. 2024. Slm meets llm: Balancing latency, interpretability and consistency in hallucination detection. *arXiv preprint arXiv:2408.12748*.

Lei Huang, Weijiang Yu, Weitao Ma, Weihong Zhong, Zhangyin Feng, Haotian Wang, Qianglong Chen, Weihua Peng, Xiaocheng Feng, Bing Qin, and 1 others. 2023. A survey on hallucination in large language models: Principles, taxonomy, challenges, and open questions, 2023. *arXiv preprint arXiv:2311.05232*.

Chaoya Jiang, Hongrui Jia, Mengfan Dong, Wei Ye, Haiyang Xu, Ming Yan, Ji Zhang, and Shikun Zhang. 2024. Hal-eval: A universal and fine-grained hallucination evaluation framework for large vision language models. In *Proceedings of the 32nd ACM International Conference on Multimedia*, pages 525–534.

Khoa Nguyen-Anh Le and Dang Van Thin. 2025. A.m.p at scihal2025: Automated hallucination detection in scientific content via llms and prompt engineering. In *Proceedings of the Fifth Workshop on Scholarly Document Processing (SDP 2025)*.

J Li, J Chen, R Ren, X Cheng, WX Zhao, JY Nie, and JR Wen. 2024. The dawn after the dark: An empirical study on factuality hallucination in large language models. arxiv, article. *arXiv preprint arXiv:2401.03205*.

Timothee Mickus, Elaine Zosa, Raúl Vázquez, Teemu Vahtola, Jörg Tiedemann, Vincent Segonne, Alessandro Raganato, and Marianna Apidianaki. 2024. Semeval-2024 task 6: Shroom, a shared-task on hallucinations and related observable overgeneration mistakes. In *Proceedings of the 18th International Workshop on Semantic Evaluation (SemEval-2024)*, pages 1979–1993.

Abhika Mishra, Akari Asai, Vidhisha Balachandran, Yizhong Wang, Graham Neubig, Yulia Tsvetkov, and Hannaneh Hajishirzi. 2024. Fine-grained hallucination detection and editing for language models. *arXiv preprint arXiv:2401.06855*.

Vipula Rawte, Swagata Chakraborty, Agnibh Pathak, Anubhav Sarkar, SM_Towhidul Islam Tonmoy, Aman Chadha, Amit Sheth, and Amitava Das. 2023. The troubling emergence of hallucination in large language models-an extensive definition, quantification, and prescriptive remediations. Association for Computational Linguistics.

Tim Schopf, Juraj Vladika, Michael Färber, and Florian Matthes. 2025. Natural language inference fine-tuning for scientific hallucination detection. In *Proceedings of the Fifth Workshop on Scholarly Document Processing (SDP 2025)*.

Yue Zhang, Yafu Li, Leyang Cui, Deng Cai, Lemao Liu, Tingchen Fu, Xinting Huang, Enbo Zhao, Yu Zhang, Yulong Chen, and 1 others. 2023. Siren's song in the ai ocean: a survey on hallucination in large language models. *arXiv preprint arXiv:2309.01219*.

Detecting Hallucinations in Scientific Claims by Combining Prompting Strategies and Internal State Classification

Yupeng Cao[1,2], **Chun-Nam Yu**[1], **Koduvayur Subbalakshmi**[2]
[1]Nokia Bell Labs
[2]Stevens Institute of Technology
https://github.com/InfintyLab/SciHal-Challenge

Abstract

Large Language Model (LLM) based research assistant tools demonstrate impressive capabilities, yet their outputs may contain hallucinations that compromise their reliability. Therefore, detecting hallucinations in automatically generated scientific content is essential. SciHal2025: Hallucination Detection for Scientific Content challenge @ ACL 2025 provides a valuable platform for advancing this goal. This paper presents our solution to the SciHal2025 challenge. Our approach combines several prompting strategies to prompt LLMs and leverages their hidden states as features to build the classifier. We first benchmark multiple LLMs on the SciHal dataset under the zero-shot prompting. Next, we developed a detection pipeline that integrates few-shot and chain-of-thought prompting. Then, the hidden representations extracted from the LLMs serve as features for an auxiliary classifier, further improving detection performance. In this paper, we present comprehensive experimental results and discuss the implications of our findings for future research on hallucination detection in scientific content.

1 Introduction

Large Language Models (LLMs) have demonstrated remarkable capabilities in generating scientific content across various domains (Le Scao et al., 2023; Thulke et al., 2024; Zhang et al., 2024; Zheng et al., 2025). LLM-powered research assistant tools further streamline scholarly workflows by answering research-related questions and output structured, concise responses. However, hallucinations may be introduced by LLMs pose a significant challenge to fully trusting these automatically generated scientific outputs (Alkaissi and McFarlane, 2023). Consequently, detecting hallucination content from the LLM-powered system is essential for their safe deployment.

Hallucination Detection for Scientific Content challenge (SciHal 2025) @ ACL 2025 provides a rigorous test platform for this problem (Li et al., 2025). The dataset contains real-user questions, retrieved scientific abstracts, LLM-generated responses, and extracted claims from responses with human annotation. The goal is to classify each claim based on the provided reference abstracts into different hallucination types. This paper describes our technical solution for the SciHal Challenge.

Our solution integrates prompting techniques with LLMs and leverages the models' internal representations for classification. We begin by benchmarking multiple LLMs on the SciHal dataset under zero-shot prompting to gauge their out-of-the-box performance. Subsequently, we develop a detection pipeline by combining domain-specific few-shot examples with Chain-of-Thought (CoT) prompting (Wei et al., 2022). Specifically, we first classify each data point into its respective domain, then pair it with corresponding domain-aware few-shot examples to construct refined CoT prompts. Then, the hidden states produced by the LLM serve as features for training a classifier, enhancing predictive accuracy. On the evaluation set, our approach achieves F1 scores of 0.59 on subtask 1 and 0.51 on subtask 2, as reported on the leaderboard. A detailed performance analysis is provided in Section 4.

2 SciHal Task Description

2.1 Problem Definition

The challenge aims to develop advanced LLMs that can identify hallucinations in scientific claims. Given a claim c to be verified, the model M will take the input query q, which includes claim c, reference r, and prompt instructions p. The model M then makes a classification $y = M(q[c; r; p])$:

- For subtask1, $y \in$ ['Unverifiable', 'Contradiction', or 'Entailment']
- For subtask2, $y \in$ ['Unrelated and unverifiable', 'Related but verifiable', 'Misrepresenta-

Proceedings of the Fifth Workshop on Scholarly Document Processing (SDP 2025), pages 316–327
July 31, 2025

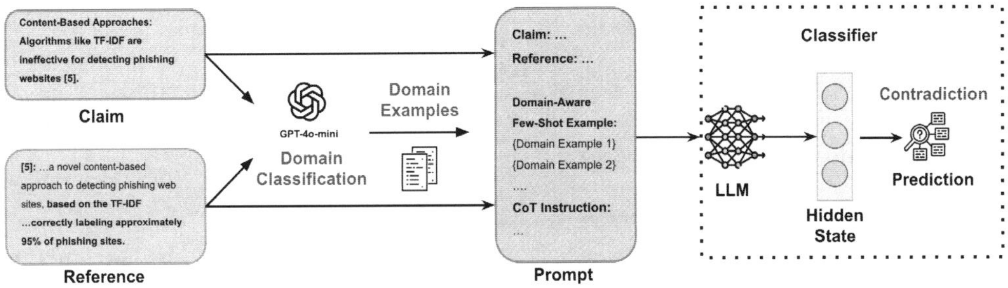

Figure 1: Overview of our method that detects the hallucination in scientific claims.

tion', 'Missing information', 'Numeric error', 'Entity error', 'Negation', 'Entailment']

Performance evaluation employs the weighted F1 score as the major evaluation metric.

2.2 Dataset

The dataset curation began with more than 50,000 real user questions spanning five domains: engineering, environmental science, medicine, agriculture & biological sciences, and computer science. After LLM paraphrasing and manual removal of sensitive information, 500 unique questions remained. For each question, the organizer fetched the 20 most relevant scientific abstracts through a retrieval-augmented generation (RAG) system. Answers were generated from these abstracts, broken into individual claims, and linked to their supporting references. Synthetic hallucinations were injected via targeted LLM prompts to balance the label distribution. Expert annotation combined with LLM labeling produced the final dataset $D = \{d_1, d_2, ..., d_n\}$ consisting of n data samples. Each data point is a six-tuple $d_i = (q, a, c, l, r, j)$ comprising the q-question, a-answer, c-claim, l-label, r-reference, and j-justification.

The organizers provided three training batches with identical data points but differing label sets for each subtask. Batch 1 data is a strict subset of batch 2 and was therefore discarded. All experiments in this paper are therefore conducted on batches 2 and 3 with a total of 3,592 data points. Table 1 presents the label distribution in the training set.

(a) Subtask 1

Label	Count	%
contradiction	1 369	38.1
unverifiable	890	24.8
entailment	1 333	37.1

(b) Subtask 2

Label	Count	%
negation	625	17.4
misinterpretation	395	11.0
related but unverifiable	738	20.5
entailment	1 333	37.1
entity error	174	4.8
unrelated and unverifiable	152	4.2
missing information	59	1.6
numeric error	116	3.2

Table 1: Distribution of ground-truth in both subtasks.

3 Methodology

In this section, we outline the proposed pipeline for hallucination detection in scientific claims (See in Figure 1). We first assign claims to their domain and select a few corresponding examples. By leveraging the in-context learning (ICL) capacity of LLMs (Radford et al., 2019; Brown et al., 2020; Dong et al., 2024), we then construct the detection pipeline that utilizes LLM's hidden states as features to train the classifier.

3.1 Domain-Aware Few-Shot Selection

Because claims and their supporting references span distinct fields, the specialized terminology and knowledge scope vary significantly. To exploit in-context learning more effectively, we first classify each data point d_i into its domain $t \in$ {engineering, computer science, environmental science, medicine, agriculture & biological sciences}. For the given data point d_i, we input the claim c and its associated reference r into the proprietary LLM (GPT-4o-mini) to determine the appropriate domain, formally expressed as $t = \text{LLM}(c, q)$.

After completing the domain assignment, each data point is updated to include its domain t, represented as $d_i = (q, a, c, l, r, j, t)$. Subtask 1 and Subtask 2 differ only in their labels, while the claim and reference remain the same. Thus, we did the domain classification once for both subtasks. After classifying all 3,592 data points by domain, we randomly sampled 100 to do a manual check for quality control. GPT-4o-mini correctly labeled the vast majority. The only notable confusion occurred between 'computer science' and 'engineering' domains, whose content often overlaps. Therefore, the domain classification accuracy is adequate for pairing each claim with the appropriate few-shot examples and is utilized in the following steps. We have listed the domain statistics results in Table 8 of Appendix A.

3.2 Few-Shot Learning with Chain-of-Thought Prompting

We first design baseline few-shot prompts for subtasks 1 and 2 (in Appendix D.2). Specifically, we randomly select two data points from each label as examples and evaluate two prompting variants:

- **Few-Shot Prompt 1:** Provide two data examples for each label, each example consisting of a claim with its corresponding reference, and instruct the LLM to output the prediction directly.

- **Few-Shot Prompt 2:** Provide two data examples, each including the claim, reference, and justification. Instruct the LLM to first generate a justification and subsequently output the corresponding prediction.

Next, we utilize the domain classification results to refine our few-shot strategy. Given a data point d_i, we randomly select two examples per label based on their assigned domain t, and incorporate these domain-specific examples into the two prompt templates described above (whole prompt in Appendix D.3).

Building upon our few-shot prompts, we further incorporate Chain-of-Thought (CoT) prompting (Wei et al., 2022) to enhance model reasoning. For subtask 1, we structure the CoT prompt in four steps: 1) Read the reference abstract(s) carefully; 2) Read the scientific claim carefully; 3) Analyze the relationship between the claim and reference abstract(s); 4) Determine which single category best describes the relationship. Subtask 2 has more complex and fine-grained labels, so we leverage its tree label structure[1] to design the CoT prompt. We require the LLM to provide a detailed justification and respond to a checklist of diagnostic questions before assigning a label. This checklist is illustrated in Figure 5. The combination of justification and checklist-based reasoning exemplifies the application of CoT prompting. All CoT prompt templates can be found in the Appendix D.4.

3.3 Prompting Strategies with Internal State Classification

The few-shot learning approach above only uses a very limited number of labeled examples, and it also doesn't take into account the relative frequencies of each target class. As a refinement of the few-shot prompting approach above, we study the use of the internal states of LLMs for hallucination detection. The internal states of LLMs have been used to detect hallucinations in many studies (Azaria and Mitchell; Marks and Tegmark). Specifically, we take the last layer hidden state vector of the LLM model at the last generated token (the customary choice for finetuning causal LLMs for classification), and train a logistic regression model on top of it. Note that we do not perform any fine-tuning on the LLM parameters. We just take the hidden state vector as a fixed representation and train a classifier on it. We use the "justification+label" template for subtask 1 and "justification+checklist+label" template for subtask 2 from above.

4 Experiments and Results

In this section, we present a detailed analysis of our experimental results and discussion. Specific details regarding experiment setup and configurations are provided in the Appendix B.

4.1 Zero-shot benchmark results

We first evaluate several widely used LLMs on subtask 1 under zero-shot prompting. This initial benchmarking enables us to gain insight into the baseline performance and comparative strengths of different LLMs on the SciHal challenge. For efficiency, we use accuracy as the evaluation metric. The results are presented in Figure 2, with the detailed prompt in the Appendix D.1.

From Figure 2, we can find that the instruct models consistently outperform their base model, and models with larger parameter sizes achieve even better performance. Consequently, for subsequent experiments, we selected Llama3.1-8B-Instruct, Llama3.1-70B-Instruct, and Llama3.3-70B-Instruct as our primary evaluation models, effectively covering a range of parameter sizes.

We also observe that in the zero-shot setting,

[1] https://www.kaggle.com/competitions/hallucination-detection-scientific-content-2025/overview

Model & Prompt	Batch 2 Data		Batch 3 Data	
	Macro-F1	Micro-F1	Macro-F1	Micro-F1
Subtask 1				
Llama3.1-8B-Instruct, ref + label (Few-Shot Prompt 1)	29.76	31.42	20.08	22.61
Llama3.1-8B-Instruct, ref + just + label (Few-Shot Prompt 2)	60.30	64.57	35.82	37.15
Llama3.1-8B-Instruct, ref + just + subj + label (Domain-Aware Few-Shot)	61.43	63.32	36.50	39.41
Llama3.1-70B-Instruct, ref + label (Few-Shot Prompt 1)	62.16	65.43	43.10	45.50
Llama3.1-70B-Instruct, ref + just + label (Few-Shot Prompt 2)	<u>**73.46**</u>	<u>**75.16**</u>	53.50	54.33
Llama3.1-70B-Instruct, ref + just + subj + label (Domain-Aware Few-Shot)	72.36	74.71	54.62	57.13
Llama3.1-70B-Instruct, Domain-Aware Few-Shot + CoT	70.03	71.63	51.02	53.28
Llama3.3-70B-Instruct, ref + just + subj + label (Domain-Aware Few-Shot)	<u>**73.61**</u>	<u>**75.52**</u>	<u>**61.20**</u>	<u>**64.79**</u>
Subtask 2				
Llama3.1-8B-Instruct, ref + label (Few-Shot Prompt 1)	31.23	36.27	-	-
Llama3.1-8B-Instruct, ref + just + label (Few-Shot Prompt 2)	43.98	48.16	-	-
Llama3.1-8B-Instruct, ref + just + checklist + label	30.50	34.15	-	-
Llama-3.1-70B-Instruct, ref + label (Few-Shot Prompt 1)	57.18	68.78	-	-
Llama-3.1-70B-Instruct, ref + just + label (Few-Shot Prompt 2)	<u>**62.97**</u>	<u>**72.88**</u>	38.10	43.25
Llama-3.1-70B-Instruct, ref + just + subj + label (Domain-Aware Few-Shot)	60.28	70.15	36.97	39.15
Llama-3.1-70B-Instruct, ref + just + checklist + label	54.48	59.24	-	-

Table 2: Few-shot and CoT results for Subtasks 1 and 2. 'ref' denotes reference, 'just' denotes justification, and 'subj' signifies domain-matched few-shot examples.

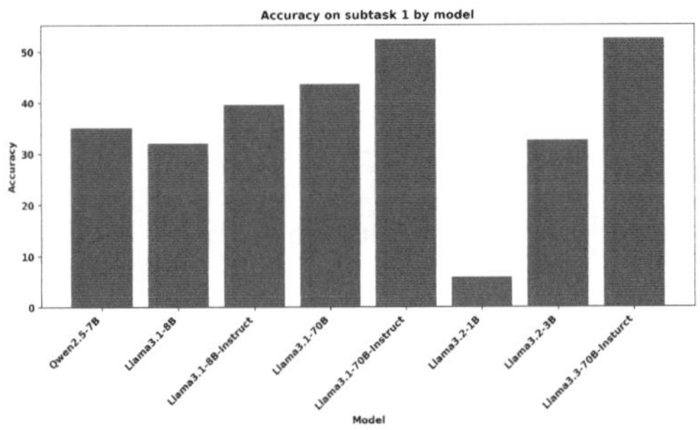

Figure 2: LLMs zero-shot performance on subtask 1.

LLMs exhibit poor performance. Even the 70B-parameter model achieves an accuracy of only around 50%, underscoring the inherent complexity of the task and emphasizing the necessity for continued development of more advanced methods.

4.2 Few-shot with CoT results

Batch 2 Results. From Table 2 'Batch 2 Data' column, we observe that requesting the LLM to provide a justification prior to outputting the label significantly enhances the F1 scores for Subtask 1, particularly for the 70B models. A similar trend is evident for Subtask 2, where prompting for justification also results in improved accuracy. Moreover, performance is further enhanced when employing domain-aware few-shot examples rather than standard few-shot prompts.

However, asking the LLM model to go through a checklist of questions before outputting the label actually degrades performance for both the 8B and 70B models in subtask 2. We examined the results more carefully and found that with the checklist, the LLM models tend to predict the class "missing information" a lot more frequently when it is only a very small class (10 examples out of 2092), leading to a drop in accuracy. We also find it very difficult as humans to distinguish between the two classes "related but unverifiable" and "missing information" in subtask 2. We tried to ask the organizers for clarification of their definitions but could not get an answer. If we merge these two classes and re-run our experiments with the 70B model, we obtain results from Table 3. We can see that there are consistent improvements from adding a checklist on top of justifications.

Model & Prompt	Macro-F1	Micro-F1
Llama3.1-70B-Instruct, ref + label	62.48	70.59
Llama3.1-70B-Instruct, ref + just + label	71.49	76.66
Llama3.1-70B-Instruct, ref + just + checklist + label	72.55	77.05

Table 3: Subtask 2 with 7 classes ('missing information' merged with 'related but unverifiable').

Batch 3 Results. From Table 2 'Batch 3 Data' column, the results are largely consistent with Batch 2, with improvements using logistic regression on the hidden state vectors, except for macro-f1 on Subtask 2 due to the smaller categories. Additionally, due to the timing of data release, constraints imposed by the competition schedule, and limited computational resources, we were unable to complete all planned experiments for subtask 2.

Comparing batch 2 and batch 3 of the training data we notice there is a large drop in the performance. We believe this is due to the differences in how batch 2 and batch 3 are collected. Both batch 2 and batch 3 are labeled by a subject matter expert (SME) and an LLM. If the SME and the LLM agree, then the data point goes to batch 2. If there is a disagreement, another SME is requested to label the example, and it goes to batch 3 and the test set. So batch 3 and the test set contain more difficult examples compared to batch 2. However, despite the labeling process by multiple SMEs, we still find some labels that we disagree with in batch 3, which we will share in the error analysis section.

4.3 Internal State Classification

We use 80% of the data as the training set, and 20% as evaluation data. Table 4 shows the result of logistic regression on top of the internal state vectors. We can see that with or without merging the two classes "missing information" and "related but unverifiable", the logistic regression improves upon the subtask 2 results based on few-shot prompting only in Tables 2. The corresponding results for subtask 1 are also much improved.

	Macro-F1	Micro-F1
Subtask 1, Llama-3.1-70B-Inst, Batch 2	86.20	87.11
Subtask 1, Llama-3.1-70B-Inst, Batch 3	60.21	62.00
Subtask 2, Llama-3.1-70B-Inst, Batch 2	70.60	82.81
Subtask 2, Llama-3.1-70B-Inst, Batch 2 (merged labels)	79.05	81.14
Subtask 2, Llama-3.1-70B-Inst, Batch 3	36.52	52.33

Table 4: Subtask 1 and subtask 2 with logistic regression on internal state vectors.

We also perform ablation studies on the token location used for extracting hidden states for logistic regression. We compare using the hidden states from the last generated token (our current proposal) with the hidden states from the last token from the prompt (i.e., no generation). Using the hidden states from the last token of the prompt is a common finetuning strategy used for adapting causal language models to classification tasks. From Table 5 we can observe that using the hidden states of the last generated token is better than using the hidden states of the last prompt token, especially for Task 2. This shows the power of combining the generation capabilities of the LLMs together with finetuning in detecting hallucinations, which is better than using few-shot learning generation or finetuning alone.

	Macro-F1	Micro-F1
Task 1, Llama-3.1-70B-Inst, last prompt token	56.84	59.33
Task 1, Llama-3.1-70B-Inst, last generated token	60.21	62.00
Task 2, Llama-3.1-70B-Inst, last prompt token	25.18	45.33
Task 2, Llama-3.1-70B-Inst, last generated token	36.52	52.33

Table 5: Comparison of logistic regression result using last prompt token and last generated token on Batch 3.

4.4 Leaderboard Results

Based on the experimental results presented above, we evaluate the proposed pipeline on the test data. The leaderboard results are shown in Table 6. Our results are at the top-2 of subtask 1 and top-1 of subtask 2 on the leaderboard as of 10 PM EST on June 20. The results obtained from the leaderboard are consistent with the trends observed in the training dataset. These results indicate that our proposed pipeline demonstrates robustness and effectiveness.

Model & Prompt	Score
Subtask 1	
Llama-3.1-70B-Inst, Few-Shot Prompt 2	0.49
Llama-3.3-70B-Inst, Domain-Aware Few-Shot	0.55
Llama-3.3-70B-Inst, Domain-Aware Few-Shot + CoT	0.54
Llama-3.1-70B-Inst, Few-Shot Prompt 2 + Log-Reg on hidd-stat	**0.59**
Llama-3.1-70B-Inst, Domain-Aware Few-Shot + Log-Reg on hidd-stat	**0.59**
Subtask 2	
Llama-3.1-70B-Inst, Few-Shot Prompt 2	0.40
Llama-3.1-70B-Inst, Few-Shot Prompt 2 + checklist	0.47
Llama-3.1-70B-Inst, Few-Shot Prompt 2 + Log-Reg on hidd-stat	**0.51**

Table 6: Leaderboard scores for each subtask.

4.5 Error Analysis

We first analyzed the experiment results by using subtask 1, Batch 3 Data with Domain-Aware Few-Shot setting, and show the result in Table 7. The analysis indicates that the *entailment* class achieved the highest recall and overall F1-score, demonstrating that it was the easiest category for the model to identify accurately. Conversely, the class *unverifiable* exhibited the lowest recall and F1-score, highlighting its difficulty for classification.

Class	Precision	Recall	F1-score
Contradiction	0.657	0.462	0.542
Entailment	0.547	0.861	0.669
Unverifiable	0.550	0.238	0.332

Table 7: Classification metrics (precision, recall, and F1-score) for each class.

Following these findings, we conducted a detailed analysis of the data and labels to assess dataset quality. The complete results of this error analysis are provided in the Appendix C.

5 Conclusion

In this paper, we present our solution to the SciHal 2025 challenge. By integrating domain-aware few-shot and CoT prompt, and the model's hidden state as the feature, our method achieved promising results. Due to time constraints, additional experiments are ongoing and will be reported later.

Limitations

First, our current experiments were conducted exclusively using open-source models; proprietary models have not yet been evaluated on this dataset. Second, due to time constraints, several fine-tuning experiments remain ongoing. We plan to continue these experiments beyond the current submission and will provide additional results and in-depth analyses later. Finally in our preliminary evaluations with training data batch 3, the macro and micro f1 scores are close to the numbers on the leaderboard but much lower than those from batch 2 reported above. This suggests our results can be sensitive to shifts in distribution and composition of different classes.

Ethics Statement

The authors take full responsibility for the proposed method. The proposed method is intended for academic and educational purposes only and is not a substitute for a professional system. The data accessed from this challenge is solely for academic purposes and will not be shared or disseminated.

References

Hussam Alkaissi and Samy I McFarlane. 2023. Artificial hallucinations in chatgpt: implications in scientific writing. *Cureus*, 15(2).

Isabelle Augenstein, Tim Rocktäschel, Andreas Vlachos, and Kalina Bontcheva. 2016. Stance detection with bidirectional conditional encoding. In *Proceedings of the 2016 Conference on Empirical Methods in Natural Language Processing*, pages 876–885, Austin, Texas. Association for Computational Linguistics.

Amos Azaria and Tom Mitchell. The internal state of an llm knows when it's lying. In *The 2023 Conference on Empirical Methods in Natural Language Processing*.

Tom Brown, Benjamin Mann, Nick Ryder, Melanie Subbiah, Jared D Kaplan, Prafulla Dhariwal, Arvind Neelakantan, Pranav Shyam, Girish Sastry, Amanda Askell, et al. 2020. Language models are few-shot learners. *Advances in neural information processing systems*, 33:1877–1901.

Qingxiu Dong, Lei Li, Damai Dai, Ce Zheng, Jingyuan Ma, Rui Li, Heming Xia, Jingjing Xu, Zhiyong Wu, Baobao Chang, et al. 2024. A survey on in-context learning. In *Proceedings of the 2024 Conference on Empirical Methods in Natural Language Processing*, pages 1107–1128.

James Goodman, Andreas Vlachos, and Jason Naradowsky. 2016. Noise reduction and targeted exploration in imitation learning for Abstract Meaning Representation parsing. In *Proceedings of the 54th Annual Meeting of the Association for Computational Linguistics (Volume 1: Long Papers)*, pages 1–11, Berlin, Germany. Association for Computational Linguistics.

Mary Harper. 2014. Learning from 26 languages: Program management and science in the babel program. In *Proceedings of COLING 2014, the 25th International Conference on Computational Linguistics: Technical Papers*, page 1, Dublin, Ireland. Dublin City University and Association for Computational Linguistics.

Teven Le Scao, Angela Fan, Christopher Akiki, Ellie Pavlick, Suzana Ilić, Daniel Hesslow, Roman Castagné, Alexandra Sasha Luccioni, François Yvon, Matthias Gallé, et al. 2023. Bloom: A 176b-parameter open-access multilingual language model.

Dan Li, Bogdan Palfi, and Colin Kehang Zhang. 2025. Hallucination detection for scientific content. `https://kaggle.com/competitions/hallucination-detection-scientific-content-2025`. Kaggle competition.

Samuel Marks and Max Tegmark. The geometry of truth: Emergent linear structure in large language model representations of true/false datasets. In *First Conference on Language Modeling*.

Alec Radford, Jeffrey Wu, Rewon Child, David Luan, Dario Amodei, Ilya Sutskever, et al. 2019. Language models are unsupervised multitask learners. *OpenAI blog*, 1(8):9.

David Thulke, Yingbo Gao, Petrus Pelser, Rein Brune, Rricha Jalota, Floris Fok, Michael Ramos, Ian van Wyk, Abdallah Nasir, Hayden Goldstein, et al. 2024. Climategpt: Towards ai synthesizing interdisciplinary research on climate change. *arXiv preprint arXiv:2401.09646*.

Jason Wei, Xuezhi Wang, Dale Schuurmans, Maarten Bosma, Fei Xia, Ed Chi, Quoc V Le, Denny Zhou, et al. 2022. Chain-of-thought prompting elicits reasoning in large language models. *Advances in neural information processing systems*, 35:24824–24837.

Yu Zhang, Xiusi Chen, Bowen Jin, Sheng Wang, Shuiwang Ji, Wei Wang, and Jiawei Han. 2024. A comprehensive survey of scientific large language models and their applications in scientific discovery. In *Proceedings of the 2024 Conference on Empirical Methods in Natural Language Processing*, pages 8783–8817.

Yizhen Zheng, Huan Yee Koh, Jiaxin Ju, Anh TN Nguyen, Lauren T May, Geoffrey I Webb, and Shirui Pan. 2025. Large language models for scientific discovery in molecular property prediction. *Nature Machine Intelligence*, pages 1–11.

A Domain-Aware classification results

We performed domain classification on the train set batch 2 and batch 3, and the results are presented in Table 8. The distribution of data points across the five scientific domains is relatively balanced, with no substantial differences in data representation observed.

Domain	Count	% of total
Computer Science	713	19.8%
Medicine	801	22.3%
Engineering	756	21.0%
Environmental Science	780	21.7%
Agricultural&Biological Science	542	15.1%

Table 8: Distribution of data across scientific domains.

B Experiment Setup

At the outset, we selected eight widely-used LLMs for our zero-shot experiments: Qwen2.5-7B, LLaMA3.1-8B, LLaMA3.1-8B-Instruct, LLaMA3.1-70B, LLaMA3.1-70B-Instruct, LLaMA3.2-1B, LLaMA3.2-3B, and LLaMA3.3-70B-Instruct. Based on their performance, we subsequently select LLaMA3.1-8B-Instruct, LLaMA3.1-70B-Instruct, and LLaMA3.3-70B-Instruct for further experiments. All models were sourced from Hugging Face.

To ensure experimental reproducibility, we standardized inference parameters as follows: maximum output tokens set to 1024, temperature set to 0.6, and top-p sampling set to 0.9. All experiments were conducted using two NVIDIA H100 GPUs.

C Error Analysis

The experiment results show that performance does not consistently improve when the advanced prompts are employed (e.g. CoT prompt). Therefore, we conducted an error analysis to better understand the results.

C.1 Error Analysis on subtask 1 results

We first use the Subtask 1 & Batch 3 Data with Domain-Aware Few-Shot results to do the error analysis.

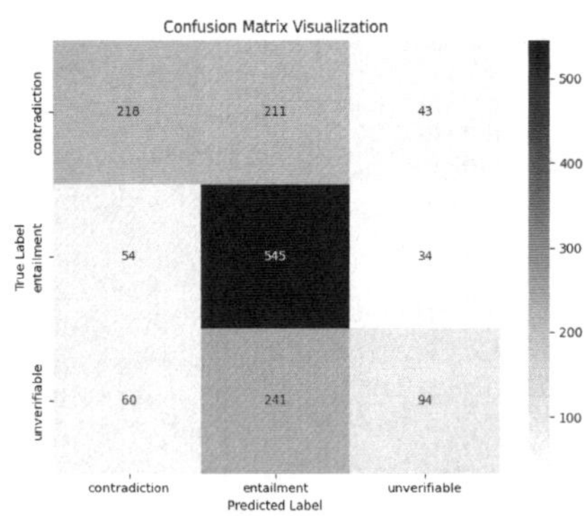

Figure 3: Confusion Matrix on subtask 1 results.

From the Figure 3, it reveals that the class *entailment* is the easiest for the model to correctly predict, exhibiting the highest accuracy. Conversely, the *unverifiable* class poses the greatest challenge, frequently misclassified as either *entailment* or *contradiction*.

C.2 Error Analysis on subtask 2 results

We then use the Subtask 2 & Batch 3 Data with Domain-Aware Few-Shot results to do the error analysis.

Class	Precision	Recall	F1-score
Entailment	0.550	0.814	0.656
Entity error	0.730	0.383	0.503
Misinterpretation	0.188	0.307	0.232
Missing information	0.333	0.041	0.073
Negation	0.447	0.328	0.378
Numeric error	0.550	0.440	0.489
Related but unverifiable	0.546	0.035	0.066
Unrelated and unverifiable	0.230	0.473	0.310

Table 9: Classification performance metrics for each class in Subtask 2.

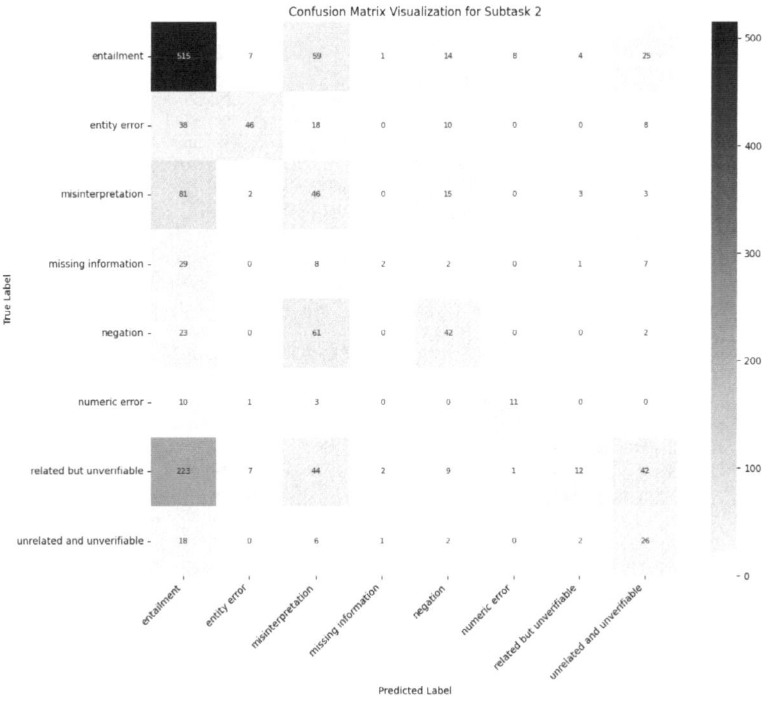

Figure 4: Confusion Matrix on subtask 2 results.

Table 9 and Figure 4 summarize the performance for Subtask 2, highlighting the strengths and challenges across different categories. Same with subtask 1, the *Entailment* achieves notably high recall (0.814) and the best F1-score (0.656), suggesting that the model effectively identifies instances belonging to this class. In contrast, the classes *Missing information* and *Related but unverifiable* exhibit extremely low recall (0.041 and 0.035, respectively), reflecting significant difficulty for accurate detection.

Additionally, Figure 4 reveals that many cases labeled as *Related but unverifiable* are misclassified as *Entailment*, likely due to subtle semantic overlaps between these categories. Similarly, the model frequently confuses *Misinterpretation* and *Negation* with *Entailment*, suggesting that nuanced distinctions among these classes pose considerable challenges. These findings underline the need for clearer category definitions and suggest that future model improvements may benefit from targeted fine-tuning or additional domain-specific examples for the most challenging classes.

C.3 Data Sample Analysis

Inspired by the confusion matrix results, we further checked the data provided by the challenge and identified instances of conflicting labels. For example, as illustrated in the figure below, both the claim and the reference discuss medical image processing; however, the content is unrelated. The claim focuses explicitly on conclusions related to ResUNet, whereas the reference addresses automatic segmentation of ultrasound breast lesions. Although they share the general domain of medical imaging, their specific topics differ significantly, rendering the reference insufficient to verify the claim. Consequently, the correct classification should be "unrelated and unverifiable." Our pipeline made the correct prediction, and subsequent validation by three human experts unanimously supported this classification. Nonetheless, the original dataset label was "related but unverifiable."

This case demonstrates that subjective understanding of the term "related" can impact classification results. Such instances underscore the inherent complexity of accurately labeling data in the task.

A data example from Subtask 2

Claim: - ResUNet, on the other hand, does not rely on such initial conditions and is more robust to variations in image quality. Level-Set Techniques: While level-set methods can capture complex boundaries, they often struggle with initialization sensitivity and computational efficiency [5, 6].

---

reference: - "[5]: Automatic segmentation of ultrasonographic breast lesions is very challenging, due to the lesions' spiculated nature and the variance in shape and texture of the B-mode ultrasound images. Many studies have tried to answer this challenge by applying a variety of computational methods including: Markov random field, artificial neural networks, and active contours and level-set techniques. These studies focused on creating an automatic contour, with maximal resemblance to a manual contour, delineated by a trained radiologist. In this study, we have developed an algorithm, designed to capture the spiculated boundary of the lesion by using the properties from the corresponding ultrasonic image. This is primarily achieved through a unique multi-scale texture identifier (inspired by visual system models) integrated in a level-set framework. The algorithm's performance has been evaluated quantitatively via contour-based and region-based error metrics. We compared the algorithm-generated contour to a manual contour delineated by an expert radiologist. In addition, we suggest here a new method for performance evaluation where corrections made by the radiologist replace the algorithm-generated (original) result in the correction zones. The resulting corrected contour is then compared to the original version. The evaluation showed: (1) Mean absolute error of 0.5 pixels between the original and the corrected contour; (2) Overlapping area of 99.2% between the lesion regions, obtained by the algorithm and the corrected contour. These results are significantly better than those previously reported. In addition, we have examined the potential of our segmentation results to contribute to the discrimination between malignant and benign lesions.[6]: In order to improve the accuracy of breast ultrasound image segmentation, an ultrasound image segmentation method using the C-V (Chan-Vese) model based on phase is proposed. First, the ultrasound image is filtered by LOG-Gabor filters in six different orientations, and the phase feature of the image is obtained by extracting the phase information in the orientation with the maximum energy. Then, the SRAD(speckle reducing anisotropic diffusion) method is used to reduce the noise of the ultrasound image, and the processed image is multiplied by the phase features to enhance the contrast of the target and background. Finally, the target of the ultrasound image is identified by the segmentation algorithm using the C-V model, and corrosion is applied to make the edge smooth and complete. The experimental results show that compared with the C-V model and GAC (geodesic active contour) model based on image gray and the ANN (artificial neural networks) method based on phase feature, the proposed method can obviously improve the accuracy of breast ultrasound image segmentation, which is 92.40%."

---

label: - "related but unverifiable"

---

prediction: - "unrelated and unverifiable"

D Prompt Set

D.1 Zero-Shot prompt

We first employed Zero-Shot prompting to evaluate multiple LLMs and establish their baseline performance on this challenge. The detailed prompts used for Zero-Shot evaluation are detailed below:

Zero-Shot prompt for subtask 1

System Prompt: - You are an assistant for claim verification. Given a claim and some reference from an academic paper, please classify the claim into three labels: contradiction, entailment, or unverifiable.
- Here is the definition of each label:
entailment: The claim is supported by the reference.
contradiction: The claim is contradicted by the reference.
unverifiable: The claim cannot be verified by the reference
- You MUST strictly output your result in the following JSON format (and nothing else).
Now it's your turn.

D.2 Baseline Few-Shot Prompts

We first designed two baseline few-shot prompts as follows. We illustrate the prompting using Subtask 1 as the example; the prompt structure for Subtask 2 is the same, selecting two examples for each corresponding label.

Baseline Few-Shot prompt 1 (ref + label)

System Prompt: - You are an assistant for claim verification. Given a claim and some reference from an academic paper, please classify the claim into three labels: contradiction, entailment, or unverifiable.
- Here are some examples:
Example 1: #Claim: {...}; #Reference: {...}; #Label: {contradiction}
Example 2: #Claim: {...}; #Reference: {...}; #Label: {contradiction}
Example 3: #Claim: {...}; #Reference: {...}; #Label: {entailment}
Example 4: #Claim: {...}; #Reference: {...}; #Label: {entailment}
Example 5: #Claim: {...}; #Reference: {...}; #Label: {unverifiable}
Example 6: #Claim: {...}; #Reference: {...}; #Label: {unverifiable}
- Now, apply the same pattern:
Input: #Claim: {...}; #Reference: {...};
Output:

Baseline Few-Shot prompt 2 (ref + justification + label)

System Prompt: - You are an assistant for claim verification. Given a claim and some reference from an academic paper, please classify the claim into three labels: contradiction, entailment, or unverifiable.
- Here are some examples:
Example 1: #Claim: {...}; #Reference: {...}; #Justification: {...}; #Label: {contradiction}
Example 2: #Claim: {...}; #Reference: {...}; #Justification: {...}; #Label: {contradiction}
Example 3:#Claim: {...}; #Reference: {...}; #Justification: {...}; #Label: {entailment}
Example 4:#Claim: {...}; #Reference: {...}; #Justification: {...}; #Label: {entailment}
Example 5: #Claim: {...}; #Reference: {...}; #Justification: {...}; #Label: {unverifiable}
Example 6: #Claim: {...}; #Reference: {...}; #Justification: {...}; #Label: {unverifiable}
- Now, apply the same pattern:
- Please output the justification and then make a prediction.
Input: #Claim: {...}; #Reference: {...};
Output:

D.3 Domain-Aware Few-Shot Prompt

We first classified each data point into its respective domain. Within each domain, we selected two examples per label to serve as domain-specific few-shot prompts. Given a claim requiring verification, we identify its domain and provide corresponding examples from that domain. Below, we illustrate this process using the domain of computer science as an example.

Domain-Aware Few-Shot Prompt (ref + justification + subj + label)

System Prompt: - You are an assistant for claim verification. Given a claim and some reference from **{Computer Science} domain**, please classify the claim into three labels: contradiction, entailment, or unverifiable.
- Here are some examples about {Computer Science} domain:
Computer Science Example 1: #Claim: {...}; #Reference: {...}; #Justification: {...}; #Label: {contradiction}
Computer Science Example 2: #Claim: {...}; #Reference: {...}; #Justification: {...}; #Label: {contradiction}
Computer Science Example 3:#Claim: {...}; #Reference: {...}; #Justification: {...}; #Label: {entailment}
Computer Science Example 4:#Claim: {...}; #Reference: {...}; #Justification: {...}; #Label: {entailment}
Computer Science Example 5: #Claim: {...}; #Reference: {...}; #Justification: {...}; #Label: {unverifiable}
Computer Science Example 6: #Claim: {...}; #Reference: {...}; #Justification: {...}; #Label: {unverifiable}
- Now, apply the same pattern:
- Please output the justification and then make a prediction.
Input: #Claim: {...}; #Reference: {...};
Output:

D.4 Details on Few-Shot learning with Chain-of-Thought prompts

Few-Shot learning with Chain-of-Thought prompt for subtask 1

System Prompt: - You are an assistant for claim verification. Given a claim and some reference from an academic paper, please classify the claim into three labels: contradiction, entailment, or unverifiable.
- Here are some examples:
Example 1: #Claim: {...}; #Reference: {...}; #Justification: {...}; #Label: {contradiction}
Example 2: #Claim: {...}; #Reference: {...}; #Justification: {...}; #Label: {contradiction}
Example 3:#Claim: {...}; #Reference: {...}; #Justification: {...}; #Label: {entailment}
Example 4:#Claim: {...}; #Reference: {...}; #Justification: {...}; #Label: {entailment}
Example 5: #Claim: {...}; #Reference: {...}; #Justification: {...}; #Label: {unverifiable}
Example 6: #Claim: {...}; #Reference: {...}; #Justification: {...}; #Label: {unverifiable}
- **When you classify a claim, please follow these steps:**
1. Read the reference abstract(s) carefully.
2. Read the scientific claim carefully.
3. Analyze the relationship between the claim and reference abstract(s).
4. Determine which single category best describes the relationship.
- Now, apply the same pattern:
- Please output the justification and then make a prediction.
Input: #Claim: {...}; #Reference: {...};
Output:

Few-Shot learning with Chain-of-Thought prompt for subtask 2 (ref + just + checklist + label)

System Prompt: - You are an assistant for claim verification. Given a claim and some reference from an academic paper, please classify the claim into three labels: contradiction, entailment, or unverifiable.
- Here are some examples:
Example 1: #Claim: {...}; #Reference: {...}; #Justification: {...}; #Label: {contradiction}
Example 2: #Claim: {...}; #Reference: {...}; #Justification: {...}; #Label: {contradiction}
Example 3:#Claim: {...}; #Reference: {...}; #Justification: {...}; #Label: {entailment}
Example 4:#Claim: {...}; #Reference: {...}; #Justification: {...}; #Label: {entailment}
Example 5: #Claim: {...}; #Reference: {...}; #Justification: {...}; #Label: {unverifiable}
Example 6: #Claim: {...}; #Reference: {...}; #Justification: {...}; #Label: {unverifiable}
- **When you classify a claim, please follow the checking list:**
1. Is the claim related to the references?
2. Does the claim contain a contradiction to the references?
3. Does the claim negate parts of the references or replaces terms with their antonyms?
4. Does the claim present logical fallacies, flawed reasoning (over-claiming, under-claiming, ambiguity, or inconsistency), or illogical conclusions?
5. Does the claim contain an erroneous numeric value?
6. Does the claim contain an erroneous entity?
7. Does the claim omit critical parts from the references, changing the meaning/intent?
8. Can the claim be supported by the references?
- Now, apply the same pattern:
- Please output the justification and then make a prediction.
Input: #Claim: {...}; #Reference: {...};
Output:

Figure 5: Checking list in Chain-of-Thought prompting.

A.M.P at SciHal2025: Automated Hallucination Detection in Scientific Content via LLMs and Prompt Engineering

Khoa Nguyen-Anh Le[1,2], Dang Van Thin[1,2],
[1]University of Information Technology-VNUHCM, Ho Chi Minh City, Vietnam
[2]Vietnam National University, Ho Chi Minh City, Vietnam
23520742@gm.uit.edu.vn, thindv@uit.edu.vn

Abstract

This paper presents our system developed for SciHal2025: Hallucination Detection for Scientific Content. The primary goal of this task is to detect hallucinated claims based on the corresponding reference. Our methodology leverages strategic prompt engineering to enhance LLMs' ability to accurately distinguish between factual assertions and hallucinations in scientific contexts. Moreover, we discovered that aggregating the fine-grained classification results from the more complex subtask (subtask 2) into the simplified label set required for the simpler subtask (subtask 1) significantly improved performance compared to direct classification for subtask 1. This work contributes to the development of more reliable AI-powered research tools by providing a systematic framework for hallucination detection in scientific content. The implementation of our system is available on GitHub. [1]

1 Introduction

Nowadays, the rapid advancement of generative AI has revolutionized academic research practices, introducing AI-powered research assistants capable of synthesizing information and responding to complex scientific queries (Glickman and Zhang, 2024). These systems leverage large language models (LLMs) such as Llama (Touvron et al., 2023) and DeepSeek (Xiong et al., 2025) to generate highly accurate answers in a very fast time. Although these tools offer efficiency in knowledge synthesis, they face a critical challenge: models generate text that sounds correct but is actually false or made up, this problem is called **Hallucination** (Ji et al., 2023). Hallucinations in scientific content are particularly problematic as they can propagate misinformation, undermine research integrity, and lead to flawed scientific conclusions.

[1]https://github.com/LeNguyenAnhKhoa/Hallucination-Detection

Question	What temperature does water boil at?
Answer	Water boils at 90 degrees Celsius which is equivalent to 194 degrees Fahrenheit
Claim	Water boils at 90 degrees Celsius
Reference	Water boils at 100 degrees Celsius
Label	Contradiction
Justification	Numeric Error, water boils at 100 degrees Celsius, not 90

Table 1: Example data point from the training dataset.

Given these problems, the SciHal2025 tasks focus on the detection of hallucination from the claim that is extracted from the answer of LLM. In this paper, we present a methodology that combines state-of-the-art language models with advanced prompt engineering techniques to identify and classify different types of hallucination.

2 Data and Task

2.1 Data

The full provided data is divided into four batches, three batches for training, and one batch for testing (batch1/batch2/batch3/test, 500/1592/1500/1000). All dataset samples have the following fields: Question (questions users ask LLM), Answer (answer generated by GenAI-powered research assistant), Claim (one or more sentences extracted from the generated answer that answers the question) and Reference (one or more references, each being an abstract from GenAI-powered research assistant). The training dataset has two additional fields: Label (classification labels are typed by SME[2] annotator) and Justification (reasoning provided by SMEs for assigning the label). SMEs received the claims, references, and detailed guidelines, including hallucination type definitions and a decision tree (as shown in Figure 1) to annotate. Every instance was labeled by one SME, ensuring baseline human judgment for all samples. Additionally, batch3 and

[2]SME = Subject Matter Expert

Proceedings of the Fifth Workshop on Scholarly Document Processing (SDP 2025), pages 328–335
July 31, 2025 ©2025 Association for Computational Linguistics

the test set are annotated by three different SME annotators. This ensures high-quality, consensus-based annotations, making batch 3 and the test set more challenging and reliable. Table 1 shows the overview of the data.

2.2 Task

This task is a multiclass classification task to determine the claim extracted from the answer containing any hallucinated content based on the references. For subtask 1, the task is to determine whether the references entail, contradict, or are unverifiable to the claim. Subtask 2 is more complex, the task is to determine whether the references entail, are unrelated and unverifiable, are related but unverifiable, misrepresentation, missing information, contain a numeric error, contain an opposite meaning, or contain an entity error to the claim. For example, in Table 1, the claim has a "Numeric Error" when water boils at 100 degrees C and not 90 degrees C, which also leads to the reference contradicting the claim. According to Figure 1, subtask 1 is a more compact version of subtask 2 with only three labels, while subtask 2 has eight labels. Weighted F1-score (Harbecke et al., 2022) is the main benchmark for this task, and we also use this score to evaluate methods.

3 System Overview

In this section, we describe the system in detail. We first noticed that the claim and reference contained quite a few encoding errors, so we used the **ftfy** library to fix these encoding errors. We then performed prompt engineering on large language models to make predictions. In addition, we discovered a simple, efficient two-step method that yields better results.

3.1 Prompt Engineering

First of all, we used LLMs as a black-box detection system, so we used the entire training set as a validation set to test the models and evaluate the methods. Next, we selected versions of the gemini models (Imran and Almusharraf, 2024), smaller versions of OpenAI's o3 and o4 (Ramachandran, 2024) models to make direct predictions.

We continued with the tuning prompt, the most optimal prompt for subtask 1 is shown in Figure 2. The first part of the prompt is to define the LLM's role and task, this helped the LLM understand the specific role to be undertaken and the task to be performed, thereby focusing on the right goal and giving feedback appropriate to the context of the request and its effectiveness has been proven at (Shanahan et al., 2023). The second part of the prompt is that we explain what each label means to help the LLM distinguish between potentially confusing concepts and apply them in the correct context for each use case, this explanation is based on the decision tree as shown in Figure 1. For the next part of the prompt, we apply few-shot learning (Schick and Schütze, 2022) to improve the model's ability to understand and perform tasks. Few-shot learning allows the model to learn from a limited number of examples, helping it quickly adapt to specific requirements and orient the model towards the desired output format. For each label, we randomly select an example for the LLM to understand better, in Figure 2 we choose the example sample for the label 'Contradiction'. Finally, we set output requirements that require the model to produce a 'justification' and an 'answer'. The 'justification' part first explains why it predicted that label, forcing the model to think before making a final decision. The 'answer' part must only respond to a single label, helping the model produce the answer with the highest probability and go straight to the point. For subtask 2, we add more explanation for the remaining labels and give more examples, we can see the sample prompt in Figure 3. The results of this approach are presented in Table 2.

Model	Subtask 1	Subtask 2
gemini-2.0-flash	0.580	0.572
gemini-2.5-flash	**0.719**	**0.635**
o3-mini	0.708	0.626
o4-mini	0.693	0.617

Table 2: Weighted F1-score on validation set among models. Best results are in bold.

3.2 Two-step approach

As shown in Figure 1, we can see that the label nodes of subtask 1 are parents of the label nodes of subtask 2 in the decision tree. So instead of directly predicting three labels for subtask 1, we can predict eight labels for subtask 2 and then reduce this result to three labels for subtask 1. The converted labels can be seen in detail in Figure 4. With this method, we reduced the direct prediction from two

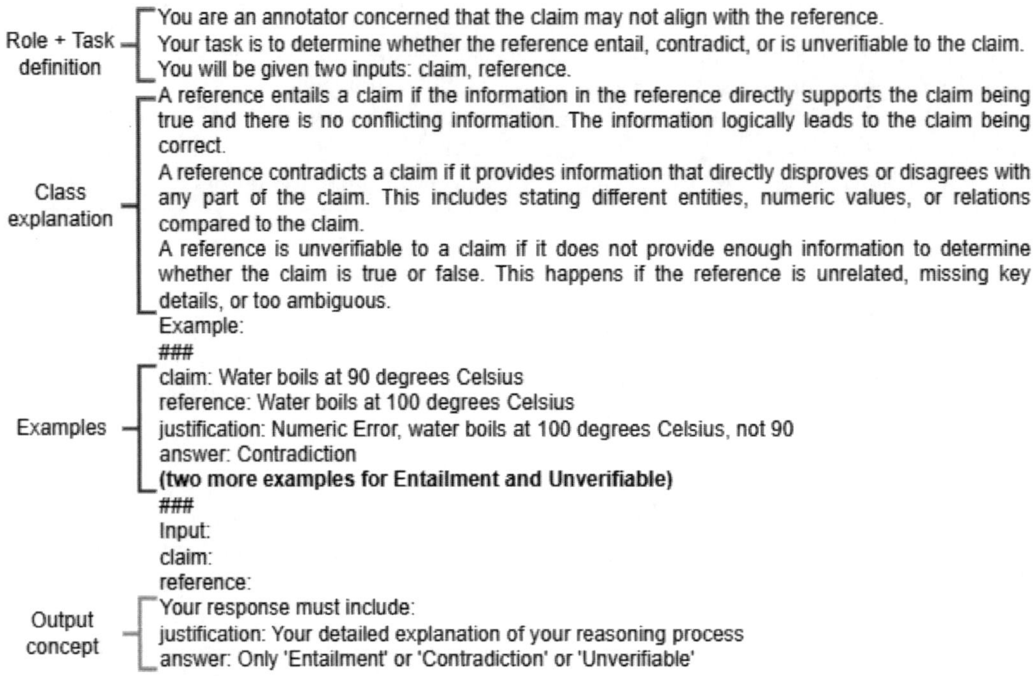

Figure 2: Example prompt with one example for each label for subtask 1.

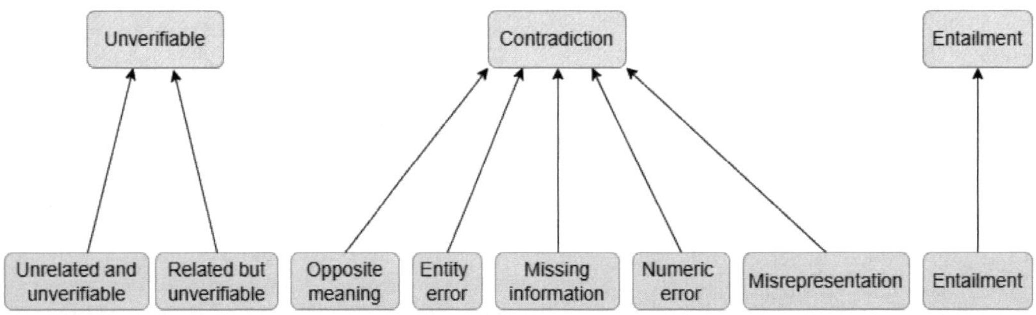

Figure 4: Two-step approach. The label of subtask 1 is light blue. The label of subtask 2 is light green.

Model	Directly	Two-step
gemini-2.0-flash	0.580	0.694
gemini-2.5-flash	0.719	0.723
o3-mini	0.708	0.714
o4-mini	0.693	0.703

Table 3: Weighted F1-score on validation set of subtask 1 between directly and two-step approach.

times (each time one subtask) to a single prediction for subtask 2, while subtask 1 only requires simple operations to be able to make the prediction. Finally, this approach gives better results in all models shown in Table 3.

4 Experimental Setup

We used large language models through APIs, which allow us to make predictions quickly and test multiple methods without the need for powerful hardware. However, sometimes due to network errors, we have to find specific patterns to re-predict, which costs a bit of money. For Gemini models, we cast the output to JSON format so that the output has a specific format and we can process the output more easily. Also, we leave the **temperature** coefficient as 0 so that the model gives the highest probability result. Gemini's API documents are available at Google AI Studio [3]. For OpenAI models, we cannot set the temperature coefficient

[3]https://ai.google.dev/gemini-api/docs

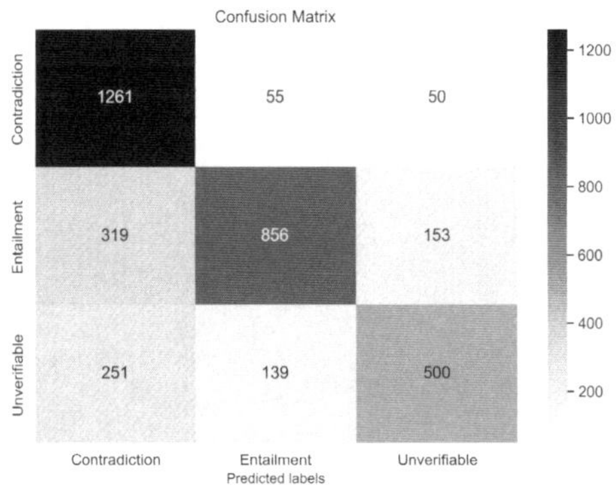

Figure 4: Confusion matrix of subtask 1 uses gemini-2.5-flash model to make prediction using two-step method.

Category	Precision	Recall	F1-score
Contradiction	0.69	0.92	0.79
Entailment	0.82	0.64	0.72
Unverifiable	0.71	0.56	0.63
Accuracy	—	—	0.73
Macro Avg	0.74	0.71	0.71
Weighted Avg	0.74	0.73	0.72

Table 4: Classification report for subtask 1 using gemini-2.5-flash model to make prediction using two-step method.

or cast the output, but instead we can adjust the **reasoning_effort** coefficient to "high" to make the model think more carefully before giving the final answer. OpenAI API documentation can be found at OpenAI Platform [4]. For all models, I set my lucky **random seed** to 13 so that each run of the models gives the same results.

5 Results

Based on Table 2 and Table 3, we decided to make a direct prediction using the prompt in Figure 3 for subtask 2 and reduce this result to predict for subtask 1. We also selected the only best model (gemini-2.5-flash) to make predictions on the test set.

5.1 Subtask 1 result

Our two-step system demonstrated moderate performance with an overall accuracy of 73% and a weighted F1-score of 0.72, exhibiting notable class-wise performance disparities according to Table 4.

[4]https://platform.openai.com/docs/overview

Category	Precision	Recall	F1-score
Entailment	0.82	0.64	0.72
Entity error	0.54	0.78	0.64
Misrepresentation	0.40	0.48	0.43
Missing information	0.00	0.00	0.00
Numeric error	0.83	0.83	0.83
Opposite meaning	0.64	0.96	0.77
Related but unverifiable	0.61	0.45	0.52
Unrelated and unverifiable	0.50	0.51	0.50
Accuracy	—	—	0.64
Macro avg	0.54	0.58	0.55
Weighted avg	0.66	0.64	0.63

Table 5: Classification report for subtask 2 using gemini-2.5-flash model to make prediction directly.

The model achieved good performance in contradiction detection, with a precision of 0.69, recall of 0.92, and F1-score of 0.79, indicating effective identification of contradictory statements with minimal false negatives. The most challenging category is unverifiable content classification, achieving the lowest F1-score of 0.63 with a precision of 0.71 and recall of 0.56. The confusion matrix (can be viewed at Figure 4) reveals significant misclassification patterns, particularly 251 unverifiable instances incorrectly predicted as contradictions, indicating the model's tendency to over-predict the contradiction class.

5.2 Subtask 2 result

Based on the classification report (as shown in Table 5) and the confusion matrix (as shown in Figure 5), our system exhibits moderate performance with 64% accuracy and a weighted F1-score of 0.63. Additionally, we have a strong performance in detecting numeric inconsistencies (F1-score: 0.83) and opposite meaning contradictions (F1-score: 0.77, recall: 0.96). However, the model encounters significant limitations with subtler hallucination types, most notably complete failure in missing information detection (zero performance across all metrics) and poor performance in misrepresentation identification (F1-score: 0.43). The confusion matrix reveals substantial misclassification patterns, with entailment cases frequently confused with other categories (856 correct and 472 misclassified instances), and notable confusion between related categories such as 'Related but unverifiable' and 'Entailment' (132 misclassifications).

5.3 Final result

In the test set evaluation, the o3-mini model demonstrated superior performance on both sub-tasks, al-

Models	Subtask 1	Subtask 2
o3-mini	**0.59**	**0.48**
gemini-2.5-flash	0.57	0.47
o4-mini	0.52	0.43
gemini-2.0-flash	0.49	0.4

Table 6: Performance of our models on the test set. Best result are in bold.

System	Subtask 1	Subtask 2
ScaDS.AI x sebis	**0.6**	0.5
YupengCao	0.59	**0.51**
Ours	0.59	0.48
Crivoi Carla	0.51	0.43
JB	0.25	0.49

Table 7: Weighted F1-score on test set on the leaderboard. Best results are in bold.

though the gemini-2.5-flash model performed better on the validation set (full models' performance in Table 6. The model achieved a weighted F1-score of 0.59 for subtask 1 and 0.48 for subtask 2, representing the highest scores among all evaluated models. We can see the results on the test set in Table 7, our system is ranked 3rd in subtask 1 and 4th in subtask 2.

6 Conclusion

In this paper, we introduced a good system to detect various types of hallucinations produced by LLMs. The key point of our system is to design an optimal prompt with the following components: role and task definition, class explanation, examples, and output concepts so that the model can understand the concept and make accurate predictions. In addition, we introduce a two-step method to make efficient and fast predictions for both subtasks. In summary, the A.M.P system was competitive with the other systems submitted for evaluation.

Acknowledgements

This research was supported by The VNUHCM-University of Information Technology's Scientific Research Support Fund.

References

Mark Glickman and Yi Zhang. 2024. Ai and generative ai for research discovery and summarization.

David Harbecke, Yuxuan Chen, Leonhard Hennig, and Christoph Alt. 2022. Why only micro-f1? class weighting of measures for relation classification.

Muhammad Imran and Norah Almusharraf. 2024. Google gemini as a next generation ai educational tool: a review of emerging educational technology. *Smart Learning Environments*, 11(1):22. Open Access.

Ziwei Ji, Nayeon Lee, Rita Frieske, Tiezheng Yu, Dan Su, Yan Xu, Etsuko Ishii, Ye Jin Bang, Andrea Madotto, and Pascale Fung. 2023. Survey of hallucination in natural language generation. *ACM Computing Surveys*, 55(12):1–38.

Anand Ramachandran. 2024. Revolutionizing research and engineering openai o3's transformative role in scientific discovery and global innovation.

Timo Schick and Hinrich Schütze. 2022. True few-shot learning with prompts—a real-world perspective. *Transactions of the Association for Computational Linguistics*, 10:716–731.

Murray Shanahan, Kyle McDonell, and Laria Reynolds. 2023. Role play with large language models. *Nature*, 623(7987):493–498.

Hugo Touvron, Thibaut Lavril, Gautier Izacard, Xavier Martinet, Marie-Anne Lachaux, Timothée Lacroix, Baptiste Rozière, Naman Goyal, Eric Hambro, Faisal Azhar, Aurelien Rodriguez, Armand Joulin, Edouard Grave, and Guillaume Lample. 2023. Llama: Open and efficient foundation language models.

Luolin Xiong, Haofen Wang, Xi Chen, Lu Sheng, Yun Xiong, Jingping Liu, Yanghua Xiao, Huajun Chen, Qing-Long Han, and Yang Tang. 2025. Deepseek: Paradigm shifts and technical evolution in large ai models. *IEEE/CAA Journal of Automatica Sinica*, 12(5):841–858.

A Decision Tree

The figure below presents the decision tree guideline used by SME annotators during the annotation process. It also adds an explanation of the classes for LLMs to make predictions.

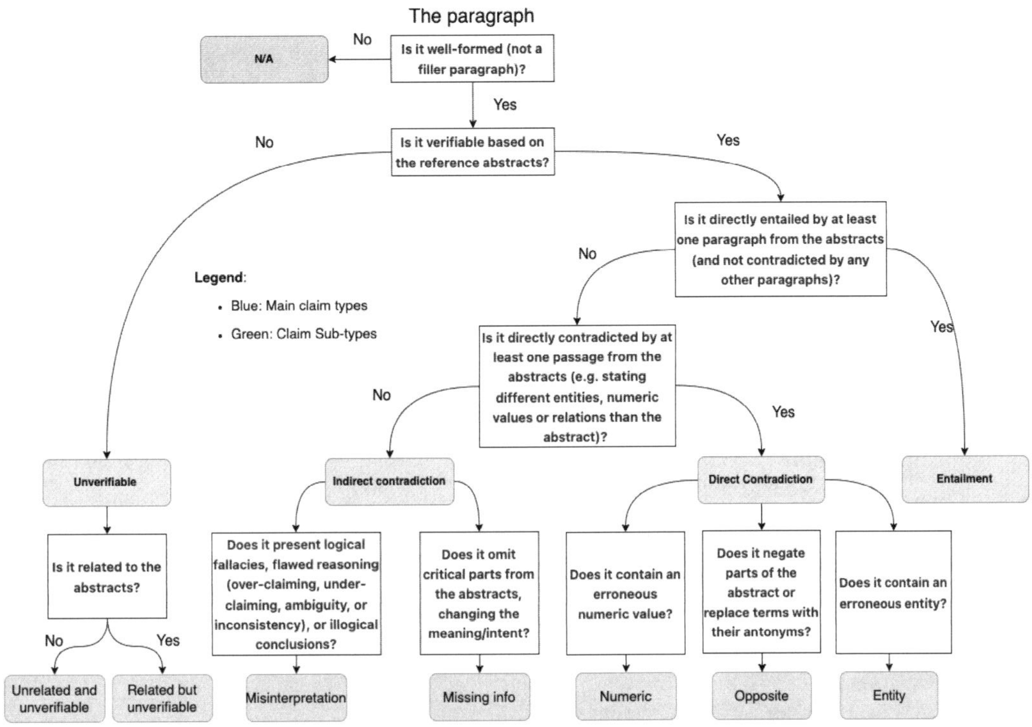

Figure 1: Decision Tree guideline for SME annotators.

B Subtask 2 prompt

Prompt for subtask 2, the components are similar to the prompt for subtask 1 and are explained in detail above. The difference is in the 'Class explanation' and 'Examples' sections as subtask 2 has more labels than subtask 1.

Role + Task definition

You are an annotator concerned that the claim may not align with the reference.
Your task is to determine whether the reference entail, contradict, or is unverifiable to the claim.
You will be given two inputs: claim, reference.

Class explanation

Entailment occurs when reference information directly supports a claim's accuracy with no conflicting information. The logical connection between reference and claim is strong enough that the claim's truth follows naturally from the reference content.
Opposite meaning identifies claims that directly contradict references by stating the contrary position. This happens when a claim negates key parts of a reference or substitutes terms with their antonyms, fundamentally reversing the reference's meaning.
Misrepresentation labels claims that present logical fallacies or flawed reasoning relative to references. This includes over-claiming, under-claiming, introducing ambiguity, creating inconsistency, or drawing conclusions that don't logically follow from the reference material.
Related but unverifiable describes claims that connect to references through shared subjects or entities but cannot be verified because the reference lacks specific information to confirm or deny the claim's accuracy.
Entity error identifies claims that incorrectly name entities (people, organizations, places) compared to reference information. Even if other claim elements are accurate, entity misidentification compromises the claim's overall accuracy.
Unrelated and unverifiable applies to claims discussing topics or information entirely absent from references, providing no basis for accuracy assessment.
Numeric error identifies claims presenting incorrect numerical values (quantities, percentages, dates) compared to reference figures.
Missing information flags claims that omit critical reference details, significantly altering the original meaning or intent of the referenced information.

Example:
###

Examples

claim: Water boils at 90 degrees Celsius
reference: Water boils at 100 degrees Celsius
justification: Numeric Error, water boils at 100 degrees Celsius, not 90
answer: Numeric Error
(7 more examples for remaining labels)

###
Input:
claim:
reference:

Output concept

Your response must include:
justification: Your detailed explanation of your reasoning process
answer: Only 'Opposite meaning' or 'Misrepresentation' or 'Related but unverifiable' or 'Entailment' or 'Entity error' or 'Unrelated and unverifiable' or 'Numeric error' or 'Missing information'

Figure 3: Example prompt with one example for each label for subtask 2.

C Subtask 2 confusion matrix

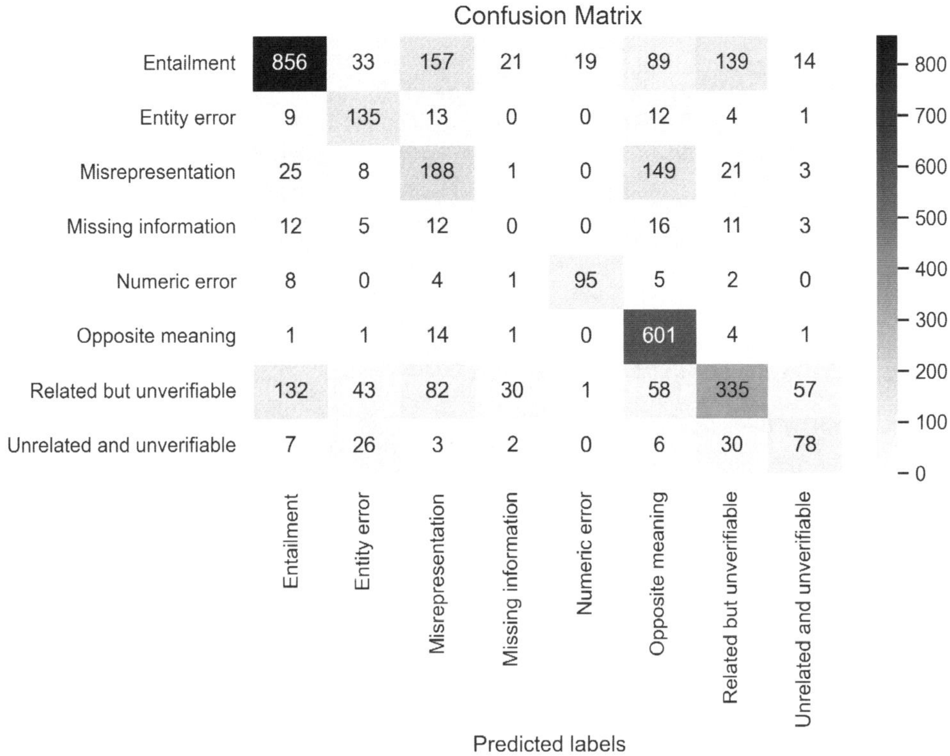

Figure 5: Confusion matrix of subtask 2 uses gemini-2.5-flash model to make prediction directly.

SciBERT Meets Contrastive Learning: A Solution for Scientific Hallucination Detection

Carla Crivoi[1] **Ana-Sabina Uban**[1,2]
[1]Faculty of Mathematics and Computer Science, University of Bucharest
[2]Human Language Technologies Research Center, University of Bucharest
crivoicarla02@gmail.com, auban@fmi.unibuc.ro

Abstract

Large language models are increasingly used to synthesize scientific literature, yet they remain prone to *hallucination* — claims that are linguistically fluent but lack support in the cited sources. We tackle hallucination detection in the SciHal 2025 challenge by augmenting SciBERT with Triplet and InfoNCE contrastive objectives in addition to cross-entropy classification. The system achieves validation macro-F_1 scores of 0.626 ± 0.004 on the coarse-grained hallucination detection task (Sub-task 1) and 0.632 ± 0.012 on the fine-grained detection task (Sub-task 2), exceeding a plain SciBERT baseline by more than three points. The official blind test set scores reach macro-F_1 scores of 0.51 and 0.43 for Sub-tasks 1 and 2, respectively, securing fifth place in both leaderboards. Confusion matrix analysis shows that contrastive learning markedly improves majority classes, whereas sparse categories, especially *Missing Information*, remain challenging despite aggressive attempts to mitigate class imbalance.

1 Introduction

Large language models (LLMs) such as ChatGPT (OpenAI, 2023) are increasingly used to support academic research by answering domain-specific questions and summarising scientific content. While their outputs are often fluent and persuasive, they may introduce statements that are not grounded in the source material — a phenomenon known as *hallucination*. Detecting hallucinated claims is especially difficult in scientific domains, where language is highly specialised and reference documents are lengthy.

In this work we present a contrastive-learning solution based on SciBERT (Beltagy et al., 2019) for hallucination detection in scientific answers. Our contributions are three-fold: (i) a systematic analysis of the SciHal corpus that highlights the linguistic and structural challenges of the task, (ii) a multi-objective optimisation scheme that couples classification with two contrastive losses, and (iii) discussion and analysis of results and errors, including confusion matrix diagnostics, demonstrating the effectiveness of the proposed model.

2 Related Work

Early studies of factual consistency focused on abstractive summarisation, where hallucinations degrade summary quality. Maynez et al. (2020) showed that even state-of-the-art models hallucinate frequently, motivating automatic detection methods such as Question Answering (QA)-based factuality probes (Kryściński et al., 2020). With the advent of large language models (LLMs) like GPT-3, hallucinations have been documented in open-domain Question Answering (Ji et al., 2023) and conversational agents (Thoppilan et al., 2022). Most approaches frame hallucination detection as either an entailment problem, requiring reference retrieval and contradiction detection, or a generation-probability anomaly task.

Contrastive objectives have proven effective at learning semantically meaningful representations from limited supervision (Chen et al., 2020). In factuality research, Liu et al. (2022) applied supervised contrastive loss to claim verification, achieving gains over cross-entropy-only training. Yuan et al. (2022) employed Information Noise-Contrastive Estimation (InfoNCE) to align biomedical entity mentions with definitions, improving downstream question answering performance. For hallucination mitigation, Shi et al. (2023) used retrieval-augmented contrastive tuning to discourage unsupported generations, while Deng et al. (2024) introduced dual-encoder contrastive pretraining to rank evidence passages. Our work differs by combining *two* contrastive losses: Triplet and InfoNCE with a cross-entropy objective inside a SciBERT backbone, targeting both coarse and fine-grained hallucination labels in scientific texts.

Proceedings of the Fifth Workshop on Scholarly Document Processing (SDP 2025), pages 336–343
July 31, 2025 ©2025 Association for Computational Linguistics

3 Task Description

The Hallucination Detection for Scientific Content (SciHal) shared task addresses a challenge in the use of generative AI-powered academic research assistants: the detection of hallucinated claims in automatically generated scientific answers. These hallucinations—claims unsupported by reliable sources—undermine the trustworthiness of AI-generated scientific content.

The task is formulated as a multi-label classification problem, where participants are required to assess the factual consistency of claims generated in response to research-related questions. For each instance, participants are provided with: a question related to scientific research, a summarized answer produced by a generative AI system, an extracted claim from that answer, and the corresponding reference abstracts cited in support of the summary.

Participants must determine whether each claim is factually supported or hallucinatory based on the provided reference materials. The task is divided into two sub-tasks: coarse-grained hallucination detection, and fine-grained hallucination detection.

3.1 Sub-task 1: Coarse-grained Hallucination Detection

In the first sub-task, each claim must be classified into one of the following categories:

- **Entailment**: the claim is supported by the references.
- **Unverifiable**: the claim cannot be verified using the provided references.
- **Contradiction**: the claim contradicts information in the references.

3.2 Sub-task 2: Fine-grained Hallucination Detection

The second sub-task requires a more fine-grained analysis of hallucination types. Each claim must be categorized as one of the following: Entailment, Unrelated and unverifiable, Related but unverifiable, Misrepresentation, Missing information, Numeric error, Entity error, Opposite meaning.

3.3 Evaluation Metrics

We evaluate models with the macro F_1 score, which assigns equal weight to every class by averaging their per-class F_1 values, irrespective of class frequency. To provide a more granular picture of errors, we also include confusion matrices for each sub-task, detailing how predictions are distributed across the true labels.

4 Methodology

4.1 Dataset and Split Strategy

The official SCIHAL release provides 3,592 labelled instances for Sub-task1 and 4,092 for Sub-task2. Following the shared-task protocol we adopt an 85:15 split, corresponding to 3,053 / 539 (train / validation) examples for Sub-task1 and 3,478 / 614 examples for Sub-task2. The test sets were not released to the participants, but the submissions were evaluated on 50% on the test data using the same metrics to obtain the team rankings for both sub-tasks.

4.2 Data Analysis

Tables 1-3 summarise descriptive statistics for the dataset. These numbers highlight linguistic and structural challenges: input sequences vary substantially in length and claims are concise, whereas references are much longer. A lexical overlap analysis provides further evidence: the average Jaccard coefficient (da F. Costa, 2021) between lemmatised claim and reference token sets is 0.092 (minimum 0.000; maximum 0.474), confirming that surface-form overlap is generally low.

Field	Max C	Min C	Avg C
Question	269	15	80.06
Claim	705	28	256.18
Answer	5649	897	3426.23
Reference	19375	190	2046.49

Table 1: Character count statistics across text fields.

Field	Avg W	Max W	Min W
Question	11.24	37	2
Claim	36.02	104	4
Answer	465.18	757	133
Reference	299.91	2824	30

Table 2: Word count statistics across text fields.

4.3 Proposed Solution

Our system tackles hallucination detection by fine-tuning SCIBERT within a contrastive-learning paradigm. The network features a dual-head design: a classification branch with two dense lay-

Field	Avg S
Question	1.01
Claim	1.70
Answer	22.00
Reference	15.66

Table 3: Average sentence count per field.

ers with layer normalization, dropout, and a softmax output, and a projection branch consisting of a two-layer MLP with ReLU and dropout whose L_2-normalised embeddings serve the contrastive objectives. We pool the final hidden states by concatenating the [CLS] vector with the mean of all token embeddings, yielding a hybrid representation that feeds both heads.

Optimisation relies on a composite loss,

$$\mathcal{L} = 0.3(\mathcal{L}_{Triplet} + \mathcal{L}_{InfoNCE}) + 0.7\,\mathcal{L}_{CE},$$

where Triplet Loss (Schroff et al., 2015) enforces distance constraints between positive and negative claim-reference pairs, *InfoNCE Loss* (Oord et al., 2018) promotes high cosine similarity among positives, and *Cross-Entropy Loss* (Bishop, 2006) supplies the multi-class signal. A grid search confirmed that the 30:70 contrastive classification weighting gives the best validation performance.

During training we adopt differential learning rates: 5×10^{-5} for the encoder, and 5×10^{-4} for the task-specific layers cosine annealing with a 15% warm-up, early stopping (maximum 25 epochs), and gradient clipping at an L_2-norm of 5 to prevent exploding updates.

We employ a weighted loss in order to mitigate class imbalance. Class weights are computed as

$$w_i = \frac{N}{K \cdot n_i}, \tag{1}$$

where N is the total number of samples, K the number of classes, and n_i the frequency of class i.

5 Experiments

5.1 Sub-task 1

5.1.1 Dataset and Preprocessing

The SciHal dataset comprises 3,592 labeled instances with class distribution: *contra* (1,369), *entail* (1,333), and *unver* (890). We employed an 85:15 train-validation split, yielding 3,053 training and 539 validation examples. Class weights were computed to mitigate the observed label imbalance during training.

5.1.2 Results

The model reached its peak validation performance at epoch 5 with a macro F_1 of 0.626 ($\pm$0.004 across five runs); the corresponding per-class F_1 scores were 0.673 for *contra*, 0.600 for *entail*, and 0.591 for *unver*.

In this run, 1,000 validation instances were classified as follows: *entail* (521), *contra* (251), and *unver* (228). The mean prediction confidence, computed as the probability output by the model for the predicted class, was 0.892, with only 17 predictions falling below a 0.60 threshold; class-specific average confidences were 0.923 for *unver*, 0.888 for *contra*, and 0.881 for *entail*.

Figure 1 presents the normalised confusion matrix obtained from a *fresh* evaluation run using the same experimental settings. Small numerical deviations from the previous report reflect the non-deterministic nature of stochastic optimisation and mini-batch sampling.

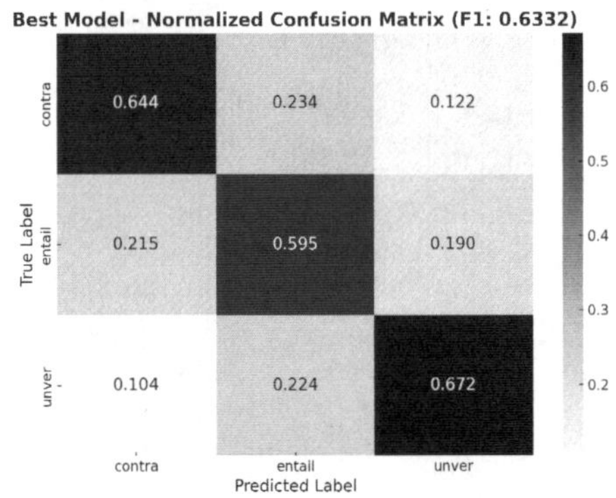

Figure 1: Normalised confusion matrix for the best validation checkpoint for Sub-task 1.

The confusion matrix shows that the *average misclassification rate*, defined as the sum of all off-diagonal cell counts divided by the total number of validation instances, is 0.1815. The *standard deviation* of these off-diagonal error proportions is 0.0505, indicating a moderate spread: while roughly 18% of inputs are assigned to an incorrect class, the class-to-class variability rarely exceeds $\pm$5 percentage points.

On the official blind test set released by the SCIHAL 2025 organisers our final submission, trained with the configuration described above, attained a macro-F_1 score of 0.51, which placed us fifth out of all participating teams.

5.2 Sub-task 2

5.2.1 Dataset and Preprocessing

Sub-task 2 employs the extended SCIHAL corpus of 3,592 annotated instances covering eight hallucination categories. The data were randomly partitioned in an 85:15 ratio, resulting in 3,053 training examples and 539 validation examples. Because the class distribution is heavily skewed (categories such as *missinfo*, *numerr*, and *unrelunvef* are markedly under-represented), we adopt inverse-frequency weighting on the training split only. The resulting weights are shown in Table 4.

Class label	Train examples	Weight w_i
Entail	1333	0.337
Related-Unverifiable	738	0.608
Opposite Meaning (negat)	625	0.718
Misrepresentation	395	1.137
Entity Error	174	2.580
Unrelated-Unverifiable	152	2.954
Numeric Error	116	3.871
Missing Information	59	7.610

Table 4: Class frequencies in the training split (3,478 instances) and the inverse-frequency weights used during optimisation for Sub-task 2.

5.2.2 Training Configuration and Results

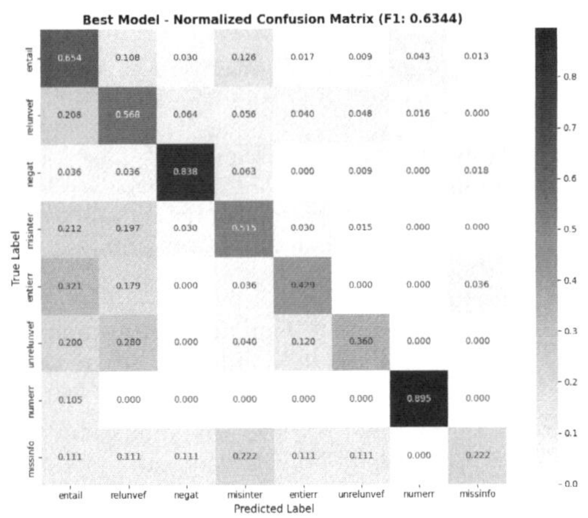

Figure 2: Normalised confusion matrix for the best validation checkpoint for Sub-task 2.

The experimental setup mirrors that of Sub-task 1; the only architectural difference is the output softmax now spans eight classes instead of three. Validation performance rose steadily and peaked at a macro-F_1 of 0.632 (± 0.012 across five runs) on epoch 19.

The confusion matrix in Figure 2 further shows that the *missinfo* category, despite receiving the largest class weight, remains; its under-representation renders it the most difficult label to learn, illustrating that even aggressive re-weighting cannot fully offset data sparsity.

For Sub-task 2 the same model configuration achieved a macro-F_1 of 0.43 on the shared-task test set, securing fifth place in the final leaderboard. While performance naturally drops in the more fine-grained, eight-class scenario, the result demonstrates that our contrastive SCIBERT approach remains competitive even when the label space is enlarged and class imbalance becomes more pronounced.

Additional experiments and results are reported in the Appendix, including results with a vanilla fine-tuned SCIBERT model using only the cross-entropy objective, which obtains poorer validation results were poorer than our final approach.

6 Conclusion

We have introduced a contrastive-learning extension of SCIBERT for detecting hallucinated claims in AI-generated scientific answers. Jointly optimising cross-entropy with Triplet and InfoNCE losses yields consistent gains on both coarse- and fine-grained settings of the SCIHAL 2025 benchmark, outperforming an unweighted baseline and a purely cross-entropy model. The improvement is most pronounced for majority and medium-frequency labels, confirming that semantic alignment objectives complement token-level supervision. Nonetheless, the model still struggles with the under-represented classes, indicating that re-weighting alone cannot fully offset data scarcity.

Future work could improve performance by model updates along three possible axes. First, coupling the encoder with a retrieval-compression module that distills each reference into a handful of salient sentences could help by thereby shortening inputs while preserving key evidence. Second, we intend to introduce a curriculum that over-samples rare labels and structurally complex claims early in training, then relaxes the sampling schedule as the model stabilizes. Third, we will examine whether parameter-efficient fine-tuning of substantially larger transformer backbones improves robustness, especially on the sparsest categories, without incurring prohibitive computational cost.

Limitations

Our approach has several practical and methodological limitations. First, all experiments were conducted using a single NVIDIA Tesla P100 GPU, which constrained the batch size and training speed, especially during contrastive learning. Due to memory limitations, we relied on models from the BERT family, which support a maximum input length of 512 tokens. This likely prevented the model from accessing the full context in cases where the reference abstracts were lengthy or complex.

Another key limitation is the relatively small size of the training dataset. While sufficient for fine-tuning, the number of examples is limited from the perspective of large language models (LLMs), increasing the risk of overfitting and limiting generalization. This was especially evident for underrepresented labels in Sub-task 2, where performance gains plateaued early. More data and better-balanced class distributions would likely improve robustness.

Lastly, our model processes claims and references independently at the input level, without explicitly modeling document structure or reasoning chains. Incorporating more advanced context handling or retrieval-augmented methods could help mitigate this in future work.

Ethics Statement

This work focuses on improving the factual reliability of AI-generated scientific content by detecting hallucinated claims. Our intention is to support responsible use of large language models (LLMs) in academic research, not to automate or replace scientific reasoning. We recognize that LLMs may still introduce errors or biased outputs, and systems built on top of them should always be used with human oversight.

We used publicly released data provided by the SciHal 2025 shared task organizers, and did not collect or annotate any additional human data. No personally identifiable information (PII) was involved. Our models were trained and evaluated only for research purposes, and we do not deploy them in production systems.

We also acknowledge the computational costs of training large models. While we used relatively modest hardware (a single P100 GPU), future work should continue to consider the environmental impact of large-scale training.

Finally, we emphasize that hallucination detection is not a solved problem, and there is a risk that users may overtrust partially automated systems. Clear communication of model limitations and transparency in design choices are essential to ensure ethical deployment.

Acknowledgements

This research was partially supported by the project "Romanian Hub for Artificial Intelligence - HRIA", Smart Growth, Digitization and Financial Instruments Program, 2021-2027, MySMIS no. 334906, and by InstRead: Research Instruments for the Text Complexity, Simplification and Readability Assessment CNCS - UEFISCDI project number PN-IV-P2-2.1-TE-2023-2007.

References

Iz Beltagy, Kyle Lo, and Arman Cohan. 2019. Scibert: A pretrained language model for scientific text. *EMNLP*.

Christopher M. Bishop. 2006. *Pattern Recognition and Machine Learning*. Springer.

Ting Chen, Simon Kornblith, Mohammad Norouzi, and Geoffrey Hinton. 2020. A simple framework for contrastive learning of visual representations. In *International Conference on Machine Learning (ICML)*, pages 1597–1607. PMLR.

Luciano da F. Costa. 2021. Further generalizations of the jaccard index.

Xiang Deng, Han Zhang, Wenhao Yu, Clare Lee, and Mohit Bansal. 2024. Factscore 2.0: Dual-encoder contrastive pre-training for factual consistency. *Transactions of the Association for Computational Linguistics*, 12:1–19.

Ziwei Ji, Nayeon Lee, Rita Frieske, Tiezheng Yu, Dan Su, Yan Xu, Etsuko Ishii, Ye Jin Bang, Andrea Madotto, and Pascale Fung. 2023. Survey of hallucination in natural language generation. *ACM Computing Surveys*, 55(12):1–38.

Wojciech Kryściński, Bryan McCann, Caiming Xiong, and Richard Socher. 2020. Evaluating the factual consistency of abstractive text summarization. In *Proceedings of the 2020 Conference on Empirical Methods in Natural Language Processing (EMNLP)*, pages 9332–9346, Online. Association for Computational Linguistics.

Zhenhao Liu, Haoran Xu, and Huan Sun. 2022. Fine-grained fact verification with supervised contrastive learning. In *Findings of the Association for Computational Linguistics: EMNLP 2022*, pages 1235–1247. Association for Computational Linguistics.

Joshua Maynez, Shashi Narayan, Bernd Bohnet, and Ryan McDonald. 2020. On faithfulness and factuality in abstractive summarization. In *Proceedings of the 58th Annual Meeting of the Association for Computational Linguistics (ACL)*, pages 1906–1919, Online. Association for Computational Linguistics.

Aaron van den Oord, Yazhe Li, and Oriol Vinyals. 2018. Representation learning with contrastive predictive coding. In *arXiv preprint arXiv:1807.03748*.

OpenAI. 2023. Gpt-4 technical report. ArXiv:2303.08774.

Florian Schroff, Dmitry Kalenichenko, and James Philbin. 2015. Facenet: A unified embedding for face recognition and clustering. In *Proceedings of the IEEE Conference on Computer Vision and Pattern Recognition (CVPR)*, pages 815–823.

Weizhe Shi, Shijie Wu, Xinyun Chen, and Xiang Ren. 2023. Replug: Retrieval-augmented black-box language models. In *Proceedings of the 61st Annual Meeting of the Association for Computational Linguistics (ACL)*, pages 1600–1618. Association for Computational Linguistics.

Romal Thoppilan, Daniel De Freitas, Jamie Hall, Noam Shazeer, Apoorv Kulshreshtha, Heng-Tze Cheng, Alicia Jin, Taylor Bos, Leslie Baker, Yu Du, YaGuang Li, Hongrae Lee, Huaixiu Steven Zheng, Amin Ghafouri, Marcelo Menegali, Yanping Huang, Maxim Krikun, Dmitry Lepikhin, James Qin, Dehao Chen, Yuanzhong Xu, Zhifeng Chen, Adam Roberts, Maarten Bosma, Vincent Zhao, Yanqi Zhou, Chung-Ching Chang, Igor Krivokon, Will Rusch, Marc Pickett, Pranesh Srinivasan, Laichee Man, Kathleen Meier-Hellstern, Meredith Ringel Morris, Tulsee Doshi, Renelito Delos Santos, Toju Duke, Johnny Soraker, Ben Zevenbergen, Vinodkumar Prabhakaran, Mark Diaz, Ben Hutchinson, Kristen Olson, Alejandra Molina, Erin Hoffman-John, Josh Lee, Lora Aroyo, Ravi Rajakumar, Alena Butryna, Matthew Lamm, Viktoriya Kuzmina, Joe Fenton, Aaron Cohen, Rachel Bernstein, Ray Kurzweil, Blaise Aguera-Arcas, Claire Cui, Marian Croak, Ed Chi, and Quoc Le. 2022. Lamda: Language models for dialog applications.

Xuanji Yuan, Tao Shen, Shawn Tan, and Min-Yen Kan. 2022. Improving biomedical question answering via contrastive learning in biobert. In *Proceedings of the 21st Workshop on Biomedical Language Processing (BioNLP)*, pages 156–167. Association for Computational Linguistics.

A Additional Training Statistics

To assess the stability of our optimisation procedure, we repeated each model training five times with different random seeds and report the best-checkpoint macro F_1.

A.1 Sub-task 1

Table 5 summarises statistics for the coarse-grained results.

Statistic	Macro F_1
Mean	0.628
Standard deviation	0.004

Table 5: Validation macro F_1 across five independent training runs for Sub-task 1.

A.2 Sub-task 2

Table 6 reports statistics for the fine-grained, eight-class setting.

Statistic	Macro F_1
Mean	0.632
Standard deviation	0.012

Table 6: Validation macro F_1 across five independent training runs for Sub-task 2.

A.3 Training Dynamics Sub-task 1

Figure 3 illustrates macro F_1 evolution across epochs, while Figure 4 shows per-class F_1 trajectories.

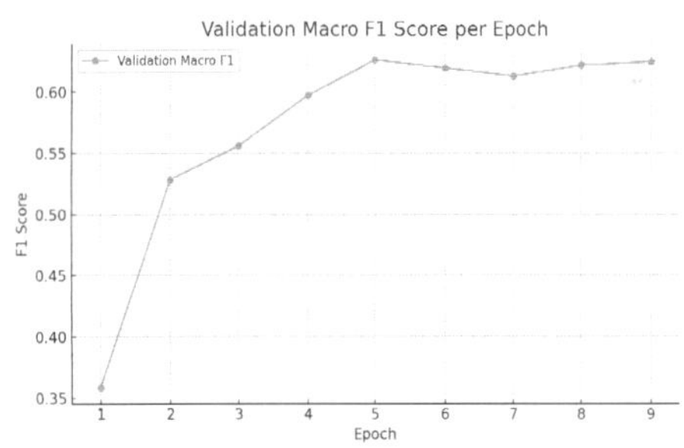

Figure 3: Macro F_1 Score Evolution

A.4 Training Dynamics Sub-task 2

Figure 5 presents macro F1 evolution across training epochs, while Figure 6 illustrates per-class F1 trajectories for representative categories.

B SciBERT Baseline (No Contrastive Learning or Class Weights)

To establish an absolute reference point, we fine-tuned a vanilla SciBERT model using only the cross-entropy objective and *no* class weighting or

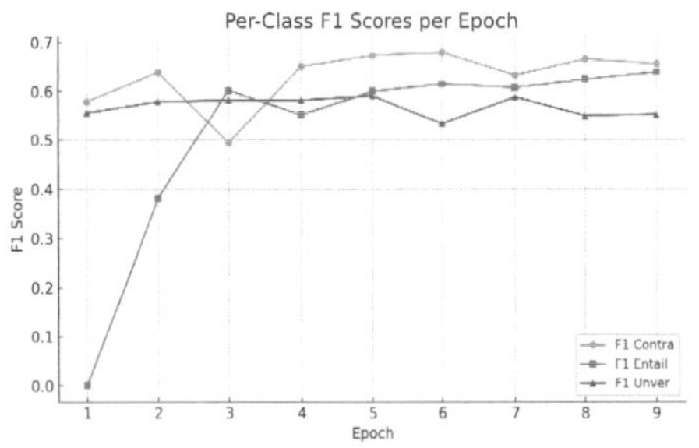

Figure 4: Per-Class F_1 Score Evolution

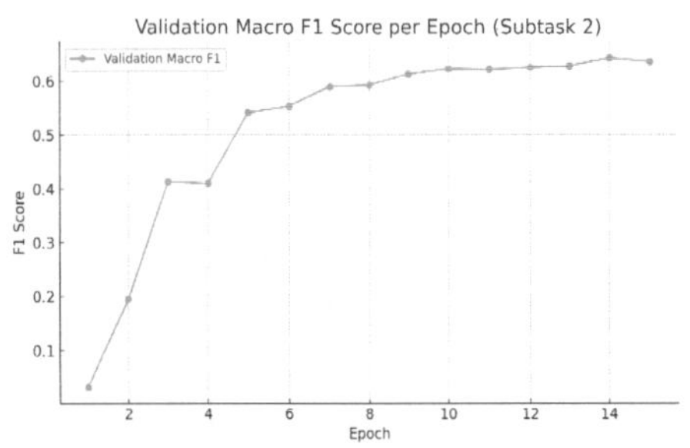

Figure 5: Validation Macro F1 Score Evolution (Sub-task 2)

contrastive losses. Training was performed with early stopping (maximum 10 epochs) and a learning rate of 2×10^{-5}. Table 7 reports the resulting macro-F_1 scores, while Figures 7 and 8 show the corresponding confusion matrices. Overall, our final approach using class weighting and contrastive loss seems to obtain improvements compared to the baseline for most classes, while the most notable difference is in the rare classes, such as *Missing Information*, for which the simple baseline does not manage to classify almost any examples correctly.

	Macro F_1	
	Sub-task 1	Sub-task 2
SciBERT (baseline)	0.601	0.586

Table 7: Validation macro F_1 for the SciBERT baseline trained without contrastive objectives or class weighting.

B.1 Confusion Matrix for SciBERT Baseline for Sub-task 1.

Figure 7 shows the confusion matrix of the vanilla SciBERT baseline, which yields a validation macro-F_1 of 0.601 on Sub-task 1.

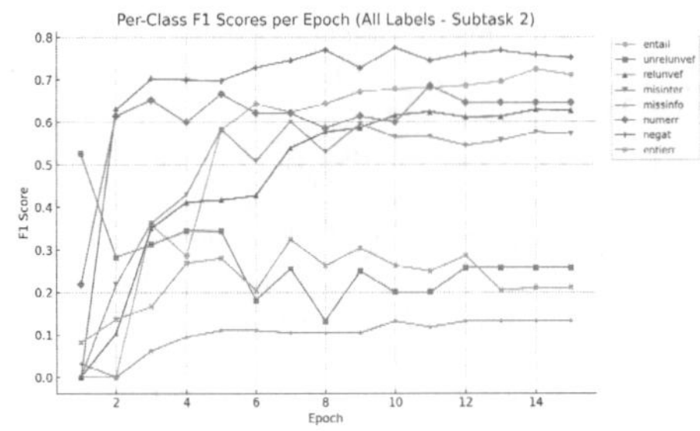

Figure 6: Per-Class F1 Score (Sub-task 2)

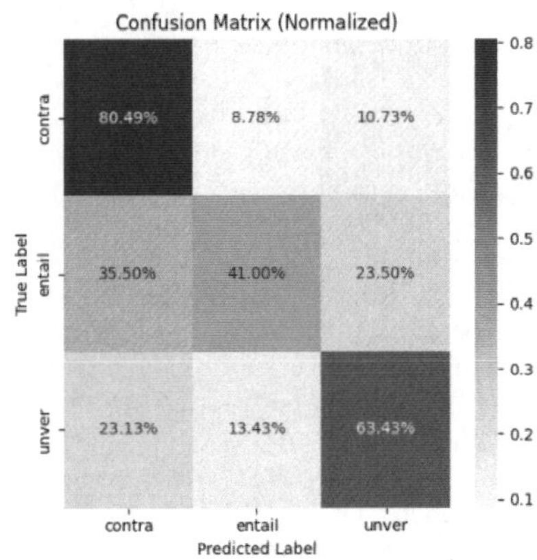

Figure 7: Confusion matrix for the SciBERT baseline on Sub-task 1 (validation macro-$F_1 = 0.601$).

B.2 Confusion Matrix for SciBERT Baseline for Sub-task 2.

Figure 8 displays the confusion matrix of the SciBERT baseline, which attains a validation macro-F_1 of 0.586 on Sub-task 2.

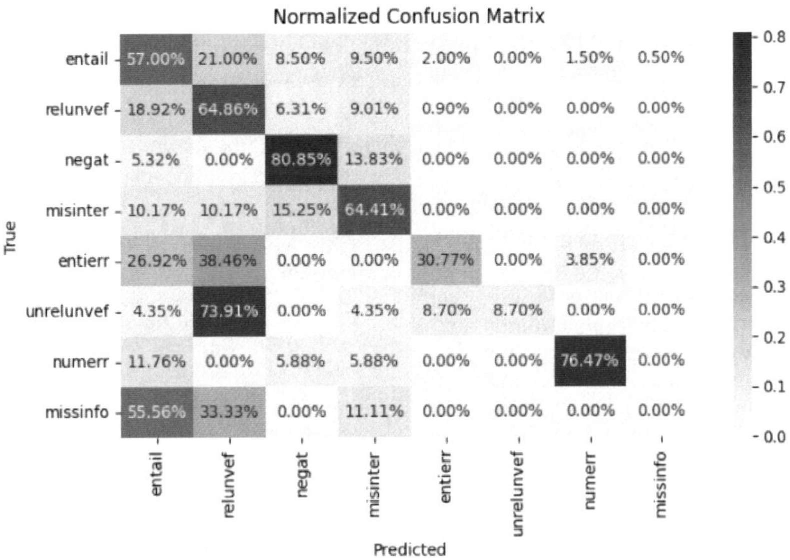

Figure 8: Confusion matrix for the SciBERT baseline on Sub-task 2 (validation macro-$F_1 = 0.586$).

Natural Language Inference Fine-tuning for Scientific Hallucination Detection

Tim Schopf♠, Juraj Vladika◇, Michael Färber♠, and Florian Matthes◇
♠ScaDS.AI & Dresden University of Technology
◇Technical University of Munich
{tim.schopf,michael.faerber}@tu-dresden.de
{juraj.vladika,matthes}@tum.de

Abstract

Modern generative Large Language Models (LLMs) are capable of generating text that sounds coherent and convincing, but are also prone to producing *hallucinations*, facts that contradict the world knowledge. Even in the case of Retrieval-Augmented Generation (RAG) systems, where relevant context is first retrieved and passed in the input, the generated facts can contradict or not be verifiable by the provided references. This has motivated SciHal 2025, a shared task that focuses on the detection of hallucinations for scientific content. The two sub-tasks focused on: (1) predicting whether a claim from a generated LLM answer is entailed, contradicted, or unverifiable by the used references; (2) predicting a fine-grained category of erroneous claims. Our best performing approach used an ensemble of fine-tuned encoder-only ModernBERT and DeBERTa-v3 models for classification. Out of nine competing teams, our approach achieved the first place in sub-task 1 and the second place in sub-task 2.

1 Introduction

The increasing availability of academic research assistants based on Large Language Models (LLMs) have revolutionized the way research is conducted, enabling users to pose research-related questions in natural language and receive structured and concise summaries supported by relevant references (Eger et al., 2025; Schmidgall et al., 2025). These systems have the potential to greatly accelerate the research process, facilitating the discovery of new knowledge and insights (Schopf and Matthes, 2024). However, the tendency of LLMs to introduce *hallucinations* – claims that are not supported or grounded in relevant evidence or established world knowledge – poses a significant challenge to the reliability of these automatically generated scientific answers (Huang et al., 2025b). Hallucinations can lead to the dissemination of misinformation, undermining the validity of research findings and the trustworthiness of AI-powered research tools (Huang et al., 2024).

To address this issue, the SciHal shared task was established, focusing on the detection of hallucinated claims in answers generated by AI-powered research assistants. The task provides a dataset of research-oriented questions, the corresponding answers and references, annotated with labels indicating the presence and type of hallucinations. By developing systems that can accurately detect hallucinations, researchers can take a crucial step towards ensuring the reliability and trustworthiness of AI-enhanced research assistants.

In response to this challenge, we developed an approach using an ensemble of fine-tuned encoder-only models DeBERTa-v3 and ModernBERT. This approach achieved the first place on sub-task 1. This paper describes our model architecture, training procedure, and results on the shared task. The performance of our approach on the task demonstrates the potential of machine learning models to identify hallucinations and improve the accuracy of generated answers. We outline our findings, challenges, and directions for future improvements.

2 Related work

Hallucinations in LLMs refer to the generation of fluent but factually incorrect or inconsistent claims (Ji et al., 2023; Zhang et al., 2023; Sahoo et al., 2024; Huang et al., 2025a; Xu et al., 2025). Factual hallucinations are outputs that deviate from real-world facts and can be addressed through fact-checking, which verifies the accuracy of claims (Guo et al., 2022; Sahnan et al., 2025). Manual fact checking is labor intensive and time consuming (Hassan et al., 2015), prompting research into automated approaches.

These approaches typically involve broad classifications (e.g., supported, refuted, not enough infor-

Proceedings of the Fifth Workshop on Scholarly Document Processing (SDP 2025), pages 344–352
July 31, 2025

mation), limiting their applicability in real-world scenarios (Vladika and Matthes, 2023a). To improve utility, finer-grained classification schemes have been proposed, reflecting degrees of truthfulness (Wang, 2017; Alhindi et al., 2018, *inter alia*). Some methods retain original fact-checking labels (Augenstein et al., 2019), while others consolidate categories for simplicity (Hanselowski et al., 2019; Kotonya and Toni, 2020; Gupta and Srikumar, 2021). Typically, scientific text classification is conducted in a supervised manner (Sadat and Caragea, 2022; E. Mendoza et al., 2022; Schopf et al., 2023), while some approaches support scenarios where labeled training data is scarce (Shen et al., 2018; Toney and Dunham, 2022; Schopf et al., 2024). Final claim veracity prediction is often modeled as a Natural Language Inference (NLI) task, where a relation between a premise and a hypothesis (entailment, contradiction, neutral) must be predicted (Vladika and Matthes, 2023b; Laurer et al., 2024). This paper investigates two sub-tasks: one using coarse-grained labels and another with finer-grained classifications to assess whether an LLM generated claim is a hallucination, given reference evidence.

3 Task Description

The SciHal 2025 shared task addresses the critical challenge of factual inconsistency in responses generated by generative AI-powered academic research assistants. SciHal formulates this problem as a classification task, focused on evaluating the factual alignment between individual claims and their supporting evidence. Given a research-focused question, an LLM generated response from a Retrieval-Augmented Generation (RAG) system, an extracted claim from the response, and a reference retrieved from a large corpus of scientific literature that is used to ground the generated response, the objective is to classify the claim based on its factual consistency with the provided reference. SciHal 2025 is structured into two sub-tasks:

Sub-task 1 involves coarse-grained classification of each claim into one of three categories: *Entailment*, *Unverifiable*, or *Contradiction*.

Sub-task 2 extends this formulation by employing a fine-grained label set. Each claim must be categorized as one of the following: *Entailment*, *Unrelated and unverifiable*, *Related but unverifiable*, *Misrepresentation*, *Missing information*, *Numeric error*, *Entity error*, or *Opposite meaning*.

4 Dataset

The SciHal dataset comprises labeled claims designed to evaluate hallucination detection in scientific assistant outputs. The data creation process involves both real and synthetic components, ensuring a diverse and balanced distribution of hallucination types.

Data Collection Over 50,000 real-user queries were collected from a live academic assistant system over a week. These questions focused on the five scientific fields Engineering, Environmental Science, Medicine, Agricultural and Biological Sciences, and Computer Science. After de-identification and refinement, 500 questions were retained. For each question, a RAG system indexed over a million scientific abstracts to retrieve the top 20 most relevant documents. The system then generated an answer, from which individual claims were extracted. Each claim was paired with the retrieved references used to justify the answer.

Synthetic Hallucination Generation To balance the dataset across hallucination types, 75% of the claims were synthetically modified using LLM prompting, simulating errors aligned with the classification labels. This method ensured controlled type distributions, where entailment accounts for less than 25% and other types each account for under 10% of the labels.

Annotation Process The annotation process for the dataset was conducted through subject matter experts (SMEs). SMEs received the claims, references, and detailed guidelines, including definitions of hallucination types, a decision tree, and a trial phase to ensure they were aligned with the task's requirements and labeling standards. To strike a balance between annotation quality and cost, both human SME annotations and an internal LLM-based hallucination detection method were used. The data was released in following batches:

- Batch 1 & 2: Instances where SME and LLM labels agreed. Batch 1 is a subset of Batch 2.
- Batch 3 & Test Set: In cases where SME and LLM labels disagreed, the claim was relabeled by a second SME. To resolve any remaining discrepancies, a third SME was involved in adjudicating the label.

5 Approaches

To identify hallucinated claims, we explore a range of approaches spanning zero-shot prompting and supervised fine-tuning, leveraging both encoder-only and decoder-only models.

DeepSeek-R1 Zero-shot We use the DeepSeek-R1 model (DeepSeek-AI et al., 2025) in a zero-shot setting to classify claims into predefined categories using the associated reference as supporting evidence. The prompt includes a task definition and detailed descriptions of each classification label. The full prompt is provided in Figure 1.

DeepSeek-R1 Zero-shot with Claim Decomposition Building on the basic zero-shot setup, we extend the prompting strategy by explicitly instructing DeepSeek-R1 to first decompose the claim into its constituent subclaims. The model then classifies each subclaim individually and aggregates the results into a final prediction for the full claim. This decomposition aims to enhance reasoning granularity. The corresponding prompt is in Figure 2.

GPT-4o Zero-shot We evaluate GPT-4o (OpenAI et al., 2023) using the same zero-shot prompt as above (Figure 1). To mitigate variance stemming from the non-deterministic behavior of the model, we generate ten independent predictions per input and derive the final class prediction via majority voting. This ensemble-like setup enhances prediction stability and robustness.

DeBERTa-v3 Fine-tuning We fine-tune a DeBERTa-v3 large model (He et al., 2023)[1], pretrained on several Natural Language Inference (NLI) datasets including MultiNLI (Williams et al., 2018), Fever-NLI (Nie et al., 2019), Adversarial-NLI (Nie et al., 2020), LingNLI (Parrish et al., 2021), and WANLI (Liu et al., 2022), comprising a total of 885,242 hypothesis-premise pairs. We also evaluate a DeBERTa-v3 base variant[2] fine-tuned on the *tasksource* dataset (Sileo, 2024). For both models, we experiment with different fine-tuning data configurations: using batch 2, batch 3, and their combination.

ModernBERT Fine-tuning We also experiment with ModernBERT[3] (Warner et al., 2024), a recent improved and optimized version of BERT (Devlin et al., 2019). We again use the version previously trained on *tasksource* data and fine-tune it on batches 2 and 3.

Ensemble We investigate an ensemble approach, where predictions of three fine-tuned encoder-only models that performed well on the leaderboard are combined using majority voting. This includes DeBERTa-v3 NLI (batch 3) and ModernBERT Tasksource (batches 2+3 & batch 3).

Llama Fine-tuning To investigate the potential of a decoder-only model, we fine-tune LLama3.1-8B-Instruct (Grattafiori et al., 2024). We train the model to generate the label annotation justifications contained in the training data before predicting the classification labels. This approach ensures that the model explicitly thinks and reasons prior to the classification. Fine-tuning is conducted exclusively on batch 3, which closely reflects the distribution of the test set.

To optimize resource usage, we initially evaluate all methods on sub-task 1. Based on the performance results, we then adapt the best-performing approach for sub-task 2.

6 Evaluation

The primary evaluation metric for the shared task is the weighted F_1 score. It is computed by calculating the F_1 score independently for each class and then taking the average, weighted by the number of true instances (support) for each class.

	Approach	F_1
prompt	DeepSeek-R1 Zero-shot	0.49
	DeepSeek-R1 Zero-shot Decompose	0.44
	GPT-4o Zero-shot	0.43
fine-tune	LLama3.1-8B-Instruct	0.50
	DeBERTa-v3 NLI (batch 2)	0.50
	DeBERTa-v3 NLI (batch 3)	0.57
	DeBERTa-v3 NLI (batch 2+3)	0.56
	DeBERTa-v3 Tasksource (batch 3)	0.50
	DeBERTa-v3 Tasksource (batch 2+3)	0.54
	ModernBERT Tasksource (batch 2+3)	0.57
	ModernBERT Tasksource (batch 3)	0.56
	Ensemble of DeBERTa NLI (batch 3), ModernBERT Taskso. (batch 2+3 & 3)	**0.60**

Table 1: Comparison of Approaches and their F_1 scores for sub-task 1 on 50% of the test data.

Each sub-task's test set comprises 1,000 examples, with 50% designated for official evaluation and leaderboard ranking during the challenge. The

[1]MoritzLaurer/DeBERTa-v3-large-mnli-fever-anli-ling-wanli

[2]tasksource/deberta-base-long-nli

[3]tasksource/ModernBERT-large-nli

remaining 50% is withheld and only evaluated after the competition concludes. Accordingly, all reported results in this paper are based on the publicly accessible 50% split of the respective test sets.

As shown in Table 1, fine-tuning the DeBERTa-v3 NLI and ModernBERT models achieves good results. When combined in an ensemble, this achieves the winning score of 0.60 on sub-task 1. For sub-task 2, we use DeBERTa-v3 NLI fine-tuned on batch 3, where it achieves a F_1 score of 0.50 and secures second place on the leaderboard.

7 Discussion

Our findings show that the dataset poses a considerable challenge and that fine-tuned models clearly outperform prompting-based approaches. Notably, the smaller encoder-only DeBERTa-v3 and ModernBERT models achieve better results than much larger decoder-only LLMs. Despite their scale, LLMs such as DeepSeek-R1 and GPT-4o struggle in prompting setups compared to fine-tuned ModernBERT and DeBERTa-v3 variants.

Interestingly, advanced prompting techniques, such as claim decomposition, do not improve classification performance. In fact, they often underperform compared to simpler zero-shot prompting. To understand this behavior, we perform a detailed analysis of both the dataset and the prediction behaviors of the model.

We observe that the test sets are inherently difficult due to the way they were constructed: they include only those instances where initial predictions by SMEs and LLMs diverged. These disagreements were later resolved by a third SME. However, the data annotations remain often ambiguous, inconsistent, and challenging. During our manual inspection, we identified multiple very similar instances with different labels. Inconsistent labels were particularly common in examples annotated as unverifiable (unver) or contradiction (contra). For instance, claims that involved information not present in the reference were sometimes labeled 'contra' and other times 'unver', even when the annotation justification was nearly identical.

Prompt-based approaches are particularly affected by this inconsistency. Given that prompts contain fixed class definitions, the models tend to adhere to those instructions. For instance, when claim content is missing from the reference, LLMs frequently predict 'unver', aligning with the prompt's class description, although the example is labeled as 'contra'. We also identified inconsistencies in the annotation of entailment (entail) cases. Some instances were labeled as 'entail' only when the claim's content was explicitly stated in the reference, while others were labeled 'entail' even when the reference only implicitly supported the claim through inference. However, the instructions provided in the prompt resulted in the LLM to rely strictly on explicit information and often misclassified such implicit entailment examples as 'unver'. Internal validation supports these observations: all prompting-based approaches demonstrated particularly low precision for the 'unver' class.

Contrary to our expectations, decomposing claims into subclaims did not improve performance. In fact, this led to overly conservative predictions. For example, the model would identify one unsupported detail within a claim and classify the entire example accordingly, even when the overall meaning was supported. The annotators, by contrast, appeared to take a more holistic view, labeling a claim as entailment based on general alignment, even when minor details were not mentioned.

Overall, these findings suggest that prompting-based methods lack the flexibility required to handle the annotation noise and implicit reasoning present in the dataset. In contrast, fine-tuned models can better adapt to such irregularities, likely because they learn implicit patterns and labeling conventions from the training data.

Finally, the strong performance of smaller encoder-only models highlights the importance of task-specific training. The ModernBERT and DeBERTa-v3 models were already trained on a diverse set of NLI datasets, whereas the Llama3.1-8B-Instruct model was not. This likely gave the smaller models a major advantage, suggesting that task-specific training on relevant datasets can outweigh model scale for downstream performance.

8 Future work

In future work, we aim to further improve the fine-tuning process of decoder-only language models considering their vast world knowledge and reasoning capabilities. Given that we achieved the best result using an ensemble, we additionally aim to experiment more with advanced ensembles and committee voting techniques, including the introduction of weighting mechanisms. Finally, we plan to incorporate hierarchical classification in the form of multi-step predictions for sub-task 2 involving fine-grained labels.

9 Conclusion

We presented fine-tuning approaches based on ModernBERT and DeBERTa-v3 that consistently outperformed baseline methods and other submitted solutions. This success is largely attributable to prior training on extensive NLI datasets, which closely align with the nature of the target tasks. Notably, the same approach demonstrates strong performance on both sub-task 1 and sub-task 2, underscoring its generalizability across related tasks.

Our findings further suggest that in scenarios where the data is inherently challenging—due to ambiguity or inconsistent labeling, fine-tuning offers a clear advantage over prompt-based LLM approaches. While prompting yields consistent predictions based on static label definitions, it lacks the flexibility to adapt to subtle patterns and inconsistencies in the data. In contrast, fine-tuned models are better able to internalize such nuances.

Moreover, our results highlight the importance of training on data that closely resembles the target task. Models exposed to large volumes of relevant data prior to task-specific fine-tuning consistently achieve superior downstream performance. Notably, this results in smaller models using this strategy outperforming larger models that lack similar task-aligned training.

References

Tariq Alhindi, Savvas Petridis, and Smaranda Muresan. 2018. Where is your evidence: Improving fact-checking by justification modeling. In *Proceedings of the First Workshop on Fact Extraction and VERification (FEVER)*, pages 85–90, Brussels, Belgium. Association for Computational Linguistics.

Isabelle Augenstein, Christina Lioma, Dongsheng Wang, Lucas Chaves Lima, Casper Hansen, Christian Hansen, and Jakob Grue Simonsen. 2019. MultiFC: A real-world multi-domain dataset for evidence-based fact checking of claims. In *Proceedings of the 2019 Conference on Empirical Methods in Natural Language Processing and the 9th International Joint Conference on Natural Language Processing (EMNLP-IJCNLP)*, pages 4685–4697, Hong Kong, China. Association for Computational Linguistics.

DeepSeek-AI, Daya Guo, Dejian Yang, Haowei Zhang, Junxiao Song, Ruoyu Zhang, Runxin Xu, Qihao Zhu, Shirong Ma, Peiyi Wang, Xiao Bi, Xiaokang Zhang, Xingkai Yu, Yu Wu, Z. F. Wu, Zhibin Gou, Zhihong Shao, Zhuoshu Li, Ziyi Gao, and 181 others. 2025. Deepseek-r1: Incentivizing reasoning capability in llms via reinforcement learning. *Preprint*, arXiv:2501.12948.

Jacob Devlin, Ming-Wei Chang, Kenton Lee, and Kristina Toutanova. 2019. BERT: Pre-training of deep bidirectional transformers for language understanding. In *Proceedings of the 2019 Conference of the North American Chapter of the Association for Computational Linguistics: Human Language Technologies, Volume 1 (Long and Short Papers)*, pages 4171–4186, Minneapolis, Minnesota. Association for Computational Linguistics.

Óscar E. Mendoza, Wojciech Kusa, Alaa El-Ebshihy, Ronin Wu, David Pride, Petr Knoth, Drahomira Herrmannova, Florina Piroi, Gabriella Pasi, and Allan Hanbury. 2022. Benchmark for research theme classification of scholarly documents. In *Proceedings of the Third Workshop on Scholarly Document Processing*, pages 253–262, Gyeongju, Republic of Korea. Association for Computational Linguistics.

Steffen Eger, Yong Cao, Jennifer D'Souza, Andreas Geiger, Christian Greisinger, Stephanie Gross, Yufang Hou, Brigitte Krenn, Anne Lauscher, Yizhi Li, Chenghua Lin, Nafise Sadat Moosavi, Wei Zhao, and Tristan Miller. 2025. Transforming science with large language models: A survey on ai-assisted scientific discovery, experimentation, content generation, and evaluation. *Preprint*, arXiv:2502.05151.

Aaron Grattafiori, Abhimanyu Dubey, Abhinav Jauhri, Abhinav Pandey, Abhishek Kadian, Ahmad Al-Dahle, Aiesha Letman, Akhil Mathur, Alan Schelten, Alex Vaughan, Amy Yang, Angela Fan, Anirudh Goyal, Anthony Hartshorn, Aobo Yang, Archi Mitra, Archie Sravankumar, Artem Korenev, Arthur Hinsvark, and 542 others. 2024. The llama 3 herd of models. *Preprint*, arXiv:2407.21783.

Zhijiang Guo, Michael Schlichtkrull, and Andreas Vlachos. 2022. A survey on automated fact-checking. *Transactions of the Association for Computational Linguistics*, 10:178–206.

Ashim Gupta and Vivek Srikumar. 2021. X-fact: A new benchmark dataset for multilingual fact checking. In *Proceedings of the 59th Annual Meeting of the Association for Computational Linguistics and the 11th International Joint Conference on Natural Language Processing (Volume 2: Short Papers)*, pages 675–682, Online. Association for Computational Linguistics.

Andreas Hanselowski, Christian Stab, Claudia Schulz, Zile Li, and Iryna Gurevych. 2019. A richly annotated corpus for different tasks in automated fact-checking. In *Proceedings of the 23rd Conference on Computational Natural Language Learning (CoNLL)*, pages 493–503, Hong Kong, China. Association for Computational Linguistics.

Naeemul Hassan, Chengkai Li, and Mark Tremayne. 2015. Detecting check-worthy factual claims in presidential debates. In *Proceedings of the 24th ACM In-*

ternational on Conference on Information and Knowledge Management, CIKM '15, page 1835–1838, New York, NY, USA. Association for Computing Machinery.

Pengcheng He, Jianfeng Gao, and Weizhu Chen. 2023. DeBERTav3: Improving deBERTa using ELECTRA-style pre-training with gradient-disentangled embedding sharing. In *The Eleventh International Conference on Learning Representations*.

Lei Huang, Weijiang Yu, Weitao Ma, Weihong Zhong, Zhangyin Feng, Haotian Wang, Qianglong Chen, Weihua Peng, Xiaocheng Feng, Bing Qin, and Ting Liu. 2025a. A survey on hallucination in large language models: Principles, taxonomy, challenges, and open questions. *ACM Trans. Inf. Syst.*, 43(2).

Lei Huang, Weijiang Yu, Weitao Ma, Weihong Zhong, Zhangyin Feng, Haotian Wang, Qianglong Chen, Weihua Peng, Xiaocheng Feng, Bing Qin, and 1 others. 2025b. A survey on hallucination in large language models: Principles, taxonomy, challenges, and open questions. *ACM Transactions on Information Systems*, 43(2):1–55.

Yue Huang, Lichao Sun, Haoran Wang, Siyuan Wu, Qihui Zhang, Yuan Li, Chujie Gao, Yixin Huang, Wenhan Lyu, Yixuan Zhang, Xiner Li, Hanchi Sun, Zhengliang Liu, Yixin Liu, Yijue Wang, Zhikun Zhang, Bertie Vidgen, Bhavya Kailkhura, Caiming Xiong, and 52 others. 2024. TrustLLM: Trustworthiness in large language models. In *Proceedings of the 41st International Conference on Machine Learning*, volume 235 of *Proceedings of Machine Learning Research*, pages 20166–20270. PMLR.

Ziwei Ji, Nayeon Lee, Rita Frieske, Tiezheng Yu, Dan Su, Yan Xu, Etsuko Ishii, Ye Jin Bang, Andrea Madotto, and Pascale Fung. 2023. Survey of hallucination in natural language generation. *ACM Comput. Surv.*, 55(12).

Neema Kotonya and Francesca Toni. 2020. Explainable automated fact-checking for public health claims. In *Proceedings of the 2020 Conference on Empirical Methods in Natural Language Processing (EMNLP)*, pages 7740–7754, Online. Association for Computational Linguistics.

Moritz Laurer, Wouter Van Atteveldt, Andreu Casas, and Kasper Welbers. 2024. Less annotating, more classifying: Addressing the data scarcity issue of supervised machine learning with deep transfer learning and bert-nli. *Political Analysis*, 32(1):84–100.

Alisa Liu, Swabha Swayamdipta, Noah A. Smith, and Yejin Choi. 2022. WANLI: Worker and AI collaboration for natural language inference dataset creation. In *Findings of the Association for Computational Linguistics: EMNLP 2022*, pages 6826–6847, Abu Dhabi, United Arab Emirates. Association for Computational Linguistics.

Yixin Nie, Haonan Chen, and Mohit Bansal. 2019. Combining fact extraction and verification with neural semantic matching networks. In *Association for the Advancement of Artificial Intelligence (AAAI)*.

Yixin Nie, Adina Williams, Emily Dinan, Mohit Bansal, Jason Weston, and Douwe Kiela. 2020. Adversarial nli: A new benchmark for natural language understanding. In *Proceedings of the 58th Annual Meeting of the Association for Computational Linguistics*. Association for Computational Linguistics.

OpenAI, Josh Achiam, Steven Adler, Sandhini Agarwal, Lama Ahmad, Ilge Akkaya, Florencia Leoni Aleman, Diogo Almeida, Janko Altenschmidt, Sam Altman, Shyamal Anadkat, Red Avila, Igor Babuschkin, Suchir Balaji, Valerie Balcom, Paul Baltescu, Haiming Bao, Mohammad Bavarian, Jeff Belgum, and 262 others. 2023. Gpt-4 technical report. *Preprint*, arXiv:2303.08774.

Alicia Parrish, William Huang, Omar Agha, Soo-Hwan Lee, Nikita Nangia, Alexia Warstadt, Karmanya Aggarwal, Emily Allaway, Tal Linzen, and Samuel R. Bowman. 2021. Does putting a linguist in the loop improve NLU data collection? In *Findings of the Association for Computational Linguistics: EMNLP 2021*, pages 4886–4901, Punta Cana, Dominican Republic. Association for Computational Linguistics.

Mobashir Sadat and Cornelia Caragea. 2022. Hierarchical multi-label classification of scientific documents. In *Proceedings of the 2022 Conference on Empirical Methods in Natural Language Processing*, pages 8923–8937, Abu Dhabi, United Arab Emirates. Association for Computational Linguistics.

Dhruv Sahnan, David Corney, Irene Larraz, Giovanni Zagni, Ruben Miguez, Zhuohan Xie, Iryna Gurevych, Elizabeth Churchill, Tanmoy Chakraborty, and Preslav Nakov. 2025. Can llms automate fact-checking article writing? *Preprint*, arXiv:2503.17684.

Pranab Sahoo, Prabhash Meharia, Akash Ghosh, Sriparna Saha, Vinija Jain, and Aman Chadha. 2024. A comprehensive survey of hallucination in large language, image, video and audio foundation models. In *Findings of the Association for Computational Linguistics: EMNLP 2024*, pages 11709–11724, Miami, Florida, USA. Association for Computational Linguistics.

Samuel Schmidgall, Yusheng Su, Ze Wang, Ximeng Sun, Jialian Wu, Xiaodong Yu, Jiang Liu, Zicheng Liu, and Emad Barsoum. 2025. Agent laboratory: Using llm agents as research assistants. *arXiv preprint arXiv:2501.04227*.

Tim Schopf, Karim Arabi, and Florian Matthes. 2023. Exploring the landscape of natural language processing research. In *Proceedings of the 14th International Conference on Recent Advances in Natural Language Processing*, pages 1034–1045, Varna, Bulgaria. INCOMA Ltd., Shoumen, Bulgaria.

Tim Schopf, Alexander Blatzheim, Nektarios Machner, and Florian Matthes. 2024. Efficient few-shot learning for multi-label classification of scientific documents with many classes. In *Proceedings of the 7th International Conference on Natural Language and Speech Processing (ICNLSP 2024)*, pages 186–198, Trento. Association for Computational Linguistics.

Tim Schopf and Florian Matthes. 2024. NLP-KG: A system for exploratory search of scientific literature in natural language processing. In *Proceedings of the 62nd Annual Meeting of the Association for Computational Linguistics (Volume 3: System Demonstrations)*, pages 127–135, Bangkok, Thailand. Association for Computational Linguistics.

Zhihong Shen, Hao Ma, and Kuansan Wang. 2018. A web-scale system for scientific knowledge exploration. In *Proceedings of ACL 2018, System Demonstrations*, pages 87–92, Melbourne, Australia. Association for Computational Linguistics.

Damien Sileo. 2024. tasksource: A large collection of NLP tasks with a structured dataset preprocessing framework. In *Proceedings of the 2024 Joint International Conference on Computational Linguistics, Language Resources and Evaluation (LREC-COLING 2024)*, pages 15655–15684, Torino, Italia. ELRA and ICCL.

Autumn Toney and James Dunham. 2022. Multi-label classification of scientific research documents across domains and languages. In *Proceedings of the Third Workshop on Scholarly Document Processing*, pages 105–114, Gyeongju, Republic of Korea. Association for Computational Linguistics.

Juraj Vladika and Florian Matthes. 2023a. Scientific fact-checking: A survey of resources and approaches. In *Findings of the Association for Computational Linguistics: ACL 2023*, pages 6215–6230, Toronto, Canada. Association for Computational Linguistics.

Juraj Vladika and Florian Matthes. 2023b. Sebis at SemEval-2023 task 7: A joint system for natural language inference and evidence retrieval from clinical trial reports. In *Proceedings of the 17th International Workshop on Semantic Evaluation (SemEval-2023)*, pages 1863–1870, Toronto, Canada. Association for Computational Linguistics.

William Yang Wang. 2017. "liar, liar pants on fire": A new benchmark dataset for fake news detection. In *Proceedings of the 55th Annual Meeting of the Association for Computational Linguistics (Volume 2: Short Papers)*, pages 422–426, Vancouver, Canada. Association for Computational Linguistics.

Benjamin Warner, Antoine Chaffin, Benjamin Clavié, Orion Weller, Oskar Hallström, Said Taghadouini, Alexis Gallagher, Raja Biswas, Faisal Ladhak, Tom Aarsen, Nathan Cooper, Griffin Adams, Jeremy Howard, and Iacopo Poli. 2024. Smarter, better, faster, longer: A modern bidirectional encoder for fast, memory efficient, and long context finetuning and inference. *Preprint*, arXiv:2412.13663.

Adina Williams, Nikita Nangia, and Samuel Bowman. 2018. A broad-coverage challenge corpus for sentence understanding through inference. In *Proceedings of the 2018 Conference of the North American Chapter of the Association for Computational Linguistics: Human Language Technologies, Volume 1 (Long Papers)*, pages 1112–1122. Association for Computational Linguistics.

Ziwei Xu, Sanjay Jain, and Mohan Kankanhalli. 2025. Hallucination is inevitable: An innate limitation of large language models. *Preprint*, arXiv:2401.11817.

Yue Zhang, Yafu Li, Leyang Cui, Deng Cai, Lemao Liu, Tingchen Fu, Xinting Huang, Enbo Zhao, Yu Zhang, Yulong Chen, Longyue Wang, Anh Tuan Luu, Wei Bi, Freda Shi, and Shuming Shi. 2023. Siren's song in the ai ocean: A survey on hallucination in large language models. *Preprint*, arXiv:2309.01219.

A Appendix

The appendix shows the prompts used for classification, including the simple zero-shot prompt (Figure 1 and the prompt for subclaim decomposition and aggregated prediction (Figure 2).

Simple Zero-shot Prompt

```
Determine whether the provided claim is entailed by the corresponding evidence
. Entailment in this context implies that all information presented in the
claim is substantiated by the evidence. If any information in the claim is
contradicted by at least one information in the evidence, the claim is
contradicted. If the claim is neither entailed nor contradicted by the
evidence, the claim is unverifiable.

Evidence: {reference}
Claim: {claim}

Assess the claim's entailment with the evidence by predicting either 'entail'
for entailment, 'contra' for contradication, or 'unver' for unverifiable.
Explain your decision and afterwards provide your prediction in JSON format as
 one of the options {'prediction': 'entail'}, {'prediction': 'contra'}, {'
prediction': 'unver'}.
```

Figure 1: Simple zero-shot prompt to instruct an LLM to detect a hallucinated claim.

Zero-shot Claim Decomposition Prompt

```
Instruction:
Decompose the claim into its individual subclaims (e.g., distinct factual
assertions or components). For each subclaim, determine whether it is entailed
, contradicted, or unverifiable based on the provided evidence. Use the
following criteria:

Entail (entail): All information presented in the subclaims are substantiated
by the evidence. Usually, this means that the information is directly included
 in the evidence. However, a subclaim can also be entailed if the evidence can
 be used to infer the subclaim.
Contradiction (contra): At least one piece of evidence explicitly contradicts
the subclaim. Contradiction in this sense also means that a claim mentions one
 thing, but the evidence only supports the claim's statement regarding a
different thing. Or it could be a contradiction (instead of unverifiably) if a
 claim is overgeneralized, oversimplified, or overstates the evidence.
Unverifiable (unver): The subclaim is neither supported nor contradicted by
the evidence.

After evaluating all subclaims, determine the overall prediction for the full
claim using these rules:
If any subclaim is contradicted, the overall prediction is "contra".
If all subclaims are entailed, the overall prediction is "entail".
Otherwise, the overall prediction is "unver".

Process:
Decomposition: Break the claim into subclaims (e.g., "Subclaim 1: [X].
Subclaim 2: [Y].").
Evaluation: For each subclaim, explain whether it is entailed, contradicted,
or unverifiable.
Aggregation: Combine subclaim results to determine the overall prediction.

Output Format:
Provide a detailed explanation for each subclaim and the overall prediction.

Return the final answer in JSON format with two keys:
"subclaims": A list of objects, each containing "subclaim" (text), "
justification" evaluation (text), and "prediction".
"overall_prediction": One of "entail", "contra", or "unver".
Example Output:
     {
"subclaims": [
{"subclaim": "Subclaim 1 text", "justification": "Explanation of evaluation
for sublaim 1", "prediction": "entail"},
{"subclaim": "Subclaim 2 text", "justification": "Explanation of evaluation
for sublaim 2", "prediction": "unver"}
],
"overall_prediction": "unver"
}

Evidence: {reference}
Claim: {claim}
```

Figure 2: Zero-shot prompt to instruct an LLM to decompose a claim into subclaims, predict the class of each subclaim and aggregate the predictions to one overall prediction.

From RAG to Reality: Coarse-Grained Hallucination Detection via NLI Fine-Tuning

Daria Galimzianova, Aleksandr Boriskin, Grigory Arshinov
MTS AI

Abstract

We present our submission to SciHal Subtask 1: coarse-grained hallucination detection for scientific question answering. We frame hallucination detection as an NLI-style three-way classification (entailment, contradiction, unverifiable) and show that simple fine-tuning of NLI-adapted encoder models on task data outperforms more elaborate feature-based pipelines and large language model prompting. In particular, DeBERTa-V3-large, a model pretrained on five diverse NLI corpora, achieves one of the highest weighted F1 scores on the public leaderboard. We additionally explore a pipeline combining joint claim–reference embeddings and NLI softmax probabilities fed into a classifier, but find its performance consistently below direct encoder fine-tuning. Our findings demonstrate that, for reference-grounded hallucination detection, targeted encoder fine-tuning remains a competitive approach.

1 Introduction

Generative AI assistants are increasingly utilized to produce reference-based answers in scientific and research contexts, particularly via retrieval-augmented generation (RAG) systems that combine large language models with external knowledge sources. While RAG can greatly improve factual coverage, it also introduces a critical problem: *hallucinations*, wherein the model generates claims that are unsupported or directly contradicted by the cited references. Detecting such hallucinations is essential for trustworthy scientific communication, yet remains a major challenge for evaluation pipelines.

The **SciHal** shared task on **Hallucination Detection for Scientific Content** (Li et al., 2025), organized at Workshop on Scholarly Document Processing at ACL 2025, formalizes this problem as a multi-label classification task. Given a research question, a model-generated summary, and an extracted claim, participants must determine whether each claim is *entailment*, *contradiction*, or *unverifiable* with respect to the provided reference abstracts (Subtask 1: Coarse-Grained Detection).

In this paper, we report our approach that was ranked fourth and share our experiments for SciHal Subtask 1. We explore three families of approaches:

1. **Cross-Encoder Fine-Tuning**: We adapt NLI-pretrained encoders (most notably DeBERTa-v3) directly on the Subtask 1 training data, achieving a competitive score of weighted F1 (0.58).

2. **Feature-Based Classification Pipelines**: We experiment with semantic similarity features and NLI probability scores to train a classifier for label prediction. While more computationally intensive, these pipelines underperform relative to specialized encoder fine-tuning.

3. **LLM Prompting**: we deploy large language models like Qwen in a few-shot setting, which do not yield any promising results for the claim classification task.

Our analysis shows that among the methods listed above, *straightforward fine-tuning of an NLI-adapted encoder* yields the best performance on the task test dataset. We conclude that, for coarse-grained hallucination detection, simpler encoder-only architectures might be an efficient choice.

2 Related work

Automatic verification of factual consistency has attracted intense attention in recent years, reflecting a surge of methods and datasets devoted to achieving this goal (Li et al., 2022). Within the scientific domain, this research tradition is grounded in claim-verification datasets such as SciFact (Wadden et al., 2020) and follow-up shared tasks like SCIVER

Proceedings of the Fifth Workshop on Scholarly Document Processing (SDP 2025), pages 353–359
July 31, 2025 ©2025 Association for Computational Linguistics

(Wadden and Lo, 2021). The NAACL SCIVER scaled verification to a 5 M-abstract corpus, systems had to retrieve evidence and assign support or refute labels. All top-3 teams combined sparse retrieval with domain specific BERT-family encoders like SciBert (Beltagy et al., 2019a), BioBert (Lee et al., 2020) and Roberta (Liu et al., 2019). Recent developments (Mor-Lan and Levi, 2024) (Sankararaman et al., 2024) show that NLI cross-encoders demonstrate the ability to discern factual claims from non-factual ones given evidence. NLI is the task of determining whether a "hypothesis" text can be inferred (entailment), contradicted (contradiction), or is undetermined (neutral) from a "premise" text. NLI cross-encoders (Mor-Lan and Levi, 2024) are a natural fit for scientific claim verification because their label space: entailment, contradiction, and neutral is isomorphic to the support, refute, unverifiable taxonomy used in SciFact, SCIVER and SciHal Subtask 1, so no label remapping is required.

3 Data

The dataset is a claim-level annotated benchmark designed to measure factual correctness and hallucination detection quality in scientific RAG systems. Data was originally sourced from logs of a scientific research assistant tool. 50,000 samples were collected over one week. Organizers used an LLM to classify user questions by domain, ensuring completeness and correctness, and filtered out non-English texts.

Given the feasibility of employing subject matter experts (SMEs) for annotation, the dataset authors included texts from multiple domains: Engineering, Environmental Science, Medicine, Agricultural and Biological Sciences, and Computer Science. All questions were rewritten using an LLM, after which human annotators removed confidential or commercial information. This process yielded a refined dataset of 500 samples. Organizers then used a RAG scientific research assistant to retrieve 20 relevant article abstracts for each question. Finally, they generated answers and extracted claims with corresponding references.

To balance class distribution, the authors prompted an LLM to synthetically falsify claims. They modified 75% of samples by corrupting claims according to predefined fallacy types (for Sub-task 2), while maintaining class balance. The resulting dataset was manually verified and annotated by SMEs. This methodology ensured only 25% of samples were marked as entailment, with other classes each representing less than 10% of samples. Synthetic corruption also reduced manual annotation costs.

In the first annotation round, one SME validated samples within their domain, establishing baseline human annotations. Samples where both the LLM and SME agreed formed Batches 1 and 2. The remaining samples were annotated by a second SME. To achieve consensus, a third SME made final label decisions after reviewing justifications from prior annotators. This process improved the quality and challenge level of Batch 3 and the test set. The resulting Batch 2 (that also includes Batch 1 data), Batch 3 and test set contain 2092, 1500 and 1000 samples accordingly. Each record contains: the original question, the AI-generated answer, one or more claims (extracted from the answer), one or more references (article abstracts from the RAG tool), a label (for training sets only; three-class scheme: *entail, unver, contra*) and justification (SME reasoning for the label; training sets only).

4 Experiments

We approach this task as a pure classification problem, namely we view it as a NLI task. All three NLI labels are identical in their sense to the labels provided in the training data of this task.

Given limited time and resources, we train three groups of models. The choice of BERT-like models fine-tuned for the NLI task is intuitive, since the labels we need to predict are directly used in NLI. To test a more complicated pipeline, we train a classification model on features extracted from the data: cosine similarity scores for the embedded claims and references and probabilities for NLI classes. The third group is LLM-based: we prompt Qwen3-8B [1] to predict the labels with two examples for each class taken from the training set. The resulting scores can be found in Table 1.

4.1 BERT-based Models

We fine-tune four BERT-based models on the training data provided by the organizers. To adapt the standard NLI annotation scheme, we map the traditional NLI *neutral* label to the *unverifiable* label used in this task. Each model has been previously fine-tuned on multiple generic NLI datasets.

[1] https://huggingface.co/Qwen/Qwen3-8B

Model	F1 Weighted
BERT-based	
SciBERT-NLI	0.35
ModernBERT-base	0.56
ModernBERT-large	0.57
DeBERTa-NLI	**0.58**
Classifiers	
SciBERT + DeBERTa-NLI	0.34
SciBERT-FT + DeBERTa-NLI	0.51
Few-shot LLMs	
Qwen3 8B	0.45

Table 1: F1 weighted scores reported on the public leaderboard for various approaches.

- **SciBERT-NLI** (Beltagy et al., 2019b)[2]: Chosen for its domain-specific vocabulary and prior adaptation to scientific NLI.
- **ModernBERT-NLI** (Sileo, 2024): Built on the ModernBERT architecture, supports long contexts (up to 8 192 tokens) and trained on a blend of NLI corpora.
- **DeBERTa-V3-large-NLI** (Laurer et al., 2023)[3]: Pre-fine-tuned on over 800 k hypothesis–premise pairs, yielding the strongest performance on the leaderboard.

4.2 Classification Models

To capture richer signals from NLI models, we construct a secondary pipeline that treats NLI outputs and embedding similarities as features for a downstream classifier:

1. **Embedding Similarity.** Embed each claim and each reference abstract with SciBERT (chosen for its scientific domain fit) and compute their cosine similarity.
2. **NLI Probabilities.** Run DeBERTa-V3-large-NLI on each (reference, claim) pair and collect the softmax probabilities for entailment, contradiction, and unverifiable.
3. **Feature Concatenation.** Concatenate the cosine similarity scores and NLI probabilities into a single feature vector for each claim.
4. **CatBoost Classification.** Train a CatBoost classifier (Dorogush et al., 2018) on these feature vectors to predict the three coarse-grained labels.

We also experiment with fine-tuning SciBERT on the claim–reference classification task prior to feature extraction. In this variant, we:

- Extract `[CLS]` embeddings from the fine-tuned SciBERT model for every claim and reference.
- Recompute cosine similarities using these task-adapted embeddings.
- Apply the same CatBoost pipeline with DeBERTa-NLI probabilities.

This enhanced feature pipeline improves over the vanilla version, but still underperforms compared to direct fine-tuning of DeBERTa for Subtask 1.

4.3 Embedding Visualization

To assess whether our joint (reference, claim) embeddings capture class-discriminative structure, we computed `[CLS]` vectors from our fine-tuned SciBERT-NLI model for each claim–reference pair and aggregated them by mean. We then measured the silhouette score on these high-dimensional embeddings (silhouette = 0.0885), indicating poor cluster separation. A 2D t-SNE projection (Figure 1) further confirms that the three classes (entailment, contradiction, unverifiable) do not form well-separated clusters. This suggests that even with task-specific fine-tuning the learned embedding space may not suffice for clear, unsupervised clustering of hallucination types.

4.4 LLMs

For the LLM setting, we apply the Qwen3-8B (Yang et al., 2025) model with few-shot demonstrations per class (entail, contra, unver) drawn from the training set. Each inference prompt consists of a question, an answer, a claim and 2 references separated by `[SEP]` tokens. We evaluate Qwen3-8B only with non-thinking mode. The prompt template can be found in Figure 2.

5 Error analysis

We conduct a qualitative error analysis on a development set comprising 360 samples (10% of the training data). Table 2 presents the classification performance of the DeBERTa-V3-large model

[2] https://huggingface.co/gsarti/scibert-nli

[3] https://huggingface.co/MoritzLaurer/DeBERTa-v3-large-mnli-fever-anli-ling-wanli

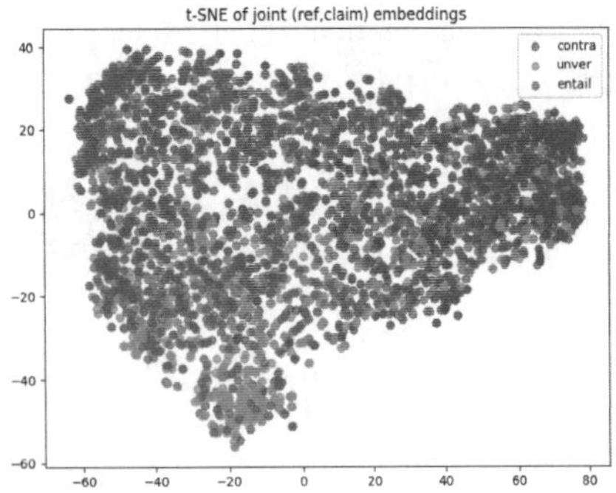

Figure 1: t-SNE projection of joint (reference, claim) embeddings from the fine-tuned SciBERT-NLI model, colored by true label (entailment, contradiction, unverifiable). The lack of well-separated clusters corroborates the low silhouette score.

fine-tuned for one epoch. The majority of errors involved confusion between the *entailment* and *unverifiable* classes, with *unverifiable* often incorrectly classified as *entailment* (32.58% of all misclassifications). This indicates that the model tends to assume textual support even in uncertain scenarios.

Class	Precision	Recall	F1	Support
Unver	0.73	0.60	0.65	89
Contra	0.84	0.82	0.83	137
Entail	0.70	0.79	0.74	134
Accuracy			0.76	360
Macro Avg	0.75	0.74	0.74	360
Weighted Avg	0.76	0.76	0.75	360

Table 2: Fine-tuned DeBERTa-V3-large model (scores on the development set).

Output Class \ Target Class	contra	entail	unver
contra	0 0%	17 37%	7 35%
entail	15 68%	0 0%	13 65%
unver	7 32%	29 63%	0 0%

Table 3: Misclassification matrix of DeBERTa-V3-large (counts).

Table 3 illustrates specific error patterns, emphasizing that misclassifications predominantly involve confusion between *entailment* and *unverifiable*. This suggests that improving the model's discrimination between supported and uncertain statements could substantially enhance performance.

We also evaluated the CatBoost-based pipeline with similarity and NLI features, which demonstrated notably lower performance (weighted F1: 0.57 on the development set), primarily due to increased confusion across classes, particularly between *contradiction* and *entailment*.

Additionally, we assessed the Qwen model, which exhibited a significantly higher error rate (43.4%) on a similar development set. The Qwen model predominantly confused *contradiction* with *entailment* and vice versa, highlighting fundamental issues in distinguishing these classes effectively. This suggests that the Qwen model requires further adaptation or training enhancements to reliably detect textual support and contradiction in scientific contexts.

Some classification examples can be found in Table 4.

6 Results

The resulting weighted F1 scores on the public leaderboard are shown in Table 1. The most efficient and highest-performing approach is simply fine-tuning NLI-adapted encoder models on the task's training data. Interestingly, DeBERTa-v3 (released in 2022 and fine-tuned on five diverse NLI datasets) outperforms the newer ModernBERT, despite the latter having seen a much larger set of NLI pairs. Our fine-tuned DeBERTa model therefore ranks fourth on the public leaderboard for Subtask 1.

By contrast, more elaborate pipelines that extract features via embeddings and NLI probability outputs incur substantial computational overhead and still underperform compared to direct cross-encoder fine-tuning.

Similarly, in-context learning with LLM that we evaluated, while a popular choice, is markedly more expensive to run and achieves lower F1 scores than the smaller, specialized encoder models.

These results resurface the importance of task-specific transfer learning and highlight the role of training data quality over multi-domain generalization abilities of a model.

```
You are a scientific claim validator for the SciHal task.
Given (1) Question, (2) Claim, (3) References (abstracts)
decide which label applies following the decision tree:
• If the paragraph is not well-formed filler → output "unver".
• Else, if claim is ENTIRELY supported by 1 abstract AND not contradicted by any other → "entail".
• Else, if claim is DIRECTLY contradicted (different number/entity/relation) → "contra".
• Else → "unver".
Return ONLY one of: entail | contra | unver
FEW_SHOT_BLOCK
Question: {row.query.strip()}
Answer snippet: {answer_snippet}
Claim: {row.claim.strip()}
References: {refs}
Label:
```

Figure 2: Prompt template used for Qwen3-8B.

7 Conclusion

We have addressed the challenging problem of coarse-grained hallucination detection in scientific question answering by framing it as a three-way NLI task (entailment, contradiction, unverifiable) on retrieved reference abstracts. We evaluated a range of methods—from simple encoder fine-tuning (SciBERT, ModernBERT, and DeBERTa-V3) to more elaborate feature-based pipelines combining joint claim–reference embeddings and NLI softmax scores, as well as few-shot prompting of large language models. Our experiments demonstrate that direct fine-tuning of an NLI-adapted cross-encoder, and in particular DeBERTa-V3-large, offers competitive accuracy in solving the hallucination detection task, achieving fourth place on the public leaderboard for SciHal Subtask 1. The modest performance of unsupervised embedding clustering and the underwhelming results of more complex pipelines underscore the inherent difficulty of reliably detecting scientific hallucinations without explicit supervision. Our findings reaffirm that, despite the task's complexity, targeted cross-encoder fine-tuning remains an effective strategy for reference-grounded hallucination detection.

8 Limitations

While our study demonstrates the strong performance of NLI–adapted cross-encoder fine-tuning for coarse-grained hallucination detection, several limitations remain:

- **Model diversity.** We evaluated a relatively small set of encoder models (SciBERT, ModernBERT, DeBERTa-V3). Exploring additional architectures, especially lighter or multilingual encoders, may yield further gains.
- **Data scale.** Although our training splits are carefully annotated and of high quality, the overall dataset remains modest in size. Larger or more varied annotated corpora could improve robustness and generalization.
- **LLM fine-tuning.** We only tested few-shot prompting of large language models. With task-specific fine-tuning and structured-output prompts (e.g. chain-of-thought templates), LLMs may ultimately surpass encoder-only approaches, at the expense of greater computational cost.

References

Iz Beltagy, Kyle Lo, and Arman Cohan. 2019a. SciBERT: A pretrained language model for scientific text. In *Proceedings of the 2019 Conference on Empirical Methods in Natural Language Processing and the 9th International Joint Conference on Natural Language Processing (EMNLP-IJCNLP)*, pages 3615–3620, Hong Kong, China. Association for Computational Linguistics.

Iz Beltagy, Kyle Lo, and Arman Cohan. 2019b. Scibert: A pretrained language model for scientific text. *arXiv preprint arXiv:1903.10676*.

Anna Veronika Dorogush, Vasily Ershov, and Andrey Gulin. 2018. Catboost: gradient boosting with categorical features support. *arXiv preprint arXiv:1810.11363*.

Moritz Laurer, Wouter Van Atteveldt, Andreu Casas, and Kasper Welbers. 2023. Less Annotating, More Classifying: Addressing the Data Scarcity Issue of Supervised Machine Learning with Deep Transfer Learning and BERT-NLI. *Political Analysis*, pages 1–33.

Jinhyuk Lee, Wonjin Yoon, Sungdong Kim, Donghyeon Kim, Sunkyu Kim, Chan Ho So, and Jaewoo Kang. 2020. Biobert: a pre-trained biomedical language representation model for biomedical text mining. *Bioinformatics*, 36(4):1234–1240.

Dan Li, Bogdan Palfi, and Colin Kehang Zhang. 2025. Hallucination detection for scientific content. `https://kaggle.com/competitions/hallucination-detection-scientific-content-2025`. Kaggle.

Wei Li, Wenhao Wu, Moye Chen, Jiachen Liu, Xinyan Xiao, and Hua Wu. 2022. Faithfulness in natural language generation: A systematic survey of analysis, evaluation and optimization methods. *arXiv preprint arXiv:2203.05227*.

Yinhan Liu, Myle Ott, Naman Goyal, Jingfei Du, Mandar Joshi, Danqi Chen, Omer Levy, Mike Lewis, Luke Zettlemoyer, and Veselin Stoyanov. 2019. Roberta: A robustly optimized bert pretraining approach. *arXiv preprint arXiv:1907.11692*.

Guy Mor-Lan and Effi Levi. 2024. Exploring factual entailment with nli: A news media study. *arXiv preprint arXiv:2406.16842*.

Hithesh Sankararaman, Mohammed Nasheed Yasin, Tanner Sorensen, Alessandro Di Bari, and Andreas Stolcke. 2024. Provenance: A light-weight fact-checker for retrieval augmented llm generation output. *arXiv preprint arXiv:2411.01022*.

Damien Sileo. 2024. tasksource: A large collection of NLP tasks with a structured dataset preprocessing framework. In *Proceedings of the 2024 Joint International Conference on Computational Linguistics, Language Resources and Evaluation (LREC-COLING 2024)*, pages 15655–15684, Torino, Italia. ELRA and ICCL.

David Wadden, Shanchuan Lin, Kyle Lo, Lucy Lu Wang, Madeleine van Zuylen, Arman Cohan, and Hannaneh Hajishirzi. 2020. Fact or fiction: Verifying scientific claims. *arXiv preprint arXiv:2004.14974*.

David Wadden and Kyle Lo. 2021. Overview and insights from the sciver shared task on scientific claim verification. *arXiv preprint arXiv:2107.08188*.

An Yang, Anfeng Li, Baosong Yang, Beichen Zhang, Binyuan Hui, Bo Zheng, Bowen Yu, Chang Gao, Chengen Huang, Chenxu Lv, Chujie Zheng, Dayiheng Liu, Fan Zhou, Fei Huang, Feng Hu, Hao Ge, Haoran Wei, Huan Lin, Jialong Tang, Jian Yang, Jianhong Tu, Jianwei Zhang, Jianxin Yang, Jiaxi Yang, Jing Zhou, Jingren Zhou, Junyang Lin, Kai Dang, Keqin Bao, Kexin Yang, Le Yu, Lianghao Deng, Mei Li, Mingfeng Xue, Mingze Li, Pei Zhang, Peng Wang, Qin Zhu, Rui Men, Ruize Gao, Shixuan Liu, Shuang Luo, Tianhao Li, Tianyi Tang, Wenbiao Yin, Xingzhang Ren, Xinyu Wang, Xinyu Zhang, Xuancheng Ren, Yang Fan, Yang Su, Yichang Zhang, Yinger Zhang, Yu Wan, Yuqiong Liu, Zekun Wang, Zeyu Cui, Zhenru Zhang, Zhipeng Zhou, and Zihan Qiu. 2025. Qwen3 technical report. *Preprint*, arXiv:2505.09388.

Claim	Justification	DeBERTa	CatBoost	Qwen	True Label
Common Antibiotics Detected: Studies have identified various antibiotics in water sources, including tetracyclines, sulfonamides, and quinolones, suggesting that all water sources are likely contaminated with these substances at harmful levels [2, 3, 4].	The claim generalized that all water sources are likely contaminated with various antibiotics; however, the cited references specifically mentioned contamination only in engineered aquatic environments.	entail	entail	entail	contra
Determination of Optimal Conditions: Use the model to determine the optimal conditions that maximize the desired responses. For example, optimal conditions might include specific temperature, time, and solvent concentration that yield the highest antioxidant activity [1, 2, 3, 5, 6].	The claim and the experimental data should fit a second-order polynomial model with a high R, aligning with the methodologies and results described in the reference.	unver	entail	entail	entail
Heat Stress and Diet Composition: The Temperature-Humidity Index (THI) significantly impacts both water intake and DMI in dairy cows, with higher THI leading to increased water intake and decreased DMI [3]. Although this study focuses on cows, similar effects can be expected in goats, suggesting that environmental conditions and diet composition are crucial factors in managing water and dry matter intake.	Both the claim and reference address how heat stress affects diet composition of livestock. The reference correlates it with lactating dairy cows. However, the claim implies that goats can have similar affects which the reference did not mention.	entail	contra	unver	unver

Table 4: Classification examples from the development dataset.

Author Index